Dress and Identity in Iron Age Britain

A study of glass beads and other objects of personal adornment

Elizabeth M. Foulds

ARCHAEOPRESS ARCHAEOLOGY

ARCHAEOPRESS PUBLISHING LTD
Gordon House
276 Banbury Road
Oxford OX2 7ED

www.archaeopress.com

ISBN 978 1 78491 526 1
ISBN 978 1 78491 527 8 (e-Pdf)

© Archaeopress and Elizabeth M. Foulds 2017

Cover: Replica of the Queen's Barrow necklace from Market Weighton, East Riding of Yorkshire. The replica was created by Tillerman Beads. Photo © Elizabeth M. Foulds

All rights reserved. No part of this book may be reproduced, in any form or by any means, electronic, mechanical, photocopying or otherwise, without the prior written permission of the copyright owners.

Printed in England by Oxuniprint, Oxford
This book is available direct from Archaeopress or from our website www.archaeopress.com

Contents

Preface xii

Sites Mentioned in Text xiii

Copyright Information and Image Acknowledgements xiii

Chapter 1
    Introduction 1
    An Introduction to Previous Studies of Glass Beads 3
    Aims of Current Research 4
    Methodology 4
        Identified Issues 4
        Study Regions 5
        Data Acquisition and Organisation 6
        Analyses 9
    Layout 10

Chapter 2
    Previous Approaches to Glass Beads 11
    Guido Typology 11
    Scientific Analysis of Iron Age Glass Beads 14
    Glass Bead Manufacturing 16
    The Wider European Context 18
    Conclusion 19

Chapter 3
    Glass Beads and Dress 20
    People and Objects 20
        Dress and Society 20
    Dress and Archaeology 22
        Dress, the Body, and Identity in Archaeology 22
        Dress in Iron Age Britain 24
        Human Iconography 25
        Death and the Body 26
    Artefacts of Dress 28
        Artefacts and Colour 29
        Artefacts as Dates 30
        Artefact Production and Exchange 31
        Artefacts and Identity 31
        Summary 33

Chapter 4
    The Nature of the Archaeological Resource in the Regions 34
    The Archaeological Resource 34
        Southwest England 34
        East Anglia 35
        East Yorkshire 35
        Northeast Scotland 36
        Impact of Developer-funded Archaeology 36
    Patterns of Iron Age Settlement 37
        Southwest England 37
        East Anglia 40
        East Yorkshire 41
        Northeast Scotland 43
        Discussion 45

Ritual/Treatment of the Dead	45
Southwest England	47
East Anglia	47
East Yorkshire	48
Northeast Scotland	49
Summary	50
Discussion	50

Chapter 5

Typological Conundrums, Quandaries, and Resolutions	52
Typological Complications	52
Critique of the Guido Typology	52
General Problems with the Guido Typology	65
Discussion	65
New Typology	65
Typology Description	66
Types in the Study Regions	68
Bead Class and Type Analysis	68
Chronology	73
Discussion	81
Conclusion	83

Chapter 6

Form and Regional Identity	84
Shape	85
Size	85
Size Analysis	89
Size Discussion	100
Colour	106
Monochrome Beads	106
Polychrome Beads	107
Discussion	125
Decorative Motif	129
Decorative Motif Analysis	129
Discussion	132
Discussion	137
Conclusion	145

Chapter 7

Archaeological Context	146
Glass Bead Distribution	147
Overall Distributions	147
Example Distributions	149
Archaeological Excavation	151
Glass Beads by Excavation Method	151
Density of excavations	153
Excavation Size and Methodology	156
Discussion	159
Site Types and Features	159
Site Type	159
Feature Type	177
Discussion	195

Chapter 8

Regional Bodily Adornment	197
Glass Bead Use	197
Inhumations	197
Non-Inhumations	210
Glass Beads in an Artefactual Context	214
Objects of Dress	215

  Wider Artefact Context..232
 Discussion..232
 Conclusion...240

Chapter 9
 Glass Beads in their Social Context...242
 Glass Beads in Iron Age Britain..242
 Dress in Iron Age Britain..245
 Areas for Future Research and Conclusion...246

Appendix A
 Terminology and Guide to Recording Glass Beads..247
 Dimensions and Shape..247
 Colour and Decorative Motif...248
 Other Aspects..250
 Photographing Glass Beads...251
 Chronology Terminology...251

Appendix B
 Guido Iron Age Glass Bead Types..254
 Class 1..254
 Class 2..254
 Class 3..254
 Class 4..255
 Class 5..255
 Class 6..255
 Class 7..255
 Class 8..256
 Class 9..256
 Class 10..256
 Class 11..256
 Class 12..257
 Class 13..257
 Class 14..257
 Group 1..257
 Group 2..257
 Group 3..258
 Group 4..258
 Group 5..258
 Group 6 and 7..258
 Group 8..258

Appendix C
 List of All New Types...259
 Class 1: Simple monochrome beads...259
  A. Simple shapes...259
 Class 2: Monochrome beads...259
  A. Complex shapes...259
 Class 3: Polychrome beads, no design motif..259
 Class 4: Beads with eyes..259
  A. Simple Eyes..259
  B. Complex Eyes...260
  C. Compound Eyes...260
 Class 5: Beads with perforation colour..260
  A. With yellow..260
  B. With blue..260
 Class 6: Beads with linear design...260
  A. Multiple circumferential lines..260
  B. Single wave/zig-zag..260
  C. Chevrons..260

- D. Criss-cross 260
- E. Diagonal criss-cross 260
- F. Pinnate 261
- G. Spirals 261

Class 7: Wrapped beads 261
- A. Simple wrapped 261

Class 8: Whirl beads 262
- A. Simple whirl 262

Class 9: Ray beads 262
- A. Simple ray 262

Class 10: Beads with spots 262
- A. Bead with spots 262

Class 11: Complex motifs 262

Guide to the Illustrated Glass Beads 264

Bibliography 276

Index 336

Data covering lists of excavated sites, glass beads and non-glass bead artefacts used in this book is available to download from http://bit.ly/2iea1Ke

List of Figures

Figure 1: Compilation map of all of Guido's (1978a) original data. 7
Figure 2: Identification of project study regions. 8
Figure 3: Guido's (redrawn after 1978a Figure 1) sixteen decorative motifs. 13
Figure 4: Schematic diagram of Guido's Iron Age and Roman glass bead classification (redrawn after 1978a Plates I and II, Figure 19, 23, 37). 14
Figure 5: Applying linear decoration during glass bead manufacture. 18
Figure 6: Haevernick's (1960) eight main types of beads (author's translation). 19
Figure 7: Details from the Gundestrup Cauldron (held in collections at National Museum of Denmark). (a) Detail of antler figure, interior Plate A, (b) Detail of panel, exterior Plate F. 27
Figure 8: Drawing of the Roos Carr figures from East Yorkshire (held in collections at Hull and East Riding Museums:Hull Museums KINCM:1991.141.10876). 27
Figure 9: Back view of chalk figurine from East Yorkshire (Hull and East Riding Museums:Hull Museums KINCM:2006.11303.4576). 28
Figure 10: Key sites in Southwest England mentioned in the text. 39
Figure 11: Key sites in East Anglia mentioned in the text. 42
Figure 12: Key sites in East Yorkshire mentioned in the text. 44
Figure 13: Key sites in Northeast Scotland mentioned in the text. 46
Figure 14: List of Guido classes and the number of examples recorded by Guido, compared to the number contained in the database that resulted from the current research. It also shows the number of beads that were studied first-hand. 53
Figure 15: List of Guido Groups and the number of examples included in her catalogue, compared to the number contained in the database that resulted from the current research. It also shows the number of examples that were studied first-hand. 53
Figure 16: (a) Scatter-graph showing the overall size of Class 1 beads by Guido sub-type, and pie-charts showing (b) the proportion of different number of eye motifs and (c) the proportion of different types of shaped Guido Class 1 beads. 54
Figure 17: Analysis of Guido Class 3 beads (a) Scatter-graph showing the overall size, and pie-charts showing (b) the proportion of beads by number of eyes, (c) the proportion of different colours used for the body of the bead, and 55
Figure 17: Analysis of Guido Class 3 beads (d) the proportion of different colours used for decoration. 56
Figure 18: Analysis of Guido Class 10 and 13 beads (a) pie-chart showing the proportion of different Guido Class 10 shapes, (b) pie-chart showing the proportion of different colours of glass used for the body of Guido Class 13 beads. 57
Figure 18: Analysis of Guido Class 10 and 13 beads (c) scatter-graph of Guido Class 10 beads showing dimensions and shape, and (d) scatter-graph of Guido Class 13 beads showing dimensions and shape. ...58
Figure 19: Comparison of Guido Class 7, 9, and 14 beads (a) scatter-graph comparing overall size. 58
Figure 19: Comparison of Guido Class 7, 9, and 14 beads (b) bar-charts comparing the proportion of Class 7 body and (c) decorative colours. 59
Figure 19: Comparison of Guido Class 7, 9, and 14 beads (d) bar-charts comparing the proportion of Class 9 body and (e) decorative colours. 60
Figure 19: Comparison of Guido Class 7, 9, and 14 beads (f) bar-charts comparing the proportion of Class 14 body and (g) decorative colours. 61
Figure 20: Scatter-graph comparing the dimensions of Guido Class 8 beads. 62
Figure 21: Scatter-graph comparing the dimensions of Guido Group 6 and 7 beads with guideline for perfect sphere (x) and 'annular' shape (x/2). 62
Figure 22: Schematic diagram of Guido typology chronology in typological order. 64
Figure 23: Schematic diagram of Guido typology chronology in chronological order. 64
Figure 24: Schematic diagram showing the hierarchy of new glass bead types. 67
Figure 25: Frequency of Class 1 beads in the study regions. 69
Figure 26: Frequency of Class 2 beads in the study regions. 69
Figure 27: Frequency of Class 3 beads in the study regions. 69
Figure 28: Frequency of Class 4 beads in the study regions. 69

Figure 29: Frequency of Class 5 beads in the study regions. 69
Figure 30: Frequency of Class 6 beads in the study regions. 70
Figure 31: Frequency of Class 7 beads in the study regions. 71
Figure 32: Frequency of Class 8 beads in the study regions. 71
Figure 33: Frequency of Class 9 beads in the study regions. 71
Figure 34: Frequency of Class 10 beads in the study regions. 71
Figure 35: Frequency of Class 11 beads in the study regions. 71
Figure 36: Summary table of presence and absence of new types. (1) Southwest England, (2) East Anglia, (3) East Yorkshire, and (4) Northeast Scotland. 72
Figure 37: Bar chart showing the frequency of total datable glass beads in study regions. 74
Figure 38: Bar chart showing (a) the frequency and (b) the percentage of total datable glass beads by study region. 75
Figure 39: Bar chart showing (a) the number and (b) the percentage of the quantity of colours of glass beads over time. 81
Figure 40: Bar chart showing (a) the number and (b) the percentage of different general motif type over time. 82
Figure 41: Number of glass beads per study region. 85
Figure 42: Bar-chart showing the frequency of shape for all study regions combined. 86
Figure 43: Bar-charts showing the use of bead shapes in (a) Southwest England, (b) East Anglia, (c) East Yorkshire, and (d) Northeast Scotland. 87
Figure 44: Bar-chart comparing (a) the frequency of glass bead shape and (b) the percentage of glass bead shape between the four study regions. 88
Figure 45: (a) Descriptive statistics for Diameter/Width measurement. 90
Figure 45: (b) Histogram of the Diameter/Width measurement of glass beads for all beads in study regions. 90
Figure 46: Histogram showing Diameter/Width measurement for (a) Southwest England, (b) East Anglia, (c) East Yorkshire, and (d) Northeast Scotland. 91
Figure 47: (a) Descriptive statistics for Height measurement. 92
Figure 47: (b) Histogram of the Height measurement of glass beads for all beads in study regions. 92
Figure 48: Histogram showing Height measurement for (a) southwest England, (b) East Anglia, (c) East Yorkshire, (d) Northeast Scotland. 93
Figure 49: (a) Descriptive statistics for Perforation Diameter measurement. 94
Figure 49: (b) Histogram of the Perforation Diameter measurement of glass beads for all beads in study regions. ... 94
Figure 50: Histogram showing Perforation Diameter measurement for (a) Southwest England, (b) East Anglia, (c) East Yorkshire, (d) Northeast Scotland. 95
Figure 51: Scatter-graph plotting the Diameter/Width measurement against the Height measurement for all beads in study regions. 96
Figure 52: Scatter-graph plotting the Diameter/Width against the Height for beads from (a) Southwest England, (b) East Anglia. 97
Figure 52: Scatter-graph plotting the Diameter/Width against the Height for beads from (c) East Yorkshire, (d) Northeast Scotland. 98
Figure 53: Scatter-graph plotting the Diam:Height ratio against the Perforation Diameter measurement for all beads in study regions. 100
Figure 54: Scatter-graph plotting the Diam:Height ratio against the Perforation Diameter for beads from (a) Southwest England, (b) East Anglia. 101
Figure 54: Scatter-graph plotting the Diam:Height ratio against the Perforation Diameter for beads from (c) East Yorkshire, (d) Northeast Scotland. 102
Figure 55: (a) Descriptive statistics for Weight measurement for beads from all study regions (grams). 103
Figure 55: (b) Histogram showing the combined Weight distribution for all study regions. 103
Figure 56: Histogram showing Weight measurement for (a) Southwest England, (b) East Anglia, (c) East Yorkshire, (d) Northeast Scotland. 104
Figure 57: Scatter-graph comparing the Diameter/Width and Height measurements for glass beads forming possible necklaces, or found in burial contexts in Southwest England. 105
Figure 58: Scatter-graph comparing the Diameter/Width and Height measurements for glass beads forming possible necklaces, or found in burial contexts in East Yorkshire. 105
Figure 59: Bar-chart comparing the frequency of colour occurrence in all four study regions. 107
Figure 60: Bar-chart comparing the (a) frequency, and (b) percentage of colour occurrence in the four study regions. 108
Figure 61: Bar-chart comparing the (a) frequency, and (b) percentage of colours on each bead between study regions. 109

Figure 62: Bar-chart showing the frequency of colours for monochrome beads for all study regions. 110
Figure 63: Bar-chart comparing the (a) frequency, and (b) percentage of monochrome beads that occur in each study region. 111
Figure 64: (a) Diagram showing the colour combinations of bi-colour beads in Southwest England, and (b) bar-chart showing the frequency of bi-colour combinations in Southwest England. 112
Figure 65: (a) Diagram showing the colour combinations of bi-colour beads in East Anglia, and (b) bar-chart showing the freuquency of bi-colour combinations in East Anglia. 113
Figure 66: (a) Diagram showing the colour combinations of bi-colour beads in East Yorkshire, (b) bar-chart showing the frequency of bi-colour glass beads in East Yorkshire. 114
Figure 67: (a) Diagram showing the colour combinations of bi-colour beads in Northeast Scotland, and (b) bar-chart showing the frequency of bi-colour combinations from Northeast Scotland. 115
Figure 68: List of colour combinations used on glass beads made from two colours of glass and the frequency in each study region. 116
Figure 69: Bar-chart showing the (a) frequency, and (b) percentage, of individual colours for polychrome beads with two colours in all four study regions. 117
Figure 70: (a) Diagram showing the colour combinations of tri-colour beads in Southwest England, and (b) bar-chart showing the frequency of tri-colour glass beads in Southwest England. 118
Figure 71: (a) Diagram showing the colour combinations of tri-colour beads in East Anglia, and (b) bar-chart showing the frequency of tri-coloured glass beads from East Anglia. 119
Figure 72: (a) Diagram showing the colour combinations of tri-colour beads in East Yorkshire, and (b) bar-chart showing the frequency of tri-coloured glass beads from East Yorkshire. 120
Figure 73: (a) Diagram showing the colour combinations of tri-colour beads in Northeast Scotland. 121
Figure 73: (b) Bar-chart showing the frequency of tri-coloured glass beads in Northeast Scotland. 121
Figure 74: List of colour combinations for glass beads with three colours of glass and the frequency in each study region. 122
Figure 75: Bar-chart showing the (a) frequency, and (b) percentage, of individual colours for polychrome beads with three colours in all four study regions. 123
Figure 76: Diagram showing the combinations of four colours found on glass beads in Southwest England. 124
Figure 77: Diagram showing the colour combinations of four colours beads in Northeast Scotland. 124
Figure 78: (a) Bar-chart showing the frequency of individual colours for polychrome beads with four colours in all four study regions, and (b) bar-chart showing the percentage of individual colours for polychrome beads with four colours in all four study regions. 125
Figure 79: (a) Bar-chart showing the combined frequency of bead body colour across all study regions, and (b) bar-chart showing the combined frequency of bead decorative colour across all study regions. 126
Figure 80: Bar-chart showing the use of body colour of polychrome beads in (a) Southwest England and (b) East Anglia. 127
Figure 80: Bar-chart showing the use of body colour of polychrome beads in (c) East Yorkshire and (d) Northeast Scotland. 128
Figure 81: List of colours and colour combinations found on the body of the bead and the frequency in each study region. 129
Figure 82: Bar-chart showing the use of decorative colour for polychrome beads in (a) Southwest England and (b) East Anglia. 130
Figure 82: Bar-chart showing the use of decorative colour for polychrome beads in (c) East Yorkshire and (d) Northeast Scotland. 131
Figure 83: List of colours and colour combinations found as decorative motif on the bead and the frequency in each study region. 132
Figure 84: Bar-chart showing the frequency of glass beads by body colour and corresponding decorative colours by study region. Colour words to the left of the hyphen indicate body colour, and colour words to the right of the hyphen indicate decorative colour. (a) Black, (b) Brown, (c) Colourless. 133
Figure 84: Bar-chart showing the frequency of glass beads by body colour and corresponding decorative colours by study region. Colour words to the left of the hyphen indicate body colour, and colour words to the right of the hyphen indicate decorative colour. (d) Blue and Bluegreen. 134
Figure 84: Bar-chart showing the frequency of glass beads by body colour and corresponding decorative colours by study region. Colour words to the left of the hyphen indicate body colour, and colour words to the right of the hyphen indicate decorative colour. (e) Green, (f) Orange, (g) Purple and Redpurple. 135
Figure 84: Bar-chart showing the frequency of glass beads by body colour and corresponding decorative colours by study region. Colour words to the left of the hyphen indicate body colour, and colour

words to the right of the hyphen indicate decorative colour. (h) White, (i) Yellow, (j) multiple body colours and no decorative colours. 136
Figure 85: Summary table correlating motif with new classification. 137
Figure 86: Bar-chart showing the frequency of general motif types for all four study regions. 137
Figure 87: Bar-chart showing the (a) frequency, and (b) percentage of general motif types in all four study regions. 138
Figure 88: List of all decorative motifs and their frequency within each study region. 139
Figure 89: Bar-chart showing the use of decorative motif in (a) Southwest England. 140
Figure 89: Bar-chart showing the use of decorative motif in (b) East Anglia, (c) East Yorkshire. 141
Figure 89: Bar-chart showing the use of decorative motif in (d) Northeast Scotland. 142
Figure 90: Bar-chart showing the (a) frequency of complex decorative motif in all four study regions. 143
Figure 90: Bar-chart showing the (b) percentage of complex decorative motif in all four study regions. 144
Figure 91: Summary table of generalised regional characteristics. 145
Figure 92: Overall distribution of glass beads in Britain. Drawing on data from the Guido (1978a) catalogue and new additions in the research database. 148
Figure 93: Maps of study regions showing density of typed glass beads. (a) Southwest England, (b) East Anglia, (c) East Yorkshire, (d) Northeast Scotland. No colour = bead absence, yellow = low density, red = high density. 149
Figure 94: Size of region, number of typed glass beads, and beads per square mile in each study region (all excavated glass beads and stray beads included). 149
Figure 95: Comparison of the distribution of Guido Class 1 beads in (a) Southwest England and (b) East Yorkshire. 150
Figure 96: Comparison of the distribution of Class 4 blue and white beads in (a) Southwest England and (b) East Yorkshire. 150
Figure 97: Distribution of colourless and opaque yellow glass beads in four study regions. (a) Southwest England, (b) East Anglia, (c) East Yorkshire, (d) Northeast Scotland. 152
Figure 98: Distribution of blue and white glass beads in the four study regions. (a) Southwest England, (b) East Anglia, (c) East Yorkshire, (d) Northeast Scotland. 152
Figure 99: Comparison of the number of records in the database, with the number of excavation events, and the number of individual excavated sites. 153
Figure 100: Chart showing the frequency of developer funded reports (included in the research) by publication year since 1991 and also showing the frequency of glass bead finds. 153
Figure 101: Table showing the frequency of excavations by type and the frequency of presence or absence of glass beads. 153
Figure 102: (a) Bar-chart showing the frequency of different types of excavations in each study region, (b) Bar-chart showing the proportion of different types of excavations in each study region. 154
Figure 103: (a) Bar chart showing the relative percentage of different types of excavations in each study region with no typed glass beads, (b) Bar chart showing the relative percentage of different types of excavations in each region with typed glass beads. 154
Figure 104: Table comparing the different types of excavations where typed glass beads were not found in the region. 155
Figure 105: Table comparing the frequency of different types of excavations where typed glass beads were found. 155
Figure 106: Maps showing the density of research and developer-led excavations within each study region. The white diamonds represent glass beads found through excavation, and the black diamonds represent other typed glass beads, usually found as stray finds. Yellow = low density of excavation, Red = high density of excavation. (a) Southwest England, (b) East Anglia, (c) East Yorkshire, (d) Northeast Scotland. 155
Figure 107: Maps showing locations of excavations. 'X' represents sites where no glass beads were found and circles represent were typed glass beads were found. Colour differentiates the type of excavation: Green=developer-led, Red=research, Blue=rescue, and black=other. (a) Southwest England, (b) East Anglia, (c) East Yorkshire, (d) Northeast Scotland. 156
Figure 108: Maps showing the size (square meters) of excavations in (a) Southwest England, (b) East Anglia, (c) East Yorkshire, (d) Northeast Scotland. 157
Figure 109: Chart showing the frequency of excavation size by study region. 158
Figure 110: Chart showing the frequency of excavation size and whether typed glass beads were present. 158
Figure 111: Bar-chart showing the frequency of different site types in all four study regions. 160

Figure 112: Bar-chart showing the (a) frequency, and (b) relative proportion of site types between study regions. 161
Figure 113: List of the number of different types of sites and whether glass beads were present. 162
Figure 114: Chi-square data for type of site and presence of glass beads. Note that some categories from Figure 113 have been condensed in order to create valid results in the chi-square test. 162
Figure 115: Bar-chart showing the frequency of sites where typed glass beads were found. 163
Figure 116: Bar-chart showing the (a) frequency, and (b) proportion of site types where typed glass beads were found by study region. 164
Figure 117: Bar-chart showing the frequency of the occurrence of activity from different periods for all study regions. 165
Figure 118: Bar-chart showing the (a) frequency, and (b) percentage of activity from different periods within each region. 166
Figure 119: Bar-chart showing the frequency of sites and general period where typed glass beads were (a) not found at, and (b) present. 167
Figure 120: Sites in Southwest England with activity dating to the Late Bronze Age/Early Iron Age with glass beads. 167
Figure 121: Sites with activity dating to the Middle Iron Age/Late Iron Age with glass beads (a) Southwest England, (b) East Anglia, (c) East Yorkshire. 169
Figure 122: Sites with activity dating to the Late Iron Age/Early Roman period with glass beads (a) Southwest England, (b) Northeast Scotland. 170
Figure 123: Sites with activity dating to the Early Roman/Romano-British period with glass beads (a) Southwest England, (b) East Anglia, (c) East Yorkshire. 171
Figure 124: Sites with activity dating to the post-Roman/Anglo-Saxon period with glass beads (a) Southwest England, (b) Northeast Scotland. 171
Figure 125: Bar-chart showing the number of colours of glass on each bead in Southwest England (a) frequency, (b) percentage. 173
Figure 126: Bar-chart showing the number of colours of glass on each bead in East Anglia (a) frequency, (b) percentage. 174
Figure 127: Bar-chart showing the number of colours of glass on each bead in East Yorkshire (a) frequency, (b) percentage. 175
Figure 128: Bar-chart showing the number of colours of glass on each bead in Northeast Scotland (a) frequency, (b) percentage. 176
Figure 129: Bar-chart showing the frequency of glass beads at different site types in Southwest England (a) frequency, (b) percentage. 178
Figure 130: Bar-chart showing the frequency of glass beads at different site types in East Anglia (a) frequency, (b) percentage. 179
Figure 131: Bar-chart showing the frequency of glass beads at different site types in East Yorkshire (a) frequency, (b) percentage. 180
Figure 132: Bar-chart showing the frequency of glass beads at different site types in Northeast Scotland (a) frequency, (b) percentage. 181
Figure 133: Chart showing the proportion of glass bead complexity rank (combining colour and decorative motif) by (a) study regions, (b) site type. Rank is from most simple (1) to most complex (5). 182
Figure 134: Glass bead feature analysis for Southwest England (a) bar-chart of glass bead frequency by feature, (b) comparison of site type and feature type, (c) comparison of feature and period of activity. 183
Figure 134: Glass bead feature analysis for Southwest England. (d) Comparison of Classes and features. 184
Figure 135: Glass bead feature analysis for East Anglia (a) bar-chart of glass bead frequency by feature, (b) comparison of site type and feature type, (c) comparison of feature and period of activity. 185
Figure 135: Glass bead feature analysis for East Yorkshire. (d) Comparison of Classes and features. 186
Figure 136: Glass bead feature analysis for East Yorkshire (a) bar-chart of glass bead frequency by feature, (b) comparison of site type and feature type, (c) comparison of feature and period of activity. 187
Figure 136: Glass bead feature analysis for East Yorkshire. (d) Comparison of Classes and features. 188
Figure 137: Glass bead feature analysis for Northeast Scotland (a) bar-chart of glass bead frequency by feature, (b) comparison of site type and feature type, (c) comparison of feature and period of activity. 189
Figure 137: Glass bead feature analysis for Northeast Scotland. (d) Comparison of Classes and features. 190
Figure 138: Bar-chart showing the number of beads found within single contexts. 191
Figure 139: List of sites where glass beads were found in pit contexts. 192
Figure 140: Table comparing the different types of objects found in pits with glass beads. 193
Figure 141: List of sites where glass beads were found in inhumations in Southwest England. 193

Figure 142: List of sites where glass beads were found in inhumations in East Yorkshire. 194
Figure 143: Frequency of inhumations in East Yorkshire. 195
Figure 144: Illustration showing four different lengths of necklaces to demonstrate the different effects of differing lengths of strands of glass beads. 198
Figure 145: Bar chart comparing the number of glass beads in each possible necklace with the estimated length of each strand of beads in East Yorkshire. 199
Figure 146: Comparison of East Yorkshire burials and bead types. Dark grey highlight indicates bead types that are repeated across necklaces, light grey highlight indicates bead types that only occur singly on one necklace and are not found elsewhere. 200
Figure 147: Scatter-graph comparing the size of all East Yorkshire glass beads from burials. 201
Figure 148: Scatter-graph comparing the size of four different bead types from East Yorkshire burials: (a) Type 102, (b) Type 417, (c) Type 421, (d) Type 901. 202
Figure 149: Comparison of different motifs found on East Yorkshire necklaces. 203
Figure 150: Hypothetical reconstruction of glass beads from Wetwang Slack: (a) Burial 209, (b) Burial 274, (c) Burial 249. 204
Figure 151: Hypothetical reconstructions using 120 glass beads. (a) 4-strand tassel, (b) 40-strand tassel with three beads per strand, (c) continuous loop of beads. 205
Figure 152: List of sites where glass beads were found in inhumations in East Yorkshire. 207
Figure 153: Comparison of different artefact types and their location on the body where known from East Yorkshire. 208
Figure 154: Bar-chart showing the frequency of dress objects within 127 inhumations in East Yorkshire (groups of beads that likely formed a necklace or other object are counted once). 209
Figure 155: Bar-chart showing the frequency of different dress objects within 127 inhumations in East Yorkshire. 209
Figure 156: Illustration of different body zones and terms. 210
Figure 157: Pie-chart showing the proportions of artefacts and the body zones that they were found in association with (beaded necklaces are only counted as one instance). 210
Figure 158: List of sites where glass beads were found in inhumations in Southwest England. 211
Figure 159: Bar-chart comparing the number of glass beads and length of glass bead strand for each possible strand of glass beads in Southwest England. 211
Figure 160: Hypothetical reconstruction of glass beads from Southwest England: (a) glass and stone beads from Chesil mirror burial, Dorset, (b) glass beads from the Cleveland Cist burial, Somerset, (c) glass, faience, and wood(?) beads from Burial 8 Whitcombe, Dorset. 212
Figure 161: Bar chart showing the frequency of the number of objects of dress within each Southwest England inhumation (27 inhumations, 40 objects). 212
Figure 162: Comparison of different object types and their location on the body in Southwest England. 213
Figure 163: Pie-chart comparing the location of 28 objects in connection with the body in Southwest England. 213
Figure 164: Bar-chart showing the number of glass beads and the length of a strand of beads if strung together. ... 214
Figure 165: Hypothetical reconstruction of possible necklace (G68, Somerset Museum) from Meare Lake Village East in Somerset. 214
Figure 166: Scatter-graphs comparing the dimensions of beads found in the same mound context at Meare Lake Village in Somerset. (a) Necklace G68 from MLVE Mound 22; (b) Necklace G69 from MLVE Mound 47; (c) MLVW Mound 7; (d) MLVW Mound 33. 215
Figure 166: Scatter-graphs comparing the dimensions of beads found in the same mound context at Meare Lake Village in Somerset. (e) MLVW Mound 34. 216
Figure 167: Proposed typologies: (a) Pins, (b) Wrist/Arm/Ankle Rings, (c) Finger- and Toe-rings, (d) Torcs. 217
Figure 168: Bar-charts comparing the frequency of different types of artefacts in each study region: (a) Frequency, (b) Percentage. 218
Figure 169: General frequency of brooches throughout the Iron Age using data from all study regions. 219
Figure 170: Bar-charts comparing the frequency of brooches by date: (a) Frequency; (b) Percentage. 220
Figure 171: Bar-chart comparing the frequency of different torc types using data from all study regions. 222
Figure 172: Bar-charts comparing the frequency of different torc types by study regions: (a) Frequency; (b) Percentage. 223
Figure 173: Bar-chart showing general frequency of different types of objects worn on either the wrist, arm, or ankle. Dark grey are types made mostly out of metal, usually iron or copper alloy, medium grey are two types of glass rings, and lightest grey are different types of objects made from stone, usually shale or jet. 224

Figure 174: Bar-charts comparing the frequency of different types of rings worn on the wrist, arm, and ankle by study region: (a) Frequency, (b) Percentage. 225
Figure 175: Bar-chart comparing the frequency of different types of finger- and toe-rings using data from all study regions. 226
Figure 176: Bar-charts comparing the frequency of finger- and toe-rings in each of the study regions. (a) Frequency. 227
Figure 176: Bar-charts comparing the frequency of finger- and toe-rings in each of the study regions, (b) Percentage. 228
Figure 177: Bar-chart showing the frequency of different types of pins using data from all study regions. 229
Figure 178: Bar-charts comparing the frequency of different pin types by study region: (a) Frequency. 230
Figure 178: Bar-charts comparing the frequency of different pin types by study region: (b) Percentage. 231
Figure 179: Bar-charts showing the frequency of objects in study regions over time: (a) All Objects, (b) Arm/Wrist/Ankle rings. 233
Figure 179: Bar-charts showing the frequency of objects in study regions over time: (c) Finger-/Toe-rings, (d) Pins. 234
Figure 179: Bar-charts showing the frequency of objects in study regions over time: (e) Torcs, (f) Brooches. 235
Figure 180: Map showing the density of all beads from database including Guido catalogue. Yellow = low density, red = high density. 236
Figure 181: Comparison of the distribution of different Iron Age artefacts from Portable Antiquity Scheme data. (a) Brooches, (b) Coins. Yellow = low density, red = high density. 237
Figure 181: Comparison of the distribution of different Iron Age artefacts from Portable Antiquity Scheme data. (c) Cosmetic Objects, (d) Horse related gear. Yellow = low density, red = high density. 238
Figure 182: Bead measurements of round and non-round beads. 248
Figure 183: Illustration of different bead shapes. 248
Figure 184: Bead shapes as determined by ratio used throughout book...249
Figure 185: Identified decorative motifs. 250
Figure 186: Example of bead colour terminology on polychrome beads with dot and linear decorative motifs......251
Figure 187: Diagram of motif placement on the beads. (a) single circumferential, (b) single alternating, (c) paired circumferential, (d) pairs and single circumferential. 251
Figure 188: Description of bead decoration terminology...252
Figure 189: Examples of Class 1, 2, and 3 beads. 265
Figure 190: Examples of Class 4 and 5 beads. 267
Figure 191: Examples of Class 6 beads. 269
Figure 192: Examples of Class 7, 8, 9, and 10 beads. 271
Figure 193: Examples of Class 11 beads. 273
Figure 194: Examples of Class 11 and un-typed beads..275

Preface

The following monograph was originally written as my doctoral thesis whilst at Durham University. I did not change substantial amounts of text, but I did adjust the organisation slightly and I completed some minor edits. The biggest change is the figures, the majority of which I remade for consistency. I have also included my site catalogue and bead catalogue as a text file, which I hope will be in a usable format and will help future researchers.

I owe a lot to the work of Margaret Guido, whose catalogue of Iron Age glass beads formed the initial data-set for this research. As much as possible, I tried to track down each bead in museum collections in order to view them first-hand. In some cases this was not possible and I have relied upon Mrs Guido's descriptions and measurements. This is clearly indicated in the data download available at http://bit.ly/2iea1Ke.

The data collection of the thesis and resulting monograph could not have been achieved if it were not for the generous grants provided by the Rosemary Cramp fund, the Prehistoric Society, and the Association for the History of Glass. I wish to thank these organisations for their financial support, as without it the resulting research would have produced a very different outcome.

I must also extend a heartfelt thank you to a number of museums, Historic Environment Record office staff, and other organisations for their patience and help during data collection. These include: The British Museum, The National Museum of Scotland, The Museum of Somerset, Wiltshire Heritage Museum, Dorchester Museum, Gloucester Museum, Poole Museum, Gillingham Museum, Bristol City Museum, Red House Museum, Corinium Museum, Stroud Museum, The Ashmolean, Norwich Castle Museum, The Yorkshire Museum, Hull Museum, the Marishcal Museum collection at the University of Aberdeen, Forres Museum, Elgin Museum, The Hunterian Museum, and Inverness City Museum. The HERs visited span the following: Dorset, Somerset, Gloucestershire, Bristol City, Norfolk, Suffolk, North Yorkshire, North Yorkshire Moor National Park, Humberside, City of York, and the Royal Commission on the Ancient and Historical Monuments of Scotland.

I would also like to thank the following individuals for their extraordinary assistance: Stephen Minnitt, Fraser Hunter, Jody Joy, John Davies, Alice Cattermole, and Paula Gentil. For access to unpublished material, thanks are due to: Jody Joy and J.D. Hill at the British Museum, Damian Evans at Bournemouth University, Steve Malone formerly at Archaeological Project Services, Paula Gentil at the Hull Museum, Fraser Hunter at the National Museum of Scotland, Ross Murray formerly at Headland Archaeology, and Angela Wardle at the Museum of London Archaeology. Thanks are also due to John Dent for answering my questions about Wetwang Slack.

For their willingness to listen to me ramble on about glass beads, a huge thank you to my husband, Freddie Foulds (who had to put up with most of it!), as well as: Fraser Hunter, Martina Bertini, Steve Minnitt, Jody Joy, Mel Giles, Arthur Anderson, Jo Zalea Matias, Mhairi Maxwell, Lindsy Büster, Rachel Reader, Paul Murtagh, Tom Crowther, Emma Cunliffe, Jocelyn Baker, Jo Shoebridge; and, of course my wonderful supervisors: Tom Moore and Richard Hingley.

Finally, a big thank you to my family and friends. I don't think I would have ever finished this work without your support! However, any errors of course remain my own.

Elizabeth M Foulds
Durham, May 2016

Sites Mentioned in Text

Southwest England (Figure 10)

1. Atworth Roman Villa, Wiltshire
2. Bagendon, Gloucestershire
3. Battlesbury Camp, Wiltshire
4. Birdlip, Gloucestershire
5. Bredon Hill, Gloucestershire
6. Burn Ground, Gloucestershire
7. Cadbury Castle, Somerset
8. Cannard's Grave, Somerset
9. Catsgore, Somerset
10. Chalbury Camp, Dorset
11. Cirencester, Gloucestershire
12. Claydon Pike, Gloucestershire
13. Clevedon, Somerset
14. Conderton Camp, Worcestershire
15. East Chisenbury, Wiltshire
16. Glastonbury Lake Village, Somerset
17. Ham Hill, Dorset
18. Hengistbury Head, Dorset
19. Chesil Mirror Burial, Dorset
20. Lidbury Camp, Wiltshire
21. Maiden Castle, Dorset
22. Meare Lake Village, Somerset
23. Salmonsbury, Gloucestershire
24. Sea Mills, Bristol City
25. Swallowcliffe Down, Wiltshire
26. Totterdown Lane, Gloucestershire
27. Whitcombe, Dorset

East Anglia (Figure 11)

1. Billingford, Norfolk
2. Caister-on-Sea, Norfolk
3. Fison Way, Norfolk
4. Grandcourt Quarry, Norfolk
5. Ipswich, Suffolk
6. Ken Hill, Norfolk
7. Santon Downham, Suffolk
8. Thetford, Norfolk

East Yorkshire (Figure 12)

1. Arras, North Yorkshire
2. Brough, East Riding of Yorkshire
3. Bugthrope, East Riding of Yorkshire
4. Burton Fleming, East Riding of Yorkshire
5. Castleford, West Yorkshire
6. Cowlam, East Riding of Yorkshire
7. Dalton Parlours, West Yorkshire
8. Dane's Graves, East Riding of Yorkshire
9. Garton Slack, East Riding of Yorkshire
10. Rudston, East Riding of Yorkshire
11. Staple Howe, East Riding of Yorkshire
12. Sutton Common, West Yorkshire
13. Wetwang Slack, East Riding of Yorkshire

Northeast Scotland (Figure 13)

1. Berryhill, Aberdeenshire
2. Birnie, Moray
3. Candle Stane, Aberdeenshire
4. Cawdor, Highland
5. Culbin Sands, Moray
6. Culduthel Farm, Highland
7. Forest Road, Aberdeenshire
8. Sculptor's Cave, Moray
9. Tap o'Noth, Aberdeenshire
10. Thainstone, Aberdeenshire
11. Wardend of Durris, Aberdeenshire

Copyright Information and Image Acknowledgements

Figures 1, 2, 10, 11, 12, 13, 92, 93, 95, 96, 97, 98, 106, 107, 108, 180, 181: © Crown Copyright/database right 2012. Contains Ordnance Survey data, an Ordanance Survey EDINA supplied service.

Figures 189 – 194: Individual Copyright/Acknowledgements for each artefact are given in the figure captions.

Author's copyright: all other images

Chapter 1
Introduction

Of all the Britons by far the most civilised are the inhabitants of Cantium, a purely maritime region, whose way of life is little different from that of the Gauls. Most of those inhabiting the interior...clothe themselves in skins. All the Britons dye themselves with woad, which produces a blue colour, and as a result their appearance in battle is all the more daunting. They wear their hair long, and shave all their bodies with the exception of their heads and upper lip.

(Julius Caesar (1st c. BC), Gallic War V, 14)

Most of (northern) Britain is marshy...For the most part they are naked... Also, being unfamiliar with the use of clothing, they adorn their waists and necks with iron, considering this an ornament and a sign of wealth, just as other barbarians do gold. They tattoo their bodies with various designs and pictures of all kinds of animals. This is the reason they do not wear clothes: so as not to cover up the designs on their bodies.

(Herodian (3rd c. AD), III, 14, 6-8)

In many ways we are at a disadvantage for understanding the people that inhabited Britain during the Iron Age (c. 800 BC - AD 43). In the past, textual evidence from classical authors has been taken for granted and presumed to be more-or-less accurate representations of everyday life in Iron Age Britain (Hingley 2011). While seemingly informative and almost ethnographic in nature, these sources are quick to belittle the inhabitants of Britain and construct stereotypes that portray their distant neighbours as outrageously different in both appearance and mannerisms. If these sources were to be taken at face value, they would have us believe that people in the British Iron Age wore no garments or, at best, covered themselves with animal pelts and hides, which of course was considered uncivilised (see above quotes). Historically, classical texts have formed a framework where the archaeological evidence has been manipulated to fit the textual narratives with little critical awareness. These classical sources have provided the basis for which studies of Iron Age tribal ethnicity and social hierarchy, as well as settlement sites, such as *oppida*, have been viewed within both Iron Age and Roman period studies of Britain (e.g. Wheeler's (1954) interpretation of Stanwick in North Yorkshire). On its own, archaeological evidence clearly points to the contrary and within recent years, this topic has been subject to a growing debate regarding the ways in which we should interpret archaeological evidence, and the applicability and validity of classical sources to supplement our understanding of the past (Collis 2003; 2011; Hill 2011; Hingley 2011; James 1999; Karl 2004; 2008; Megaw and Megaw 1998; Moore 2011; Pitts 2010; Woolf 1993).

If it is not possible to rely solely on the written classical texts in order to understand how the people living in Iron Age Britain dressed, then what kind of evidence do we have available? How can we answer the question: how was visual appearance materialised? The most obvious sources of information for appearance in the past is the representation of humans in art and the placement of people and objects within burials. Unfortunately for the study of the Iron Age period in Britain, neither of these sources are found abundantly, as there is very limited evidence for human representation in material form, and formal inhumation was limited geographically and to specific periods of time (Carr and Knüsel 1997; Whimster 1981). However, we can at least draw on evidence for appearance from preserved bog bodies, such as Lindow Man (Stead, Bourke et al. 1986) and others from Britain (Turner and Scaife 1995). Bog bodies are extremely rare, but none-the-less provide an unparalleled line of evidence.

Instead, a study of dress for this period requires a mélange of archaeological sources utilising differing avenues of evidence from which we can piece together an approximation of how people may have looked. For example, in contrast to the classical author's assertions, there is evidence that people wore textile garments. The actual fibres do not often survive in the archaeological record, but can be found as impressions in metal corrosion.

Indirect evidence comes from the manufacturing tools used to produce textiles, for example: spindle whorls, loom weights, and weaving combs (DeRoche 1997). Other evidence for dress is derived from the objects that were worn on the body. Two of the best known artefacts from this period are both objects that were worn: the torc and the brooch. Other artefacts include finger-rings, beads, and bracelets. These objects were made from a variety of materials, including copper alloy, iron, glass, jet, and shale. In contrast to earlier and later periods, materials such as gold, silver, and amber were not used extensively in the Iron Age, but do figure in some limited geographical areas and periods. Artefacts, such as tweezers, and 'nail cleaners' hint that the body was carefully managed (Eckardt and Crummy 2008; Hill 1997), while small mortars and pestles are thought to have been connected to woad-based body paint or tattoos (Carr 2005).

Some of these objects would have been worn in close juxtaposition to the body and communicated information to the viewer about the identity of the wearer, perhaps regionality, community, family, and even the individual, such as gender or age (Roach-Higgins and Eicher 1995). Finally, there is evidence that the manipulation of hair and its presentation in different styles would have been important during this period (Aldhouse-Green 2004). Connections between objects and the human body are not restricted to these objects of dress, as other artefacts worn or utilised by a person may also have communicated information about the individual's identity. For example: a blacksmith wielding their hammer, a farmer holding a plough, an individual holding a sword or shield, or even a person holding a weaving comb would have imparted an immediate notion of the person's identity and role within society. While these objects are no less symbolic of a person's identity, they are tools or utilitarian objects that are much larger in size than the objects that attach to or otherwise modify a person's appearance. This research is primarily concerned with the objects sometimes referred to as objects of adornment, bodily adornment, or body ornaments, although their sole purpose may not have been to adorn the body.

Materiality during the Iron Age is generally considered to increase throughout the period as evidenced by the somewhat scarce numbers of artefacts in the earlier period, and the larger frequency and broader range of artefacts in the later Iron Age (Hill 1995a). For example, a greater range of pottery is available in the Later Iron Age of southeast Britain compared to earlier periods along with changes in the level of production intensity (Hamilton 2002), and in earlier periods cosmetic implements were relatively scarce compared to the number that are known from the Later Iron Age and Early Roman period (Eckardt 2008). Brooches too have been shown to follow this general trend as Early and Middle Iron Age brooches are fewer in number compared to the examples from Late Iron Age and early Roman Britain (Haselgrove 1997; Jundi and Hill 1997). However, recently excavated sites, such as at Grandcourt Quarry in Norfolk, may contradict this pattern. An exceptionally high number of brooches were found at this site in a deposition act(s) that may have occurred as early as the Middle Iron Age. Part of a wider change in foodways and eating habits, these brooches, along with the cosmetic equipment articles, are thought to indicate a changing attitude towards the body and establishing identity through the manipulation of appearance (Carr 2005; Hill 1997). This comes at a time when the archaeological record suggests greater contact with Europe in southern Britain and the circulation of a larger body of material culture after the Caesarian invasion in 55 BC and eventual conquest in AD 43. However, a comprehensive analysis of the differing types of artefacts of dress that cross type and material boundaries is currently lacking.

While many studies of Iron Age material culture related to dress frequently focus on metallic objects (e.g. brooches, pins, torcs, mirrors, cosmetic and toilet equipment), glass beads provide an interesting contrast as they are made from a different raw material. Glass, as with copper alloys, melts when heated to approximately 1,000°C, depending on the exact composition (Henderson 1985, 272). Although, from a modern standpoint it would be agreed that glass (being silica based) is different from copper alloy (derived from tin and copper ores), the melting properties of both materials may have meant, within the Iron Age world-view, that these two materials were more closely related than iron (un-meltable at this time, but still manipulated through heat) and copper alloy. This association is supported by the combination of these two materials on objects, such as some brooches and horse equipment. As a material, glass is made through the combination of three key ingredients: silica, soda, and lime. Unlike other meltable materials, the colour and opacity can be manipulated through the addition of oxides and minerals.

Beads are one of the earliest glass objects to be found in Britain. They are found in very small numbers from contexts that date to as early as the Bronze Age, for example, at the Wilsford G42 Bell Barrow (Guido, Henderson *et al.* 1984). Some Bronze Age beads are made from another 'glass-like' substance called faience, sometimes referred to as 'Egyptian faience' to distinguish it from a type of modern pottery. It is also a silica-based material, although not heated to a molten state as with true glass. Both Bronze Age and Roman period examples (the ubiquitous melon beads) are coated in a glaze, but they have a rougher texture than true glass and are always opaque. Beads made from true glass, however, are different. They range in size from very small (only a few millimeters in diameter) to very large (several centimeters in diameter). They come in several shapes, are made from different colours of glass, and some are decorated. They are found in Iron Age contexts in extremely large numbers (100+) at three key sites discussed throughout this work: Meare Lake Village in Somerset, Wetwang Slack in East Yorkshire, and Culbin Sands in Morayshire Scotland. However, these are unusual compared to the majority of sites discussed throughout the book where between one and twenty glass beads would be more usual. Unfortunately, many of the beads that have been recorded to date are old stray finds and can only be generally attributed to a known Iron Age site, or sometimes only to a village or parish.

This study has specifically chosen to focus on glass beads, as opposed to beads made from other materials, or other glass objects, for a number of reasons. Other glass objects, namely vessels, are confined to the very latest Iron Age and began to flourish from the Early Roman period (Frank 1982). Roman period glass vessels in Britain have been the subject of a long-standing history of study (e.g. Price and Cottam 1998). Glass beads, on the other hand, date to a much earlier period, as they have been found in Bronze Age contexts (albeit in extremely limited numbers) and the Iron Age, where they occur in relatively larger numbers (Guido 1978a). Beads made from other materials (i.e. clay, jet, amber, other types of stone; and possibly wood or bone), however, are problematic. They are found in very small numbers throughout the Iron Age and because they lack stylistic characteristics, they are very difficult to date without contextual information (c.f. the 62 examples from Grandcourt Quarry (Malone 2010), which may change our perspective on this). In cases where they appear to be deposited within Iron Age contexts, it is unclear as to how they were used in society at that time, or perhaps as to whether they were manufactured at an even earlier date. Interestingly, there does not seem to be a strong tradition of using beads made from other materials that was eventually replaced by what became a tradition for using glass beads. The previous significant period of major bead use in Britain dates back to the Early Bronze Age and the utilisation of intricate jet necklaces (Sheridan and Davis 2002). Therefore, it seems that the use of glass beads during the Iron Age was an entirely new type of bodily adornment, as it not only drew upon a new raw material, but was also formed into a new type of object that was not used in significant numbers immediately prior to this period. In the future, a study that includes beads of other materials will be an interesting area of further research.

Despite the recognition of glass beads from Iron Age contexts, there is a limited appreciation of their broader implications. Why were they made in specific colours? How were they used? Where are they found? And more generally, how can we incorporate them into a wider understanding of Iron Age dress in Britain? This chapter will introduce some of the background to the previous approaches to the study of glass beads, followed by a discussion of the aims of research, research methodology, and finally a roadmap to the contents of the work.

An Introduction to Previous Studies of Glass Beads

In comparison to other Iron Age artefacts (pottery, coins, brooches), the study of glass beads has been largely neglected. Some of the earliest mentions of Iron Age glass beads come from records of donations published in society proceedings (e.g. *Proceedings of the Society of Antiquaries of Scotland*), but they were also listed within early excavation small finds reports. However, it seems that glass beads were not considered to be important for dating or understanding site chronology in the same way that other objects, such as brooches or pottery, were used. In most early site reports glass beads were simply listed with other objects, but analysis or interpretation did not often go beyond this, for example at Glastonbury Lake Village (Bulleid and Gray 1917).

In the mid-twentieth century, Margaret Guido (1978a) undertook a project to catalogue prehistoric glass beads from Britain and Ireland. This subsequently led to the creation of a typology based on visual characteristics. The corpus has been the only major published work on glass beads from Britain as a whole. Drawing on Guido's typology, Julian Henderson (1982) examined the chemical composition of Iron Age glass beads using x-ray fluorescence (XRF). One of the aims of his research was to use his scientific analyses to expand on Guido's visual classification by adding a composition component. More recently, Martina Bertini (2012) has pioneered work on Iron Age glass beads by combining several different types of analyses. This has allowed her to examine the chemical composition and to map the morphology of Guido Classes 13 and 14 beads, which indicates the process of manufacture (all three studies are discussed in more detail in Chapter 2).

Guido's work was an important foundation for all subsequent studies of glass beads. Her catalogue alone is a valuable resource, as it presented a fairly accurate list of all known Iron Age glass beads at the time of publication, except for contemporary ongoing excavations. Her distribution maps suggest that the concentration of glass beads across Britain was varied (discussed further in Chapter 2). Generally, southern Britain was distinguishable from the rest of Britain in terms of overall density, but the Somerset area has long been identified as an area where glass beads have been found in particularly large numbers. However, other areas have been recognised as areas of high glass bead density, such as East Yorkshire and Northeast Scotland. Although, recent finds (e.g. Llandygai in North Wales in Kenney 2008; and Grandcourt Quarry in Norfolk in Malone 2010) suggest that the Britain-wide distribution is continually changing and re-assessment is necessary.

The manufacturing origin of glass beads continues to be an enigma. Comparisons with known European material by Guido suggested that some glass beads found in Britain were not found in Europe, leading to the hypothesis that some of these beads were actually manufactured in Britain. Guido (1978a, 32-7) proposed several possible major production centres (Meare Lake Village, Somerset; Culbin Sands, Morayshire; Glastonbury Lake Village, Somerset; Glenluce Sands, Dumfries and Galloway; Traprain Law and Newstead in the Scottish Borders, and Wilderspool near Warrington), and a number of less probable sites (Covesea Cave, Morayshire; and Caerhun, Clwyd). Her suggestions appear to be based solely on the higher frequency of glass beads at these particular locations. A number of glass beads, however, bear a striking resemblance to examples found in European Iron Age contexts. The similarity was taken to indicate that the movement (migration/invasion) of people could be tracked by the dispersal of glass beads. At the time of her publication, there was very little in the way of other archaeological material that could support her hypothesis that glass bead manufacturing occurred in Britain (see Chapter 2).

Despite the assertion in the Iron Age research framework that the subject of glass beads is an area where a 'substantial understanding has been achieved' (Haselgrove, Armit *et al.* 2001, 22), as with any research, the time that has elapsed since Guido's publication has resulted in many unanswered questions. Since her publication, there has been an explosion in archaeological excavation resulting primarily from the implementation of PPG16 in England in 1990 and NPPG5 in Scotland in 1994. Despite the increasing amount of data regarding prehistoric settlements and material culture that this has produced (Bradley 2007), there has been no recent published attempt at creating a major synthesis of recently discovered glass beads, nor has there been any critical discussion of the Guido typology and interpretations (cf. Armit 1991 for Atlantic Scotland).

Aims of Current Research

As introduced above, a comprehensive understanding of Iron Age dress in Britain is currently lacking. In order to address this issue, the present study focuses on glass beads from this period, to provide a useful contrast to the often metal-dominated studies of artefacts related to dress (e.g. Fox 1958; Garrow and Gosden 2012; Jacobsthal 1969; Jope 2000; MacGregor 1976; Piggott 1970). However, it is essential to go beyond one type of object and instead to draw on many types in order to understand the full assemblage of material culture used in dress throughout Iron Age Britain. Therefore, there are three main aims to this research:

1. To undertake a systematic review of the appearance, chronology, and deposition of glass beads;
2. To place glass beads within the wider context of other objects used in dress;
3. To develop a narrative of dress in Iron Age Britain.

The first aim not only draws on data regarding the physical appearance of glass beads, but also on the wider circumstances of where they were found. It seeks to answer questions about glass beads, such as: their appearance, the date of the context that they were found in, and the kinds of sites they were found at. The second aim examines how the beads were used and how they relate to other objects of dress. For this comparative aspect, five other key types of objects are included: brooches, bracelets, finger-rings, torcs, and pins. Finally, the third aim seeks to contextualise beads by drawing together multiple lines of evidence from artefacts, and burial data as it is recognised that artefacts should not be seen in isolation.

Methodology

This section discusses the methodology employed prior, during, and after the collection of data. The material presented here is pertinent to understanding the following data analysis chapters. It will first examine a number of issues identified during two pilot studies. Then it will discuss how the four study regions were selected, followed by a discussion of how the data was obtained and organised within a database. The terminology used throughout the analysis chapters is then detailed, and finally, this chapter will discuss the methods used during analysis.

Identified Issues

The methodology and terminology used here was developed out of preliminary work on glass beads and other artefacts during a pilot study conducted between 2008-09 for a Masters degree (Schech 2009). This study examined the use of glass beads during the Iron Age and Roman period within the Tyne-Forth region. One of the interesting results from this preliminary study was that glass beads were more numerous at Roman forts rather than at other settlements, whether Roman or non-Roman in style. From the bead data, there was not a strong difference between 'Roman' identities in this region and what have sometimes been referred to as 'native' identities. However, compared to other types of objects related to dress, they were the most abundant object. A second, smaller, pilot-study was conducted during the initial stages of the present research, which focused on Northeast Scotland. The aim was to test the proposed methodology that developed out of the MA research over a different region. The methodology was further refined and subsequently used over three additional regions.

It is from these initial analyses that some issues became apparent that would need to be addressed during the course of the research. Although this study is about glass beads and Iron Age dress, it also seeks to bring to light a number of issues with the study of artefacts. In the past, studies have often been limited to catalogues, description of types, and descriptions of their distributions (e.g. Fowler 1960; Fowler 1953; Mackreth 2011; Stead 2006). While these basic studies are clearly needed to provide fundamental information about material culture during the Iron Age (Haselgrove, Armit *et al.* 2001), they need to move beyond these tools in order to develop an understanding of not only production and methods of distribution, use, and finally deposition, but also what we can learn about society from artefacts.

A second topic that was identified during the pilot-studies was the use of terminology used to designate chronology or cultural periods. This includes terms, such as 'native', 'Roman', and 'Romano-British', which at times refers to the date of the artefact (i.e. pre-Roman or post-Roman conquest), and at other times refers to the culture of the object (i.e. pre-Roman, post-Roman conquest but non-Roman, or Roman). The issues of identity and cultural interaction during this period has long been a topic of discussion (e.g. Haverfield 1915; Mattingly 1997a; Millett 1990; Webster and Cooper 1996), and while these labels might be convenient, it does create confusion as to how the occupants at these sites thought of themselves. In addition, the idea of degrees of Romanisation further complicates this issue as it is often implied that this was something desirable and the natural course of society. In the case of glass beads, what would usually be considered typical 'Iron Age' examples that have been found on 'Roman' sites are explained as being residual, rather than suggesting that social interactions at such sites may have been more complex than a native/Roman duality (e.g. Hunter 2001b; 2007a; b).

Another area that was identified as potentially problematic was in the quality of the descriptions in written artefact reports. This was encountered during the MA pilot-study, where written descriptions were primarily relied upon. The pilot-study conducted during the initial stages of the current research was able to test the quality of published descriptions by viewing the artefacts first hand. It was quickly discovered that descriptions and illustrations do not always adequately describe the artefacts to the level of detail needed for the analyses to be conducted in subsequent chapters. In part this is due to an unclear understanding of the standards necessary for reporting many later prehistoric artefacts: a clear framework would be of benefit (see Appendix A). Furthermore, discussions with museum staff often brought to light glass beads that were previously unpublished and thus unknown.

One other issue identified was the impact of developer-funded excavations. The MA pilot-study investigated all unpublished reports held in the Historic Environment Record offices in County Durham and Northumberland, and the RCAHMS that contained evidence for Iron Age or Roman period archaeological evidence from excavation. Although very few new beads were identified in this way, it was unclear if this was a reflection of regional material culture, as only limited numbers of Iron Age glass beads were known from this region as recorded in the Guido catalogue. In contrast, the initial pilot-study conducted over Northeast Scotland identified several glass beads that were found during developer-led excavation, including the nationally important site of Culduthel Farm near Inverness (Murray 2007a). This suggested that there was potential for discovery of glass beads through a review of developer-led excavation.

In order to address these issues a clear and consistent methodology was needed in order to perform a detailed and rigorous analysis of the data. This included the identification of key aspects of glass beads that would be informative through analysis and the terminology needed in order to record data. One of the outcomes of this was the recognition that the Guido (1978a) typology is not suitable for the detailed analyses needed here in order to complete the aims of the study. Chapter 5 presents an analysis of the Guido typology and explains the development of the new typology. However, the aim of this research is not simply to devise a new typology and catalogue, but to put glass beads into a social context through an examination of their use and deposition. This has been a growing theme in on-going and recently completed doctoral theses as seen at recent student conferences[1] and new approaches to understanding Celtic Art (Garrow and Gosden 2012; Garrow, Gosden *et al.* 2008). It is these approaches that the analysis of glass bead context draws upon in Chapter 7.

Study Regions

Guido's original catalogue contains entries for over 1,000 glass beads that were found from a variety of circumstances up until about the 1970s. During the data collection phase of the present work, it was found that the actual quantity of glass beads within the study regions (to be discussed below) as recorded by Guido, was relatively accurate. Thus, her catalogue could be said to be a reliable reflection of glass beads thought to be of Iron Age date in the 1970s. However, the catalogue has been the only data-set available for glass beads throughout Britain (Henderson's (1982) catalogue was based on Guido's). Although both Guido and Henderson studied glass beads on a Britain-wide scale (and Guido included Ireland), considering the level of detail utilised in the current study this wide-scale geographic approach would be inappropriate. Instead, the selection of small geographic areas of study was vital.

---

[1] Iron Age Research Student Symposium/Seminar held in 2010 at Bradford, 2011 in Durham, 2012 at Southampton, and 2013 at Hull/Bradford.

To understand the available data better, distribution maps were created using Guido's catalogue. This allowed areas of high and low bead density to be identified (Figure 1). Drawing on this summary distribution map, Guido's class based distribution maps and her interpretations (1978a), four regions were selected for in-depth study: Southwest England, East Anglia, East Yorkshire, and Northeast Scotland (Figure 2). 'Southwest England' covered most of Dorset, Somerset, North Somerset, South Gloucestershire, Gloucestershire, Northeast Somerset and Bath, Bristol City, and Wiltshire; and 'Northeast Scotland' covered the old counties of Aberdeenshire, Banffshire, Morayshire, and Inverness-shire. These two regions were chosen for similar reasons. They are both areas of high bead density and each contained a site where more than 100 beads were found. In Southwest England this was Meare Lake Village, Somerset, and Culbin Sands, Morayshire in Northeast Scotland. Guido considered both of these sites to be possible locations of glass bead manufacturing. However, glass beads were not restricted to these single sites. They have been recorded from many other sites within the region.

East Yorkshire was also chosen as a region of study due to the large number of glass beads that were known from this area. In contrast to Southwest England and Northeast Scotland, the beads in this region were found from a very small number of human burials and were very much isolated to these occurrences. Although Guido only included the Queen's Barrow at Arras and Barrow L at Cowlam in her 1978 catalogue, it was also known at the time of the research design that the excavations at Wetwang Slack also uncovered many glass beads and that this added to the numbers from this region. This area was chosen as another study region due to the significant number of beads and the context they were found in (which is markedly different from the other regions). The boundaries of the region were extended further west to the A1(M) in the hope of being able to place the burial evidence into a wider context within the surrounding region.

The first three regions were chosen for study because of the high frequency of glass beads and the likelihood that they constituted a significant element of dress during the Iron Age in those areas. In order to assess whether Guido's distributions remain an accurate reflection of bead prevalence, a final region was chosen. The distribution map formed from Guido's original catalogue highlights a number of seemingly blank areas where glass beads apparently did not occur. This posed an interesting question: might the increasing amount of archaeological investigations since the 1970s, particularly as a result of developer-funded archaeology, mean such variations in distributions were no longer accurate? At the time, initial data from the recent Celtic Art project led by Duncan Garrow (2008) had been published with tantalising distribution maps of Celtic Art, coins, and other objects.

These distribution maps indicated East Anglia as an area where metalwork was most widespread. In comparison, Guido's distribution maps of glass beads showed that very few glass beads (many of which were Roman) were found in this region. Due to the discrepancies between the number of metal and glass artefacts in East Anglia (defined here as Norfolk and Suffolk), this region became an ideal subject for further investigation.

Data Acquisition and Organisation

A regional approach to glass beads was undertaken using the four study regions set out in the preceding section. As the Guido catalogue already suggested that a large numbers of glass beads would be involved, it was imperative that a consistent method be used in order to obtain accurate and quality data. This was achieved through the use of a database. Detailed information was recorded for both artefacts and sites using the following parameters:

1. **Sites:** all sites with Iron Age and/or Roman activity that have been excavated (purposefully excluding non-excavated (i.e. surveyed) sites);
2. **Artefacts**: all artefacts related to bodily adornment from the sites identified by parameter 1.

Data was obtained from three main sources: published research excavation reports, published and unpublished ('grey-literature') developer-funded reports, and from first-hand observations of artefacts. In order to cover as many sites as possible, entire runs of local/regional journals were surveyed for any excavation reports that encountered Iron Age and/or Roman period material. While many of the larger and more significant developer-led excavations are published either as monographs or as journal articles, the majority are not easily available. Therefore, unpublished grey-literature was accessed at Historic Environment Record (HER) offices in England, and at the Royal Commission on the Ancient and Historical Monuments of Scotland (RCAHMS). In total, it was possible to visit 10 HER offices in England, including: Dorset, Somerset, Gloucestershire, Bristol City, Norfolk, Suffolk, North Yorkshire, North Yorkshire Moor National Park, Humber Archaeology Partnership, and City of York. Where it was not possible to visit an HER in the study region (Wiltshire, North Somerset), grey literature reports were accessed through the OASIS database available on the *Archaeology Data Service* website.

The final main source for data came from actual examination of artefacts in museums, which included stray finds. In total, it was possible to visit twenty-one museums, including: the British Museum, National museum of Scotland, Museum of Somerset, Wiltshire Heritage Museum, Dorchester Museum, Gloucester Museum, Poole Museum, Gillingham Museum

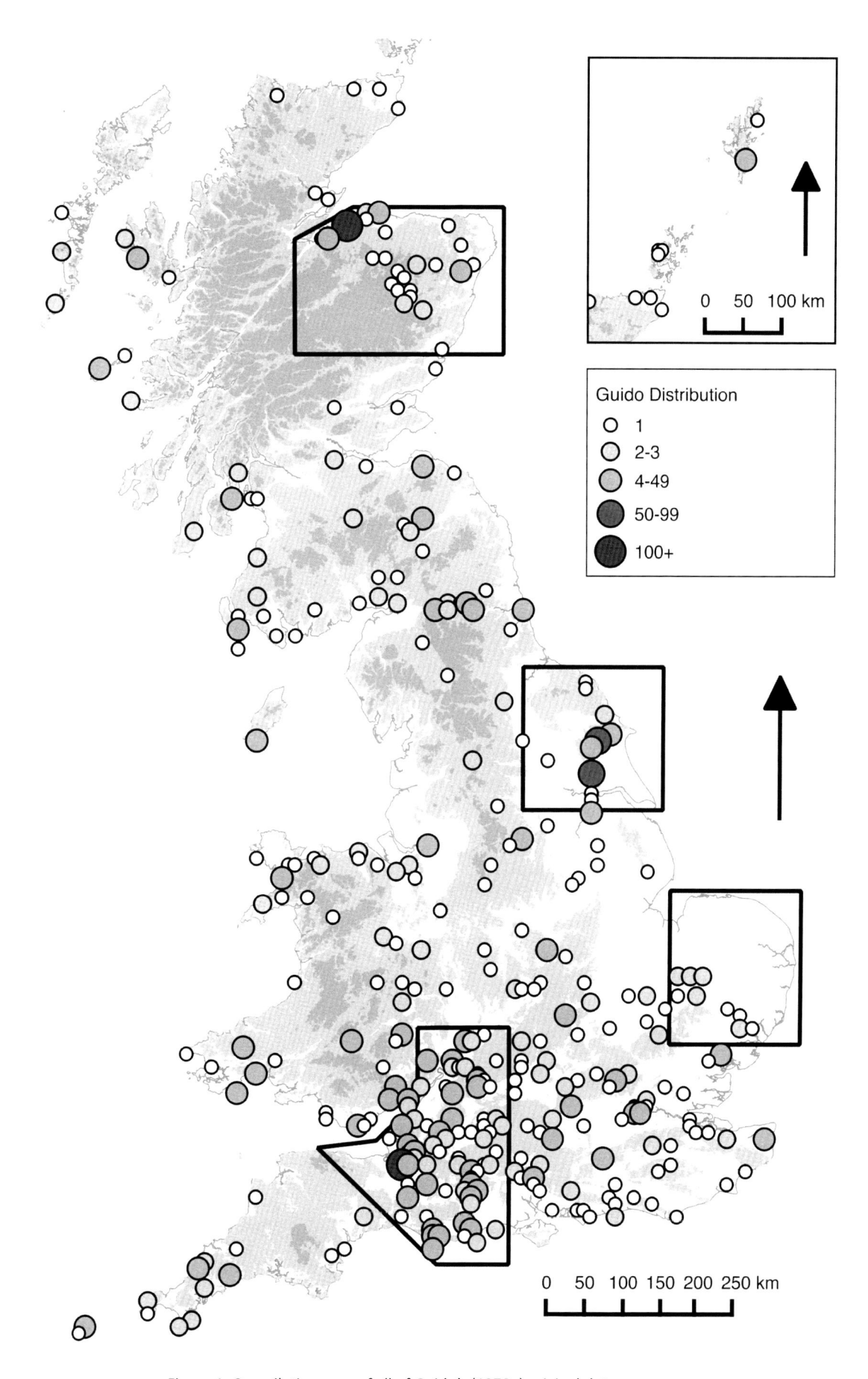

Figure 1: Compilation map of all of Guido's (1978a) original data.

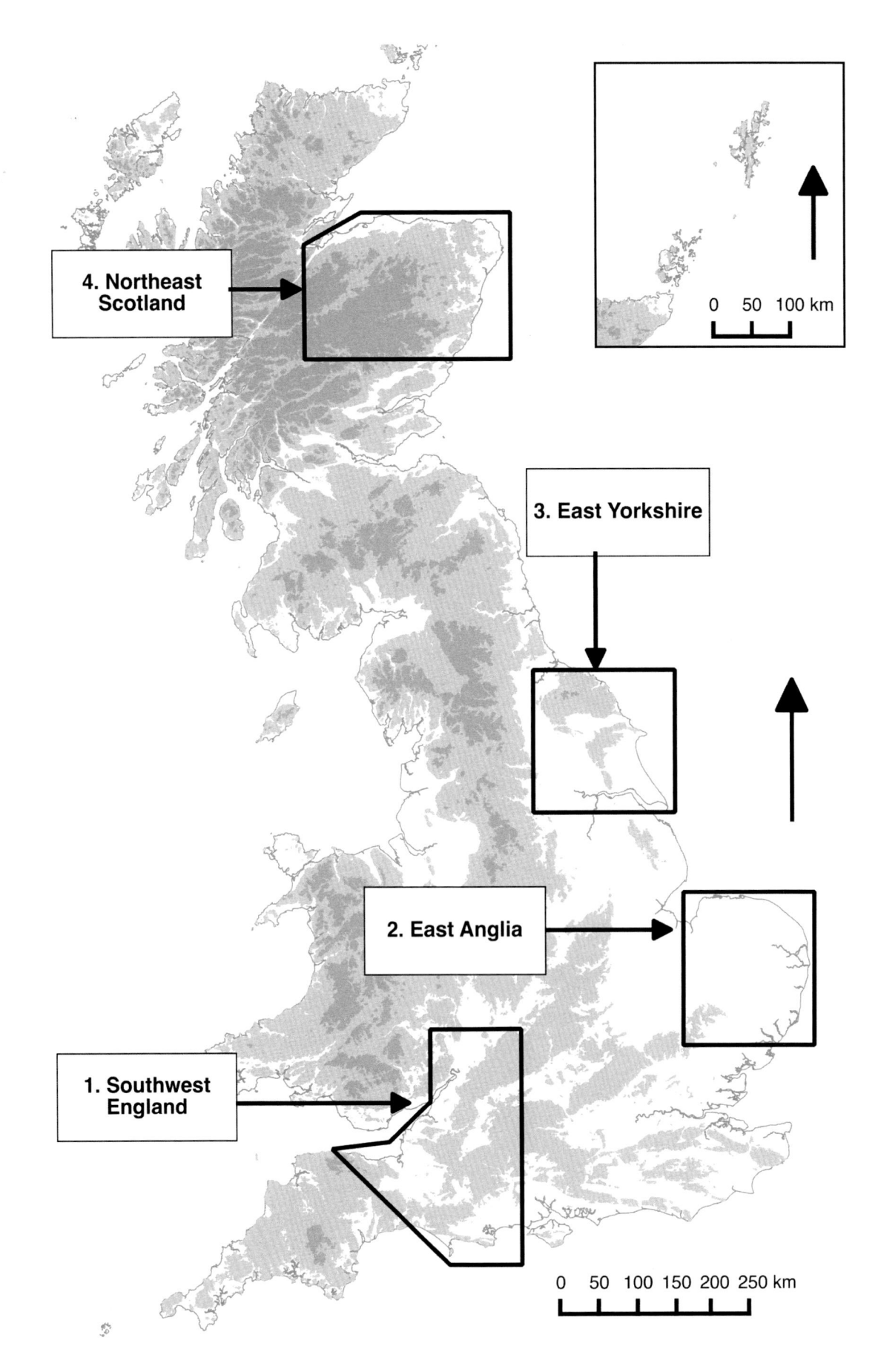

Figure 2: Identification of project study regions.

(Dorset), Bristol City Museum, Red House Museum (Christchurch), Corinium Museum, Stroud Museum, Ashmolean, Norwich Castle Museum, Yorkshire Museum, Hull Museum, Marischal Museum, Forres Museum, Elgin Museum, Hunterian Museum, and Inverness City Museum. Although all museums in the study regions could not be visited, first hand analysis of glass beads was extremely beneficial. In some cases published descriptions only needed to be verified, but for others additional details could be gathered. Methods of recording data were continually improved over the course of the data-collection, while insuring that consistency was maintained. Key data included: dimensions, weight, description of colour and decorative motif, shape of perforation, modifications, and completeness (see Appendix A). This was accomplished through the use of a digital caliper with a resolution of 0.1mm and an accuracy of ±0.2mm. A digital scale was used with an accuracy of 0.01g up to 100g. Finally, multiple high-resolution digital photographs were taken of each bead from multiple angles in order to ensure full coverage.

All of the data from both written sources and visual analysis was compiled into the database. Each artefact had a separate entry even when found together, such as in burial features. Through firsthand analysis and studies of context, it became clear that each individual bead was, or could have been, treated separately and would have had its own individual biography. The recording method ensures that each individual object is considered on its own merits and permits comparison in statistical software.

In addition to the glass beads that were recovered, other artefacts related to dress that were found during excavation were also recorded (e.g. brooches, pendants, bracelets, etc.). In addition, other data sources were added, as many significant artefacts were not found during excavation. This primarily included relevant artefacts from the Portable Antiquities Scheme database (2003), MacGregor's (1976) catalogue of Northern Celtic Art, and the Celtic Art Database (Gwilt, Joy et al. August 2010).

As with any research methodology, there were a number of issues encountered during the data collection. The following describes some of the issues encountered during data-collection, which may have some bearing on final interpretations:

1. **Inconsistencies in excavation reports.** The data-collection process dealt with 1,699 excavations reports produced over a period of at least 100 years. Over this period, both the excavation and recording methodology employed changed drastically, and the quality varied between reports.

2. **Lack of illustrations in reports.** Reports often contained very vague descriptions of artefacts discovered and did not always include an illustration.
3. **Additional data on supplemental material.** Technological changes have rendered some data inaccessible (e.g. micro-fiche).
4. **Developer-funded excavation reports.** For consistency, a request was made to each Historic Environment Record Office for all excavations that recovered Iron Age and/or Roman period activity. Due to differences in recording practices in HER databases and the sheer quantity of reports, in some cases only a sample could be included in the analyses (e.g. a 40% sample of reports at Gloucester and a 75% sample at Suffolk).

While these issues may have some bearing on the data and final interpretations, it seems likely that, by completing either a 100% survey at each HER, or by visiting the missing HERs, the final interpretation would not be significantly different. The primary reason for including every site that had been excavated where Iron Age and Roman material was found was to assess whether new Iron Age glass beads had been found during developer-funded excavation. In the few cases that this did happen, the reports had already been published either as monographs or in local journals, or knowledge was passed on by museum curators, local HER staff, and through other networks. There were in fact very few glass beads encountered in the developer-funded excavation reports that were added to the database in the first instance due to discovery at the HER offices. However, the second reason for including every excavation with Iron Age and Roman period evidence was to contrast sites where glass beads had been found, with the negative evidence showing where excavations had taken place, but no Iron Age glass beads had been discovered (see Chapter 7).

Analyses

Prior to analysis, the data was checked for consistency and accuracy. For example, Guido's catalogue contained several duplicate entries that needed to be deleted. Following database cleanup, an extraction from the database was converted into SPSS files (Windows, version 19.0.0) for analysis. Using SPSS, it was possible to evaluate the data that is discussed in later chapters. This was done using a variety of means, depending on the types of data. Bead size analyses were conducted using ranges, averages, and standard deviations. They were also plotted through the use of histograms and scatter-graphs. Other categorical descriptive data, such as colour, decorative motif, and types were compared through the use of bar charts and tables showing frequencies. Bar charts and tables were also used to compare sites and material culture. In a few instances, it was possible to carry out a Chi-square test using the data, but in order to make the data valid smaller categories were combined (Fletcher and Lock 2005, 131).

Although every effort was made to examine as many glass beads as possible, as already highlighted in this chapter, this was not always feasible. The number of possible beads for analysis in the follow chapters amounts to 1,788 individual specimens. Many of these were seen first-hand, but for others written descriptions needed to be relied on. In some cases, data was not available to the detail needed for analysis. In order to be as explicit as possible for each analysis, the number of beads that are included is stated, as some were necessarily left out due to missing data.

Spatial data was explored through the use of mapping software. These maps show the locations, distributions, and density of sites and objects and were created using QGIS (For Mac, 2.4.0 Chugiak). While exact find spots or sites are known for many examples, unfortunately, there is a large number of stray that rely on villages or towns to describe provenance. In some cases, these are only known at the parish or administrative district/county level. In these cases, beads have been left out of distributional maps, as their area of origin is too vague. In each section the analysis carried out is described in detail.

Layout

The following three chapters form the background to the analyses. Chapter 2 provides an in-depth discussion on the Guido typology, and the context of other Iron Age glass bead typologies and glass bead studies that cover the European Iron Age. Chapter 3 introduces many of the theoretical concepts that the interpretations are based upon, especially in terms of dress and object studies. Finally, the last of these preliminary chapters (Chapter 4) addresses the nature of the archaeological resource in each region and implications for a study of glass beads.

Following these introductory chapters, Chapter 5 follows on from the discussion of the Guido typology presented in Chapter 2, by critiquing its use and some of the inherent issues in its construction. With these issues in mind, as well as the aims of this research, a new typology is proposed that is utilised throughout the remainder of the book. Chapter 6 uses data obtained for glass beads and analyses regional characteristics of beads, including: size, shape, colour, and decorative motif. This is followed by Chapter 7, which explores the archaeological contexts in which glass beads have been found. Then, Chapter 8 places glass beads into a wider discussion of dress in the Iron Age by examining at the evidence for how glass beads were used. Finally, Chapter 9 summarises the analysis and presents a final interpretation about dress, identity, and Iron Age objects.

To supplement the main text, there are a number of appendices. Appendix A is a glossary of terms used throughout the book and guidelines for reporting on glass beads. Appendix B describes each of the Guido types for reference, while Appendix C is a complete list of types proposed by the new typology. 'A full catalogue of the sites and glass beads discussed throughout is included on the accompanying data download. Some of these are also illustrated in Figures 189-194.

Chapter 2
Previous Approaches to Glass Beads

Despite their colourful appearance, Iron Age glass beads did not extensively preoccupy antiquarians. One of the earliest discussions is that of Akerman (1852), who published a drawing of some glass beads from a private collection, with descriptions of the items. These were noted to be from a variety of different sites from Britain and elsewhere, but there was little recognition of any differences in date. In 1906, Greenwell published a summary article that illustrated many of the finds excavated in East Yorkshire. The remarks on beads in these earlier publications are generally descriptive. The best example of consistent recording in publication comes from Scotland, where the *Proceedings of the Society of Antiquaries of Scotland* regularly recorded objects that were donated or bought and subsequently became a part of the National Museum of Scotland's collections. The entries of these acquisitions were often limited to the name of the donor/seller, a brief description, and the town or parish that the bead was found in. Sometimes a description of the activity that led to the discovery was also included such as 'peat-digging' or 'trench-digging'. Finally, two articles were also published in the proceedings that discuss charms and amulets (Black 1891; Simpson 1862). Both articles discuss glass beads, which seem to refer to beads that were later speculated to be of Iron Age date.

Within the early antiquarian published literature, there is very little additional indication of interest in Iron Age glass beads. In contrast, many examples within museums were acquired during this antiquarian period, so they were clearly known. It seems that there was very little initiative to study them in greater detail at this time. The remainder of this chapter will explore the major approaches to the study of glass beads and some critiques that can be made. It will also discuss evidence for glass bead manufacturing and craft and begin to place the British evidence within a wider European context.

Guido Typology

Prior to Guido's (1978a) study, a comprehensive understanding of Iron Age glass beads in Britain was non-existent (although for regional/site typologies see: Bulleid and Gray 1917; Dent 1984; Stead 1979). For the first time, her study provided an overview ranging from the Late Bronze Age, through the Iron Age, and into the Roman period. At the time, there was no consistent research that separated prehistoric and early historic beads. This presented a problem for her research, and a second volume followed her initial publication, which dealt with Anglo-Saxon beads (Guido 1999). Bringing together this large quantity of evidence for beads from prehistory through to the early historic period was clearly a massive undertaking, as she was working for the first time with an artefact that had seen little more than anecdotal descriptions within the literature. Her study provided the first systematic method for cataloguing and describing glass beads.

As an archaeologist, Margaret Guido in part remains a mystery. She was married to Stuart Piggot, and together in the 1930s they were a part of the team that uncovered Sutton Hoo in Suffolk (Guido 1999, x). Later, after Stuart's appointment in Edinburgh, she undertook excavations at Hownam Rings in Roxburghshire Scotland in 1948 (Piggott 1947-48), followed by other excavations in the region (Piggott 1948; 1949; 1953). These excavations drew heavily on the Hawkes/Piggott (Hawkes 1958; Piggott 1966) framework for the Iron Age and attempted to test them (ScARF 2012, 6). The aims of this excavation were framed in terms of cultures that built and used this hillfort, and would later serve as a model for hillforts in eastern Scotland (Armit 1999). Although she encountered very few glass beads during these excavations, she later credited her study to suggestions by Dr Donald Harden (Guido 1978a, vi), who commented on the small glass bead from Bonchester Hill (Piggott 1949, 129). As Guido's data collection ended some time in the 1970s, prior to publication in 1978, she potentially spent some twenty years on the catalogue and typology. The influence of the Hawkes and Piggott model are clear within her study, as she often references invasions of different cultures, and the equation of artefacts with particular cultural groups. By the time of publication, much had changed in studies of Iron Age Britain, including Graham Clark's (1966) critique of the invasion hypothesis and the introduction of the 'New Archaeology'. It is unfortunate that despite being such an important foundational work on Iron Age material culture studies, that in terms of the changing theoretical approaches at the time, Guido's publication was already out of date.

Guido's work in effect drew the line between the end of prehistory and the beginning of history for British glass bead studies. This became an overarching theme that pervaded her typology. At its heart, the typology is based on a meaningful and clear distinction between culturally pre-Roman, Roman, and early historic period beads. Although she admitted that there were a few cases where prehistoric beads were found at Roman period sites, these were a minority of cases (Guido 1978a, 26). Due to the perceived limitation in cross-over of types and extended use of beads, it was thought that the beads could be useful to the archaeologist, which in turn meant that they could be used as type-fossils to date excavated contexts (Guido 1978a, vi). In addition to ascertaining the chronological limits of each type, Guido (1978a, 26) suggested that beads could also be used to '…indicate tribal concentrations, folk movements, and commercial contacts, both within Britain itself and in the wider context of Europe'. Thus, she assumed that not only was each type limited by the length of time it was used, but also by the people that used them.

Within the Guido typology, there is a clear distinction between two main types of Iron Age or 'native' glass beads. There are those from the c. third century BC onwards that were manufactured in Britain, and a group of earlier beads that were manufactured in continental Europe and imported either through commercial contacts or migration (Guido 1978a, 30). Somewhat confusingly, she proposed that some of the beads that resemble the continental examples may in fact have been later copies made in Britain (Guido 1978a, 25). Therefore, the second major division within her typology is dependent on assumptions about where particular beads were manufactured. Throughout the typology, it is suggested, though never explicitly stated, that movement of beads and people was uni-directional: always from continental Europe *to* Britain. The possibility that beads manufactured in Britain might have been a desirable commodity in Europe is a topic that was never discussed. This may be due to a number of reasons, such as the number of reports on Iron Age excavations in Europe that were available to Guido, which placed limitations on her interpretation (1978a, 4). However, in the case of one particular class of 'British' bead (Class 13) she did suggest that similar types can be found on the continent, but she suggested they were only superficially similar (Guido 1978a, 85).

The unidirectional movement of glass beads also enveloped Guido's interpretation of the value of glass beads. She considered them to be highly valuable, luxury items (Guido 1978a, 28). Iron Age Britons had to trade something in exchange for glass beads, but only after their basic living needs had been met (Guido 1978a, 28). Thus, in areas that were poor, this could not happen, although this impoverished state could be the result of two factors: natural environment or enforced by outsiders (i.e. Romans). For example, despite a thriving trade in tin, the miners in Devon and Cornwall were unable to afford luxuries due to their poor environmental conditions and difficulty in acquiring nourishment, while in Norfolk and Suffolk the Romans suppressed the inhabitants after the Boudican rebellion, who then had no resources to trade for glass beads (Guido 1978a, 28). Therefore, Guido suggested that the presence and quantity of glass beads directly reflects the social and political environment. In contrast, today we would discuss other mechanisms by which material culture could be exchanged, using both archaeological and ethnographic evidence; for example, through gift exchange (Gosden 1985; Mauss 1990 (1950); Sharples 2010), the importance of artefact biography (Appadurai 1986; Gosden and Marshall 1999; Kopytoff 1986), and the idea that material culture does not reflect poverty, but instead reflects social choices (Moore 2007a).

Despite the apparent impoverishment of some areas, Guido (1978a, 28) suggested that there was nevertheless a thriving trade of glass beads amongst the more socially interconnected areas of southern Britain, especially around the Bristol Channel. However, Guido suggests that the influx of glass beads from the continent was unable to keep up with demand. Thus, local manufacturing developed (1978a, 27-8), probably around the third century BC. In this case, relative glass bead density was used to propose possible locations of manufacture. Two major sites with the largest number of glass beads at the time of Guido's research were Meare Lake Village, Somerset, and Culbin Sands, Morayshire. As the number of finds at both locations exceeded 100 beads and multiple types were present, these sites were considered to be the most significant for manufacture in Britain. In fact, Guido suggested that, due to the similarity in beads from both locations, glassworkers migrated from Somerset to Morayshire to continue their craft, albeit at what she considered to be a lower standard of quality (Guido 1978a, 35, 76, 85-9). Other locations considered to be possible centres of manufacture due to the prevalence of beads include: Glastonbury Lake Village, Somerset, Glenluce Sands, Wigtownshire, Traprain Law, East Lothian, and Newstead, Scottish Borders (Guido 1978a, 32-7). Only a few sites have been considered to be glass manufacturing centres based on alternative evidence, such as the raw glass at Hengistbury Head, Dorset (Guido 1978a, 29). Although there is no evidence to suggest that raw glass was manufactured in Britain at this time, other sources have been suggested, such as the re-use of glass armlets, as well as Roman vessel glass (Guido 1978a, 30-1).

By the time of the Roman occupation in Britain, Guido proposed that the use of glass beads changed dramatically. The thriving bead manufacturing industry in Britain diminished and eventually ended around the time of the Roman conquest (Guido 1978a, 29). In addition, the use of 'native' beads also ended and, by the mid-second century AD, only the standardised Roman types were used (Guido 1978a, 37). Large, decorated, and colourful beads only returned after the end of the Roman occupation (Guido 1978a, 29) in the Anglo-Saxon period. This is emphasised by the distinction between pre-Roman, Roman, and early historic glass beads within Guido's framework. The implication

PREVIOUS APPROACHES TO GLASS BEADS

Figure 3: Guido's (redrawn after 1978a Figure 1) sixteen decorative motifs.

of these divisions is that there were distinct 'native' identities portrayed through the use of 'native' beads, while 'Roman' identity was displayed using Roman types. There is little consideration of the heirloom effect and the possibility that these beads continued to have use and significant meaning post-conquest.

Turning now to specifically examine Guido's typology, she was explicit regarding her method. Although there were already a number of seemingly universal approaches to categorising this type of artefact (e.g. Beck 1928; Kidd and Kidd 1970; Van der Sleen 1967), Guido chose not to utilise any of these methods as 'a badly made bead can very easily be removed from the Class or type to which reason and experience tell us it more properly belongs' (Guido 1978a, 4-5). This suggests she thought that a rigorous method for determining the type would have been too strict. Instead, she borrowed from Beck's classification system: form, perforation colour, material, and decoration (Beck 1928), to which she added 'dimensions, translucency or opacity, method of manufacture…some kind of analysis…approximate or exact date of archaeological context in which it was found…and its position in relation to a burial…' (Guido 1978a, 5). As part of these criteria, she identified 16 different decorative motifs (Figure 3), 7 methods of manufacture (after Van der Sleen 1967), and a range of opaque and translucent glass colours.

The results of Guido's data collection led to the creation of 14 Classes and 8 Groups of Iron Age glass beads, and 16 types of Roman glass beads (Figure 4). Classes 1 to 7 are Iron Age glass beads types that she considered to be manufactured on the continent, or potential British copies. Classes 8 to 14, on the other hand, are British beads manufactured according to local tastes and aesthetics. The Classes have chronological and spatial significance, and can be used to date contexts. In contrast, the eight Groups are less precise as some examples date to the Iron Age, while other examples even within the same type may date to the Roman period or potentially even later. Group 8 was specifically designated as 'exotic beads of Iron Age date', which seems to have served as a category for examples that did not fit in with the other beads. A complete description of each of Guido's classes and groups is given in Appendix B.

Decorative motif is the main characteristic that defines the different groups and classes, with colour playing a secondary role. This is especially apparent in Class 7. This class is defined by similarity in decorative motif (rays or whirls), but divided into sub-types based on

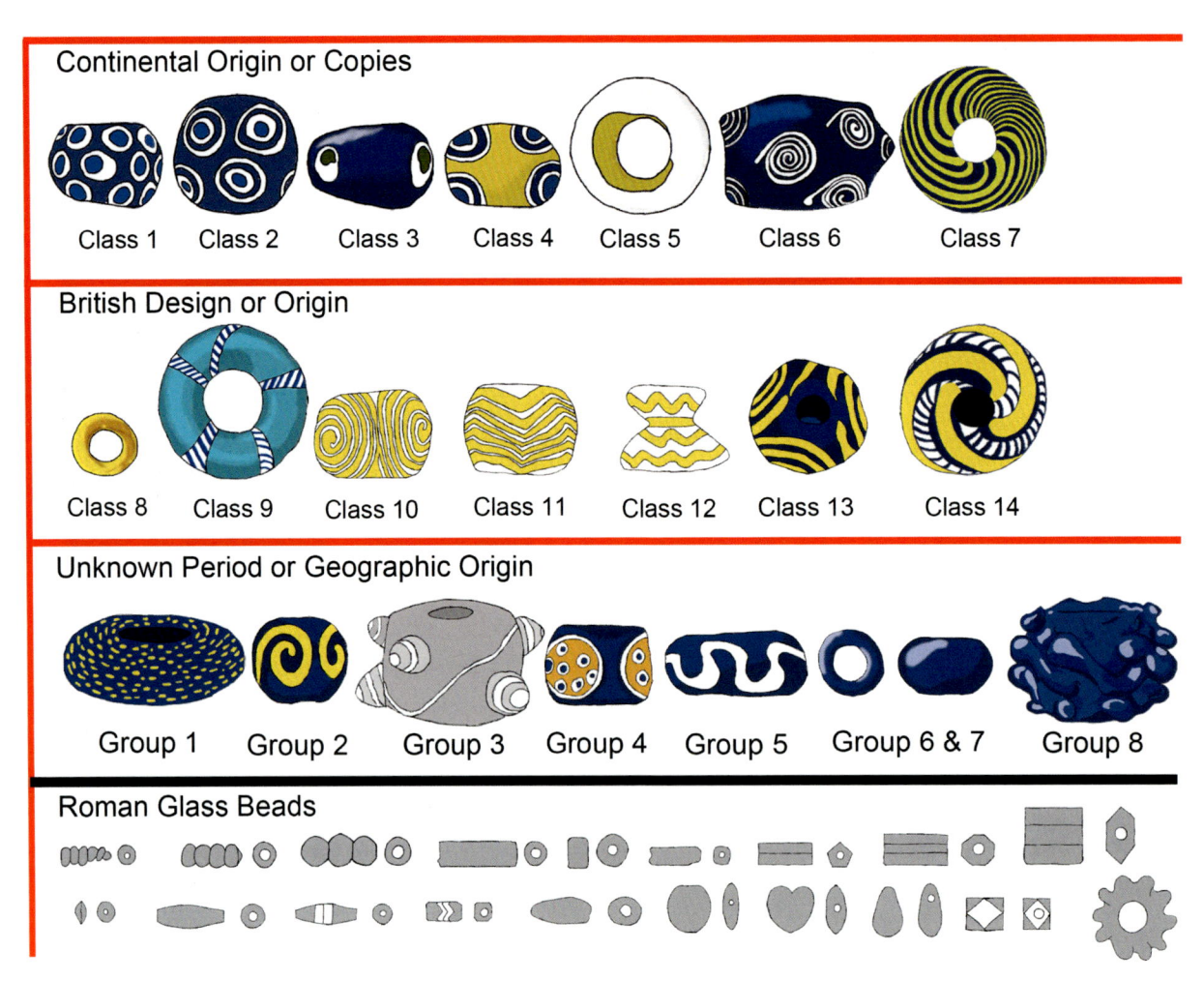

Figure 4: Schematic diagram of Guido's Iron Age and Roman glass bead classification (redrawn after 1978a Plates I and II, Figure 19, 23, 37).

colour: Class 7a – blue or purple, Class 7b – brown or yellowish-brown, and Class 7c – other colours. Although Guido expressed that form, perforation shape, and dimensions should be included within the criteria for each type, this was not applied consistently, something that is especially evident in the description of the Class 7 beads.

For Guido, and other researchers, the typology accomplished a number of goals:

- Beads that appeared to be visually similar were assigned to the same type, and each type had a description. Newly discovered specimens could be added to a type.
- All Guido classes had chronological relevance and could be used to date contexts of sites (Guido 1978a, vi). Each type had a discrete temporal appearance, geographic distribution, and cultural affiliation.

Further complicating this is that many current researchers do not *critically* apply the typology to their own interpretations. Instead, each type description is used as canon, or truth (Hill and Evans 1972, 235). Guido herself considered her typology to be in no way final (Guido 1978a, 4). Despite this, the classification system has been a valuable tool for archaeologists and does provide a useful starting point for comparing beads. Chapter 5 explores each type and the broader issues with the structure. These analyses show that there are two main problems with the typology: first, the types are imprecise, and are unable to draw out real differences that are evident in assemblages; and second, new types have been discovered that do not fit within the existing typology.

Scientific Analysis of Iron Age Glass Beads

Although much of Henderson's (1982) work on Iron Age glass beads remains unpublished, his PhD thesis used x-ray fluorescence (XRF) to measure the chemical composition of Iron Age glass beads. At this time, Guido's catalogue and typology had been recently published, and Henderson used XRF to determine the extent to which beads within each type were made from similar types of glass (Henderson 1982, 4). This tested the visual classification of beads proposed by Guido through an examination of the homogeneity and variance of glass composition within each type. In addition to approaching beads from a typological point of view, he also examined chemical composition on a regional basis, again to identify homogeneity or discrepancy (Henderson 1982, 4-5). Through these two approaches, Henderson searched for signatures in the chemical composition that could indicate production at different workshops. Theoretically, he proposed that beads with similar chemical compositions were manufactured at the same (or regional) manufacture site.

While this section will not go into the details of Henderson's data and results, it will instead discuss some methodological issues with the technique used for scientific analysis, which may have impacted his interpretations, and his interpretation of the data. Recent work (Bertini 2012: see especially Chapter 4) has highlighted some of these. The results presented in his thesis have also led to papers discussing the nature of workshops and craft within Iron Age Britain and Europe (Henderson 1992), possible glass working or bead manufacture locations within Britain (Henderson 1989), as well as contributing to an intense debate on the methods for manufacturing particular glass beads, which Henderson suggests was accomplished with moulds (Henderson 1978; 1980; 1995; Lierke 1995; Lierke, Birkhill *et al.* 1995). This is a topic that will be returned to later.

Drawing on the conclusions from his XRF analyses, Henderson (1992) later developed the concept of industrial specialisation within the production of objects in late Iron Age Europe. His argument suggests that society at this time became more centralised, as did production. Iron Age glass working was preformed by craft specialists, meaning that they used specific or rare raw materials, specialised processing methods were introduced, and products were standardised in quality and appearance (Henderson 1992, 104-5). In his interpretation, glass beads were a rare and valuable artefact, because of the distance that the raw material, and in some cases finished beads, travelled from their point of manufacture. Developing this idea of value further, Henderson (1992) examined the frequency of complex beads in relation to the type of site that they were found at. He showed that large quantities of complex decorated glass beads occurred at high-status sites, while lower status sites had fewer examples. There are several critiques that could be made of this method and analysis:

1. The data that is examined here is unclear. Presumably data from his PhD thesis was used, but his selection criteria for inclusion in this analysis is unclear (e.g. did he excluded stray beads from known archaeological sites?).

2. The site types do not take the changing nature of a site's enclosure into account. For example, sites that fluctuated between enclosed and unenclosed, and where the size of the enclosure changed over time.

3. Henderson included the plain yellow annular beads (Guido Class 8/this study Type 1 Class 10) with the decorated beads in his analysis, but this distorts the data and interpretation. By removing these beads from the lake village category, the percentage of decorated beads at this type of site is reduced to around 42% rather than the 88% total he gives.

4. It is unclear how he derived the total (n=423) glass beads from the Square Ditched cemeteries. The dataset in which this book is based includes approximately 700 glass beads from the East Yorkshire square burials (that would have been published at the time of Henderson's publication: Cowlam burial L, Queen's barrow at Arras, Wetwang Slack burials), of which only 33% were decorated with a secondary colour. This contrasts with the 91% of decorated glass beads from square-ditched cemeteries reported by Henderson.

5. Henderson's analysis generalised all sites based on morphology alone and does not consider the temporal differences between sites.

6. Although the analysis reports a 'N' value for the frequency of each site type, he does not explore the number of sites where glass beads were not found during excavation. For example, presumably the Farming or Minor Settlement category refers to lowland unenclosed sites. Here, 30 beads were found over 19 sites, but the number of excavated sites at the time of publication is not clear.

7. Finally, he does not consider regional differences in site location and artefact deposition, or regional differences in archaeological enquiry.

These seven points suggest that there are some flaws with Henderson's approach, and the research presented in this book will address the relevant issues by discussing the number of sites excavated compared to the presence of glass beads, and the changing nature of settlement sites over time (see Chapter 7).

In this paper, Henderson (1992) also developed a model for glass production. Drawing on ethnographic evidence from the Yuroba of West Africa, he suggests that Iron Age glass beads reflect characteristics of identity to the observer. Furthermore, in his example of the beads from Meare Lake Village, he proposed that, because the earlier distribution of glass beads is the same distribution of later coins, it is possible to back-date the tribal boundaries to the period of glass bead manufacture at Meare (Henderson 1992, 125). This is a potentially hazardous conclusion, especially in light of recent research, which suggests a different explanation for the so-called tribal boundaries based on evidence from coins (Leins 2008), and the recognition that there are other possible reasons for social cohesion between settlements (Moore 2011, 351).

Recent scientific work by Bertini has used LA-ICP-MS to analyse the chemical composition of Guido's Class 13 and 14 beads from northeast Scotland (Bertini 2012; Bertini, Shortland *et al.* 2011). This micro-destructive method, along with rigorous methodology, has resulted in a highly accurate method of scientifically analysing the chemical composition of glass, including major, minor, and trace elements. This produces consistent and repeatable results that allows for further discussion of glass typology and provenance, as well as understanding the raw material and the pigments used to alter the colour and opacity of glass. Coupled with 3D-microcomputer-tomography and Synchraton light, Bertini has pioneered a new and innovative way to understand technical aspects of glass bead manufacture. Combined with analyses of both archaeological and experimentally made glass beads, she was able to objectively determine the similarities between archaeological and experimental samples to understand whether the outcome of her glass making techniques yielded similar results. Although her work was limited to only two types of later Iron Age glass beads found in Scotland (many of the same beads are discussed throughout the analysis chapters), future work hopes to incorporate earlier glass beads from Britain into a larger study.

Glass Bead Manufacturing

Glass is a material created through the combination of silica, soda, and lime under high amounts of heat (approximately 1,000°C). Most glass will be a pale translucent green due to the natural presence of iron oxides within the sand. Manipulation of glass colour and opacity can occur at the raw glass forming stage, or later during subsequent melts, through the addition of oxides, minerals, chunks of previously coloured glass, and in some cases by manipulating the atmosphere of the furnace. For example, the addition of cobalt causes glass to turn to a dark translucent blue, while copper oxide makes a green-blue glass (although, cuprous oxide (Cu_2O) causes glass to turn opaque red), and manganese can result in either purple or decolourised (true colourless) glass (Henderson 1985).

The process of glass manufacture and object manufacture is very different, and the two processes need not occur in the same location. The actual manufacture of glass can combine different materials from a variety of different sources, and once made, need not require any additional materials other than the tools to work it. In this form, it is possible to transport glass long distances, as suggested by the approximately 175 glass ingots found on the Late Bronze Age Uluburun shipwreck (Pulak 1998). However, glass beads could also be traded in their finished form, as suggested by the thousands of faience and glass beads found in ceramic vessels amongst other cargo on the Uluburn (Ingram 2005; Pulak 1998).

Although Guido formed her typology based on the assumption that some were made on the continent and others were made in Britain, there was very little evidence that this occurred at the time Guido published her study. Instead, she drew on the frequency and distribution of glass beads throughout Britain to suggest key possible areas of manufacture, most notably, the copious amount of beads from Culbin Sands in Morayshire and from the Meare Lake Villages in Somerset. Other evidence to suggest glass working, although not necessarily glass manufacture, included the large chunks or 'raw glass' (unformed) that were recovered from Hengistbury Head in Dorset, which further attested to the possibility that this activity occurred in Iron Age Britain.

Building on Guido's conclusions, Henderson's (1982) comparison of glass bead chemical composition found that local bead manufacture could be supported at these dense-bead sites. Additional evidence at the time included an unusual bead at Meare Lake Village West in 1979, which led to his hypothesis that decorated beads were formed using a mould (Henderson 1981). This particular example (SF2501) is a possible Guido Class 11 chevron bead that was encased in a layer of clay mixed with opaque red glass. He suggested that, through a combination of the *cire perdue* (lost wax method) and the *pâte de verre* technique (applying layers of glass over grooves and then grinding it off to expose a pattern), it would be possible to make these beads. However, it is unclear how this would have worked (Lierke, Birkhill *et al.* 1995), and publication on his experiments that support this method never came to fruition (as cited in: Henderson 1978) and only referred to in later work (Henderson 1981).

Up until recently, the evidence and theories behind glass bead manufacture have changed very little beyond the hypotheses of Guido and Henderson. New evidence has come to light after two sites excavated as a part of developer-funded projects, which have provided new evidence for glass working in Britain. In the south, at 10 Gresham Street in London (Casson, Drummond-Murray *et al.* 2014), glass working and probable bead making evidence was found in mid-first century AD contexts. The evidence comprises a broken eye bead (with a clay core), bead wasters, glass waste cullet, and white and blue threads ('stringer'). Much of this material was found around a hearth situated in a rectangular building, which was set amid contemporary roundhouses. Interestingly, despite the evidence for glass working, there were no associated tools or equipment that could be connected with the glass industry. In the north, at Culduthel Farm in Inverness (Murray 2007a; forthcoming) a range of glass beads were found along with chips and other fragments of glass (many found through sampling) in opaque red (commonly used for 'enamelling' on metal objects), and other colours was discovered, along with a rod of twisted blue and white glass. While initially thought to be later in date due to the presence of beads that Guido dated to the first and second century AD, the radiocarbon dating suggests that the beads were found in contexts as early as the fourth century BC, although a second century BC to second century AD date seems more likely (Headland Archaeology, pers. comm.).

Currently, the actual manufacturing process and 'industry' of glass bead making remains wholly unclear for much of Iron Age Britain. Assuming that raw glass manufacturing did not occur, how was bead making organised? Were there in-fact workshops that specialised in the production of glass beads as suggested by Henderson (1992)? Or, were they smaller, local affairs by occasional craftspeople? As discussed further in Chapter 5 and 6, there are glass beads that exhibit very similar qualities, but it is not clear to what extent this indicates that the beads were made by the same person, or in the same workshop, or even in the same region. Did craftspeople make the same bead repeatedly? And, how were they made? What sort of tools and equipment did the Iron Age craftsperson have available to them? There are a lot more questions that need to be answered on this subject. To this we can also extend the questions to the nature of exchange. Were glass beads manufactured for personal consumption, or were they exchanged with local and distant neighbours? Chapter 7 explores the question of exchange by looking at the distribution of glass beads. However, further work and possible comparisons with other artefact types, such as pottery, are needed to explore this further.

As much of the archaeological evidence is unclear, and glass bead making is not a process that many people today would be familiar with, it is useful to discuss this process in a modern setting. Many of the principles would be the same as in the past, as there are fundamental necessities for working glass, such as a heat source. By reviewing this process, the terminology presented in Appendix A and the analyses presented in the following chapters will be more comprehensible. Today, modern bead makers create beads through a process referred to as 'lampwork'.[2] This is in reference to the 'lamp' that was used as a heat source to melt the glass (Lierke 1990; Lierke 1992), although today a torch that burns propane, natural gas, or MAPP gas is used to create a flame. This heat source sits on the edge of the workbench closest to the artist, who sits in front of it. The torch is placed so that the flame is directed out from their chest. The artist holds a metal mandrel coated in a silica release agent in one hand, and in the other a pre-formed glass rod is held. The artist heats the mandrel and glass rod simultaneously in the flame while slowly twisting them between their fingers. Once the mandrel is hot and the glass rod has softened to a molten state, they gently apply the glass to the mandrel while twisting the mandrel between their fingers. Continually rolling it while applying molten glass achieves an even application. During this process it may be necessary to continue to heat the glass rod to have enough molten glass to apply, as well as keeping the glass on the mandrel warm. This results in a layered glass disc on the mandrel, which when heated by the flame will become spherical as long as the mandrel is continually rolling between the fingers.

Different types of decorations can be applied by using very thin pieces of glass, called 'stringer'. These are made by producing a molten glob of glass at one end of a large glass rod. Pliers are then used to pinch the molten glass and quickly pulled away to produce very fine rods. Twists or cables of multi-coloured glass are easily made by twisting together two different colours of stringer with a small amount of heat. This is a feature on some Guido Class 9 and 14 glass beads. These thin glass rods can be applied to the main surface of the bead by carefully applying heat. It is the basis for creating simple decoration, such as straight or wavy circumferential lines, or simple dots or complex layered dots ('eyes'). Initially, these decorative elements will sit raised on the bead surface, but when re-heated it absorbs into the surface and creates a smooth finish (Figure 5). Alternatively, they can be left raised on the surface for a textured effect. Raised dots are not often seen on Britain Iron Age beads, but are a feature of other prehistoric beads found elsewhere in Europe.

Without further manipulation, bead shape will naturally be more disc-like (annular) or spherical (globular) depending on the amount of glass added to the mandrel, the amount of re-heating, and the amount of rotation during heating and cooling. Use of a 'marver',[3] or graphite block, can further alter the shape of the bead by rotating the molten bead over the flat surface. This can create a cylindrically shaped bead. Grooves can be impressed into the surface of the bead using the corner of the marver, creating melon beads and other shapes. When the bead is finished, it is allowed to slowly cool to prevent shattering. The release agent on the mandrel allows the bead to be removed from the mandrel easily

---

[2] This is based on experienced gained in Spring 2009 while working with bead maker and independent lampwork artist Mike Poole, in Todmorden, West Yorkshire. Mike is familiar with Iron Age glass beads and is often commissioned by museums to make replicas for museum exhibits.

[3] Guido (1978a) made frequent references to marvering, especially in connection to the application of different designs to the beads. For example, she would say a simple eye is marvered into the surface of the bead, meaning that the applied decorative glass is made flush with the surface of the bead by rolling the molten bead onto a smooth stone or other material. However, the use of a marver may not have been necessary in the late prehistoric period, because it would have visibly altered the shape of the bead. Modern glass bead-artisans use a marver, or smooth flat graphite block, to manipulate the surface of the bead to change the shape of the bead (Mike Pool, pers. comm.).

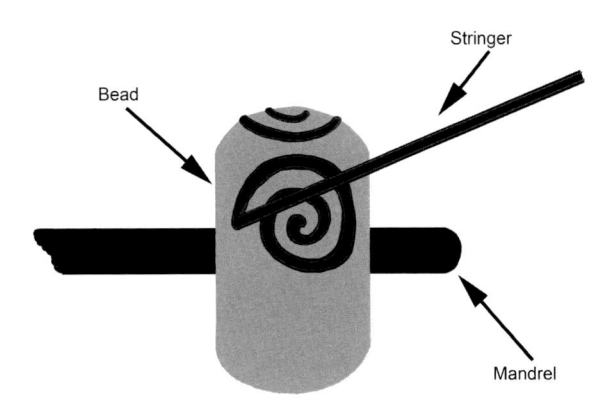

Figure 5: Applying linear decoration during glass bead manufacture.

at this point. To finish the bead, modern bead makers anneal them in a kiln. The kiln slowly heats and then cools allowing the surface tension of the glass to be diminished, which reduces the chances of cracking or breaking. Finally, the bead perforation must be reamed with a tool, which removes any excess release agent from the perforation.

Although the technology used today is not the same as in the past, and we still do not understand the social meaning of glass technology (Lemonnier 1992), the basic principles would still apply. It is essential to have a heat source. Lierke (1990) has suggested the use of oil lamps with a small mouth-blown bellows to create a heat source hot enough to melt glass. Alternatively, Jacqui Wood (1991) has suggested that a small clay lamp, originally thought to be a prehistoric cheese mould, may be connected with small craft work. Her experiments have shown that the flame that is created by burning plant matter is intense enough to solder metal. Further testing is needed in the future to determine if this was a viable heat source for glass working. What is clear, however, is that there is no evidence for a heat source used for making glass beads in Britain.

Other tools that were necessary for making glass beads are the mandrels. These objects might be difficult to recognise, because they could have been simple iron rods (copper alloy may have melted due to similar melting points). Analysis of a dark substance on the interior perforation of a bead from Culduthel Farm in Inverness revealed the presence of iron (Headland Archaeology, pers. comm.), while a recently discovered bead from 10 Gresham Street, London from a possible bead manufacture site had a clay core (Casson, Drummond-Murray *et al.* 2014).

In summary, it remains unclear as to the extent that glass beads were manufactured in Britain. Recent evidence certainly points to the possibility that at least some were in fact manufactured in Britain, as well as the presence of glass on copper alloy objects. Even the nature of the manufacturing technology is under debate, as there is very little clear evidence. It is hoped that experimental work, continued scientific analysis, and new archaeological discoveries will help to explain this process more fully in the future.

The Wider European Context

As with Guido's study, studies of glass beads from the European Iron Age also focused on typology. In contrast to the continent, most glass objects found in British Iron Age contexts tend to be beads, although there are a very small number of examples of bangles that likely originated in Europe (e.g. at Hengistbury Head, Dorset). With the European material, it is difficult to determine the balance of glass bangles versus beads. However, given the amount of published material (e.g. Feugère and Py 1989; Gebhard 1989a; b; c; Guillard 1989; Haevernick 1960; Kaenel and Müller 1989; Roymans and Verniers 2010; Tilliard 1989; Vanpeene 1989; Venclová 1989), it seems that it might be a regional matter, and bangles may at least be found in larger quantities (and variety) than in Britain. Historically, two researchers stand out as the most prolific authors to discuss European Iron Age glass beads: Haevernick and Venclová. Both have focused on glass beads and bangles from a typological point of view.

Haevernick's research on both glass beads and bracelets from the middle to late La Tène in Europe has formed a substantial backbone to archaeological research into these objects. Her primary publication (Haevernick 1960) described eight main types of beads, displayed in Figure 6. As with Guido's work, the study was focussed on typology, distribution maps, and a catalogue of beads throughout Europe. However, Guido drew on Haevernick's study of glass bangles and beads and, although there is very little overlap, Guido's Class 5 is the same as Haevernick's Gruppe 21 and Guido's Group 1 contains many of the beads Haevernick would describe as Gruppe 24.

Unfortunately, Haevernick was unable to fully publish her research, resulting in four posthumous publications (Dobiat, Matthäus *et al.* 1987; Frey, Matthäus *et al.* 1983; Hunter and Haevernick 1995; Zepezauer 1993) that further expand on her 1960 publication. Again, they primarily consist of descriptions of bead typologies, rather than further interpretation. These publications described beads that were not noted in her 1960 publication and included typologies for beads decorated with zig-zag designs, ring eye beads, spiral eye beads, and eye beads.

Venclová's (1990) work continues to follow this typological approach, though she examined glass objects from as early as the Bronze Age. Her work is

Type	Original Description	Translation
Gruppe 19	Ringperlen mit Grat	Beads with bur or edge
Gruppe 20	Klare Ringperlen mit gelber Folie	Clear annular bead with yellow film
Gruppe 21	Einfarbige Ringperlen	Monochrome or single coloured beads
Gruppe 22	Kleine zarte Ringperlen	Small delicate ring-bead
Gruppe 23	Ringperlen mit Schraubenfäden	Ring beads with 'screw-threads'
Gruppe 23a	Ringperlen mit mehrfachem zichzackfaden	Ring beads with multiple zig-zag thread
Gruppe 24	Ringperlen mit hellgesprenkelter Oberfläche	Ring bead with bright speckled surface
Gruppe 25	Ringperlen mit Gitternetz	Ringbead with net

Figure 6: Haevernick's (1960) eight main types of beads (author's translation).

primarily concerned with glass objects from the Czech Republic and addresses beads, bangle, rings, gems, pendants, and vessels. Venclová's study is important to glass bead researchers, because she is explicit in regards to the creation of her typology, and included copious illustrations and watercolours to pictorially describe the appearance of each type, as well as the assemblages of objects. The organisation of her typology was taken as the inspiration for the typology presented in Chapter 5.

There are smaller typologies based on single characteristics, such as the spiral beads described by Zepezauer (1989), and more site based typologies like that described for the Manching oppidum (Gebhard 1989a), and the catalogues for the ongoing excavations at Bibracte (Bride 2005). However, a systematic synthesis for all glass beads in the wider European context, even from a basic typological or catalogue approach, appears to be lacking. This renders a modern comparison of British Iron Age glass beads to continental glass beads difficult without further extensive research to compile data across Europe.

Conclusion

Study of glass beads does not derive from a long-standing tradition. Antiquarian engagement with glass beads was limited to collections of 'ancient' objects, or formed donations to museums. Any serious study did not occur until Margaret Guido undertook her research. Her approach has laid a necessary foundation for all future work, as she was able to distinguish glass beads into prehistoric, Roman, and Anglo-Saxon categories. Long-lived designs, such as a simple white wave on a translucent blue bead, caused some amount of difficulty from a visual analysis perspective, as it is difficult and in some cases even impossible to distinguish beads of differed periods. Subsequent studies, such as Henderson's work on analytical approaches to glass composition, has provided an alternative view to glass beads. However, in both Guido and Henderson's cases, critiques of their methodology suggest that there is some degree of refining that could be done to ensure an accurate sample is reflected.

Chapter 3
Glass Beads and Dress

Until recently, the study of artefacts was often taken as a given: artefacts simply reflect past activity. But can artefacts be understood simply as the passive by-product of human activity? Or can we use them to understand the past in other, more dynamic ways? It has been argued that not only do objects become intrinsic to meeting the needs of everyday life, but they can develop their own biographies and even their own agency (Gosden 2005; Gosden and Marshall 1999). Thus, artefacts are much more than a passive reflection of the past. There is an active social relationship between objects and people. This chapter explores the relationship that is built between objects and people through dress. Although defined more thoroughly below, dress refers to both modifications of the natural body, such as hairstyles or nail maintenance, as well as objects that are worn on it, such as textile garments or decorative objects. However, the way in which dress is studied within archaeology and in the wider social sciences disciplines varies. Following this discussion, this chapter will examine the approaches to artefacts within Iron Age studies.

People and Objects

This study is not just about objects, nor is it only about people; it is about the relationship built between people and objects. Actor-Network-Theory (ANT) provides a useful way of thinking about interactions between people and objects. While some approaches preference one over the other, ANT puts both on level footing (Knappett 2011). It examines the connections between people and objects and the way in which they interact. However, within archaeology, both of these subjects are usually approached separately. Although this could be viewed as a hurdle for understanding the symbiotic relationship between two seemingly opposed foci of study, by borrowing this concept from ANT we can bring together different aspects of studying people and objects as a way to understand how they interrelate. This book is particularly concerned with objects that are worn on the body that form a person's dress. These objects become bound up in the everyday discourses of social interaction and may relate to communicating information about the wearer's identity.

While this study focuses especially on one type of artefact, it is necessary to place it within its wider theoretical context. Recent object based studies have begun to move beyond form or style (e.g. Dunnell 1978; Sackett 1977; Sackett 1985; Wiessner 1983; 1985) as passive reflections of the past, or passive participants within a system of exchange (e.g. Macinnes 1989). Instead, they have begun to explore new questions that interpret artefacts in a different light. Many of these approaches see artefacts as active, almost living, in which they not only had a biography and agency, but also real meaning during their life, no matter how mundane (Gell 1998; Gosden 2005; Gosden and Marshall 1999; Hoskins 1998; 2006). Expanding on form and style, other studies have recognised the importance of colour and the significance of the use of some colours over others (Scarre 2002; Young 2006). This of course varies from object to object, as well as between materials, but it is no longer possible to ignore the importance of colour and the choices that it reflects. Objects and their colour did not exist on their own outside of the social processes in which they were bound up. Instead they played an integral role in human relations. Here, two main ideas become important. How do objects relate to the socially constructed body? And, how are objects used in order to build dress and identity?

Dress and Society

One of the most tantalising aspects for studying glass beads and other material culture, such as bracelets and brooches, is that these objects were probably worn on the body. Although the evidence for this is limited (see Chapters 7), it does suggest they were used in this way. For example, there are a number of burials from Wetwang Slack, and elsewhere in East Yorkshire, where other dress items (i.e. finger-rings, beads, brooches) were found within individual inhumations, in a way that may reflect how they were used in life (see Chapter 8). However, it remains a possibility that some of the glass beads were not worn on the body throughout the entire span of their life cycles. This research works on the assumption that glass beads were used in this way because they were found in burials, although it is acknowledged that they may have been used for other purposes during the life of each object.

Another commonly held assumption is that beads were worn as a strand placed around the neck. Again, there is little evidence to suggest that all glass beads were used in this way. There are many alternative ways they could have been worn on the body. For example, they could have been worn as a strand on either the wrist or ankle. There are also examples of beads being placed onto copper alloy rings, for example at Sandwick, Unst in the Shetlands Islands (Fraser Hunter, pers.comm.), and Portable Antiquities Scheme find: LON-041951 from Greater London. They may also have been placed onto other metal objects, such as bracelets, or they could have been sewn onto garments alone or as part of a larger conglomerate object. They could also have been attached to the ear or placed in the hair as decoration. Ethnographic evidence has shown that bead use varies across cultures, as does its social significance (Sciama and Eicher 2001). Thus we should expect to see some differences in bead use, as well as differences in the interpretation of their significance. Regardless of how Iron Age beads were placed on the body, they would have helped to constitute a person's dress, although to varying degrees. This section will explore different approaches to understanding the interplay between dress and the body.

There are many different terms related to how an individual or a group of individuals manipulate the body for the senses. Literature may refer to 'dress', 'fashion', 'adornment', 'clothing', 'apparel', or 'costume' when referencing this act. As Entwistle (2000) points out, the terminology employed by various authors often depends on the discipline of study and the goals of their research. Anthropological studies, as she states, are more likely to be concerned with dress or adornment, while sociology is often more focused on fashion as an industry. However, throughout the twentieth century, these perspectives have also changed, even from author to author. For example, two anthropologists, Roach[4] and Eicher (1965, 1), described the words referring to a person's appearance as synonymous, although they emphasised that 'dress' both refers to the 'apparel' worn by people and to the act of 'dressing', while 'adornment' stresses 'the aesthetic aspects of altering the body'. However, their perspective later changed and instead of describing all of these possible terms as synonyms, they preferred the use of the word 'dress' in terms of an individual's "…assemblage of modifications of the body and/or supplements to the body" (Roach-Higgins and Eicher 1992; Roach-Higgins, Eicher *et al.* 1995). This includes everything from changes that modify the body directly, including tattoos, piercing, maintenance of nails, and the way in which hair is arranged, to the supplements, which modify the body through the addition of objects, such as garments and jewellery. They argue that this word suffers least from ethnocentric views of methods of dress and at the same time includes all circumstances for dress, rather than emphasising the extraordinary over the ordinary. Despite their changing definition, it demonstrates some anthropological desire for defining a term that can describe what has assumed to be a universally human ability to modify or dress the body (Entwistle 2000, 42-3).

Utilising their definitions of dress, Roach-Higgins and Eicher take a symbolic interactionist approach to understanding dress. This is one of the dominant approaches to understanding the ways in which people dress, especially within anthropology (Entwistle 2000, 58), which is also common in archaeology. This method of inquiry sees dress primarily as a symbolic mode of non-verbal communication, particularly regarding identity (Roach-Higgins and Eicher 1995, 12). Dress, therefore, symbolises membership to particular groups, such as ethnicity, status, age, or gender.

For the anthropologist, it is perhaps the so-called "universal words" that have been of most interest (Barnes and Eicher 1993; Eicher 1995; Roach and Eicher 1965; Roach-Higgins, Eicher *et al.* 1995). As dress is seen as a system of symbols, this approach 'reads' dress as if it were a text with a straightforward interpretation. For example, in Nigerian Kalabari dress, female dress reflects the five stages of Kalabari womanhood (pre-puberty, puberty, maturity, marriage, and motherhood), while male dress reflects achievements, whether personal, economic or political, and age (Michelman and Erekosima 1993). Because dress directly represents various stages in Kalabari life and their identity, this status can be communicated non-verbally to the viewer.

While dress could be argued to communicate identity, the symbolic interactionist approach tends to be the dominant interpretation of dress across the social sciences. The approach has been criticised because it focuses on the 'why' questions (Entwistle 2000, 57), for example: 'why do we wear clothes?' and 'why is male fashion different from female fashion'? These types of questions are simplistic in a descriptive sense, as well as reductive in their attempt to be all-inclusive and comparable across the world, and do not examine the complex relationship between both dress and body (Entwistle 2000, 56-7). Instead, Entwistle (2000, 12) proposes a different approach that draws on structuralism and phenomenology in order '…to understand the body as a *socially constituted object…*' and '…dress as an *embodied experience*' (original emphasis).

By drawing on the experience of dress, Entwistle (2000, 11) builds a framework for understanding dress on the premise that it is a '[socially] situated bodily practice' by exploring the relationships between body, dress, and culture. In this sense, dress will vary depending on the social situation, where for example, one might dress differently when going out on a Friday night with friends compared to staying home and doing housework on the weekend. Entwistle does not reject the idea that dress communicates ideas about a person's individual or social identity. Instead, she recognises that dress is far more complex. Fashion is a constant contradiction between the desire to fit in socially, and the need to stand out as an individual (Entwistle 2000, 116). This complex relationship between dress and identity derives from two sources; first, Entwistle draws on Foucault's

---
[4] Mary Ellen Roach is later cited as 'Roach-Higgins'.

work, especially on power and knowledge, and second, on Merleau-Ponty's work on phenomenology.

Foucault's work on discourses specifically relates to the body and the power/knowledge dichotomy. Prior to exploring how discourse is used in relation to dress, it will be useful to turn to the body and what is meant by it. In his review of the major approaches towards understanding the body, Shilling (2003) outlines some of the major theoretical trends that have attempted to address what the body means within society. It is only recently that such studies have become more 'explicit' rather than 'implicit' as the body has often been taken for granted rather than providing the centre of study (Shilling 2003, 8, 17). Different approaches have led to different interpretations of bodies within society. For example, the 'naturalistic' approach emphasises the biological basis and especially the biological reasons for differences between the male and female bodies and how this manifests within society.

In contrast to the naturalistic body, Foucault's work and others, such as Mary Douglas and Erving Goffman, are the extreme opposite: the socially constructed body (Shilling 2003). Central to Foucault's work is the idea of *discourse*, meaning communication, especially in relation to knowledge. For Foucault, knowledge creates power, but power does not exist without knowledge (Entwistle 2000, 16). He is interested in '…the body and the effects of power on it' (Foucault 1980, 58), which manifests particularly in his studies on the penal system (Foucault 1979). Although, as Entwistle notes (2000, 20), Foucault was not explicitly concerned with dress or fashion, his understanding of the body and its relation to power has implications for how dress is understood. For her, 'Foucault's account…offers one way of thinking about the structuring influence of social forces on the body as well as offering a way of questioning commonsense understandings about modern dress' (Entwistle 2000, 20). For example, dress is closely linked to ideas of power and gender, even on the fundamental level where concerns about dress can be considered a female attribute and sometimes to be frivolous, whereas men do not concern themselves to the same level (Entwistle 2000, 21-2).

To balance Foucault, Entwistle drew on Merleau-Ponty's work on embodiment and agency (Entwistle 2000, 23-8). Rather than seeing the body as passive, through Merleau-Ponty's view we '…come to understand our relation in the world via the positioning of our bodies physically and historically in space' thus allowing us to see that '…our bodies are not just the place from which we come to experience the world, but it is through our bodies that we come to be seen in the world' (Entwistle 2000, 29). For Merleau-Ponty, space is an important concept, because bodies move through space. For dress, this is a useful concept, as 'dress in everyday life is always located spatially and temporally: when getting dressed one orientates oneself to the situation, acting in particular ways upon the body' (Entwistle 2000, 29).

By drawing on these ideas of embodiment, it is possible to understand practices of dress as socially and culturally situated, whereby everyday dress is negotiated between the fashion system, social norms, and the agency to make individual choices (Entwistle 2000, 37). Therefore, Entwistle's structural/phenomenological framework for understanding dress draws, on the one hand, from discourses of the body and power and, on the other hand, from the embodied experience of dress, which results in a study of dress that reflects a situated practice. In relation to the previously mentioned 'reading dress' approach, or symbolic interaction, Entwistle does not entirely reject the possibility that particular approaches to dress can be read or seen as symbols. Instead, she sees dress as being more than this; dress constitutes the embodiment of many different aspects of an individual, which is not limited to their categorical identity such as age, gender, or ethnicity, but can also include a projection of a person's mood, anticipated social setting, or agenda, to name a few possibilities.

Dress and Archaeology

Having reviewed two theories of dress, both found in anthropological literature, it is now time to turn to archaeology. In contrast to the studies discussed above, archaeologists are interested in past societies rather than modern Western, non-Western, or recent historical societies. While these contemporary studies have the benefit of fieldwork within living communities, or access to text and pictorial material, a study of prehistoric dress is at a distinct disadvantage. Those that inhabited Britain during the Iron Age left us with no written texts, the representation of human form is rare, and when it does occur there is little indication of dress. This section will first review how dress and identity have been approached in Iron Age studies and archaeology more generally, and will then discuss the evidence for dress in Iron Age Britain.

Dress, the Body, and Identity in Archaeology

Despite the growing diversity of approaches in the social sciences, studies of dress and objects related to dress in archaeology have a tendency to be limited to two types of discussion. The first is artefact based, typically where only a single type of artefact is researched in depth. For example, when examining Iron Age material culture, studies focus on brooches (e.g. Hull and Hawkes 1987), pins (e.g. Dunning 1934b), or regional artefacts, such as massive armlets in Scotland (e.g. Hunter 2006c; Simpson 1968). These often manifest either as extensive catalogues or lists of objects (e.g. MacGregor 1976), or classificatory studies that attempt to order the variability seen in the artefacts, often within a chronological dimension (e.g. Fowler 1960; Haselgrove 1997; Hull and Hawkes 1987). Other studies take a scientific approach to better understand the technology and chemical composition of the objects themselves (e.g Dungworth 1996; Henderson 1982). The results of these studies see artefacts as passive by-products of human activity and they simply serve to investigate artefacts on a superficial level sometimes without the archaeological context. They do not necessarily answer questions about objects such as: how was it used? Or, what did it mean to different people? However, recently there has been a move towards seeing decorated objects, especially metalwork, as more than just chronological markers (e.g. Garrow and Gosden 2012; Joy 2011b), but rather active participants within Iron Age society. Although these studies have examined a variety of objects, not all are connected to dress, and their aims tend not to explore the understanding of dress as a whole.

The second major type of study found in archaeology, is the application of the 'reading' dress approach, as discussed in an anthropological context previously. In these studies, a variety of different types of data are used for interpretation where possible (textual, visual representation, artefacts), although data from inhumations has generally come to be seen as a reflection of a person's age, gender, status, and any other affiliation. For example, Sørensen's (1991; 1997) work draws on European Bronze Age burial evidence to explore connections between age and biological sex and how dress was constructed through the placement of artefacts in relation to the body.

Despite the previously mentioned criticisms of simply reading dress as a reflection of an individual's identity, this continues to be the primay way in which dress is understood within archaeology (e.g. Marcus 1993).[5] When a burial is taken to be a clear reflection of an individual's identity in this way, there is little consideration of who buried the individual and the social meaning of the inclusion of the artefacts, the possibility of disguise or altered identity, or whether the artefacts reflect the individual's identity in life. Furthermore, as identity is often discussed in terms of categories of identity, such as gender, age, ethnicity, status, we cannot assume that these categories explicitly existed in the past, but rather need the data to demonstrate that they did.

Thus far, identity has been mentioned, but has not been discussed in detail. From the archaeological standpoint, Díaz-Andreu and Lucy provide a cogent working definition of identity as "…[an] individuals' identification with broader groups on the basis of differences socially sanctioned as significant" (Díaz-Andreu and Lucy 2005, 1). When we talk about identity, we mean an individual person's sense of belonging or attachment to different social groups. Although identity is often studied in terms of categorical identity (e.g. age, gender, or ethnicity), it is recognised that a person's identity is not just one of these categories, but many. These categories are not permanent once they are attached to a person, as they can change over a lifetime. Despite organising their book into the identity categories of gender, age, status, ethnicity, and religion, Díaz-Andreu and Lucy emphasise the need for studies of identity to move beyond this singular approach and examine how an identity is determined from multiple aspects of a person (Díaz-Andreu and Lucy 2005, 9). While it seems that this proposition would be a positive move for identity studies, they continue to limit their ideas to combinations of these identity categories. This creates a very simplistic view of identity, as it is unable to take into account the agency of the individual, or even a group, to act outside of their identity category. Nor does it consider a person's experience in the world and how they construct, maintain, or actively change their identity. As archaeologists work with the remains of past societies, it is often anticipated that the effects of these past social processes will fit into neat, discreet categories. Why should we expect all adult females in Late Iron Age Britain to dress the same, or use the same material culture? And, for that matter, why should males?

One of the problems with trying to build an understanding of dress in the past is that we, as archaeologists, are not removed from the contemporary perceptions of body or dress. While they are clearly linked from a modern standpoint, our interpretation of the body in the past is bound to reflect our contemporary viewpoint of its importance within our own societies (Borić and Robb 2008, 2; Shilling 2003). Similarly, Entwistle (2000, 78-81) has stressed that our modern understanding of dress, and especially of fashion, is the result of centuries of development of a specific manner of dress, with the purpose of becoming socially mobile. It is, therefore, crucial to recognise where our own culturally intuitive understandings of body and dress originate from, to allow us to be critically reflective when interpreting the past.

Further complicating the relationship between dress, identity, and body are artefacts themselves. Unlike studies of classification and typology, all artefact types cannot be treated the same. Each individual object will undergo a different life pathway, and there is no reason to assume that all objects should be treated in the same way in life or death. This results in differing artefact biographies as objects are used, exchanged, gifted, modified, broken (Gosden 2005; Kopytoff 1986), and finally left in intentional or accidental deposits, later to be subsumed into the archaeological record. Therefore, despite apparent similarity, no two artefacts are ever truly alike.

---

[5] Although very recent literature has shown that this perspective has began to change (e.g. Gleba, Munkholt et al. 2008; Harlow 2012)

Bringing together the theoretical concepts of artefact biographies, the body, identity, dress, and studies of artefacts, is the 'reading' dress approach as far as we can take a study of prehistoric dress? Can we take it further using Entwistle's framework for seeing dress as a situated practice? Judging from recent workshops and conference sessions, this is beginning to happen,[6] yet there is still a lack of published literature that critically reflects on the study of dress in the past, and in particular prehistory. This book aims to incorporate these new ideas and interpretations by drawing on current approaches to understanding the body, dress, and identity. In this way, it will move beyond reading dress as the goal of study.

Thinking about late prehistoric Britain, would a person's dress be a straightforward display of an individual's identity? Or could they have manipulated it in the ways that Entwistle recognises during the modern period? But perhaps more relevant is the question of the sort of identities that people displayed in Iron Age Britain. Here I want to move away from the strict categories of identity that are so often used. Instead, I will draw on Bourdieu's concept of *habitus,* as it not only envelopes the categories of identity, but it also extends to include much more. For Bourdieu, this is the experience of everyday life in all aspects, where there is interaction between the individual *habitus* (self-identity), and that of the group (group-identity), such as social class (Bourdieu 1990, 60). However, within this shared group identity, the individual *habitus*, or 'personal style' marks out an individual, while at the same time maintaining membership to the group *habitus*. Although Bourdieu (1984) was particularly interested in the effect of different class systems on *habitus*, we can extend this to the more traditional concepts of identity categories. In this way, we can talk about these identity categories, while at the same time recognising that they are multiple in nature and transformational, and are also subject to the actions of the agent as an individual. Therefore, when thinking about identity in Iron Age Britain, I am examining identity in these less strict categorical terms.

Dress in Iron Age Britain

Studies of dress, the body, and identity in Iron Age Britain have been undertaken through a more piecemeal approach, for example, study of a single regional perspective (e.g. Giles 2012; Hunter 2007a), or the examination of a particular artefact type (e.g. Hill 1997; Hunter 2006c). These studies particularly emphasis the status displayed by individuals through the use of material culture, such as emphasising differences between Romans and the native inhabitants of Scotland in the case of Hunter's work. Giles, on the other hand, interpreted the evidence in terms of age and gender as well as status within a regional identity. Yet there remains an absence of a method for analysing the construction of dress across the whole of Britain that brings together evidence for textiles, artefacts, human representation, and classical sources (when appropriate) in an effort to understand the changing dynamic of dress during the Iron Age. A Britain-wide approach does not preclude the opportunity for discussions of regional dress; quite the opposite, as it allows us to compare and contrast the evidence in differing regions. This section will review the evidence for dress in Iron Age Britain and the implications for a study of glass beads.

One of the major trends seen in evidence for Iron Age Britain is a general sparseness of material culture at first, followed by incremental increases in the number and variety of artefacts towards the end of the period (Hill 1995a). This is a pattern seen in the study of pottery (Pollard 2002), grooming objects (Eckardt and Crummy 2008; Hill 1997), brooches (Haselgrove 1997; Jundi and Hill 1997), and other objects (e.g. horse equipment, coins, etc.). Changes in material culture, settlements (e.g. *oppida*), methods for treatment of the dead, and possible developments in social stratification have led to the suggestion that there was a dramatic change in society, around the first century BC (Hill 1995a, 78-89). This has been described by some as the result of increased contact with the continent and the importation of exotic or luxury goods (Fitzpatrick 1990; Haselgrove 1982; Sharples 1990), as well as the Claudian conquest in the mid-first century AD, the initial effects of which were particularly felt in southern Britain. Whether these new objects were the cause of social change, or merely a reflection of changes already occurring, has been a major area of debate (Fitzpatrick 2001; Hill 2007, c.f. Cunliffe 2005). Nevertheless, the increase in artefacts, especially those related to dress, has been interpreted as reflecting a wider change in attitudes towards the body.

Not only do we find more artefacts related to the care and maintenance of the body, but brooches change in style, become more numerous, and perhaps reflect an increased desire to adorn the self (Eckardt 2008; Hill 1997). However, these ideas primarily reflect the Iron Age of southern Britain and cannot necessarily be said to reflect contemporary changes in the rest of Britain (i.e. Northern Britain, Wales, Scotland). In the case of Northeast Scotland, changes in material culture did occur, although at a slightly later date, within the first few centuries AD (Hunter 2001a; 2006c; 2007a). Therefore, from a Britain-wide perspective, a degree of caution is needed, as it is not possible to say whether changes in perceptions to the body and the increased use of dress objects occurred in all regions, or if all objects follow this pattern. The following section will consider the

---

[6] For example: Rags to Riches: dress and dress accessories in social context, Reading University, 21 April 2012; 'Dressing Sensibly: sensory approaches to dress for archaeologists' session at TAG 2012, Liverpool University; and the session 'Gender Identities in the Making - prehistoric dress and network patterns in a supraregional perspective' at the 19th Annual EAA Meeting, 4-8 September 2013.

various types of evidence for dress in Iron Age Britain, and the implications for its understanding.

Human Iconography

Representation of the human form could potentially provide an indication of the types of cloth used and the manner in which textiles and other objects were worn, and the way in which the hair was styled. Human imagery was prevalent during the Iron Age on the continent (Megaw 1970). For example, the figures on the Gundestrup Cauldron display several individuals on its panels, in addition to figures of animals (Figure 7). The extent that these figures were human, rather than supernatural is unclear, although the large size of some figures (Aldhouse-Green 2001, 114) and the antlers worn by another certainly suggest that the object might depict interactions between humans and divine beings. However, not only do these images show individuals in human form, but also they wear torcs around their necks, an object that is found in the archaeological record. Several of the figures also wear close fitting garments (for example see the antler individual in Figure 7a), similar to a modern unitard. This suggests that at least some people wore very tightly fitted garments and the detail shown in the repoussé depicts fabric woven in stripes, or an alternating twill/herringbone pattern (see: DeRoche 2012; Mannering, Gleba *et al.* 2012 for examples from both Britain and Dennmark). This seemingly contradicts any assumption that early garments were 'simple' in construction, utilising only large pieces of cloth. The other figure (central individual in Figure 7b) is shown with long, possibly arranged hair. There is a smaller figure to the right, who appears to be in the process of grooming the larger figure. This may depict the importance of social grooming, perhaps as a part of everyday life, or possibly in a ritual or servile sense if the figures are divine.

Human iconography from Iron Age Britain, on the other hand, seems to be a much rarer occurrence. The human figure was largely absent in much of the surviving material until the third century BC (Jope 2000, 92). Clear representations of the human form have been found on the remains of the Marlborough bucket, the Baldock bucket, and the Aylesford bucket, while some are more ambiguous, such as the possible face from the 'Grotesque torc' from Snettisham (Garrow and Gosden 2012, 2 and Figure 1.4) and the 'sheet bronze head' from Stanwick in Yorkshire (Jope 2000, Plates 150-1 e-o). These representations focus on the head or the face, which may suggest that this was an important aspect of the body in these representations.

A very small number of human figurines from Britain represent the whole body. These include wooden figures from various contexts, and a number of chalk figurines found predominately in East Yorkshire. Of the wooden figures, the Roos Carr find is the most elaborately constructed. It consists of four individuals attached to a boat, one of which holds a shield. The eyes of the figures are inlaid with white quartz (Piggott 1951, 17), giving the figures a piercing, yet strange appearance (Figure 8). Other wooden figures have been found individually, such as those from Ballachulish in Argyllshire, Dagenham in Essex, and Teigngrace in Devon. Other comparable examples have been found at Shercock, Co. Cavan in Ireland and at Montbuoy, Loiret in France. Although the date of these different figures is unclear, similarities in style between these different figures tie them together, such as the detachable penis on the Shercock and Dagenham figures, and the quartz eyes on the Balachulish figure, which is a feature that is shared with the Roos Carr figures.

Additional details for these figures remain largely elusive, including their date (although Piggott (1951) suggested a Late Bronze Age date) and purpose. However, it appears that most, if not all, of these figures were nude, as evidenced by their visible male genitalia. This suggests that they were not painted or otherwise clothed and that their naked appearance was important and intentional. There does not seem to be any surviving indication that these figures were represented with hair, which is at odds at least with Late Iron Age European depictions of males. If these figures do represent humans, or divine beings in human form, then it is possible that these figures represent the importance of the unclothed body. Although if these figures were created in relation to ritual acts or periods of time, then it may be that the nakedness had situational importance.

In contrast, the chalk figurines, although crudely formed, do illustrate a different level of detail. There are approximately 40-50 figurines, including fragments (Stead 1988). Where their provenance is known, they have been connected with later Iron Age ladder-type enclosures in East Yorkshire (Giles 2007a; Stead 1988). Examples that are complete, or mostly complete, show details either embossed on the main surface, or engraved into the chalk. For example, Figure 9 shows the back of one figure where an arm is reaching for a sword attached to a belt. Others, such as Stead's (1988) nos. 7, 28, 40, have repeated scratch marks on the surface that may indicate a textile garment or perhaps a woven belt, as on no. 28. However, Stead's no. 38 is the only example where gender has been clearly marked out and this individual is depicted as wearing a belt with sword. Nudity, it seems, does not negate the ability to wear a sword, suggesting that this may have been an important feature of the individual's identity.

The wood and chalk figures were likely created for different purposes. Textile evidence is known from Late Bronze Age Britain (DeRoche 2012); therefore the wooden figures (if Late Bronze Age) appear to be deliberately nude, while some of the chalk figures are clothed and naked. As very few of these wood and chalk objects have been found in clear dated contexts, it is unclear whether we are seeing regional differences, period differences, or differences of situation. However, it is interesting that of the wooden figures, only those from Roos Carr have any accompanying objects (shields), while the chalk figures often displayed a sword in scabbard, and possibly garments.

Finally, a combination of head and body iconography can be found on some Gallo-Belgic coins. Allen (1958) has proposed that they can be used to understand aspects of daily life in Late Iron Age (pre-Roman) Britain, including both men's and women's garments and hairstyles. However, some of this imagery is clearly borrowed from early Roman styles, and some of the individuals may be deities (Allen 1958, 55-9). Therefore, it is difficult to determine whether these display Roman, Gallo-Belgic, or British individuals. For example, Allen (1958, 56) pointed out that it is rare for men to be shown with moustaches or beards on these coins, while this feature figures prominently on other representations of the human form. Given that we have limited representations of the human form in Britain during this period, it is difficult to support the coins as evidence for everyday life.

Death and the Body

Turning now to the body in death, Iron Age Britain is usually characterised as a period without a widespread burial tradition (Carr and Knüsel 1997). When compared to inhumations and cremations from the Bronze Age, and the formal cemeteries of the Roman and succeeding periods, this may seem to be the case at first. However, there is clear evidence that methods for treating the dead during this period were highly complex and varied regionally, as well as over time (Whimster 1981). Formal inhumations begin to appear in the Middle Iron Age, as shown by cists and other inhumations from southwest Britain (Dudley 1961; Johns 2006), and crouched pit inhumations in southern Britain (Cunliffe 1984a).

By the end of the Middle Iron Age radiocarbon dates suggest that, in East Yorkshire, the extensive regional square barrow tradition and so-called 'chariot burials' appear (Jay, Haselgrove *et al.* 2012). One exception to this is the Newbridge chariot burial outside Edinburgh (Carter and Hunter 2003), which has been dated to substantially earlier (Jay, Haselgrove *et al.* 2012), making it both a regional and temporal anomaly. The East Yorkshire burials are often found clustered in cemeteries, such as at Wetwang Slack and Arras. Many of these inhumations have simple grave-goods, such as joints of meat and ceramic vessels. However, some are more elaborate and contain brooches, glass beads, and bracelets. By the Late Iron Age, the 'Durotrigian' crouched burial style was practiced in Dorset, while in other regions, such as in the southeast, cremation became a regional practice. Some of the burials in Dorset also included mirrors (e.g. the Chesil mirror burial), while others occasionally contain swords (e.g. Whitcombe burial no 9). Both mirrors and swords are thought to represent high-status burials (Joy 2011a).

The excavated inhumations and cremations by no means form the dominant methods for treatment of the dead. It is clear that not all bodies were placed in inhumations or were cremated prior to burial. Articulated limbs, skulls, and single human bones are not uncommon in pits, which are commonly thought to have been used previously for grain storage. The collection of skulls, whether whole or fragmentary, has been used to suggest the idea of a 'head-cult' in Iron Age Britain (Armit 2012), while human remains in pits may have been an act of propitiation (Cunliffe 1992). In other cases, fragmentary human remains are often attributed to a different treatment of the body - excarnation (Carr and Knüsel 1997). In this process, the body is left exposed to the elements, and it may be that, after natural processes of decomposition have taken place, the remaining bones were collected either for burial or curation. Finally, in a limited number of known cases, certain individuals may have been intentionally placed in bogs at death (Stead, Bourke *et al.* 1986; Turner and Scaife 1995).

The body is clearly not a static entity during this period and differences in practice appear to reflect changes in meaning, both regionally and chronologically. In some instances, it was treated as a whole and remains intact, while in others the body is found in varying degrees of fragmentation. In the majority of cases, it seems that the body does not enter the archaeological record in a visible way. The flexibility and variety in the practice of treatment of the dead attests to the idea that there was not a prescribed practice throughout Britain, but that people were treated in a multitude of different ways. This may have even have been a source of conflict between groups. The body then becomes very important in the discussion of Iron Age Britain, because of the multiplicity of human actions. Burial practice and the treatment of the dead may have been decided within the community, with every decision a deliberate act. Studies of human remains, however, tend to focus on the skeletal evidence itself (e.g. age, sex, health, etc.), as well as the layout of the burial, such as the orientation and position of the body (e.g Whimster 1981). There is little explicit consideration of how differing burial practices reflect Iron Age ideas about the body. Why are these differences present? And what do these different burial practices express? Do they reflect identity, or are there other circumstances that determine the way in which a person is buried?

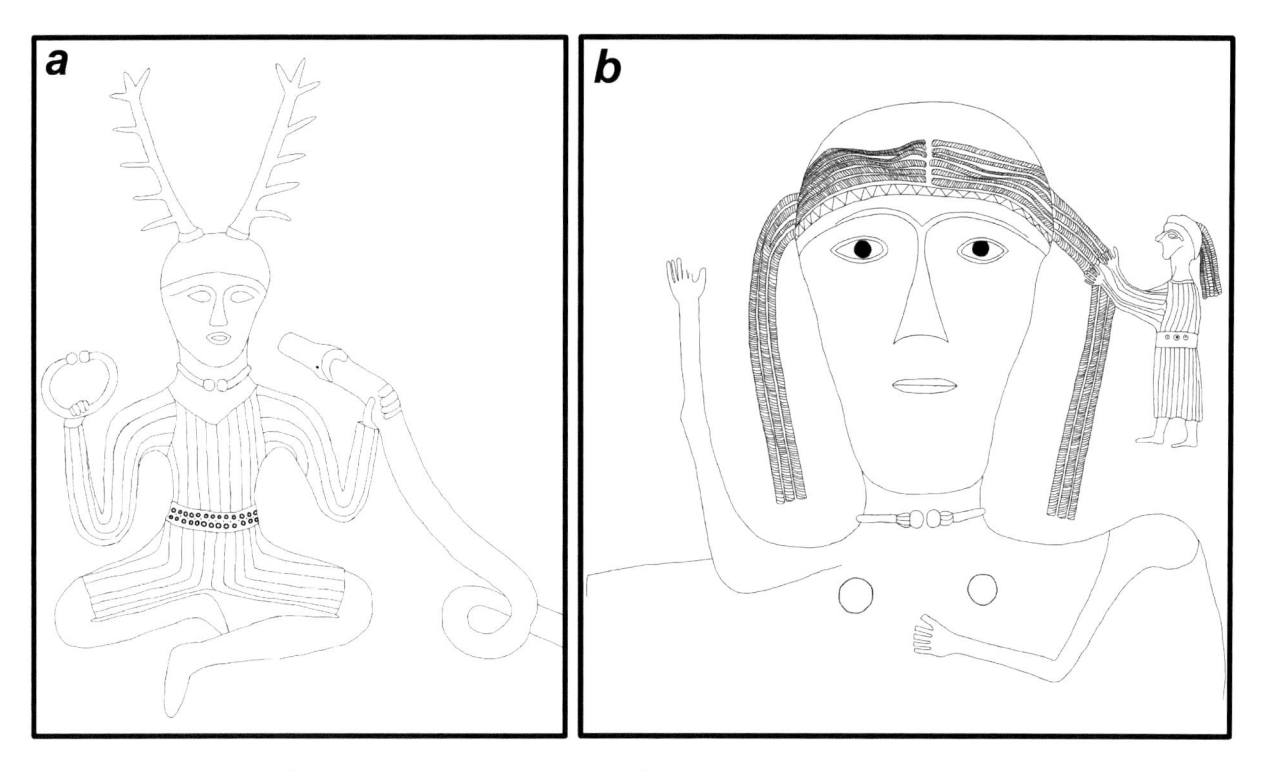

Figure 7: Details from the Gundestrup Cauldron (held in collections at National Museum of Denmark).
(a) Detail of antler figure, interior Plate A, (b) Detail of panel, exterior Plate F.

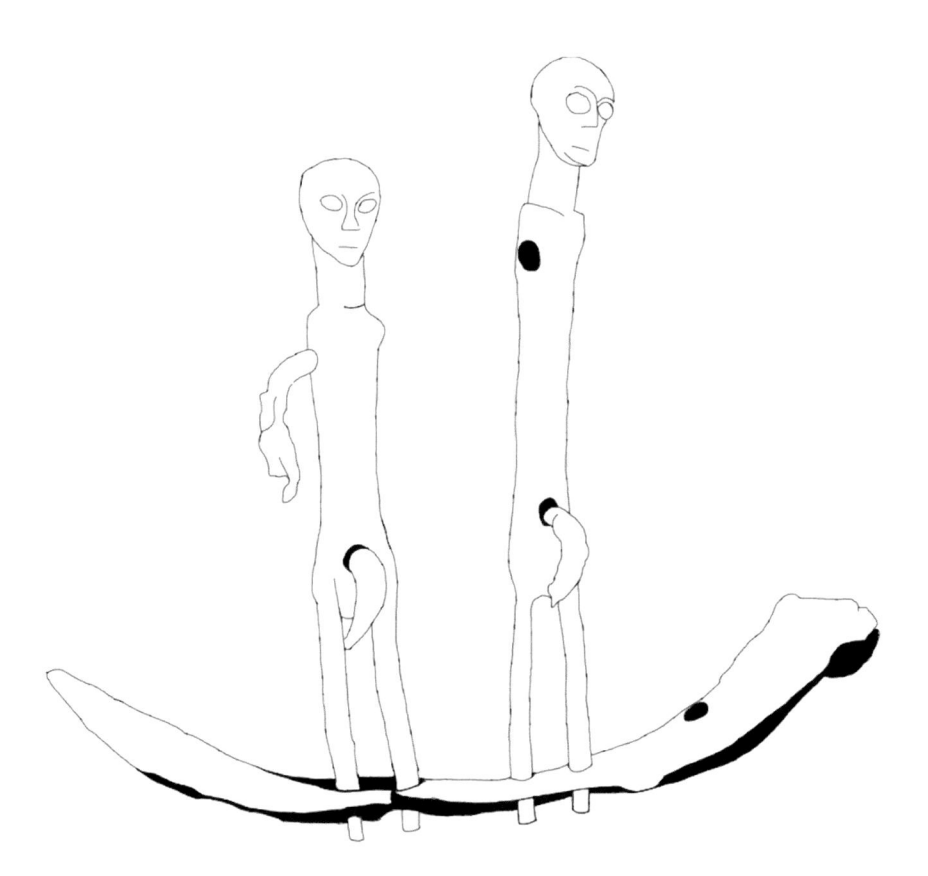

Figure 8: Drawing of the Roos Carr figures from East Yorkshire
(held in collections at Hull and East Riding Museums:Hull Museums KINCM:1991.141.10876).

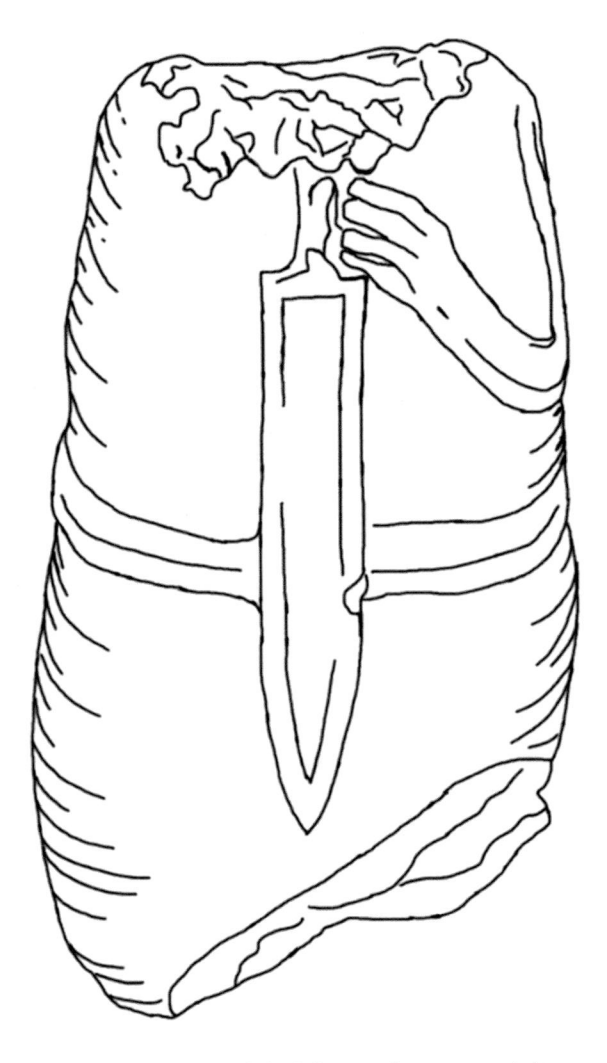

Figure 9: Back view of chalk figurine from East Yorkshire (Hull and East Riding Museums:Hull Museums KINCM:2006.11303.4576).

Although we have evidence for how the body was treated during death, how then do we extrapolate from this to the experience of the body during life? This is especially difficult given that we do not fully understand the differences between how the body was treated in these two states. Artefacts form one physical type of evidence that we can draw on. Although not exclusive to artefacts of dress, these objects by their nature would have been created, held, used, and transformed by an individual or moved between groups, although some (e.g. pots in East Yorkshire, Rigby in Stead 1991a, 105) may have been made specifically for deposition within burials. Artefacts found with an individual have often been used comparatively to understand the status of the deceased. For example, the lavish 'princess/lady' inhumation at Vix has been described as high-status in-part because of both the quantity and different types of objects contained within the burial (Pope and Ralston 2011, 383). Examples of high-status burials from Britain include the cart or chariot burials from East Yorkshire, as well as other mirror burials (Chesil mirror burial and Portesham both in Dorset, and Birdlip in Gloucestershire), the tumulus burial at Lexeden, and the Welwyn Garden city burial. If the objects that accompanied the body represent the deceased's belongings in life, then perhaps they do reflect status. However, the selectivity of an inhumation rite suggests that there is much more at play. Does inhumation in itself imply a higher status in comparison to others? To what extent do rare or exotic objects amplify the status of the individual? One last issue is that the archaeological record is biased towards materials that survive better within the ground. This, perhaps, has led to a distorted view of a material hierarchy in the past, coupled with the use of our modern hierarchical systems during our interpretations.

Artefacts of Dress

Artefacts related to dress have been found from contexts throughout the Iron Age in Britain. The brooch is perhaps one of the most extensively studied artefacts, as its evolution over time can be shown to follow a more or less linear pattern (Fowler 1953; Haselgrove 1997; Hattatt 1985; Hattatt 1989; Mackreth 2011). However, there has been less focus on how they were used. Other types of artefacts that were worn on the body includes: bracelets, finger-rings, toe-rings, anklets, arm-rings, armlets, pendants, necklaces, neck-rings, and collars. Objects worn on the head as part of a crown or headdress are very rare, although one notable exception is the crown from the Deal Warrior in Kent (Parfitt 1995). Other artefacts were used for the care and maintenance of the body, such as shears, tweezers, ear-scoops, 'nail-cleaners', mirrors, and small pestle and mortars that may have been used for grinding woad.

These artefacts are sometimes found in inhumations, as well as settlements, and occasionally in dry-land hoards. When found in association with human remains they may indicate the way that they were used (e.g. small rings found on the finger-bones), but it is unclear if the body was prepared in a specific way for burial, or appeared as it did in everyday life. Artefacts found as stray finds or within settlements are more ambiguous, as they do not directly indicate the manner in which they were used. While the way that some objects were employed seem obvious, such as bracelets worn on the wrists and brooches pinned together garments, the manner in which they were specifically displayed or used is unclear, and may even have changed over time according to regional traditions.

Textiles and garments made from leather or hide may also indicate aspects of dress. However, evidence for textile production is extremely rare for this period (DeRoche 2012). It is best indicated by spindle whorls and loom-weights found on settlements, although no looms have been recovered (except possibly from Glastonbury

Lake Village (Bulleid and Gray 1917, Plates LII-LVII)). Very few scraps of textiles remain (e.g. Somerleyton in Suffolk, and Skipworth Common in Yorkshire (DeRoche 2012)), but the best evidence is found in the corrosion of metal objects, which were in contact with either plant or animal fibres. However, while these scraps can be analysed in terms of the quality and direction of the spin, and the pattern of weave, the small size of the fragments makes determining the type of garments worn unclear. Brooches were presumably used to connect different garments, but it is also unclear how this was done.

Artefacts and Colour

One aspect of these objects that has not been discussed is that they all have different forms and were made from a variety of materials. Each of these materials has a different quality, some of which can be manipulated, while others cannot. For example, jet is a naturally black substance, but can be polished to create a lustrous surface or abraded to produce a matt surface. Meltable metals (i.e. gold, silver, and copper alloy) were combined to create different metallic colours that range from reds, to yellows, and silvers as displayed by the coin evidence (Creighton 2000). Fitzpatrick (2005) connects these yellow or golden colours with the embodiment of deities on earth or other connections to the heavens or celestial beings. Complicating some of these objects further is the decoration created through areas of texture, such as hatching juxtaposed with sinuous designs (e.g. mirrors). It is this play with colour, reflectivity of light, and play with shadow through texture that may have created a sense of confusion or even awe when viewed (Gell 1998).

There are two materials that can be directly manipulated to exhibit a full spectrum of colour. The first are textiles, which can be dyed through the use of a variety of oxides and plant materials, including the famous woad blue. The fragment textile from Skipworth Common in Yorkshire is suggested to be between 20-30% dyed, while a fragment from Burton Fleming burial 20 is thought to be the earliest example of embroidery in Britain and probably employed dyed wool to render the design visible (DeRoche 2012). Colour can also be manipulated on a second type of material: glass. Through the addition of oxides and minerals, glass can change in both colour and opacity from its often natural pale translucent green colour (Henderson 1985; 2000). While glass objects or objects containing glass are found in Iron Age Britain (e.g. beads and inlay on some copper alloy objects), and it has been suggested that localised production of some objects occurred in Britain (Davis and Gwilt 2008; Henderson 1987; 1989), it is unclear if colour and opacity were manipulated at the time of object manufacture, or whether glass was primarily coloured at an earlier stage with no later alterations. While the colour of some materials can be directly manipulated, and the texture of others can sometimes be altered, it is through the combination of multiple objects that colour and texture come together to create appearance.

The connections between colour and human society have been studied from various perspectives. Development of methods to measure and describe colour is an area of study to itself, as is the study of the biological capacity to perceive colour (Fortner and Meyer 1997). Other approaches seek to understand the connection between colour, language, and cognition. Berlin and Kay's (1999) seminal work has laid the foundation for later studies on this topic, including those in archaeology (Spence 1999). The basic premise is that colour descriptive word development follows a universal evolutionary pattern from a simple dichotomy between light (white) and dark (black) to more complex language where terms exist for ten or more colours. There have been numerous critiques of their study from both within the linguistic discipline (Saunders and Brakel 1997), and from the archaeologist's perspective (Chapman 2002).

A third approach to the study of colour examines the symbolic aspects of colour, where a particular colour can represent or communicate an idea. However, Young (2006, 179) critiques this approach as it limits colour to simply reflecting meaning and does not take context into consideration, or consider colour in flux. In contrast, she studies the materiality of colour, which seeks to understand why objects have a particular colour and what the colour does for the object (Young 2006, 175). Through a materiality approach, it is possible to consider the changing nature of colour over time, its context, and the juxtaposition of different colours. Young's (2005b; 2010) ethnographic work on the colour of cars and cultural synaesthesia in Western Australia is a good example of this approach to the study of colour.

Within studies of Iron Age Britain, Giles (2008a) has examined the effect of decoration on copper alloy objects. Some of these were decorated by the inclusion of either coral or red glass. While this decoration would not have been visible from a distance, at shorter range it would have stimulated a culturally learned reaction and interpretation, possibly leading to states of dazzlement, confusion, or even fear (Giles 2008a, 60), especially when viewed on martial objects, such as swords. In contrast, blue glass beads are found in mature female inhumations, which she suggests reflected the age and seniority of the individual (Giles 2008a, 72). Because the context of colour is important, it may be that the use of red on items other than martial objects, such as pins, pendants, and bracelets, or blue used outside of glass beads, such as woad, may have had a different effect on the viewer.

The idea of painting or tattooing with woad is also recognised as a practice during this period. A recent examination of evidence by Carr (2005) suggests that there may have been a change in the use of woad, first as an 'all-over' body paint and then later through the application of intricate designs. This change would have created visible differences in practice perhaps between an older and younger generation. In addition, there may have been an element in terms of resistance against the Romans, whereby individuals concealed their identity or political associations through the application of temporary woad dye applications. Alternatively, its use could proclaim an allegiance to a particular group (Carr 2005, 284-5).

Artefacts as Dates

Artefacts have long been instrumental in understanding the phases of prehistory. Prior to the development of scientific dating methodologies (e.g. C^{14} dating), the organisation of artefacts into periods of use and disuse provided a relative framework from which to describe the past. Since the development of radiocarbon dating, coupled with dendronchronology, it has been possible to pinpoint the dates of artefacts, features, and other material within calendrical date ranges. Within Iron Age studies, absolute dates have not replaced artefact chronologies, and both remain integral to interpreting archaeological evidence. In part, this is due to the radiocarbon plateau between 800 and 400 BC, which results in large error margins and wide date ranges. However, it is also due to the increasingly recognised complexity of both archaeological features in Iron Age Britain (Collis 2008; Hill 1995b), and the concept of time more generally (Lucas 2005).

Understanding the archaeological complexity of time is integral for interpreting evidence and developing chronologies for interpreting the past, as it is the result of human action. For example, the infill of a pit can be a slow natural accumulation, deliberate complete infill, slow deliberate infill over time resulting in many layers, or a combination of these factors. It can be the result of actions undertaken within the space of a few hours, weeks, months, years, or even decades. In contrast, given the intact nature of many formal inhumations, it is more likely that these were short-lived events that were completed within a few hours to a few days (Collis 2008). The way that we visualise these events is imperative for our interpretation (Collis 2008, 92).

Artefacts have been used to date features and sites in a number of ways. First, there is the horizon, where the presence of certain objects or materials indicates a fundamental change in either technology or material culture. For example, some materials can only be used through the use of new technology (i.e. metal objects would not be expected in Palaeolithic contexts), and coinage developed during a particular period in time (i.e. would not be expected in Neolithic contexts). Long-running types of artefacts can also be seen to change over time, and the manifestation of these changes can be used to date features. For example, pottery is perhaps one of the longest established types of material culture with good survivability. From the macro-scale perspective, we can see it change from the Neolithic to the modern day; however, it is often the micro-scale that is the most beneficial for archaeologists. Iron Age pottery has been heavily relied upon for dating settlements and burials. Brooches, which first appeared in Britain during the Iron Age, have also been shown to steadily change in appearance throughout this period (Haselgrove 1997). However, the premise of artefact chronology and resulting typologies is that they expect artefacts to develop in a linear pattern and that they will be deposited in roughly contemporary features.

This brings us to two issues with using artefacts for dating. First, the assumption that artefacts naturally develop linearly; and second, that they will be deposited within a contemporary feature that reflects their manufacture and short use period. Both of these areas are problematic. While some artefacts, such as brooches (Haselgrove 1997), have been shown to develop linearly, Garrow and Gosden (2012) have suggested that the decoration on Celtic Art does not follow a linear development, but instead is an accumulation of patterns and designs. Therefore, caution is needed when studying artefacts and their dates and linearity should not be assumed. In addition, artefact chronologies and their use for dating features and sites are complicated partly by the complexity of time in the past discussed above, but also by the issue of artefacts out of their temporal period. This is often referred to as 'residuality', however, this antiquated term suggests that such an appearance was abnormal and that the practice of artefacts being used outside of their time period goes against the natural consumer behaviour to dispose of 'old' objects and acquire 'new' versions. These so-called residual objects have been discussed recently in two different contexts: Hingley's (2009) discussion of Bronze Age objects found in Iron Age depositions, and Lockyear's (2007; 2012) study of Roman coins. Lockyear's study demonstrated the problems with coin hoards by graphing the date ranges of the coin issues contained within each hoard. In several cases, there were hoards with Republic issues along with late first or early second century AD coins, which suggest that these objects circulated for very long periods of time. Together, these studies suggest that we should not necessarily expect objects to be deposited within representative features, and care needs to be taken when extending artefact chronology dates to features, as well as scientific dates to artefacts.

Guido's (1978a) typology was based on the assumption that glass beads could act as type fossils to date archaeological features (as discussed in Chapter 2). Each of her classes was thought to form discrete period packages of beads that were manufactured, used, and deposited within a short period of time. 'Residual' Iron Age examples sometimes manifested in Roman period contexts, but she interpreted these as having little meaning. For example, one of her 'Class 2 Welwyn Garden City type' beads, which exhibits complex eyes (see Appendix B) was found in a pit with Romano-British pottery and a Vespasian coin, however she dismisses it as having come from an earlier occupation at the site, rather than the possibility that it continued to play a role within society (Guido 1978a, 48).

Artefact Production and Exchange

While the previous sections discussed evidence for dress, the relationship between artefacts and colour, and artefacts as dates, this section will examine what we can learn about exchange and production through studies of artefacts. Here, production refers to the resources and steps taken in order to produce an object, while exchange refers to the mechanisms by which they changed hands.

Production of objects has been suggested to be the culmination of a suite of factors: raw materials, location of raw materials, location of production, time investment, and construction; although other socially mediated factors have also been identified, such as the selection of raw materials (DeRoche 1997; Hamilton 2002). The scale that different production occurs at is linked to the level of exchange. Thus, a small household level production will utilise only local resources, requires little equipment investment, utilises only family labour, and produces objects used by the household or perhaps within the community (DeRoche 1997, 20). However, a larger production scale might draw on a larger resource base, perhaps choosing specific resource types over others, might have a more specialised or dedicated workforce, occurs within a designated area, and there is both a larger time investment in production and in tools. DeRoche (1997) suggested that in order to understand the mode of production, it is crucial to understand the technology needed to produce objects, as each will have different requirements.

Exchange then can range from the household/local level to the larger long-distance exchange network. For example, Moore has shown that within the Severn-Cotswolds, Malvern pottery, May Hill querns, and Droitwich briquetage occur at similar sites, which suggests that they may have been exchanged within similar networks (Moore 2007a, 50). Functional models explore exchange in economic terms where items have value and are exchanged for similarly valued objects; however, the actual mechanism for exchange, and the social processes involved remains unclear (Moore 2007a, 50-1). Recently, anthropological literature has been explored to understand exchange less as an economic process, but instead as the social processes and the social bonds that it can create. For example, interpretation of exchange through gift-giving draws upon the work of Mauss (1990 (1950)). Although, as Sharples (2010, 74) points out, it is impossible to see gift-giving in the archaeological record, Moore (2007a, 53-5) shows that by examining the settlement pattern and artefact distributions, it is possible to explore the relationship that inhabitants had with their neighbours through the archaeological record.

In comparison to pottery (Hamilton 2002), metalwork (Dungworth 1996), and querns (Peacock 1987), there has been little study of the evidence for glass bead manufacture in Britain (c.f. Henderson 1992). Evidence for raw glass manufacture in Britain is non-existent, and evidence for glass-working is extremely limited and in many cases unsubstantiated. However, an analysis of the key requirements for glass working suggests that in many ways the process requires similar conditions and tools to those needed for working with copper alloy. Both materials need to be heated to a similar temperature, and both may have been melted in crucibles at some stages.

Artefacts and Identity

The connection between people and artefacts has long been a topic of discussion. Within the Culture History approach to interpreting the past, artefacts were used to define different culture groups and their boundaries (e.g. Childe 1929; Childe 1940). However, although this approach to interpreting the past has fallen from favour, the connection between material culture and identity has continued to be an area of study (Hodder 1982; Miller 2010; Shanks and Tilley 1987). Hunter (2007a) has argued that within Iron Age Scotland and Northern Britain, patterns in the artefactual record do exist. Rather than viewing these patterns as a static reflection of the past or tribal/cultural boundaries, they are instead interpreted as evidence for different regional identities. Different patterns can be seen at different scales, and also within different groups of artefacts or by the materials utilised (Hunter 2007).

Patterning in the material culture is particularly important for the present project. This study has examined four very distinct geographic regions by considering the patterns at the macro-level through a comparison of types and characteristics. As is shown in the following chapters, there are patterns in the different types used, the colours, and in the different decorations on glass beads. This may suggest that there were distinct regional identities that were displayed through the use of material culture. This is further supported in Chapter 8 through a comparison of other types of material culture found in the study regions. However, not only are there regional patterns of material culture, but patterns also manifest in the organisation of settlement, boundaries, and in the treatment of the dead (explored further in Chapter 4).

Other types of identity are discussed in terms of the individual identity, such as age, gender, or status. Although burial data varies throughout Iron Age Britain, they have nonetheless formed the basis for discussions of identity. For example, in their discussion of sex and status evidence from burials in Iron Age Britain, Pope and Ralston (2011) suggest that by using grave wealth as an indicator of social status, women were just as likely to attain high status as men, but that these status-based identities were marked out through the gendered use of different types of material culture. Interestingly, they suggest that sex was not a major structuring principle in Middle Iron Age burials (Pope and Ralston 2011, 409), which suggests that men and women both had an opportunity to obtain a differentiated status through other means. Glass beads, it seems, forms a part of this gender package for marking out female identity, as where osteological examination has been carried out, they are never found with individuals thought to be male (discussed further in Chapter 8).

While regional and individual identities form core areas of study, another subject is the changing nature of identities around the first century BC, coupled with the Caesarian and Claudian invasions in southern Britain. It is these events that led to people from the Mediterranean and northern Europe arriving in Britain. Many of them inhabited Britain, some as soldiers with the Roman army, as well as others that came to support the army and later settled (James 2001). They brought with them a different material culture and religious practices, new ways for treating the dead, and alternative styles of building, all of which are represented in the archaeological record.

In the past, this has led to an interpretation of a strict dichotomy between the inhabitants of Britain. On the one hand, there were the 'native' inhabitants of Britain, who were barbaric and uncivilised. On the other hand, there were those who identified themselves as Roman and brought their civilised culture to Britain. It was proposed that the native inhabitants took up the Roman way of life and in effect, became more 'Roman'. This process has been referred to as Romanisation (Haverfield 1915; Millett 1990). The implications of this change suggest that the people of Britain wanted to change and adopt a Roman way of life to become more civilised (Hingley 1996, 39). Criticisms of this explanation for social change suggested that the theory of 'Romanisation' was too simple, that it was elite focused, and interpreted the identities during this period in simplistic terms (Hingley 1996; 2005, 14). Some have challenged this perspective by considering resistance to Roman enforced change (Mattingly 1997b). It is also becoming increasingly apparent in our post-colonial world that cultures are not simply one or the other, and we have begun to explore cultural changes in reference to hybridisation and creolisation (Carr 2003; 2006; Webster 2001).

Issues of identity after the conquest become particularly interesting, especially in terms of material culture. Outside of the areas that were more directly impacted by the Roman conquest, the situation is even more complex. Much of the material culture in Northeast Scotland is largely attributed to the first few centuries AD, despite the lack of absolute dates for most of the artefacts. Due to their relatively late date in the Iron Age, artefacts are often described as:

- 'Roman' artefacts in a 'native' context,
- Artefacts of 'native' design, but stylistically influenced by 'Roman' artefacts, sometimes made by recycling Roman objects.

Thus, this interaction between the inhabitants of Northeast Scotland and the Romans becomes an important dynamic for understanding the material culture through contact networks and relationships. It is also interesting, however, that while the settlement architecture suggests continuity during this period and there is an emphasis on limited direct contact between Iron Age and Roman people in Northeast Scotland (except for in violent encounters (Macinnes 1989, 108)), that the material culture does not reflect limited interaction (Hunter 2001c). Instead, it has been noted that much of the Roman material culture found in Scotland is of a very high quality (Hunter 2001c, 301; Robertson 1970, 200). The Roman objects fall into two main categories: artefacts related to feasting and drinking (e.g. pottery, metal vessel), and ornaments, such as beads, brooches, and toilet instruments (Hunter 2001c, 299). In contrast, objects thought to have been made to local tastes, but with a 'Roman' flavour, include the massive metalwork tradition, which consists of a number of armlets, and a few finger-rings and strap-junctions (Hunter 2001c, 291). The glass bangles and beads may also be a part of this assemblage, as some have suggested that they were made from recycled Roman vessel glass (Bertini 2012; Stevenson 1956; 1976), although the degree to which the designs were influenced by Roman styles is unclear.

One of the issues with the Roman or Roman influenced material is in the interpretation. What is the significance of these objects north of Hadrian's Wall, in an area that saw only limited permanent Roman occupation? Were they exotic objects that displayed status (Harding 2007, 234)? Or were they merely trinkets or curios (Macinnes 1989, 114)? Again, this relates back to the question of social organisation and hierarchy in Scotland, especially by the time Hadrian's Wall was established. Do artefacts simply reflect status and ethnicity? This not only is an issue in Scotland, but also becomes an interpretive issue for glass beads found in Early Roman or Romano-British contexts in the rest of Britain. What does the presence of these beads say about the identity of the wearer, were they either 'native' or 'Roman'? It seems likely that their identity was a complex combination of identity from multiple aspects of society and cannot be defined in this strict dichotomy.

Summary

Evidence for dress in Iron Age Britain derives from several sources. Pictorial representations of the human figure are rare, and the burial record is limited and exhibits a large amount of variability throughout the Iron Age. Textile evidence is also limited, as are other artefacts made from organic materials, leaving the most prolific types of evidence to be objects made from metals, glass, and stone. So, where does identity originate during this period? Evidence from the human body, or lack thereof, suggests that identities were based on a changing set of criteria that varied regionally and over time, and drew on other socially defined attributes beyond age/sex/ethnicity that we cannot measure or see within the archaeological record. General patterns from artefactual evidence suggest that increasing materiality throughout the Iron Age is indicative of not only changing concepts of the body and how it should be taken care of or displayed, but also an increasing desire to decorate it. The analyses in Chapter 8 will approach dress from a regional perspective, and examine the different types of evidence for dress in each region to understand how dress changed over time, the way in which dress was regionally constituted, and finally provide suggestions on the experience of wearing these objects.

Chapter 4
The Nature of the Archaeological Resource in the Regions

Study of the Iron Age period has not been equally pursued throughout Britain. Instead, for different reasons and circumstances, some areas or time periods are studied more than others. This varies not only throughout the history of research, but also in the methods utilised to approach the study of this period. Despite these differences, it is becoming increasingly clear that there was not a single unifying Iron Age culture, as there is a considerable degree of difference in regional practices (Haselgrove, Armit *et al.* 2001, 22). Four study regions were briefly introduced and defined in Chapter 1: Southwest England, East Anglia, East Yorkshire, and Northeast Scotland (Figure 2). Before turning to an analysis of objects and their contexts in Chapters 5 through 8, it is prudent to ground these interpretations in an understanding not only of the evidence for human activity in each of the study regions, but also differences in the history of research that may affect the interpretations of the available evidence.

This chapter will briefly explore each region under study. It begins by introducing the archaeological resource in terms of the history of research and the impact of developer-led excavations. Then, it turns to different patterns of settlement in each region. For some regions, this is well established, but for others evidence is scarce. Finally, this chapter will examine variances in the patterns for ritual and for the treatment of the dead. Although it is generally considered that the domestic world and ritual aspects of Iron Age life were not separate, but instead intimately intertwined (Fitzpatrick 1997b), this division has been utilised here because it provides a way to organise the material in order to emphasise some of the differences in the dominant sources of evidence. It should not be taken to reflect a point of view on the organisation of the Iron Age world.

Throughout this chapter, it should be clear that the impact of different research strategies and interests of antiquarians and archaeologists have much to do with both the quality and quantity of archaeological data available for analysis, which impacts the analyses presented in the following chapters. For example, relatively few research excavations have been carried out in East Anglia when compared to Southwest England. Yet, the preponderance of artefacts, especially metalwork in the form of coins and torcs in Norfolk, stand out as significant (see especially Garrow 2008). It is the extent that these extreme regional differences reflect real patterns in past societies, or whether it is simply the result of different archaeological practices and recovery strategies in the recent past, that remains the question.

The impact of developer-funded excavation after the implementation of Planning Policy Guidance (PPG) 16 in 1990 (currently replaced by the National Planning Policy Framework (NPPF) and its equivalents in the rest of the UK) can also be seen to affect each region differently (explored further in Chapter 7). This is a result of not only the quantity of the work undertaken, but also the placement of the investigations. With the exception of road or pipeline schemes, excavations are often centred on high-density urban areas and their neighbouring countryside. One of the benefits of developer-funded excavation is that excavations and other archaeological investigations are occurring in areas that would not normally be the subject of research projects (Moore 2006a). Of course the impetus for developer-funded excavation is entirely dependent on the location intended for development and not on the ideal location for filling in gaps in our knowledge. In some areas, such as Northeast Scotland, research excavations have been comparatively rare, and it is only through the very small number of developer-funded excavations that we can even begin to discuss settlement patterns and artefacts with context. Research and developer-funded excavations do not provide complete answers on their own, but instead provide a useful counterbalance of data.

The Archaeological Resource

Within each of the four study regions considered here, there are a number of factors that affect both how and what we know about the Iron Age. Much of this is to do with the history of research, but also the development of archaeology as a discipline. Excavation, and other means of assessing archaeology, has never been as widespread and frequent as it is today, as a result of the need for excavation prior to development. This section will discuss the ways in which the history of research and developer-funded excavation have shaped our understanding of these four regions of Britain, followed by a discussion of some of the key regional themes.

Southwest England

Upstanding monuments have historically been one of the prime areas of focus for the earliest antiquaries, such as William Stukely and Richard Colt Hoare. These remnants of the past are particularly visible in southwest

England, with monuments such as Stonehenge, Avebury, Silbury Hill, and Iron Age sites, such as Maiden Castle. It is thus probably unsurprising that some of the earliest controlled excavations were undertaken in this region, such as those by Pitt-Rivers (1887-1898) on his estates in Cranborne Chase in Wiltshire, where he uncovered Iron Age material. It was also around this time that Arthur Bulleid and Harold Gray excavated the Iron Age lake villages, first at Glastonbury (Bulleid and Gray 1917), and later at Meare (Bulleid and Gray 1948a; Coles 1987). The aim of the excavations at Glastonbury was to discover a lake village in Britain similar to the same type of site found in Switzerland (Bulleid and Gray 1917a, 5). Through these excavations, a wealth of material culture was uncovered, especially organic materials that do not normally survive.

Throughout much of the twentieth century, this region has continued to be one of the most thoroughly studied regions in Britain, as well as the test-bed for different excavation techniques and the use of aerial photography. It was particularly through the excavations in southern Britain that Hawkes (1931; 1958; 1959) developed his model of British Iron Age prehistory: the 'ABC' model. Through this framework, he divided England and Wales into 5 provinces, which were further sub-divided into 30 regions. Within each of these regions, he identified a number of cultures, whereby 'A' was replaced by 'B', which was subsequently replaced by 'C'. The mechanism of these changes was the result of migrations and invasions into Britain. Although this framework, and the reliance on invasion as the prime motivator of change, was later critiqued (Clark 1966); the model made a significant impact on the interpretation of sites excavated during the mid-twentieth century.

It may be that we can attribute the overall density of glass beads, as shown in Guido's 1978a catalogue and distribution maps, to the early and intense focus in this region. Although quality of contextual data is variable, many of the glass beads from this region were found through excavation, rather than as chance or stray finds through development or agriculture.

East Anglia

Until relatively recently, there had been only one major study of the Iron Age in Norfolk and Suffolk (Clarke 1939), as it seems that antiquarians took little interest in this region. This may be due to the differences in visible monuments as the geography of East Anglia is very flat and hillforts do not exist here in the same way as they do in Wessex (Davies 1996, 63). Interest and acknowledgement of the archaeological record in this region began to change at the end of the twentieth century, as evidenced by publications resulting from two conferences (Davies 2011; Davies and Williamson 1999a).

Despite the general lack of both amateur and research excavations in this region, it nevertheless boasts a wealth of material culture. This is primarily attributable to the impact of metal-detecting and intensive agricultural production (Davies 1996, 71). The importance of metal-detecting activity is well acknowledged, as is the relationship between metal-detectorists and archaeologists, which has enabled a good practice of recording finds (Hill 2007, 34; Portable Antiquities Scheme 2003; Worrell 2007, 272-3).

Interestingly, the difference in the level of study between this region and others plays out in the way in which glass beads from this region were understood. Guido (1978a) attributed very few examples to this region, many of which were of non-diagnostic or potentially later types anyways. Perhaps this was partly due to differences in archaeological focus, yet the intense agricultural practice in this area, through which stray beads are often found in other regions, had little impact of our understanding in this area. Despite the good practice of recording material in this region, very few glass beads have been found in this way. This pattern will continue to be seen throughout the book, but with one noted exception that is discussed in the following sections of this chapter.

East Yorkshire

The archaeological resource for East Yorkshire in the Iron Age is considered to be rich, but in a different way when compared to the previous two study regions. Lacking hillforts, except for the far western area covered here (e.g. Staple Howe (Brewster 1963)), this region is known for the large numbers of barrow inhumations. It is these barrows that held the attention of antiquarians, such as Stillingfleet (1848), Mortimer (1905), Greenwell (1872; 1906), and others. These early excavators recorded the contents of the inhumation barrows at Arras, Cowlam, and Danes Graves. Although these were some of the larger cemeteries to be excavated, a number of smaller investigations were also undertaken and are summarised by Stead (1965). More recently, two notable excavation programmes have added significant data to the foundations laid by the antiquarians, as these archaeological inquiries were conducted utilising modern techniques and recording practices. First were the excavations at Wetwang and Garton Slack, prompted by impending quarry extraction, which revealed over 400 inhumations, and a contemporary settlement (Brewster 1980; Dent 1984). Second, Stead undertook excavations at Rudston, Burton Fleming, Garton Station, and Kirkburn (Stead 1991a). Supplementing these excavations has been the recent discovery of an additional chariot/cart burial with mirror at Wetwang Slack (Hill 2001; The Guildhouse Consultancy 2002). In comparison to the antiquarian excavations, these recent excavations have benefited from osteological analysis of both human and animal bones, scientific analyses of finds, and environmental analyses.

In addition to the excavation data, a major landscape project identified cropmarks through aerial photography (Stoertz 1997). This project has added a significant data-set for understanding the wider landscape, as it has become clear that the excavations in East Yorkshire have been relatively limited in number compared to the number of identified cropmarks (Bevan 1997, 182). From this macro-approach, by examining the entirety of the Yorkshire Wolds long tracks of earthwork boundaries, or dykes, can be seen to cut across the landscape.

The glass beads from the antiquarians' discoveries, as well as those from the more recent excavations in East Yorkshire, continue to be very important for the study of glass beads: more beads were found here than in any other region. Interestingly, most examples were found with inhumations in large numbers, but they were found from very few sites compared to Northeast Scotland or Southwest England.

Northeast Scotland

The nature of the archaeological resource is very different in this region compared to the others examined here. In the past, study of the Iron Age in Scotland has been focused on the borders region (Traprain Law in East Lothian (e.g. Curle 1914; 1915; Haselgrove 2009), and other sites (Childe 1933; Childe and Forde 1932; Piggott 1947; 1957; Stevenson 1948)), and in Atlantic Scotland, particularly in connection with the brochs and other megalithic dwellings (e.g. Armit 1991; Barrett 1981; Henderson 2008; MacKie 1965b; 1974; 2008; 2010; Parker Pearson, Sharples *et al.* 1996). This has led to a number of knowledge 'black holes' that have been identified in Scotland (e.g. Cavers 2008; ScARF 2012, 72). Northeast Scotland could be considered partly as a 'black hole' and partly as 'un-sorted' (Haselgrove, Armit *et al.* 2001, 25; ScARF 2012, 88).

While there was some antiquarian interest in Northeast Scotland (e.g. Anderson 1883; Christison 1898), it was really in the twentieth century, when Childe (1935; 1940; 1946) arrived in Edinburgh in 1927 that a narrative developed. Looking at settlement form characteristics in Northeast Scotland, Childe (1935) identified the 'Abernathy culture' based on their characteristic 'Gallic fort' structures. By the time that the Hawkesian model became established as a way to frame the archaeological evidence for the Iron Age in England and Wales, it did not include Scotland. Piggott (1966) later developed this model to include Scotland, but acknowledged that the Claudian invasion had less meaning in Scotland and he developed a later period of the chronology that extended further into the first millennium AD. The area studied in the present research was comprised of Piggott's 'Northeast Province', but overall interpretation had not changed drastically since Childe's synthetic publications, even with the advent of radiocarbon dating (c.f. MacKie 1969).

The result of the last century of archaeological inquiry in this region has led to an unclear understanding of the settlement of this region. Many of the glass beads and other artefacts here have been found through casual or accidental means and lack contextual information. This renders many of the characteristic artefacts for this region, including glass beads, very difficult to interpret in the context of wider social meaning.

Impact of Developer-funded Archaeology

The current state of developer-funded archaeology has advanced out of a long-term concern for the effect of development and leisure on cultural heritage since the mid-twentieth century. Government legislation was introduced in November 1990 as PPG16 (later replaced by Planning Policy Statement (PPS) 5 in 2010). Through this government initiation, the developer-funded sector of archaeology has changed the dynamics of excavation in England (and similarly in Wales and Scotland). For example, Croft (2000, 131) has shown that there was a 900% increase in development between 1986 and 1999 as seen by the number of planning applications made, which suggests a similar development in developer-led projects.

Similar legislation was enacted in Scotland in 1994 (NPPG5), and a coinciding dramatic change can be seen in here. In 2002, it was reported that more than half of the excavations carried out in Scotland were the result of developer-funded initiatives (Carter 2002). In 1990, Historic Scotland funded over 70% of the excavations, but this shifted dramatically by 2000 to only 25% of excavations when non-government funders provided the remaining 75% (Carter 2002).

Developer-funded excavation impact is mostly seen in urban areas, where new building construction or development is more likely to take place. Other large-scale works, such as road schemes or pipelines, also prompt archaeological investigation, often covering large areas of land (e.g. Brown, Howard-Davis *et al.* 2007). Thus, its effect is different in each study region (explored in Chapter 7). However, despite the increased amount of excavation and resulting data, timely synthesis of this information is not always undertaken, which in turn results in archaeological stagnation. This was an issue highlighted in the archaeological framework for the Eastern Counties (Medlycott 2011).

Out of all the study regions included in this study, Northeast Scotland has undergone the fewest research excavations. It has really only been through developer-funded excavations that an understanding of the Iron Age has begun to become clear (Phillips and Bradley 2004), such as the growing number of excavations at domestic sites, such as at Kintore (Cook and Dunbar 2008) and Candle Stane (Cameron 1999) both in Aberdeenshire. These studies have involved excavation of both enclosed and un-enclosed sites. This is proving to be especially important for adding depth to an understanding of Iron Age material culture previously based on stray finds. It is through these developer-led excavations that glass beads have finally been found in good contextual circumstances, and some even with radiocarbon dates (e.g. Thainstone and Culduthel Farm).

Patterns of Iron Age Settlement

Our interpretations of the Iron Age in Britain are linked to the history of research, research questions, and the nature of the archaeology itself. For example, drawing on the study regions investigated here, the greatest contrast is between the archaeology of Southwest England and East Yorkshire. Both regions have historically been important for research, due to the visible monuments, but the practices represented are very different. In Southwest England, settlements have become the main areas of research, while in East Yorkshire the focus has been on the square barrow inhumation practice. Burials are not absent from Southwest England and neither are settlements from East Yorkshire, but there were clearly different regional practices occurring in the Iron Age. This regionality is important when considering the glass beads from each region. Although further details are provided in Chapters 6 through 8, Southwest England, East Anglia, and Northeast Scotland are regions that were already identified by Guido (1978a) as being areas where large numbers of glass beads have been found. Although the amount of contextual data varies, these beads have been found in different types of archaeological features that form a part of a regional pattern. In contrast, very few beads were identified in East Anglia by Guido (1978a), although this chapter discusses one important site that has begun to change this perception.

While it is evident that there is a certain amount of regional practice that results in differing material remains, by the Late Iron Age this regionalisation is sometimes viewed as tribalisation. Tribal names have been taken from various classical texts that sometimes describe specific regions that were inhabited by specific groups of people. These tribal groupings have been suggested to be reflected in the coinage distribution evidence (Cunliffe 2005, 190-1). However, there is a danger that using the word 'tribe' uncritically does not permit a wider analysis of the social complexities at the end of the Iron Age (Moore 2011). While some of the discussions in this section mention tribes, or evidence connected with tribes, this is mainly in a descriptive sense, as some practices are specifically referred to as their tribal name, such 'Durotrigian burials', or 'Dobunni coins'.

Southwest England

In Southwest England (see Figure 10 for major sites mentioned in text), it has recently been suggested that the traditional three period division of the Iron Age is not as meaningful in this region as it is in others (Fitzpatrick 2007; Moore 2007a). Instead, it has been proposed that a two-part division, based on available pottery and settlement evidence and further supported by radiocarbon dates, more accurately reflects the evidence (Moore 2006b). Thus, there is an earlier component that refers to the Late Bronze Age and Early Iron Age transition, and a later Iron Age period covering approximately the fourth century BC until the first century AD. The term 'Late Iron Age' is specifically reserved for referring to the first century BC/AD.

Settlement in the earlier Iron Age is characterised by contemporary occupation at both upland and lowland sites. The lowland settlements are found in river valleys and unlike their upland counterparts, they are not surrounded by a boundary or enclosure. These settlements are often single roundhouses, such as at Lechlade at Roughground Farm (Allen, Darvill *et al.* 1993). Although these settlements were unenclosed, different types of boundaries are found across the landscape. These include large scale field systems, but also pit alignments, as at Ashton Keynes near Shorncote (Hey 2000). In the uplands, however, a number of enclosures are attributed to this period. The earliest of these, often termed 'hill-top' enclosures are early in date and are very slight, but with large defences (Cunliffe 2005, 378; Fitzpatrick 2007, 124). Examples are found at Bindon Hill, Norbury, and Ham Hill. It is unclear what these early hill-top enclosures were used for, as there is little domestic structural evidence; however, there is evidence for four-post structures, which may have been used for storing grain (Fitzpatrick 2007, 134). By the sixth century BC, a different group of enclosures located on hill-tops appear: hillforts. These were different from the earlier hill-top enclosures, as they are smaller, with a single ditch and rampart, but the biggest difference is that the defences are more substantial. Examples include the earliest phase at Maiden Castle, Chalbury Camp, and Yarnbury Castle. Very few glass beads are found at these early period settlement; although, one of the earliest examples was found in a midden feature (McOmish, Field *et al.* 2010).

By the fourth century BC, settlement in Southwest England changes. In general, this later period is characterised by a need to enclose, but this is manifested in a different way than in the previous period. Many of the hill-top and early hillfort enclosures were abandoned during this period, while others were not only enlarged, but they were developed into a complex system of enclosure defences with elaborate entryways. The later phases at Maiden Castle, Dorset is probably the best-known example of developed hillforts, with an extremely complex and ornate entrance. These sites have traditionally been seen as the homes of elites or other ruling class and formed the core of Cunliffe's (1984b) model for social organisation. However, Hill (1996) has posited that there is very little evidence to suggest that hillforts were any different in status from lowland settlements. Interpretations of hillforts are also engulfed in discussions of warfare and the need for defence (James 2007), while alternative interpretations have suggested that they fulfilled a more symbolic role (Armit 2007; Sharples 1991). Perhaps related to these changes in settlement during this period is the increased appearance of glass beads at this time.

During the later Iron Age, settlements in the lowlands also changed. Excavated sites, such as Cleveland Farm (Powell, Jones *et al.* 2008), Claydon Pike (Miles, Palmer *et al.* 2007), and Thornhill Farm (Jennings, Muir *et al.* 2004) in the Upper Thames Valley, show evidence for very dense settlement (Hey 2007, 167). In contrast to the earlier Iron Age period, these settlements were primarily unenclosed (Fitzpatrick 2007, 131). However, within these large and dense settlements, boundaries were used to mark out individual households (Moore 2006b, 69). Elsewhere in this region, in the north Cotswolds and Severn Valley, small rectilinear enclosures bound households and are sometimes found clustered, as at Birdlip (Parry 1998) and Temple Guiting (Vallender 2005). It may also be at this time that banjo enclosures were built; although their use is unclear, they may have been for stock control (Moore 2006b). Interestingly, very few glass beads have been found at these sites, although the example from Thornhill Farm is a notable exception.

By the Late Iron Age in the first centuries BC and AD, the southwest is described by some as being inhabited by the Dobunni tribe in Gloucestershire and north Somerset, and the Durotriges in modern Dorset. Traditionally, it is also during this period that the urban or proto-urban centres of political organisation, settlement, and centralised manufacturing appear, forming a different type of enclosed settlement, the *oppida*. There are many critiques over the use of this term for these sites, as well as about their purpose (Moore 2012; Pitts 2010; Woolf 1993). However, it is significant that they do not develop out of established sites, but were instead built in peripheral previously uninhabited areas (Moore 2007a). In the southwest, two sites in particular are considered to be *oppida*: Bagendon and Salmonsbury, both in Gloucestershire. Although these sites are associated with an increase in urbanisation, glass bead finds are limited. In addition, the beads from Bagendon are very characteristic of the Early Roman period and other similar examples have been found at Roman towns.

The promontory fort at Hengistbury Head in Dorset is also considered to exhibit characteristics similar to these *oppida* sites, such as the evidence for cross-channel trade, although it is earlier in date (Fitzpatrick 2001).

At many of the sites already discussed in this section, the material culture evidence is limited in part from preservation factors, but also by practices in the past that allowed the material to enter the archaeological record. However, there are two unusual sites in this region that stand out due to the diversity of material culture (Fitzpatrick 2007; Minnitt 2000): Glastonbury Lake Village (Bulleid and Gray 1917; Coles and Minnitt 1995) and Meare Lake Village (Bulleid and Gray 1948a; Bulleid and Gray 1948b; 1966; Coles 1987). Both of these sites are located in the Somerset Levels, a coastal wetland region.

Although the two sites were broadly contemporary (Glastonbury Lake Village approx. 200-50 BC; Meare Lake Village approx. 300-50 BC, although the precise dates are the subject of debate (Moore 2003, 33)) and only 5km apart, their relationship is unclear. The sites were excavated at the end of the nineteenth century and into the early twentieth century, which unfortunately means that, although Gray brought new excavation techniques that he learned from working with Pitt-Rivers, the recording practices and excavation techniques were not as precise as today's standards. Therefore, interpretation of the site is hampered by these limitations. However, it is still possible to get a general sense of the sites. These sites are vastly different from any other Iron Age settlement in Iron Age Britain. They were characterised by their many mounds in the wetlands, which presumably formed the foundations for structures kept out of the marshland. The material culture that was excavated was incredibly diverse and objects that would not normally survive, such as woodwork, were preserved. In addition, the sites are well known for the hundreds of glass beads found amongst the mounds. The combination of colourless and opaque yellow glass has been considered to be characteristic of the beads found here, and because of their large numbers, Guido (1978a) thought that they may have been manufactured there. Despite other excavations in the similar environmental locations within the nearby Avon Levels (Gardiner, Allen *et al.* 2002), it is the quantity of glass beads, the diversity of other material culture, and the size of the lake villages at Meare and Glastonbury that makes these wetland settlements incomparable to other Iron Age settlements.

The hundreds of glass beads found at the lake villages skews the data for Southwest England somewhat, but despite this, glass beads from this region are known from a greater range of site types than any other region considered here. However, when they are found at these other sites, they are found in very small numbers and often not together in the same contexts. This makes it very difficult to understand how they were used, as we

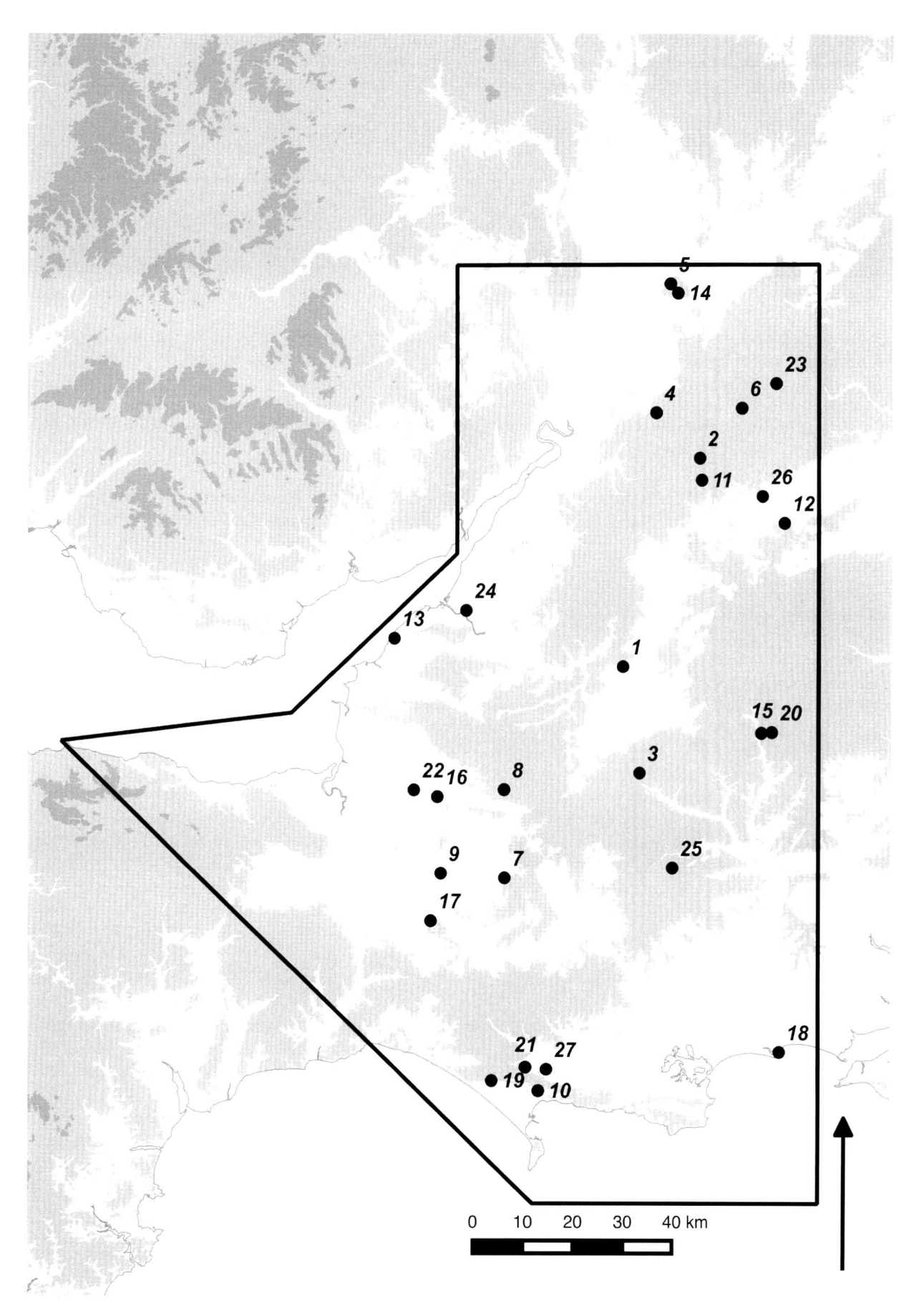

The Nature of the Archaeological Resource in the Regions

Figure 10: Key sites in Southwest England mentioned in the text.

have no way of connecting them to the body. Some of the glass beads from the lake villages were found together in clusters, which suggest some possible associations between them.

This section has primarily discussed the different settlement patterns in Southwest England. These patterns in settlement are best exemplified by the nature of the settlements in Gloucestershire, however, it is the history of research in this area that helps to provide a balanced view. There are localised differences in the character of the evidence for settlement as highlighted in the resource assessment and research agenda (Fitzpatrick 2007), yet, it is clear that the history of research and contribution of developer-funded archaeology has not contributed equally to all counties. Despite these potential biases, it is the quantity and quality of archaeological data from this region that has enabled researchers to move beyond strict reporting of finds and features, and to really engage with the data in order to explain human behaviour during the Iron Age (e.g. Cunliffe 1984c; Moore 2007b; Sharples 2010).

East Anglia

In comparison to Southwest England, very few sites have been excavated in Norfolk and Suffolk (see Figure 11 for major sites mentioned in text). Despite a growing number of developer-funded excavations in the region, interpretations of sites are unable to go beyond a very general 'late prehistoric/Iron Age/Roman' interpretation. As syntheses of the available data have been limited, a cyclical pattern emerges where an increasing number of sites are excavated, but the lack of syntheses means that they cannot be further incorporated into a growing framework of site morphology and chronology (Davies 1996, 64). Further complicating the interpretation of the evidence is the relegation of Norfolk and much of Suffolk to the periphery in the core-periphery model of Later Iron Age Britain (Hill 2007).

The limited excavations have suggested a general pattern in the settlement of this region. In the Late Bronze Age, artefactual evidence in the form of hoards, are found throughout the landscape covered by these two counties (Davies 1996; Martin 1999), which may suggest that the settlements also followed this pattern. Davies' (1996; 1999) model suggested that by the Early Iron Age that settlements were concentrated in the west and gradually moved eastward. The limited identification of Early Iron Age settlement sites is suggested to be due to the unenclosed nature of most sites (Martin 1999, 49-51). However, Davies *et al.* (1999b) and Martin (1999) have identified a few enclosed sites in Norfolk and Suffolk, some of which have been excavated. These are variable in shape, size, and nature of the enclosure. For example, Narborough in Norfolk is an irregular oval, univallate and encloses approximately 6.0ha, while Warham Camp (also in Norfolk) is circular, bivallate, and encloses 1.5ha (Davies 1999, 30-1). In Suffolk, the roughly rectangular double bank and ditch enclosure at Burgh covers 7ha (internally 3.4ha), and at the Barnham, there is a square double ditched enclosure that is much smaller and only covers 1ha (Martin 1999, 59-62). The relationship between these assumed unenclosed sites and enclosed sites is unclear.

Rectangular enclosed Iron Age sites have also been identified in this region, although most have only been excavated on a very small scale, except for the extensive excavations at the unusual site at Fison Way, Thetford (Gregory 1991). Beginning as early as the Middle Iron Age, this site saw a number of successive building phases. Each phase was more grandiose than the previous until the final phase where the ornate enclosure is suggested to have formed an artificial oak grove. The lack of general domestic debris has led to the interpretation of this site as somehow being connected with ritual activity, rather than as a farming based settlement. Davies (1999) and Martin (1999) have extended the interpretation to other rectangular enclosures in both counties and see parallels with similar rectangular enclosures from continental Europe.

Other evidence for Iron Age settlement in Norfolk is derived from extensive evidence from key areas such as at Thetford, Saham Toney, and Caistor St. Edmund (Davies 1999). This evidence is mainly from find concentrations, rather than bounded settlement evidence, but it suggests that these areas may have been heavily populated (Davies 1999, 33-5). Davies (1999, 33) interprets this evidence as connected with the Late Iron Age *oppida* found elsewhere in southern Britain at this time. Although these sites lack the linear earthworks that define the *oppida,* Davies suggests that the similarities in material culture, such as large numbers of coins and coinage production, could mean that they served a similar purpose. This interpretation may be falling into the trap of trying to define the evidence in Norfolk and part of Suffolk in terms of the Late Iron Age activity that occurred elsewhere in Souther Britian and may be an attempt to de-peripheralise northern East Anglia. Rather than trying to connect these sites to the *oppida*, Hill (2007) refers to these sites as open villages. These were long lasting farms or hamlets that in some cases show consecutive shifting structures suggesting a complex site history formed by unbounded settlements that can cover areas between 10 and 15 km across (Hill 2007, 20).

Hill's interpretation of Northern Anglia differs from the traditional explanations, such as Davies' (1996; 1999) and Martin's (1999). Despite the criticism of the use of core-periphery models to explain the change in material culture and settlement that occurred in southeast England, Hill (2007, 16-7) noted that there has been little attempt to replace the model with interpretations that fit the archaeological evidence more closely. He suggests that the extreme changes that manifested in material culture, burial treatment, and settlement over the course of the Late Iron Age were not driven by increased contact with the continent and the importation of new and exotic material culture, but instead can be traced back into the Middle Iron Age. Thus, the increase in material culture was not the cause of social change, but was a symptom (Hill 2007, 37). The narrative that Hill developed for Northern Anglia and the East Midlands is different from the west to east movement proposed by Davies and Martin. He suggests that open settlements were found extensively in the river valleys from the Middle Iron Age. He describes society at this time as:

> ...[giving] the impression of successful agricultural communities practicing mixed farming in landscapes with large open areas of arable and pasture suggesting that the land itself was communally owned or controlled. They tended to have undifferentiated ways of eating, few 'luxuries', and little overt indication of marked distinctions between households or individuals. There is not much evidence for long-distance exchange, except for basic commodities such as iron, salt, or quernstones (Hill 2007, 21).

While permanent settlements were established, not all inhabitants occupied the site throughout the year, as seasonal transhumance would have necessitated members living elsewhere, such as while making salt or herding animals (Hill 2007, 21-2). By the Late Iron Age, other settlements began to fill in the areas between the long established open settlements (Hill 2007, 33-4). These settlements may have begun as satellite settlements from the main occupation, or could have been driven by other social factors, or control over resources, but the key difference is that they were enclosed. Perhaps the move towards enclosure was the stimulus for other social changes that manifested in the Late Iron Age, such as changes in material culture. In Suffolk and Norfolk, these changes did not occur to the same extent as they did in Essex and Kent. However, Hill (2007, 23-37) stressed that rather than seeing the lack of development of exotic material culture as indicating a static passive culture, we should interpret this region as having developed its own region social practices that did not require the same types of material culture as was used elsewhere in the south.

Despite the models of settlement put forth by Davies and Hill, interpretation of social change and structure and the material culture continues to be hampered by the lack of excavation and synthesis in this region. Glass beads have not been found at any of the sites discussed above. Yet, there is one recently excavated site that has the potential to completely change the perception of this area. This is Grandcourt Quarry near King's Lynn (Malone 2010). Final publication of the excavations at this site is forthcoming, however, it is already becoming clear that the site is of national importance and will have a resounding effect on studies of ritual and material culture, due not only to the quantity, but also the variety, of artefacts. The nature of the activity is not currently clear, as the excavations revealed only part of an enclosure. Outside of the enclosure were a large number of intercutting pits with a pottery-rich fill that also contained an unusually high number of brooches and other decorated metalwork, which along with the radiocarbon dates are key for dating the site. No roundhouse features were discovered through the course of the excavation, although the interior of the enclosure was not the prime target of the excavation, so it may still have a wider settlement context. As will be discussed throughout the following analyses chapters, a large number of glass beads were also recovered through excavation where previously very few examples are known from this region.

East Yorkshire

Keeping issues with biases in our understanding of the Iron Age in East Yorkshire in mind, this section discusses the limited available evidence for settlement in this region (see Figure 12 for major sites mentioned in text). Understanding the nature of settlements and social relations is not only derived directly from the settlements themselves, but also from the large-scale dyke boundary systems. These linear earthworks are thought to have been built in the Late Bronze Age. Some of these structures are simple, composed of a single ditch and bank, while others are more complex and are composed of multiple strands of banks and ditches (Bevan 1997, 183). Overtime, the space within these large boundary dykes became increasingly divided and sub-divided until small rectangular parcels of land were sectioned off. Another type of boundary was formed by trackways. Perhaps significantly, these boundaries often incorporated pre-existing monuments such as Bronze Age round barrows or springs, possibly serving as useful landmarks in the landscape (Bevan 1999, 128). It is unclear if these boundaries served a purely functional purpose, such as animal management, restriction of land, or avenues for communication, but it has been suggested that the divisions of the landscape were connected to ideas of community identity and perhaps even reflected social organisation (Bevan 1997; Giles 2007b).

Contemporary settlements within the dyke building period (i.e. the Late Bronze Age) are thought to have been primarily enclosed sites (Bevan 1997, 184). Four sites on the Wolds have been excavated, including: Grimthorpe, Staple Howe, Devil's Hill, and Thwing. These settlement sites enclose a small area with palisades, earthworks or ramparts, with evidence for roundhouses on the interior, although Thwing was enclosed by a hengiform ditch and only enclosed one roundhouse. There is also evidence for 4- and 6-post structures within these sites, and

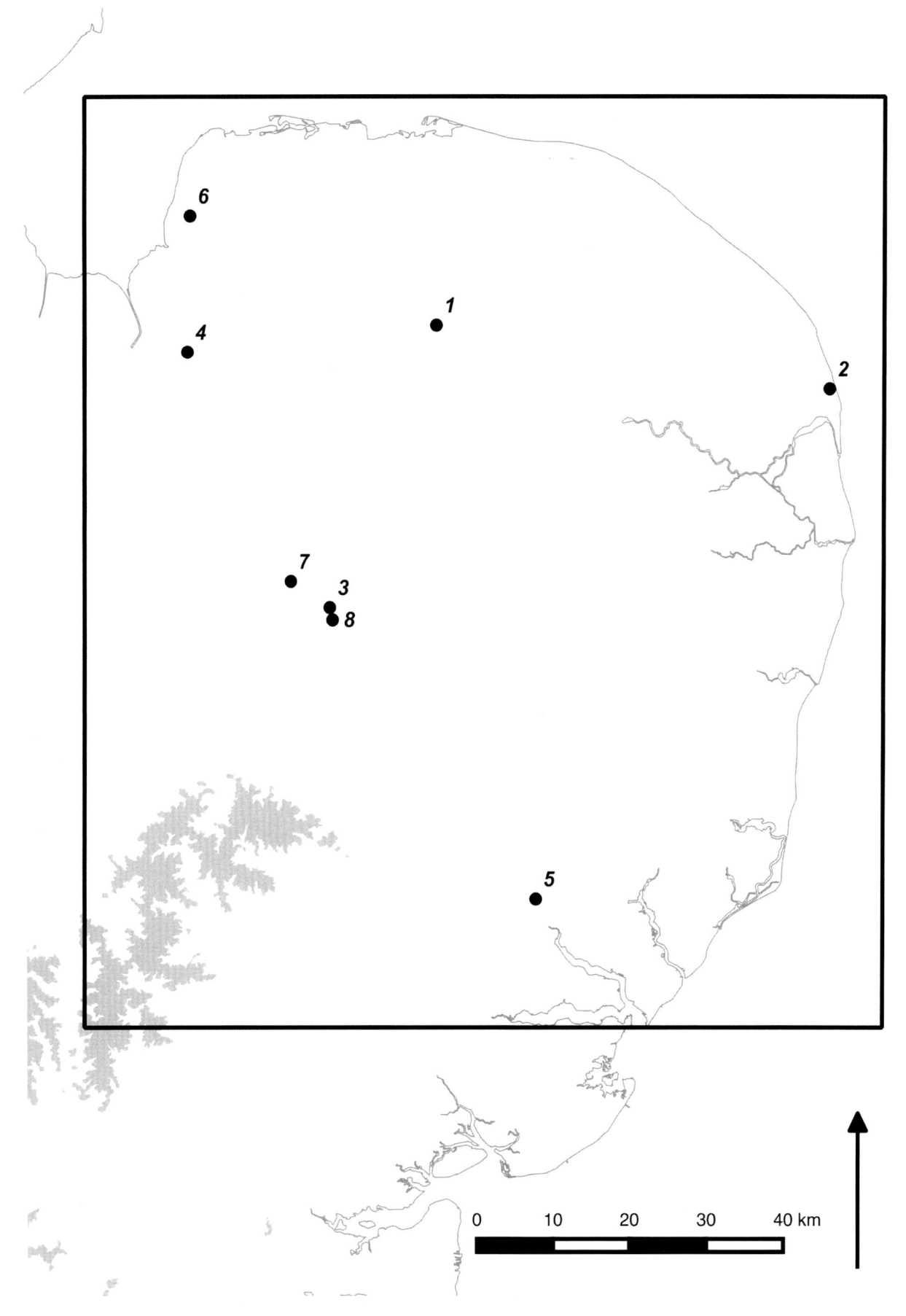

Figure 11: Key sites in East Anglia mentioned in the text.

possible storage pits at Staple Howe and Devil's Hill. These sites are all located at the junction between the upland and lowland, and Bevan (1997, 185) suggested that this may relate to the acquisition of resources from different environments. An open settlement in the Vale of Pickering at Heslerton has also been excavated and was contemporary with the dykes. This site has evidence for seven roundhouses, several 4-post structures, and an east-west pit alignment was also revealed.

Bevan (1997, 186) suggested that the dyke building and enclosed settlements were abandoned at the same time that the square barrow inhumation practice began. This change in settlement form may reflect a wider social change around the Middle Iron Age. However, as Bevan (1997, 186) points out, the only known settlement to be contemporary with the square barrow inhumations is the settlement at Wetwang Slack/Garton Slack. Settlement at this site began as an open settlement. There is evidence for 80 roundhouses/round-structures, although it is not clear if they were all in use simultaneously. Interestingly, as the square barrow inhumation practice ended, enclosed settlements return, which again may indicate social change. In this Late Iron Age period, before the Roman invasion, settlements in this region formed a distinctive pattern. These settlements are referred to as 'droveway' or 'ladder' settlements and are sets of small rectilinear ditched enclosures placed along both sides of ditched trackways. This can be observed in the later settlement period at Wetwang/Garton Slack, as well as at Rudston, Bell Slack, Brantingham, and North Cave. They are found to overlay square barrows, which Giles (2007a, 239) suggested may indicate a disregard for existing monuments. Some of these rectilinear enclosures continued to be inhabited into the Roman period, and in some cases, as at Rudston, villas overlay the droveway settlement (Giles 2007a, 239). Thus, there seems to be a change in practice in the earlier Iron Age compared to the later Iron Age. It is unclear what the relationship was between the Early Bronze Age round barrows and the Iron Age square barrows, if any, but up until the end of the Iron Age inhumation practice, the round barrow seems to have been respected in terms of the placement of Iron Age boundaries and square barrows. However, by the end of the Iron Age, there seems to have been a complete disregard for square barrows as settlements were situated on top of inhumations. It is unclear why these practices changed.

In contrast to the glass beads from other regions, where they have been primarily associated with settlements or other 'sphere of the living' contexts, glass beads in this region are not associated with these features. In fact, there are very few glass beads found outside of burial features, and these date to the Roman period, such as at Rudston Roman Villa, or at Castleford. Even the glass beads from Sutton Common have been found in contexts that suggest some sort of practice to do with the dead, rather than the living. This may demonstrate a regional practice with material culture when compared to other parts of Britain.

Northeast Scotland

Unlike the other regions discussed in this chapter, settlement in Northeast Scotland is primarily explored through survey data (see Figure 13 for major sites mentioned in text), which makes interpreting social change and structure more difficult. Extensive surveys were conducted throughout the region, notably in Moray (Jones, Keillar et al. 1993). A recent synthesis of various survey work in Donside in Aberdeenshire has highlighted the rich nature of this data, but also demonstrated the wider distribution of identified sites (Halliday 2007).

The settlement architecture in Northeast Scotland is characterised by hut-circles (roundhouses), enclosures, forts or hillforts, and souterrains. In this region, circular structures have been used as early as the Mesolithic period, which may demonstrate a long period of continuity of settlement patterns. The Iron Age domestic structures are found singly and in groups (Halliday 2007, 109). There is also a range of different types of enclosures, including lowland enclosures made from stone walls, and forts or hillforts, and they range in size from very small (e.g. Maiden Castle 0.07ha) to very large (e.g. Tap o'Noth 16.4ha) (Halliday 2007, 92-100).

Although extensive survey data of sites exists for the Northeast, it is unclear how sites relate together in the wider landscape, nor is it often clear how features relate within a given site. In the absence of a specific chronology for Northeast Scotland, the limited excavations and radiocarbon dates are interpreted within the wider trends seen elsewhere in Scotland during the Iron Age (Cook and Dunbar 2008, 11-6). As is characteristic of most of the British Iron Age, settlements in this region appear to be both enclosed and unenclosed (Halliday 2007; Hingley 1992). The general interpretation is that most early settlements were not enclosed, but throughout the first millennium BC they became enclosed, with some even becoming complex enclosures (Cook and Dunbar 2008, 11). In this earlier period, dendrochronology evidence suggests that roundhouses were not maintained over several generations, but rather only represent a period of occupation of about 15 years (Cook and Dunbar 2008, 12). Cook (2008, 12) suggested that this is most likely evidence for a single household moving around the landscape over several generations rather than the inhabitation of larger settlements that lasted for 1-2 generations.

By the end of the first millennium BC, enclosures became less complex and roundhouses were occupied for longer periods with evidence for structure superimposition (Cook 2008, 12). For example, at Wardend of Durris

Dress and Identity in Iron Age Britain

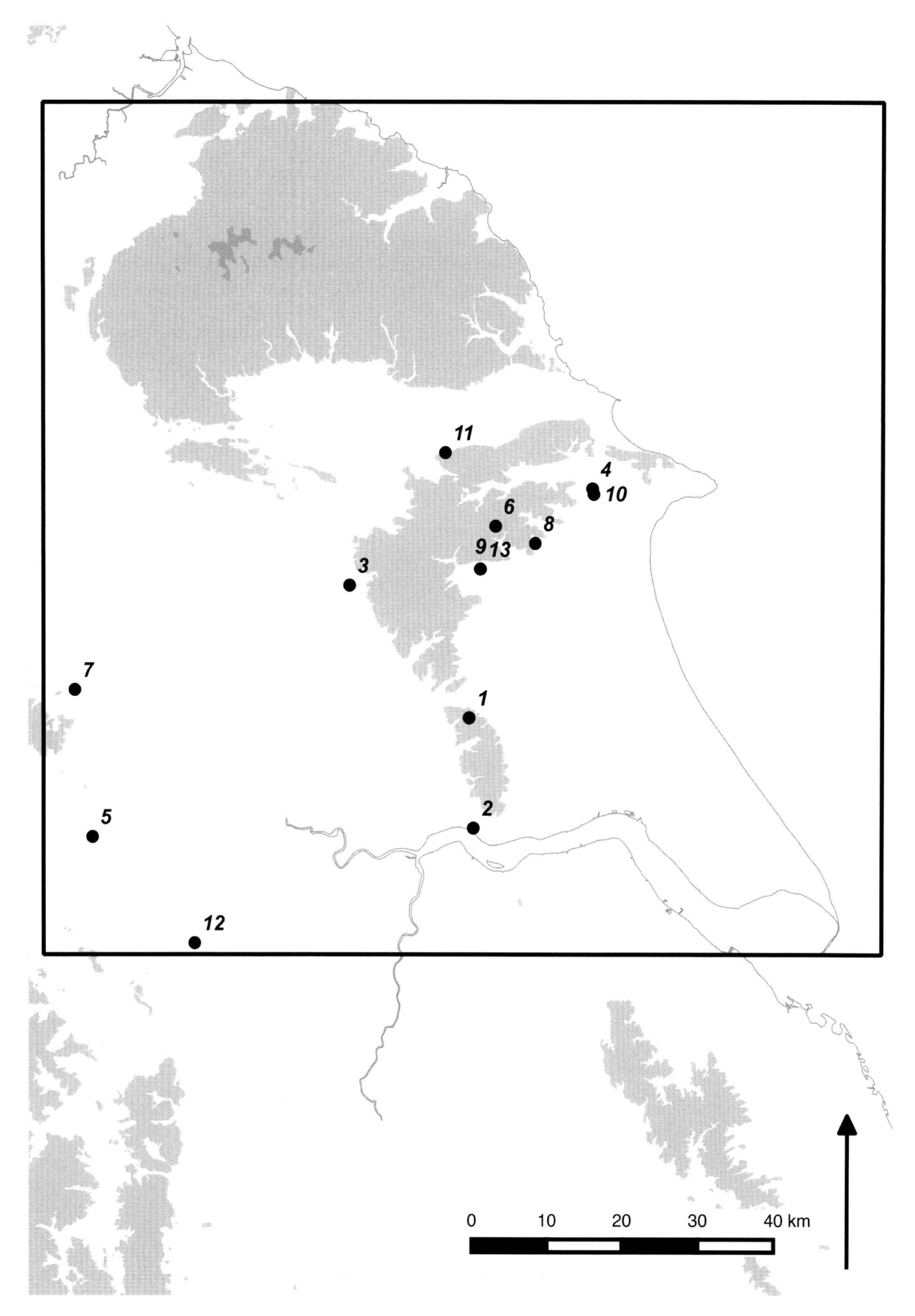

Figure 12: Key sites in East Yorkshire mentioned in the text.

in Aberdeenshire, radiocarbon dates and overlapping features suggest that this was a multi-phase site with occupation ranging from 400 BC to AD 240 (Russell-White 1995). Other settlement sites that date to the end of the first millennium include the successive post-rings at Romancamp Gate, Moray (Barclay 1993) and the post-built roundhouse at Tavelty, Aberdeenshire (Alexander 2000). In contrast, sites, such as Culduthel Farm near Inverness exhibit evidence for a much longer period of occupation from the Middle Iron Age into the Roman period (Murray 2007a, and forthcoming). Settlement sites with evidence for longer periods of occupation may coincide with continual landscape clearance, agricultural intensification, and the use of souterrains for surplus storage (Cook and Dunbar 2008, 12-4; Halliday 2007, 108). Halliday (2007, 109) suggested that the earliest fort enclosures were the largest, and that throughout the Iron Age they became progressively smaller. However, as with most of this settlement evidence, there is very little absolute dating to support this chronology.

The impact of the Roman invasion was very different in Northeast Scotland than in southern Scotland and the difference is especially drastic in comparison to southern Britain. Various campaigns in this region, from those of Agricola in the first century AD to Septimus Severus's campaign in the third century AD, left a series of camps throughout the region (Cook and Dunbar 2008, 16-8), for example, at Deer's Den in Kintore (Alexander 2000; Cook and Dunbar 2008). A single radiocarbon date taken from underneath an enclosure at Berryhill in Aberdeenshire suggested that it was built sometime after AD 20-85, which is tantalising given that it is located only a few kilometres from a known Roman camp (Murray 2002). However, there is a noted gap in the settlement record between the third and sixth centuries AD, which might be the result of the Roman presence in this region (Hunter 2007b, 49).

Interpretations of Iron Age social organisation are dependent on equating large enclosures with higher-status and power (Armit 1997; Cook and Dunbar 2008, 14; Halliday 2007, 109). It is thought that by the time the Romans campaigned in Scotland that the social system became more hierarchical due to organised raiding parties and growing elites (Cook and Dunbar 2008, 14). Metalwork, or coinage hoards, such as those found at Birnie in Morayshire, have been described as bribes (Hunter 2007b, 27-32), which may indicate that the settlements were seats of some authority. In contrast, Hingley (1992) discussed social organisation in terms of the household unit, rather than trying to equate different types of sites and their enclosures with social hierarchy. He suggests that it may be the interplay between 'substantial' roundhouses and enclosures that demarcate status (Hingley 1992, 39). The interpretation of the possibly contemporary unenclosed settlement at Birnie and the enclosed settlement at Culduthel Farm, will be particularly interesting as enclosure is often connected with ideas of power and control, but the range of artefacts found at both sites would normally be interpreted as high-status. As Hunter (2007b, 49) pointed out, if society at this time was hierarchical, we cannot rely on sites and artefacts to straightforwardly determine which sites were high- or low-status.

Key important excavated sites discussed throughout the following analyses chapters include: Culduthel Farm near Inverness (Murray 2007a, and forthcoming publication; 2007c), Birnie in Morayshire (Hunter 2002a, although final publication is forthcoming, a series of interim reports are available), and Thainstone in Aberdeenshire (Murray and Murray 2006b). Glass beads have been found in all three of these settlement sites through excavation. As the majority of glass beads in this region were stray finds, these sites are particularly important as they help to firmly establish that these beads do date to the Iron Age, rather than later periods. However, as will be discussed in Chapters 5 and 7, not all bead types that are characteristic of this region have been found in excavated contexts, leaving some question about the date of other types. The excavation at Culduthel Farm is important on a national scale, as some of the most convincing evidence for glass working, and in particular glass bead making, has been found at this site. This sort of evidence is very rare in Britain for the Iron Age. In contrast, glass beads were not found during the excavations of the other major sites in this region, but other material culture at these sites was also very rare.

Discussion

This section has given a brief overview of the settlement evidence for each of the study regions and a brief summary of the evidence for glass beads. Patterns suggest that there were periods of enclosure and unenclosure. Although the state of enclosure has often been linked with the status of the site, this is a difficult argument to sustain. As will be shown in Chapter 7, glass beads were only found at a small minority of settlement sites in each region. However, where they are found, they were often associated with roundhouse or pit features, although it is not always clear if this was the result of casual loss, intentional discard of rubbish, or intentional deposition for ritual related reasons.

Ritual/Treatment of the Dead

The Iron Age is at odds with both the preceding period (the Bronze Age) and the succeeding period (the Roman Period). In these other periods, places of ritual and locations for the burial of the dead were clearly differentiated from areas of settlement, such as cemeteries, temples in the Roman period, and in the Bronze Age there are round barrows and henge monuments. Instead, in the Iron Age, aspects of ritual life and domestic life are seen

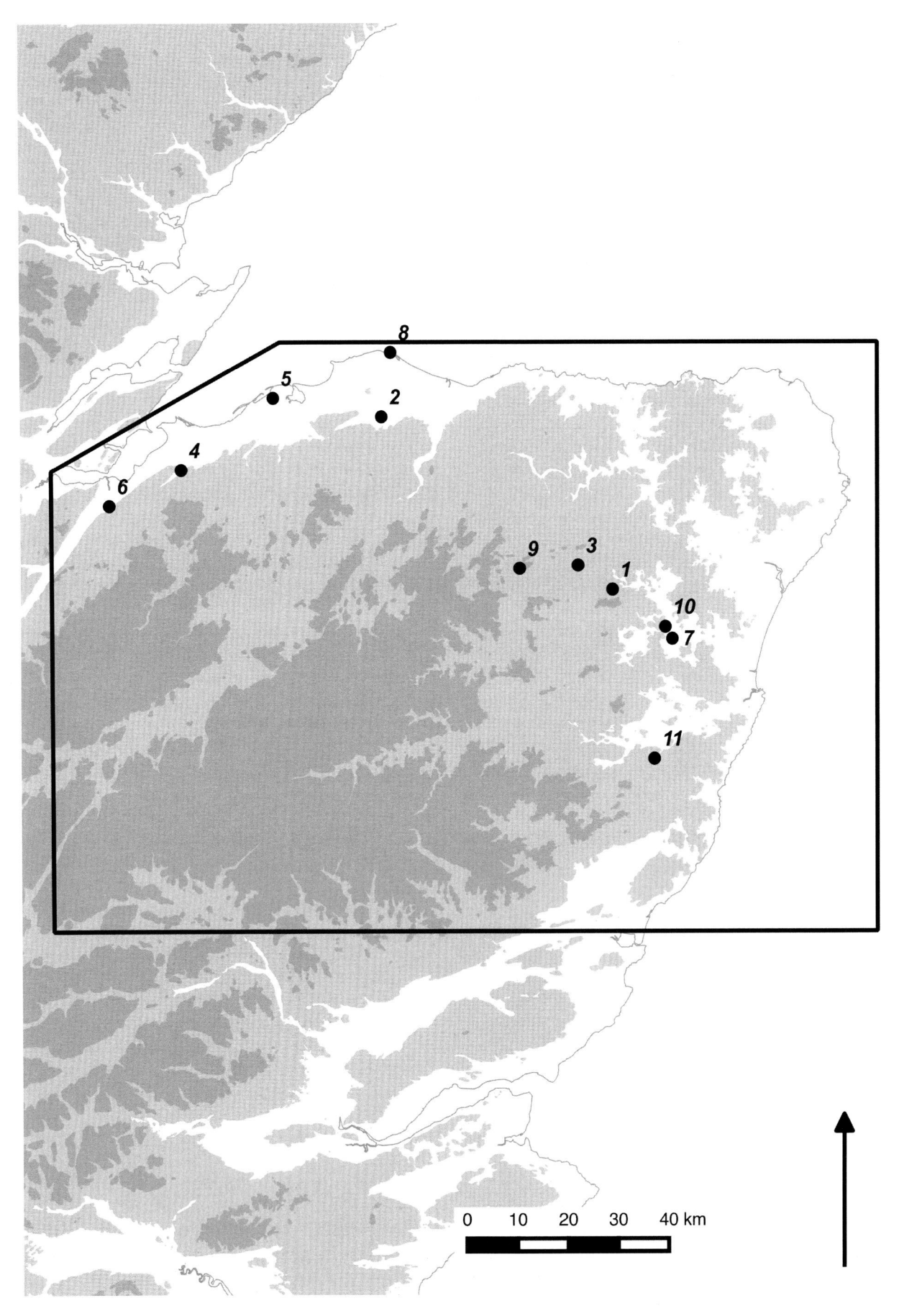

Figure 13: Key sites in Northeast Scotland mentioned in the text.

as having been intimately linked (Fitzpatrick 1997b). For example, analysis of doorway orientation has shown that there is often a preference for such openings to be oriented to the southeast (Oswald 1997). In addition, the occurrence of inhumation is a rare regional practice that manifests during specific periods (Whimster 1981). However, even the way in which the burial occurs is not a standard practice, as there are strong regional patterns (Whimster 1981). The evidence ranges from complete skeletons, to articulated segments, to single bones or fragments. Pit burials are defined as inhumations where the body is placed in a pit that probably had some other former function, such as grain storage (Whimster 1981, 10). This has led some to suggest that there may have been some additional element of ritual connected with the placement of human (and animal) remains into pits (Cunliffe 1992; Hill 1995b).

The limited number of such inhumations has led to the suggestion that not everyone was buried during the Iron Age. Some people may have been treated in other ways that did not leave an archaeological trace, and may also explain incomplete articulated portions or isolated human skeletal finds (Carr and Knüsel 1997). When excarnation, or other archaeological invisible treatments of the dead (i.e. river disposal) were practiced, we have very limited evidence to understand past populations through osteological examination, isotopic analysis, or even individual identity through a study of grave goods. The implication is that a study of material culture during the Iron Age must explore the ways in which artefacts were found or not found in association with people. However, there is a danger that only some people were specifically chosen for particular practices, and the reasons behind these decisions may not be obvious.

Southwest England

Burial evidence in the Southwest has been shown to be incredibly varied (Moore 2003). There are a limited number of single inhumations, such as the Birdlip burial in Gloucestershire (Bellows 1881; Green 1949) or the Clevedon cist burial in Somerset (Gray 1942). Other human remains were found in pits, such as the female crouched inhumation at Bourton-on-the-Water in Gloucestershire (Nichols 2006). Others were found on boundaries, and may have been connected with ideas of land ownership (Moore 2003, 154).

In Dorset, a particular type of burial emerged at the end of the first century BC (Whimster 1981, 39) and lasted until the first century AD. Commonly referred to as 'Durotrigian burials', these inhumations are found in southern Dorset, often clustered together in cemeteries (Papworth 2011, 53). These are considered to be a more formal type of burial because the bodies were not placed into pits previously used for grain storage, but instead were placed in pits that were deliberately dug. These individuals were accompanied by grave goods, which often included a pottery vessel (Whimster 1981, 50). Two inhumations from this region stand out: the Chesil and Portesham burials, both found along the Dorset coast. These two inhumations each contained a mirror, along with other artefacts. The inclusion of a mirror with a burial is often taken to indicate that the individual was high-status (Joy 2011a).

Other evidence for ritual in Later Iron Age southwest Britain comes from a small number of possible shrines or temples. For example, a small rectangular enclosure with a porch at Cadbury Castle (Barrett, Freeman et al. 2000) and small enclosure as Uley West Hill (Woodward and Leach 1993) have both been interpreted as possible shrines.

Glass beads have been found in a very small proportion of known burials in this region. Most important were the glass beads from the Clevedon cist burial and the Chesil mirror burial. It is interesting that despite the similar date between the Chesil and the Portesham burial, and that they both contained a mirror, the remaining artefacts within the burials are quite different (e.g. the Roman copper alloy strainer). Equally different is the Birdlip burial, which also contains a mirror and other Late Iron Age material (the brooch and copper alloy vessels), but there was also several large amber beads, jet beads, and a stone bead. This is extremely unusual for Iron Age Britain, as this is a period for which there is very little evidence for the use of amber (Beck 1991).

East Anglia

Owing to the sparse excavation data, there is very little evidence to suggest how the dead were treated in this region. The general lack of evidence, including very few discoveries made during agricultural activities, may suggest that throughout the Iron Age in Norfolk and Suffolk, the inhabitants of this region primarily engaged in practices that left very little physical evidence (i.e. excarnation). The young adult human skull retrieved from an enclosure at Burgh along with raven bones may indicate that in some circumstances certain bones were retrieved for later burial (Martin 1999, 59-60). However, without further excavation, it is not possible to determine the extent at which this was the general trend. Interestingly, a cart or chariot burial was discovered in 1814 in Suffolk (Martin 1999, 71). Although the nature of this find is extremely unclear, it is tantalising because it could be an extremely southern occurrence of the East Yorkshire style burials, or perhaps it was an earlier vehicle burial as with the Newbridge example (Jay, Haselgrove et al. 2012), which may in fact have continental affinities.

The evidence for wider ritual practice is generally obscured by the lack of excavation data. In terms of sites for ritual activity, one of the possible explanations for the rectangular enclosure at Fison Way near Thetford, Norfolk is that it was a ritual centre (Cunliffe 2005, 565). However, it is the material culture from hoards, or other supposedly votive deposits, that really stand out in this region. The most famous of these are the torcs from Ken Hill near Snettisham. Whether these torcs were deposited in a more functional sense for safe-keeping, or in the ritual sense as a votive deposit has been key for interpreting the activity and the legal status of the finds (Stead 1991b). However, the idea that these torcs were deposited either for functional reasons or for ritualistic purposes is really detrimental and limiting to understanding Iron Age practice, as Fitzpatrick (1992) argued that the reasons for deposition do not need to be one or the other. As with much of the evidence for Iron Age Britain more generally, there is a mix of both the domestic and ritual in everyday life (Fitzpatrick 1997b). However, in the case of the torc depositions at Snettisham, the site lacks this domestic activity and it seems that there is no nearby settlement. Instead, nearby excavations have identified the area as having some ritual significance from the nearby Roman temple (Hutcheson 2011).

The practice of hoarding or votive deposits is a widespread occurrence in Norfolk as shown by Hutcheson's (2004) work on coins, horse trappings and torcs. She has shown that in the Later Iron Age there were three main phases of hoards (Hutcheson 2004, 34). The first phase lasts from about the second century to the mid-first century BC. These hoards were composed primarily of torcs. It is during this time that the Snettisham and other torcs were probably deposited, although they were likely manufactured at different times. Dating evidence for deposition is derived from the Gallo-Belgic coins found with the Snettisham hoards. In addition, a very limited number of objects related to horses were deposited at this time. The nature of the hoards in the second phase (mid-first century BC - mid-first century AD) changes, and the objects that were deposited primarily include gold and silver coins of British types. Again, a very small amount of horse equipment is deposited. Finally, the third phase (first century AD) sees an explosion of horse equipment that is found, both as single finds and in hoard features. There have been a variety of interpretations for the reasoning behind hoarding in particular, including both functional and ritual. However, changes in both the location of the deposition and the objects to be deposited led Hutcheson to conclude:

> ...that the practice of burying metalwork and coins in the ground in this region is a continuous, if mutable tradition; the material changes, the perceptions of the landscape changes, but the essential practice remains the same. (Hutcheson 2004, 93)

It may be that in the future, as excavations increase in number and attempts are made at synthesising the data, that the general pattern for domestic ritual in connection with roundhouses (Fitzpatrick 1997b; Oswald 1997) will also be shown to extend to this region.

Glass beads have not been found in either burial or ritual deposition features within this region, except for a much later Romano-British votive pit at Billingford (Wallis 2011) and at Santon Downham (Smith 1908-09). This may be further evidence for the different roles of material culture in this region, as metalwork seems to have been of high importance given the quantity from this region. However, as the pottery-rich layers from Grandcourt Quarry with glass beads remain unclear, it may be that this unusual deposit was ritual in nature.

East Yorkshire

The treatment of the dead through inhumation provides a particularly rich resource in East Yorkshire beginning in the Early Bronze Age, as round barrows are found throughout the landscape. However, this practice was not continuous from the Early Bronze Age to the Iron Age. Use of round barrows ended in the Middle Bronze Age, by the later Bronze Age there are no contemporary inhumations with the enclosed settlements. As mentioned previously, inhumation was practiced around the Middle Iron Age around the same time that enclosed settlements were abandoned and unenclosed settlements were established.

These Iron Age barrows had a distinct appearance compared to the Bronze Age barrow practice. As with the round barrows, the Iron Age barrows were formed by a central mound that was placed over the inhumed body. However, they were markedly different in that the mound was bordered by a square ditch (Dent 1999). The actual size of the barrow varied between 3 and 15 meters across and usually only contained the remains of a single individual (Bevan 1997, 186). Within the grave the body was often oriented north-south with the head to the north and facing east and in a crouched position (Bevan 1999, 132). Both male and female inhumations occurred in approximately equal numbers (Bevan 1999, 134). These barrows are found singly or in groups that formed a cemetery.

While the square barrow tradition accounts for many of the inhumations found in East Yorkshire, there appear to have been two other less widespread practices. First, there is evidence for a small number of inhumations under small barrows or flat graves that were oriented east-west. In these examples, the body was not placed in a crouched position, but was instead laid flat. The second practice is the famous chariot or cart burials. These elaborate burials were substantially larger than most square barrows and were often placed separately from the main group of inhumations. As with the more frequent burial rite, the interred bodies were often oriented north-south and placed in a crouched position. However, it is the objects that were placed in the inhumations that make these inhumations different from the majority of other burials.

Within the East Yorkshire square barrow tradition, artefacts or grave goods are sometimes found within the grave. In both square burial practices (vehicle and non-vehicle) where the body was oriented north-south a range of different artefacts are found. It is common to find La Tène style brooches, a ceramic pot, and either a joint of sheep or pig, while uncommon finds include tools, vehicles, glass beads, bracelets, rings, spearheads, mail tunic, swords, shields, and mirrors (Bevan 1999, 134). In the east-west oriented graves, a smaller range of objects were found. More common are weapons, tools, and a joint of pig, while less common are ceramic vessels and joints of sheep (Bevan 1999, 134). Bevan (1999) suggested that although males and females are represented equally in the cemeteries, the placement of grave goods within the inhumations was very structured. For example, in female graves, ceramic vessels and joints of meat were placed near the head, while in male graves objects were placed near the pelvis and feet.

The date of the square barrow inhumation tradition has frequently been suggested to last from the fifth to first centuries BC (Bevan 1997; 1999; Dent 1999). Many of the barrows that have been excavated were explored by antiquarians prior to radiocarbon dating. Thus, artefact typologies have been important to ascertain rough dates for the inhumation practice. Brooches are one of the most common artefacts found in individual barrows, although dating is complicated by the fact that they exhibit both continental and insular characteristics (Haselgrove 1997; Hull and Hawkes 1987). In addition, it has been suggested that within cemetery sites a chronology of inhumations can be discerned by the size and placement of the burial. For example, earlier barrows will be larger and widely dispersed with a shallow cut grave, and later barrows were smaller, clustered, and the grave was placed deeply in the ground (Bevan 1997, 187).

Early radiocarbon dates were taken from the excavations at Wetwang Slack (Dent 1984) and Stead's (1991a) excavations in East Yorkshire. Recently, a comparative study examined the available radiocarbon dates from inhumations in East Yorkshire and published 21 new radiocarbon dates from Wetwang Slack (Jay, Haselgrove *et al.* 2012). The results suggest that the inhumations at Wetwang Slack occurred over a very limited time frame, from the third to early second centuries BC, while cart or chariot burials formed an even shorter lived practice and were all deposited around 200 BC. This suggests that these burials occurred approximately 200 years after similar practice flourished in France, and thus are unlikely to represent the inhumations of migrants or invaders (Jay, Haselgrove *et al.* 2012, 182). Because this reassessment also included material from Stead's (1991a) excavations, it seems likely that these dates could be extended to other square barrow inhumations, although further analysis is really necessary. As many glass beads were found in these inhumations, the implication is that they were later in date than originally thought, and that they are not necessarily the objects worn by migrants from the continent. It does not rule the possibility of incomers out completely, but it renders it less likely.

Finally, as there is little evidence for the treatment of the dead just prior to or after the square barrow tradition, a practice of excarnation is often suggested (Bevan 1997; 1999). In contrast to the extensive inhumation evidence that primarily centres on the Yorkshire Wolds, the site at Sutton Common suggests a different practice (Noort, Chapman *et al.* 2007). This site, suggested to date to the fourth century BC, is composed of two opposing multivallate enclosures with a causeway connecting them. Evidence for domestic activity was sparse, but it has been suggested that the site was somehow connected to the dead, perhaps in relation to a cremation practice. This is significant not only for its earlier date, but in that it provides evidence for the treatment of the dead outside of the Yorkshire Wolds core area of study. The process of excarnation itself during the Iron Age, such as where the body is placed in order to undergo the process of exposure is unclear, but has been suggested to take place within the settlement itself (Carr and Knüsel 1997). Therefore, evidence for a possible deliberate enclosure for the dead and cremation in a specified location is significant for understanding a particular regional practice.

This region is especially important for understanding glass beads in connection with individuals, as it is from a small number of these burials that glass beads are found in both small and large numbers. This is a very regionalised practice in comparison to the other areas of study discussed here, not only because of the number of burials, but also for the sometimes large numbers of beads found with the inhumations. This has particularly important implications for understanding how the beads were being used, which is discussed further in Chapter 8.

Northeast Scotland

As there has been very little research excavation in Northeast Scotland, elements of ritual and the treatment of the dead are not understood in any great detail. Given that there is little evidence for burials either as mounds, cairns, or cists that are attributable to this period, it seems that the dead were not buried in features that are recognisable through land survey. It may be that either the dead were not treated in this way, or that any upstanding monuments have been misattributed to other periods.

Other aspects of ritual in the Iron Age are often connected with daily domestic practices and domestic architecture and this may explain the scarcity of evidence for burials in this area (Oswald 1997; Parker Pearson 1996). However, due to the limited amount of excavation in this region, it is unclear to what extent the roundhouses in Northeast Scotland follow this pattern. Hoarding or ritual deposition is another practice that is often interpreted as having ritualistic purposes, particularly in the context of metalwork (Hunter 1997). It is worth mentioning that this practice does occur in Northeast Scotland. Notable hoards include the Roman coin hoards at Birnie in Moray (Hunter 2007b, 27-31) and the deposition of the Deskford trumpet in a peat bog (Harding 2007, 221; Hunter 2001a; ScARF 2012, 102-3).

Most of the glass beads from this region are stray finds, and the few examples there are have been found in settlement contexts. However, the glass bead found in a post-hole at the entrance to the roundhouse at Thainstone in Aberdeenshire (Murray and Murray 2006b) may suggest that these beads are more than just casual losses within a domestic environment, but instead may have been intentionally deposited in a ritualistic sense.

Summary

This overview of the different practices connected with ritual and with the dead has emphasised the regional variability. Although grave goods were sometimes included with inhumations throughout Britain, the selectivity of individuals chosen for burial makes interpretations about the person's status difficult as it seems likely that there were specific reasons behind decisions to bury some people and not others. The internments of the population at Wetwang Slack and presumably at the others sites, such as Arras and Cowlam, appears to be one of the most consistent practices, at least for a limited period of time, but elsewhere the situation remains unclear.

Discussion

Each of the regions under study has a distinct archaeological character. For example: Southwest England has been shown to be a region of dense settlement through extensive surveys and excavations. There is a relatively clear understanding of the changing nature of settlements over time, and evidence for technology and manufacturing of objects. In addition, the rich assemblages from the lake villages form an unprecedented, and as yet incomparable, body of artefacts. In contrast, the archaeology of East Anglia is limited by the number of excavated sites, but is overwhelmed by the wealth of metal artefacts. East Yorkshire provides yet another different perspective. Here, archaeological enquiry has focused on the Iron Age inhumation tradition, especially in and near to the Wolds. There has been little research undertaken to place the Yorkshire Wolds into a wider context, except from the linear boundary evidence. Finally, there has been very little excavation in Northeast Scotland, but there is survey data available. In addition, many artefacts found in this region are old finds from the nineteenth and early twentieth century and are the result of agricultural or building activities.

With these differences in mind, two questions become pertinent to the discussion. First, how has the history of research created biases in the data; and second, how does the archaeological resource impact on dress, identity, and the types of beads that occur? To tackle the first question, there is no escaping the fact that different levels of antiquarian interest, archaeological research excavations, and developer-funded excavations have all impacted these regions differently (explored in Chapter 7). Additional data is derived from accidental discoveries through farming and now metal-detecting. Would any patterns in the data be a reliable and accurate reflection of the past? In the context of metalwork found through metal-detection, Hutcheson (2004) tackled this question by examining the distribution of metalwork in Britain and concluded that these were real patterns reflecting past practices, they were not the result of different metal-detecting practices or different recording strategies in different counties. Perhaps for other material we could make a similar conclusions; however, further research needs to be undertaken that covers all of Britain to explore this.

This research tackles these questions in several ways. In terms of the regional glass bead data, Chapter 6 shows that there are differences in the number of glass beads found in each region, and Chapter 7 further explores the differences in terms of stray finds versus finds from excavated context. It also tries to answer this question by looking at the number of research excavations in comparison to developer driven excavations, and also takes their size and distribution into account. The results of these analyses will be discussed more fully in the appropriate chapters; however, it is worth noting here that these factors could indeed be affecting our understanding of glass beads and the Iron Age more widely. But again, as Hutcheson demonstrated, there seems to be an underlying pattern in Iron Age activity that differs regionally.

The second question, regarding the archaeological resource and how it impacts the evidence that we have for material culture related to dress, is very complex. The evidence that we have is the result of choices made in the past for intentional deposition, accidental loss, and survival of materials. For many of the finds discussed in this study, it is unfortunate that so many lack context. However, material culture found outside of inhumations is perplexing. How did glass beads come to be deposited in pits or within roundhouses? How much of the material that we have came from intentional acts? And, how representative is this of what people wore? The inhumation evidence on the other hand, provides a different level of detail, but, there is still no shortage of questions. Given that so many glass beads were found in such a small proportion of East Yorkshire burials, how representative of the population were these individuals? Did the objects deposited with the individual even reflect their identity?

It may be that the differences in burial practice, and their associated material culture, throughout Britain is demonstrating differing perceptions of the body at this time. For example, the widespread use of inhumation in East Yorkshire may attest to a tradition where the body as an intact burial was important. The inclusion of a range of artefacts may suggest that identity in this region was just as important in life as it was in death, which may be related to a widespread belief in this region. In contrast, in areas where there is not a strong burial tradition for entire populations, and the body may be left for exposure, the body presumably became fragmented. It was not important for the memory of these individuals for them to remain whole and at a fixed point within the landscape. However, for other individuals this was important. Again, this may be due to a widely held belief, but perhaps in these areas material culture played a different role in portraying identity, as it was not fixed to them in death. Perhaps the buried individuals held a markedly different identity within the community, or their burial marked a specific memory or event.

This chapter has provided a critical synthesis of the Iron Age in each of the four regions under study in this work. The history of research and the evidence for Iron Age activity can be seen as defining vastly different regions, however, it is these variances that defined distinctive traditions and diverse identities. Interestingly, the evidence does suggest that there were regional practices that varied over time. The implications for this are that there were regionally based identities, which in turn may have manifested in the use of different material culture related to dress (discussed in Chapter 8). The glass bead evidence as discussed in the following chapters, as well as patterns found with other artefacts of dress, supports this hypothesis.

Chapter 5
Typological Conundrums, Quandaries, and Resolutions

The typological approach has been, by far, the most influential method for interpreting Iron Age glass beads. Although there are minor regional typologies, such as Stead's (1979) and Dent's (1984) for East Yorkshire, it is Guido's (1978a) typology for Britain and Ireland that has had the most influence. This approach covers glass beads during the Iron Age and Roman period that were found throughout Britain, and is cited most often in excavation reports. It is also the foundation for the limited number of subsequent scientific analysis studies on glass beads, such as that of Henderson (1982) and more recently Bertini (2012). However, since the publication of the Guido typology, there has been little critical awareness of the issues surrounding the interpretations of each type. This has become increasingly problematic over the last several decades for a number of reasons. For example, synthetic interpretations of the Iron Age have changed dramatically (e.g. Haselgrove, Armit *et al.* 2001; Hill 1995a), and the centralisation of stray finds through the Portable Antiquities Scheme has made some data publicly available and encourages public engagement with artefacts. In addition, areas not normally targeted by research archaeologists have been excavated through rescue and developer-funded archaeology (Moore 2006a) and have contributed significant data, which could potentially alter our understanding of glass beads from Iron Age Britain.

It is therefore necessary to examine the efficacy of the Guido typology to determine how coherent the types are, as well to determine whether it holds up in light of recent discoveries. In order to do this, an analysis was undertaken to test each type and then to explore the typology as a whole. The overall conclusions suggested that there are a number of issues with the typology both on the type level, and also with the typological structure as a whole. Thus, a new typology is needed to replace the Guido classification scheme. The background of the typology was discussed in detail in Chapter 2, and the following section will explore some of the issues that have been encountered during the analysis. This section will be followed by a more general discussion of the typological issues. It will then propose an interim typology to be used throughout the remainder of this book.

Typological Complications

A discussion of the Guido (1978a) typological approach to glass beads and the background to her study was presented in detail in Chapter 2. This section presents a critical discussion of her types. It draws on the data contained within her catalogue (corrected where necessary), and data from new finds (Figures 14 and 15). New additions to the data-set have, in some cases, significantly altered the quantity within each type (e.g. Class 3), although other types have had few or no new additions (e.g. Class 4, Group 3, and Group 4). While some new finds could easily be fitted into the existing typology, others were more difficult, and needed to be assigned based on best fit. Rather than discussing each type in order, this analysis has grouped together types based on shared characteristics, as it is often the case that problems encountered in one type are shared by the other types (see Appendix B for a description of each Guido type).

Critique of the Guido Typology

Eye Beads (Guido Classes 1-4, Group 4)

Five types are included in Guido's classification for beads with an 'eye' motif (see Figure 190a-ab). These are beads where dots of glass have been layered in order to create a 'ring-dot' motif. Some are simple and combine two layers of glass, which is a feature on most of these beads (Figure 190a-w); others are more complex and are made from four layers of glass (Class 2; Figure 190w-aa). The most complex eye bead is the Group 4 type where a large eye is created with two layers of glass, and then many smaller eyes are placed on top of this (Figure 190ab). Class 1 is the only type that is further sub-divided into smaller groupings: Type I and Type II.

As all of these bead types use the eye motif, the primary areas of analysis included dimensions, shape, colour, quantity of eyes, and the placement of the eyes on the beads. As only one example of Group 4 could be examined for this analysis, and none of Class 4, there is currently little more that can currently be said of these types. The type definition for Class 1 beads and division into sub-types is too vague, as it in no way accounts for the level of variability seen in size, shape, and the number of eyes on each bead (Figure 16). Rather than two sub-types, many more types could be defined. The variability in terms of physical appearance is discernible from Figure 190a-ab.

While there were only two known Class 2 beads at the time Guido's catalogue was published, a recently discovered example clearly fits this description (Figure 190z, DB 9965). However, there are an additional two

Typological Conundrums, Quandaries, and Resolutions

Type	Guido Quantity	Database Quantity	Increase (%)	No. Viewed in Museum	Viewed in Museum (%)
Class 1	76	82	7.9	65	79.3
Class 2	2	5	150	4	80
Class 3	29	62	113.7	19	30.6
Class 4	3	3	-	0	0
Class 5	12	17	41.7	7	5.9
Class 6	56	75	33.9	19	25.3
Class 7	27	45	66.7	15	33.3
Class 8	361 (approx.)	488	35.2	366	75
Class 9	49	65	32.7	13	20
Class 10	57 (approx.)	88	54.3	55	62.5
Class 11	42	74	76.2	54	72.9
Class 12	2	4	100	2	50
Class 13	48	93	93.8	66	70.9
Class 14	31	44	41.9	28	63.6

Figure 14: List of Guido classes and the number of examples recorded by Guido, compared to the number contained in the database that resulted from the current research. It also shows the number of beads that were studied first-hand.

Type	Guido Quantity	Database Quantity	Increase (%)	No. Viewed in Museum	Viewed in Museum (%)
Group 1	11	14	27.2	4	28.6
Group 2	15	16	6.7	4	25
Group 3	14	14	-	0	0
Group 4	8	8	-	1	12.5
Group 5	133	299	124.8	167	55.9
Group 6 and 7	609	1949	220	609	31.2
Group 8	20	22	10	11	50

Figure 15: List of Guido Groups and the number of examples included in her catalogue, compared to the number contained in the database that resulted from the current research. It also shows the number of examples that were studied first-hand.

examples from Wetwang Slack that exhibit a more complex four-layer eye motif (Figure 190x-y), but in contrast to the other three examples, these are sub-triangular in shape and were deposited at an earlier date. As this type is primarily defined by the use of colour and the motif type, the definition no longer works in light of these recent discoveries and revision is needed.

Finally, Class 3 beads are loosely defined by the use of the eye motif, and they clearly do not fit with the other types of eye beads (Figure 190h-m). Some are very large and very small, others had a mixed number of eyes, and others were made from colours other than the blue and white glass that makes up most other eye beads (Figure 17). In addition, some of the finds from Wetwang Slack best fit this class definition; however, on their own they are a tightly clustered and consistent group of beads. Therefore, this Class is in need of revision in order to account for the new finds.

Spiral Beads (Guido Classes 6, 10, 13, Group 2)

There are three main types of beads that exhibit the spiral motif: Class 6, 10, and 13, while Group 2 makes up a miscellaneous group of spiral and spiral-like beads. These beads are perhaps some of the most easily recognisable type of Iron Age beads; however, where Classes 10 and 13 are very similar and may have been manufactured in Britain, the Class 6 beads are very large and there are similar beads found in Europe.

The Class 6 beads are primarily defined by their large blue annular body, and the multiple white spirals placed around the bead (Figure 191p-q, s-v). Guido further subdivided this class loosely into the 'B variant' for examples that had a double yellow swag in-between the spirals (none of which could be examined in the present research). Despite some of these differences in design, these beads are largely homogeneous in size and shape, but in general there are two main areas of difference. First, on some examples, the spiral is placed on a protrusion (as in Figure 191t-v). On some examples, this protrusion is very pronounced, and others it is only very slight. Second, although these beads are visually very similar, the actual execution of each bead varies considerably. Some appear to be more finely made (as with Figure 191t), while others are less so (for example Figure 191u-v). It is not clear what the significance of

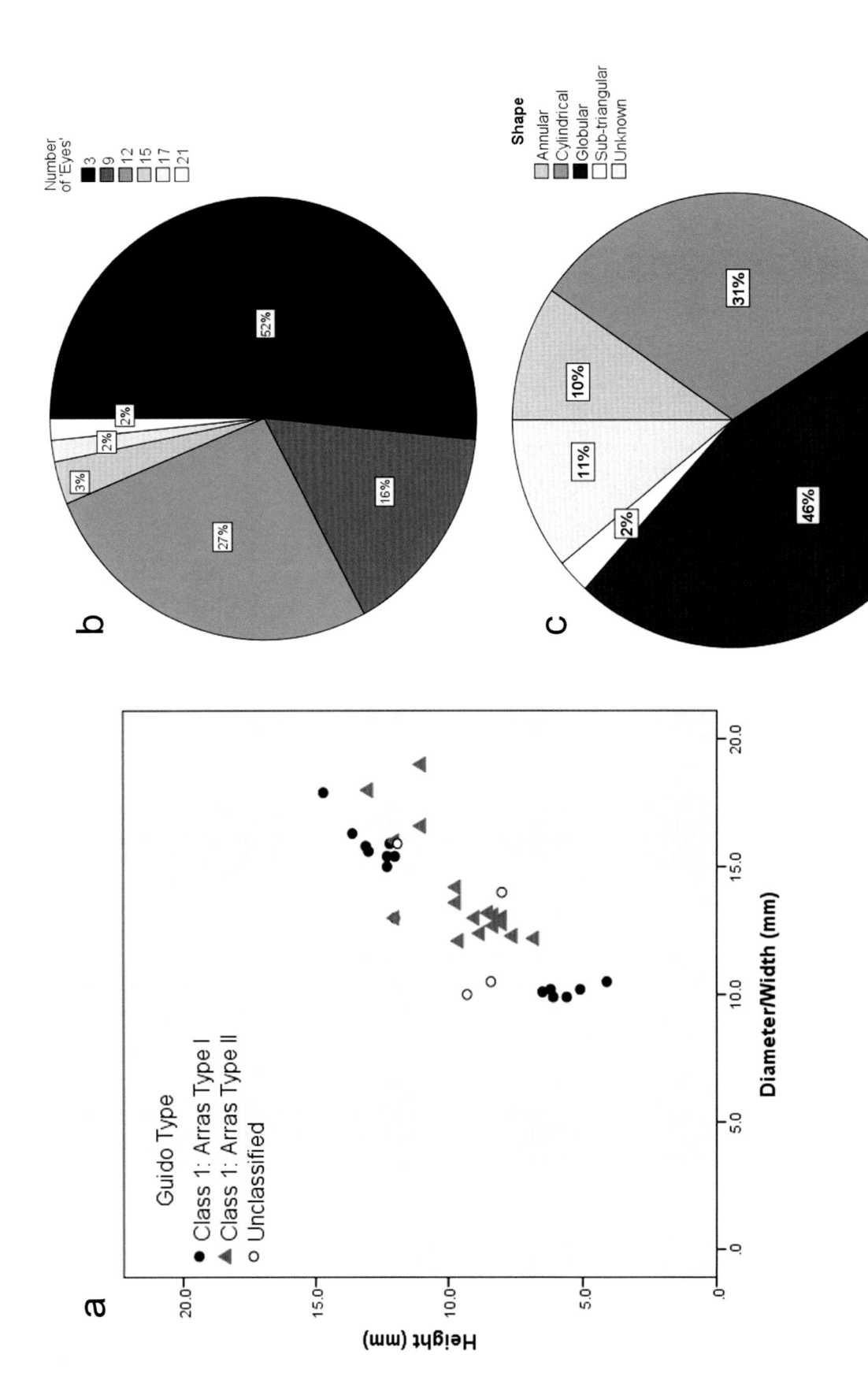

Figure 16: (a) Scatter-graph showing the overall size of Class 1 beads by Guido sub-type, and pie-charts showing (b) the proportion of different number of eye motifs and (c) the proportion of different types of shaped Guido Class 1 beads.

Typological Conundrums, Quandaries, and Resolutions

Figure 17: Analysis of Guido Class 3 beads (a) Scatter-graph showing the overall size, and pie-charts showing (b) the proportion of beads by number of eyes, (c) the proportion of different colours used for the body of the bead, and

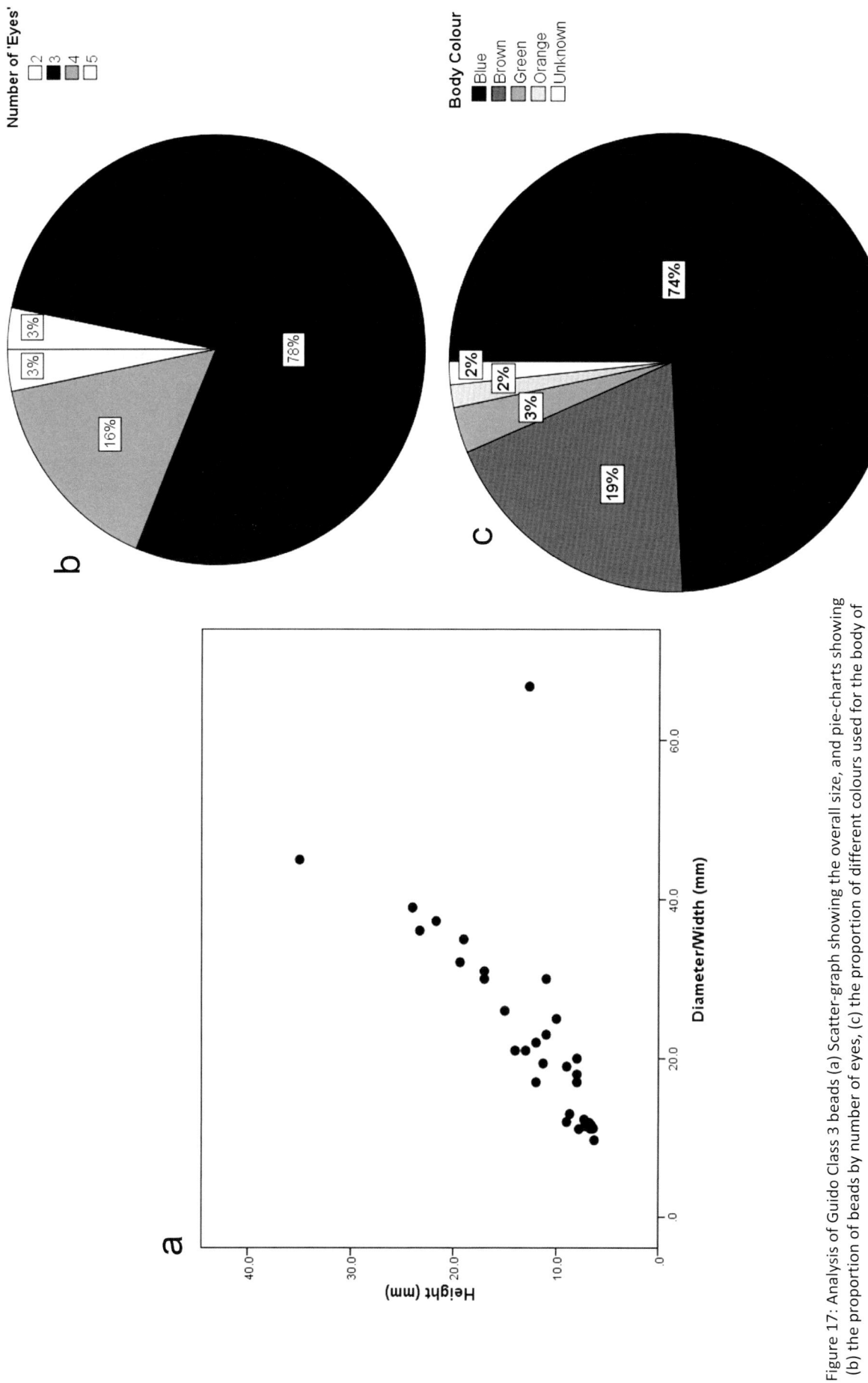

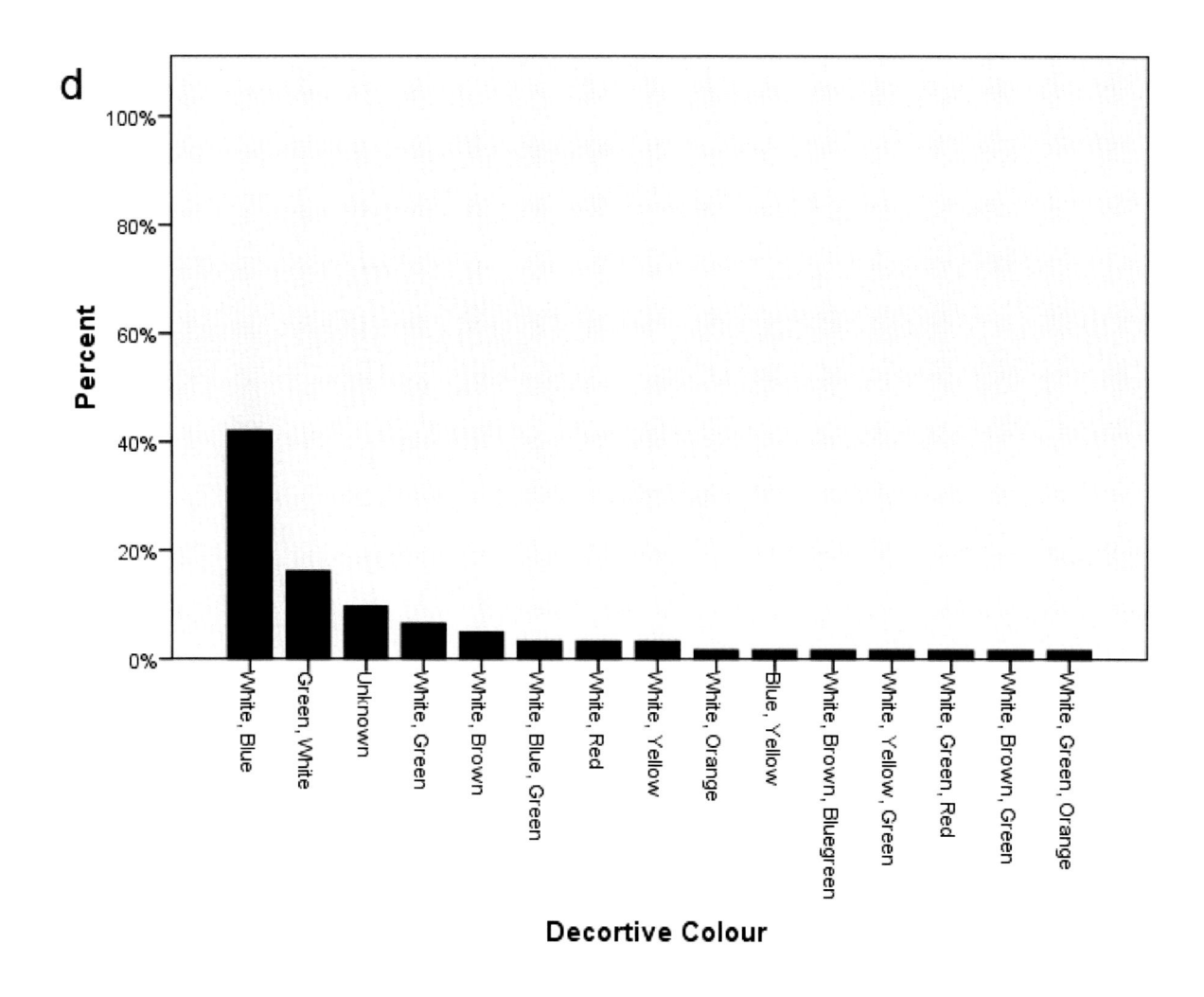

Figure 17: Analysis of Guido Class 3 beads (d) the proportion of different colours used for decoration.

these differences is, nor is there a way to objectively measure this feature. Finally, while most of these beads follow a 2-1-2 alternating pattern, Guido also included blue annular beads with spirals around the circumference to this type (for example Figure 191p-q). Therefore, this class of beads requires consistent analysis and revision in order to account for the variability.

Classes 10 and 13 beads are very similar in their appearance, although Class 10 beads are defined as utilising only colourless and opaque yellow glass (Figure 191ae-ai), while Class 13s can have a body made from any other colour (Figure 191x-ac) and are found primarily in Northeast Scotland. For both classes, Guido does not take the range of shapes into consideration, nor does she take the body colour of Class 13s into account (Figure 18a-b). For both types, it is interesting that they are both very regional types: the Class 10s are found in large numbers in Somerset and elsewhere in the region, while the Class 13s are found throughout Northeast Scotland, but a larger number have been found at Culbin Sands in Morayshire. It has only been in the last few years that examples of these Class 13 beads have been found during excavation in the Northeast Scotland, which confirms their Iron Age date. In terms of typology, both types need to be redefined in terms of their size ranges and shapes that they occur in (Figure 18c-d). For both types, there are very few examples that could be considered to be the 'same' as they demonstrate some variability.

Large Decorated Annular Beads (Guido Classes 7, 9, 14)

These three types of glass beads are all larger decorated annular beads, where most examples are unique. Class 7 beads by definition have 'whirl' or 'ray' designs (Figure 192m-n, Figure 194c,q), while Class 9 beads are decorated with a cable twist (Figure 194d-e, g-l). In some cases this cable twist appears to be more of a wave design, while in other cases it appears very similar to the whirl motif. Both of these types are further sub-divided into different types by the body colour. Guido suggested that Class 7 beads were manufactured on the continent, while Class 9 beads were manufactured in Britain. Close examination of Class 14 beads show some similarities

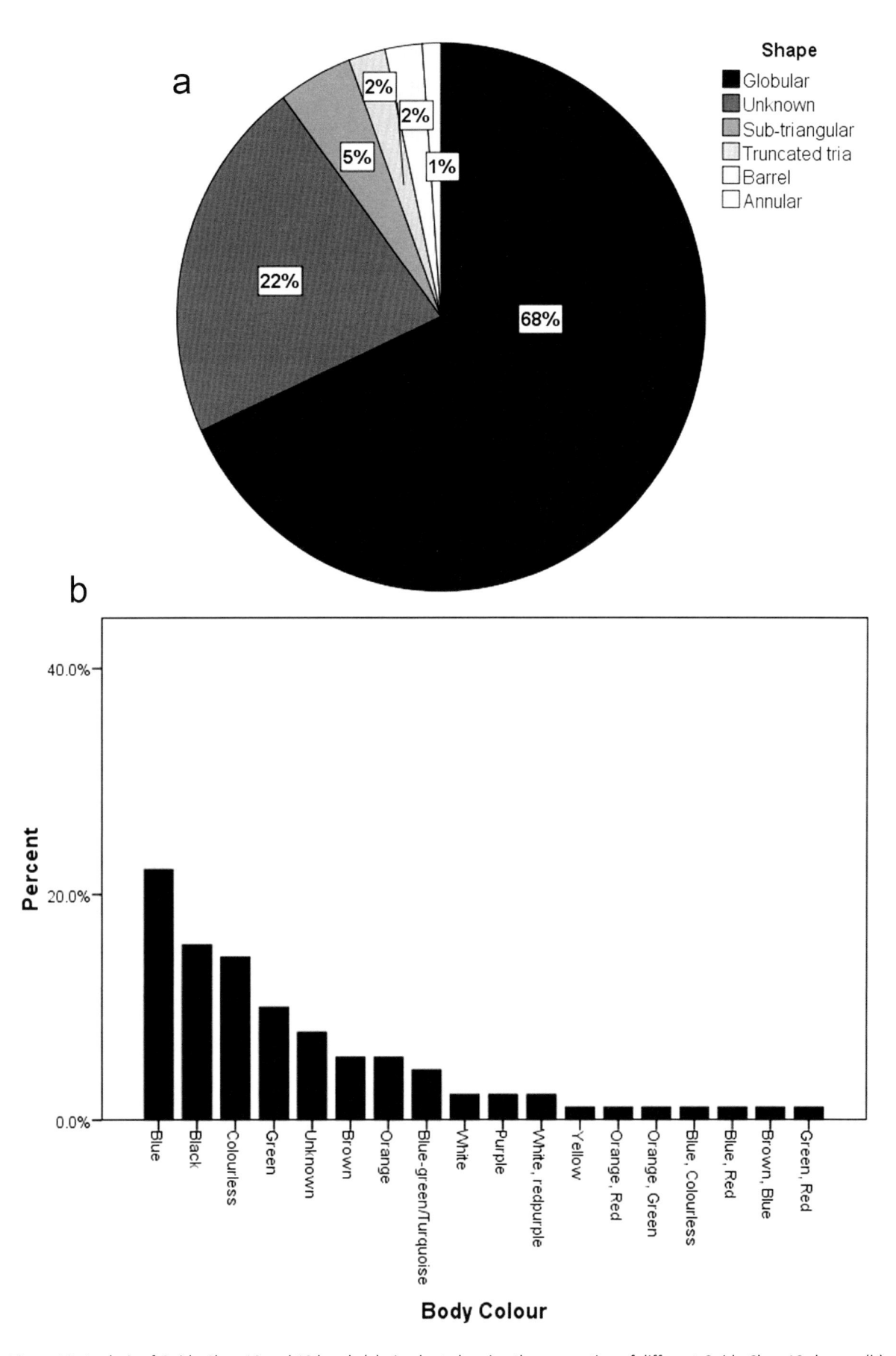

Figure 18: Analysis of Guido Class 10 and 13 beads (a) pie-chart showing the proportion of different Guido Class 10 shapes, (b) pie-chart showing the proportion of different colours of glass used for the body of Guido Class 13 beads.

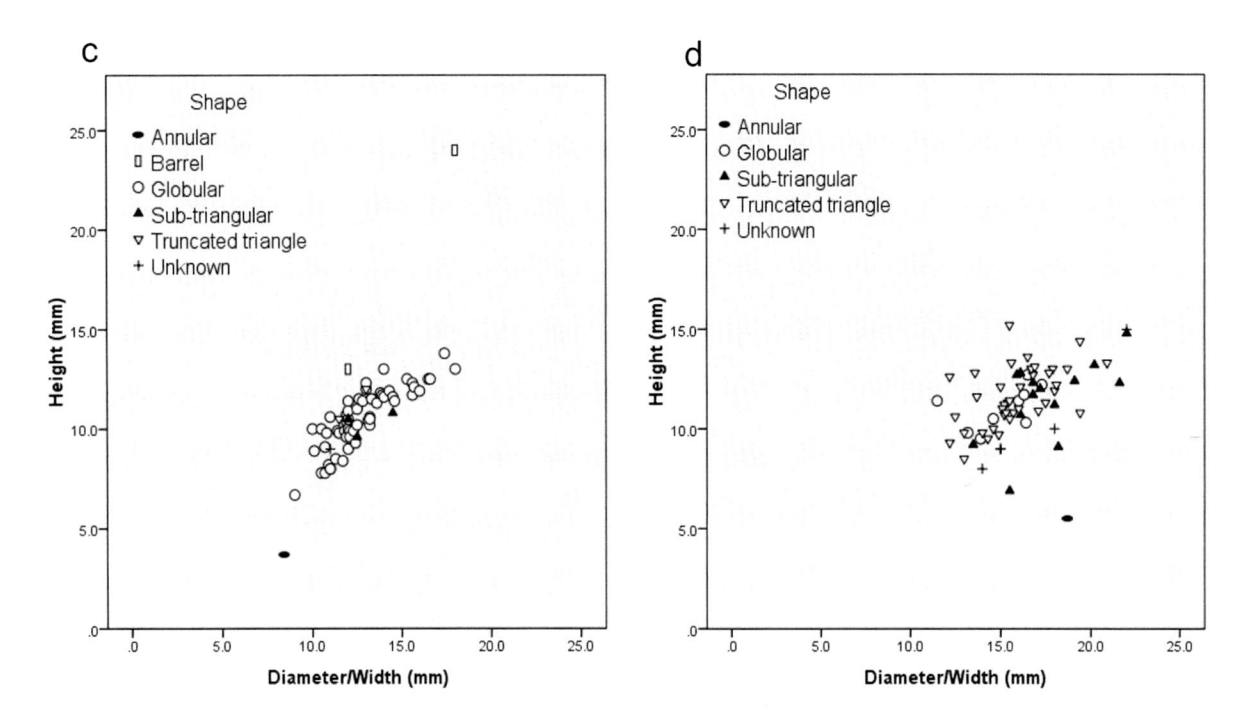

Figure 18: Analysis of Guido Class 10 and 13 beads (c) scatter-graph of Guido Class 10 beads showing dimensions and shape, and (d) scatter-graph of Guido Class 13 beads showing dimensions and shape.

with Classes 7 and 9, while others are very different. Although these Class 14 beads were not differentiated into sub-types, it is clear that there are two general groups, but in most cases, each bead is unique. The first possible subgroup is for beads that appear to be very similar to the Class 7 beads, with whirl motifs (Figure 192e-f, j). In some cases, these beads also incorporate a cable as seen in the Class 9 beads (Figure 193t-u, Figure 194a-b). The other possible sub-group are those beads that appear to be made from a multi-coloured cane wrapped around a mandrel (Figure 192a-c). In many cases, the seam where the glass joined together can still be seen, which supports this hypothesis for the method of manufacture.

One of the difficulties with these three types of beads is that despite the similarities in general motif (i.e. 'whirl', 'ray', 'cable', etc.), they exhibit a high level of variability in terms of dimensions (Figure 19a), the colours utilised (Figure 19b-g), and the actual execution of the bead. Guido's typology does not take all of these variations into consideration. In addition, despite their high frequency in Northeast Scotland, there have been no examples of Class 14 beads from excavated contexts in this region as all have been found as stray finds, rendering it currently difficult to maintain an Iron Age date. The region is also known for the Class 13 beads discussed above (for which we now have examples from clear Iron Age contexts). However, Class 13 beads have only been found at the same site as Class 14 beads in four instances: Tap o'Noth, Cawdor Castle, Culbin Sands, and Smithston, none of which were found during excavation. There is a possibility that these beads are later in date.

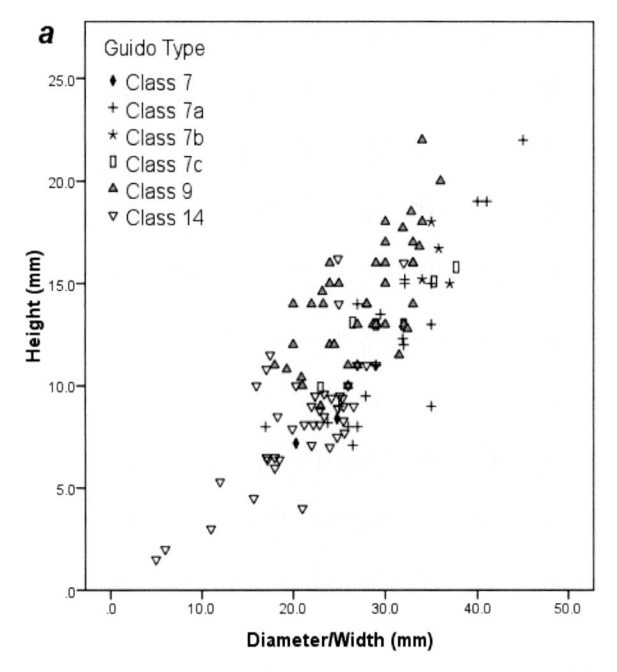

Figure 19: Comparison of Guido Class 7, 9, and 14 beads (a) scatter-graph comparing overall size.

Monochrome Beads (Guido Class 8, Groups 6, 7)

These three types of beads are all monochrome in colour and exhibit no other decoration. It is only the Class 8 beads that Guido could positively attribute to the Iron Age period. Examples of Groups 6 and 7 were sometimes found at Iron Age sites, but their lack of physical

b

c

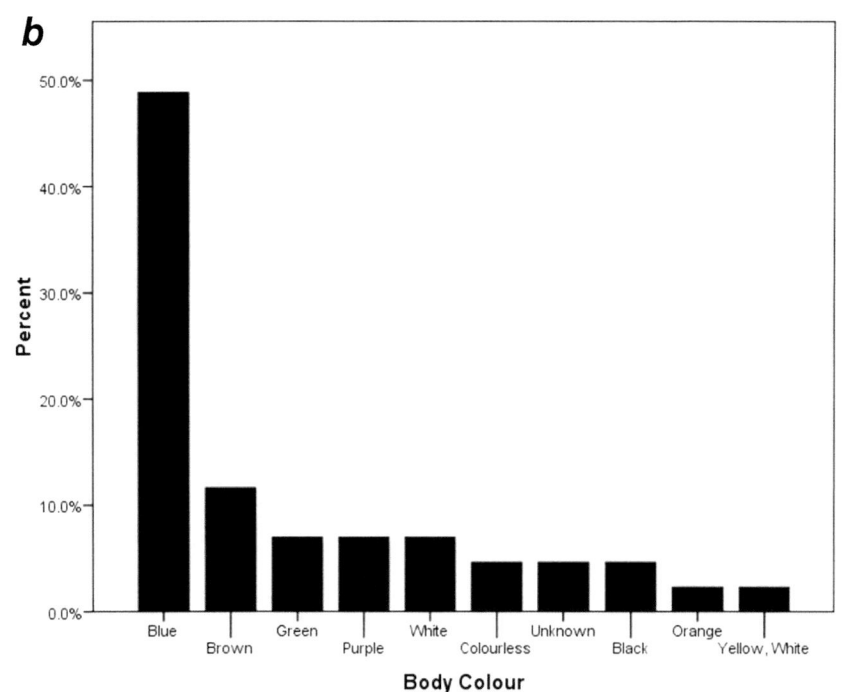

Figure 19: Comparison of Guido Class 7, 9, and 14 beads (b) bar-charts comparing the proportion of Class 7 body and (c) decorative colours.

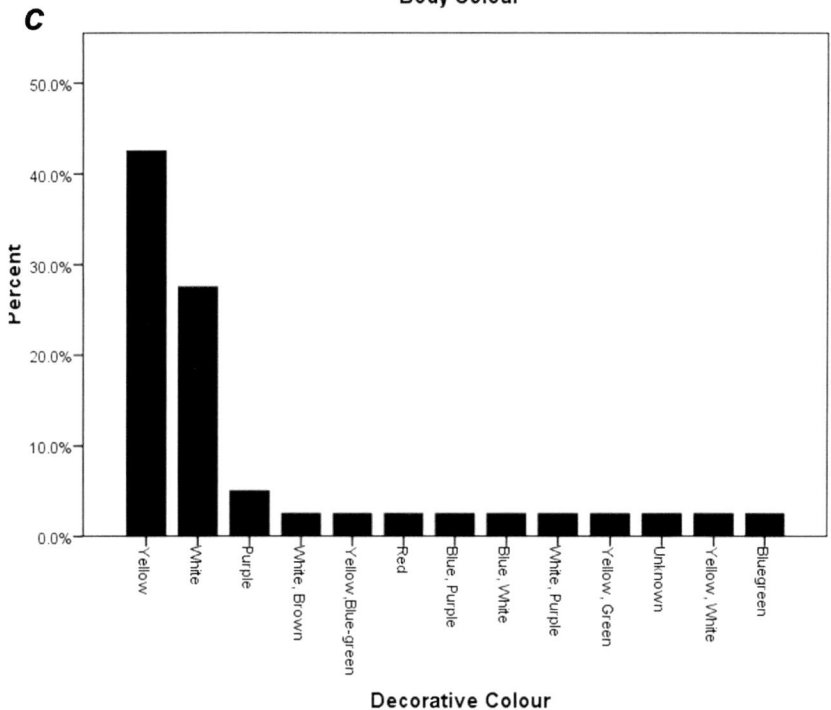

attributes rendered identifying them as Iron Age in origin difficult. Many of these plain beads have also been found in Roman and Anglo-Saxon contexts. In these cases, it could be that they were Iron Age beads that were re-used in later periods, or they could have been manufactured at a much later date.

The majority of Class 8 beads are remarkably very similar (Figure 189u-ab). They are defined as being annular in shape, and of opaque yellow glass. Despite their apparent homogeneity, two size groups emerge: a smaller group and a larger group (Figure 20). Many of these very small examples have only been discovered recently, so it may be that excavation method and environmental sampling may affect the recovery of smaller sized beads.

The overwhelming number of Group 6 and 7 plain beads highlights the desperate need for critical analysis of these types in order to determine measureable characteristics that may help to indicate date (Figure 189a-t). Many of the recent additions to these types are blue examples that were found during the excavations at Wetwang and Garton Slack.

Other than the dating issue, there are a few other problems with these two types. First, types are defined by shape

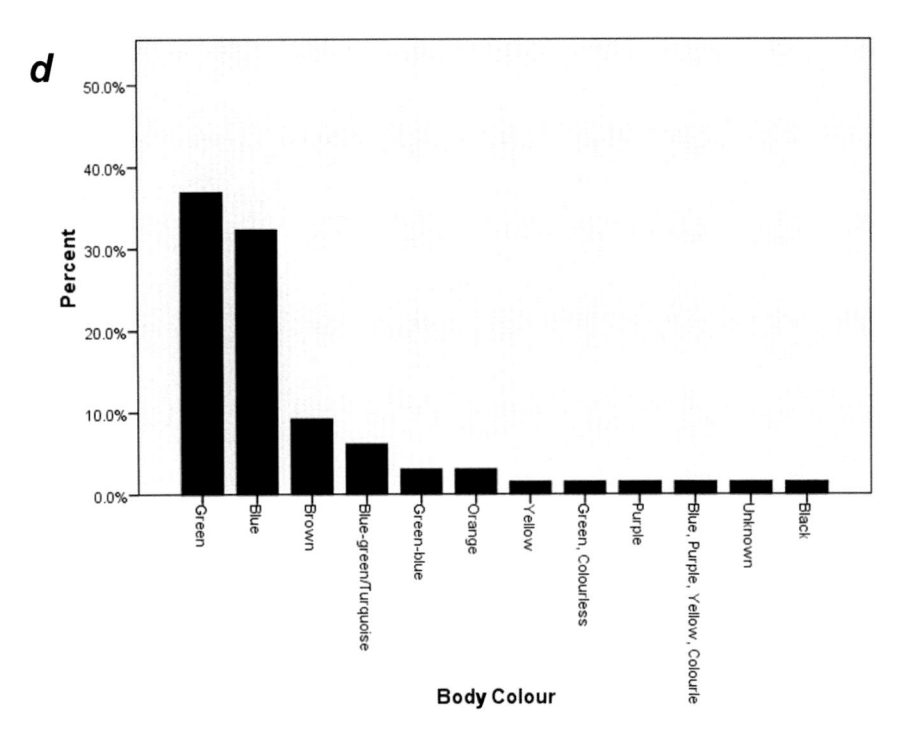

Figure 19: Comparison of Guido Class 7, 9, and 14 beads (d) bar-charts comparing the proportion of Class 9 body and (e) decorative colours.

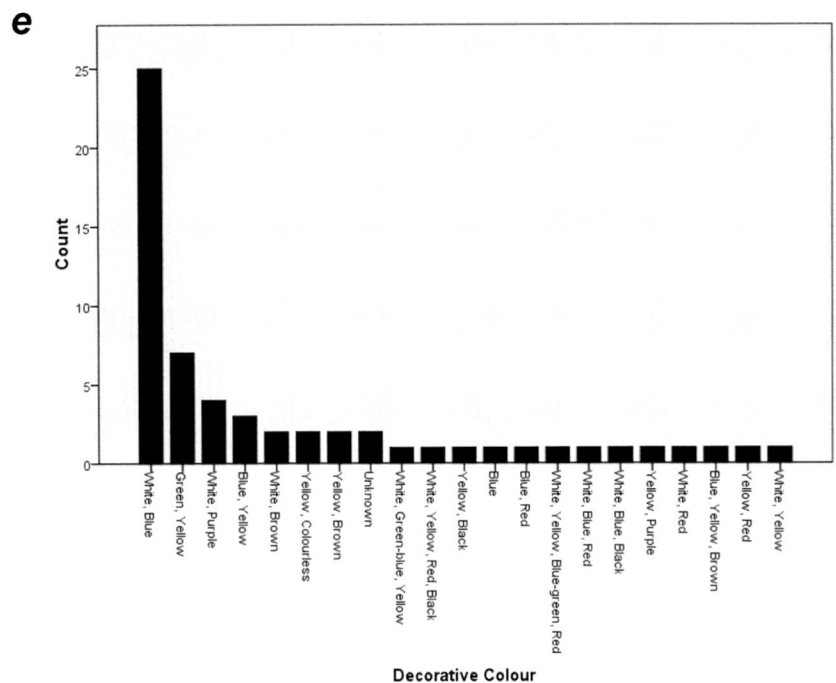

(annular or globular), then sub-types are defined first by colour, and then by size. However these divisions (other than colour) are more arbitrary than they might initially seem. For example, when all beads of Group 6 and 7 are plotted on a scatter graph (Figure 21) clear groups of beads based on shape or size do not emerge from the data as seen for Class 8 beads. Instead, there is a continuum of beads ranging from the very small to the very large, and some are more annular and others are more globular. Most beads cluster around the 1.5 ratio (x/2) line that Guido suggests as the division between these two shapes. This suggests that in many cases, the exact shape may have been less important during the manufacturing phase of many of these beads, and a strict definition of shape having implications for how a bead is classed may have less significance.

Linear Motifs Beads (Guido Class 11, Group 5)

These two Guido types utilise different linear designs for the decorative motif. Guido's Class 11 beads feature a range of different designs, but they are all made from colourless and opaque yellow glass (Figure 19 1a, g-i, k-o, ad). These beads were called 'Meare variant' beads,

f

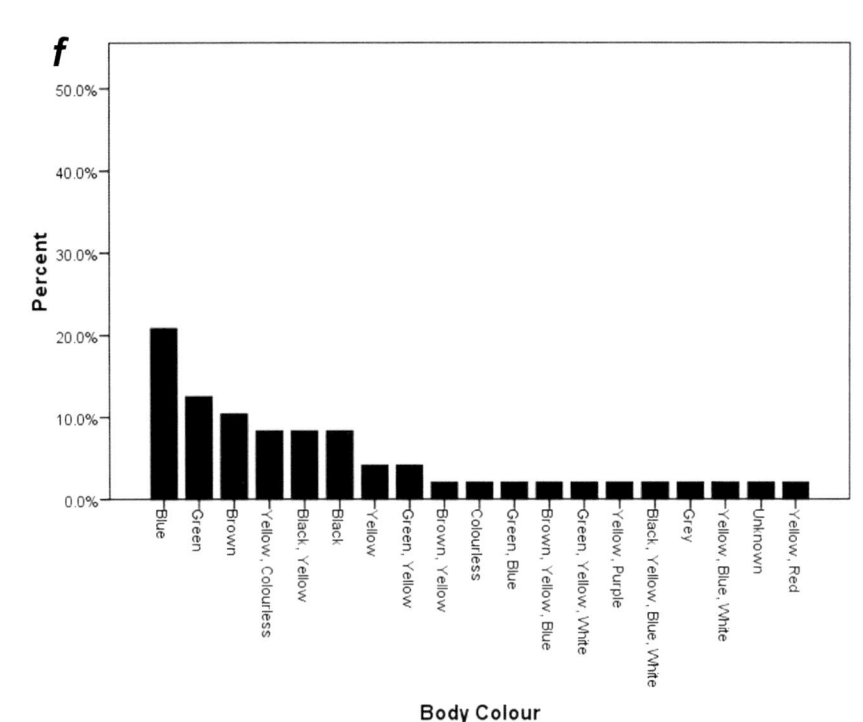

Figure 19: Comparison of Guido Class 7, 9, and 14 beads (f) bar-charts comparing the proportion of Class 14 body and (g) decorative colours.

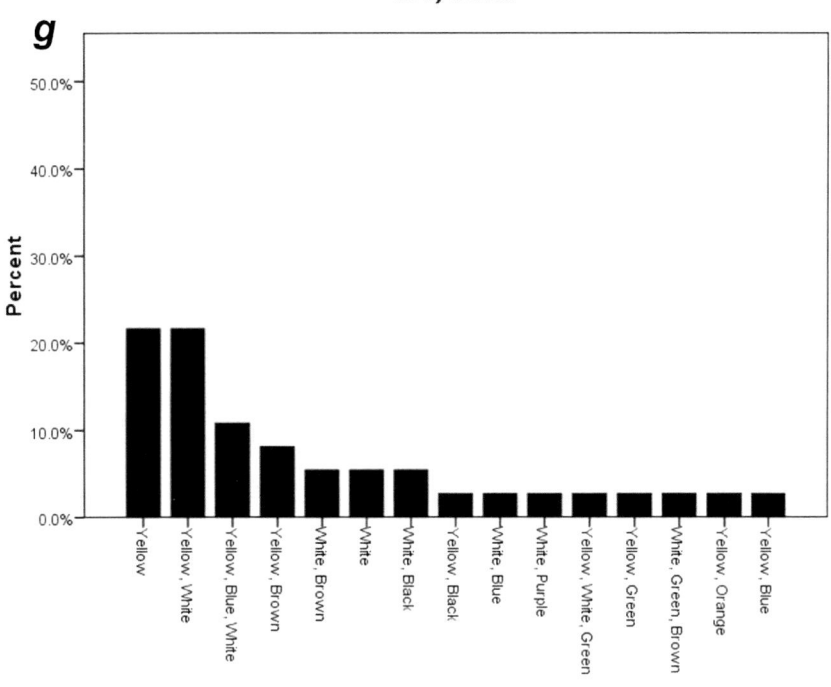

g

due to their similarity to the spiral Class 10 beads, which were presumably manufactured at Meare Lake Village. While this type was consistent in terms of colour, and the breakdown of sub-types is relatively consistent, the definition of a type by colour is inconsistent with many of the other types, especially given that the Guido Class 5 bead types are also made from colourless and opaque yellow glass. In addition, the motif based sub-division of this type is not mutually exclusive. Class 11g beads are colourless with an opaque yellow wave motif around the circumference, but Group 5 beads also feature a wave motif and are sub-divided further by colour. In this case, it is unclear whether all wave beads made from colourless glass and opaque yellow glass should be typed as a Class 11 bead, which implies that they were manufactured at Meare Lake Village; or whether they should be typed as Group 5 beads, which have few chronological associations.

Group 5 (Figure 191b-e, j) beads have a similar situation as with the Group 6 and 7 examples. Despite their abundance, the Guido typology offers little more than a way to describe wave beads. With the discovery of large numbers of this type from Wetwang Slack, it is at

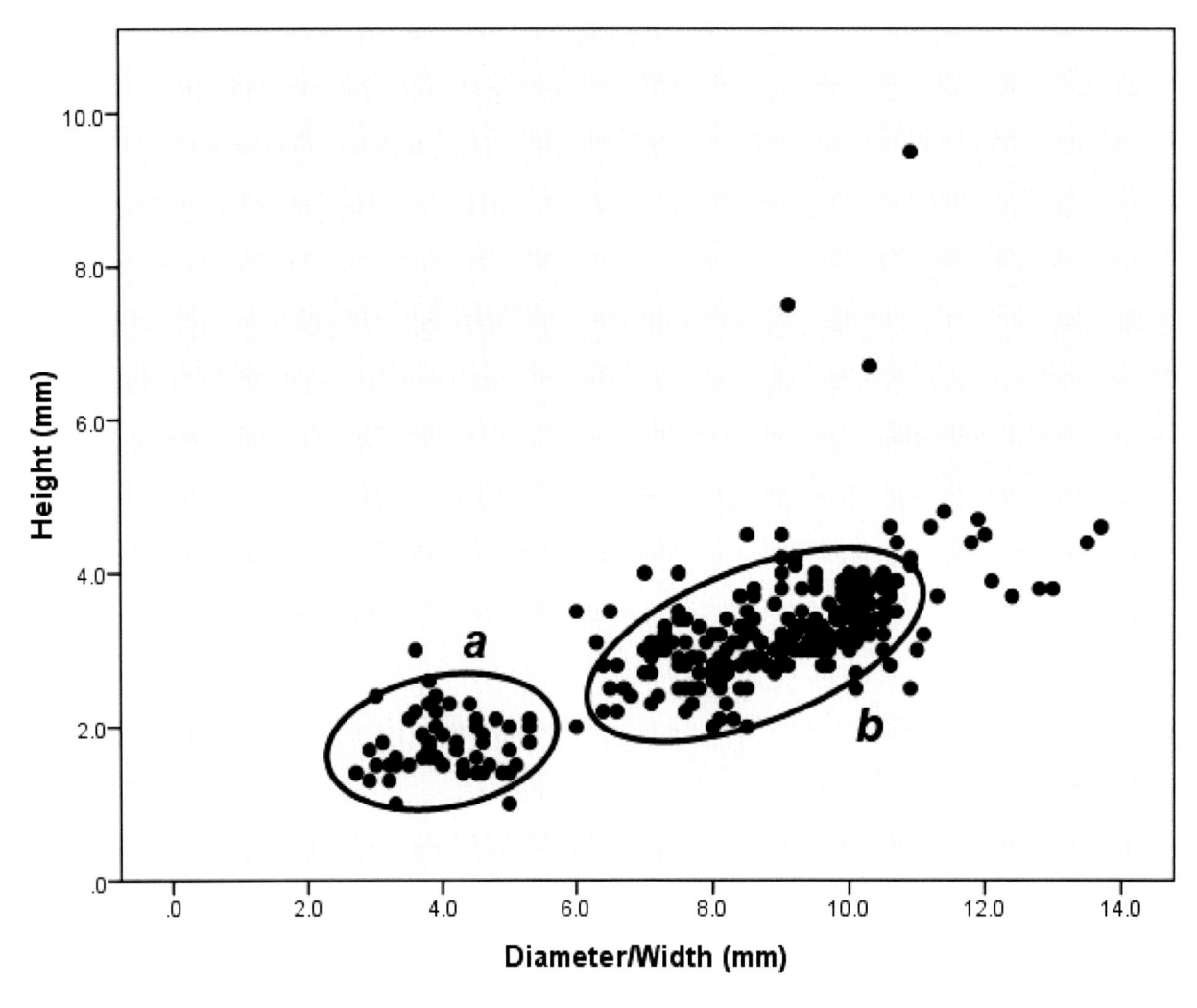

Figure 20: Scatter-graph comparing the dimensions of Guido Class 8 beads.

least possible to date some beads to this period. Further analysis is needed to determine whether all of these beads date to the Iron Age, and whether colour remains the best way to sub-divide these beads into sub-types.

Other Beads (Guido Class 5, 12, Groups 1, 3, 8)

These final glass bead types form a sort of random mixture that do not necessarily relate to each other. The Class 5 beads make up the most coherent group (Figure 190ac-ad). These beads are a large annular bead made primarily from colourless glass, but with a layer of opaque yellow around the inside of the perforation. This gives this type of bead a unique property as when it was new and the surface was unweathered, the colourless glass would have magnified the yellow and it would have appeared to glow. From the available data, examples of these beads are all quite similar, and it is a known continental bead type (Haevernick 1960). However, one new find is significantly different as it is made from colourless and opaque blue glass rather than opaque yellow (Figure 190ae). This unusual bead is the only know example from Britain thus far, and similar types

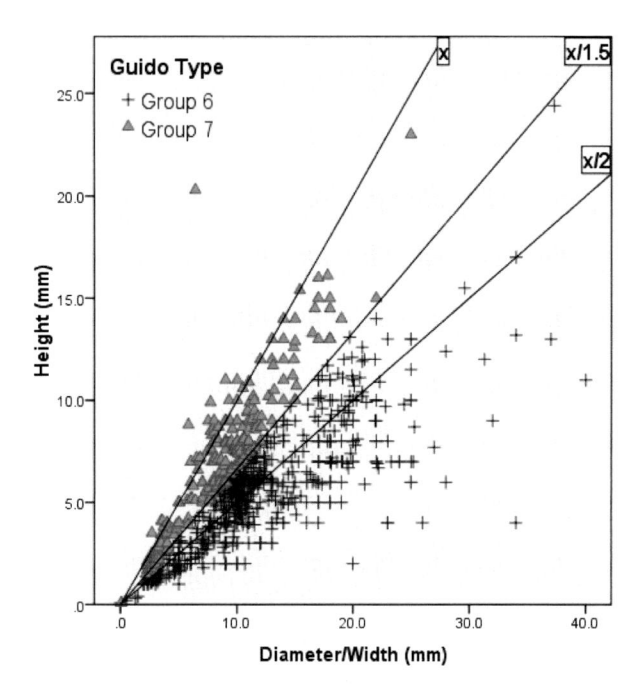

Figure 21: Scatter-graph comparing the dimensions of Guido Group 6 and 7 beads with guideline for perfect sphere (x) and 'annular' shape (x/2).

have not been identified from continental Europe. This example renders it necessary to redefine this bead type.

The Class 12 beads are inconsistent as they are loosely defined as 'stud' shaped beads (Figure 193g). Of Guido's two examples from her catalogue, one was made entirely from opaque yellow glass (DB 4228), and the other was made from colourless glass with multiple opaque yellow waves around the circumference (DB 4296). This bead type is primarily defined by the shape, rather than motif or use of colour. To this class, Henderson (1982, 113) added an example from Scotland (DB 16813), which he described as 'dumbbell' shaped, but the illustration shows that it does not resemble the two stud beads that Guido identified (Guido 1978a). Another possible example was found at Meare Lake Village West; however, this bead fragment also does not resemble the other two (Figure 189ae). The uniqueness of each of these examples suggests that rather than defining the type by the 'stud' shape, it should be redefined to reflect the segmented nature of the beads.

Group 1 beads were defined as being the same as Haevernicks' (1960) Gruppe 24 (Figure 194p). These beads have an all-over speckled appearance. This is true for some of the beads that Guido included in her catalogue (DB 4022, DB 7512), but others that she included do not fit the type description (Figure 194m). Therefore, based on the survey of beads from this type, it would be beneficial for an audit of all examples included under this type in order to determine whether they all resemble Haevernick's Gruppe 24 definition.

Unfortunately, it was not possible to view any of the Group 3 beads through the course of the data-collection. In addition, it was only possible to view a few examples of Guido Group 8 beads. From a review of the catalogue and first-hand examination of some examples, Group 8 beads became a designation for miscellaneous beads, where the date was generally unclear. However, this is misleading as the eight beads from the Clevedon Cist burials (Figure 189af-ag) can be suggested to date to about the Middle Iron Age or perhaps the end of the Middle Iron Age due to the inclusion of a Guido Class 10. There are also now two known examples of a bead that are similar to some European-style bangles from Haevernick's (1960) Gruppe 14 (Figure 189ac). Thus far, it has not been possible to find a comparable bead in Europe, but the similarity to glass bangles suggests that it may be of a similar date. Other examples of Guido's Group 8 are unclear as to whether they date to the Iron Age, or if they are from later periods.

Chronology

One of the goals that Guido saw her typology achieving is that the resolution of glass bead chronology would be fine enough that it could subsequently be used to date archaeological sites and features. This is based on the assumption that glass beads follow a chronology of typological development similar to that established for brooches where a particular type appears in fewer numbers at first, then a type becomes more popular and appears in greater numbers, and finally its use declines, which is indicated by fewer finds (e.g. Haselgrove 1997). Guido used data from archaeological excavations, site chronology based on the morphological changes of settlements over time, and assumptions about time-lag for objects to be transported from the continent to Britain in order to establish bead dates. Her earliest beads are the continental beads, while the British beads are generally later, but this is not a strict feature of the typology (Figure 22). Guido's scheme shows that more of her bead types appeared in Britain prior to the first century BC, although fourteen of her bead types continued in use during this period. Prior to exploring the chronology of bead types utilising the new typology, this section will review the chronology of Guido bead types.

The earliest type of bead was her Class 1 Type I beads, appearing as early as the fifth century BC, and her Class 4 beads appearing in the fourth century BC (Figure 23). The first of the possible British-made beads then appeared: the unusual Class 12 beads. At this same time, Guido's Class 1 Type II beads came into use, followed by the British-made Classes 8, 10, and 11 in the mid-third century BC. The early second century saw the introduction of the Class 5 beads, and at this point, the Class 1 Type I beads and Class 4 beads were no longer in use. Classes 6a and 6b as well as Class 7a beads began to be used in the mid-second century BC, but it was not until the beginning of the first century BC that Class 7b and Class 9a-c began to be used. By the end of the first century BC, a number of different bead types discontinued in use: Class 12, Class 1 Type II, Class 6a, Class 6b, Class 7a, and Class 7b. It was also during this period that the Class 2 beads were briefly introduced and quickly discontinued.

In the mid-first century BC the Class 13 beads began to be made in Scotland, and by the end of the first century BC and early first century AD the Class 14 beads began to be manufactured as well. Class 7c beads appeared in the early first century AD, but did not last beyond that century. Finally, the Class 3 beads began to be used by the end of the first century AD and lasted until the end of the second century AD. Most remaining types in use to this point disappeared: Class 5, Class 9a-c, Class 13, and Class 7c. The typology implies that most bead types were in use or were deposited in first century BC/AD contexts, which is a key point that will be returned in Chapters 7 and 8.

Again, one of the problems with this interpretation is that the Guido typology is not detailed enough for this sort of analysis. In addition, it places too much emphasis

Dress and Identity in Iron Age Britain

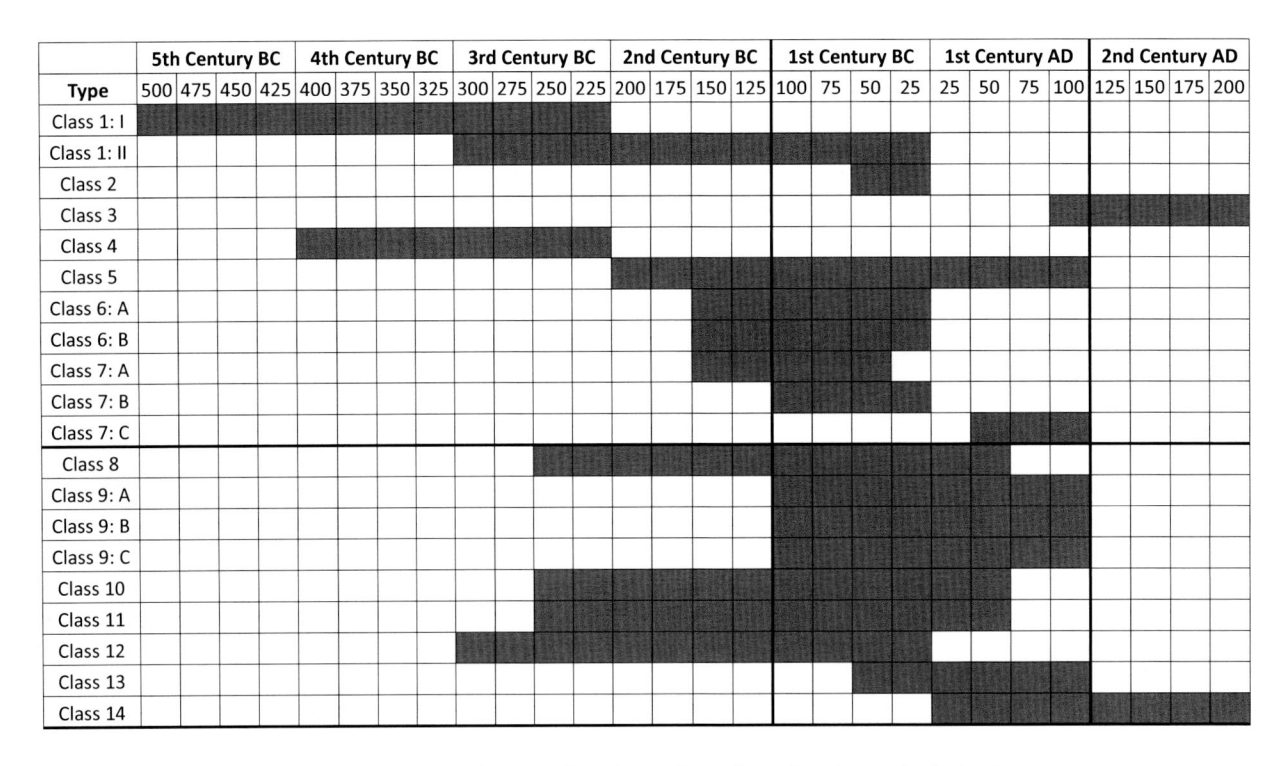

Figure 22: Schematic diagram of Guido typology chronology in typological order.

Figure 23: Schematic diagram of Guido typology chronology in chronological order.

on the idea of time lag from the continent, which is an idea that Collis (1994) and others have demonstrated is no longer supported by dating evidence. Finally, as has been demonstrated with Celtic Art (Garrow and Gosden 2012), there is no reason that glass beads must follow a strict progression of types given that they are small and portable. There is some evidence to suggest that the Guido Class 6 beads (Type 1407) had continued significance into later periods. For example, there is the broken example with a secondary perforation from Rudston

Roman Villa (DB 11630), and two examples from the Anglo-Saxon period: the pendant from Cow Low in Derbyshire (Sheffield Museum J93.704 (Ozanne 1962)) and the pendant recently found with an inhumation at Street House in Cleveland (Sherlock 2012). These finds support the hypothesis that at least some beads were in circulation for long periods of time, or perhaps were manufactured over a longer period of time. In addition, several of the necklaces from East Yorkshire combine beads that are lightly weathered and heavily weathered. This may indicate that the necklaces combined beads that were manufactured with different types of glass perhaps at different times and/or locations, and perhaps they were even passed down as heirlooms. As most beads are not found in inhumation contexts, the regional chronological evidence below suggests that several types have been in use for very long periods of time. Assuming that they were manufactured at relatively similar dates, this could indicate that they were passed through the generations.

General Problems with the Guido Typology

The result of this analysis suggested that in a few instances the types and their descriptions remain valid and useful tools of analysis (e.g. Class 8, 10 and mostly Class 5). However, for the majority of the types there are a number of issues that suggest that the typology needs to be restructured and re-created. This section will bring to light five of the major issues found during the classification analysis.

1. **Not all newly discovered beads fit into the typology.** Some beads can be said to be 'similar' to Type x, or 'bear resemblance to' a particular type, but they do not fit the type description. In some cases, there is no relevant type despite a clear Iron Age date (e.g. DB 9966).
2. **Types contain too much variability, they are not specific enough, and not all types are mutually exclusive.** This is an issue for a number of types. Upon viewing a number of examples, it was evident that beads within a Guido Class or Group were different enough that they could be considered to be different types. In effect, the typology over-generalises and makes it appear as if there are a limited number of different bead types and that they are perfect duplicates of each other. This is clearly not the case. In addition, the typology is problematic in places because a bead's physical characteristics could place it into more than one type, rendering any sort of type-based analysis impossible.
3. **Some sub-types have been arbitrarily divided and do not allow for meaningful analysis.** This is particularly a problem for Guido Classes 7 and 9, where beads are simply typed by their body colour, rather than any other characteristic, when it is clear that not all beads within a sub-type are the same. At the same time, this relates to the first issue, as not all newly discovered beads fit within the sub-types. In addition, some types need to be further sub-divided in order to clearly express the amount of variability within them (e.g. Guido Class 14).
4. **There is little evidence to support chronological periods.** Only a minority of beads and bead types were found in well dated excavated contexts, while many have been found as stray finds. In the case of continental bead types, Guido often takes the dates of similar beads from these locations, adds a lag-time to their arrival in Britain, and applies this date to the Class or Group. In the case of British-made beads, she argues southern types, such as those found at Meare Lake Village, will be earlier than those from Scotland because they were dependent on the technology transfer from south to north.
5. **Types do not equal people.** Although Guido avoided the use of tribal names in Iron Age Britain, the way she split the Iron Age beads from Roman beads, and even the 'imported' and 'local' beads, portrays the idea of very different and separate identities between the Romans, the people that inhabited Iron Age Britain, and those in continental Europe.

These five major issues pertain to the typology as a whole. Within each type, the specific issues vary depending on the type definition, the characteristics of the beads, and the available data for each bead.

Discussion

These analyses have highlighted some of the difficulties encountered with the Guido classification and chronology of glass beads. The implications are that Guido's typology cannot be used for meaningful analysis of the archaeological record, or questions of chronology, distribution, deposition, or use. Instead, much of the typology actually masks the details that make these objects so interesting.

New Typology

As the Guido typology is inadequate for analysing the complex diversity of beads in Iron Age Britain, a new typology was created for use throughout this book. This typology necessarily draws on data that is restricted to the four study regions as set out in Chapter 1. As this limits the available data for the typology, it should be considered an interim typology, but it nonetheless will explore one of the ways in which a new all-encompassing typology could be created. It is also necessary to point out that while this typology will have direct relevance to the research questions presented in the current work, it may not apply to other research questions or agendas. However, it is necessary to be explicit in regards to the organisation of the typology so that future researchers can determine whether it fits their needs.

Typology Description

The typology was constructed using data from the four research regions; however, not all beads encountered during the data collection stage have been included here. All beads that are clearly a part of Guido's classes have been included for analysis as it is reasonably certain that they date to the Iron Age, even if some were found in what might be considered Roman period contexts. Beads that would normally be a part of Guido's groups have been included only if they come from archaeological contexts that suggest an Iron Age date. Thus, many stray beads have been necessarily left out of this analysis as it is possible that they may post-date the Iron Age and Roman period. In addition, beads that cannot be classified as one of Guido's types, but come from clear Iron Age contexts, have also been included.

Utilising these criteria, 1,788 individual glass beads have been included in the creation of the typology. This covers all but two Guido types: Class 4 Findon type beads, and Group 2 Miscellaneous horned beads. Both of these types were recorded in Guido's catalogue in extremely small numbers (and were supposedly Iron Age), but none were found in the study regions under consideration. Using shape, colour, and decorative motif as the characteristics for defining types, 11 major classes of glass beads have been distinguished, with 162 mutually exclusive types. The structure takes some inspiration from Venclova's (1990) classification of prehistoric glass beads from the Czech Republic, where the simplest beads are considered first, and then they become increasingly more complex in terms of their decorative motif. Within each class are one or more types that vary in a number of attributes. Each type and class is numerically named. Although naming bead types as Guido did after a specific find (the type-find, or ideal form) provides an aid to memory, by using numerical references for each bead type it is possible to remove some of the culture history consequences that have accumulated within the study of glass beads associated with tracking cultures through artefacts. In addition, it removes the idea that there is an ideal form, and that any derivation from this is simply variation, sub-form, or poorly made. By using numerical type designations, it also allows the addition of new types within a certain class to be included with ease rather than forcing beads into types that clearly do not belong together.

In order to design this typology it was necessary to envisage a hierarchy of traits (Figure 24). At the top are the simplest traits, such as differentiating polychrome and monochrome, while at the bottom are the more complex traits such as specific colour combinations, shape, and specific design motifs. This has resulted in two classes for monochrome beads: Class 1 is defined by a simple shape (annular and globular), while Class 2 beads have more complex shapes (i.e. melon, stud).

The remaining classes are polychrome. As the simplest polychrome type, Class 3 beads are different from the remaining classes as they exhibit no particular design or decorative motif. Polychrome beads with a clear design are split into simple motifs and complex motifs. Simple motifs exhibit only one type of motif, such as eyes, or one type of linear design (Classes 4-10). Complex motifs exhibit two or more motifs (Class 11).

By creating different levels of grouping, analysis can be carried out at both the general and specific level. For example, using this method of classification, it is possible to examine all beads with eye motifs together (Class 4), or to examine one particular combination of characteristics together, for example Type 411. In some cases, it is impossible to know the full details of a specific bead, which is sometimes due to the quality of the report, or because the bead has subsequently been lost. In order to be able to include these beads even at a general level, each class has a dummy type ending in a double zero (*00), which designates beads that can generally be assigned to this type, but there is missing information. In this way, the usefulness of the data is maximized despite an inability to access individual examples.

Size does not play a role in the current interim typology. This is in part due to missing data, either through difficulty in accessing objects or poor objects descriptions in written reports, hindering the use of this variable. Although this will not be explored further here, it is worth noting that in many cases, within each type, the beads cluster according to size. If the framework of this typology has a long-lasting applicability for other researchers, it may be worth exploring size data in greater detail. However, as was shown for Guido Group 6 and 7 beads earlier in this chapter, it should be cautioned that size terms such as 'large' and 'small' can be misleading and different size groups needs to be demonstrated within the data rather than arbitrarily assigned.

A full list of each type in this interim typology is available in Appendix C. It was not possible to view and measure all beads in detail, and it is likely that further detailed work even within the study regions could substantially alter the organisation. For example, it has not been possible to fully differentiate different types of whirl and ray beads that make up classes 8 and 9 as not enough examples have been viewed and descriptions are often not precise enough to fully impart the exact nature of the motif. In addition, as this typology is only limited to the areas under consideration, further research will add additional types. However, the general structure will provide a framework that can easily be expanded to accommodate them. Overall, the typology set out will provide a tool for which to explore the variability of decorative motif, shape, and colour of glass beads throughout the study regions.

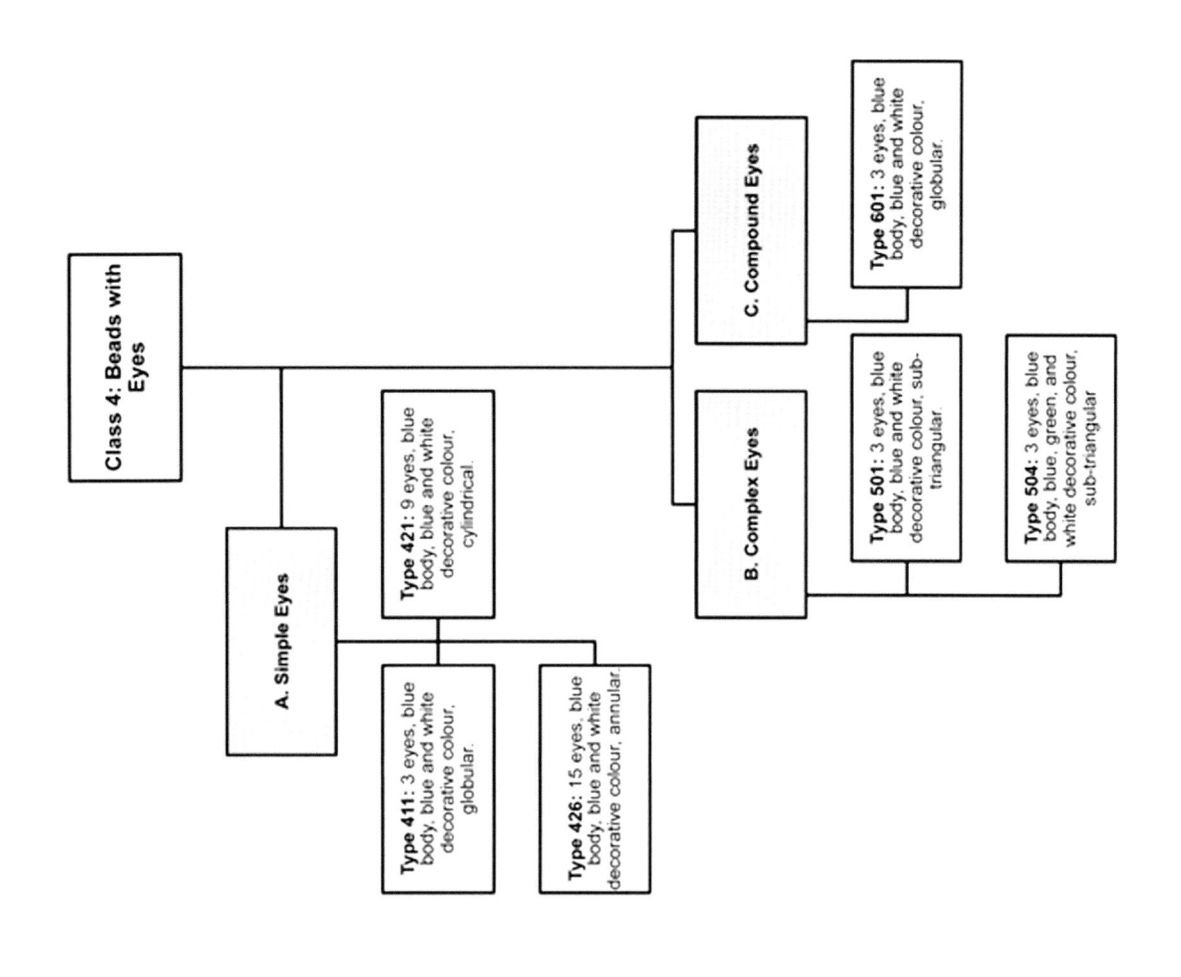

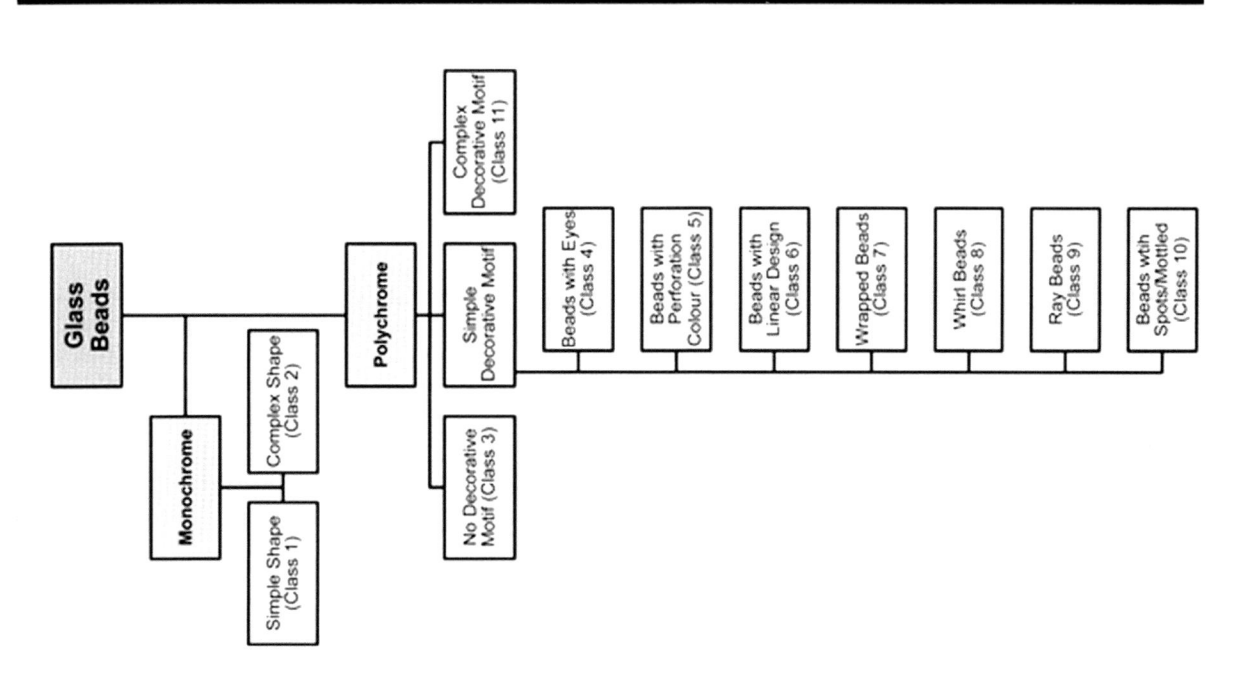

Typological Conundrums, Quandaries, and Resolutions

Figure 24: Schematic diagram showing the hierarchy of new glass bead types.

Types in the Study Regions

Southwest England has by far the largest number of types found within the study regions, which account for 54% of the total identified types. The most frequently occurring types are Types 110 (n=157, monochrome yellow beads), 102 (n=68, monochrome blue beads), and 1417 (spiral bead with 1 row of 3 yellow spirals on a colourless body, n=53). There are also a number of Type 1003 (n=36) colourless globular beads with multiple yellow chevrons. Other beads are found much less frequently, such as Types 106: monochrome green beads (n=12), 107 monochrome orange beads (n=15), and 410 beads with simple eyes but missing details (n=13). Other types of beads are less frequent.

In contrast, glass beads from East Anglia make up the smallest number of types (n=19), but there are also a small number of beads from this region (n=26). They account for 11% of the total number of identified types. The most frequent type of bead is Type 1407: blue with three rows of white spirals. All other beads even rarer, and most have only single examples of each type.

Beads from East Yorkshire are part of 32 different types of beads, which make up 18% of the total number of types. Type 102: monochrome blue beads, are the most frequent type (n=603). Also frequent is Type 901: blue bead with white wave/zigzag (n=121). All other types of beads are found in smaller numbers such as Type 202 (blue melon beads, n=16), 411 (blue globular beads with three eyes made from blue and white glass, n=26), 417 (blue with three eyes formed with green and white glass, n=13), 420 (globular brown bead with three eyes made from blue and white glass, n=12), and 424 (blue with 12 eyes formed from blue and white glass, n=14). The remaining types are rare.

Finally, the assemblage from Northeast Scotland makes up 56 different types of beads, making up 34% of the total number of types. The most prolific one being Type 110 (monochrome yellow beads, n=239). All other beads are comparatively rare. However, the uniqueness of many of these beads demonstrates just how diverse beads can be in one area.

Bead Class and Type Analysis

While the above analysis examined the types of beads in each region, the next analysis will examine each class together and compare the frequencies within each study region in order to examine regional characteristics. Class 1 beads are those that are simple monochrome beads made into simple shapes and varying by colour (Figure 25). Types 102 and 110 are by far the most frequent. However, they are only found in large quantities in Southwest England and Northeast Scotland. While some of these types are found in multiple regions, only Types 104 (brown), 105 (colourless), 108 (purple), and 109 (red) are found in Southwest England.

Classes 2 and 3 are groups of unusual beads. Class 2 beads are monochrome, but with complex shapes, and are much more limited in number than Class 1 beads (Figure 26). Type 201 is a blue bead with bumps all over that was found in East Anglia and Southwest England. Type 202 are unusual Iron Age blue melon beads found only in East Yorkshire. Finally, Type 203 and 204 represent two unusual beads. The first is a segmented yellow bead, and the second is a stud-shaped yellow bead. Both examples were found in Southwest England.

Class 3 beads are polychrome in colour, but lack a design motif. Some have a mottled colour, and others have layered colours. They also have restricted quantities (Figure 27). Type 301, 302, 305, and 306 are only found in Southwest England, while Type 303 and 304 are only found in Northeast Scotland.

Class 4 beads are the first of the simple decorated bead classes, and have eyes made from dots of glass (Figure 28). Class 4a have simple eyes, but in varying numbers placed around the bead. Interestingly, only Type 412, 415, 416, 419, 422, 427, and 429 are found in Southwest England, while Types 411, 413, 414, 417, 418, 420, 421, 423, 424, 425, and 428 are only found in East Yorkshire. The only one of these found in both regions is Type 426. None of these simple eye beads have been found in Northeast Scotland. Class 4b beads are complex eye beads and Types 501 and 503 are found in East Yorkshire, while Type 502 is only found in East Anglia. Finally, Class 4c are compound eye beads and the only example included in this study is from Southwest England.

Class 5 beads are colourless annular beads with a contrasting colour along the inside and side of the perforation (Figure 29) Two types have been identified: Class 5a (Type 701) with yellow as the contrasting colour, and Class 5b (Type 702) with blue as the contrasting colour. Type 701 has been found in Southwest England and East Yorkshire, while the only example of Type 702 known in all of Britain has been found in East Anglia.

Class 6 beads are described as beads with linear design; however, all of these are simple (Figure 30). More complex combinations of linear motifs are attributed to Class 11. As 53 different types of beads with this motif type have been identified, this class will be explored in sections. Class 6a are beads with multiple circumferential lines. There are two examples of Type 801 blue annular beads with either white or yellow circumferential lines. One of these is from East Anglia, and the other was found in East Yorkshire. Type 802 are colourless with yellow circumferential lines and are found in Southwest England. These are the only examples of beads with multiple circumferential lines in the study regions.

Type	Southwest England	East Anglia	East Yorkshire	Northeast Scotland	TOTAL
101	3	-	1	-	4
102	68	2	603	5	678
103	1	-	1	-	2
104	4	-	-	-	4
105	2	-	-	-	2
106	11	2	1	-	14
107	15	1	-	-	16
108	2	-	-	-	2
109	3	-	-	-	3
110	157	-	7	239	403
TOTAL	266	5	613	244	1128

Figure 25: Frequency of Class 1 beads in the study regions.

Type	Southwest England	East Anglia	East Yorkshire	Northeast Scotland	TOTAL
201	1	1	-	-	2
202	-	-	16	-	16
203	1	-	-	-	1
204	1	-	-	-	1
TOTAL	3	1	16	0	20

Figure 26: Frequency of Class 2 beads in the study regions.

Type	Southwest England	East Anglia	East Yorkshire	Northeast Scotland	TOTAL
301	6	-	-	-	6
302	2	-	-	-	2
303	-	-	-	1	1
304	-	-	-	1	1
305	1	-	-	-	1
306	1	-	-	-	1
TOTAL	10	0	0	2	12

Figure 27: Frequency of Class 3 beads in the study regions.

Type	Southwest England	East Anglia	East Yorkshire	Northeast Scotland	TOTAL
410	13	2	9	-	24
411	-	-	26	-	26
412	1	-	-	-	1
413	-	-	4	-	4
414	-	-	2	-	2
415	1	-	-	-	1
416	1	-	-	-	1
417	-	-	13	-	13
418	-	-	1	-	1
419	1	-	-	-	1
420	-	-	12	-	12
421	-	-	8	-	8
422	2	-	-	-	2
423	-	-	4	-	4
424	-	-	14	-	14
425	-	-	2	-	2
426	1	-	1	-	2
427	1	-	-	-	1
428	-	-	1	-	1
429	1	-	-	-	1
501	-	-	2	-	2
502	-	1	-	-	1
503	-	-	1	-	1
601	1	-	-	-	1
TOTAL	23	3	100	0	126

Figure 28: Frequency of Class 4 beads in the study regions.

Type	Southwest England	East Anglia	East Yorkshire	Northeast Scotland	TOTAL
701	6	2	-	-	8
702	-	1	-	-	1
TOTAL	6	3	0	0	9

Figure 29: Frequency of Class 5 beads in the study regions.

Class 6b are beads with a single wave. Type 901 is the most numerous and is found predominately in East Yorkshire. Other East Yorkshire versions of this motif include Type 907 and 905. All other examples (Types 902, 903, 904, 908, 909, and 910) are exclusive to Southwest England. Class 6c beads have chevron motifs and cluster according to shape, thus Types 1001-1003 are differentiated by shape. Type 1001 (annular) are found in Southwest England, East Anglia, and East Yorkshire. Types 1002 (barrel) and 1003 (globular) are found exclusively in Southwest England. None of these types of beads have been found in Northeast Scotland. Classes 6d, e, and f are each very distinct examples of specific motifs that have only been found in Southwest England. They all have a colourless body and yellow decoration. Type 1101 has a criss-cross motif made by the yellow glass, Type 1201 has a diagonal criss-cross, and Type 1301 has a pinnate motif.

Finally, Class 6g beads are spiral beads. Thirty varieties of spiral beads have been identified that vary by shape and colour, while more complex spiral beads are listed under Class 11. Out of all the different combinations, only Types 1407 and 1417 occur in three of the study regions. Type 1407 is significantly different to the majority of these beads. It is annular/globular in shape with a blue body and three rows of white spirals placed around the circumference of the bead. Examples of this type have been found in all study regions except Northeast

Scotland. Type 1417 is more similar to the remaining spiral beads. This particular type is distinctly globular in shape, has a colourless body, and a single row of three yellow spirals placed around the circumference of the bead. Examples of these beads have been found in all study regions except East Anglia, and large numbers have been found in Southwest England. The remaining beads are similar to Type 1417, but vary in shape and colour. Most types are found exclusively in either Southwest England or Northeast Scotland, but Types, such as 1418, 1419, and 1420, are found in both of these regions. These are all colourless beads with yellow spirals, but 1418 is sub-triangle in shape, 1419 is truncated triangle shaped, and the shape of 1420 is unknown.

Classes 7, 8, and 9 are somewhat related as they seem to be mostly formed from either wrapping or twisting a cane around a mandrel. Most examples do not have additional linear or dotted designs applied afterwards, as the design is contained within the cane. Class 7 beads are simple, multi-coloured wrapped beads (Figure 31). There is no consistency in the colours used to form the beads, but they are only found in Northeast Scotland. Class 8 beads are simple whirl beads that are found only in Southwest England and Northeast Scotland (Figure 32). Although most varieties are exclusive to either of these regions, suggesting possible regional types, there may be some overlap between Types 1603 and 1604. Finally, Class 9 beads have a ray design (Figure 33). There is one example from East Anglia, and the remaining examples are exclusive to Southwest England. All these beads from Classes 7 to 9 are annular in shape while any variety is derived from the colours utilised. In the case of the wrapped beads, there does not seem to be any distinction between colours used for the body of the bead, and colours used for decoration, while for whirl and ray beads there is a dominant body colour and smaller amounts of decorative colour. In most cases, with these two Classes the body colour is darker, while the decorative colour is white, yellow, or both.

Class 10 beads are the last of the beads with simple decoration (Figure 34). These unusual beads have an all-over spotted appearance that is different from the use of dots seen in Class 4. There has been one example each from East Anglia, East Yorkshire, and Southwest England, but none from Northeast Scotland. Unfortunately, the colour data are not available for the East Yorkshire example; however, the other two are both blue with white or white and yellow spots.

Class 11 beads are made from more complex motif combinations, and 49 different combinations of motif and use of colour have been identified. Due to their complex nature, many of these beads at this time appear to be unique. This may indicate a number of possible explanations such as invention, experimentation, or even long distance movement of objects. So, for example

Type	Southwest England	East Anglia	East Yorkshire	Northeast Scotland	TOTAL
801	-	1	1	-	2
802	1	-	-	-	1
900	-	-	6	-	6
901	10	2	121	3	136
902	1	-	-	-	1
903	1	-	-	-	1
904	1	-	-	-	1
905	-	-	1	-	1
906	5	-	-	-	5
907	-	-	13	-	13
908	1	-	-	-	1
909	1	-	-	-	1
910	1	-	-	-	1
1000	3	-	-	-	3
1001	4	1	1	-	6
1002	1	-	-	-	1
1003	36	-	-	-	36
1101	3	-	-	-	3
1201	1	-	-	-	1
1301	1	-	-	-	1
1400	9	-	-	15	24
1401	-	-	-	1	1
1402	-	-	-	2	2
1403	-	-	-	8	8
1404	-	-	-	1	1
1405	4	-	-	-	4
1406	1	-	-	-	1
1407	8	3	4	-	15
1408	1	-	-	-	1
1409	-	-	-	2	2
1410	-	-	-	3	3
1411	-	-	-	7	7
1412	-	-	-	2	2
1413	-	-	-	1	1
1414	-	-	-	1	1
1415	-	-	-	1	1
1416	2	-	-	-	2
1417	53	-	1	2	56
1418	3	-	-	2	5
1419	1	-	-	6	7
1420	1	-	-	1	2
1421	-	-	-	1	1
1422	-	-	-	2	2
1423	-	-	-	4	4
1424	-	-	-	1	1
1425	-	-	-	4	4
1426	-	-	-	1	1
1427	-	-	-	1	1
1428	-	-	-	1	1
1429	-	-	-	1	1
1430	1	-	-	-	1
1431	1	-	-	-	1
TOTAL	156	7	148	74	385

Figure 30: Frequency of Class 6 beads in the study regions.

Type	Southwest England	East Anglia	East Yorkshire	Northeast Scotland	TOTAL
1601	-	-	-	1	1
1602	2	-	-	-	2
1603	1	-	-	1	2
1604	2	-	-	1	3
1605	1	-	-	-	1
1606	1	-	-	-	1
1607	-	-	-	2	2
1608	1	-	-	-	1
1609	-	-	-	1	1
1610	1	-	-	-	1
1611	-	-	-	1	1
TOTAL	**9**	**0**	**0**	**7**	**16**

Figure 31: Frequency of Class 7 beads in the study regions.

Type	Southwest England	East Anglia	East Yorkshire	Northeast Scotland	TOTAL
1501	-	-	-	9	9
TOTAL	**0**	**0**	**0**	**9**	**9**

Figure 32: Frequency of Class 8 beads in the study regions.

Type	Southwest England	East Anglia	East Yorkshire	Northeast Scotland	TOTAL
1702	1	1	-	2	4
1703	1	-	-	1	2
1704	1	-	-	1	2
TOTAL	**3**	**1**	**0**	**4**	**8**

Figure 33: Frequency of Class 9 beads in the study regions.

Type	Southwest England	East Anglia	East Yorkshire	Northeast Scotland	TOTAL
1800	-	-	1	-	1
1801	-	1	-	-	1
1802	1	-	-	-	1
TOTAL	**1**	**1**	**1**	**0**	**3**

Figure 34: Frequency of Class 10 beads in the study regions.

Type	Southwest England	East Anglia	East Yorkshire	Northeast Scotland	TOTAL
2101	1	-	-	-	1
2201	1	-	-	-	1
2202	1	-	-	-	1
2301	-	-	1	-	1
2302	-	1	-	-	1
2303	-	1	-	-	1
2304	-	1	-	-	1
2306	1	-	-	-	1
2307	1	-	-	-	1
2401	1	-	-	-	1
2501	-	-	-	1	1
2502	-	-	-	1	1
2503	-	-	-	1	1
2504	-	-	-	1	1
2505	-	-	-	1	1
2506	-	-	-	1	1
2507	-	-	-	1	1
2601	-	-	-	2	2
2602	-	-	-	1	1
2603	-	-	-	1	1
2604	-	-	-	1	1
2605	-	-	-	1	1
2701	-	-	-	1	1
2702	-	-	-	1	1
2703	-	-	-	1	1
2704	-	-	-	1	1
2705	-	-	-	1	1
2706	-	-	-	1	1
2801	1	-	-	-	1
2802	-	-	-	1	1
2901	1	-	-	-	1
3000	3	-	-	-	3
3001	1	-	-	-	1
3002	1	-	-	-	1
3003	4	1	-	-	5
3005	1	-	-	-	1
3006	1	-	-	-	1
3008	-	-	1	-	1
3009	1	-	-	-	1
3010	1	-	-	-	1
3011	1	-	-	-	1
3012	2	-	-	-	2
3014	4	1	-	-	5
3015	1	-	-	-	1
3016	1	-	-	-	1
3017	2	-	-	-	2
3018	1	-	-	-	1
3019	1	-	-	-	1
TOTAL	**34**	**5**	**2**	**20**	**61**

Figure 35: Frequency of Class 11 beads in the study regions.

Class	Type	1	2	3	4
Class 1	101	x		x	
	102	x	x	x	x
	103	x	x		
	104	x			
	105	x			
	106	x	x	x	
	107	x	x		
	108	x			
	109	x			
	110	x		x	x
Class 2	201		x		
	202			x	
	203	x			
	204	x			
Class 3	301	x			
	302	x			
	303				x
	304				x
	305	x			
	306	x			
Class 4	410	x	x	x	
	411			x	
	412	x			
	413			x	
	414			x	
	415	x			
	416	x			
	417			x	
	418			x	
	419	x			
	420			x	
	421			x	
	422	x			
	423			x	
	424			x	
	425			x	
	426	x	x		
	427	x			
	428			x	
	429	x			
	500				
	501			x	
	502		x		
	503			x	
	600				
	601	x			

Class	Type	1	2	3	4
Class 5	701	x	x		
	702		x		
Class 6 (A)	800				
	801		x	x	
	802	x			
Class 6 (B)	900			x	
	901	x	x	x	x
	902	x			
	903	x			
	904	x			
	905			x	
	906	x			
	907			x	
	908	x			
	909	x			
	910	x			
Class 6 (C)	1000	x			
	1001	x	x	x	
	1002	x			
	1003	x			
Class 6 (D)	1100				
	1101	x			
Class 6 (E)	1200				
	1201	x			
Class 6 (F)	1300				
	1301	x			

Class	Type	1	2	3	4
Class 6 (G)	1400	x			x
	1401				x
	1402				x
	1403				x
	1404				x
	1405	x			
	1406	x			
	1407	x	x	x	
	1408	x			
	1409				x
	1410				x
	1411				x
	1412				x
	1413				x
	1414				x
	1415				x
	1416	x			
	1417	x		x	x
	1418	x			x
	1419	x			x
	1420	x			x
	1421				x
	1422				x
	1423				x
	1424				x
	1425				x
	1426				x
	1427				x
	1428				x
	1429				x
	1430	x			

Class	Type	1	2	3	4
Class 7	1501				x
Class 8	1601				x
	1602	x			
	1603	x			x
	1604	x			x
	1605	x			
	1606	x			
	1607				x
	1608	x			
	1609				x
	1610	x			
	1611				x
Class 9	1701			x	
	1702	x			
	1703	x			
	1704	x			
Class 10	1800			x	
	1801			x	
	1802	x			
	2101	x			
	2201	x			
	2301			x	
	2302		x		
	2303		x		
	2304		x		
	2306	x			
	2307	x			
	2401	x			
Class 11	2501				x
	2502				x
	2503				x
	2504				x
	2505				x
	2506				x
	2507				x
	2601				x
	2602				x
	2603				x
	2604				x
	2605				x
	2701				x
	2702				x
	2703				x
	2704				x
	2705				x
	2706				x
	2801	x			

Key:
- Present in one study region
- Present in two study regions
- Present in three study regions
- Present in four study regions

Figure 36: Summary table of presence and absence of new types. (1) Southwest England, (2) East Anglia, (3) East Yorkshire, and (4) Northeast Scotland.

	Type	1	3	3	4
Class 11	2802				x
	2901	x			
	3000	x			
	3001	x			
	3002	x			
	3003	x	x		
	3004				
	3005	x			
	3006	x			
	3007	x			
	3008			x	
	3009	x			
	3010	x			
	3011	x			
	3012	x			
	3013				
	3014	x	x		
	3015	x			
	3016	x			
	3017	x			
	3018	x			
	3019	x			

Figure 36: continued.

Figure 35 shows the frequency and regions where each of these types have been found. Significantly, Southwest England (n=19) and Northeast Scotland (n=16) have more unique complex beads compared to East Anglia (n=3) and East Yorkshire (n=2). However, there are some bead types for which multiple examples have been found, such as Type 2601 (n=2), 3003 (n=5), and 3014 (n=5). The first is a wrapped black and yellow bead with a cable formed from black and white glass, the second is a blue bead with a blue and white cable wave, and the last is a green bead with a blue and white cable wave. In the case of Type 2601, the two examples were found in Northeast Scotland, but for Types 3003 and 3014, four were found in Southwest England plus an additional example of each from East Anglia.

Through the use of this more detailed typological approach, it has been possible to make relevant comparisons between the material found within different regions that was not previously possible. There are of course some aspects of the beads that have not been taken into consideration at this point, such as the number of turns on spirals, the direction of spirals, the number of lines forming chevrons, or thickness of linear decoration, or size. However, it is possible to continually refine these analyses in the future to look for particular characteristics of beads, which may indicate similar styles of manufacture.

As each of the new types represents unique combinations of decorative motif, colour, and in some cases shape (where there is a clear distinction), they can be used for exploring not only similarities between the study regions, but also differences. Figure 36 shows a presence/absence chart of every bead type for each study region. Each type is colour coded depending on the number of regions within which it occurs. The majority of bead types (87%) are exclusive to single regions, suggesting that there are many localised types or local variations on types. The most unique types are found in Southwest England (n=66), and Northeast Scotland (n=44), but only 18 from East Yorkshire, and 7 from East Anglia. But there are also 12 types that are found in two regions, 6 types found in three regions, and 2 types found in four regions. In comparison, there are very few types that are found in multiple regions (13%).

Chronology

The following sections will explore the chronology of glass beads on a regional basis. It draws only on excavated examples and utilises a combination of feature, context, artefact associations and radiocarbon dates to assist in establishing earlier and later occurring bead types. Specific contexts will be explored further in Chapter 7. It should be stressed, however, that these dates primarily relate to the deposition date, not the manufacture date or the length of time that these beads were in use. Keeping this in mind, it is interesting to note that the majority of beads were deposited in the Middle Iron Age (Figure 37). Prior to this period, only a small number of beads are attributable to earlier contexts. In the Late Iron Age and Early Roman period, almost equal numbers of beads can be confidently attributed to these contexts. Perhaps unsurprisingly, the majority of the Middle Iron Age beads are from the inhumations at Wetwang Slack in the East Yorkshire study region (Figures 38). On a general note, one of the patterns emerging shows that glass beads were deposited in Southwest Britain throughout the Iron Age and Early Roman Period, while they occur in East Anglia primarily during the Middle/Late Iron Age, but also in the Early Roman/Romano-British period. Glass beads from Northeast Scotland have only been found deposited in contexts that date to this later period.

Southwest England

The glass beads from Southwest England have been found at 20 key sites that have been excavated and published with a reasonable amount of detail making it possible to assess the date of the context or site as a whole. From these sites, 16 bead types were identified as occurring within excavated contexts. This accounts for 58 glass beads in total. These sites cover activity from the Late Bronze Age/Early Iron Age (East Chisenbury, Wiltshire) until the Late Iron Age/Conquest era (Whitcombe, Dorset burials). Interestingly, there was very little overlap in

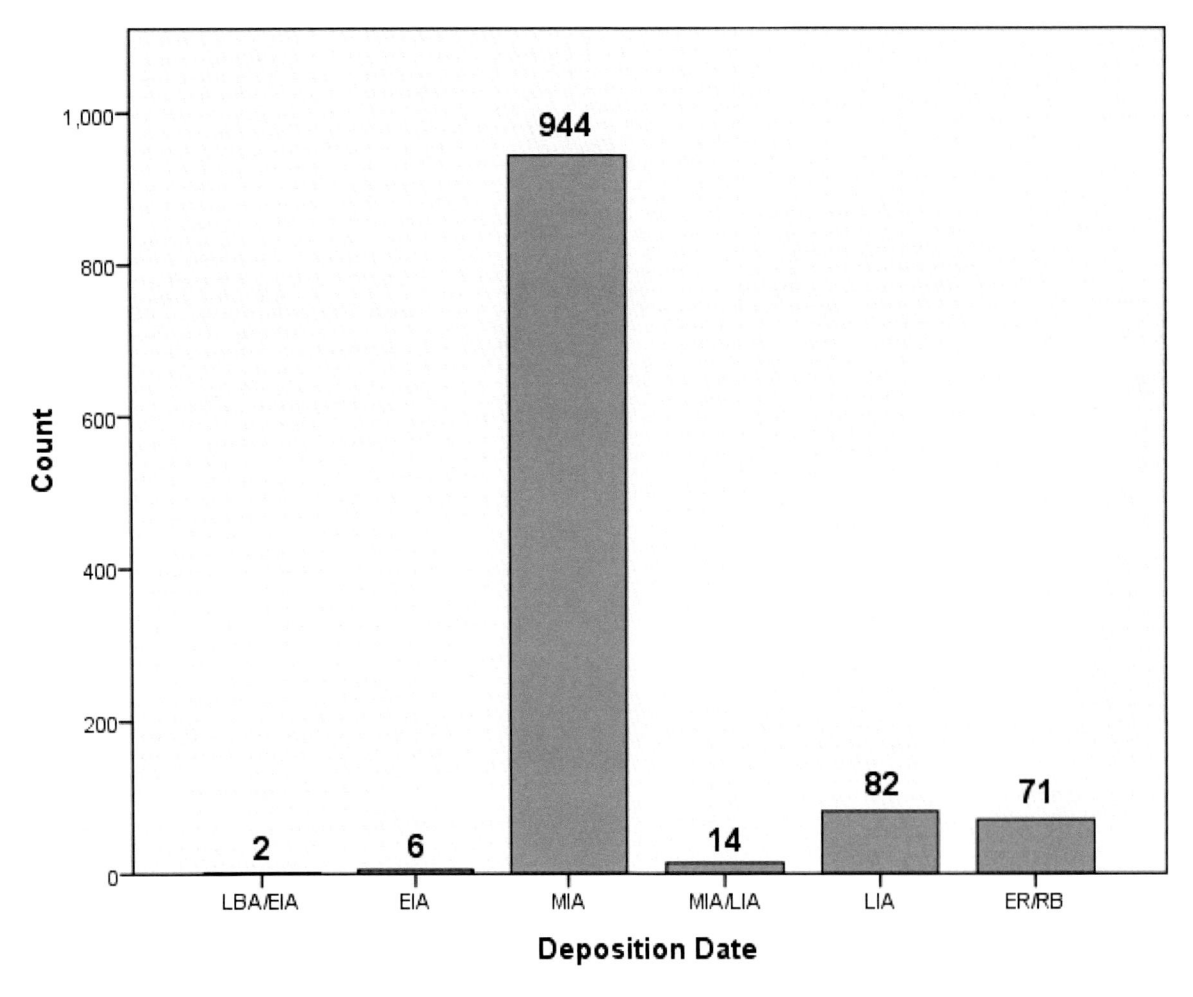

Figure 37: Bar chart showing the frequency of total datable glass beads in study regions.

terms of types, making it difficult to establish sequences without the association of either pottery or brooches. Nonetheless, it was possible to establish some trends in terms of chronology.

Earlier beads in this region include Types 204 and 427. This can be established through associations with Early Iron Age pottery for the first, and for the second with a La Tène I brooch and La Tène I/II pottery.[7] Following this are Types 426, 1431, and 901 through associations with Middle Iron Age pottery. At Maiden Castle, a very unusual bead (Type 2202) was found with Middle Iron Age pottery and Late Iron Age pottery, perhaps indicating a slightly later date. Beads associated with a very late first century BC to mid-first century AD date are those from the Chesil mirror burial (Types: 108, 1604, 1704, 2801, and 701). Finally, associated with a range of Late Iron Age and early Roman period brooches and pottery are Types 3003, 3010, and 103.

Through this analysis, it became apparent that there were three types of beads that were not diagnostic for dating purposes: Types 102, 107, and 110. Both of the first two types would have fallen into Guido's Group 6 and 7 beads that lack decoration and a specific date but in this case they appear in Middle/Late Iron Age contexts and into the early Roman period. Type 110 on the other hand, is approximately equivalent to Guido's Class 8 beads. Although Guido proposed that they were manufactured at Meare Lake Village between the mid-third century BC to mid-first century AD there is now evidence to suggest that they date to an earlier period. One example, from the Wheeler excavations at Maiden Castle, Dorset was found with "Iron Age A" pottery (although the context is not clear, the haematite bowls suggest an Early Iron Age date (Gibson 2002, 118)). The other comes from East Chisenbury, Wiltshire where it was found in the Late Bronze Age/Early Iron Age midden with pottery of the same date. Although the East Chisenbury bead has subsequently been lost, the description fits the Guido Class 8/New Type 110 description. Interestingly though, this type, plus the Type 102, which is found in Middle

---

[7] Although, it is also possible that the brooch was also curated for some time prior to deposition.

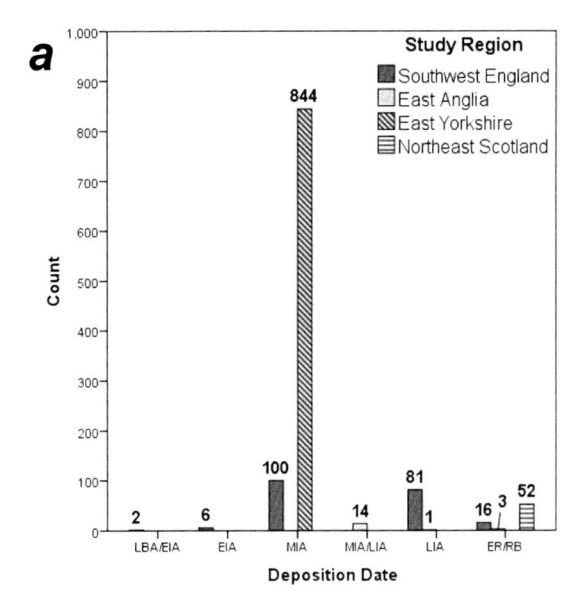

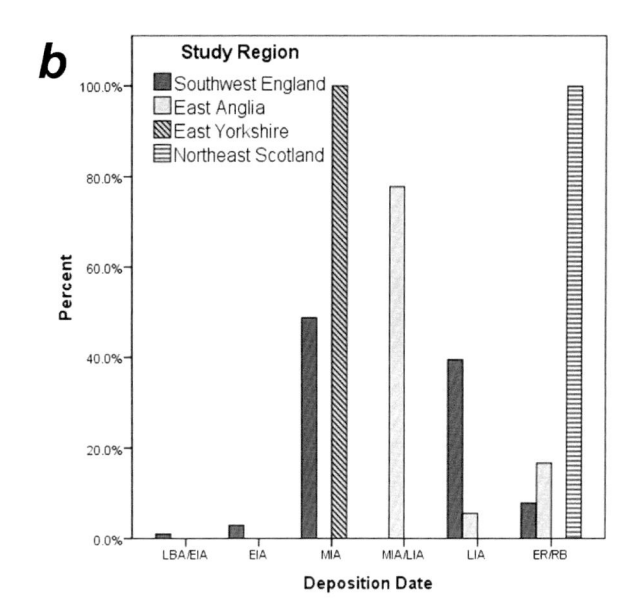

Figure 38: Bar chart showing (a) the frequency and (b) the percentage of total datable glass beads by study region.

Iron Age contexts and Type 107 and is found in Late Iron Age contexts, all continue in use into the early Roman period. Despite earlier dates as proposed for Type 110 and 102, this may be evidence to suggest that beads in this region were circulating throughout society for longer periods of time before finally entering the archaeological record.

Two sites that have so far not been discussed extensively in this analysis of chronology are Meare Lake Village and Glastonbury Lake Village. Almost 300 beads with known contexts have been found at Meare Lake Village, and twenty-four beads with contexts were found at Glastonbury Lake Village. These beads account for thirty-nine different types of beads and they were found in fifty-eight individual contexts. The recording at both sites, and at both east and west excavations at Meare Lake Village, often consists of a mound number, a level, and in some cases the distance and direction outside of the mound. The general interpretation at both sites is that they were lakeside settlements built upon mounds and that each mound represents a building that was continuously built upon (Coles and Minnett 1995). Unfortunately, this makes interpretation of the site very difficult because brooches of La Tène I, II, and III date can be found within a single mound (e.g. Meare Lake Village East Mound 17), and beads characteristic of an earlier date have been found in the same mound as Roman period brooches (e.g. Meare Lake Village West Mound 35). In general, dating these sites through a combination of pottery, brooches, and radiocarbon dates suggests that the activity at both Meare Lake Village West and East was earlier than at Glastonbury Lake Village. Haselgrove suggests a late fourth century or third century BC start date for Meare Lake Village East from the brooch evidence, while the West Village may have been slightly earlier (Haselgrove 1997, 60). Although it is generally agreed that the occupation at Glastonbury Lake Village dates to a period after settlement started at both Meare Lake Village East and West, Coles and Minnett (1995, 178) give a 250-50 BC date, while Haselgrove (1997, 60) has proposed a smaller period of occupation, from the mid-second to the mid-first century BC. Moore's (2003, 33) re-analysis of the radiocarbon dates taken from samples from all three sites is inconclusive about the settlement start dates, but seems to support the end dates. It is unfortunate that only one sample for radiocarbon dating purposes was taken from a mound associated with a glass bead (Glastonbury Lake Village Mound 38), however, not only was this bead not very diagnostic in terms of its physical characteristics, but Coles and Minnett (1995, 178) used this mound as an example of some of the difficulties in interpreting dates from artefacts and absolute dating. Therefore, it is unclear how these absolute dates relate to the glass beads themselves, but instead the site needs to be thought of in terms of broad date spans, rather than as earlier or later phases (c.f. Coles and Minnitt 1995) until further analysis can suggest otherwise.

Despite the issues with dating these sites, there are some patterns that can be observed that are worth exploring. As Guido pointed out, her Class 8 (new Type 110) and Class 10 (most typical is new Type 1417, but there are others), are the most numerous types. Although they are found associated with La Tène I brooches, these also happen to be mounds where they occur with La Tène III brooches (MLVW (Coles and Minnitt 1995) mound 9, MLVE mound 10). However, they do occur together at mounds associated only with La Tène II brooches (MLVE mound 13 and 22). It is with La Tène II brooches that there is a clear association between not only Types 110 and 1417, but also simple monochrome beads 101, 102, and 106, single wave bead Type 908, chevron bead 1003, spiral beads 1407, 1416, 1419, and complex bead 2401. Then, within the La Tène III brooch period, half of these bead types continue and simple monochrome Type 105, 109, simple polychrome Type 305, simple eye bead Type 429, perforation colour Type 701, single wave Type 901, and spiral bead Types 1405, 1418, and 1430 were deposited. Beads from mounds with only Roman brooches are only associated with beads from the La Tène II period. There are 21 other bead types that occur either in mounds without any other diagnostic artefacts or with brooches from multiple periods, making it difficult to assess. The problem here of course is that mounds do not always seem to represent one distinct period of time, but rather are stratified layers of time, as shown by Coles and Minnitt (1995) for Glastonbury Lake Village. However, it does demonstrate that some types of beads were earlier than others, and that one blanket period of bead manufacturing at both sites as suggested by Guido is not an accurate representation of bead manufacturing chronology. In addition, as several bead types are found with both La Tène II and III brooches, this suggests that these beads were in circulation for long periods of time, and that their depositional date probably has little to do with the length of time they were in use, especially given the early date Type 110 at East Chisenbury.

East Anglia

Out of the 26 glass beads that are likely to date to the Iron Age or Early Roman period, 18 come from contexts with an indication of when they were deposited. Most (n=14) come from the Middle/Late Iron Age contexts from the recently excavated site at Grandcourt Quarry. This site, which is currently awaiting publication, is unusual in that a large amount of metalwork was deposited along with very rare amber beads, and one of the largest depositions of glass beads at a single site apart from the lake villages in Somerset and the inhumations in East Yorkshire. Most glass beads were found amongst the dense pottery and metalwork deposition layer. Analysis of the metalwork suggests a Middle/Late Iron Age date (Colin Haselgrove, pers. comm.), which is supported by a radiocarbon date taken from the residue on a piece of pottery suggesting a 210-38 cal BC depositional date (Steve Malone, pers. comm.). This includes some very rare types of glass beads such as Types 201, 702, and 1801. Interestingly, there was also an example of a Type 1001 (chevrons), which is a type that has been found primarily at Meare Lake Village. However, it seems that it may have been part of a slightly later deposition at the site. In addition, it is interesting that the two specimens of Type 1407 are vastly different in appearance. One appears to be brand new as the surface retains the shiny gloss of fresh unweathered glass, while the other is very dull and appears to have greater surface weathering, potentially indicating it was manufactured at an earlier date. In general, this site represents the combination of twelve different types of beads at a single site, at a potentially limited period in time.

The remaining beads come from substantially later depositions at two different sites. The first is a Type 3014 from the Santon Downham hoard discovered in 1897. The hoard is generally interpreted as containing a mix of both Iron Age artefacts (enameled horse equipment) and Roman artefacts (steelyard, patera handle, jug) and thus is dated to the mid-first century AD (Manning 1972). A bead was also found with the hoard. It is green (presumably translucent) with a cable wave design (presumably opaque) made from blue and white glass. This is a typical colour combination, and one of the more frequently discovered types; however, it is usually found in Southwest England. The final site with beads from a datable context is the Romano-British site at Billingford, Norfolk. Here, an unusual hoard of objects was found in a pit containing a copper alloy torc, a ring (finger-ring?), an unknown ring object (possibly broken), a key, a large stone ring/bead and three glass beads. Two of the glass beads are Type 901, while the remaining one is a Type 106. The pit is associated with a nearby Romano-British settlement, but due to the inclusion of the torc, the pit deposition is dated to the first/second century AD (Wallis 2011).

Despite the limited evidence for glass beads in this region, it is interesting that there is virtually no crossover of bead types between sites. But this also renders it difficult to understand whether there is a glass bead chronology as glass beads do not really seem to have had a strong role in this area prior to the late third century BC.

East Yorkshire

Most glass beads from East Yorkshire are found in inhumation features. Two of the most recent excavated cemeteries not only revealed large numbers of burials, but the recording methods also preserved detailed information about the context. This includes the excavations at Wetwang/Garton Slack (Brewster 1980; Dent 1984), and the excavations directed by Ian Stead (1991a) that extended between Rudston and Burton Fleming. Interestingly, these excavations have shown that despite the large number of burials at both of these, at Wetwang Slack (400+) and in the Rudston/Burton Fleming area (200+ inhumations), only 21 had glass beads, of which only seven contained single beads rather than the 'necklaces' found in Cowlam Barrow L or Wetwang Slack burial 284. So, although the East Yorkshire Iron Age is regarded as an area where we can really begin to understand Iron Age society (Jay, Fuller *et al.* 2008; Jay and Richards 2006) and as an area with copious numbers of glass beads that rivals Meare

Lake Village in Somerset, their occurrence is actually significantly limited.

Chronology at these sites has depended in part on stratigraphic relationships, but also on brooch chronology. Unfortunately, brooches are not found in every inhumation, and in the case of Wetwang Slack 40 stratigraphic sequences could be defined; the large number of isolated burials creates an increasingly difficult situation for internal site chronology (Jay, Haselgrove et al. 2012, 164). Dent (1984, 81-2) proposed that there were four phases, and that general patterns in deposition could be observed, especially in relation to the Bronze Age barrow that was incorporated into the cemetery. Chronology in this region has been the subject of a recent paper exploring radiocarbon dates obtained from samples at Wetwang Slack, along with radiocarbon dates from other inhumations and chariot/cart burials in the region (Jay, Haselgrove et al. 2012). They conclude that whilst the radiocarbon dates for the Newbridge chariot burial date to before c. 400 cal BC and it more plausibly has connections with Iron Age continental Europe (Carter and Hunter 2003, 533; Jay, Haselgrove et al. 2012, 182-3), the burials at Wetwang Slack are confined to a period from the third to early second century BC and thus are clearly later than the similar practice on the continent (Jay, Haselgrove et al. 2012, 181-2).

This work has also allowed for the regional brooch chronology to be re-assessed, which renders some inhumation sequences more accurate. One of the other issues to come out of this dating re-assessment is that it appears that some objects were already old when placed in the inhumations (Jay, Haselgrove et al. 2012, 183). This is not a reflection of a time lag as has been assumed before (Jay, Haselgrove et al. 2012, 169), but it does point out that an artefact's manufacture date is not always contemporary with its depositional date. While Jay et al (2012, 162) point to the repairs on the Kirkburn scabbard as evidence that it had heirloom status, the combination of beads with both little and heavy weathering in some East Yorkshire burials may indicate that not all beads were manufactured at the same time and with the same raw material.

Out of the twenty-one inhumations in East Yorkshire with glass beads, it is the Queen's Barrow near Market Weighton that has the greatest variety of glass beads (discussed further in Chapter 7 and 8). Unfortunately, some of the beads are in extremely poor condition. Nonetheless, nine different types can be distinguished. Of these, six are different types of eye beads (Types 411, 421, 424, 425, 426, and 428) while the remaining three are different types of beads with a wave motif (Types 901, 905, and 907). No other group of beads in East Yorkshire inhumations is this diverse and there are very few connections between the types on this necklace with those on other necklaces. The necklace from Barrow L in Cowlam is made up primarily of Type 901 beads with one Type 425 bead. Wetwang burials 274, 284, and 209 all have Type 901 wave beads along with some others, and burial 249 shares Type 421 with the Queen's barrow. However, it is interesting that neither Barrow L, nor the Queen's barrow, utilises Type 102 (monochrome blue) beads that feature in nine Wetwang burials and five Garton Slack/Burton Fleming burials, most often singly, or with no other types of beads. This makes Wetwang burials 284 and 249 significant as they both combine bead types from the Queen's barrow and Cowlam barrow L with the dominant bead type at Wetwang Slack.

Between the Wetwang and Garton Slack/Burton Fleming inhumations, there are six types of beads that do not occur on more than one necklace. For example in Wetwang burial 376, although the unusual melon shaped blue beads (Type 202) are shared with burials 64 and 209, the complex eye beads (Types 501 and 503) do not occur in any other inhumation. It does not seem to be unusual that bead types that do not occur in multiple burials are slightly more complex in design or exhibit traits that are very different to the other beads. For example, while most beads that exhibit a wave/zigzag motif are simple in that they only have one line going around the circumference, Wetwang burial 274 contained a bead (Type 2301) with two zigzags going around the circumference; and burial 236 contained several unusual eye beads (Type 420) made from brown glass with three eyes made from blue and white glass. Both of these bead types are unusual and do not occur in other burials.

In terms of chronology, the Bayesian analysis of radiocarbon dates at Wetwang suggests a very limited period of use between the third and early second centuries BC (Jay, Haselgrove et al. 2012, 181). Despite both La Tene I and II brooches occurring at both Wetwang Slack and at Cowlam Barrow L (Hull and Hawkes type 1Aa, dates to mid-fifth century to early fourth century BC) it seems that this later date could generally be applied to all of the East Yorkshire burials, as the earlier types of artefacts were curated for extended periods of time. Thus, with few radiocarbon dates to go on, all of the beads in these burials are roughly contemporaneous, potentially even the two unusual beads. In burial 268 there was a single Type 1417, and in burial 102 there was a single Type 1001. Both of these types are generally considered to have been manufactured in the Meare Lake Village area. Although Jay (2006, 661) did not include either of these inhumations in her analysis of stable isotopes, her general conclusion was that most people at Wetwang Slack were not differentiated by the foods that they consumed, and thus likely were all of local origin. This implies that these were not immigrants from elsewhere that brought their bodily adornment with them. However, in the future, these specific human remains would be ideal subjects for further stable isotope study to identify whether they are of local origin or otherwise.

Northeast Scotland

Despite Guido's assertion for the date of several types of glass beads that are found in large numbers in this region, none of the beads she looked at came from excavated contexts. The situation has not improved greatly since then, but there have been some positive developments. At present, 48 glass beads, representing nine types from six different sites have added significant data to the chronological understanding of this region. Unfortunately, only two beads have been fully published or made available through grey literature reports. This includes a Type 102 from the Forest Road excavation (Cook and Dunbar 2008) and a Type 1419 from Thainstone (Murray and Murray 2006b). The Midtown Farm bead (Type 1400) is poorly described in a note in *Discovery and Excavation in Scotland* (Anon. 1975), and the Clarky Hill bead (Type 110) was found during excavations that are currently underway and interim reports were not available. The excavations at Birnie recently ended; however, final analysis and interpretation are still in preparation. Finally, the glass beads and evidence for glass working at Culduthel were found during developer-led excavation at the site (Murray 2007a). Unfortunately, they are also awaiting final interpretation and publication, but radiocarbon data has been made available for this research (Headland Archaeology, pers. comm.).

Despite the issues with establishing a relative or absolute chronology in this region at the moment, there are some trends that can be observed. First, the most commonly occurring type is Type 110. These are found at Birnie, Culduthel, and Clarky Hill. Their presence is not surprising given the 200+ examples reported as stray finds at Culbin Sands. Both Birnie and Culduthel have five different types of beads present at each site, but they overlap in only two types: Type 110 and 1418 (the latter is a colourless bead with three yellow spirals placed around the circumference of the bead of more sub-triangular shape). Although they are not exact parallels, both are similar to three beads from Meare Lake Village West. Other beads at Birnie include a Type 303, an unusual sub-triangular bead made from translucent green glass with yellow glass mixed in, and Types 1403 and 1419 (a type also found at Thainstone), which are both types of spiral beads. Culduthel also has Type 102, a plain blue bead; Type 1418, another type of spiral bead; and Type 2501, a complex form of spiral bead that incorporates a cable of two colours of glass.

Although the context of the Thainstone Type 1419 bead was not directly dated, a radiocarbon date for a similar primary fill post-hole of the same roundhouse gives a date of 30 cal BC – cal AD 130 (2σ, 1940±40, Beta-181169, Murray *et al.* 2006, 11). The overall interpretation of the site suggests that activity was at its peak between the first and second centuries AD. A similar date can be proposed for the late prehistoric activity at Birnie from the brooches, coin hoard, and Roman pottery found at this site (Hunter 2007b, 23-32, and also interim reports). In contrast, the glass evidence for Culduthel Farm now points to a substantially earlier date (Headland Archaeology, pers. comm.). Contexts for a number of glass beads from this site have been radiocarbon dated, which often suggest a pre-first century AD date. The earliest date obtained points to a fourth century BC deposition date. This suggests that the beads in Northeast Scotland could have been in use substantially earlier than the first/second century AD date suggested by Guido.

This section has so far focused on the beads that have been found in Northeast Scotland; however, it is very interesting that one of Guido's other types of glass beads by which she characterises this region has not been found in any excavated contexts. This is Guido's Class 14 'North Scottish Decorated Annular' bead (covered by new types Class 7, Class 8, and Class 11). This Guido type is incredibly poorly defined (described in Appendix B), however, in general, no two are alike. Because they lack similarity other than possibly their manufacturing method and in general a preference for incorporating the colour yellow, they are difficult to pinpoint in date. Excavated examples from Dun Mor Vaul (MacKie 1974), on Tiree, have suggested a second century AD date; however, the dates of brochs are highly contested (Armit 1991; Dockrill, Outram *et al.* 2006; MacKie 1965a; b; 2008; 2010; Outram, Batt *et al.* 2010; Parker Pearson, Sharples *et al.* 1996). Nonetheless, despite the increasing preponderance of glass beads from excavated contexts in Northeast Scotland, it may be significant that none of Guido's Class 14 beads have been found. It is possible that some date to a much later period.

Chronology Discussion

The section above addressed the chronology of glass beads within each region using the new bead typology. It highlights a number of issues and trends within the data; however, the main question to be addressed is: does the archaeological evidence support a chronology of beads? This is to ask, can we see the ebb and flow of bead types gradually coming into use, flourishing, and finally diminishing? The answer, in a word, is no. However, the answer to this question is much more complicated than a simple 'yes', or 'no'. In fact, there are a number of factors at work that complicate a straightforward interpretation from a given dated context that somehow equates to a grand scheme from manufacture to deposition. It is these dated contexts that provides us with a *terminus ante quem*, which is normally expressed as a date range. It is extremely beneficial for determining the approximate date of deposition, but it gives no indication as to when the individual bead was created or how long it was in use prior to its final deposition. This is complicated by processes whereby artefacts were curated by later generations, as has been suggested by the Kirkburn sword (Jay, Haselgrove *et al.* 2012, 62), but also demonstrated with Iron Age glass beads found in Anglo-Saxon contexts such as those from Street House in Cleveland and Cow Low in Derbyshire. Although these could be considered to be extreme examples, especially in the case of Anglo-Saxon re-use of Iron Age glass beads, the context makes it clear that these objects were curated for long periods of time until they were finally intentionally deposited in inhumations.

Beads found in settlements do not always benefit from the support of the surrounding context that demonstrate that they have been curated for long periods of time. Instead, interpretation typically happens whereby a bead that is considered to be Iron Age is found amongst other artefacts (often pottery or brooches) that support this Iron Age date. The date of these other objects is used to date both the context and the bead (this also happens with radiocarbon dates). Thus, a bead that is found with Late Iron Age pottery is said to date to the same period, as if the depositional act is somehow representative of associated objects. As in the case of glass beads found outside of their designated period, they are explained away as purely 'residual' (e.g. Guido Class 7a beads from post-conquest contexts), rather than actively participating and appreciated within society. This becomes an increasingly significant issue towards the end of the Iron Age and into the Roman period where beads of 'native' tradition are found on 'Roman' sites. But, it is these 'residual' beads that support the idea that they were a curated object and continued to have meaning within post-conquest society, a period that Guido perceived as being an influx of material culture, ideas, and people, and thus an end to pre-Roman ways life.

Instead of creating neat types with discrete periods of beginnings and endings of use, the available data suits a very different mode of thought. Instead of attempting to use the *terminus post quem* as an end date for the use of each type and inferring the original manufacture date for types, it is much more appropriate to use this data to explore depositional practices. Interestingly, there seems to be regional differences in the chronology of glass bead deposition. Taking each region as a whole, there are some general characteristics. In Southwest England, glass beads were deposited in contexts that date to as early as the Late Bronze Age and more commonly the Early Iron Age, and were deposited into the Early Roman period. In stark contrast, glass beads in East Yorkshire are restricted to deposits in the Middle Iron Age. In both Northeast Scotland and East Anglia beads were deposited in the Mid-Late Iron Age/Early Roman period, although there is also a possibility that they were deposited earlier in Northeast Scotland, but they differ not only in appearance, but also in that the East Anglian beads demonstrate a greater possible European connection, while the Scottish examples do not (an area for future research). Of course, one of the issues in such an interpretation is the differences in deposition: i.e. either intentional or unintentional loss, and this will be explored further in Chapter 7.

Despite the issues of deposition, and both visible and invisible heirloom effects, using the *terminus ante quem* we can begin to understand glass bead chronology in a general sense. However, caution is necessary. By examining the date of deposition for each bead type where this data is available for multiple beads, it is immediately noticeable that in the case of two types of bead (Types 102 and 110, corresponding to Guido Group 6/7 and Class 8) there is a considerable degree of variability in terms of depositional period. While Guido described Groups 6 and 7 as difficult to ascribe to a fixed period of use, Class 8 beads were thought to have belonged to two production centres from two different periods of time. The Meare Lake Village examples were thought to have been made at this site between the third and second centuries BC (Guido 1978a, 75), while the Culbin Sands examples were thought to date to the first and second centuries AD (Guido 1978a, 76). However, while there are examples found deposited in both earlier and later contexts, some examples can probably be said to date to an earlier period. The single example from East Chisenbury, Wiltshire was found with Late Bronze Age/Early Iron Age pottery (McOmish, Field *et al.* 2010), and an example from Maiden Castle, Dorset was found with Early Iron Age pottery (Wheeler 1943). To this can be added the example from Cannards Grave, which may have been deposited as early as the beginning of the fourth century BC (Birbeck 2002). Thus there are three examples that have been suggested to pre-date the assumed date of manufacture at Meare Lake Village. This has implications for interpreting this type of bead as a whole.

Typologies, at least in terms of Guido's typology, and the new typology presented here, act as a way to label beads and communicate the fact that two or more objects have a very similar appearance. While this can be extremely useful, there is an assumption that beads that do in fact appear to be similar were made at the same site, possibly even at the same period of time (or within a 200 year period of each other). This seems to be a reasonable explanation on the surface, but given the range of deposition dates in the case of the Type 110/Guido Class 8 beads, can this really be said to be the case? A few possible alternative explanations are that Type 110/Guido Class 8 beads:

- They were manufactured at Meare Lake Village, but the date of this activity needs to be pushed back (possibly supported by some of the earlier seemingly anomalous radiocarbon dates (Coles 1987)); later versions were manufactured at Culbin Sands.
- They do not form a useful diagnostic bead type, because they were made (and deposited) periodically

during the Iron Age, possibly even at multiple locations.
- They were manufactured somewhere in the Late Bronze Age/Early Iron Age possibly in Britain, but equally possibly from continental Europe, and continued to be used throughout the Iron Age and into the Early Roman period, and some were deposited/lost periodically during this time.

While the first two options are reasonable explanations, the third explanation is more likely. This might seem far-fetched at first glance, but is less so given that the nature of the activity remains somewhat unclear at Glastonbury and Meare Lake Villages, and that some of the earliest occurring brooches date from the La Tène I period. Interestingly, Venclová (1990, 55) noted that hundreds of these small opaque yellow annular beads occur in Hallstatt D/La Tène A graves at sites, such as Vače and Stinča in Slovenia, although they continued to be deposited in La Tène C1-C2 contexts, including at Manching. She proposed that they may have been manufactured in this region. Given that more than 100 beads of this type were found at Meare and Culbin Sands, they may have been used in similar ways as the Slovenian Beads. Venclová (1990) suggested that they were used as necklaces or sewn on textiles. These beads are traditionally considered to have been manufactured in Britain, but this type of bead existed outside of Britain much earlier than was previously suggested, and further demonstrates some of the issues with dating glass bead use. Although his sample was small, Henderson's analyses of opaque yellow glass show that there is a similarity between examples in Britain with those from sites, such as Staré Hradisko and Magdalenska Gora (Henderson 1992, Figure 10), which may support an argument for similar sources of raw glass.

This may conclude as a cautionary tale for archaeologists. However, using depositional dates we can establish some general trends throughout the Iron Age. In Early Iron Age contexts, there are several types of plain monochrome beads (Types: 102 and 110, but also 204. The earliest deposited decorated beads are two types of blue and white eye beads (Types 426 and 427), although they were deposited as early as the end of the Early Iron Age. Both of these eye beads have 15 eyes made from blue and white glass on a blue body, but one is more cylindrical in shape while the other is more globular. All of these earlier beads occur in the Southwest England study region, and there are no examples of glass beads deposited in the other study regions.

This changed dramatically in the Middle Iron Age, as all the beads from the East Yorkshire burials were probably deposited during this time. This included a large number of plain monochrome beads (Type 102), the unusual blue glass melon beads (Type 202), a number of decorated beads: eye beads (Types 411, 413, 414, 417, 418, 420, 421, 423, 424, 425, 426, 428, 501, and 503), wave/zigzag beads (Types 901, 905, and 907), other linear design beads (Types 1001, 1417), and a complex decorated bead (Type 2301). While these beads are thought to have been deposited in the earlier part of the Middle Iron Age, other beads in Southwest England were deposited generally at some point during this period as well; however, their occurrence is much more limited. This includes a simple monochrome bead at Maiden Castle, Dorset (Type 107), another at Cannard's Grave, Somerset (Type 110), and a bead from Birdlip, Gloucestershire with an unusual spiral motif (Type 1431).

By the Middle Iron Age, some of the earliest (more reliable) deposits of glass beads occurred at Meare and Glastonbury Lake Villages. This included a range of simple types (Types 101, 102, 106, and 110), as well as a number of decorated types: wave/zigzag (Type 908), chevrons (Type 1003), spiral (types 1407, 1416, 1417, and 1419), and a complex chevron bead (Type 2401). Interestingly, this is potentially problematic as one of Guido's "Meare" type beads was found at Wetwang Slack where it may date to an earlier period than the dates given for their manufacture at Meare Lake Village.

By the end of the Middle Iron Age, or possibly early in the Later Iron Age, the rich bead deposits at Grandcourt Quarry, Norfolk were made. A number of the beads that occur here are not found elsewhere in Britain, or are extremely rare. Again, there are a number of monochrome beads (Types 106 and 201), but the majority are polychrome (Types 502, 701, 702, 801, 1001, 1407, 1801, 2302, 2304). In the Late Iron Age, several bead types found in earlier contexts at Meare and Glastonbury continue to be deposited (Types 102, 106, 110, 1003, 1417, and 2401) but a few other types are not found in this later period (Types 101, 908, 1407, 1416, 1419). In addition, there are some new types that appear at this time (Type 105, 109, 305, 429, 701, 901, 1405, 1418, 1430). Notably, outside of Meare and Glastonbury, most other reliably dated beads from this period tend to be simple monochrome beads such as those from Bredon Hill and Salmonsbury (Types 102 and 107). In contrast, in inhumations such as the Chesil mirror burial, four decorated beads were found (Types 701, 1604, 1704, and 2801) along with an unusually coloured simple monochrome bead (Type 108).

Finally, in the first two centuries AD there are dated examples of bead deposits in Northeast Scotland at Birnie, Clarky Hill, Thainstone, and Culduthel. These beads are restricted mainly to Type 110 and spiral beads such as 1403, 1418, and 1419. There are some more unusual beads such as Type 303 at Birnie, and Type 2501 at Culduthel. Elsewhere in Britain, this is also the period when clearly dated examples of annular beads with cable motifs are deposited such as Type 3014 at Santon Downham, Suffolk, and Type 3010 at Catsgore, Somerset.

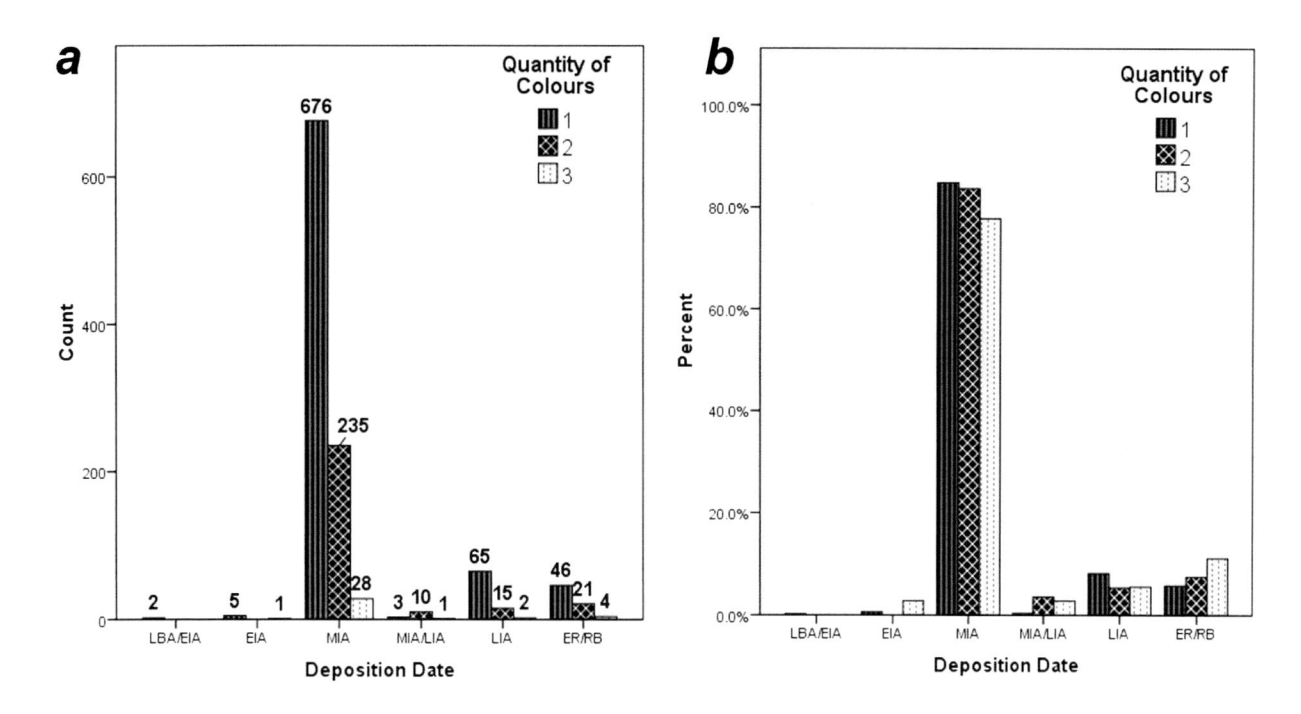

Figure 39: Bar chart showing (a) the number and (b) the percentage of the quantity of colours of glass beads over time.

At this time, a dated example of a Type 110 bead is also deposited at Sea Mills near Bristol. Examples of Type 901 beads have been found at Billingford, Norfolk and in Whitcombe burial 8 in Dorset. There are no clearly dated examples of glass beads from depositions at this time in East Yorkshire.

The relationship between chronology and glass bead deposition is clearly a complicated topic. Not only is there evidence for the potential long-term use of glass beads prior to deposition, but the available evidence suggests that there are key regional differences. There are patterns in both the types of beads used and the periods in which they were deposited, and these do vary regionally. Despite these differences, there are some bead types that have been found in multiple regions, although they are not always deposited contemporarily. Interestingly, there does not seem to be a strict chronology in which the earliest beads were the simplest or the plainest, progressively becoming more complicated through the period (Figure 39). Instead, plain beads existed alongside the more complex examples. This can also be said more generally of the decorative motifs used (Figure 40).

Discussion

Two main themes have been presented in this chapter. The first relates to typology. Despite the inherent problems with a typological approach to understanding artefacts (Adams 1988; Adams and Adams 1991; Cowgill 1990; Dunnell 1986; 2002; Ford 1954; Ford and Steward 1954; Hill and Evans 1972; Klejn 1982; Read 2007; Rouse 1960; Spaulding 1953; Topping 1987; Whittaker, Caulkins *et al.* 1998), it can provide a useful tool. The benefit is that it allows researchers to communicate about artefacts, as it often acts as a shorthand method for describing certain characteristics and allows the comparison of both similarities and differences. In this sense, typology is an effective means that allows researchers to collaborate, and expand on different aspects of artefact-based research. The danger with typology, however, is that it is not necessarily a one size fits all tool. Differing research questions and aims will give preference to certain aspects over others, thus there is a potentially unlimited number of different typologies that could be created (Hill and Evans 1972). This can also be problematic as typology can become a source of conflict within the research community as competing methods of classification are promoted. It is important to remember, however, that there is no right or wrong way to classify, but it should suit the research questions and avoid classification for the sake of classification.

The present research is concerned with exploring the diversity of glass beads, which probably accounts for the substantially larger number of types than previous typologies. Three prime characteristics were chosen that are thought to contribute greatest to the overall appearance of glass beads, thus allowing differences and similarities to be effectively and consistently explored. A typology in this sense is very different from the goals of the culture history typologies. Although criticisms of the Guido typology have been presented in this chapter, it must be stressed that the new typology presented is not

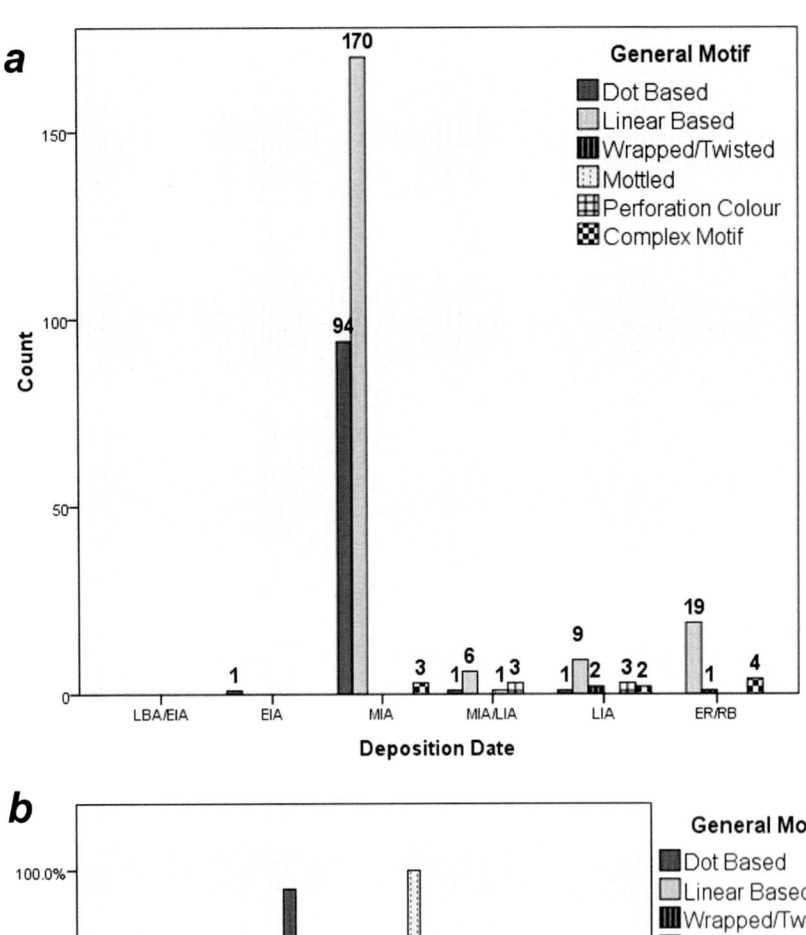

Figure 40: Bar chart showing (a) the number and (b) the percentage of different general motif type over time.

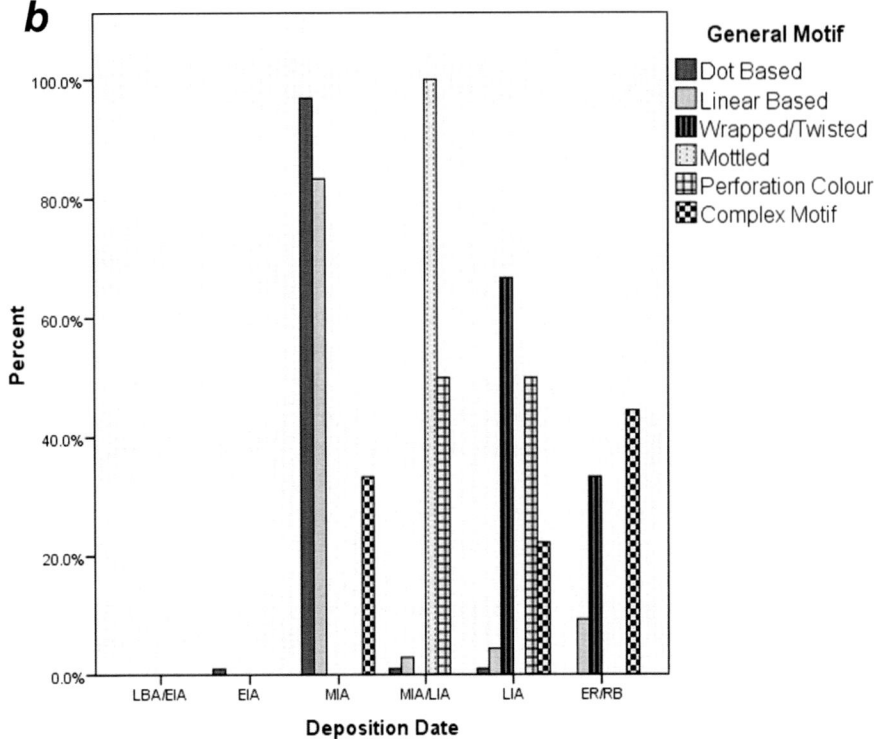

necessarily meant to replace the old typology. Rather, it provides a new way of approaching the material that allows the research questions to be addressed in subsequent chapters.

The second theme of this chapter has been that of dating, chronology, and to a lesser extent, context (further explored in Chapter 7). As the analysis of dates associated with glass beads above suggested, dating is far from straightforward. Instead, there is a complex variety of factors that affect when a bead is deposited into the archaeological record. The depositional date is not necessarily a close reflection of the manufacture date, nor does it indicate the length of time it was in use.

This of course is not just an issue with glass beads, as it has recently been shown (Lockyear 2012, 197) that coin hoards that were deposited in the first century AD contained coins that were around 200 years old. Although there are differences between coins and other artefacts (as he points out, coins do not break), nonetheless, as long as an Iron Age glass bead remained intact, they could remain in use or in circulation unless social factors suggested otherwise. An analogy between Roman coin hoards and Iron Age glass beads in Britain might not be perfect for a number of reasons, but there is also evidence for copper alloy hoards of Bronze Age artefacts that were deposited in the Iron Age and the Roman period (Hingley 2009). Whether these objects were curated continuously from the Bronze Age before their deposition is another question; however, it is clear that people in the Iron Age made sense of the past and ancestors in terms of both the landscape and the objects with which they interacted. Again, this emphasises the issue between typology and date. As Hingley (2009, 148) points out, artefacts must be understood not only through typology, but also in terms of the context in which they are found. Despite the issues with the dating and chronology of glass beads, there are clear patterns of temporally different regional depositional practices.

Conclusion

Typology is just one of the ways to understand the material here under consideration. Although the typological approach will be utilised throughout the remaining chapters, it is felt that it is necessary to understand regional patterns of different characteristics, rather than solely relying on individual types. Thus, Chapter 6 will explore regional uses of the three main characteristics used to create the typology, in an attempt to understand regional variations in shape, colour, and decorative motif. Size, in terms of both dimensions and weight, will also be analysed as it relates to how glass beads were made or how they were used, and this may also vary regionally. As discussed above, the context of the artefacts is of importance, not only in understanding the use, but also in terms of understanding when, how, and why an object was deposited into the archaeological record. This will be explored further in Chapter 7.

Chapter 6
Form and Regional Identity

In contrast to many of the other types of late prehistoric British artefacts, glass beads exhibit a range of colours and designs. Perhaps most emblematic of this period is the use of eye and spiral motifs, the colour blue, and a combination of both colourless and opaque yellow glass. Yet, even the most cursory investigation of glass beads would lead to the conclusion that there are specific areas where glass beads are abundant in number, and that some characteristics appear to be regional. However, investigations of these patterns have been limited to those undertaken by Guido (1978a) and Giles (2012). While Guido's study was limited to the use of typology, which Chapter 5 has shown is problematic; Giles' study focused only on the East Yorkshire material and so did not put it into a wider context. This chapter applies a consistent approach to an examination of four key characteristics (namely: size, shape, colour, and decorative motif), with the aim of developing a regional understanding of glass bead traits.

These four traits were chosen because they have the greatest impact when viewed. When not obscured by other garments, or (perhaps) by hair, larger beads could potentially have a greater visual impact when viewed compared to smaller beads. The delicate construction of some of the smallest beads, however, might have elicited a response of awe from the viewer, especially when strung together. Some of the smallest beads are those from the 2001 Wetwang Slack chariot burial; these are only several millimeters in diameter and height, and if strung together on a single strand of material could have been damaged with little effort. Larger beads, on the other hand, would have been heavy, potentially cumbersome, and may have caused discomfort or restricted movement.

Colour deserves a special mention here, as all of these beads are at least one colour, and a proportion were even multi-coloured. Some colours would have stood out to the viewer compared to others, but the context within which they were used would also have had some bearing on their visibility. Darker colours, such as translucent blue, are often so dark that they appear to be black.[8] Although there is little evidence for textiles and even less evidence for the garments worn during this period (DeRoche 2012), if worn against dark coloured clothing (i.e. darkly coloured natural wool fibres, or artificially coloured through a dye process), these dark beads would have blended in and would have been difficult to distinguish. If worn against lightly coloured textiles (i.e. lightly coloured natural wool fibres, lightly dyed wool, or flax), however, these dark beads would have stood out. Other beads combine dark and light colours that have been applied as a decorative motif to the surface of the bead. It is through these combinations of colour and the creation of patterns (and sometimes also through shape) that these glass beads are most visually stunning.

By bringing together separate analyses of size, shape, colour, and decorative motif of glass beads, it is possible in examine whether there are patterns in bead selection and/or use. Why do some motifs occur in some regions and not in others? Were there regional colour preferences? Did these beads reflect a local or regional identity? As shown in Chapter 3, a sense of identity derives from a number of sources, but there is evidence for different regional identities in Britain during the Iron Age related to concepts of the body and dress. An investigation of the ways in which these identities were expressed in terms of colour may help to illuminate the clothing they were worn against, or the different designs that were suitable for wear.

While this analysis focuses on four characteristics, there are a number of other specific details that must currently remain unexplored. These include the perforation shapes of the beads, the width of the glass used for linear designs, and the number and direction of turns in spiral motifs. These, and others, are aspects that can be studied at a later date in order to provide additional details on their physical appearance.

Prior to examining these topics, it is necessary to outline the nature of the data concerning beads from the study regions. 1,788 glass beads were included in these analyses, which were all taken from the four regions described in Chapter 1 and Chapter 4 and the restrictions of the dataset were described in Chapter 5. Even when examining the number of beads within each region on a very general level, immediate differences are apparent (Figure 41). For example, East Anglia yielded the smallest number of beads (n=26), which is highly unusual compared to the rest of the regions chosen for study (Southwest England n=517, Northeast Scotland n=363), with East Yorkshire contributing the largest total (n=882). Indeed, out of the total number of beads discussed in this chapter, about half are from East Yorkshire (differences in depositional practices, excavation bias and study region size are discussed in Chapters 7 and 8).

---

[8] There are some cases where this very dark effect may be the result of the weathering action that has occurred on the surface of the bead. However, while this does affect them to some extent, it is frequently the case that some beads would have appeared to be very dark in the past.

Study Region	Frequency	Percentage of total
Southwest England	517	28.90%
East Anglia	26	1.50%
East Yorkshire	882	49.30%
Northeast Scotland	363	20.30%
TOTAL	1.788	100%

Figure 41: Number of glass beads per study region.

As the previous chapter highlights, there are some significant problems with discussing glass beads in terms of Guido's typology, as it really does not adequately express the true diversity existing within this object class. Thus, this chapter will first examine differences in bead shape and make comparisons between the study regions, followed by similar examinations of size, colour, and decorative motif. This will render a better understanding of regional glass bead characteristics possible, which have implications for understanding regional identity, dress, and the materiality of colour.

Shape

An examination of shape is essential for understanding the regional use of glass beads. Despite the fact that very little evidence exists for bead-making workshops or tools, it is at least possible to infer from some beads that many were made by winding molten glass around a mandrel. Thus, the simplest bead shapes are created: barrel, globular, and annular (see Chapter 2 and Appendix A). In some cases these beads have received some post-furnace alternations, probably by grinding them on a stone to create a flat surface on each perforation end. In contrast, the cylinder, segmented, stud, sub-triangular and truncated triangle shapes underwent additional manipulation of the molten glass in order to create each shape. This was probably achieved through the use of additional tools, such as a marver. These shapes were deliberate alterations of molten glass. Discussion of the shape of glass beads is very closely related to aspects of size, notably in relation to the Diam:Height ratio discussed previously.

By far the most common shape among the beads included in the present analysis is annular (Figure 42), accounting for 72% of the glass beads from these study regions. This percentage reflects the large numbers of yellow and blue annular beads found in three of the study regions. Globular beads account for 16.6% of the total number of glass beads, and the remaining shapes account for even fewer. There are a large number of unknown bead shapes due to the lack of detail in many archaeological reports or inability to gain access to objects in museums. In these cases they were excluded from the analysis.

Each individual region has a bead shape trend similar to that of the overall data set. In Southwest England, for example, the primary shapes are annular and globular (Figure 43a). There are also a number of barrel-shaped beads, as well as a few cylindrical and sub-triangular. Southwest England has the greatest variety of glass bead shapes compared to the other regions. In East Anglia, almost all beads found could be classed as annular, except for three individual examples (Figure 43b). Again, East Yorkshire beads are primarily annular, although a significant number of them are globular (Figure 43c). In this region there is also a rare group of Iron Age melon shaped beads. Finally, beads from Northeast Scotland are predominately annular in shape (Figure 43d), however, there are a number of sub-triangular and truncated triangle beads that are not found in significant quantities in other regions.

The overall impression is that annular and globular beads are most numerous, principally in Southwest England and in East Anglia (Figure 44). Having said this, however, although annular beads are also found in large numbers in Northeast Scotland, globular beads are found in much smaller numbers. Instead, other shapes, such as the truncated triangle, are found in greater numbers. Within the regions studied, there are three shapes that are unique to specific regions. The double segmented bead and the 'stud' shaped bead are both unique to Southwest England, while the melon beads (from Iron Age contexts) are found only in East Yorkshire. In addition, although sub-triangular and truncated triangle beads are found in multiple regions, they are found in large numbers in Northeast Scotland. A similar situation exists for barrel and cylindrical shapes, with barrels mainly found in Southwest England and cylindrical examples usually confined to East Anglia, despite examples existing in other regions.

This data shows that beads that are simplest to make, here the globular and annular beads, are found in large numbers in all study regions. Beads requiring greater manipulation are found in fewer numbers, and in some cases are found in only one region, or are more frequent in one region than in others. This may suggest that the annular/globular shape may be more 'universal', and that other complex shapes were the products of local manufacture. In some cases, the presence of particular shapes may indicate some element of exchange or communication with other regions.

Size

Iron Age glass beads greatly range in size. Some are very delicate beads, in some cases less than two millimetres in diameter and less than one millimetre in height,

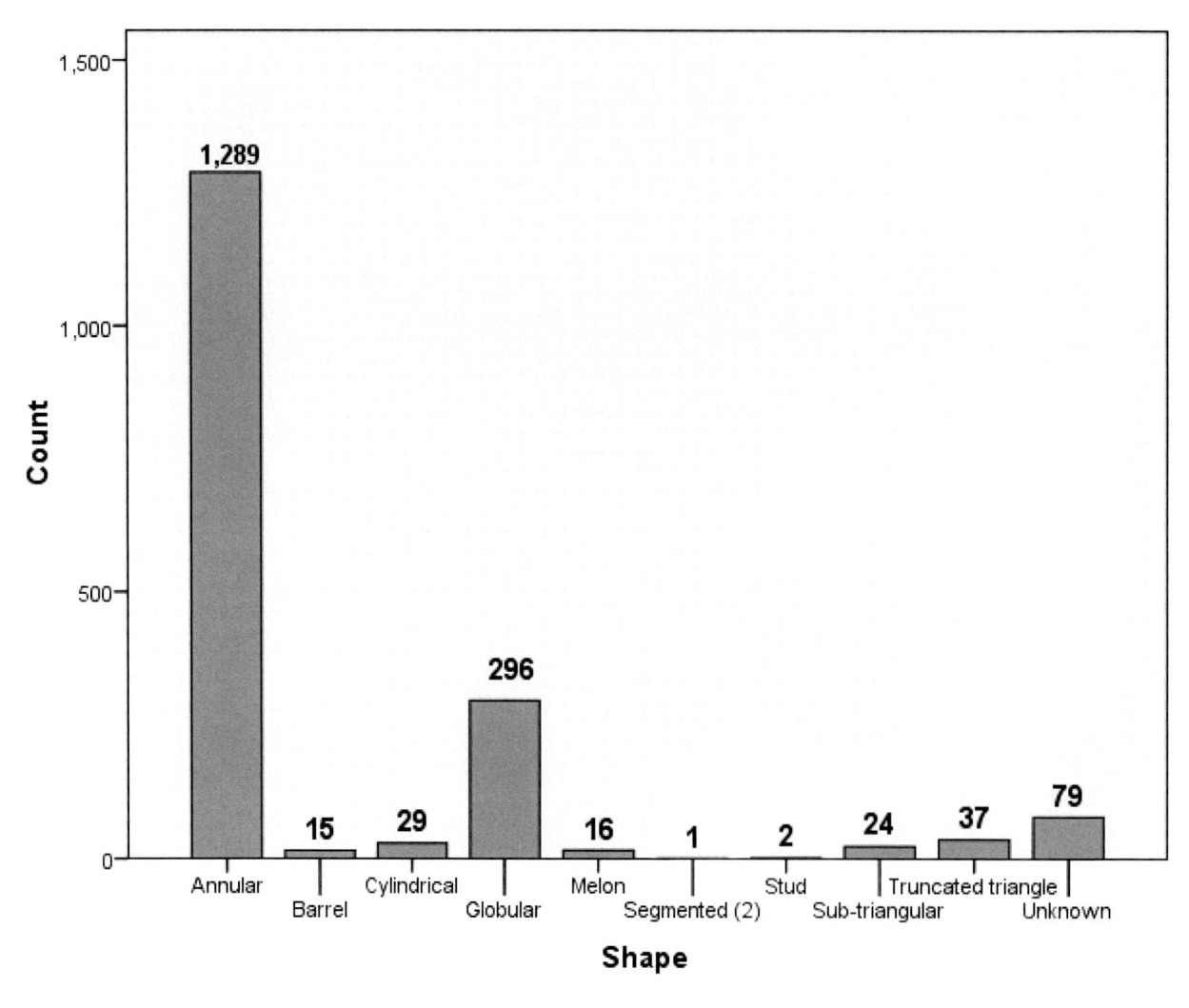

Figure 42: Bar-chart showing the frequency of shape for all study regions combined.

while others are very large and measure more than 50 millimetres in diameter. Despite these extremes, most examples fit into a middle size range: approximately 10-20mm in diameter and height. Here, four primary dimensions of size will be explored: the Diameter/Width, Height, Perforation Diameter, and Weight (see Appendix A for definitions and methodology).

Bead size can indicate a number of different things. For example, it might indicate availability of or access to raw materials. This in turn may have implications for the question of glass bead manufacture. Although there is some limited evidence that glass working occurred, there is no evidence to suggest that raw glass was being manufactured in Britain. Nonetheless, if we can at least assume that some 'glass working' as opposed to 'glass manufacturing' was occurring within Britain, then there must have been some sort of access to raw glass. This is often assumed to have come from continental Europe, or in the Later Iron Age and Roman period from the reuse of broken Roman glass vessels (Guido 1978a; Stevenson 1956, 215; 1976, 50-1). Therefore, some regions in Britain may have had better access to these raw materials than others, meaning that beads were more numerous and perhaps larger where glass was more readily available, and less frequent and smaller where it was difficult to acquire.

If size reflects the availability of raw materials, then it may also be related to status. Glass as a material could be considered a high-status material based on the rarity of glass beads at most sites. Guido (1978a, 28) suggested that glass was a luxury object that could only be obtained by those who had met their basic living necessities. Unfortunately, glass objects are generally not found in hoard contexts, as with coins or torcs. There are some noteworthy exceptions, such as the glass bangle 'hoard' at Broxmouth in East Lothian (Armit and McKenzie 2013). Another example is the much later 'votive pit' deposition at the Romano-British site at Billingford in Norfolk, containing glass beads, a fragment of a torc, and other objects (Wallis 2011). Adding to the interpretative difficulty, the general lack of cemeteries in Iron Age Britain makes a comparison of grave goods and dress problematic. Nonetheless, in the cemetery at Wetwang Slack (which may or may not be representative) only 17

FORM AND REGIONAL IDENTITY

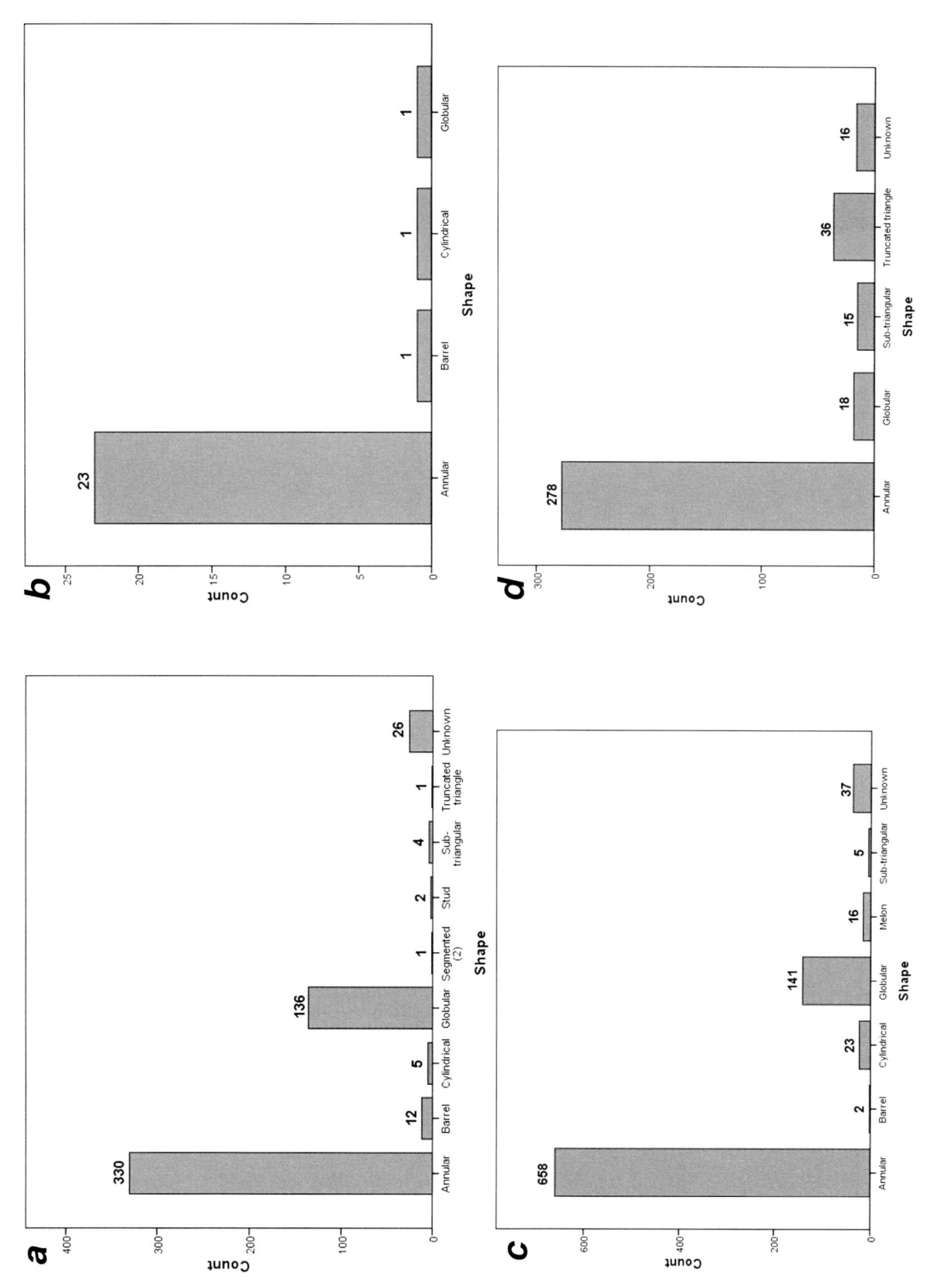

Figure 43: Bar-charts showing the use of bead shapes in (a) Southwest England, (b) East Anglia, (c) East Yorkshire, and (d) Northeast Scotland.

87

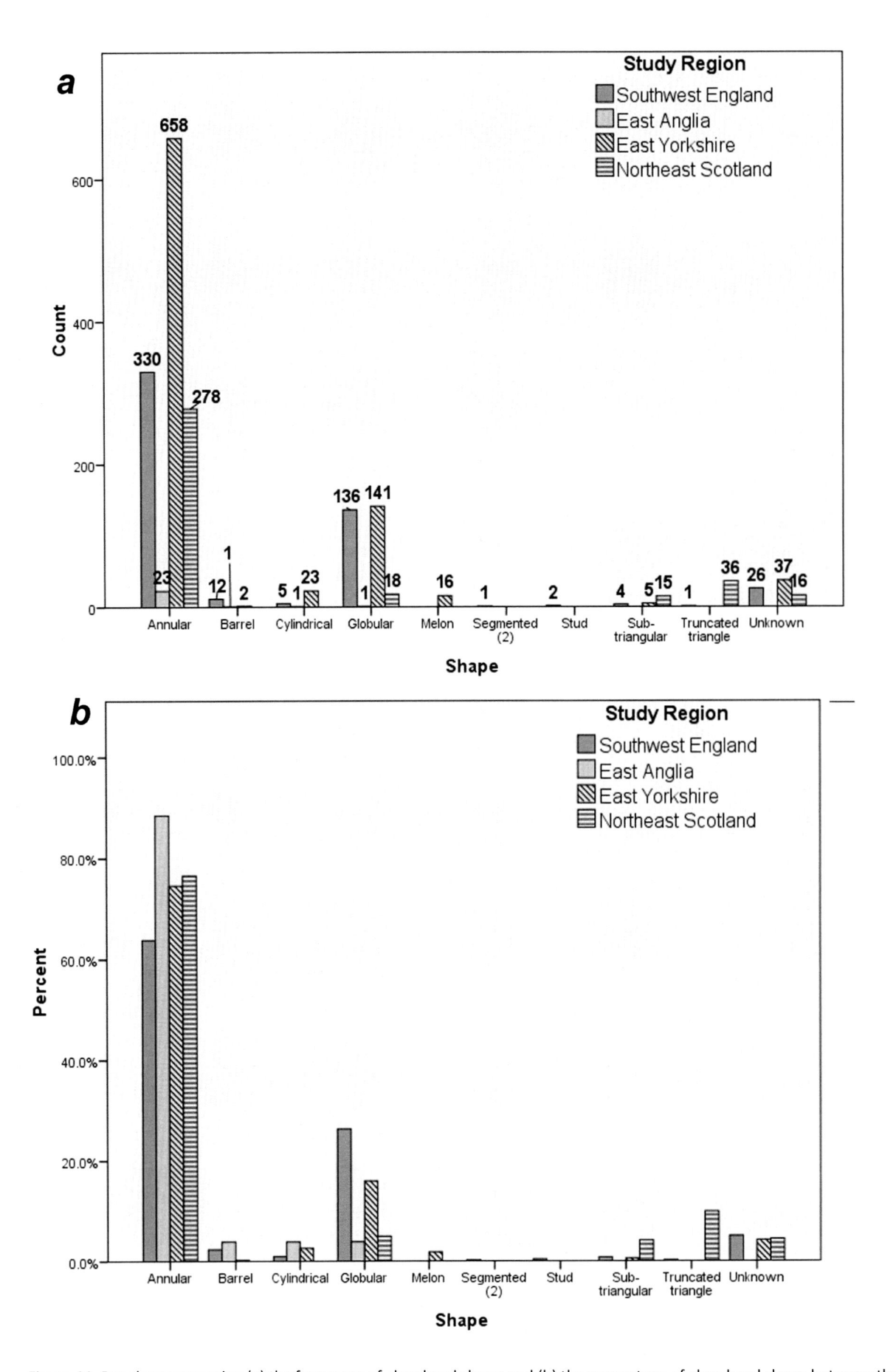

Figure 44: Bar-chart comparing (a) the frequency of glass bead shape and (b) the percentage of glass bead shape between the four study regions.

out of the over 400 inhumations contained glass beads. This is a very small proportion of inhumations, and in most cases these beads ranged from small to medium size in both dimensions and weight, rather than examples of beads at the large end of the size spectrum. On the other hand, 120 minuscule (approx. 1-2mm in diameter) blue glass beads were recently found in a female chariot burial along with a mirror (Hill 2001). Thus, in a region that is relatively bountiful in glass beads, it is the smallest examples of this craft that were found within one of the most lavishly furnished inhumations. It may be that these minuscule beads were recovered because they were excavated under laboratory conditions, and that in general, small beads are more likely to be missed under normal excavation circumstances. Whether these small beads are the norm for this region or for all of Britain is still uncertain, but it is worth considering that larger beads may not indicate higher status simply because they used more glass.

The size of the glass bead can also indicate use or potential uses. Although the term 'bead' usually implies that the object is used primarily for adorning the human body, there is no reason why this must be its only function, or that there needs to have been only one method of usage throughout the bead's entire life. There is evidence in Britain for glass beads having been strung on natural fibre string or leather cord, such as the necklaces from Wetwang Slack (Dent 1984) and the possible necklaces from the Clevedon Cist burial (Gray 1942), and Meare Lake Village in Somerset (Coles 1987) may have been treated in the same way. Within the European context there is further evidence for beads being used as necklaces (e.g. the Reinheim burial), as well as being strung on copper alloy bracelets (e.g. Couilly, Les Jogasses, Grab 72) and their use on fibula (e.g. Roveri, Grab 30). However, these beads are most often small- to medium-sized. In Britain, larger beads (i.e. over 10mm) are not usually found in burial contexts, except for the Chesil mirror burial in Dorset. In this case, the circumstances of the find and later excavations were not able to preserve the placement of the beads in relation to skeletal remains. Thus, it is entirely possible that these rather larger 'beads' were not meant as bodily adornment, but potentially used in some other capacity.

Finally, on a more functional note, it may be that some glass beads have been misidentified and are actually spindle whorls. In shape, whorls differ only slightly from beads, as both are perforated and commonly occur in circular shapes. Size can be of some help here, although it can be very difficult to tell the two apart (Liu 1978, 90). The size and weight of a spindle whorl is dependent on the material of the object, but also on the material being spun (Liu 1978, 90-1). Liu states that some of the smallest whorls can be just 8mm in diameter and less than a gram in weight, while larger ones can be 73mm in diameter and 140grams in weight (1978, 90). He also suggests that most beads tend to be smaller than 15mm-20mm in diameter, as they would be too heavy for spinning if they were made any larger (Liu 1978). The perforation diameter is also significant in this case. For beads this measurement refers to the largest size of cord or wire that the bead can be strung onto, while for spindle whorls it refers to the diameter of the spindle that is passed through the perforation. Again, from Liu's (1978, 97) data this measurement ranges from 3mm to 10mm, but most measured between 7mm and 8mm. For Liu, however, the most important way to tell the difference between a whorl and a bead is the context of the find. This is problematic for Iron Age Britain as most of these perforated objects outside East Yorkshire are not found in burial contexts, nor with other fibre or textile processing equipment; nevertheless, this does highlight some of the issues associated with the interpretation of late prehistoric artefacts. It is also entirely possible that some perforated objects were used as adornments, charms, and spindle whorls concurrently, or on separate occasions.

Size Analysis

Having discussed some of the reasons for investigating regional use of size, the data collected in analyses of glass beads can now be considered. When examining the data set in light of the Diameter/Width, it is clear that there are differences in the size of beads used within each region. The smallest Diameter/Widths are found in East Yorkshire (1.3mm) while the largest are found in Northeast Scotland (55.0mm), as is the largest size range (between 2.2mm and 55.0mm, Figure 45a). In all regions except for East Anglia, the smallest beads are under 5.0mm in length. The Southwest England data set has the largest standard deviation, suggesting a high level of variability. The combined histogram (Figure 45b) confirms that the Southwest England beads have a larger size range than other regions, as do the Northeast Scotland beads; however, it also shows that the most common diameter size for all beads is between 9.0mm and 12.0mm.

Examining the Diameter/Width measurement for each region, we can see that although the Southwest England beads cover a large range, most fall between 7.0mm and 14.0mm (Figure 46a). In contrast, although the East Anglia beads form a very small assemblage, most beads are larger in size, between 22.0mm and 26.0mm (Figure 46b). East Yorkshire, on the other hand, has two distinct sizes of beads: the first between 2.0mm and 4.0mm, the second between 10.0mm and 15.0mm (Figure 46c). Finally, most beads from Northeast Scotland measure between 9.0mm and 11.0mm although there are two smaller sub-groups, on measuring 3.0-4.0mm, and another 15.0-17.0mm (Figure 46d). Aside from East Anglia, it is interesting that the assemblages from most regions cluster around 10.0mm, although most have a

Region	Qty. Glass Beads	Minimum (mm)	Maximum (mm)	Mean	Standard Deviation
Southwest England	462	3.0	37.7	13.135	6.7943
East Anglia	25	7.7	30.0	20.788	5.2678
East Yorkshire	466	1.3	31.5	9.557	4.6738
Northeast Scotland	343	2.2	55.0	11.708	5.8372

Figure 45: (a) Descriptive statistics for Diameter/Width measurement.

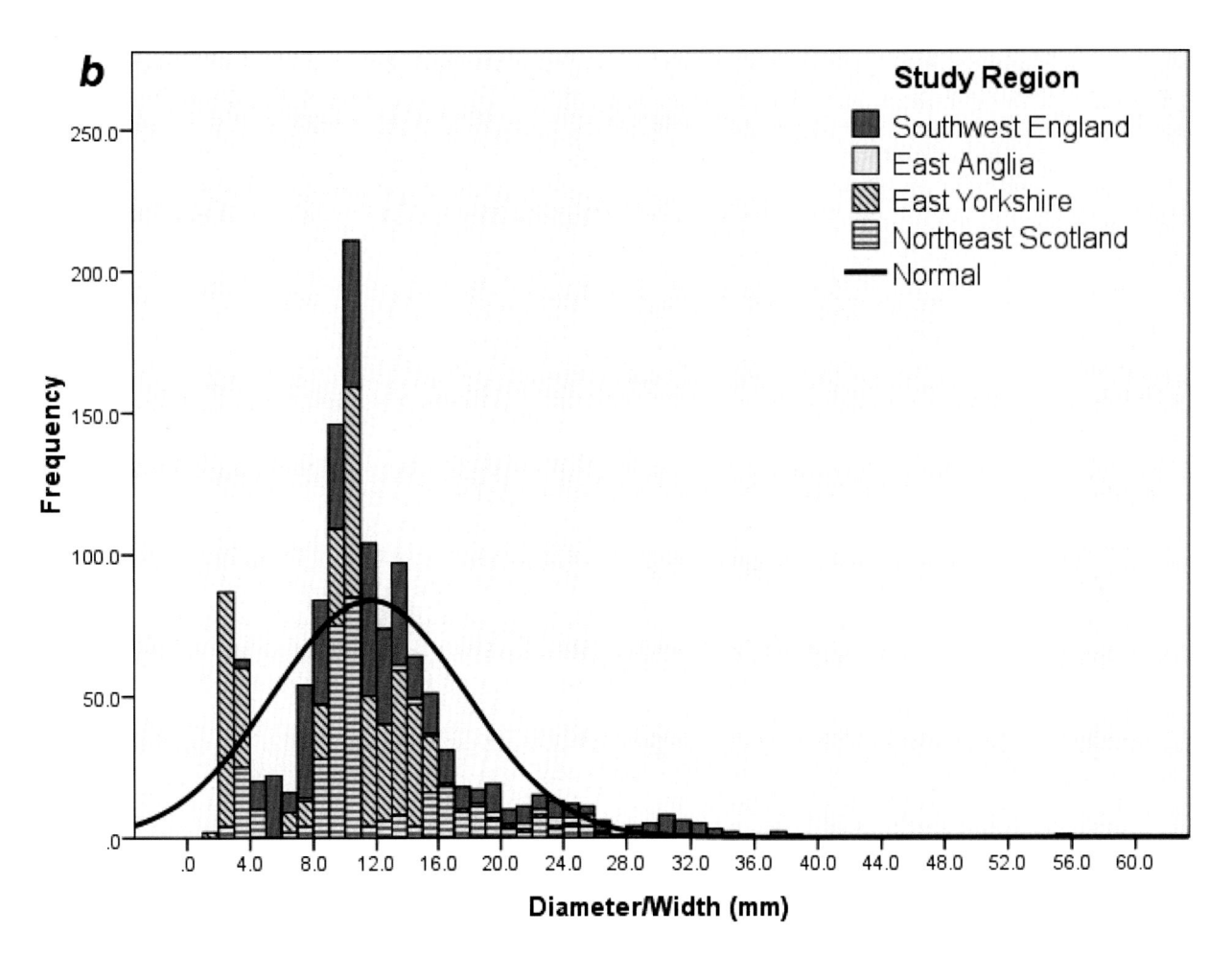

Figure 45: (b) Histogram of the Diameter/Width measurement of glass beads for all beads in study regions.

smaller peak around 4.0mm. This suggests that in three of the four study regions there are groups of both smaller and larger beads in use. Possibly owing to its small sample size, the East Anglian beads include a larger proportion of large-sized beads, with only one measuring less than 10mm in length.

A comparison of glass bead height shows a similar level of difference between the four regions (Figure 47a). East Yorkshire again has the smallest height measurement at 0.3mm, while East Anglia has the largest at 34.0mm, as well as the largest range of measurements. Although each region has beads with a minimum height measurement less than 4.0mm, and large standard deviations, the mean is very different. Again, East Anglia has a larger average sized height, while East Yorkshire has the smallest average sized height. This may be partially explained by the overall shape of the beads and the relation between the diameter and the height (explored below). Combining all the regional data suggests that most beads have a height of 1.0mm to 4.0mm (Figure 47b).

Examining the height measurements found within each region individually shows a slightly different picture.

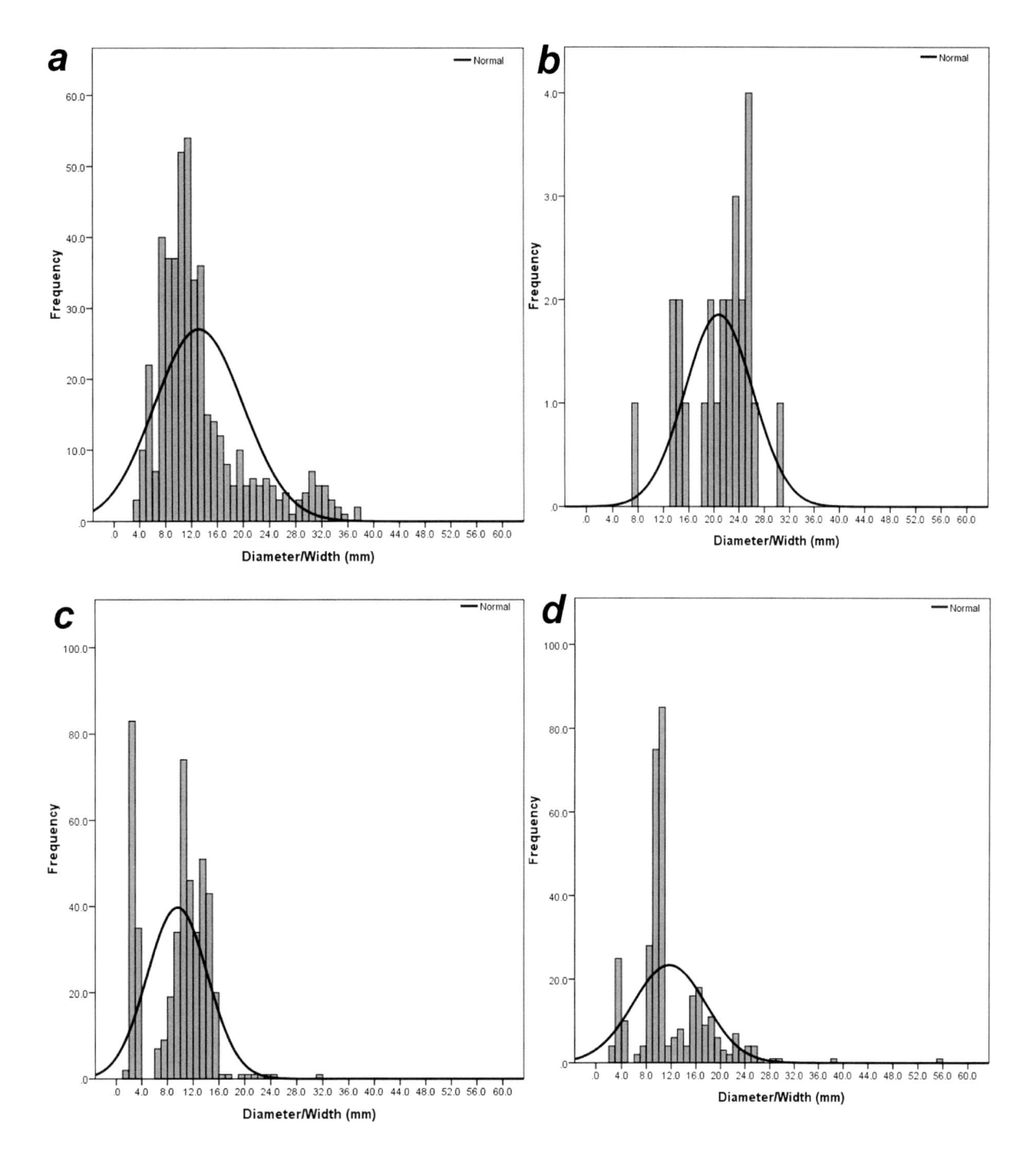

Figure 46: Histogram showing Diameter/Width measurement for (a) Southwest England, (b) East Anglia, (c) East Yorkshire, and (d) Northeast Scotland.

Glass beads from Southwest England fall markedly between the 2.0mm and 4.0mm range, but there is a secondary, although less pronounced cluster between 9.0mm to 11.0mm (Figure 48a). In addition, there are two very large examples that fall between 22.0mm and 24.0mm. East Anglia has a similar range of bead heights, between 7.0mm and 10.0mm (Figure 48b). This overlaps slightly with the beads from Southwest England. The histogram shows a very irregular range of sizes, but this is probably due to the small sample size. Similar to the Southwest England beads, the East Yorkshire and Northeast Scotland beads have two clusters (Figures 48c-d). In East Yorkshire, the smaller peak is between 1.0mm and 2.0mm, suggesting a very tight cluster of very small beads, while the Northeast Scotland beads are slightly larger, between 3.0mm and 4.0mm, also forming a tight cluster. The larger beads from East Yorkshire fall predominantly between 5.0mm and 8.0mm, while in Northeast Scotland, they fall roughly between about 9.0mm and 13.0mm. The larger Northeast Scotland bead

Region	Qty. Glass Beads	Minimum (mm)	Maximum (mm)	Mean	Standard Deviation
Southwest England	462	3.0	37.7	13.135	6.7943
East Anglia	25	7.7	30.0	20.788	5.2678
East Yorkshire	466	1.3	31.5	9.557	4.6738
Northeast Scotland	343	2.2	55.0	11.708	5.8372

Figure 47: (a) Descriptive statistics for Height measurement.

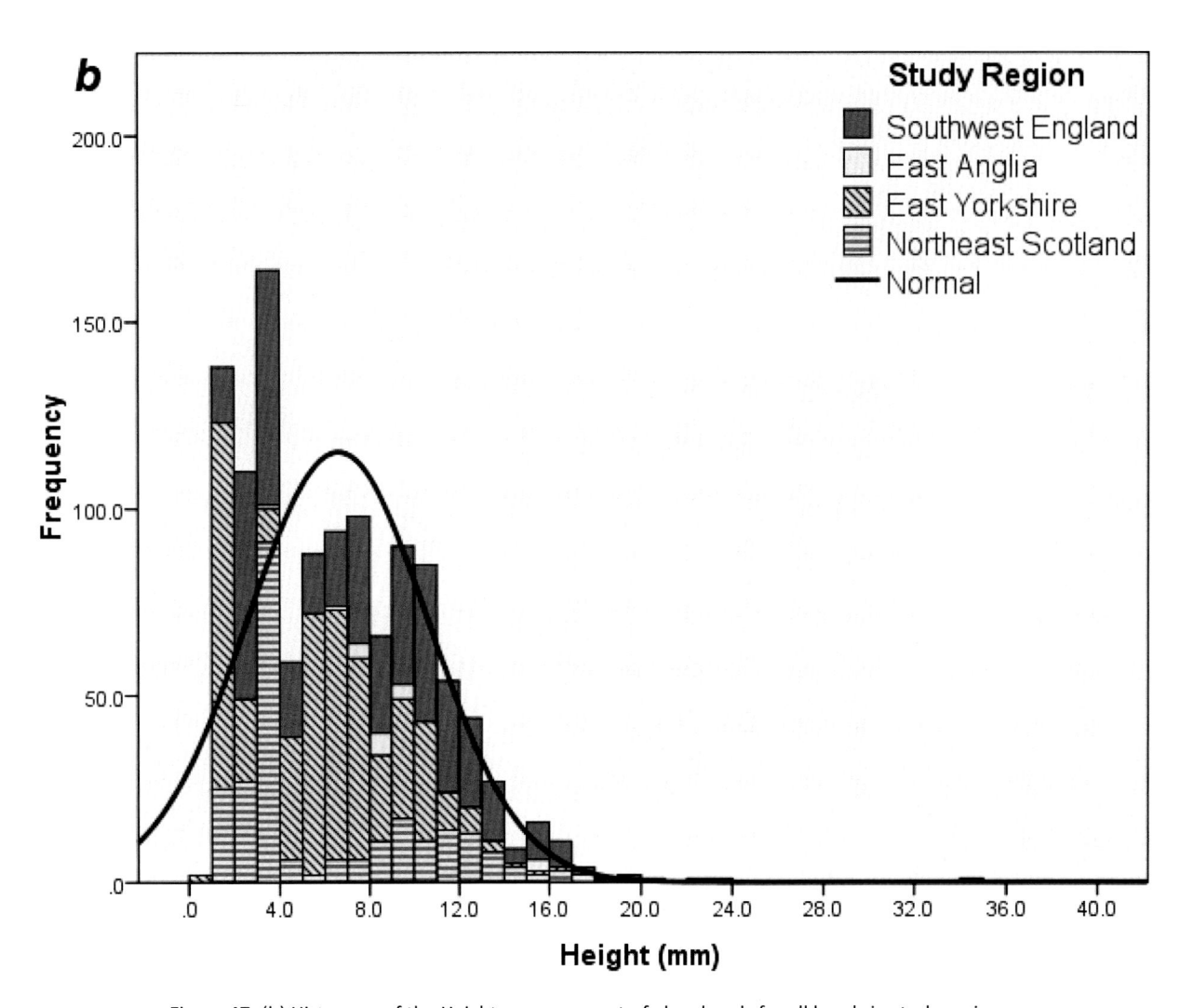

Figure 47: (b) Histogram of the Height measurement of glass beads for all beads in study regions.

height is not only larger than the East Yorkshire beads, but covers a larger range.

The last dimension analysed in this study is perforation diameter. The smallest perforation diameters are found in Northeast Scotland (0.9mm), while the largest is found in Southwest England (27.0mm, Figure 49a). The beads from Southwest England also have the largest perforation diameter range, covering 25.9mm; however, the other three regions have similar ranges. Interestingly, each region has very different average perforation diameters. Northeast Scotland has the smallest at 3.7mm, and East Anglia has the largest average at 9.1mm. While most perforation diameters overall fall between 3.0mm and 6.0mm (Figure 49b), the differing regional averages suggest that there may be different regional uses of beads, or that they are being strung onto different sized materials.

While the averages suggest that there are different sizes of perforation diameters within each region - indicating different sized mandrels were used when forming the

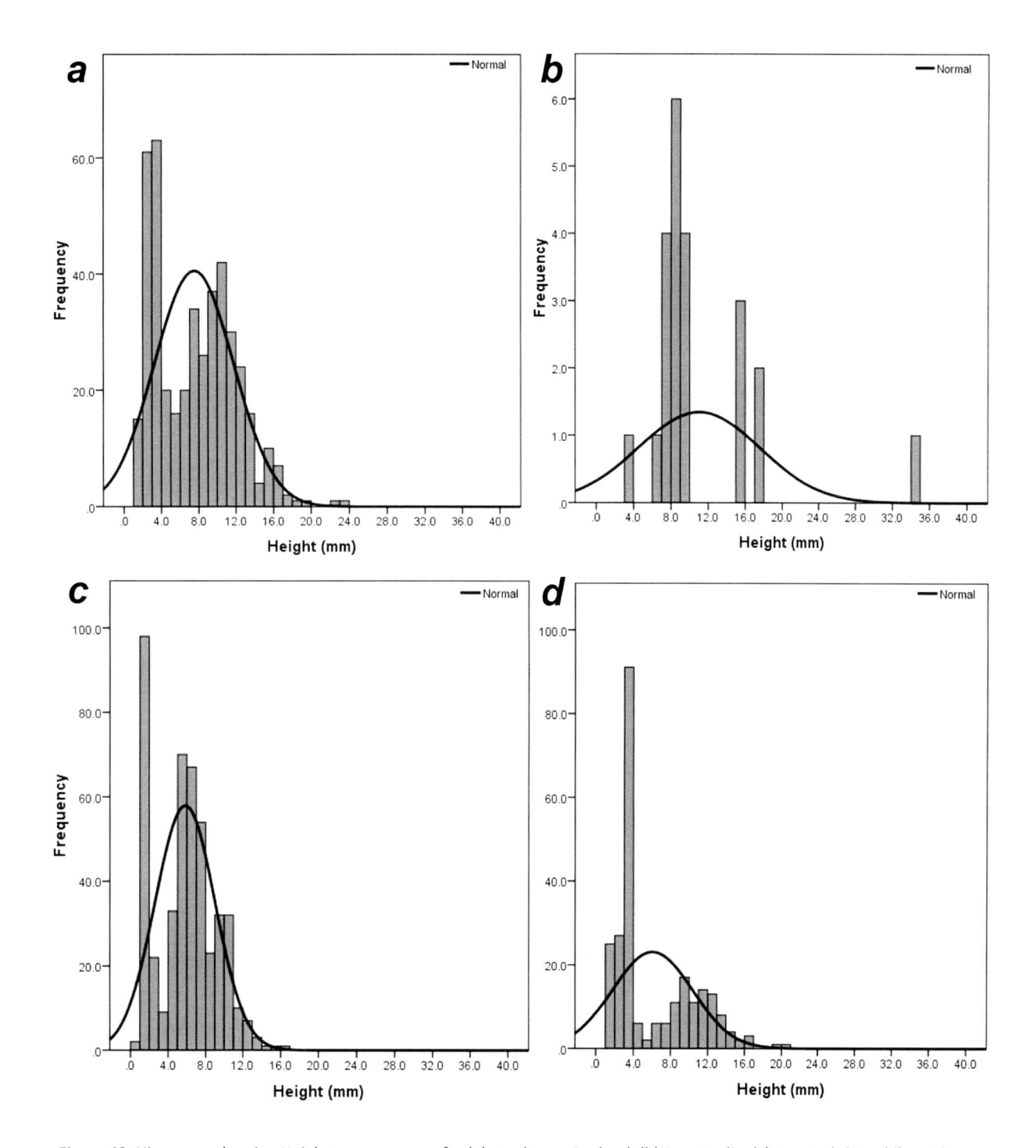

Figure 48: Histogram showing Height measurement for (a) southwest England, (b) East Anglia, (c) East Yorkshire, (d) Northeast Scotland.

beads during the manufacturing process, and possibly different uses - by examining individual histograms of the perforation diameters it is clear that there is actually much more homogeneity within the data than is initially apparent. The most frequently occurring measurements within the Southwest England, East Yorkshire, and Northeast Scotland assemblages fall between about 3.0mm and 6.0mm (Figures 50a, c, d). The most frequent range of perforation diameters for East Anglian beads falls between 11.0mm and 12.0mm (Figure 50b). This is slightly larger than the major trend seen in the other regions. Again, this could still indicate differences in glass bead use between East Anglia and the other three regions.

While these analyses have examined individual aspects of size, it is also possible to examine combinations of these measurements to gain an understanding of the overall size of beads by region. By plotting the Diameter/Width and Height measurements for all beads within the study

Region	Qty. Glass Beads	Minimum (mm)	Maximum (mm)	Mean	Standard Deviation
Southwest England	395	1.1	27.0	5.629	2.8911
East Anglia	19	2.0	12.3	9.079	2.9213
East Yorkshire	337	1.0	14.0	4.487	1.389
Northeast Scotland	235	0.9	12.7	3.661	1.6822

Figure 49: (a) Descriptive statistics for Perforation Diameter measurement.

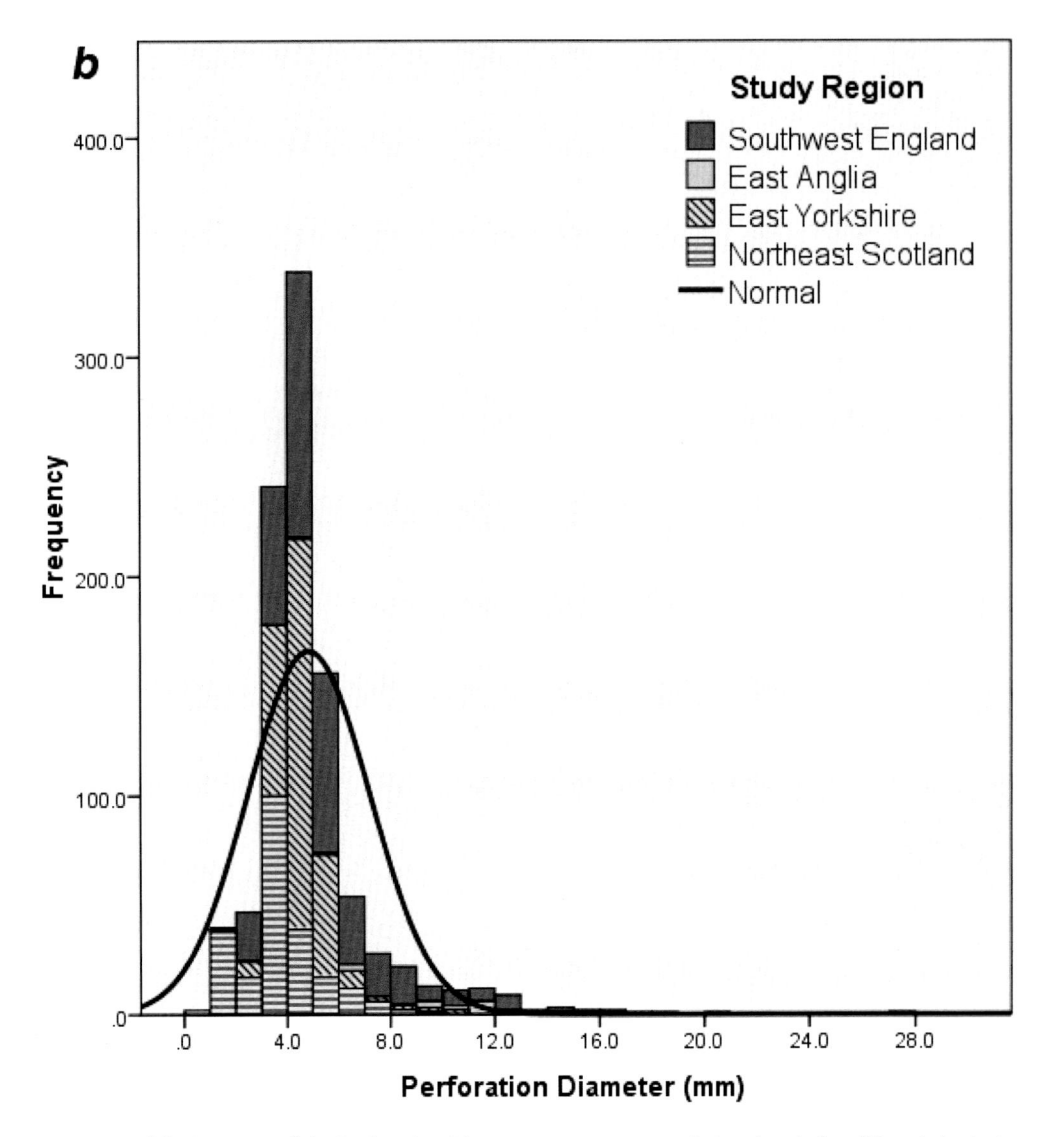

Figure 49: (b) Histogram of the Perforation Diameter measurement of glass beads for all beads in study regions.

regions on a scatter-graph, we can see that while there is overlap between the regions, there are also distinct clusters within the data (Figure 51). This graph shows two major groupings within the overall data. The first is very small (*a*) and incorporates measurements of 2.0mm to 6.0mm in Diameter/Width and <5.0mm in Height. The second major grouping (*b*) has a larger range involving a Diameter/Width between 7.0mm and 16.0mm and a Height ranging from 3.0mm to about 12.0mm. This is the main cluster that most beads fall within, and although it is wide-ranging, it shows that rather than occupying distinct and consistent size clusters (except for cluster *a*), most beads fall along a more general size continuum instead. It may also be significant that this major cluster

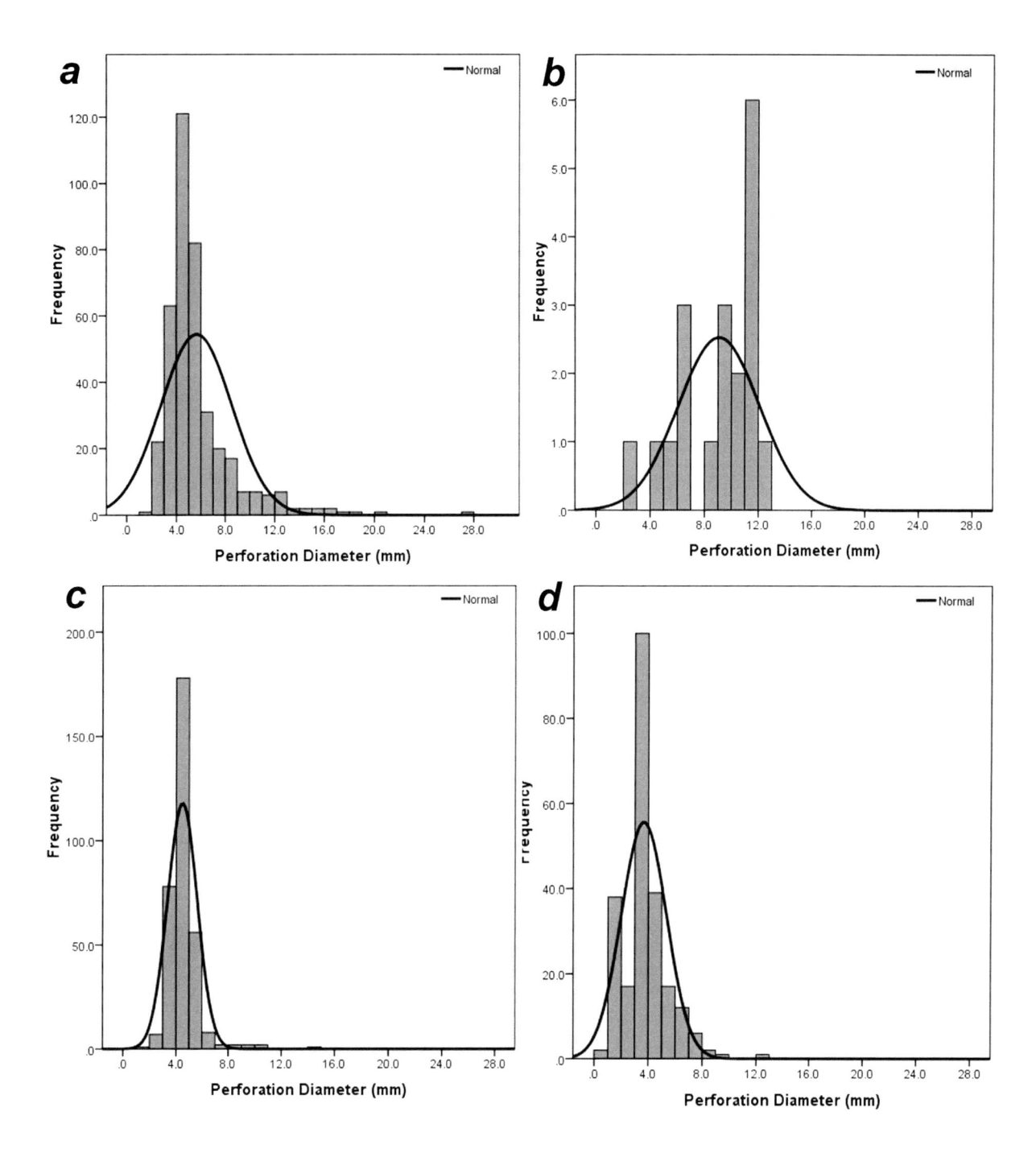

Figure 50: Histogram showing Perforation Diameter measurement for (a) Southwest England, (b) East Anglia, (c) East Yorkshire, (d) Northeast Scotland.

is positioned below the 1:1 ratio line, but crosses both the 1:1.5 and 1:2 ratio lines. This suggests that the terminology used to distinguish between 'globular' (spherical) shaped beads and 'annular' (ring or doughnut) shaped beads does not agree with the data. If there were clear-cut distinctions between globular and annular beads, then we would expect to see very distinct clusters on either side of the ratio guidelines. This is not the case. In addition, there are a number of larger outlier beads that neither fit with the main *b* cluster nor form their own large bead cluster. Future research needs to take this into consideration when defining bead shapes.

Using these scatter-graphs, it is possible to examine size trends within each region. In Southwest England, there are two major size groups (Figure 52a). Here, both of these groups (labeled *a* and *b*) fall within clear size distinctions. Group *a* has a smaller Diameter/Width and a smaller height, and is just below the 1:2 ratio line. Group *b* is specifically more globular in shape and,

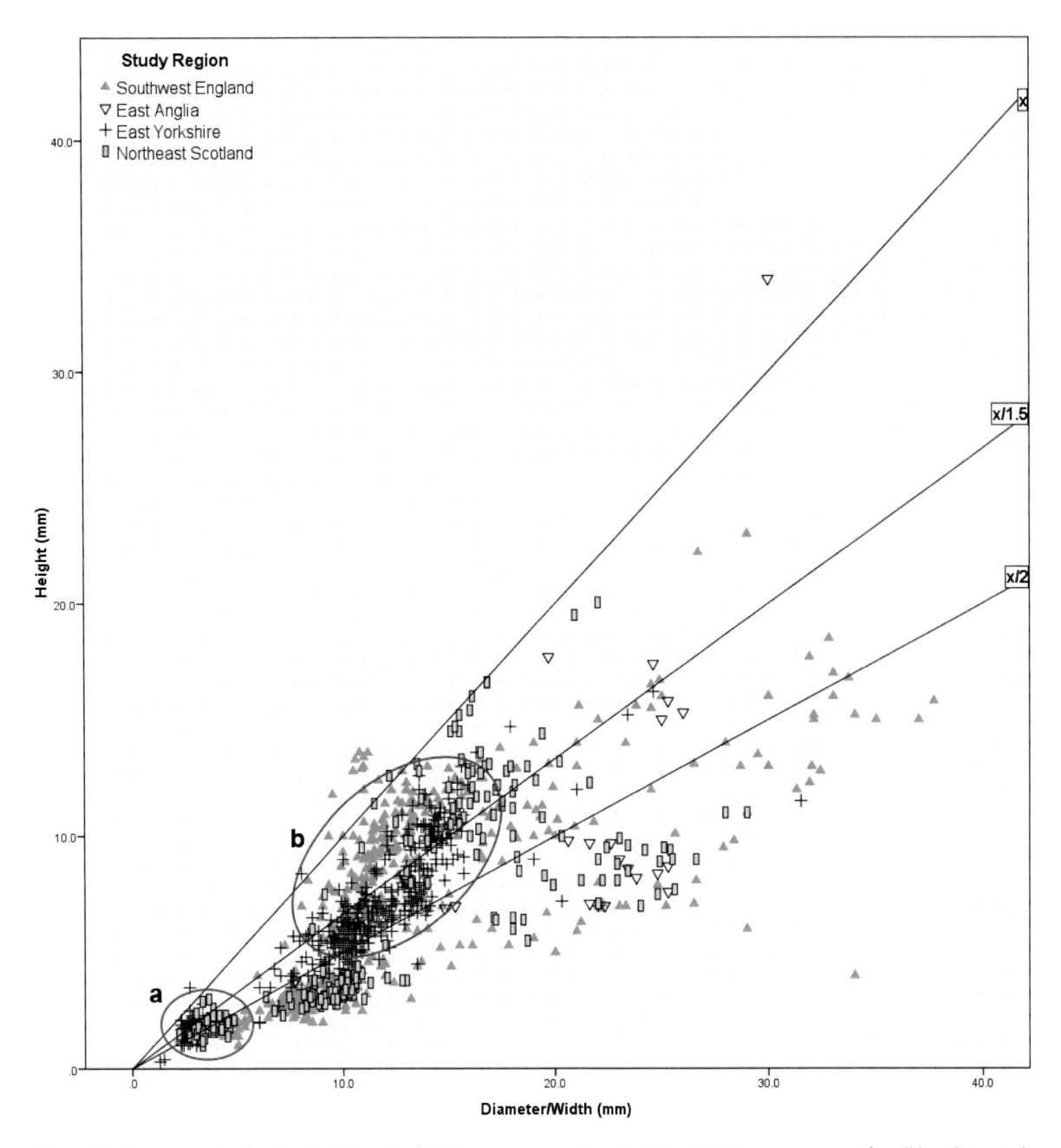

Figure 51: Scatter-graph plotting the Diameter/Width measurement against the Height measurement for all beads in study regions.

although it has a larger size range, it occurs primarily between the 1:1 and 1:1.5 ratio guidelines. Within this region, it seems that there is a clear distinction in terms of both ratio and size. There are, of course, a number of other beads that do not cluster within these groups, some of which are very annular and others that are more ambiguously categorised. In East Anglia, there are two clusters, one below the 1:2 ratio line (*a*) and another that is much larger and crosses the 1:1 and 1:1.5 ratio guidelines (Figure 52b). In this case, it seems that there is a clear distinction between annular beads and larger beads. However, interpretation is hampered by the small sample size.

Scatter-graphs for East Yorkshire and Northeast Scotland also demonstrate clear size groups. East Yorkshire clearly has a group of smaller beads (*a*) and a larger size (*b*) group (Figure 52c). Both of these groups cross the ratio guidelines, again suggesting that the distinction between shapes is not clear from the data, but rather that they form a continuum. In contrast, the small group of Northeast Scottish beads also crosses these guidelines, but the medium size group (*b*) tends to be more annular (Figure 52d). A substantial number of the Northeast Scotland beads are not a part of these clusters, but are much larger and form a loose cluster spreading from the 1:1 to 1:2 ratio guidelines. Again, it seems that for these

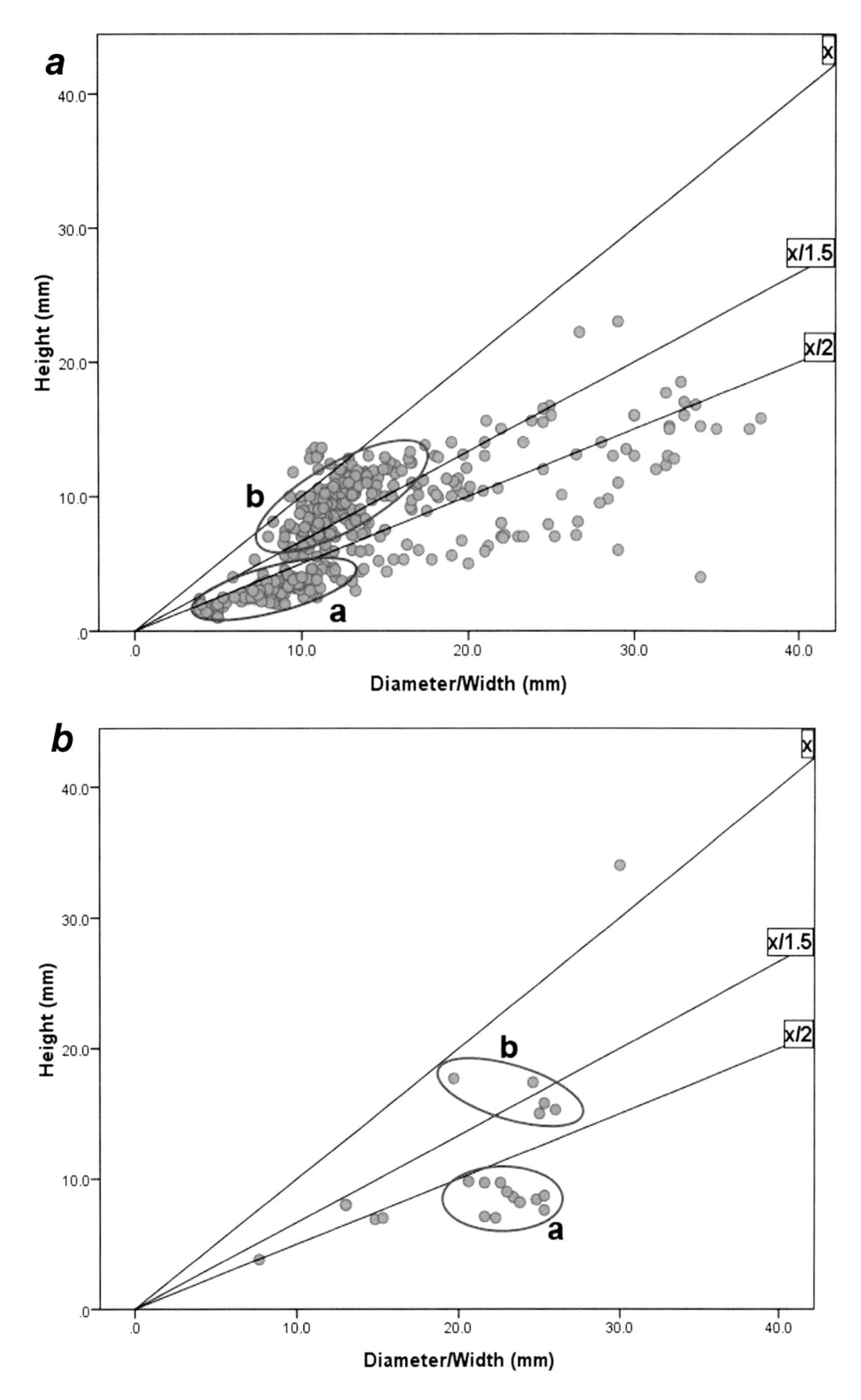

Figure 52: Scatter-graph plotting the Diameter/Width against the Height for beads from (a) Southwest England, (b) East Anglia.

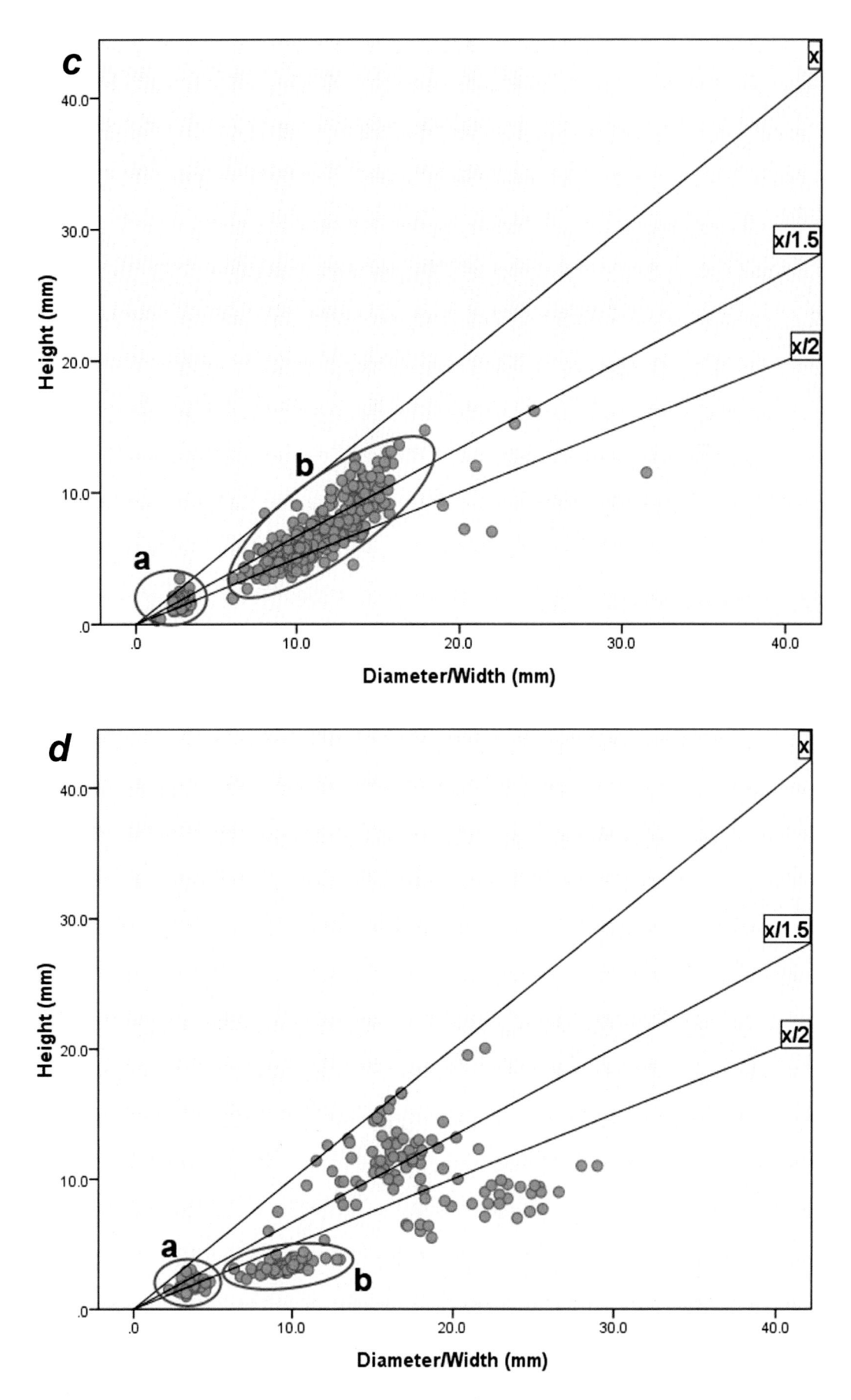

Figure 52: Scatter-graph plotting the Diameter/Width against the Height for beads from (c) East Yorkshire, (d) Northeast Scotland.

larger beads, the important message is that they are large, but do not necessarily conform to a standard size or ratio.

The second type of scatter-graph specifically examines the Diam:Height ratio and perforation diameter. In this case, horizontal clustering indicates similar perforation size, while vertical clustering indicates a similar ratio between diameter and height. The combined regional data shows that there are two major clusters and some examples that do not cluster (Figure 53). Cluster *a* is formed from beads with a ratio ranging from nearly 1.0 to nearly 3.5, but their perforation diameter is very small (between 1.0mm and 2.0mm). Cluster *b* has the same ratio range, but with a larger perforation diameter (between 2.0mm and 6.0mm). Cluster *b* has the largest number of beads by far, and it is interesting that it includes beads from multiple regions; Cluster *a* on the other hand, is primarily composed of beads from Northeast Scotland alone. There are also some additional beads that do not fit with the two main clusters or form clusters of their own. Most of these beads also have a ratio between 1.0 and 3.5, but their perforation diameters are much larger and range from 6.0mm to 27.0mm. These beads are also found in all study regions.

Despite some examples that do not fit the dominant ratio range and perforation diameter range, the normative size range for all regions has a ratio between 1.0 and 3.5 and a perforation diameter between 2.0mm to 6.0mm. In conjunction with the overall size graph shown in Figure 51, this implies that similarly shaped and sized beads are found in all the regions under study. Nonetheless, there are also certain regional trends, and these can be explored by producing graphs of beads by individual study region. For Southwest England there are two main clusters labeled *a* and *b* (Figure 54a). Both clusters have perforation diameters that range between 2.0mm and 6.0mm, but cluster by Diam:Height ratio. Cluster *a* ratios range between 1.0 and 2.0, while cluster *b* has a ratio range between 2.0 and 3.5. This suggests that in Southwest England, there may be some real differences in shape, although rather than using 1.5 as the dividing line between globular and annular shaped beads, 2.0 may be more apt. Again, there are a number of beads with much larger perforation diameters that do not cluster together.

The East Anglian beads do not follow this pattern. The majority of beads have a larger perforation diameter, between 9.0mm and 12.0mm (Figure 54b). There is one small cluster that includes five beads of similar ratio and perforation diameter (labeled *a*), but on the whole there is little evidence to suggest a dominant trend. In contrast, the beads from East Yorkshire and Northeast Scotland present a very different picture. The majority of the East Yorkshire beads cluster into one group defined by both ratio (between 1.0 and about 2.5) and perforation diameter (between 3.0mm and 6.0mm) (Figure 54c).

There are very few beads that do not cluster within this group, suggesting that within this region the distinction between what we would call annular and globular is not clear and that most beads have a very similar perforation diameter. It should be noted that it was not possible to include the 2001 Wetwang Slack chariot burial bead data in this instance as the perforation diameter could not be measured. However, while the ratio of these beads is very similar to those already shown on previous graphs, their perforation diameters are less than 1.0mm. This would have formed a separate cluster by perforation diameter. The Northeast Scotland beads, on the other hand, fall within three main clusters. The first cluster has ratio values ranging between 1.0 and 2.5, but with a very small perforation diameter measuring between 1.0 and 2.0mm (labeled *a*, Figure 54d). The second group has a very strict ratio between 1.0 and 1.5 and a perforation diameter between 3.0mm and 5.0mm (labeled *b*). The third group has a ratio between 2.5 and 3.5 and perforation diameters ranging mostly between 2.0mm and 4.0mm, but which can be as large as 9.0mm (labeled *c*). This clustering suggests that there are three major groupings within the beads and that they are based on both proportional data and the perforation diameters.

The last size-based measurement to be examined here is weight. Unfortunately, the sample size for this measurement is very limited as weight is almost never recorded in excavation reports. In addition, many museums string together glass beads for display, but doing so makes it impossible to weigh individual beads. Lastly, only the weight of whole or nearly whole beads has been included here. According to available data, each region has beads that weigh as little as <0.5grams (Figure 55a). Beads from East Yorkshire appear to be the most consistent, with a standard deviation of 0.8436. Interestingly, the mean of these beads also suggests that this region has the smallest beads and that East Anglia has the largest. The combined regional histogram shows that beads lighter in weight are most common and that there are fewer heavy-weight beads (Figure 55b). By comparing this data according to the study areas shows that there are regional characteristics for weight. In Southwest England, most beads fall between 0.1g and 2.0g, but there are also a number of beads that fall between 2.0g and 4.0g and very few that are heavier than this (Figure 56a). However, there are also examples of beads from Southwest England that could be considered to be very heavy (at 21.9g). In contrast, the East Anglia beads mainly weigh between 2.0g and 5.0g, with the heaviest between 12.0g and 13.0g (Figure 56b). Similar to the Southwest England beads, the East Yorkshire and Northeast Scotland beads weigh predominantly between 0.1g and 1.0g (Figure 56c-d). The range of East Yorkshire beads is much more limited as they rarely weigh more than 4.0g, whereas the Northeast Scotland beads have a second peak between 3.0g and 5.0g. This suggests that the East Yorkshire beads are more consistent (something

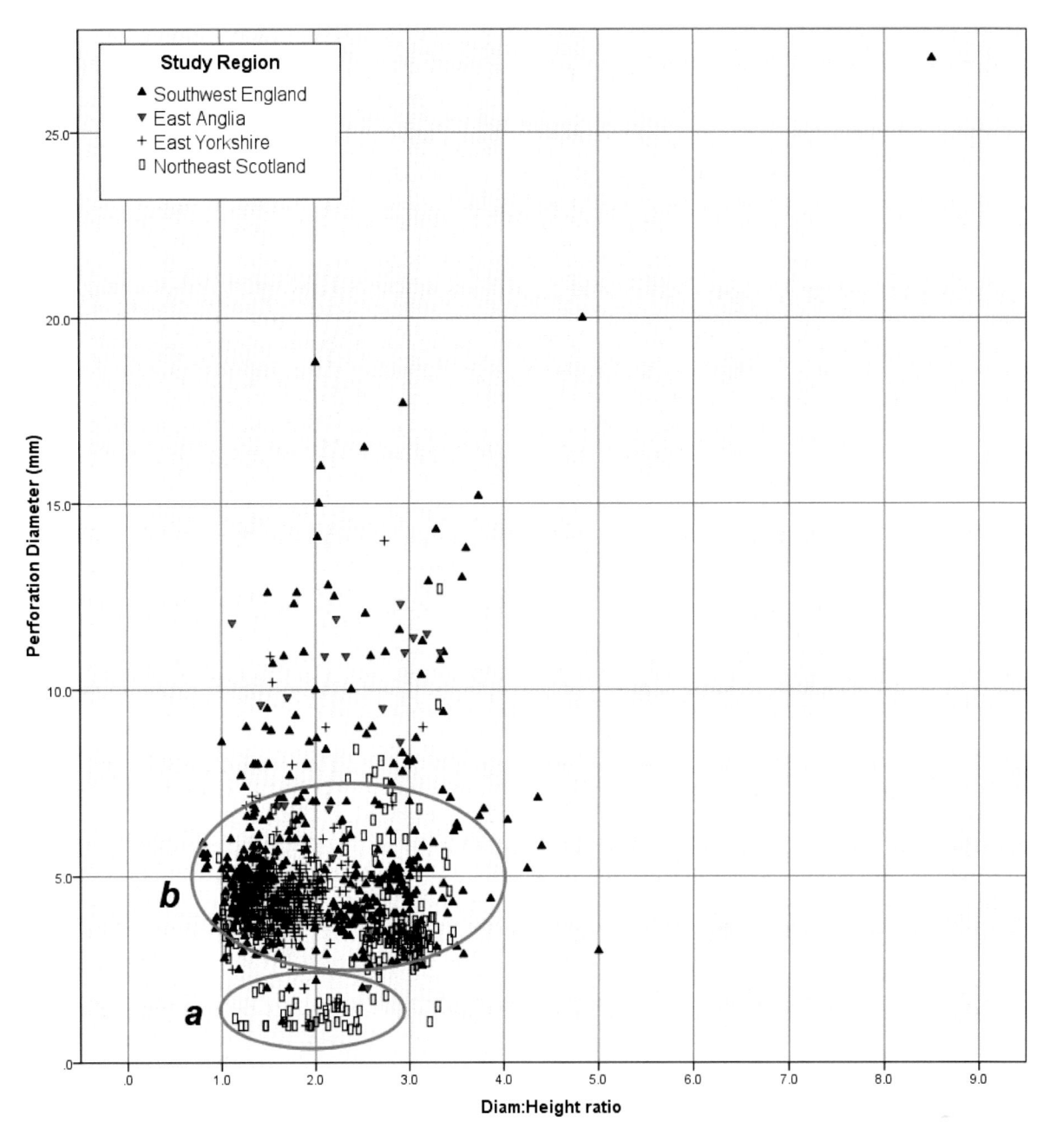

Figure 53: Scatter-graph plotting the Diam:Height ratio against the Perforation Diameter measurement for all beads in study regions.

also seen with the dimension data), while there are two weight ranges for the Northeast Scotland beads.

Size Discussion

Overall, the data for bead size suggests a number of things. While there are several similarities between the study regions, as shown by the overlap in the data, there are also some marked differences. First, the East Yorkshire beads are very consistent in terms of their dimension and weight. There is no clear distinction between beads that would normally be termed annular and those that are globular. This may be related to the context of the finds, which will be explored further in Chapter 8. Second, the Northeast Scotland beads often form multiple clusters based on size and weight. This suggests that there were clearer distinctions between size and shape in this region compared to other regions. The beads from Southwest England also form size-based groups; however, like the East Yorkshire beads, they do not form clear size based clusters. Finally, it is interesting that the East Anglia beads do not consistently follow the general trends seen in the other three regions. This may be due to the small sample size and it may be that, given time for the acquisition of new data, this will change. Alternatively, it may be that this region will have its own characteristics of bead size and weight.

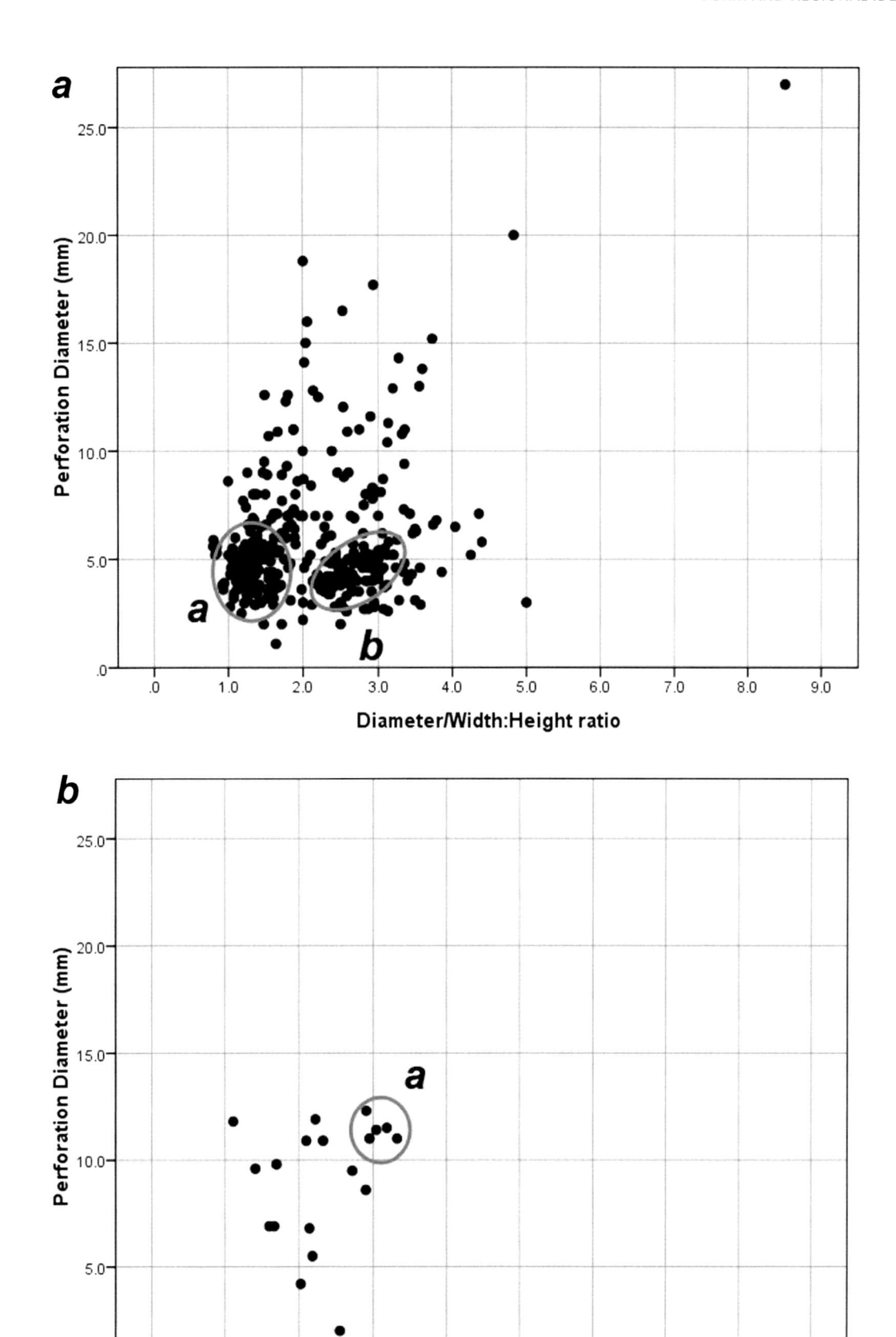

Figure 54: Scatter-graph plotting the Diam:Height ratio against the Perforation Diameter for beads from (a) Southwest England, (b) East Anglia.

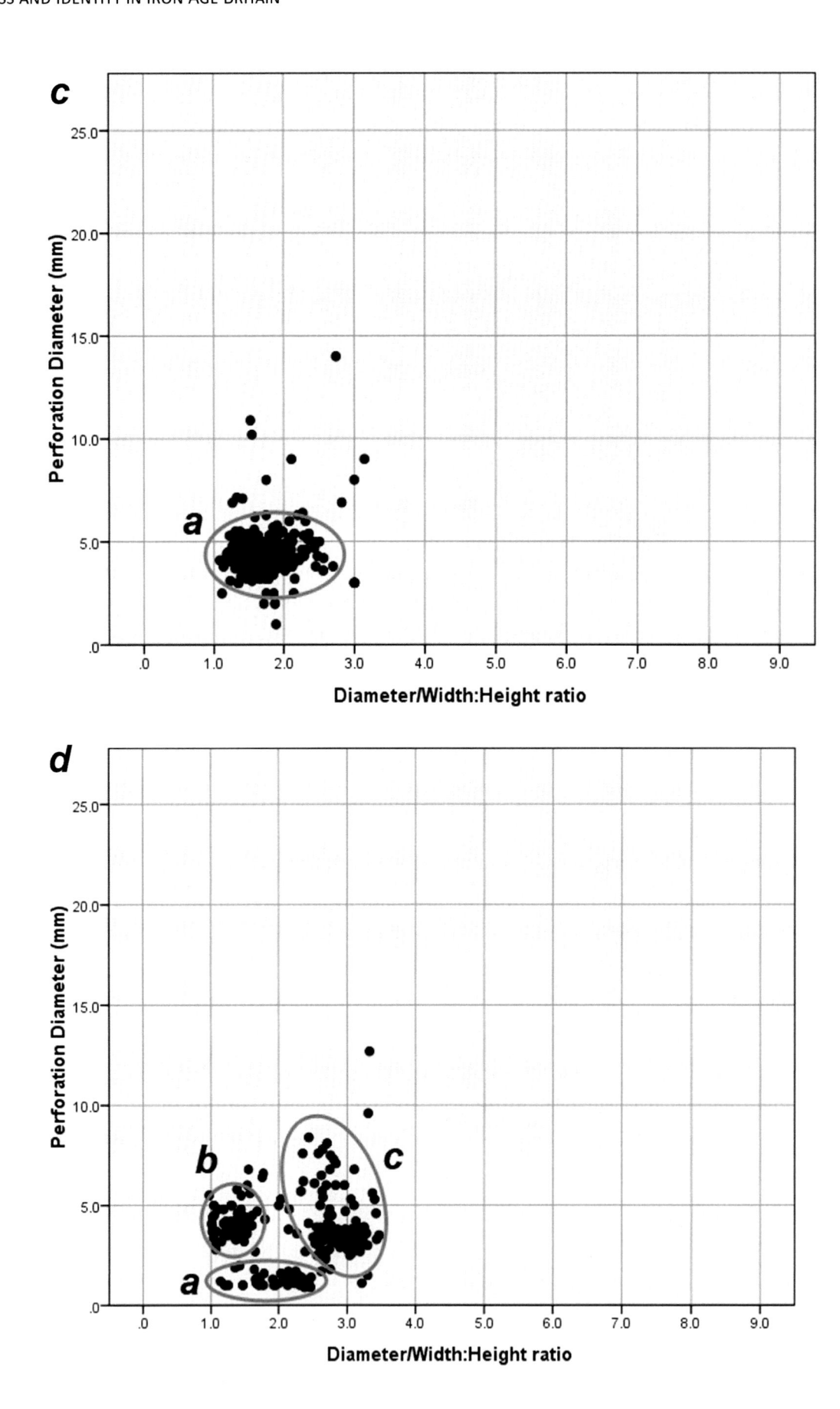

Figure 54: Scatter-graph plotting the Diam:Height ratio against the Perforation Diameter for beads from (c) East Yorkshire, (d) Northeast Scotland.

Region	Qty. Glass Beads	Minimum (g)	Maximum (g)	Mean	Standard Deviation
Southwest England	347	0.1	25.1	1.801	2.59
East Anglia	19	0.3	12.3	4.505	3.0623
East Yorkshire	167	0.2	5.1	1.16	0.8548
Northeast Scotland	122	0.1	12.5	3.05	2.6903

Figure 55: (a) Descriptive statistics for Weight measurement for beads from all study regions (grams).

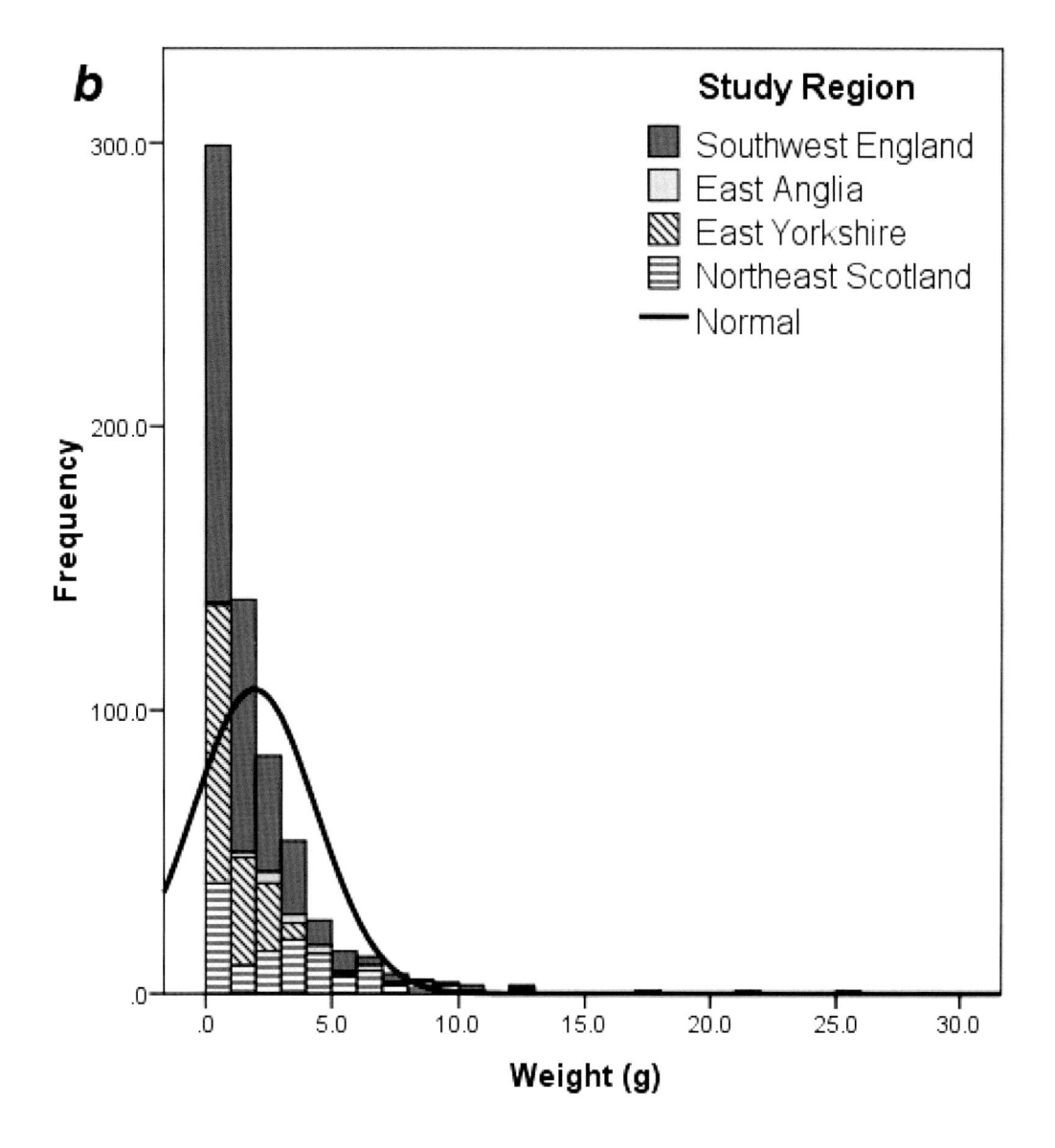

Figure 55: (b) Histogram showing the combined Weight distribution for all study regions.

What do these analyses tell us about glass beads? At the beginning of this section, several topics were raised. These include: the issues of regional access to raw materials for those beads manufactured in Britain; potential indications of status and the idea that glass beads were a luxury; and the ways in which glass beads may have been used as indicated by size. The key question to this research is what does the size of a glass bead indicate about manufacturing, use, and the identity of the people that used them?

The answers to these questions all depend on the context of glass bead finds. This will be addressed more fully in the following chapters; however, it is worth briefly

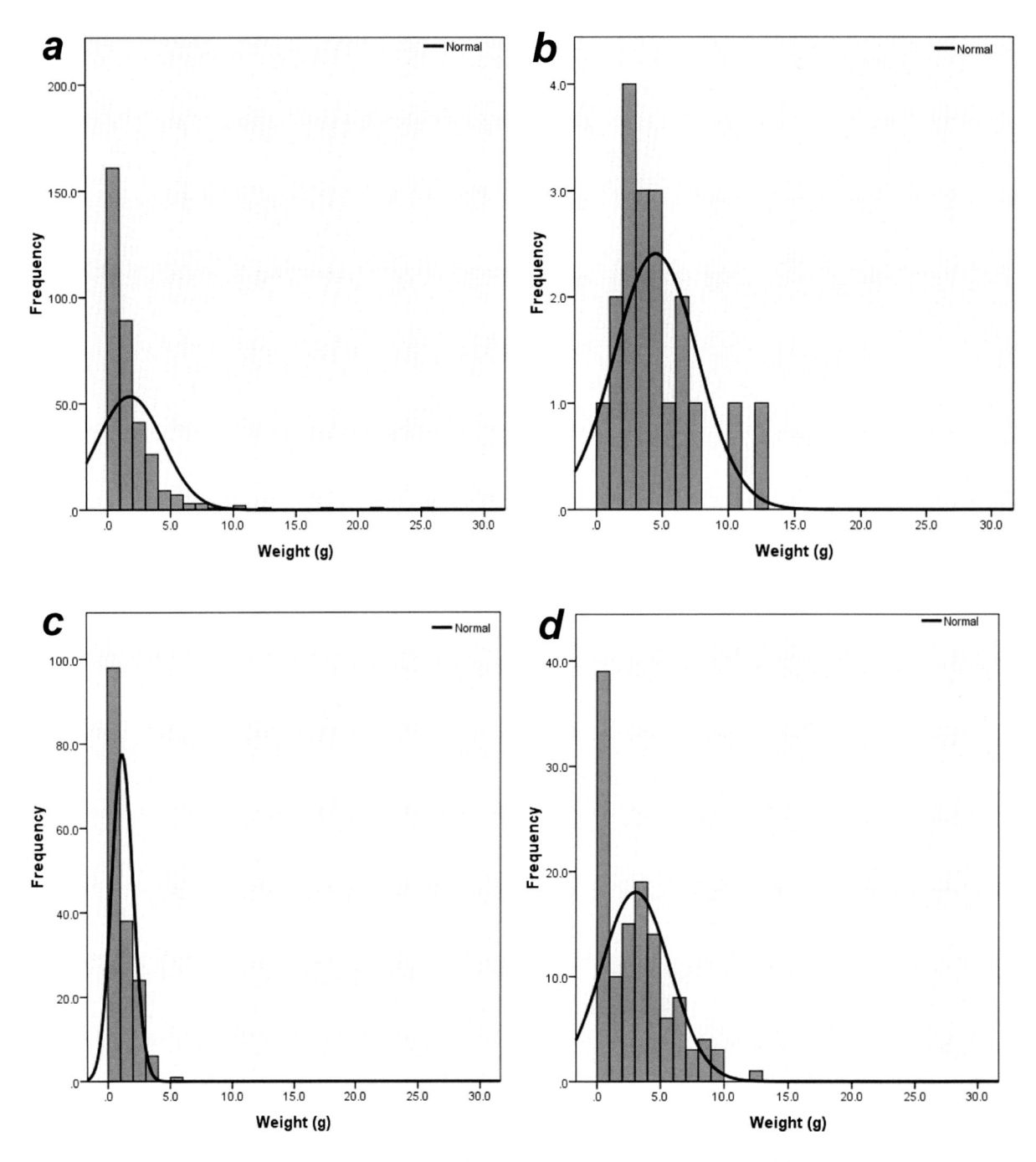

Figure 56: Histogram showing Weight measurement for (a) Southwest England, (b) East Anglia, (c) East Yorkshire, (d) Northeast Scotland.

discussing these issues here. Many of these beads have turned up as stray finds throughout Britain, and those excavated from settlements are rarely found in multiples in the same context. However, in the few cases for beads found in the same context, either within a settlement or in an inhumation, it can be shown that glass bead size is meaningful. Figures 57 and 58 show scatter-graphs of glass beads clustered according to their context. The first graph shows beads from Southwest England from five different contexts (three from burials and two from a settlement). The beads from some of these contexts cluster according to similarity in size (e.g. Clevedon Cist burial, MLVE G68), while others do not cluster to the same extent (e.g. Langdon Herring burial).

The East Yorkshire beads are taken from 13 inhumations. In the cases of the Wetwang Chariot burial, Cowlam Barrow L, Wetwang Burial 274, and Wetwang Burial 209, clear clusters are formed. The beads from the remaining inhumations (Wetwang Burials: 376, 284, 257, 249, 236, 210, 155, 139, and the Queen's Barrow) form an overlapping cluster of beads that are smaller

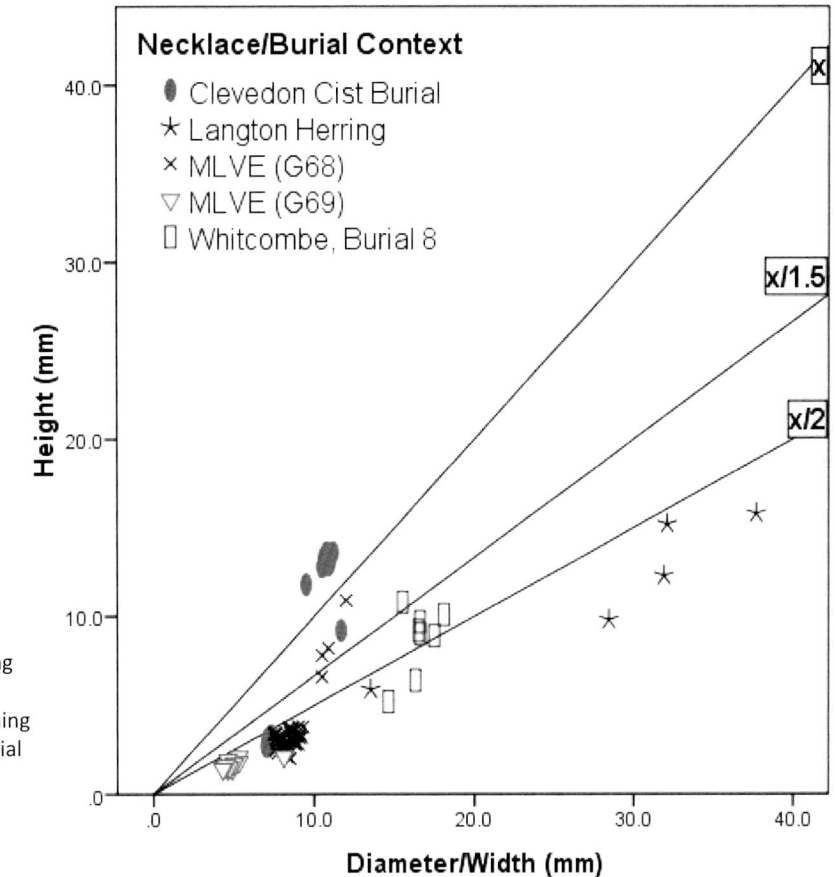

Figure 57: Scatter-graph comparing the Diameter/Width and Height measurements for glass beads forming possible necklaces, or found in burial contexts in Southwest England.

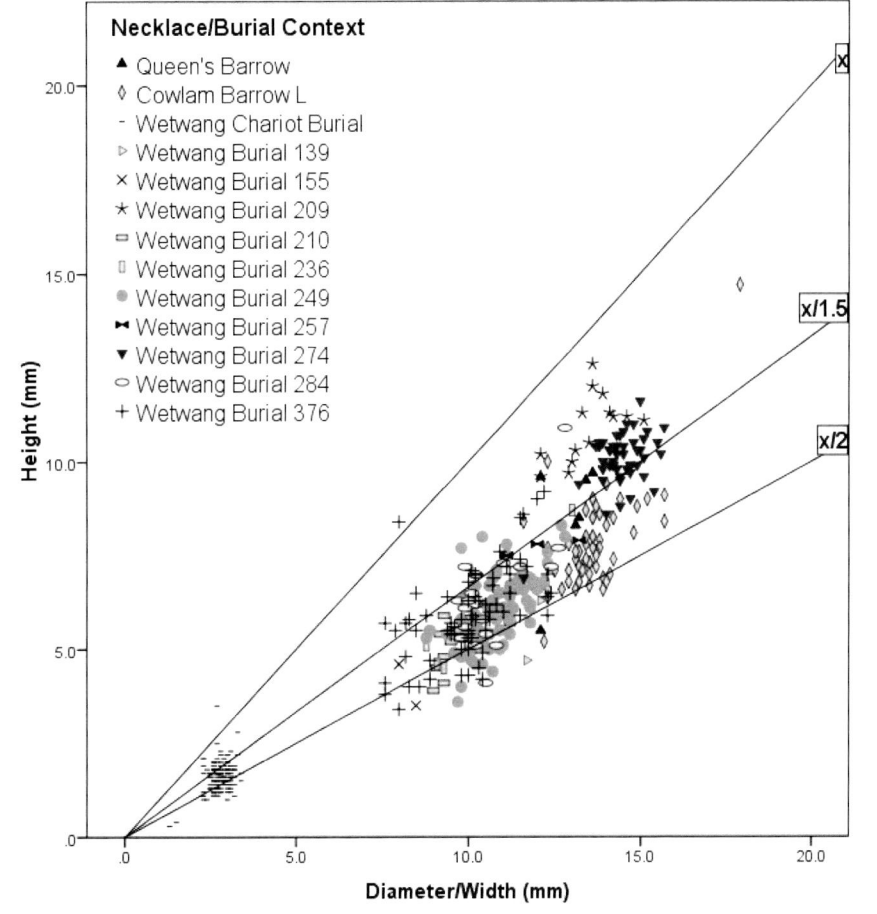

Figure 58: Scatter-graph comparing the Diameter/Width and Height measurements for glass beads forming possible necklaces, or found in burial contexts in East Yorkshire.

than many of the beads from Wetwang burials 209 and 274 and the Cowlam Barrow L.

While this section only briefly delves into the contextual side of analyzing bead size, these clusters of beads found in close association suggest that beads were specifically chosen for their size. Dense clusters represent beads that are all roughly the same size, while outliers would have stood out; not only for their difference in size, but often because of their difference in appearance. On the other hand, looser scatters often form a linear spread, suggesting that there may have been some element of gradation when the beads were strung. Building on this idea, it may also be that these beads were manufactured at the same or a similar time, perhaps purposefully for use in necklaces.

Colour

One of the most interesting aspects of glass beads compared to other artefacts is that the colours of glass are vibrant and bold (colour terminology described in Appendix A). Other authors have already hinted at colour use on a regional basis. Guido (1978a, 79-84) emphasised the combination of colourless and yellow glass in Southwest England by naming two types of beads after Meare Lake Village (Class 10 and 11), as beads with this combination are found in large quantities there. Furthermore, Giles has suggested that the colour blue in East Yorkshire may have some meaning, as this is the dominant colour found at Wetwang Slack (Giles 2008a, 72; 2008b, 72). However, so far there has not been a Britain-wide quantification of glass bead colour for comparison. This section will first examine the general data for the four study regions as a whole, and then will specifically examine monochrome beads, polychrome beads, and finally the different uses of colour by region.

Many studies of colour depend on historic and modern linguistic data in order to understand how a population conceives of and internally structures the colours it sees, for example through the utilisation of Berlin and Kay's (1999) colour and language theory. As this is not feasible for the study of Iron Age Britain, it is necessary to use artefacts as a lexicon for understanding the way in which late prehistoric people understood colour during this period. Through such a study, we can attempt to answer a number of questions, including: issues surrounding the colours late prehistoric glass workers had access to, colour combinations, and the ways use varied by region. This is made more complicated, because some beads are monochrome and others are polychrome, leading to difficulties in assessing how frequent a colour is in each region. For example, a bead that has a blue body with eyes made by layering white and blue glass is made from two colours of glass, but there are three instances of colour. In addition, in some cases, such as wrapped beads, it is not possible to separate how the colour was used into categories, such as body colour and decorative colour. This is because the multiple colours used to form the bead are a part of the bead itself rather than being a separate element. Therefore, during these analyses, wrapped bead (Class 7 Type 1501) colours are all considered to be body colours. There are cases where wrapped beads also incorporate a cable element (Class 11 Types 2601-2605). In these cases, the colours used to create the cable are considered decorative, and the remaining colours are categorised as body colours.

Given the difficulties in providing a quantification of colour use in each region, only a very crude analysis can be provided. By counting instances of colour on the body or as part of the decoration, we can see some general trends emerge from the 1,788 beads for which colour data was available (Figure 59). Among all the study regions, blue is by far the most frequently found colour and accounts for nearly half of the data recorded. The next most frequently used colour is yellow, followed by white. Colourless and green beads are also numerous, but some colours, such as blue-green, brown orange, purple, red, and red-purple, are very infrequent. In terms of regional comparisons, while blue is found in all regions, it is particularly characteristic of East Yorkshire beads, along with the use of white (Figures 60a-b). Yellow is used mostly in Southwest England and in Northeast Scotland. Colours such as black, brown, green, orange, and red are found in small quantities in most or all regions, while blue-green, purple and red-purple are found exclusively in specific regions. Although this is perhaps a simple method for measuring differences in the usage of colour, it provides an overview of the variety and differences in colour between each of the study regions.

The following sections will specifically examine how colour is used on monochrome and polychrome beads. First, however, it is worth exploring the frequencies of the number of colours on each bead. By analysing the number of colours, it is also possible to explore some of the complexities within bead manufacture. Monochrome beads are by far the most frequent type (Figures 61a-b). This is true for Southwest England, East Yorkshire, and Northeast Scotland. Interestingly, despite a small sample size, most beads from East Anglia use two or more colours. As might be expected, there is a relationship between the number of colours and the size of the available samples; there are many examples of beads with one and two colours, and fewer examples with three and four colours. There are no known beads with more than four colours present.

Monochrome Beads

Many simple beads are made using only one colour of glass (e.g. Figure 189a-ae). This means that any variability is tied to their size and shape. Although most tend to be annular or globular in shape, this is not always

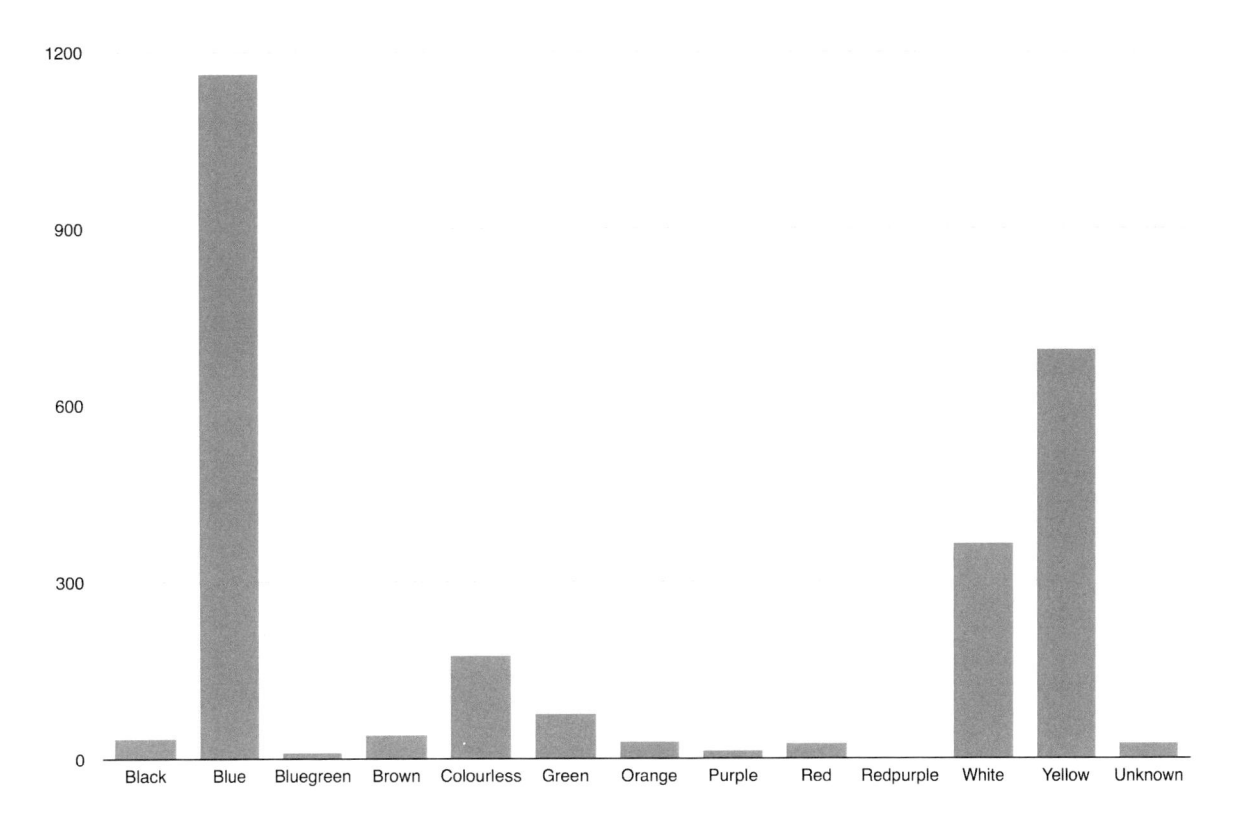

Figure 59: Bar-chart comparing the frequency of colour occurrence in all four study regions.

the case. Out of the 1,788 beads with available colour data, 64% are monochrome; of these, the majority are either blue or yellow (Figure 62). Other colours that occur are green and orange, but these appear in much lower quantities. However, there are differences seen between the regions (Figures 63a-b). For example, blue beads are found in large numbers in East Yorkshire, while a much smaller number is found in Southwest England. Yellow beads are also found in the Southwest region, but are found more frequently in Northeast Scotland. This suggests that there may have been regional preferences for monochrome beads, or that there was variable access to raw materials if they were manufactured in Britain.

Polychrome Beads

Polychrome beads are much more complex than monochrome beads. This is due to a number of factors. Firstly, numerous colour combinations have been recorded. As noted above, in the case of the four regions under study, beads used between two and four colours. Second, in many cases, some colours comprise the main part of the bead, or the 'body', while other colours are used in the decorative motifs. Therefore, this section will provide three analyses:

1. A general colour combination analysis for beads from each study region. This will examine colour use regardless of how it is employed on each bead;
2. A more specific analysis of polychrome beads, which examines the colour(s) used on the body of the bead and the colour(s) used as decorative colour within each region. In this case body colours and decorative colours are analysed separately;
3. A very detailed analysis of the colour combinations, which specifically examines the combinations of body colour(s) and decorative colour(s) together from a regional perspective.

Colour combinations

The simplest form of analysis of polychrome beads is an examination of the different colours that are combined, regardless of how they are used. Glass beads that incorporate two colours (bi-colour) are the most frequent type of polychrome bead (e.g. Figure 190a). Southwest England and Northeast Scotland have the largest number of colour combinations, with 11 and 13 different arrangements respectively. In Southwest England, colourless-yellow beads are found in large numbers; however, there is also a substantial number of blue-white beads (Figure 64). Other combinations which are much less frequent include blue-yellow, colourless-red, and green-yellow. Some combinations are unique and only occur once, such as black-white, blue-green, and red-white. Most colour combinations include yellow or white in some way, although it may be significant there have been no examples of yellow and white combined on the same bead.

Similar to those from Southwest England, beads from the East Anglia are also often blue-white or colourless-

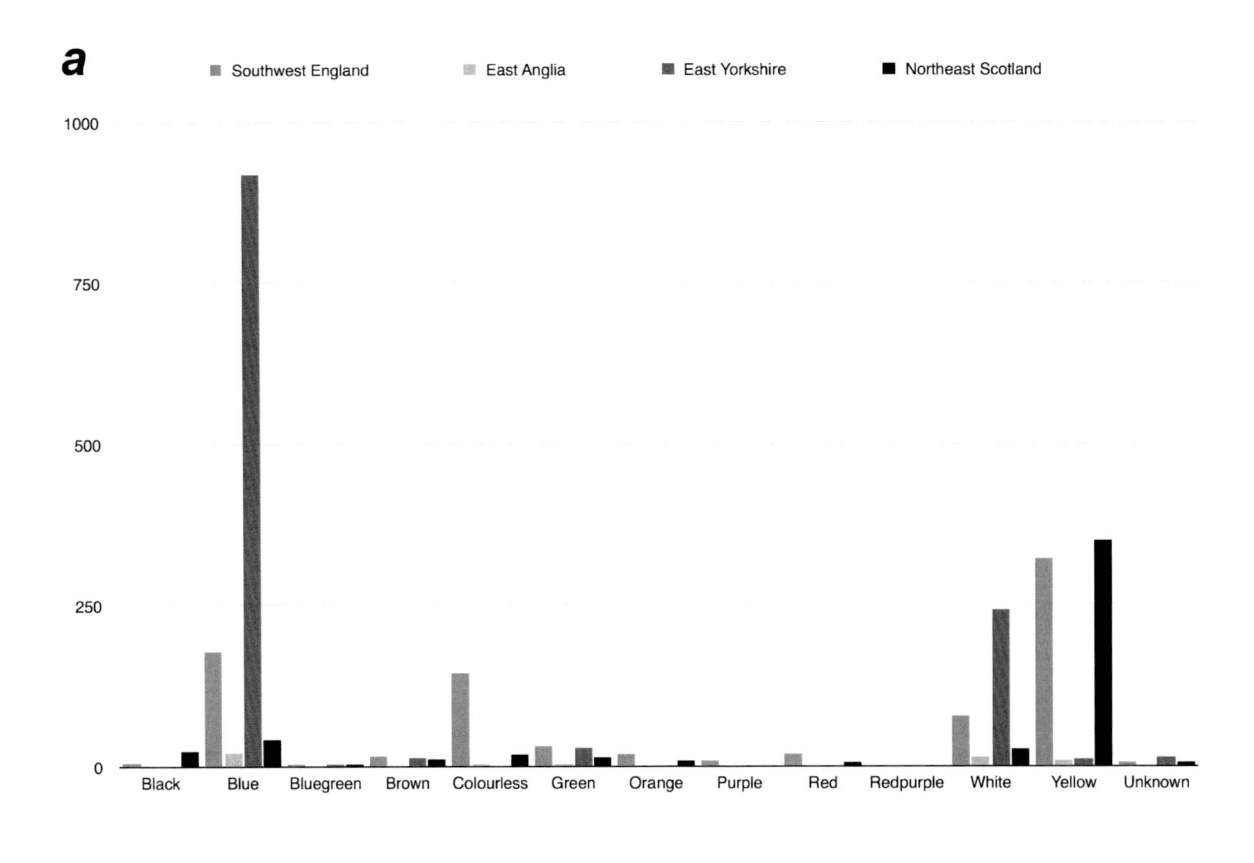

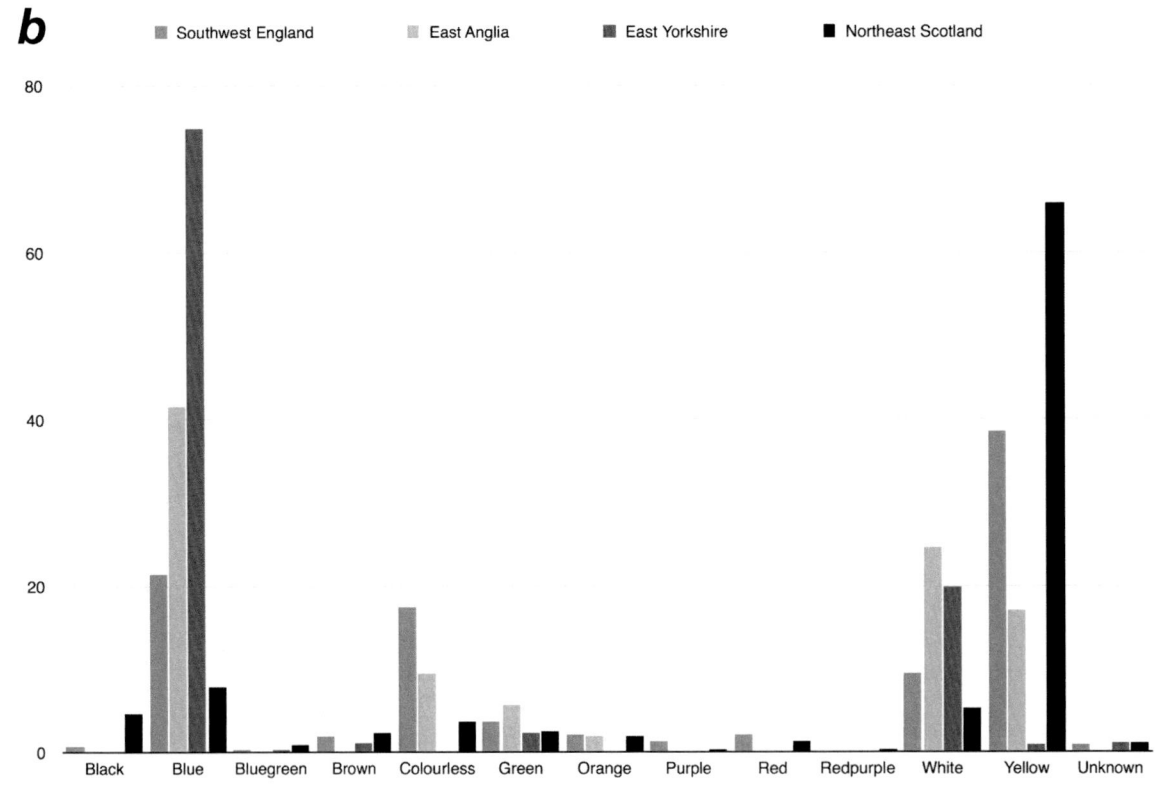

Figure 60: Bar-chart comparing the (a) frequency, and (b) percentage of colour occurrence in the four study regions.

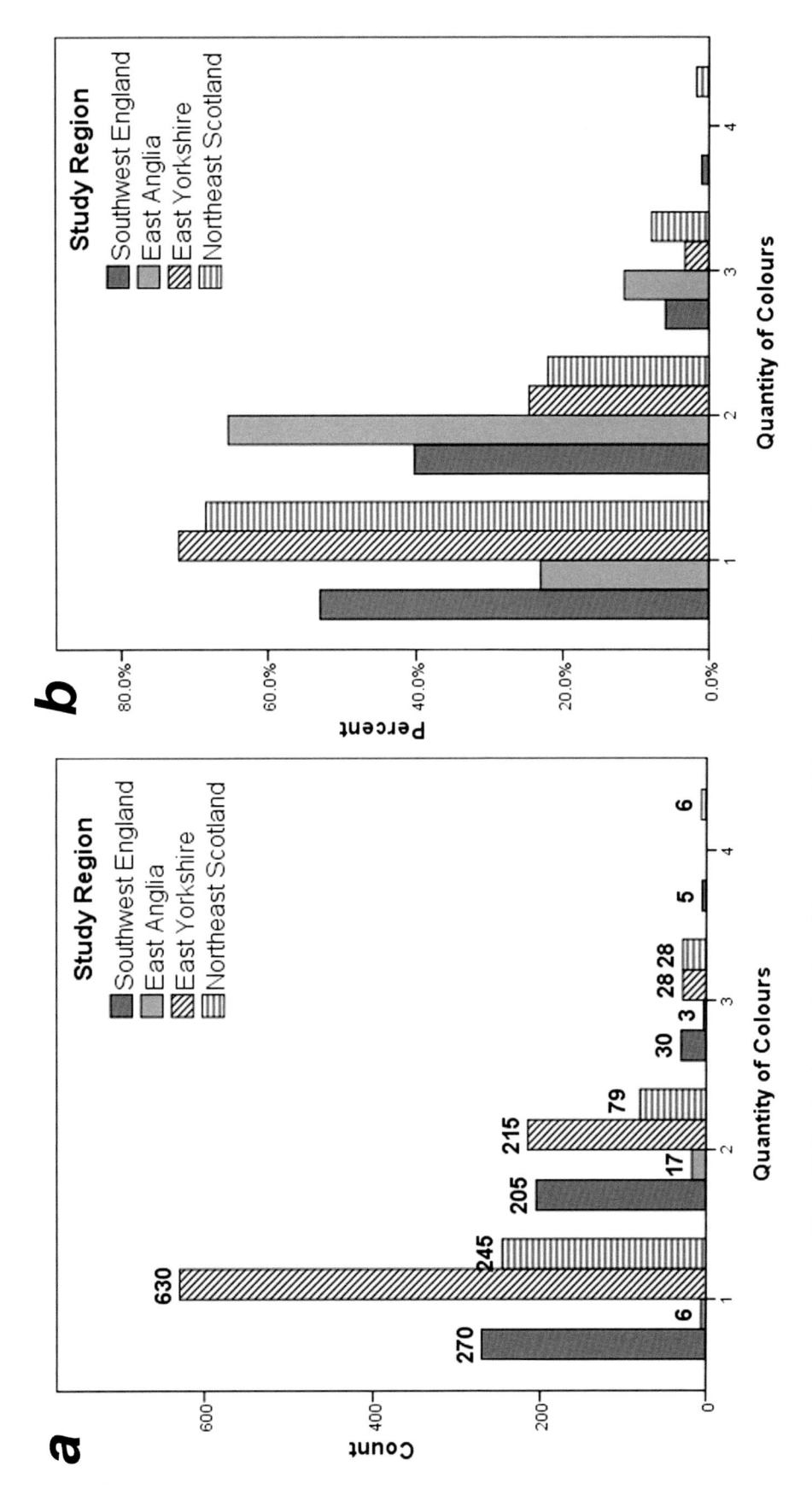

Figure 61: Bar-chart comparing the (a) frequency, and (b) percentage of colours on each bead between study regions.

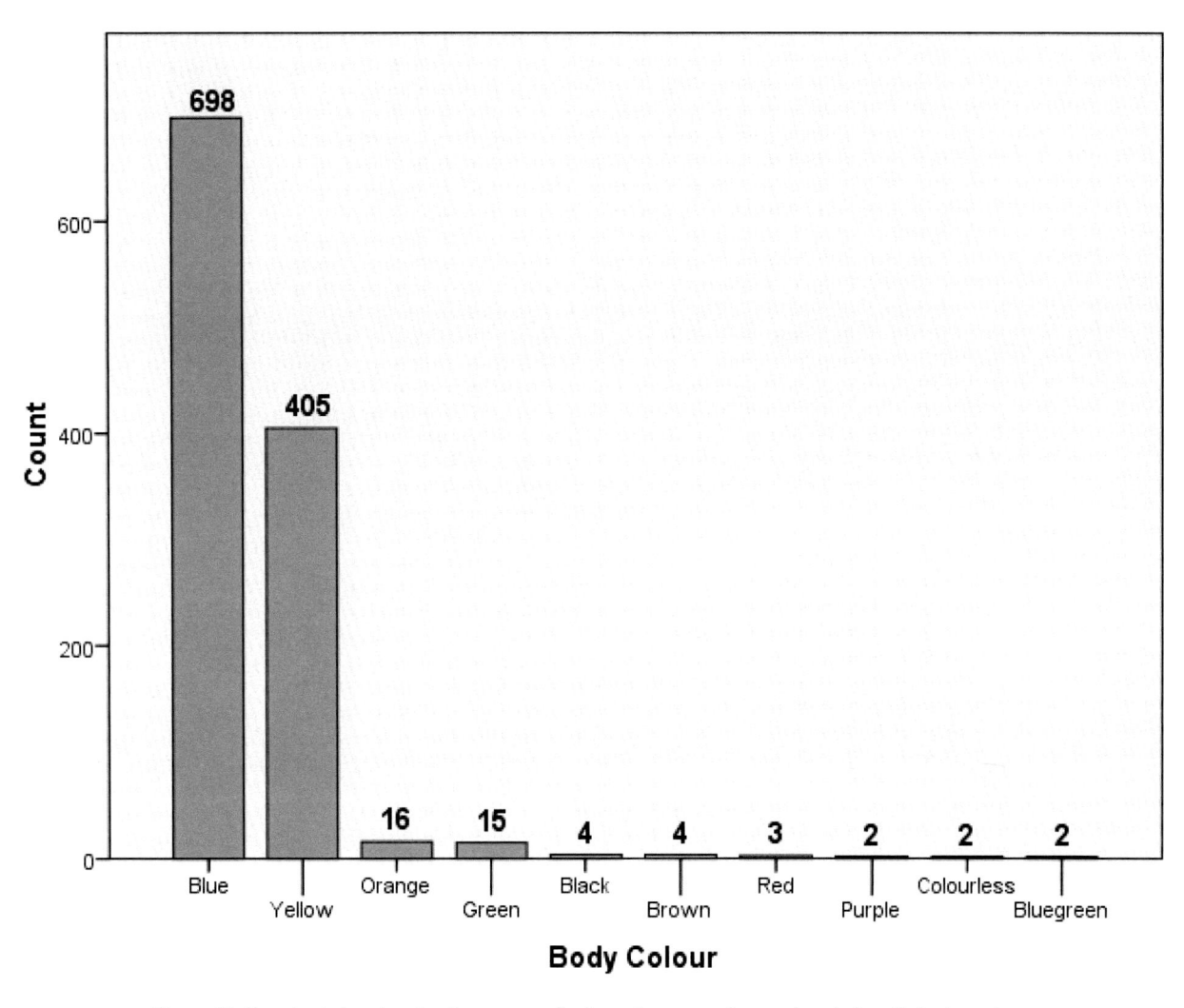

Figure 62: Bar-chart showing the frequency of colours for monochrome beads for all study regions.

yellow, but there are far fewer combinations and they are found in much smaller quantities (Figure 65). In this study region, blue-colourless, blue-yellow, and white-yellow are unique finds. Again, all beads incorporate yellow, and there is only one bead that does not. As with most aspects of East Yorkshire beads, there is very little variability in colour (Figure 66). The majority of these beads are blue-white, but there are also a small number of green-white beads. All of these beads incorporate either white or yellow, although interestingly yellow does not occur as frequently in this region. Finally, the beads from Northeast Scotland are highly variable in terms of their colour (Figure 67). Again, every bead uses either yellow or white glass, but predominately yellow glass. In addition, yellow and white do occur on the same bead together. The most frequently occurring combination is blue-yellow, followed by black-yellow, and colourless-yellow. Other combinations also occur, including four instances of unique combinations such as red-yellow, white-yellow, and brown-white.

Some of these combinations of bi-colour beads are unique to their study region and are not found elsewhere. For example, the 13 beads made from green-white glass, or the single example of blue-colourless or blue-green glass from Southwest England (Figure 68). Other combinations are frequent in all study regions, the most obvious being blue-white and colourless-yellow. Almost all of these beads incorporate either yellow or white glass, and the exceptions nearly always have blue glass in them. A study of the frequency of individual colours shows that blue and white are frequent colours in each study region (Figure 69). Colourless glass occurs most frequently in Southwest England, but makes up a large proportion of bead finds in East Anglia. Yellow is frequently found in Southwest England and in Northeast Scotland, and proportionately in East Anglia, but not in East Yorkshire. It is clear, from a bi-colour analsysis that blue and white occur as an important combination in beads from all study regions. Colours such as colourless and yellow are frequent in all but East Yorkshire. Other colours play minor roles in all regions.

There are fewer beads with three colours (tri-colour) of glass (e.g. Figure 190h). Southwest England and Northeast Scotland have the largest number of tri-colour

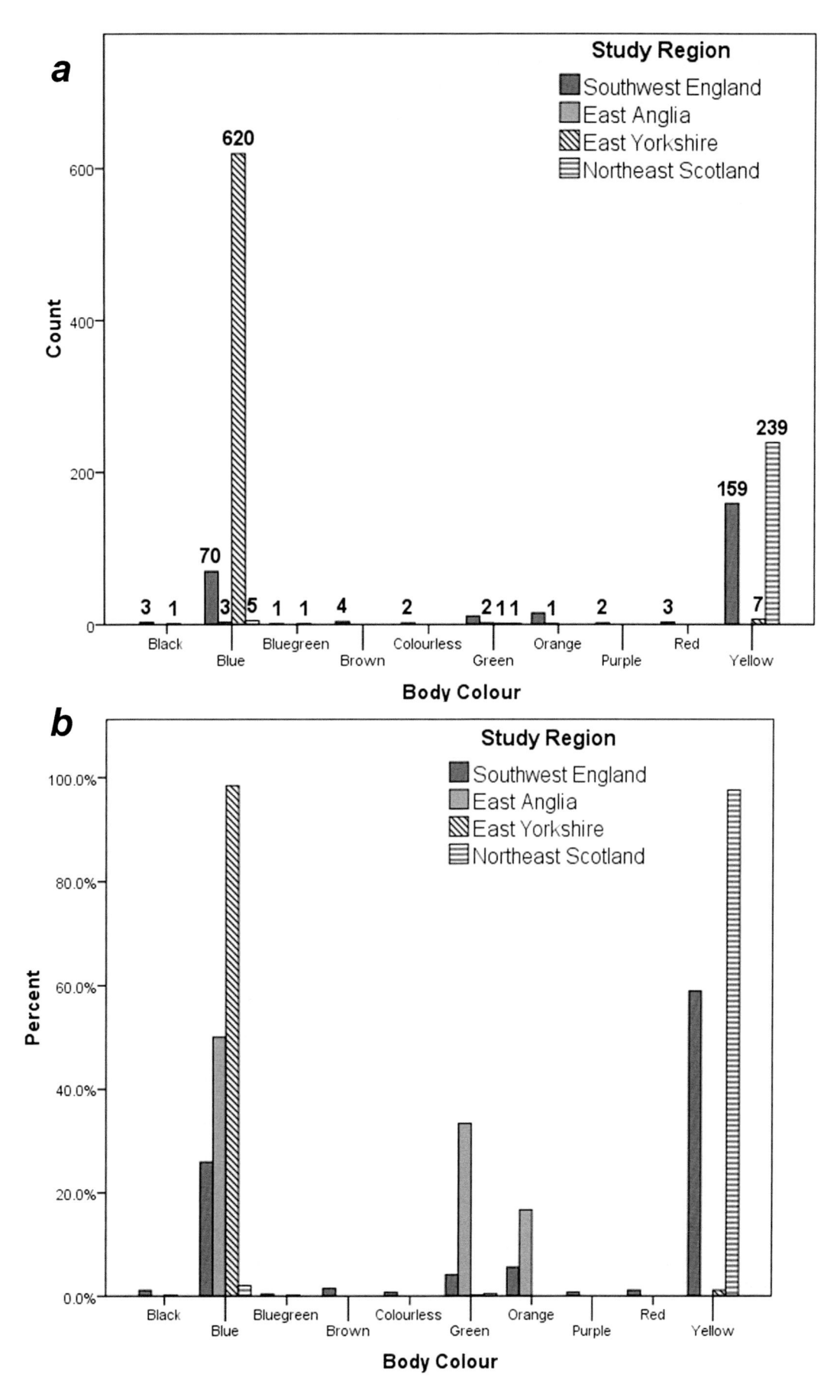

Figure 63: Bar-chart comparing the (a) frequency, and (b) percentage of monochrome beads that occur in each study region.

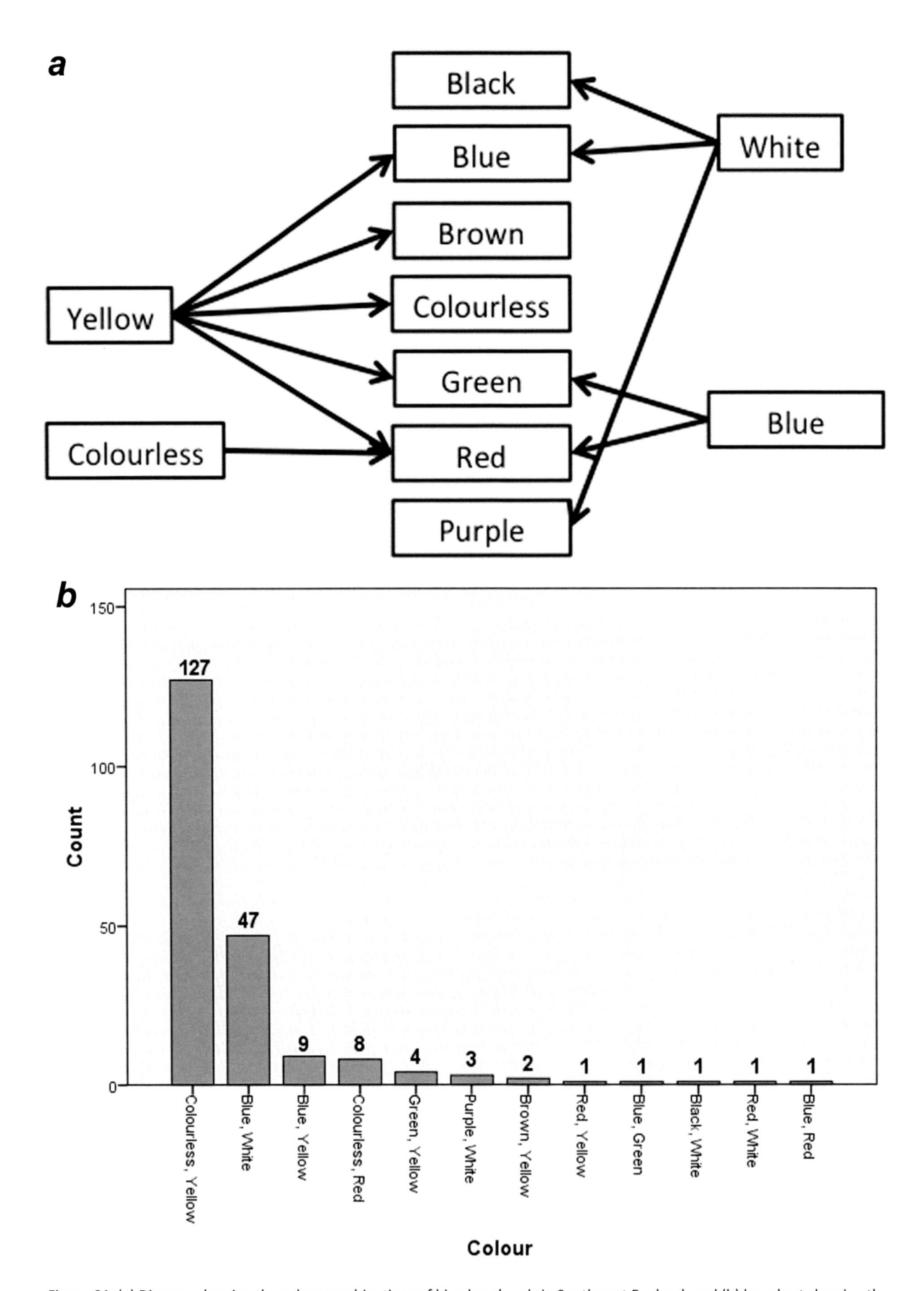

Figure 64: (a) Diagram showing the colour combinations of bi-colour beads in Southwest England, and (b) bar-chart showing the frequency of bi-colour combinations in Southwest England.

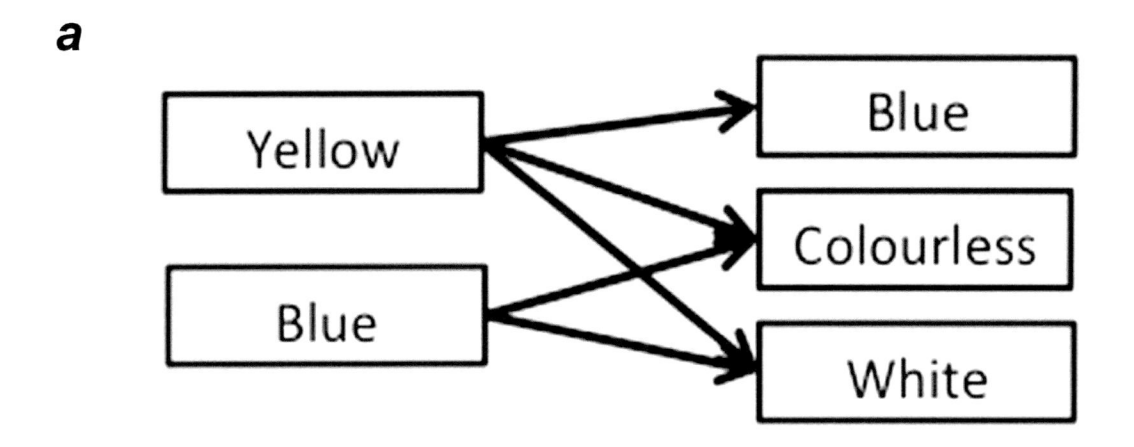

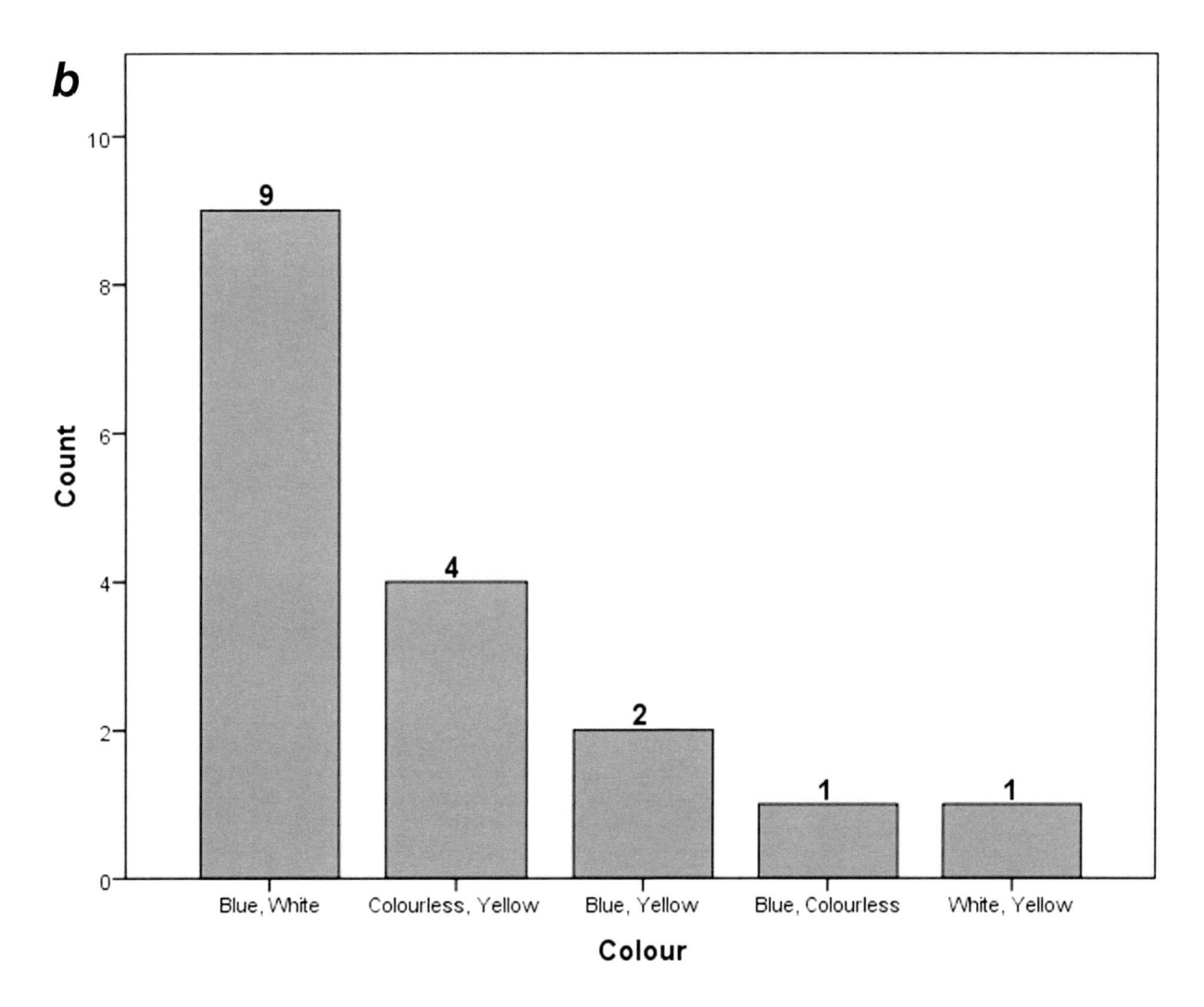

Figure 65: (a) Diagram showing the colour combinations of bi-colour beads in East Anglia, and (b) bar-chart showing the freuquency of bi-colour combinations in East Anglia.

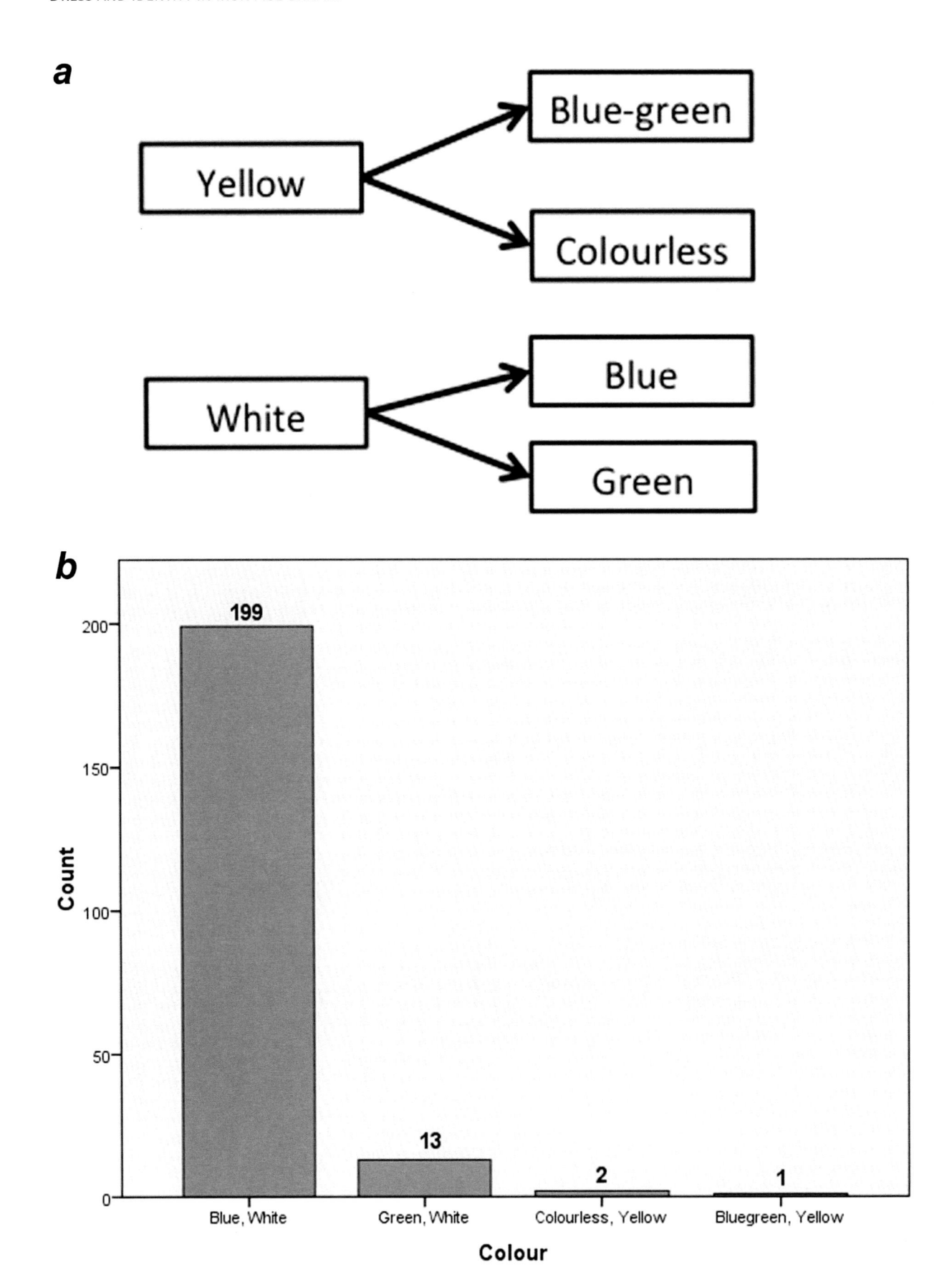

Figure 66: (a) Diagram showing the colour combinations of bi-colour beads in East Yorkshire, (b) bar-chart showing the frequency of bi-colour glass beads in East Yorkshire.

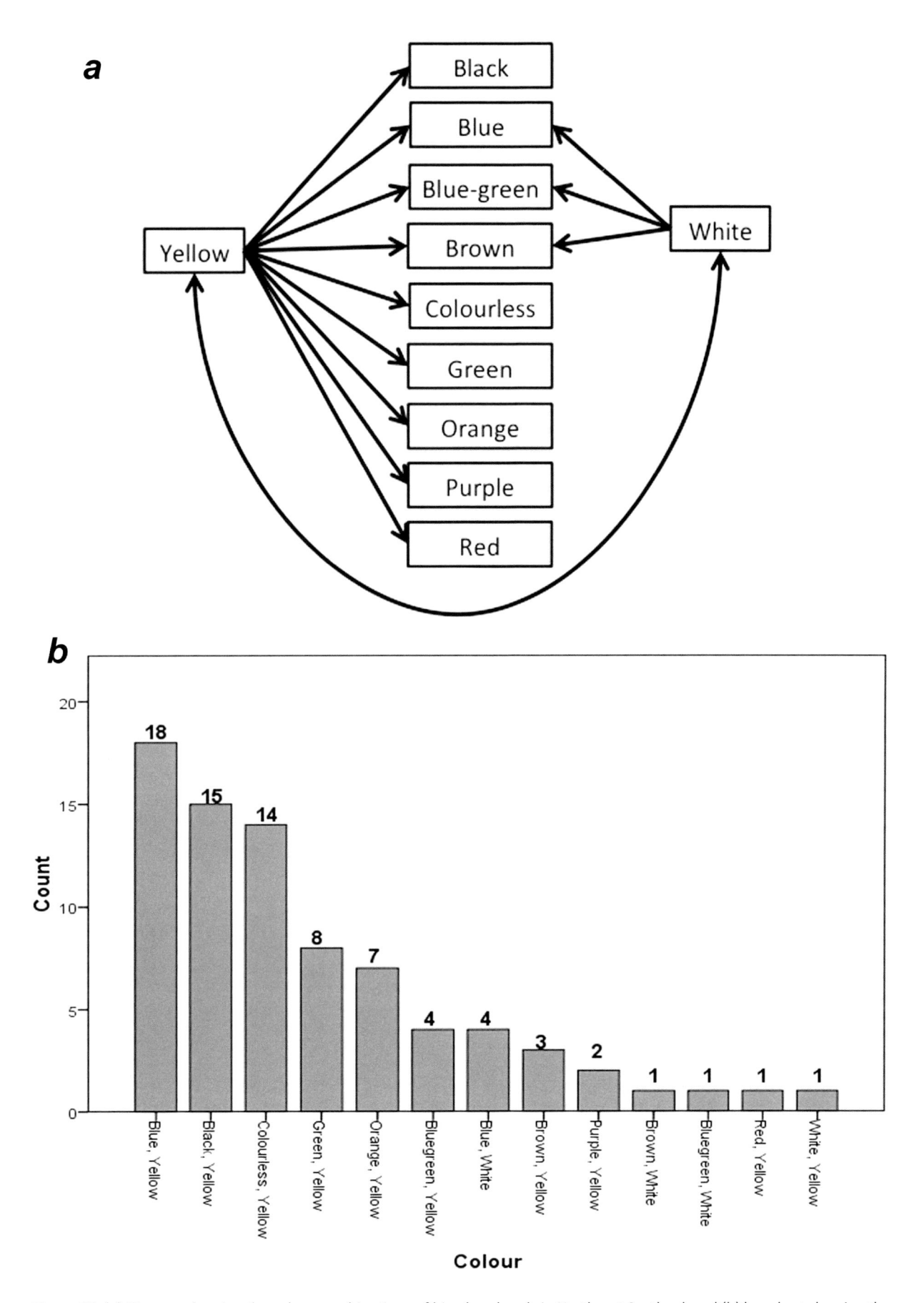

Figure 67: (a) Diagram showing the colour combinations of bi-colour beads in Northeast Scotland, and (b) bar-chart showing the frequency of bi-colour combinations from Northeast Scotland.

combinations (16 and 18 respectively). In Southwest England, the most frequently found colour combinations are blue-brown-white and blue-green-white (Figure 70). Other combinations occur, and there are 10 different combinations that are unique to the region. Every combination includes yellow, white or both. The other dominant colours are blue and green. Beads from East Anglia with three colours are more limited and include one white-blue-green, and two white-blue-yellow beads (Figure 71). Although there are very few examples of glass beads from this region, most are either monochrome or polychrome with two colours, as three colour beads are very infrequent and there are no East Anglian examples with four colours of glass. Again, East Yorkshire presents a rather conservative picture, with only three combinations of tri-colour beads (Figure 72). They are white-blue-brown, white-blue-green, or white-bluegreen-brown.[9] In all cases, white and blueish glass was combined with a third colour: either brown or green. The white-blue-green combination occurs most frequently, but white-blue-brown was also found. There was only one example of the white-bluegreen-brown bead. Finally, most of the large number of colour combinations from Northeast Scotland (Figure 73) are unique in the region and not found elsewhere. Combinations such as white-yellow-green and white-yellow-black occur most frequently, although there are a few examples of five other combinations. Similar to the other beads, white and yellow are prominent members of these colour combinations.

Overall, it is the blue-brown-white and blue-green-white combinations that are found most frequently (Figure 74). Most colour combinations are unique, even inter-regionally. In terms of individual colour frequency, blue, green, and white occur in all four regions and proportionately frequently (Figure 75). Yellow also occurs frequently, but as with the bi-colour combinations it does not occur in East Yorkshire. Interestingly, some colours that are not dominant in bi-colour combinations are more frequent in tri-colour ones; brown, green, and (in some regions) black and red. In addition, the use of colourless glass dramatically declines in tri-colour combinations.

Finally, there are 11 beads with four colours of glass. Five of these examples were found in Southwest England (Figures 76), and six in Northeast Scotland (Figure 77). In each case there is only one bead displaying these characteristics, making each bead unique. As with most other colour combinations, white and yellow are common. In the case of the Northeast Scotland beads they occur together, but do not in the Southwest England beads. Overall, as was seen in the other combinations,

2 Colour Combination	Southwest England	East Anglia	East Yorkshire	Northeast Scotland	TOTAL
Black, White	1	-	-	-	1
Black, Yellow	-	-	-	15	15
Blue, Colourless	1	-	-	-	1
Blue, Green	1	-	-	-	1
Blue, Red	1	-	-	-	1
Blue, White	47	9	199	4	259
Blue, Yellow	9	2	-	18	29
Bluegreen, White	-	-	-	1	1
Bluegreen, Yellow	-	-	1	4	5
Brown, White	-	-	-	1	1
Brown, Yellow	2	-	-	3	5
Colourless, Red	8	-	-	-	8
Colourless, Yellow	128	4	2	14	148
Green, White	-	-	13	-	13
Green, Yellow	4	-	-	8	12
Orange, Yellow	-	-	-	2	2
Purple, White	3	-	-	-	3
Purple, Yellow	-	-	-	2	2
Red, White	1	-	-	-	1
Red, Yellow	1	-	-	1	2
White, Yellow	-	1	-	1	2
TOTAL	207	16	215	74	512

Figure 68: List of colour combinations used on glass beads made from two colours of glass and the frequency in each study region.

the colours blue, white and yellow appear most frequently on four-colour beads (Figure 78). There are three occurrences of green, and the remaining colours only appear once or twice.

Body Colour and Decorative Colour

The above analysis specifically investigates the combinations of colours utilised on glass beads and explores the frequency of individual colours. It does not specifically examine how the colours were implemented on the beads. Most beads have a linear design, meaning that the body of the bead is formed out of one colour of glass, and the design is formed out of another colour of glass – often contrasting (Figure 191). The following analysis will examine the differences in the ways colour was used on beads within the study regions and compare use between the regions. It will also necessarily incorporate some of the colour combination data used in the previous section, as it sometimes happens that glass beads have multiple body colours or contain more than one colour within their decoration.

Overall, there are only a few colours used frequently for the body of polychrome beads. Of these, blue and

---
[9] Visual analysis of blue and bluegreen suggested that the difference between the two colours was significant enough to use different colour categories here.

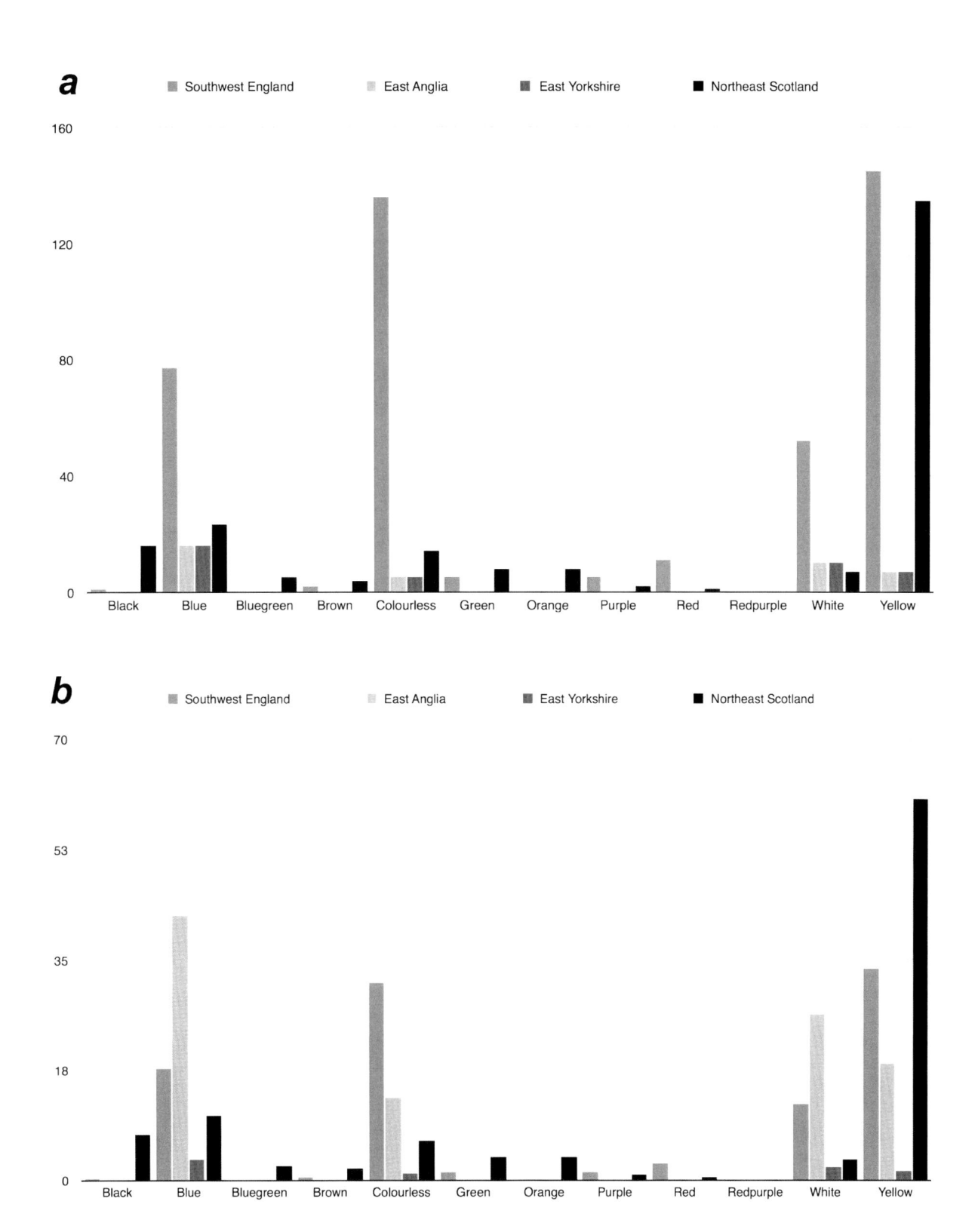

Figure 69: Bar-chart showing the (a) frequency, and (b) percentage, of individual colours for polychrome beads with two colours in all four study regions.

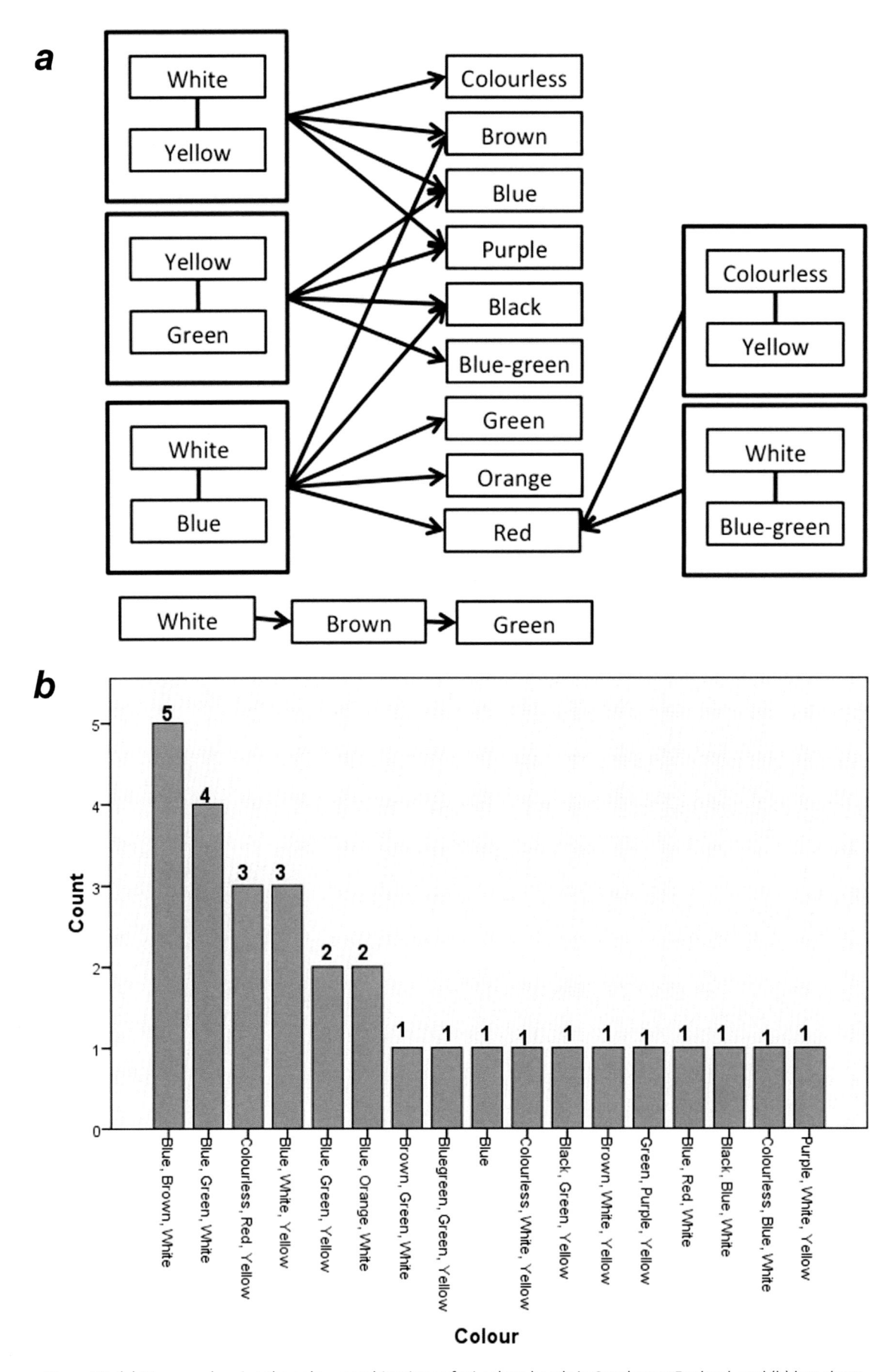

Figure 70: (a) Diagram showing the colour combinations of tri-colour beads in Southwest England, and (b) bar-chart showing the frequency of tri-colour glass beads in Southwest England.

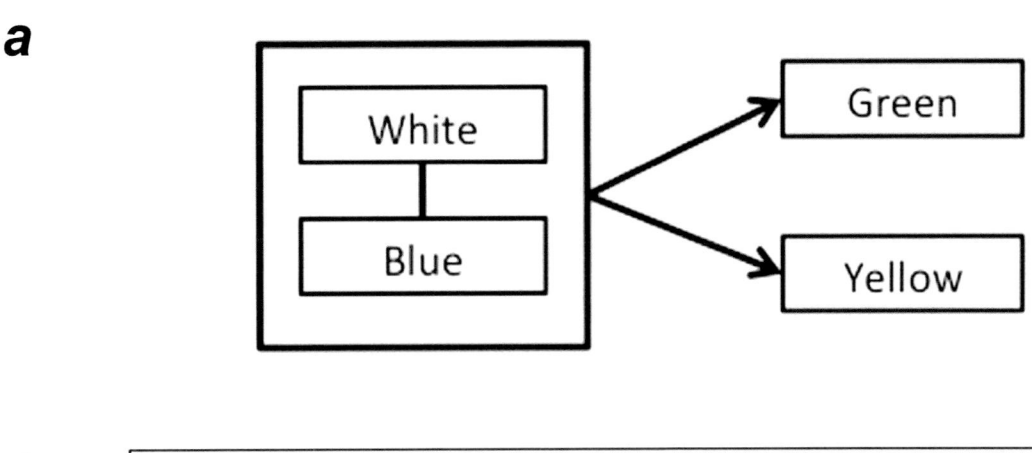

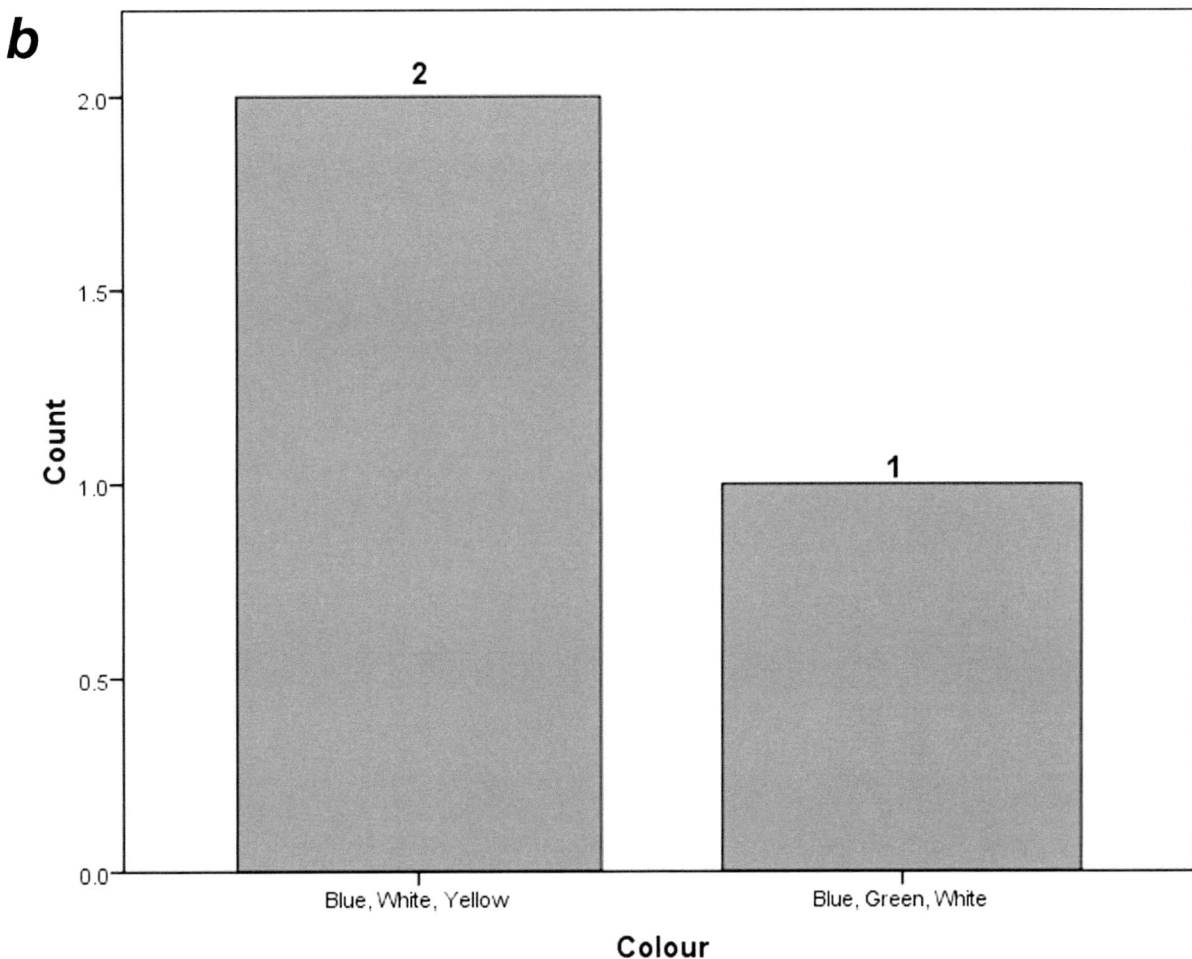

Figure 71: (a) Diagram showing the colour combinations of tri-colour beads in East Anglia, and (b) bar-chart showing the frequency of tri-coloured glass beads from East Anglia.

colourless appear to be the most abundant based on an examination of regional assemblages (Figure 79a). In this analysis, blue-bodied beads account for 53% of the beads under study, while colourless-bodied beads account for 27% of beads under study. Other colours, such as green, black, and brown are found occasionally and account for 7.3%, 3.9%, and 3.7% respectively of the studied assemblage. There are a number of colours that are rarely found, including purple, orange, yellow, and white. Unsurprisingly, the colours most frequently used as decorative elements on glass beads are yellow (37.1%), followed by white (30.5%) and a combination of blue and white glass (19.8%) (Figure 79b). As with bead bodies, there are several other decorative colours

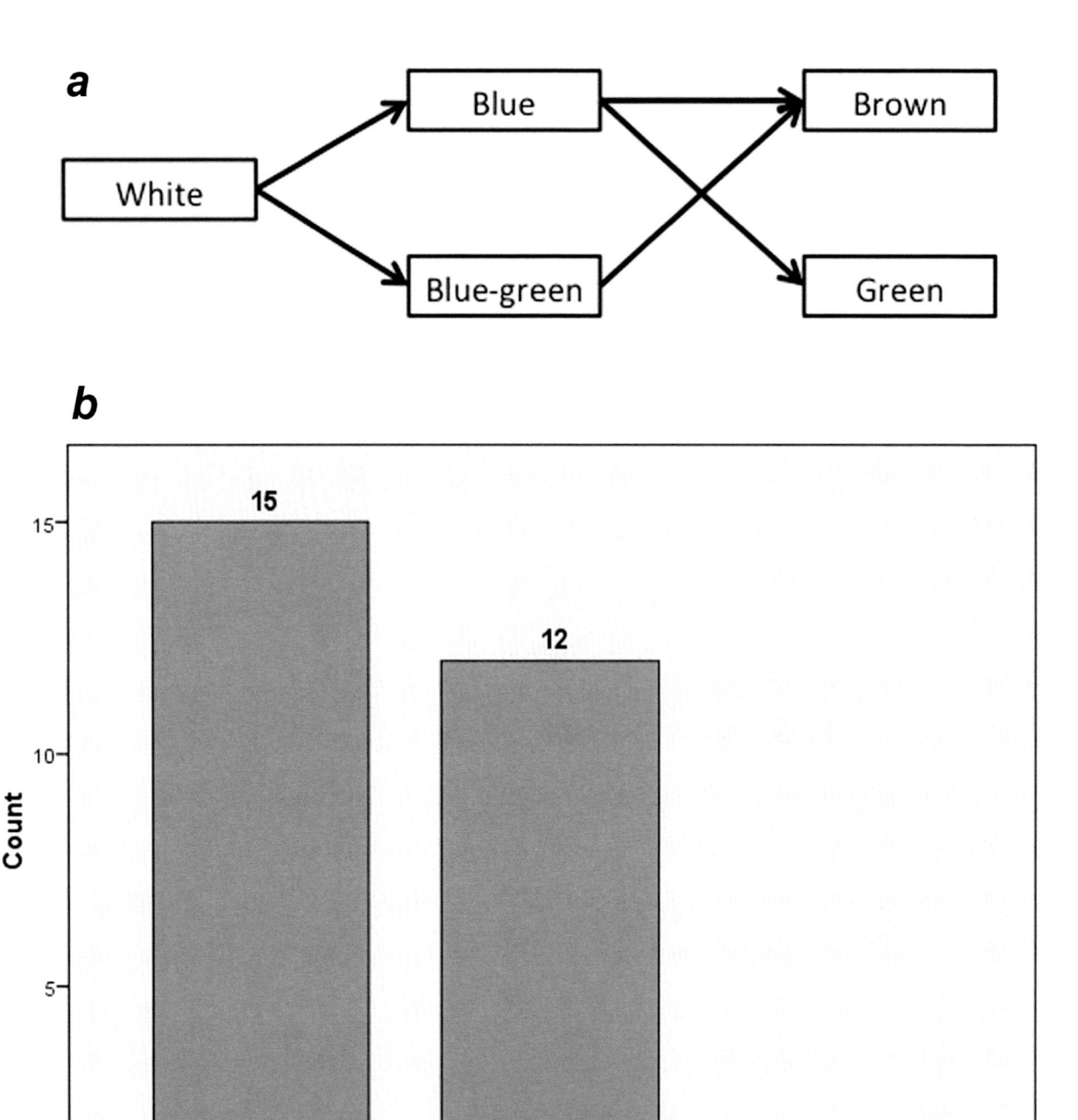

Figure 72: (a) Diagram showing the colour combinations of tri-colour beads in East Yorkshire, and (b) bar-chart showing the frequency of tri-coloured glass beads from East Yorkshire.

used, most of which are rarely found more than once. However, decorative colours, such as a green-white and brown-white combinations, occur several times.

The above assessment provides a very general view of glass beads from Britain as a data set for the regions selected for study. While there are dominant trends seen on a wider scale, it is also possible to examine the study regions independently in order to determine whether there are regional trends in the use of both body colour and decorative colour. This was done by creating bar charts that show the frequency of each colour in each study region for both body colour and decorative colour. This next section will explore the use of body colour between regions and then decorative colour.

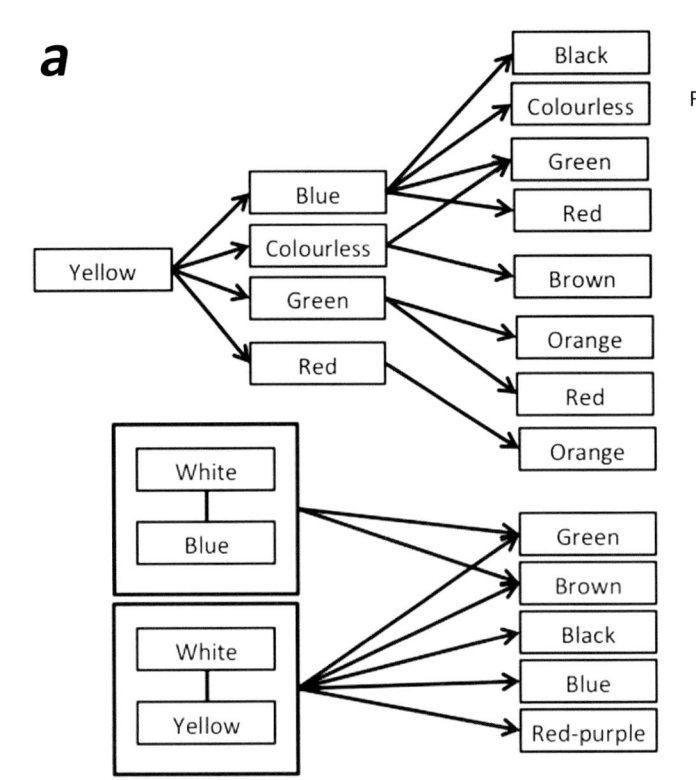

Figure 73: (a) Diagram showing the colour combinations of tri-colour beads in Northeast Scotland.

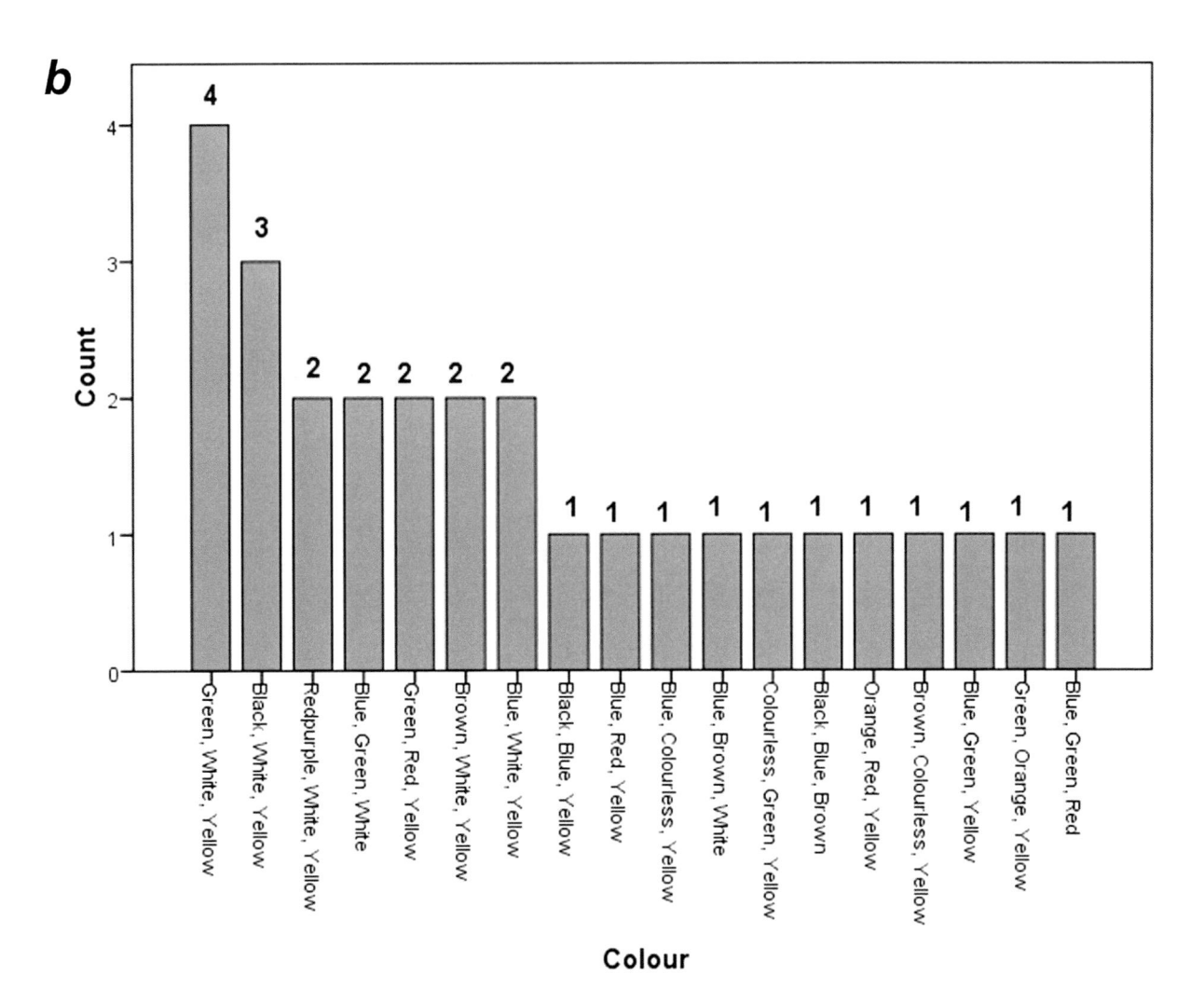

Figure 73: (b) Bar-chart showing the frequency of tri-coloured glass beads in Northeast Scotland.

3 Colour Combination	Southwest England	East Anglia	East Yorkshire	Northeast Scotland	TOTAL
Black, Blue, Brown	-	-	-	1	1
Black, Blue, White	1	-	-	-	1
Black, Blue, Yellow	-	-	-	1	1
Black, Green, Yellow	1	-	-	-	1
Black, White, Yellow	-	-	-	3	3
Blue, Brown, White	5	-	12	1	18
Blue, Colourless, Yellow	-	-	-	1	1
Blue, Green, Red	-	-	-	1	1
Blue, Green, White	4	1	15	2	22
Blue, Green, Yellow	2	-	-	1	3
Blue, Orange, White	2	-	-	-	2
Blue, Red, White	1	-	-	-	1
Blue, Red, Yellow	-	-	-	1	1
Blue, White, Yellow	3	2	-	2	7
Bluegreen, Brown, White	-	-	1	-	1
Bluegreen, Green, Yellow	1	-	-	-	1
Bluegreen, Red, White	1	-	-	-	1
Brown, Colourless, Yellow	-	-	-	1	1
Brown, Green, White	1	-	-	-	1
Brown White, Yellow	1	-	-	2	3
Colourless, Green, Yellow	-	-	-	1	1
Colourless, Red, Yellow	3	-	-	-	3
Colourless, White, Yellow	1	-	-	-	1
Green, Orange, Yellow	-	-	-	1	1
Green, Purple, Yellow	1	-	-	-	1
Green, Red, Yellow	-	-	-	2	2
Green, White, Yellow	-	-	-	4	4
Orange, Red, Yellow	-	-	-	1	1
Purple, White, Yellow	1	-	-	-	1
Redpurple, White, Yellow	-	-	-	2	2
TOTAL	29	3	28	28	88

Figure 74: List of colour combinations for glass beads with three colours of glass and the frequency in each study region.

The dominance of blue and colourless glass used in the body of beads can be seen in most regions; indeed in Southwest England this is the main trend (Figure 80a), where these colours were used in the majority of beads. Other colours, such as green and a colourless-red combination, occur less frequently. Despite a small sample size, blue and colourless glass are also the most frequent colours in East Anglia, although in this area blue beads are more numerous than colourless beads (Figure 80b). In East Yorkshire, however, the body of beads are most frequently blue rather than any other colour (Figure 80c). Other colours, such as brown and green beads, are less frequent than blue beads, while bluegreen and colourless beads are the least frequent. Finally, beads in Northeast Scotland have the largest range of different colours and colour combinations in the bodies of the beads (Figure 80d). While blue and colourless glasses play a major role in the assemblage of polychrome beads, other colours, such as black, green, and orange, are also frequent. However, there are many colour combinations that are unique to this region, such as blue-brown and green-red.

Although the general view (outlined above) of the combined data suggests that blue and colourless glasses are most frequent, this analysis shows that it differs by region (Figure 81). While blue-bodied beads are found in frequent numbers in all study regions (most notably in East Yorkshire), colourless beads are most frequent in Southwest England. In addition, colourless glass has a minor presence in East Yorkshire, where only two colourless glass beads have been found. Moreover, while it is easy to point out the high frequency of blue and colourless glass, green beads also occur in all study regions, although in much smaller numbers, while black and brown glass is found in three out of four study regions. Finally, where multiple colours are combined for the body of the beads, they are unique to the different regions, possibly suggesting the reuse of available glass or use of scraps.

Turning now to the use of decorative colour, the general analysis above suggests a high frequency in the use of yellow, white, and a blue-white combination. This trend is well illustrated in Southwest England (Figure 82a). Yellow is by far the most frequent colour used as a decorative element, followed by white and the blue-white decorative combination. Other colours and colour combinations are very infrequent, chiefly those combining three different colours. This trend is also found in East Anglia where yellow is also most frequent, and where white and the blue-white combination are also found in relatively large numbers (Figure 82b). The other decorative colours differ little from the dominant colours, such as the use of blue by itself or a combination of white and yellow glass. Yellow glass, however, has very little presence in East Yorkshire; instead the colour white and the blue-white combination are the most

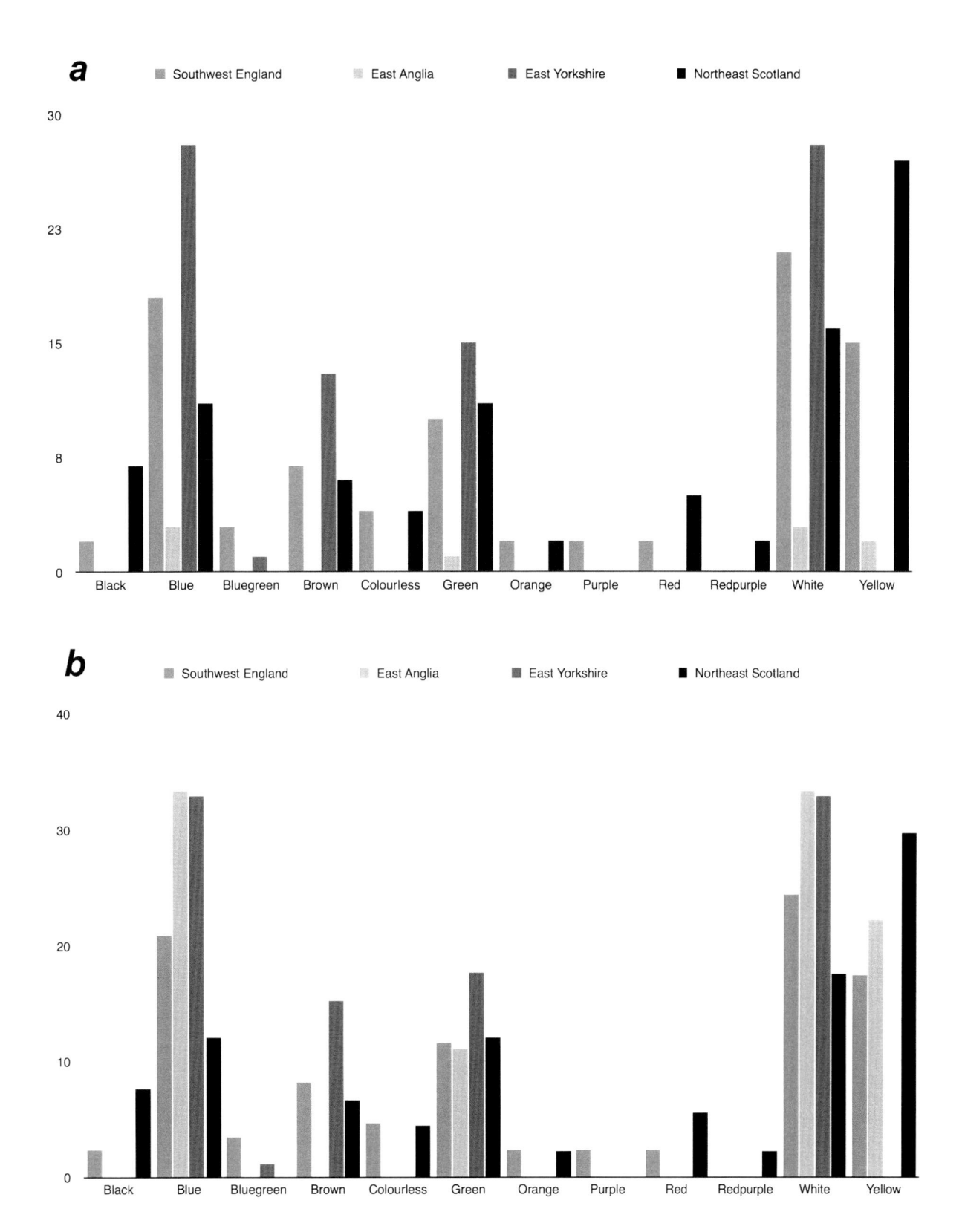

Figure 75: Bar-chart showing the (a) frequency, and (b) percentage, of individual colours for polychrome beads with three colours in all four study regions.

DRESS AND IDENTITY IN IRON AGE BRITAIN

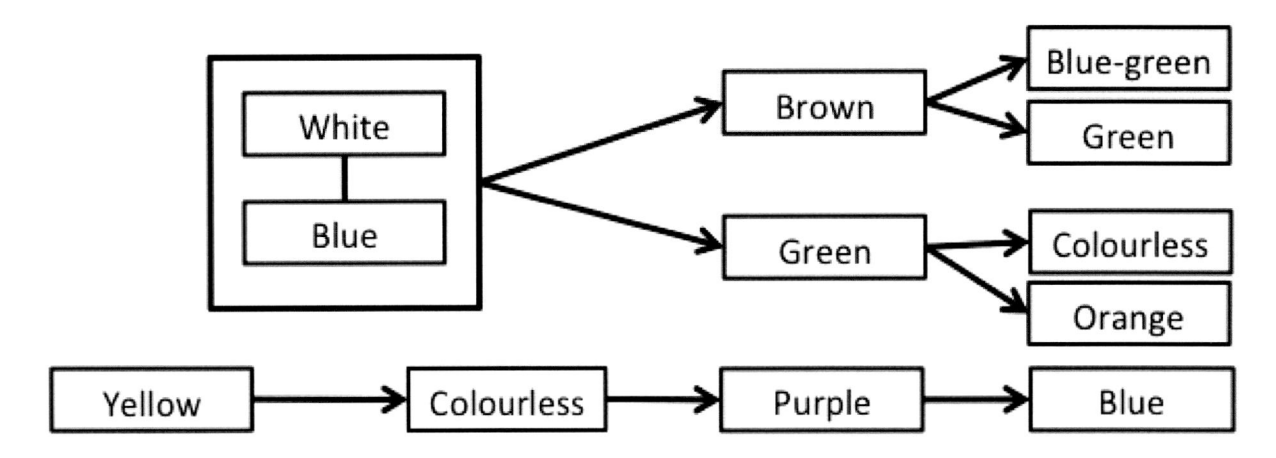

Figure 76: Diagram showing the combinations of four colours found on glass beads in Southwest England.

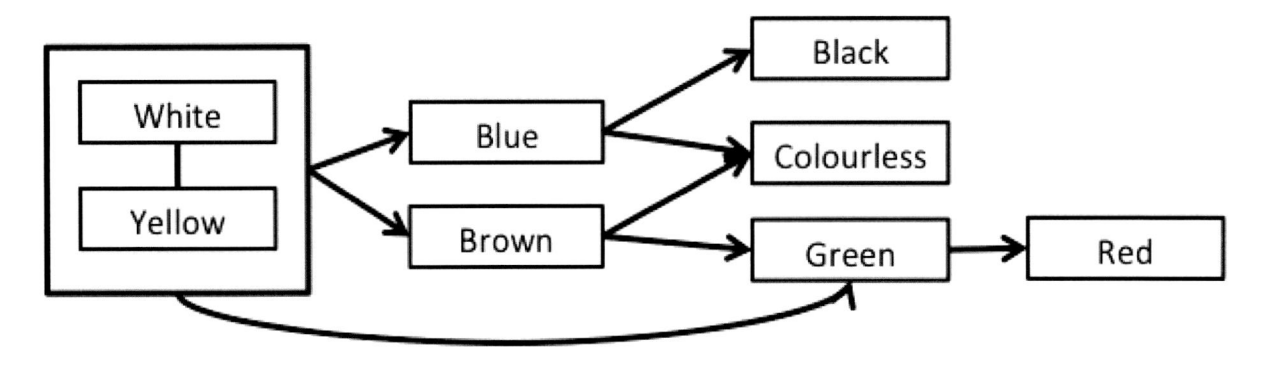

Figure 77: Diagram showing the colour combinations of four colours beads in Northeast Scotland.

frequent (Figure 82c). A green-white combination also occurs, but most combinations, such as blue-green-white and brown-white, are very infrequent. Finally, Northeast Scotland again has the highest variety of colours and colour combinations used for decorative elements (Figure 82d). Yellow is by far the most frequent colour used there and even white and the blue-white combination are comparatively rare. Again, for this region, most other colours and combinations are unique or only share similarities with a few other examples. As is also true for bead body colour, although most regions follow the general trend explored above, there is a certain amount of regional variability in the use of decorative colour (Figure 83). For instance, white and the blue-white colour combination are frequent in all study regions except for Northeast Scotland, and yellow does not play a large role in the decorative colour used in East Anglia. Other colours used for decoration are found less frequently, but occur in most study regions; the use of a brown-white or green-white colour combination, for example.

Body and Decorative Colour Combinations

The final method used to examine bead body and decorative colour is a more specific investigation of the ways different colours are combined. The previous section on colour combination took a general approach to exploring this; however, this section will explore how colour was used. This analysis was carried out by creating a list of all beads according to their body colour or colours and the colour or colours used as decoration; bar charts were then generated which display the frequency of each combination of both body and decorative colour. These calculations resulted in charts (Figures 84a-i) showing 85 different combinations of polychrome beads, including 12 polychrome combinations of colours without an applied linear motif (Figure 84j). These charts show that there are two combinations that are equally frequent (n=129 in both cases); beads that have a blue body and white decoration, found predominantly in East Yorkshire; and beads with a colourless body and yellow decoration, which are found predominantly in Southwest England. Another frequently occuring use of colour is a blue bead body with a combination of blue and white decoration; these are also found predominantly in East Yorkshire (n=72). Most other combinations of colour are comparatively infrequent, rare, or unique to a specific region. This is true for several specimens in East Yorkshire such as, beads with a green body and white decoration (n=13) or beads with an orange body and yellow decoration from Northeast Scotland (n=6).

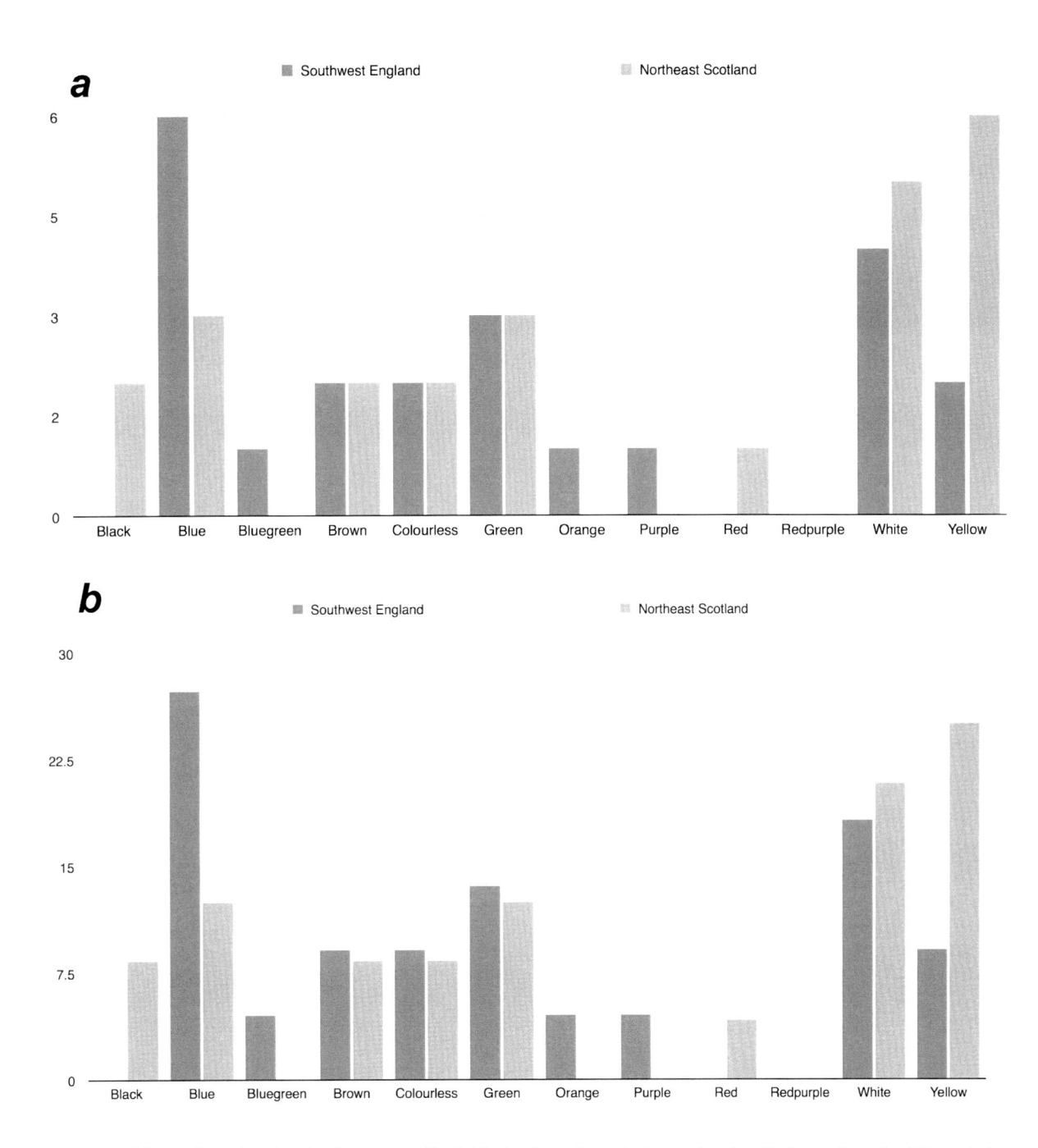

Figure 78: (a) Bar-chart showing the frequency of individual colours for polychrome beads with four colours in all four study regions, and (b) bar-chart showing the percentage of individual colours for polychrome beads with four colours in all four study regions.

Discussion

As suggested by the above analysis of decorative colour, the majority of the combinations studied have either yellow or white glass as the decorative colour. Another interesting result of this analysis is that, out of the 85 different combinations of body colour and decorative colour, there are only six that do not use either white or yellow glass. It may be that white and yellow glass was used as a contrasting colour to make the bead's design stand out to viewers. The other beads that do not use white or yellow glass on them have either red or colourless glass somehow incorporated into the bead. This may have been an alternative method for attracting a viewer's attention.

This section began with the following research objectives: what colours did late prehistoric glass workers have access to? What combination of colours did they use? Most importantly, how does this use of colour vary by region? These analyses have examined use of colour at a general level to understand the frequency of individual

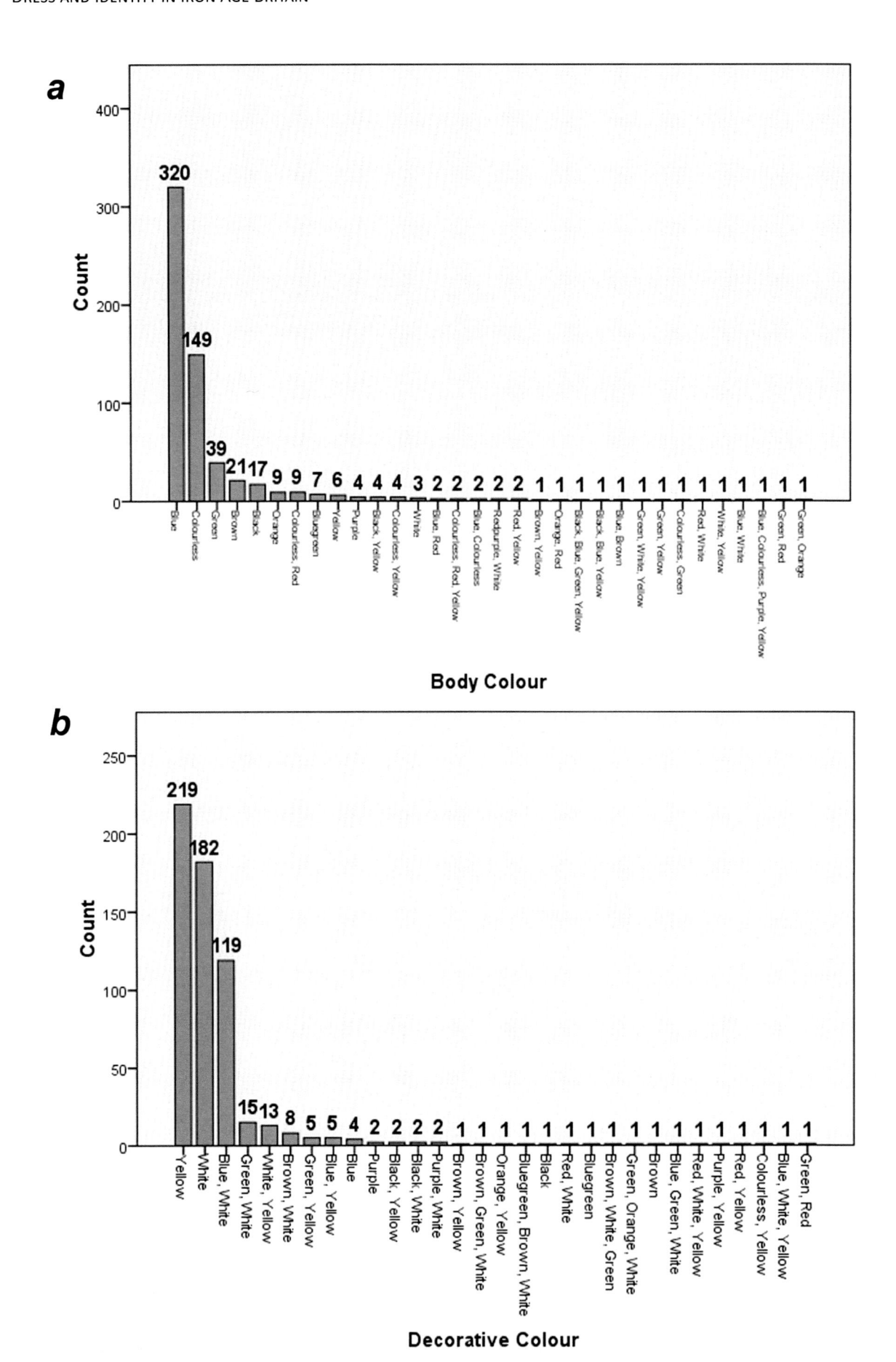

Figure 79: (a) Bar-chart showing the combined frequency of bead body colour across all study regions, and (b) bar-chart showing the combined frequency of bead decorative colour across all study regions.

FORM AND REGIONAL IDENTITY

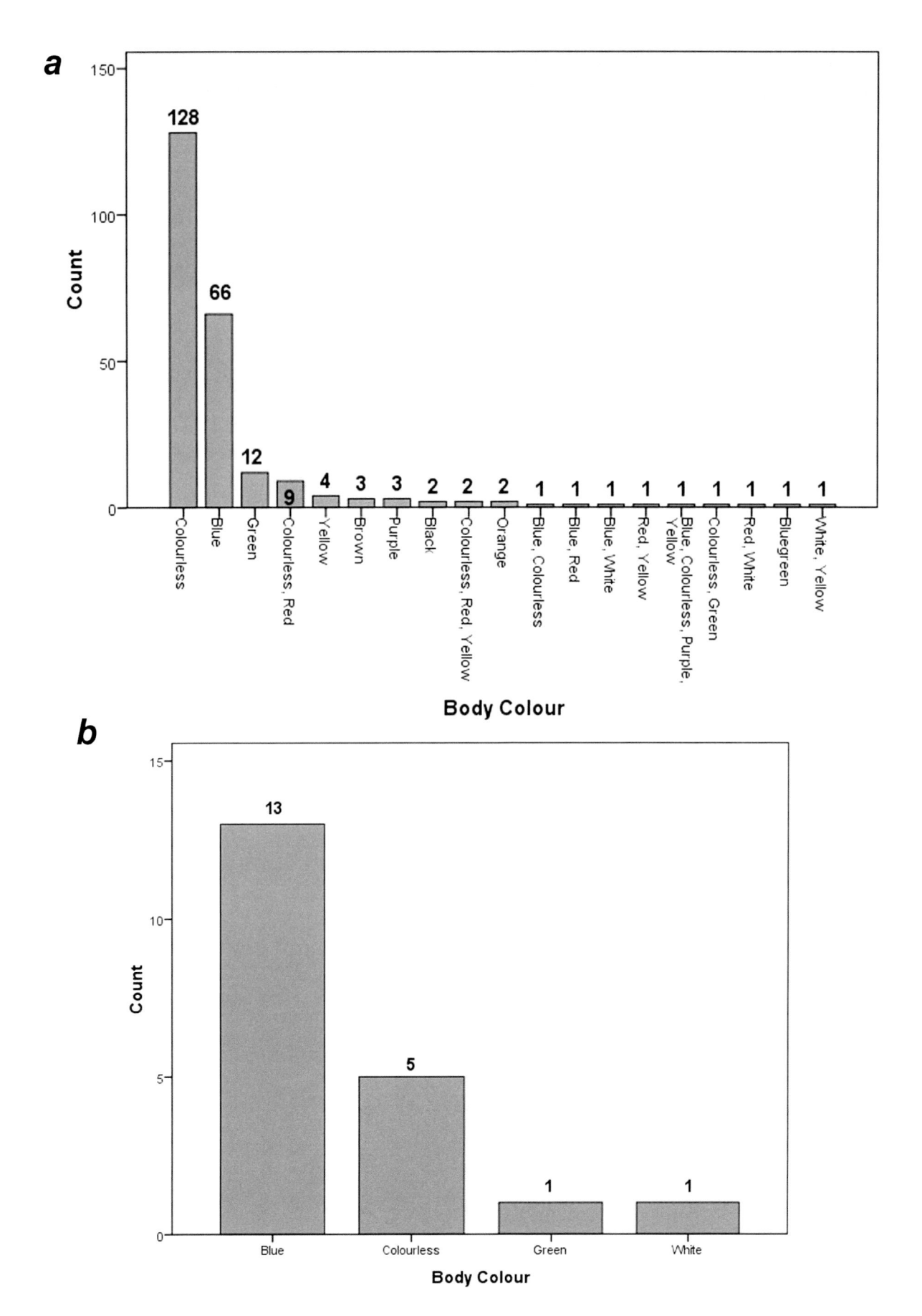

Figure 80: Bar-chart showing the use of body colour of polychrome beads in (a) Southwest England and (b) East Anglia.

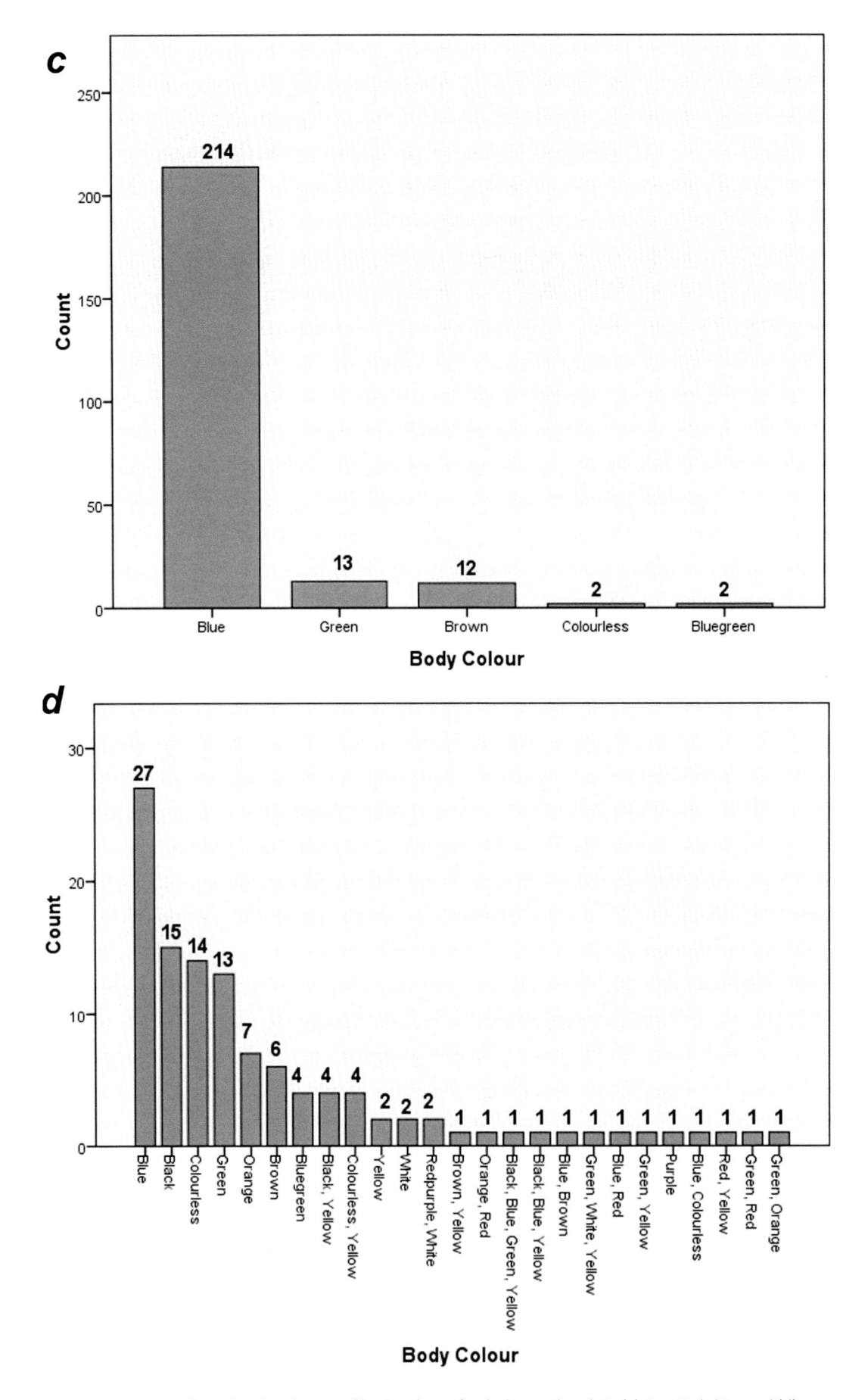

Figure 80: Bar-chart showing the use of body colour of polychrome beads in (c) East Yorkshire and (d) Northeast Scotland.

Body Colour	Southwest England	East Anglia	East Yorkshire	Northeast Scotland	TOTAL
Black	2	-	-	15	17
Black, Blue, Green, Yellow	-	-	-	1	1
Black, Blue, Yellow	-	-	-	1	1
Black, Yellow	-	-	-	4	4
Blue	66	3	214	27	310
Blue, Brown	-	-	-	1	1
Blue, Colourless	1	-	-	1	2
Blue, Colourless, Purple, Yellow	1	-	-	1	2
Blue, Red	1	-	-	1	2
Blue, White	1	-	-	-	1
Bluegreen	1	-	3	4	8
Brown	3	-	12	6	21
Brown, Yellow	-	-	-	1	1
Colourless	129	2	1	14	146
Colourless, Green	1	-	-	-	1
Colourless, Red	10	-	-	-	10
Colourless, Red, Yellow	2	-	-	-	2
Colourless, Yellow	-	-	-	4	4
Green	12	1	13	13	39
Green, Orange	-	-	-	1	1
Green, Red	-	-	-	1	1
Green, White, Yellow	-	-	-	1	1
Green, Yellow	-	-	-	1	1
Orange	1	-	-	4	5
Orange, Red	-	-	-	1	1
Purple	3	-	-	1	4
Red, White	1	-	-	-	1
Red, Yellow	1	-	-	-	1
Redpurple, White	-	-	-	2	2
White	1	-	-	2	3
White, Yellow	1	-	-	-	1
Yellow	4	-	-	2	6
TOTAL	242	6	243	110	601

Figure 81: List of colours and colour combinations found on the body of the bead and the frequency in each study region.

colours within the data-set. It has also specifically examined colour combinations, as well as the use of colour for both body and decorative elements on the beads. There is strong evidence for local variability in the preference for some colours over others, as each region has different patterns for the use of colour. For example, beads from Northeast Scotland had the most variability in terms of colour combinations used for both body and decorative colours; in contrast, the East Yorkshire beads demonstrate a more consistent, but otherwise limited, use

of colour and colour combinations. As the evidence for bead manufacture in Britain is sparse and it is unclear to what extent glass colour or opacity could be manipulated at this time, it is unclear if this is in part a reflection of the access to raw materials to alter the glass or access to different colours and opacity of glass. If glass bead making did not occur, then this may be a reflection of different networks of exchange with other communities that did manufacture glass beads. Of course, at this time in Britain, it may not have been one or the other, but if bead manufacturing did occur, some areas could have made glass beads, while others were a part of an exchange network. In either scenario, it is interesting that each region does have a characteristic use of colour, although some are more varied while others are less so. Regardless of how the glass beads were obtained, there was clearly something affecting the colours that were available within a region, either in raw form or finished form.

Decorative Motif

The final aspect of bead appearance under investigation is the use of decorative motifs on glass beads. Unlike manipulation of shape, the motif is a deliberate modification of the appearance of a bead through the application of at least one, usually contrasting, glass colour. In most cases, a secondary colour was applied in one of the combinations discussed in the previous sections. Some were created through the use of layered dots that created an 'eye' effect. Other motifs were created through the application of linear designs, such as circumferential lines or waves. There were also more complex beads that lack these dot-based or linear decorations; rather the motif is formed through the actual manufacture of the bead. This is the case with some whirl beads, ray beads, and wrapped beads. Many of these beads were formed by creating a cane or rod of multi-coloured glass, which was then wrapped around a mandrel. Finally, some beads exhibit a combination of these three types of decoration, thereby creating a much more complex motif, such as the whirl-with-cable beads found in Northeast Scotland.

Decorative Motif Analysis

Out of the 1,781 glass beads for which data regarding motif is available, 1,165 (65%) are undecorated. Any variability within these beads is introduced by differences in shape and colour. The remaining 616 beads (35%) exhibit some sort of decorative motif, most of which are very simple, although a small proportion of them are more complex. Most motifs can be described as 'dot-based', 'linear-based', 'wrapped/twisted', 'mottled', 'perforation-colour', or as having a combination of these motifs, which is subsequently defined as a 'complex-motif' (a summary of how general motif types relate to specific type classes is shown in Figure 85). In the

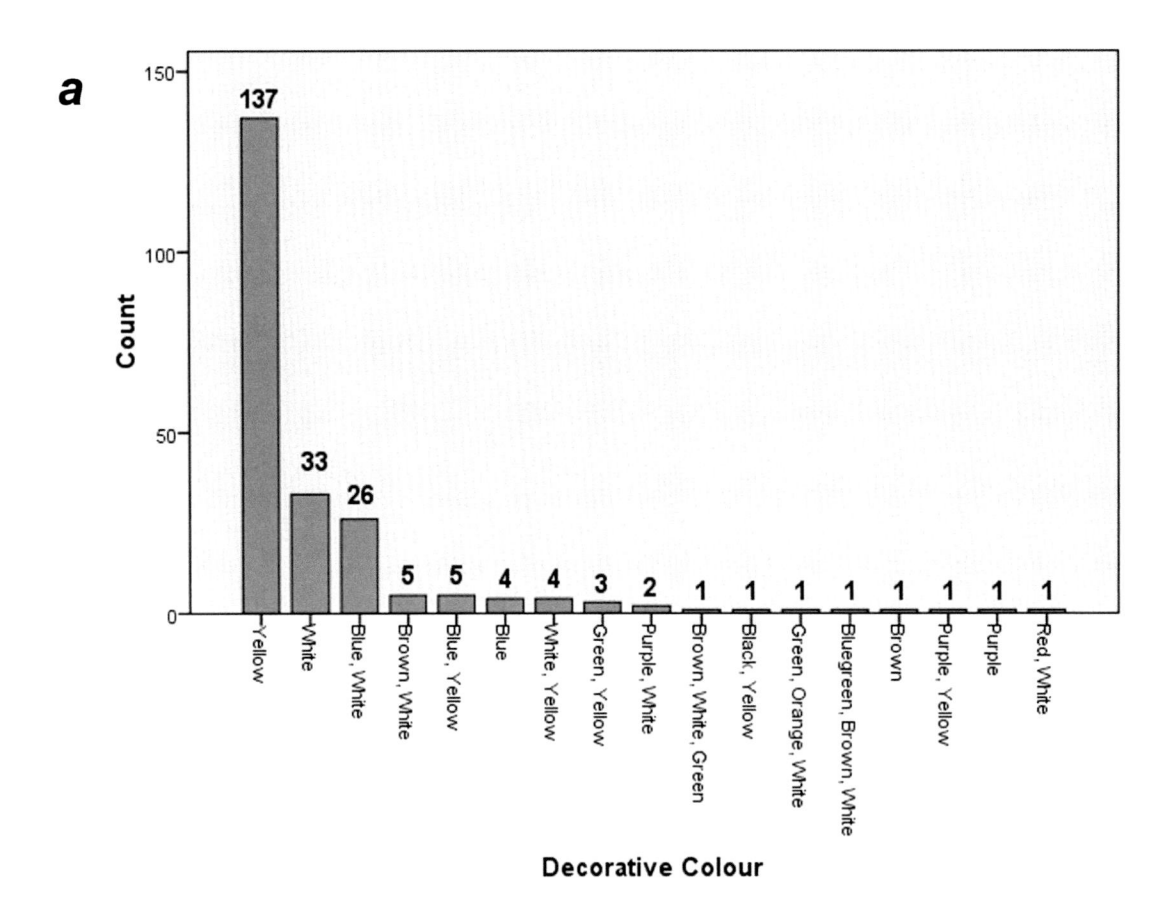

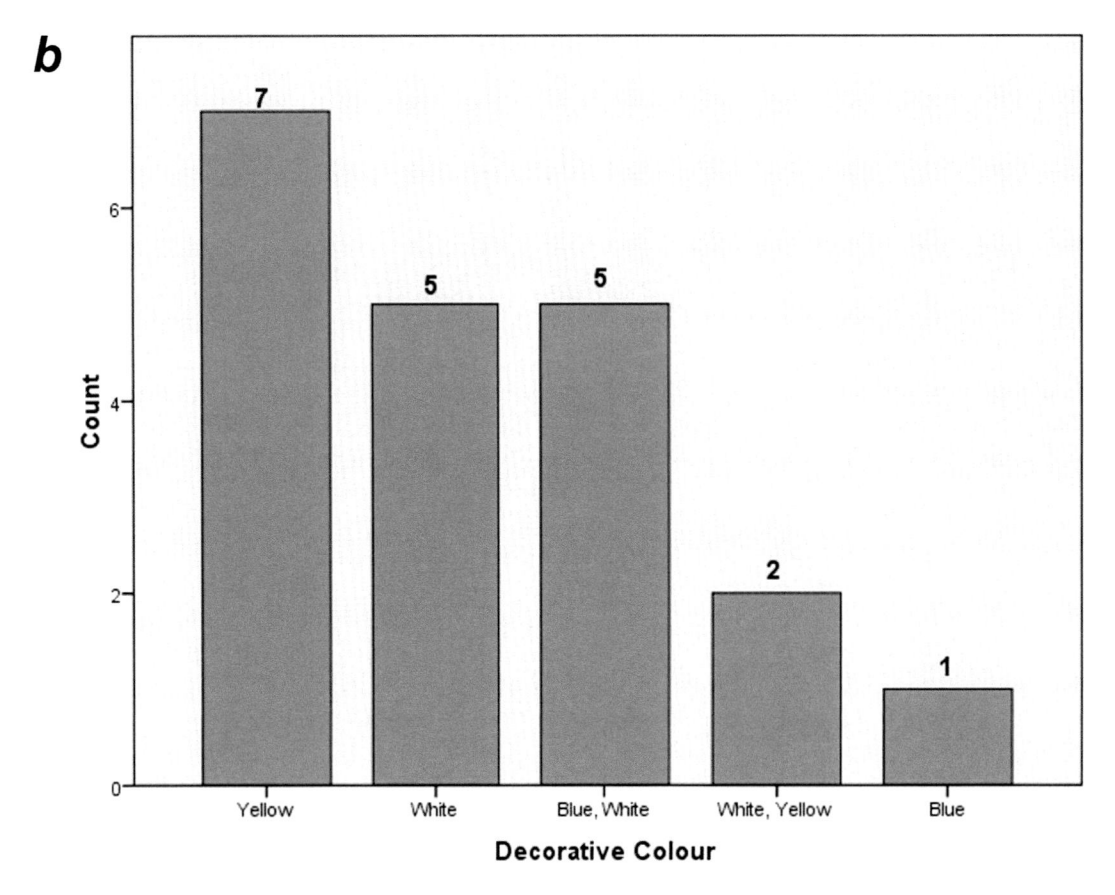

Figure 82: Bar-chart showing the use of decorative colour for polychrome beads in (a) Southwest England and (b) East Anglia.

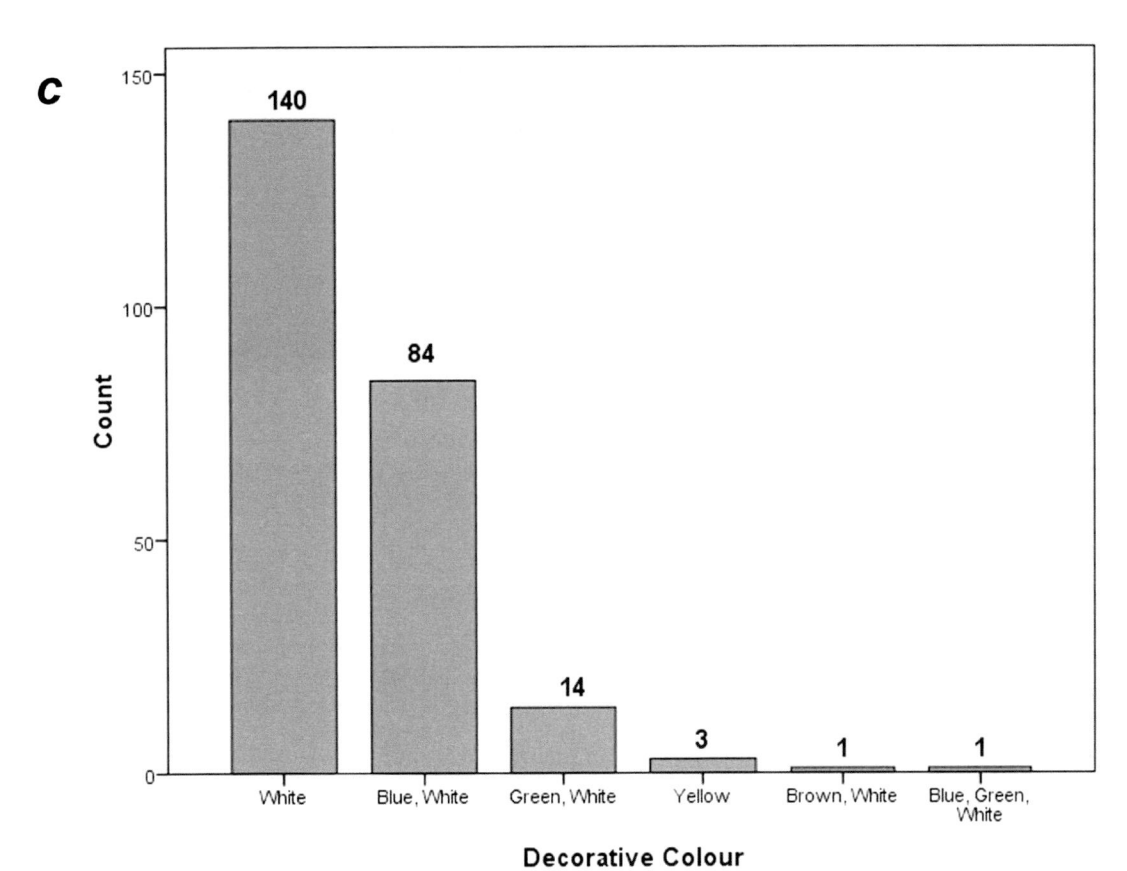

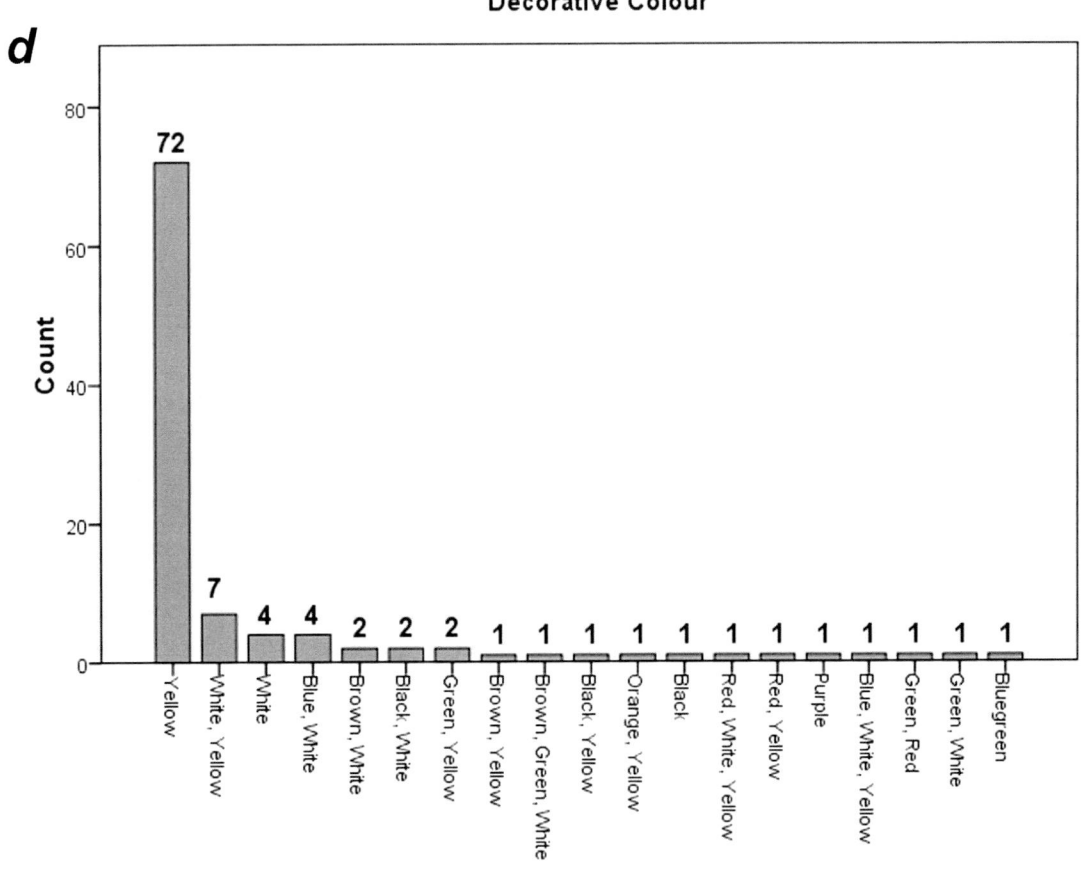

Figure 82: Bar-chart showing the use of decorative colour for polychrome beads in (c) East Yorkshire and (d) Northeast Scotland.

Decorative Colour	Southwest England	East Anglia	East Yorkshire	Northeast Scotland	TOTAL
Black	-	-	-	1	1
Black, White	-	-	-	2	2
Black, Yellow	1	-	-	1	2
Blue	3	1	-	-	4
Blue, Green, White	-	-	-	1	1
Blue, White	26	5	84	4	119
Blue, White, Yellow	-	-	-	1	1
Blue, Yellow	3	-	-	-	3
Bluegreen	-	-	-	1	1
Bluegreen, Brown, White	1	-	-	-	1
Brown	1	-	-	-	1
Brown, Green, White	-	-	-	1	1
Brown, White	5	-	1	2	8
Brown, White, Green	1	-	-	-	1
Brown, Yellow	-	-	-	1	1
Green, Orange, White	1	-	-	-	1
Green, Red	-	-	-	1	1
Green, White	-	-	14	1	15
Green, Yellow	3	-	-	2	5
Orange, Yellow	-	-	-	1	1
Purple	1	-	-	1	2
Purple, White	2	-	-	-	2
Purple, Yellow	1	-	-	-	1
Red, White	1	-	-	-	1
Red, White, Yellow	-	-	-	1	1
Red, Yellow	-	-	-	1	1
White	33	5	140	4	182
White, Yellow	3	1	-	2	6
Yellow	138	7	2	72	219
TOTAL	224	19	241	101	585

Figure 83: List of colours and colour combinations found as decorative motif on the bead and the frequency in each study region.

overall data set from all four study regions, the simple dot based and linear based motifs are by far the most frequent (Figure 86). However, it is clear that there are differences in the types of motifs employed on beads in different regions (Figures 87). The least common motifs are the perforation colour and mottled colour based motifs, although proportionately the perforation-colour motif occurs frequently on the beads from East Anglia. There is also a strong polarity between dot-based motifs and linear-decorated beads in Southwest England and East Yorkshire. From the raw frequency and percentage graphs (Figure 88), it is clear that both regions make use of linear designs, while East Yorkshire beads also displays high frequency of dot-based motifs.

In contrast, both wrapped/twisted and complex-motif beads are found almost entirely in Southwest England and Northeast Scotland, but are rare or even nonexistent in East Anglia and East Yorkshire.

Interestingly, all six types of decorative motif are found in the Southwest England beads, but the wrapped/twisted, mottled, and perforation colour beads are not found in all study regions. East Yorkshire has no examples of wrapped/twisted and perforation colour beads, while dot-based, mottled and perforation colour beads are not found in Northeast Scotland. This may indicate some differences in local bead manufacture or differences in trade or exchange of goods and the networks through which they were moved. The following analysis will closely examine the specific motifs found within each region, and will then take a comparative approach to examine where specific motifs are found or not found. This will give an indication of the types of motifs used within each region.

In Southwest England, there are 23 different types of decorative motifs; 12 of these are simple motifs, while the rest are more complex (Figure 89a, 90). As mentioned above, all types of motif are present in this study region. The most common motifs are applied-spirals (n=77), chevrons (n=44), and the cable-wave motif (n=26). In most cases, there was only one example of each complex motif, which may suggest that they were one-off productions. In East Anglia (Figure 89b), there are 12 different types of motifs, all of which are simple. The most common motifs are applied-spirals (n=3), perforation colour (n=3), and zigzags (n=3). Ten different motifs, all of which are simple, have been found in East Yorkshire (Figure 89c). The majority of beads, however, are either simple concentric-rings or waves.

Finally, in Northeast Scotland, there are 12 different types of decorative motifs present, only four of which are simple (Figure 89d, 90). Interestingly, compared to Southwest England, the frequency of each type of complex motif in Northeast Scotland is different. Whereas in Southwest England there was only one example of each complex design, there were multiple examples of complex designs found in Scotland. The applied-spiral motif is much more frequently found than any other design.

Discussion

In studying the decorative motifs found in all four study regions, it is clear that there are both similarities and differences among the different designs that occur (Figure 89). First, the only simple motif to occur in all four study regions is the wave motif. Although there are only a few examples of the wave in both East Anglia and Northeast Scotland, this motif has a strong presence in Southwest England, and a predominant one in East Yorkshire.

FORM AND REGIONAL IDENTITY

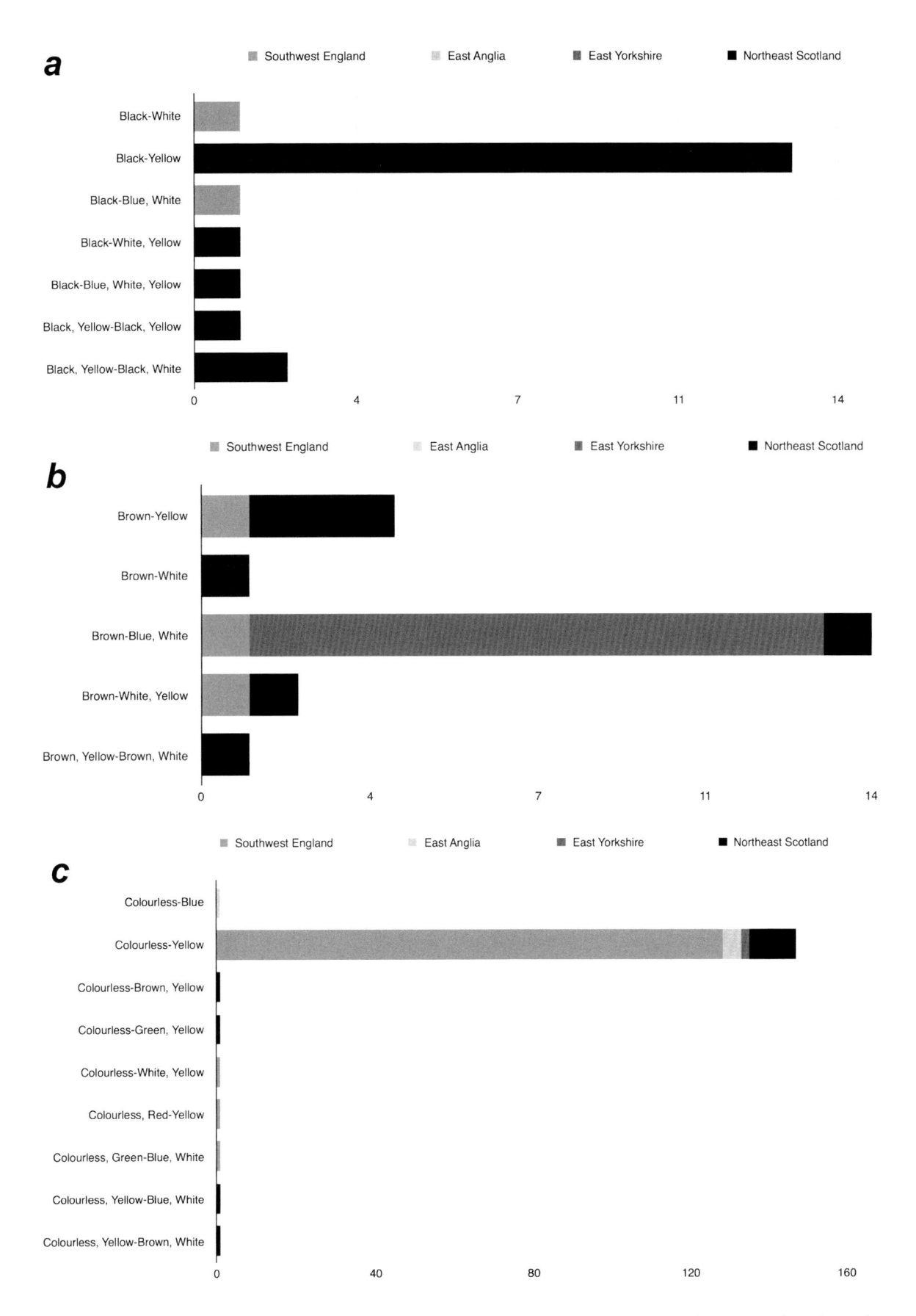

Figure 84: Bar-chart showing the frequency of glass beads by body colour and corresponding decorative colours by study region. Colour words to the left of the hyphen indicate body colour, and colour words to the right of the hyphen indicate decorative colour. (a) Black, (b) Brown, (c) Colourless.

d

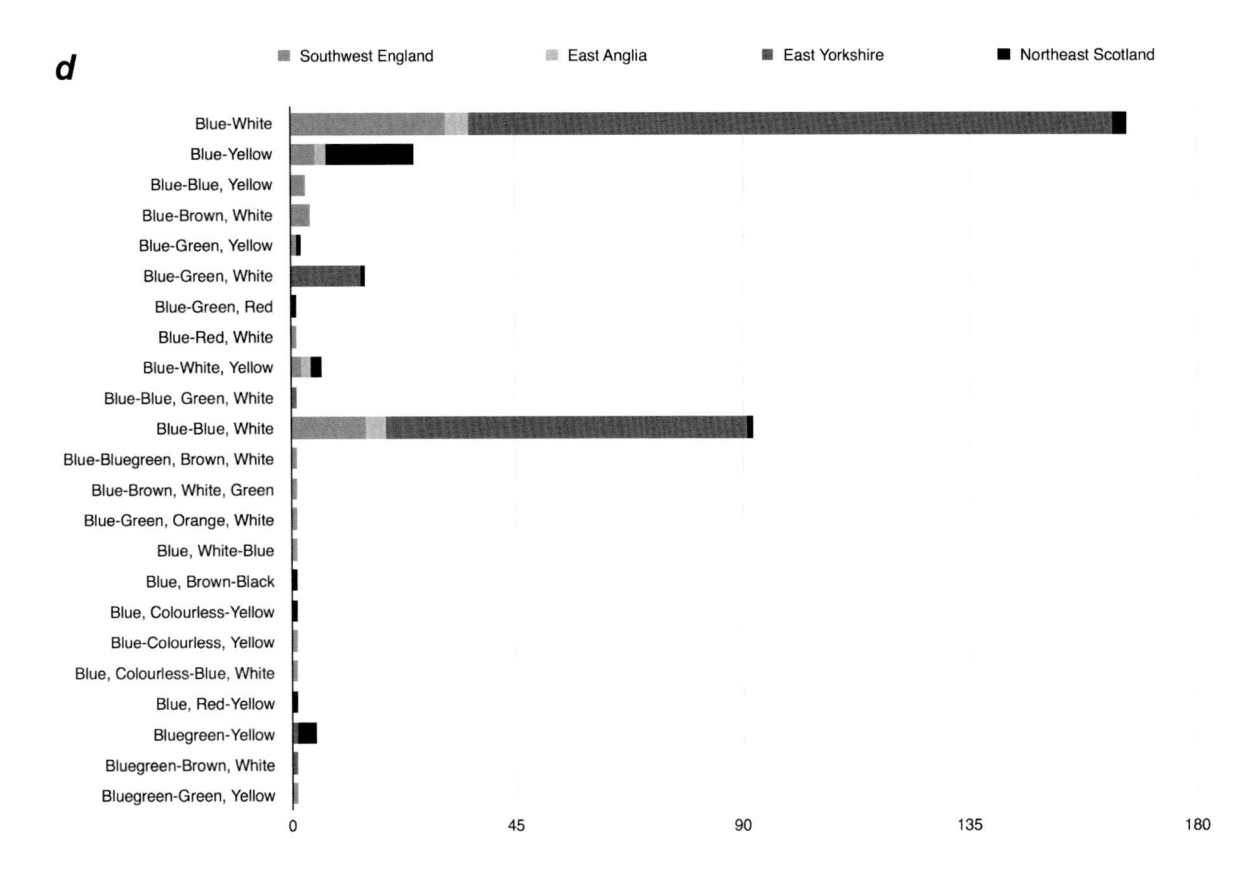

Figure 84: Bar-chart showing the frequency of glass beads by body colour and corresponding decorative colours by study region. Colour words to the left of the hyphen indicate body colour, and colour words to the right of the hyphen indicate decorative colour. (d) Blue and Bluegreen.

Most other motifs, such as chevrons, circumferential line, mottled colour, and simple concentric-ring, occur in at least three study regions: Southwest England, East Anglia, and East Yorkshire. The applied-spiral, on the other hand, occurs in all but East Anglia. There are also a number of motifs that only occur in one study region: compound concentric-ring, criss-cross, diagonal criss-cross, spiral-whirl, and pinnate motifs only occur in Southwest England, while wrapped beads only occur in Northeast Scotland. This indicates that there are differences in the types of motifs that occur in each study region, perhaps even a north/south divide.

Complex motifs follow a similar pattern of distribution (Figures 90). Thirteen of the 14 different combinations of complex motifs only occur in one study region, most often in Northeast Scotland. The complex cable wave motif, however, occurs in all study regions, except Northeast Scotland. In addition, there are examples of applied-spiral beads with mottled colours occurring in both Southwest England and in Northeast Scotland. It is also significant that the majority of the complex motifs from Northeast Scotland involve applied-spirals in combination with other additional motifs. In Southwest England, the complex motifs incorporate circumferential lines with other motifs, some linear and others wrapped/twisted. A bead with a combination of both dots and waves was also found in this region, which is a combination not encountered elsewhere.

This analysis of decorative motifs suggests there are a large number of simpler motifs that occur in Southwest England, while a greater number of complex motifs occur in Northeast Scotland. Bead motifs in East Yorkshire are by far the most limited in terms of complexity compared to all regions; even in East Anglia, which despite the very small assemblage, there is a greater variety of motifs. There are also strong trends seen within some of the regions; in terms of simple motifs, applied-spiral beads are found chiefly in Northeast Scotland, while simple concentric-rings and wave beads are found particularly in East Yorkshire. Both Southwest England and East Anglian beads have a wider range of variability. Complex motifs, with the exception of the cable-wave, are a product of Southwest England and Northeast Scotland. However, this analysis has only examined four regions within Britain. Although there does seem to be differences between motifs occurring in different study regions, Guido's (1978a) catalogue shows that additional examples of some motifs appear in other regions not studied here, so there could be other trends in other regions.

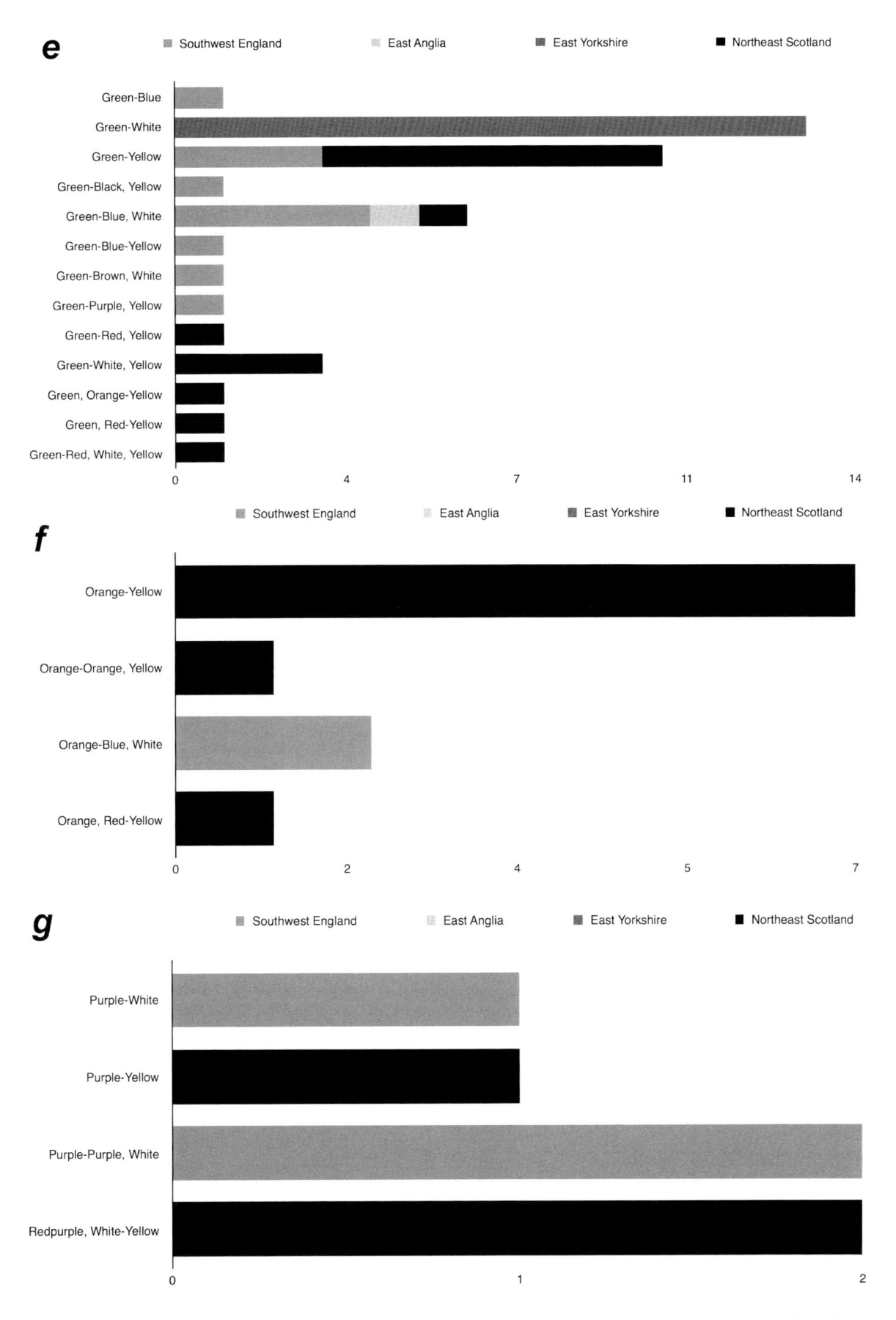

Figure 84: Bar-chart showing the frequency of glass beads by body colour and corresponding decorative colours by study region. Colour words to the left of the hyphen indicate body colour, and colour words to the right of the hyphen indicate decorative colour. (e) Green, (f) Orange, (g) Purple and Redpurple.

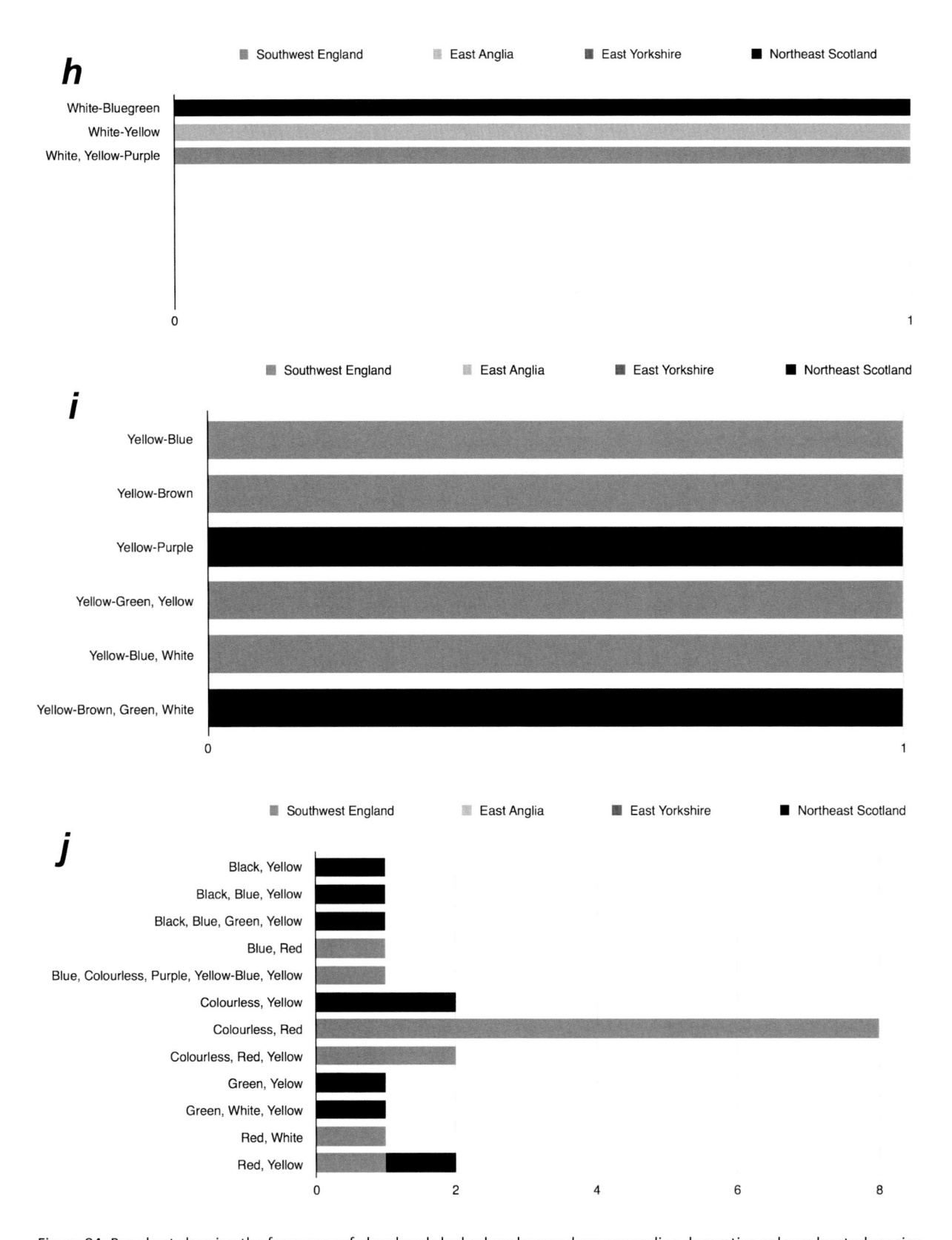

Figure 84: Bar-chart showing the frequency of glass beads by body colour and corresponding decorative colours by study region. Colour words to the left of the hyphen indicate body colour, and colour words to the right of the hyphen indicate decorative colour. (h) White, (i) Yellow, (j) multiple body colours and no decorative colours.

Form and Regional Identity

Simple Motif Type	New Types
None	Class 2, Class 2, Class 3
Dot Based	Class 4
Linear Based	Class 6
Wrapped/Twisted	Class 7, Class 8, Class 9
Mottled/spotted	Class 10
Perforation Colour	Class 5
Complex Motif	Class 11

Figure 85: Summary table correlating motif with new classification.

Discussion

The analyses presented in this chapter have individually explored different aspects of glass beads and made regional comparisons. From this, we can begin to build a picture of each region incorporating this data, in order to understand trends in size, shape, colour, and decorative motif.

Dominant overall regional trends are summarised in Figure 91. It shows that every region has at least two size categories, but annular beads are the most frequent shape. However, there are not always clear distinctions in shape when it comes to annular and globular/spherical beads. Instead, there is a continuous spread from small to large that covers both of these size ratios. The most frequently occurring colours are blue and white, although yellow is also frequent in all regions except in East Yorkshire. While monochrome beads are the most frequent in all regions except East Anglia, the applied-spiral motif is found in large numbers in both Southwest England and Northeast Scotland. By contrast, in East Yorkshire the wave and simple concentric-ring motifs are found more often. Finally, there is some overlap between the most frequently occurring types. For example, Type 110 is found in large numbers within both Southwest England and Northeast Scotland, and Type 901 is found in both East Anglia and in East Yorkshire.

In contrast to the most frequent regional trends, there are many nuances in all aspects of the beads that occur in less frequent numbers within the regional assemblages. For example, two bead shapes are unique to Southwest England: the double segment and stud. In contrast, while the colour blue makes up a significant proportion of the

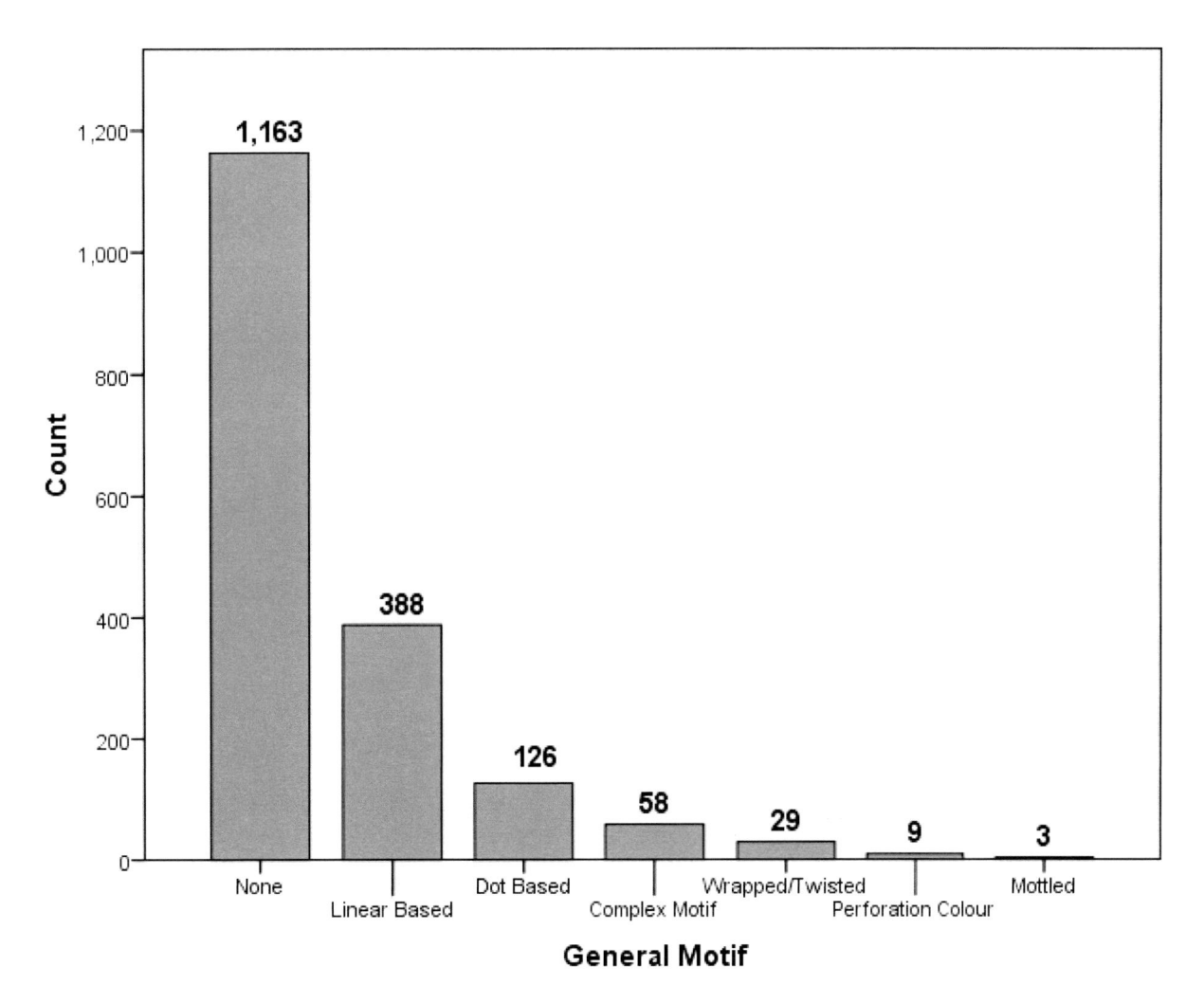

Figure 86: Bar-chart showing the frequency of general motif types for all four study regions.

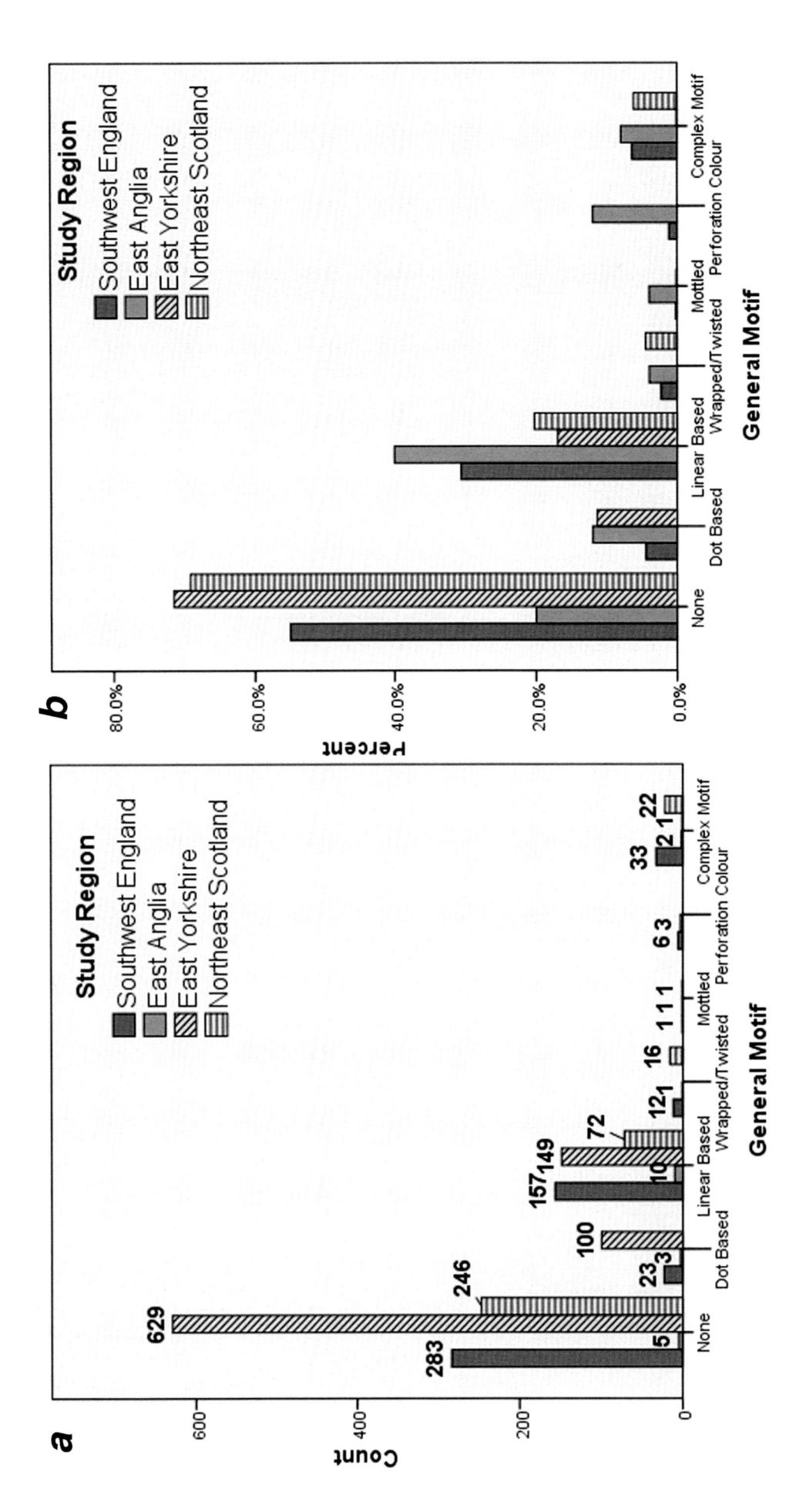

Figure 87: Bar-chart showing the (a) frequency, and (b) percentage of general motif types in all four study regions.

Decorative Motif	Southwest England	East Anglia	East Yorkshire	Northeast Scotland	TOTAL
Applied-spiral	77	-	2	69	148
Applied-spiral, Protrusion	5	3	3	-	11
Chevrons	44	1	1	-	46
Circumferential Line	1	1	1	-	3
Complex Concentric-ring	1	3	-	-	4
Compound Concentric-ring	1	-	-	-	1
Criss-cross	3	-	-	-	3
Diagonal Criss-cross	1	-	-	-	1
Mottled Colour	1	1	1	-	3
Perforation Colour	5	3	-	-	8
Pinnate	1	-	-	-	1
Ray	3	1	-	-	4
Simple Concentric-ring	22	2	97	-	121
Spiral-whirl	1	-	-	-	1
Wave	24	2	141	3	170
Whirl	9	-	-	7	16
Wrapped	-	-	-	9	9
Zig-zag	-	3	1	-	4
TOTAL	199	20	247	88	554

Figure 88: List of all decorative motifs and their frequency within each study region.

beads found in East Yorkshire, the blue melon-shaped beads in this region have not been found in any other Iron Age context outside of this region. And finally, within Southwest England and Northeast Scotland, there are a number of complex multi-coloured beads that mix four different colours of glass, although each bead is unique.

With these differences in mind, the question becomes: Why are there such differences between study regions? In part, this may relate to where the beads were manufactured. At least some of these beads were probably manufactured in continental Europe. This seems likely for at least some bead types, given their similarities to European glass beads (e.g. Dobiat, Matthäus et al. 1987; Frey, Matthäus et al. 1983; Gebhard 1989a; Haevernick 1960; Hunter and Haevernick 1995; Venclová 1990; Zepezauer 1993). Exact parallels for some of the beads, even Guido's 'Continental Types', remain elusive.

Regardless of when and where the beads were manufactured, there are several stages at which point individuals made a choice. First, at the manufacturing stage, the craftsperson would have chosen the colour, shape, and decoration (if any) to be used. Was only one colour available, or was there a choice between several? Was there an opportunity to change the colour or opacity of the glass before actually creating the bead? Why do some beads have decorative motifs while the majority did not? How were these motifs chosen? Iron Age glass workers continue to be archaeologically invisible, so it is unclear whether they were making the beads for their own use, for use within their own kin-based network, or for others, either more distant kin or those outside of their immediate community network (DeRoche 1997; Hamilton 2002). Second, after manufacture, someone would have used the bead. How did they choose which beads to use? Was it dependent on the colour of the bead, the weight, the size, or the decoration? Was there an idea of fashion, in the sense that particular colours or decorations were more desirable than others, and these were later replaced by other patterns and/or colours? As beads can be combined to create larger objects (e.g. necklaces or bracelets), were multiple beads purposely combined immediately after manufacture to make a single object? Alternatively, were beads partible, i.e. could they be removed from a larger object and exchanged or gifted (Fowler 2004)? Were 'fancier' beads, such as those with combinations of glass colour and use of motifs more desirable than plainer beads? Another aspect of bead selection may relate to the movement of people to Britain or even individuals who traveled to continental Europe and back, perhaps even bringing with them 'exotic' glass beads. At the final stage of a bead's biography, why were beads chosen for intentional deposition? Did the physical aspects of beads affect the fact that they were chosen for inclusion in burials or pits?

Despite our inability to answer many of these questions, it is clear that if we take this data as reflecting real choices and use in the Iron Age, some clear patterns do emerge. Contextual analysis will follow in the succeeding chapter. However, it becomes clear that many of the beads that have been found either through excavation, or as stray finds, are the result of the object entering the archaeological record through deliberate depositional practices. It may be that some bead specimens were neither intentionally nor accidentally deposited, but that they were later melted and reworked into something else, or that they were destroyed through intentionally or accidentally breaking them into small fragments, which then become difficult to identify. Therefore, the examples of beads available for analysis may simply be those objects deemed important or appropriate enough to be buried intentionally in the ground, or those which were interred as a result of chance loss. Chapter 4 showed that the Iron Age activity in each study region differs and is reflected in different regional practices, it may be that the possibility of glass bead deposition within each of these regions is variable. Nonetheless, based on available data we can say with certainty that there are patterns in the use of different glass bead sizes, shapes, colour, and decorative motifs.

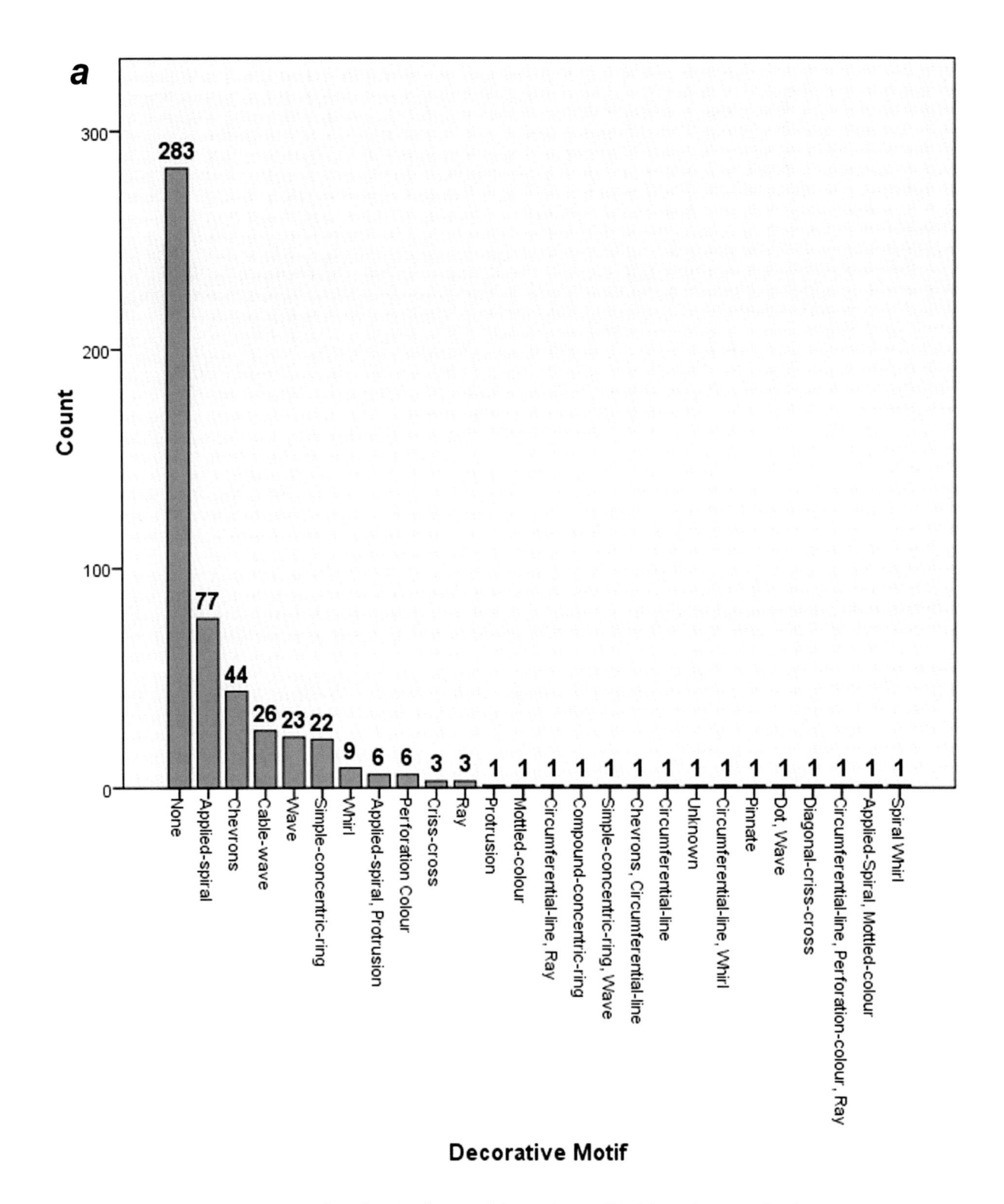

Figure 89: Bar-chart showing the use of decorative motif in (a) Southwest England.

One implication of patterns of glass bead characteristics is that they may be reflecting regional patterns or tastes in dress. In Southwest England and in Northeast Scotland there is an emphasis both on the colour yellow (used on different types of beads from both regions), and the use of the spiral motif. In East Yorkshire, however, the colour blue is prevalent and often occurs on plain beads, wave beads, and eye beads. Giles (2008a, 72; 2008b, 72; 2012, 150) has suggested that in East Yorkshire the colour blue is associated with mature women as blue beads were found primarily in burials with remains that have been determined to be female and more advanced in age. Other inhumations that were excavated, but where an osteological examination of the remains was not possible (e.g. Barrow L at Cowlam, and the Queen's Barrow at Arras), have been assumed to be female due to the other

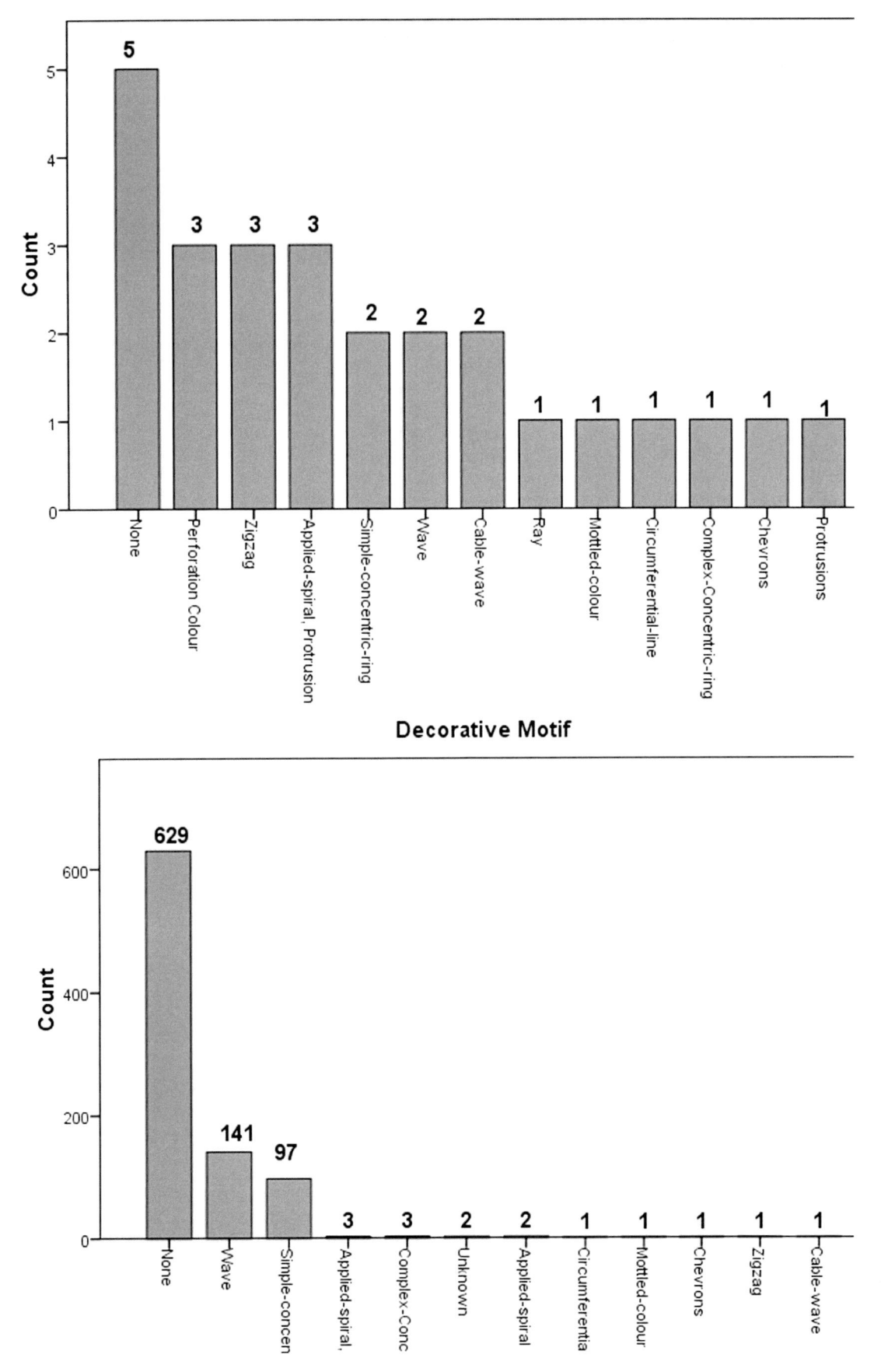

Figure 89: Bar-chart showing the use of decorative motif in (b) East Anglia, (c) East Yorkshire.

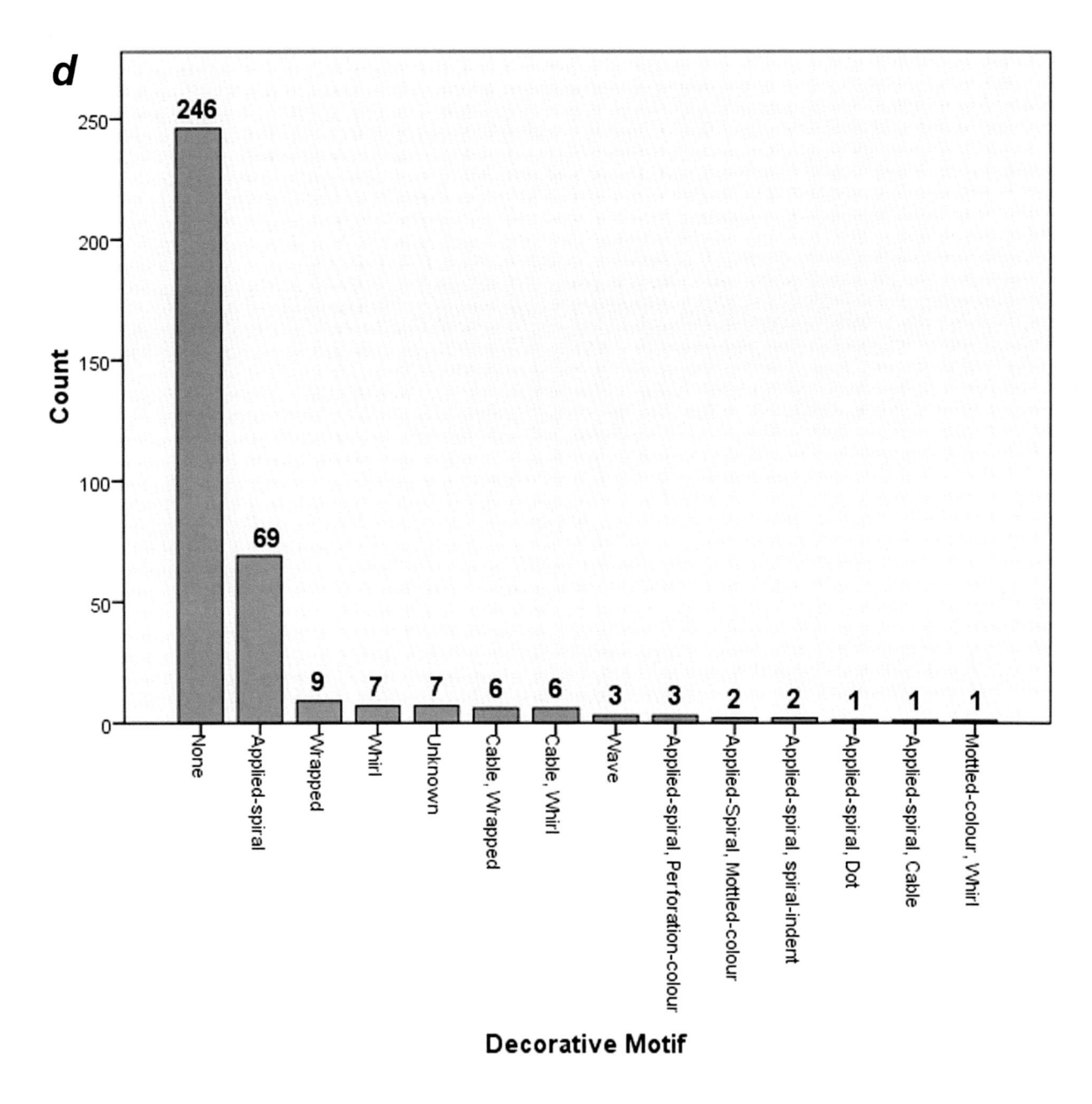

Figure 89: Bar-chart showing the use of decorative motif in (d) Northeast Scotland.

grave goods that were included. However, do these blue beads simply reflect age and sex? Within this region, there are very few beads found that were not mostly blue, except for the few translucent green beads found with the Queen's Barrow and one of the inhumations at Wetwang Slack, which had a number of brown beads. In both cases, these were mixed in with other blue examples. Assuming that these beads belonged to the individual that they were buried with, could they have meant something more about the individual who owned them?

The rarity of these beads in inhumation contexts, especially compared to the single finds at Rudston and Burton Fleming versus larger numbers of beads at Wetwang and Garton Slack, suggest that the individuals buried with the beads, would have stood out against the remainder of the community due to their dress. Whether this style of dress was because they were women, or because they were mature (or both), is not readily apparent. However, perhaps what is being reflected is the connectivity of networks between individuals. This is supported especially by the Queen's Barrow necklace, which has the widest range of beads compared to the other necklaces, and by the beads found at Rudston and Burton Fleming, which are not only found singly, but also are furthest away from Wetwang Slack and the inhumations at Arras. Connectivity in this region is further attested by the scale of earthworks, ditched boundaries, and trackways that parceled up the region and probably provided avenues for travel (Bevan 1997, 129).

FORM AND REGIONAL IDENTITY

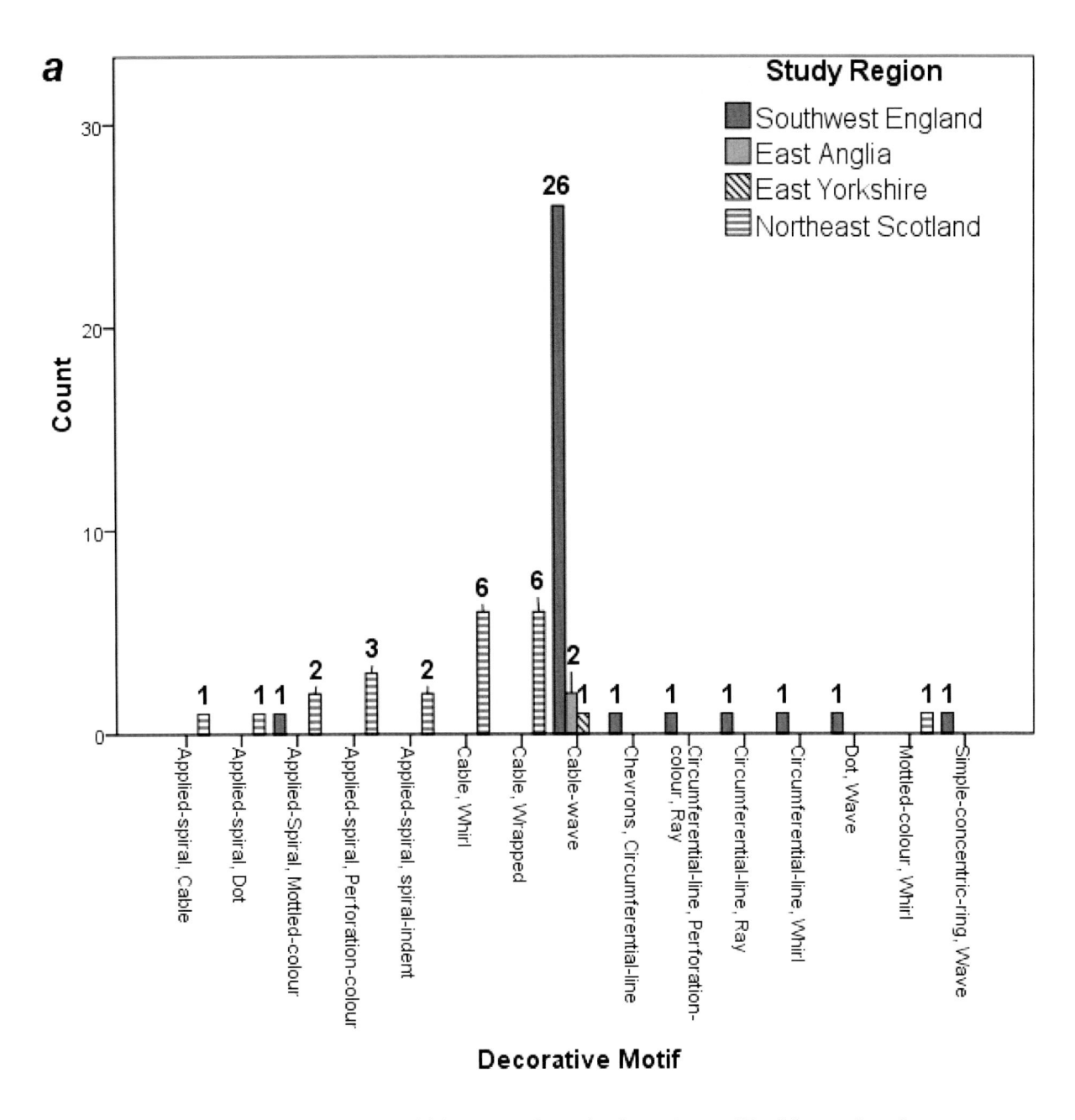

Figure 90: Bar-chart showing the (a) frequency of complex decorative motif in all four study regions.

As an element of dress, it is likely that these beads only made up part of an individual's assemblage of objects worn, as suggested by the textile evidence and other objects of dress discussed in Chapter 3 attested in the East Yorkshire burials. When worn against differently coloured garments, the colours of the beads would either render them extra-visible through the use of contrast, or allow them to blend in. For example, a dark blue bead with a white wave design would blend into a darker textile or hide garment (although the design would stand out), but if worn against a lightly coloured garment the entire object would both gain visibility and be illuminated by the light background. This idea is developed further in Chapter 8. The different colours of beads that dominate each region suggest that dress may have been constructed differently, and these differences would have led to different regional- or community-based identities through dress.

The motifs used on glass beads are still not entirely understood; there has been much casual speculation on the meaning of the eye motif (Guido 1978a, 22). This motif is not unique to Britain, and is seen on other glass beads (Eisen 1916), and pottery decoration (Gomez de Soto 2003) throughout later prehistoric Europe. It has been shown that this idea of the eye as protector is very old and features in some classical (e.g. Pliny the Elder Book 7 chapter 2) and biblical texts (Dundes 1992). There may be some connection between the eye beads found in the archaeological record and 'evil eye' charms that reflect away bad thoughts. It is not clear if these ideas extend to their use in Iron Age Britain. These beads

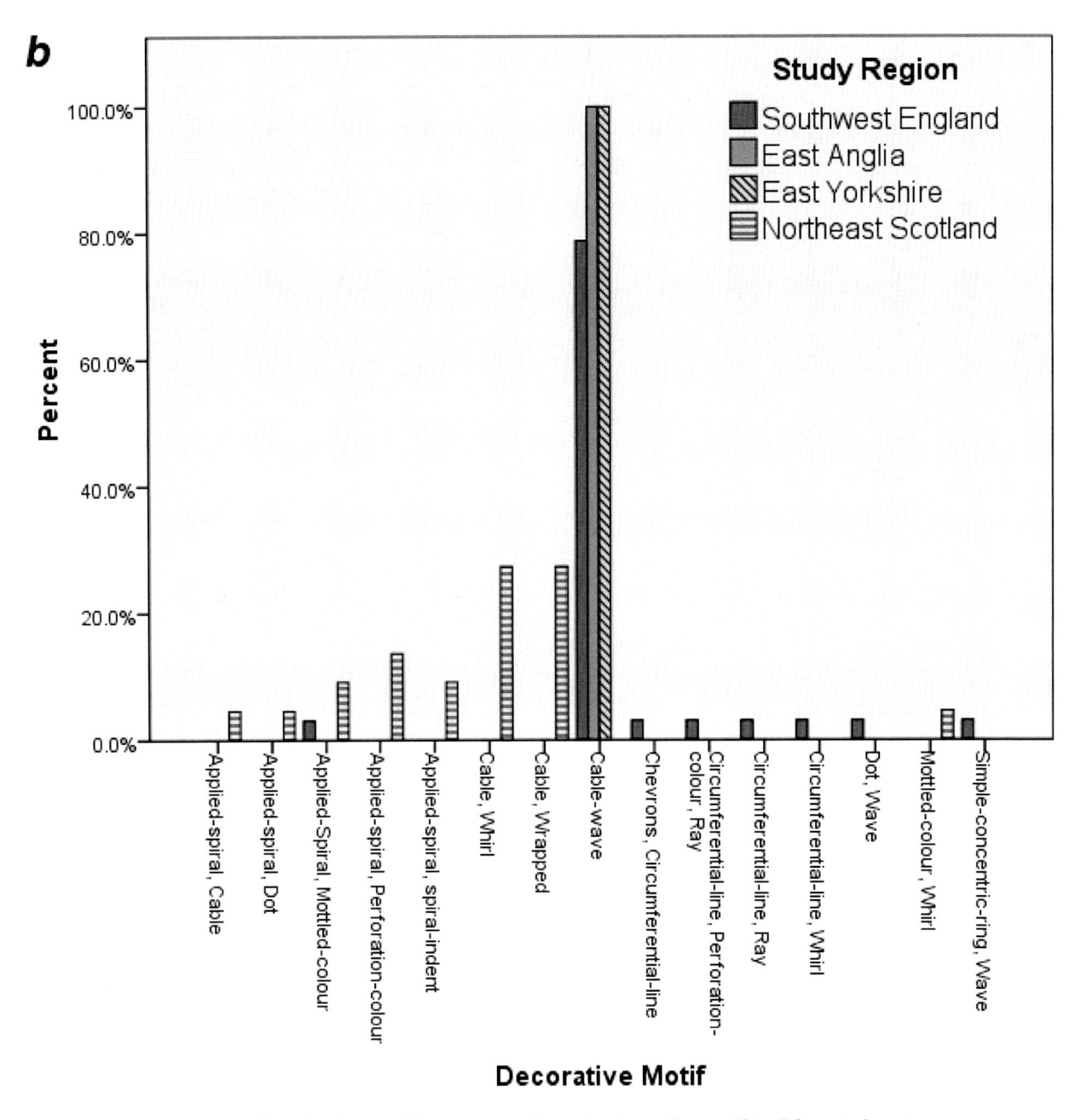

Figure 90: Bar-chart showing the (b) percentage of complex decorative motif in all four study regions.

have also been likened to Phoenician 'head' beads, and the concentric-ring motif may be an anthropomorphism of the human eye. The concentric-ring, however, may be the same ring-and-dot motif that is found inscribed onto bone objects, such as weaving combs, in Britain and on objects from earlier prehistoric periods in continental Europe (e.g. Herring 2003; Jope 2000 Plate 305f, 313k, n; Joy 2011b). On other objects this motif is repeated over the surface of the item in both regular and irregular patterns, whereas for beads they are most often placed around the circumference or in a 2-1-2 pattern. The spiral motif found on beads, however, does not seem to be employed on other objects made from bone or metal (e.g. Fox 1958; Jope 2000). While much of the highly decorated metalwork of this period (Celtic Art) employs a range of sinuous designs that sometimes draw on classical foliage motifs (Fox 1958; Jope 2000), this spiral motif is not found on these objects.

It may be that these motifs form part of an Iron Age symbology, in which different symbols had a specific meaning, or it may be that their use was flexible and open to interpretation (Garrow and Gosden 2012). Many of the motifs found on these beads depict multiple flowing and moving lines that encircle the object, perhaps causing dizziness or confusion (Garrow and Gosden 2012; Gell 1988). The larger whirl- and ray-type beads would have been hypnotic when spun (perhaps strengthening the idea for their use as a spindle whorl). It may also be significant that these simple designs are also found

Study Region	Size	Shape	Colour	Motif	Type
Southwest England	Small	Annular	Yellow, Blue, Colourless, White	Applied Spiral, Chevrons, Cable Waves, Waves, Simple Concentric Rings	102, 106, 107, 110, 410, 1003, 1417
	Medium-Large				
	Medium-Large	Globular			
East Anglia	Large	Annular	Blue, White, Yellow, Colourless	Applied Spiral, Perforation Colour, Zig-zag	102, 106, 410, 701, 901, 1407
	Large	Globular			
East Yorkshire	Small	Annular	Blue, White, Green	Wave, Simple Concentric rings	102, 901
	Medium-Large				
	Small	Globular			
	Medium-Large				
Northeast Scotland	Small	Annular	Yellow, Blue, White	Applied Spirals, Wrap/twisted, Complex beads	110, 1400, 1501
	Medium				
	Large				
	Small	Globular			
	Large				

Figure 91: Summary table of generalised regional characteristics.

in the first few stages of entoptic phenomena, which are seen during altered states of consciousness (Lewis-Williams 1997; Lewis-Williams, Dowson *et al.* 1988; Lewis-Williams and Pearce 2005). However, it seems more likely that at least some of the motifs draw on a much earlier decorative tradition stretching back into the prehistoric period (Wilkins and Herring 2003).

Conclusion

This chapter aimed to explore on an individual basis the data related to four key characteristics of glass beads: size, shape, colour, and decorative motif. The analyses have indicated that while there are some general trends found between regions, and even within each region, a closer examination of the evidence is necessary to truly comprehend the levels of inter-regional difference and similarity. This contrasts with other studies, notably Giles' study of bodily adornment from East Yorkshire (Giles 2008a, 72; 2008b, 72). Giles' conclusions emphasised the use of the colour blue and the correlation between this colour and mature women in burial contexts. However, by examining the data by region, it is apparent that while blue does form a significant proportion of the material in East Yorkshire, it also frequently occurs in other regions, thus demonstrating that colour cannot be studied in one isolated region. Unfortunately, burial evidence is scarce for the remainder of Britain; however, the contexts of deposition will be explored further in the next chapter.

Chapter 7
Archaeological Context

To understand past human behaviour, it is vital to go beyond simply describing material culture, and begin to engage with an object's context. In the broadest sense of the word, context here refers to the biography of the object, from raw material and production, to use, and finally to deposition. While material evidence can sometimes provide clues about some of these aspects, it is in the depositional feature where we can often see the result of human action. The aim of this chapter is to present the find contexts at different levels: distribution, site type, and feature type, in order to understand patterns and differences in glass bead deposition.

In the past, the distribution, presence, and absence of glass beads from Iron Age sites has been wrapped up in the idea of social hierarchy and status during Iron Age Britain. Chapters 3 and 4 introduced some of these concepts and some of the key arguments surrounding these ideas. Glass has been considered to be an inherently high-status material (Guido 1978a; Henderson 1992; e.g. as at Thainstone in Aberdeenshire: Murray and Murray 2006b). Thus, objects made from this material were argued to be used by the elites of Iron Age Britain, as they were placed in a limited number of inhumations, and the presence of these elites is reflected in the discovery of these objects at settlements.

There have been several arguments for the relatively high-status nature of glass beads. First, this specific type of object does not immediately contribute towards meeting survival needs, such as food, water, and shelter (Guido 1978a, 28). Therefore, these glass objects would have been a luxury. Second, whether glass beads were manufactured in Britain, or in continental Europe, the original raw material is likely to have originated from very distant locations. In this case, the farther the distance a material travelled from its origin, the higher the status (Henderson 1992, 110). A similar phenomenon can be seen with pieces of coral found in copper alloy metalwork in Britain, which presumably came from Mediterranean sources (Henderson 1992). Finally, some of the actual oxides and minerals that were added to the glass to manipulate both colour and opacity could render some beads more desirable than others. For example, Henderson examines the frequency of decorated glass beads (which he argued were higher-status than plain beads), by site type in order to determine a hierarchy of different categories of site (Henderson 1992, Table 1). A full critique of this analysis has been provided in Chapter 2; however, it is relevant to point out here that Henderson included plain opaque yellow annular beads with the decorated types in his analysis, as he argued the high-lead glass would have been of high-status (Henderson 1992, footnote on his Table 1). Unfortunately, he has not provided an explanation as to why lead-oxide was high-status.

In conjunction with other types of objects, glass artefacts have been used to demonstrate that the items found at supposedly high-status Wessex sites, such as hillforts, are little different from the sites considered to be lower in status (Hill 1996). This suggests that the interpretation of artefacts as an indication of inhabitant status is far from clear and that care is needed when discussing an individual's or a site's status through the presence or absence of certain artefacts. One of the problems with these approaches to status is the assumption that both sites and objects manifested an inherent and constant status, when the role of both potentially varied regionally and throughout time (Haselgrove 1997; Hill 1995b; Hingley 2006). In addition, there is the idea that all examples of an object would have the same meaning, when each individual example would have developed its own life history and meaning. Instead, akin to other studies of Iron Age artefacts (e.g. Joy 2007), we need to consider the biography of the individual object. As will become clearer throughout the following analyses, beads are not all found at the same types of sites, neither are they found in the same features. Rather, it seems that each find is the result of a different biography from the time of manufacture until the final deposition.

Not only does the hypothesis that glass was a high-status material become a problematic argument to sustain, but it also limits our understanding of the interactions between people and objects. The goal of artefact studies is not simply to find high-status examples of objects or people, especially given that there are other factors that affect our visibility of the archaeological record, such as preservation of materials. Ceramics, stone, metals, and glass all have preference in many studies of the past, as they are more likely to survive. Organic materials, such as wood, fur, hide, and textiles, on the other hand, will only survive in specific conditions. This distorts the evidence for materiality in Iron Age Britain. Other factors include the re-use of materials: glass and some metals can be re-melted and used again, iron can be reworked, and pottery can be broken for use in new pots as temper. Finally, there is a growing body of evidence to suggest that the artefacts that were recovered are the result of intentional deposition (Cunliffe 1992; Giles 2007a; Hill 1995b). Hence, our data is dependent on the act of deposition in the past.

With these issues in mind, this chapter explores data related to context in order to understand the nature of human behaviour during this time. It begins by examining the wider distribution of glass beads and the patterns in glass bead distribution utilising the typology set out in Chapter 5. Then, it closely examines beads found through excavation. Before examining this dataset, this chapter examines the nature of the data in order to determine whether there are biases related to the motivation for excavation. Then, a contextual analysis examines patterns of site type and specific features. Through these analyses, it will be possible to understand how glass beads were treated in Iron Age society, how and where they were deposited, and by using the typology, it will be possible to suggest networks between communities.

Glass Bead Distribution

Distribution maps are a useful method for understanding the geographic locations of artefact finds. In addition, they allow simple comparisons to be made between different types of artefacts or even different sub-types. Guido (1978a) relied on maps to demonstrate the overall distribution of each of her types across Britain and Ireland, and inferred different ideas about the beads from this type of analysis. For her beads of continental origin (Classes 1-7), she used these maps to suggest where the beads were introduced into Britain, and how they subsequently spread across the country. For beads without continental parallel, which she assumed had been manufactured in Britain, she used distribution maps to demonstrate areas where glass beads were densest, and suggested possible locations for manufacture based on their concentration. She then examined the spread of glass beads as they radiated and diffused out from these areas to suggest how they were moving across Britain and inferred a direction of flow. In some cases, when beads of the same or similar type were found in very distant locations (e.g. Class 8 beads and Class 10/13 beads), she suggested that people migrated from south to north. Henderson has similarly used distribution maps to show the disbursement of opaque yellow glass from Meare and Culbin Sands outwards (Henderson 1982, Figures 37 and 38).

One of the problems with these approaches to artefacts is that they assume that high densities of beads reflect the origin point (manufacturing centre) and that these beads were subsequently deposited in the same location that they were created. The best example is Guido's Class 10 beads, which were found in large numbers at Meare Lake Village and consequently it was suggested that they were manufactured on site (Guido 1978a, 79). Examples found outside of Meare, such as at Maiden Castle in Dorset, South Shields in Tyne and Wear, Culbin Sands in Morayshire, and even an example from Orkney, were explained as a reflection of contact between groups, or spread of people out of Meare (Guido 1978a, 80-1). It is not explained why so many of these beads were deposited at this site supposedly soon after their manufacture. This continues to be the interpretation used in recent reports (e.g. Towrie 2005), which draws on Guido's discussion, with limited critique on the implications for such an interpretation.

The next section will present some general background data regarding the distribution of glass beads and the nature of the archaeological record that will underpin much of the analyses presented in the following sections. Rather than seeing the frequency of glass beads in each study region as a reflection of the status of the inhabitants, or the distributions reflecting the origin and spread of beads, this section aims to identify areas of presence and absence, and large-scale patterns of bead characteristics.

Overall Distributions

Each of the study regions that are examined here were chosen for specific reasons. The resulting distribution map draws on both the Guido (1978a) catalogue and newly discovered examples in the database (Figure 92), and highlights a number of changes in our understanding of this object in comparison to the Guido distribution (Figure 1). New examples of glass beads continue to be found in the Southwest England region, further building on the already established distribution of beads in this area. In East Anglia, where Iron Age glass beads were previously lacking, there are now not only examples that are typologically identified as Iron Age, but there are also examples that were found in securely dated features. In East Yorkshire and Northeast Scotland, continued excavation and accidental finds through metal-detection have both added to the known examples along with excavation context and clear spatial data.

With the overall British distribution of glass beads in mind, within each study region the actual distributions differ (Figure 93). The distribution of beads in Southwest England is the most dispersed, although the largest clusters are at the lake villages of Glastonbury and Meare. Smaller clusters are visible on the Dorset coastline and along the south side of the Bristol Channel. Other finds add to the overall density for the region, but in general they are from a small number of sites. In contrast, the concentrations of glass beads in the other three study regions are more localised. In East Anglia, this is primarily in northwest Norfolk at Grandcourt Quarry, and in East Yorkshire, the primary cluster runs between Arras, Wetwang, and Cowlam. In Northeast Scotland, the main clusters are at Culbin Sands and Birnie, and at Culduthel Farm. This pattern is derived in part from the research history of each region as discussed

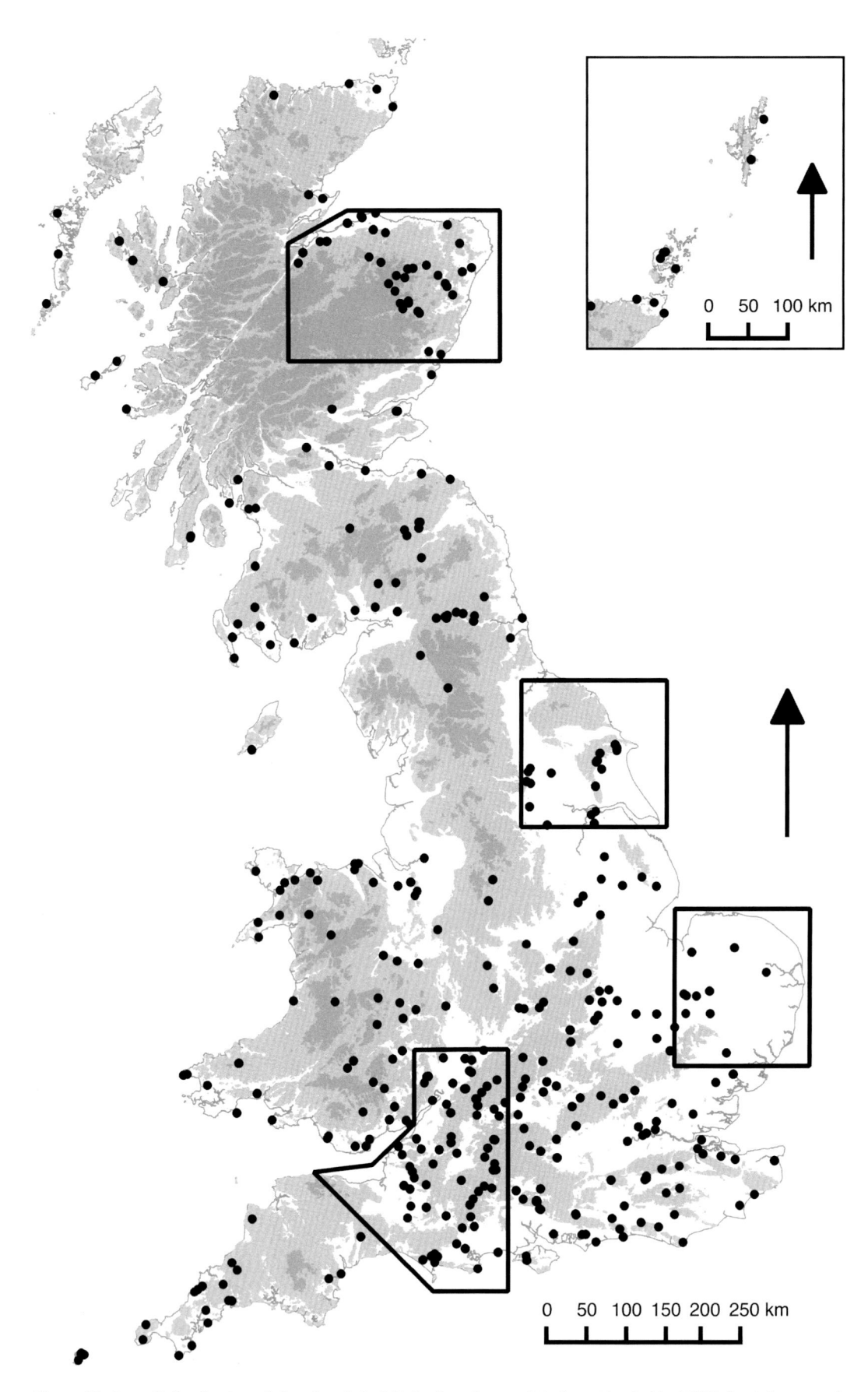

Figure 92: Overall distribution of glass beads in Britain. Drawing on data from the Guido (1978a) catalogue and new additions in the research database.

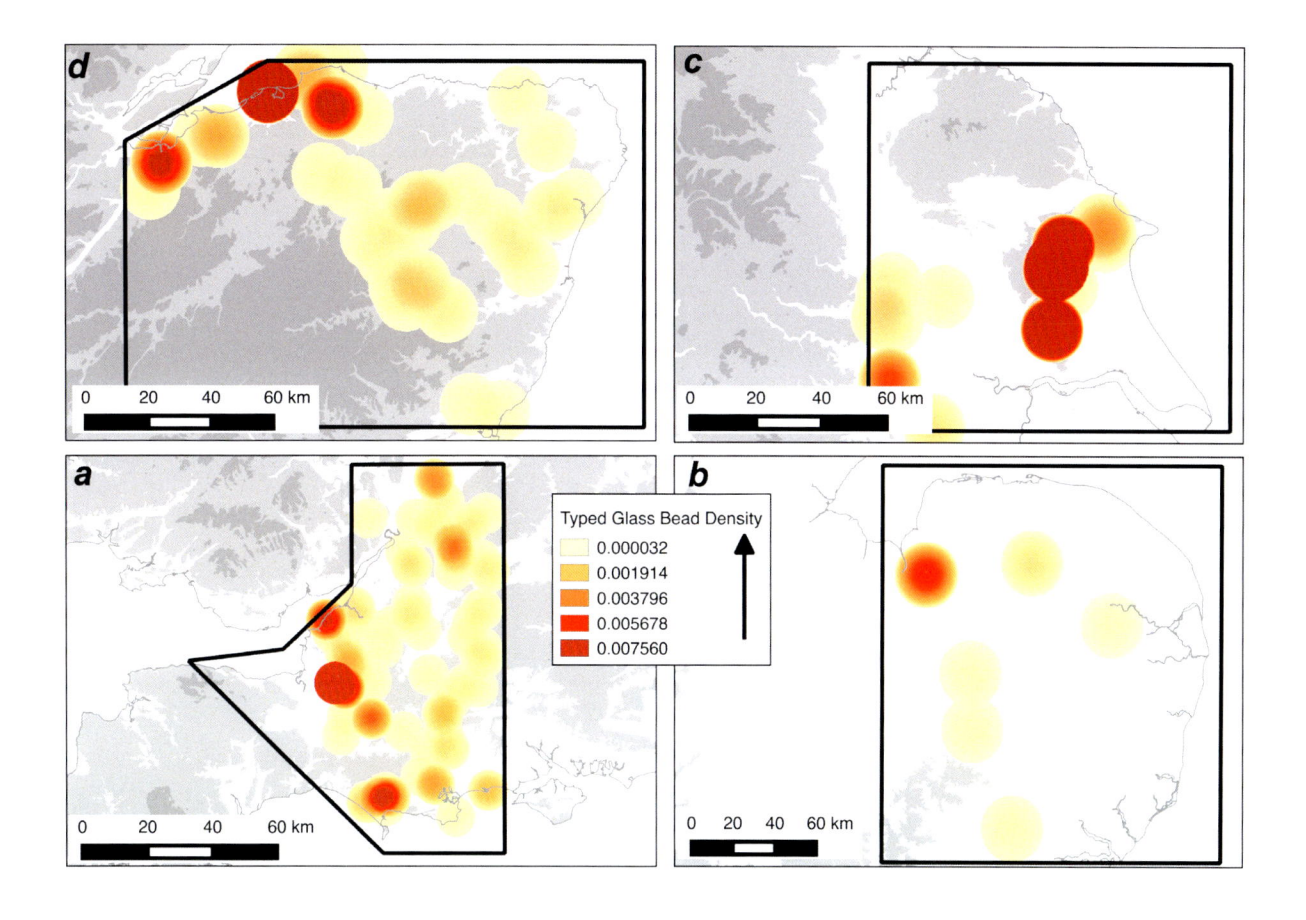

Figure 93: Maps of study regions showing density of typed glass beads. (a) Southwest England, (b) East Anglia, (c) East Yorkshire, (d) Northeast Scotland. No colour = bead absence, yellow = low density, red = high density.

in Chapter 4, but also from the nature of archaeological excavation as discussed in later in this Chapter.

The regions under study here are not equal in size (Figure 94). Interestingly, Southwest England is the largest region, but East Yorkshire has the largest number of beads, which also happens to be the smallest region and has the highest number of beads per square mile (0.2704 beads/mi^2). This suggests that larger areas of study do not necessarily yield an increased quantity of beads, but rather it may reflect differences in regional material culture and perhaps differences in depositional behaviour. Although only a limited number of glass beads have been found in East Anglia, this region is far from devoid of material culture. Instead, it is rich in coins, torcs, and horse equipment (Hutcheson 2004). In comparison, the area covered by the Northeast Scotland study region is well known for its number of glass beads, yet other material culture, such as pottery, is generally lacking. The implications of this analysis suggest that the occurrence of glass beads is not equally spread throughout Britain, but that it is tied to regional patterns of material culture.

	Size of study region (mi²)	Typed glass beads (n)	Beads/mi²
Southwest England	5.701.32	517	0.0907
East Anglia	3,938.22	26	0.0066
East Yorkshire	3,262.34	882	0.2704
Northeast Scotland	5,692.65	363	0.0638
TOTAL	18.594,53	1788	0,09616

Figure 94: Size of region, number of typed glass beads, and beads per square mile in each study region (all excavated glass beads and stray beads included).

Example Distributions

Rather than discuss distribution maps for each type, instead I would like to highlight two examples of how a detailed analysis utilising distribution maps can help to illustrate patterns in the dataset. As shown in Chapters 5 and 6, the eye motif is a particularly common design found on glass beads, as is the colour combination blue and white. Using Guido's (1978a) subdivision of Class 1 beads, the distribution in the study regions would appear

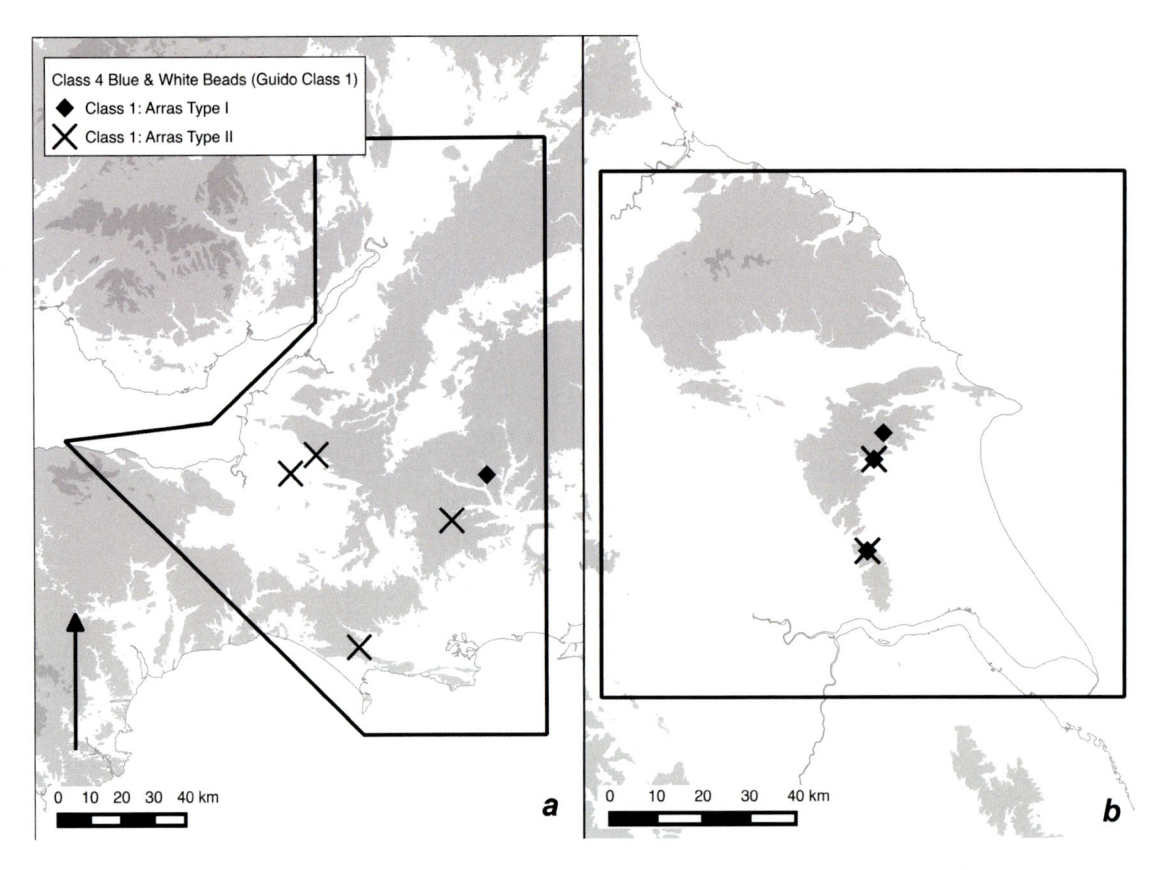

Figure 95: Comparison of the distribution of Guido Class 1 beads in (a) Southwest England and (b) East Yorkshire.

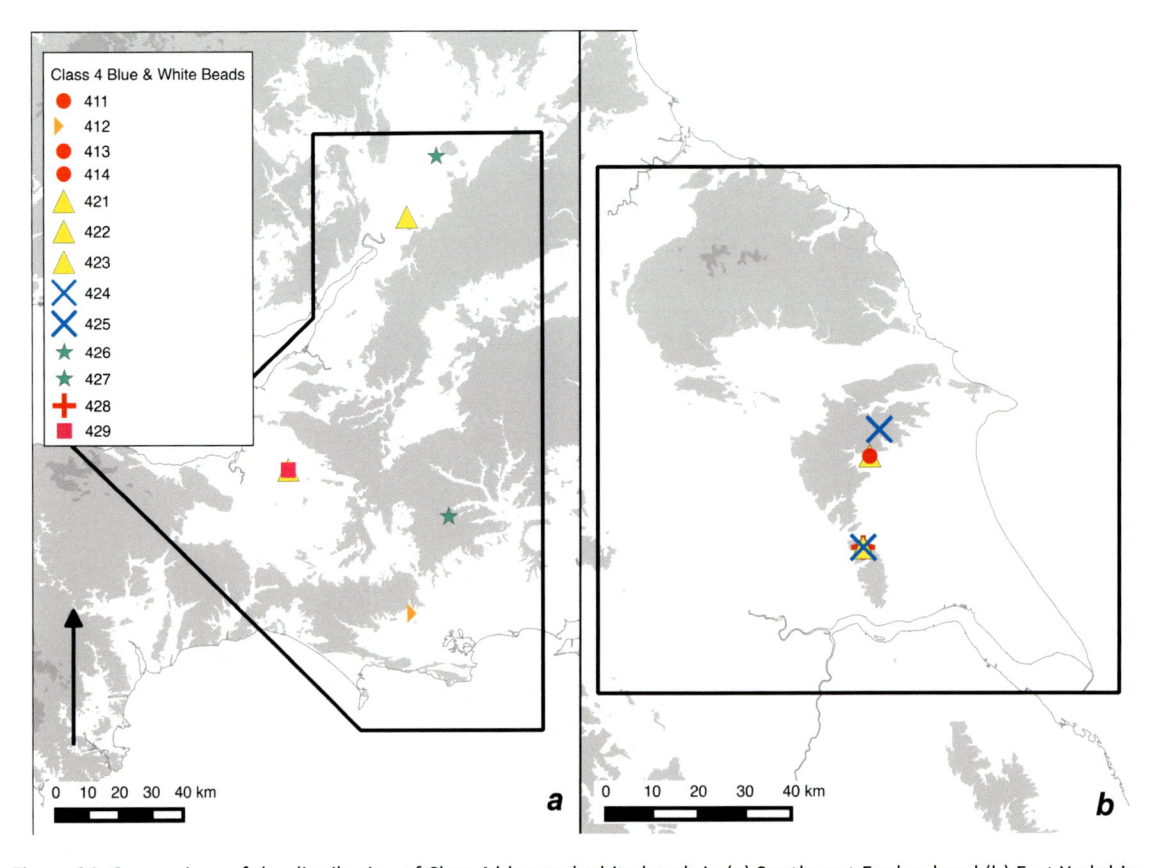

Figure 96: Comparison of the distribution of Class 4 blue and white beads in (a) Southwest England and (b) East Yorkshire.

as in Figure 95.[10] This shows that there is some overlap of both Type I and Type II beads. This might lead to the conclusion that not only are the beads used in these two regions the same, but that there might be some interaction between these distant areas. For Guido, explanations would probably suggest that this was the result of trade, as this type moved from the Bristol Channel or Dorset coast north and eastwards.

In comparison, through the use of the new typology proposed in Chapter 5, a different pattern emerges (Figure 96). Here, the distributions suggest that the blue and white eye beads found in East Yorkshire are distinctly different from those in Southwest England. Out of the thirteen types mapped, one group may exhibit some overlap between the regions. These are Types 421, 422, and 423, which are blue beads with nine eyes made from blue and white glass and the only potential area of variety here is in the shape of the beads. Other types, including: 412, 426, 427, and 429 are all distinct to Southwest England, while Types 411, 413, 414, 424, 425, and 427 are restricted to East Yorkshire. So while Guido's interpretation would suggest that perhaps there was communication between these regions, a more detailed analysis suggests that these regions may have been more isolated or at least had limited direct contact.

The second example breaks away from these typological based distributions to examine the patterns of a particular trait. Chapter 6 demonstrated the preponderance of the colourless and opaque yellow glass combination and the translucent blue and opaque white combination on some decorated beads. By comparing these two different combinations, different patterns in the use of colour emerge (Figures 97 and 98). Although the colourless and opaque yellow glass combination is characteristic of the finds from Meare Lake Village in Somerset, there nonetheless are other examples from the study regions, in particular those in Northeast Scotland. In contrast, beads with the blue and white combination are found in dense concentrations particularly in East Yorkshire, but also in Southwest England. Interestingly, only a few examples have been found in East Anglia, and they are almost absent from Northeast Scotland. This may suggest that this colour combination was preferred in two out of four study regions.

Although these distribution maps do not take chronological or other contextual data into consideration, they nonetheless aid in illustrating general patterns. While it is difficult at this point to extract general patterns throughout Britain as only four regions were investigated, the above analyses have demonstrated that

by querying particular attributes of glass beads, it is possible to begin to see some patterns.

Archaeological Excavation

Chapter 4 briefly discussed the archaeological resource in each of the study regions, along with some of the key debates and research questions. As shown, not only has there been an increase in the awareness of the diversity of practice, but also that archaeological inquiry has followed diverse paths in different regions. This section will examine the nature of excavation and the data within each region and how it affects the analyses contained in the following sections. In terms of understanding why glass beads are found at some sites rather than others, this section also aims at determining whether this is related to excavation methodology.

As developer funded excavation is a relatively recent development, not every excavation fits into a neat research versus developer-funded dichotomy. Prior to city planning and heritage management initiatives, sometimes archaeological remains were exposed through construction. These isolated object, feature, or site discoveries and/or resulting rescue excavations, have been included in an 'other' category: the resulting excavations are not always comparable to research and developer-funded excavations and reports. The analyses in this chapter specifically do not include sites that have not been excavated (i.e. survey), or random/chance finds from known or presumed prehistoric sites.

The database of sites was compiled by adding a separate record for each text, thus there were 1,699 records in the database that refer to publications or other literature within all four study regions. As some of these records duplicate information from other publications, these entries were summarised into 1,558 excavation events and 1,329 individual sites (Figure 99). These records form the basis for the subsequent analyses in this section and the remainder of the chapter. All of these excavated sites have met the guidelines for site inclusion as described in Chapter 1, namely that they exhibited activity dated to the Iron Age (or late prehistoric), Roman period, or a combination of both periods.

Glass Beads by Excavation Method

Data for excavated sites comes from both research-based reports and largely unpublished developer-funded reports. The growing number of developer-funded excavations (Figure 100) since the implementation of PPG16 in 1990 is reflected in the number of developer-funded excavations compared to research based excavations. Despite an increase in the number of excavations occurring, there is not a comparable increase in the number of glass beads that have been found. Out of all the excavations included in the database, 13.0%

---

[10] Only Southwest England and East Yorkshire are illustrated here as these were the only regions studied where these types of beads have been found.

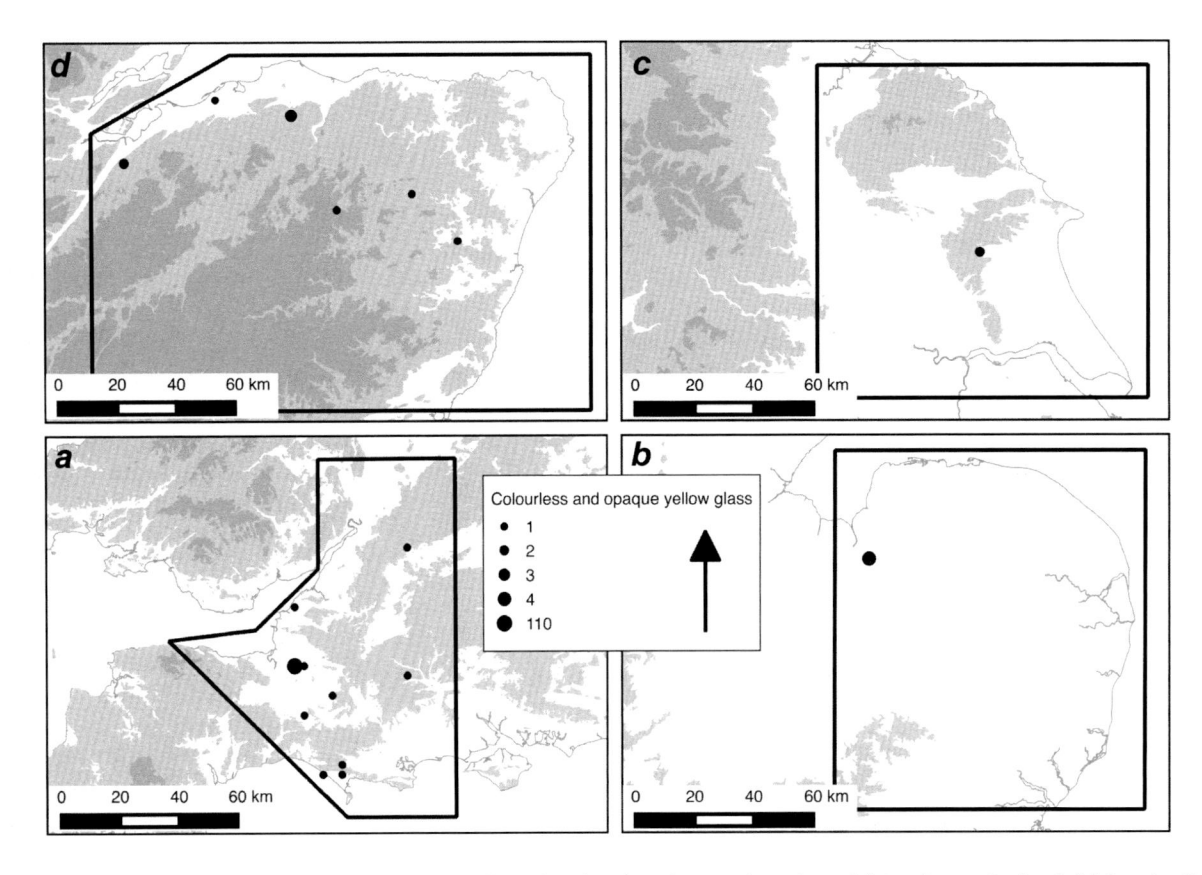

Figure 97: Distribution of colourless and opaque yellow glass beads in four study regions. (a) Southwest England, (b) East Anglia, (c) East Yorkshire, (d) Northeast Scotland.

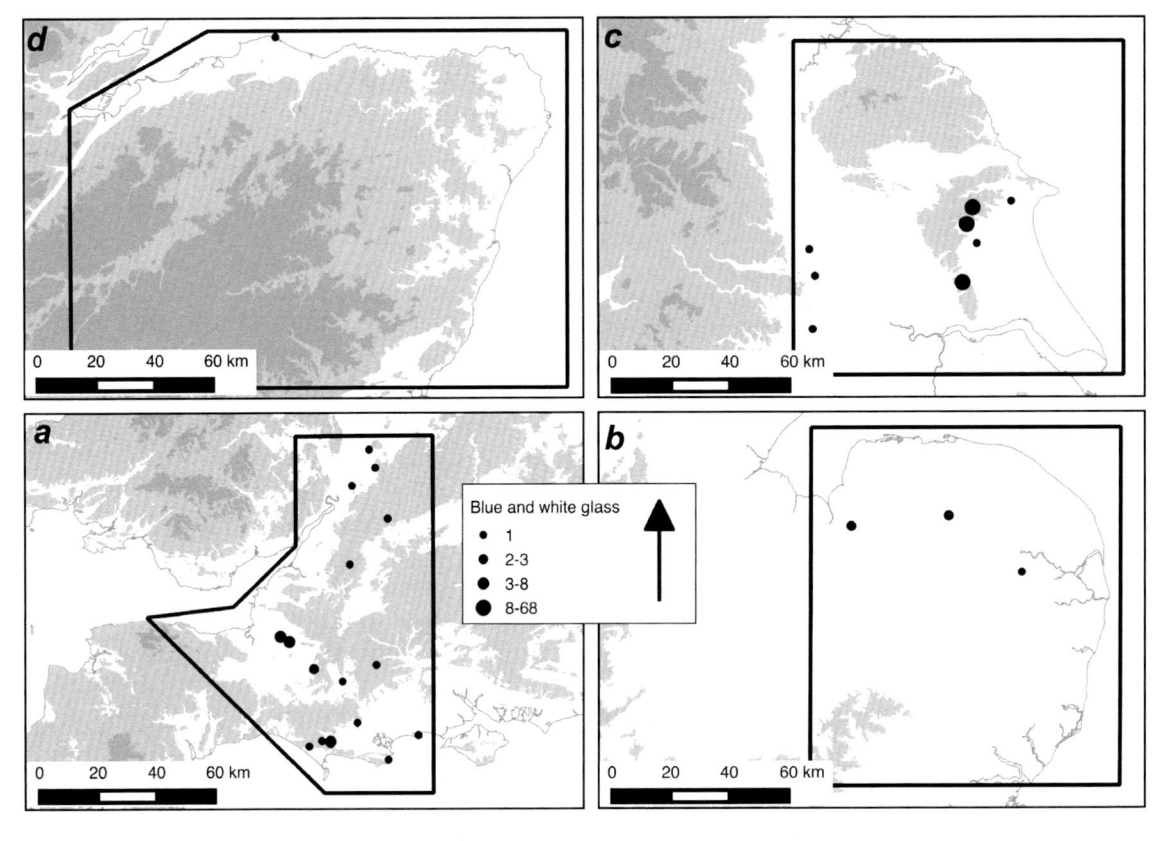

Figure 98: Distribution of blue and white glass beads in the four study regions. (a) Southwest England, (b) East Anglia, (c) East Yorkshire, (d) Northeast Scotland.

of research-based excavations found typed glass beads, while only 1.1% of developer-funded excavations found typed glass beads (Figure 101). This suggests that developer-funded excavations are less likely than research-based excavations to have an Iron Age glass bead occurrence. It is possible that this may be the result of different types of sites targeted through research and developer-funded excavations.

The impact of developer-funded archaeology can be seen in all study regions (Figure 102). In all regions except Northeast Scotland, these excavations account for more than 60% of the excavations in which Iron Age and/or Roman period activity was found. In Northeast Scotland, 'other' excavation types, such as rescue excavations, made up nearly 60% of the excavations, while developer-funded excavations made up 27% of the excavations. As might be expected, typed glass beads were absent from the majority of developer-funded excavations (Figure 103a and Figure 104).

However, the presence of typed glass beads is noted from research-based excavations in Southwest England and East Yorkshire, but from proportionally more developer-funded excavations in East Anglia and Northeast Scotland (Figure 103b). The quantity of sites in all cases is very small (Figure 105). The hypothesis that typed glass beads are more likely to be found during research-based rather than developer-funded excavations is confirmed by a Chi-square test, which suggests that there is strong evidence of an association between the presence of beads and the method of excavation (using data from Figure 101 X^2=150.726, df=4, p<0.01). The reasons why this should be the case are discussed in below.

Density of excavations

The history of research and development within each study region affects how and where excavations occur. For example, past research excavations in Southwest England have specifically targeted hillforts and Roman villas, rather than others sites. In contrast, developer-funded excavations are not necessarily intentionally directed at a specific type of site, but are more likely to excavate those that are less monumental, such as enclosed settlements and other/unenclosed settlements. As this chapter combines data from both excavation motivations, it is possible to cover a wider and more varied range of both prehistoric activity and geographic area.

Through a combination of developer-led and research-based excavation, there is the potential to evenly cover a wider geographic area. Instead, excavations cluster, and currently in some of the regions chosen for study here, blank areas remain (Figure 106). By mapping the density of excavation events it becomes possible to overlay the locations where glass beads have been found through excavation and as stray finds. Interestingly, despite the dense coverage of excavation events in

	Records in database	Excavation events	Excavated sites
Southwest England	929	857	702
East Anglia	401	387	347
East Yorkshire	251	247	226
Northeast Scotland	118	67	54
TOTAL	1699	1558	1329

Figure 99: Comparison of the number of records in the database, with the number of excavation events, and the number of individual excavated sites.

	Qty. Glass Beads Present	Glass Beads Present (not-typed)	Glass Beads Present (Typed)	TOTAL
Developer-funded	995	37	12	1044
Research	228	31	40	299
Other	162	36	16	214
TOTAL	1386	104	67	1557

Figure 101: Table showing the frequency of excavations by type and the frequency of presence or absence of glass beads.

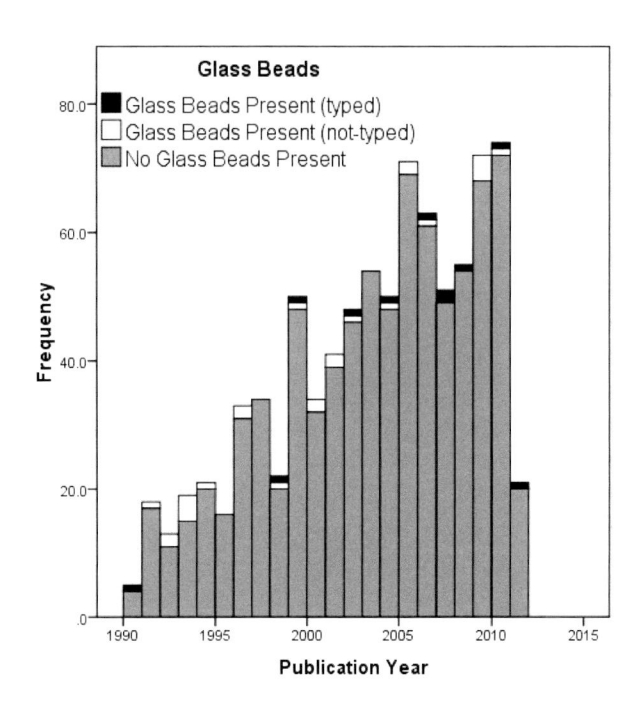

Figure 100: Chart showing the frequency of developer funded reports (included in the research) by publication year since 1991 and also showing the frequency of glass bead finds.

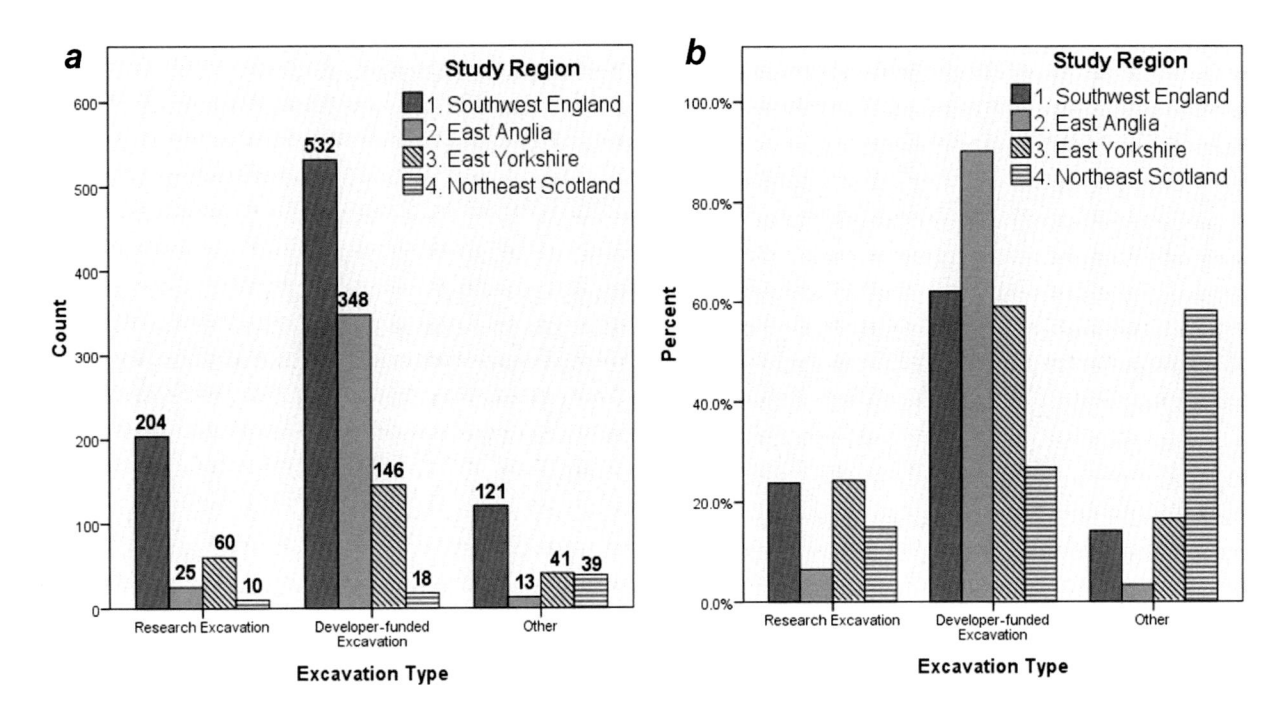

Figure 102: (a) Bar-chart showing the frequency of different types of excavations in each study region, (b) Bar-chart showing the proportion of different types of excavations in each study region.

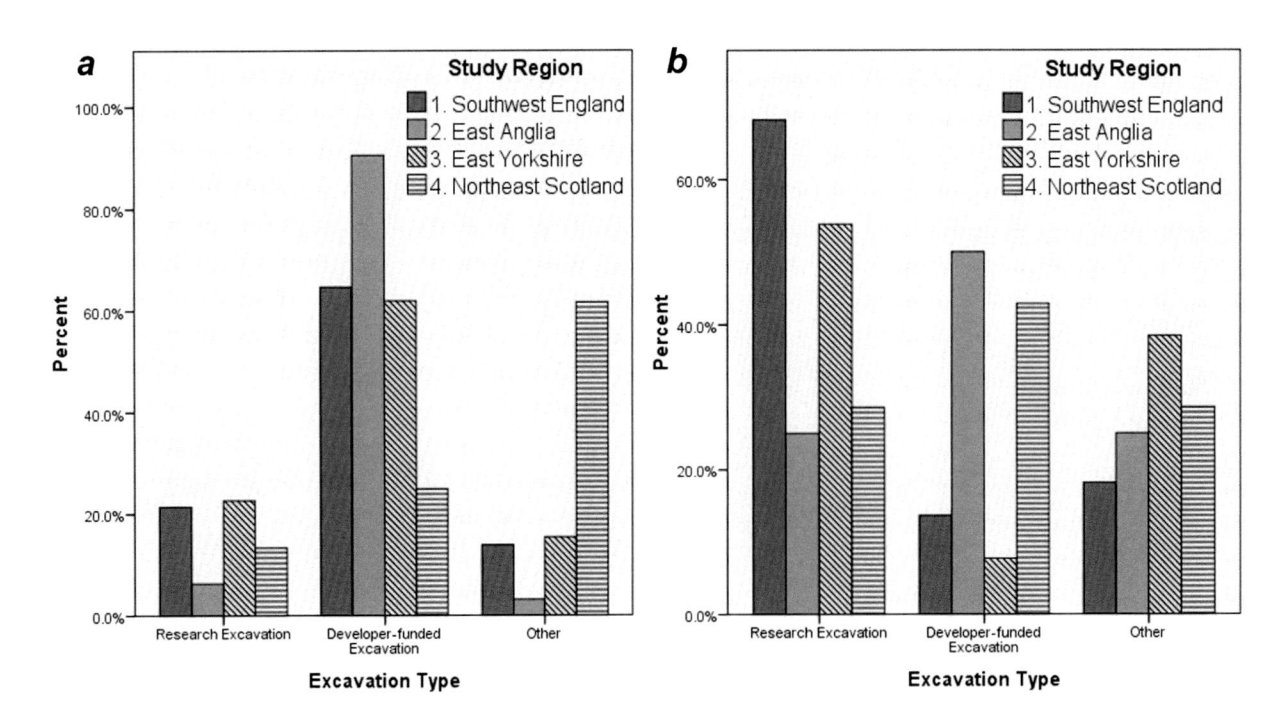

Figure 103: (a) Bar chart showing the relative percentage of different types of excavations in each study region with no typed glass beads, (b) Bar chart showing the relative percentage of different types of excavations in each region with typed glass beads.

ARCHAEOLOGICAL CONTEXT

	Southwest England	East Anglia	East Yorkshire	Northeast Scotland	TOTAL
Developer-funded	526	346	145	15	1032
Research	174	24	53	8	259
Other	113	12	36	37	198
TOTAL	814	382	234	60	1489

Figure 104: Table comparing the different types of excavations where typed glass beads were not found in the region.

	Southwest England	East Anglia	East Yorkshire	Northeast Scotland	TOTAL
Developer-funded	6	2	1	3	12
Research	30	1	7	2	40
Other	8	1	5	2	16
TOTAL	43	4	13	7	68

Figure 105: Table comparing the frequency of different types of excavations where typed glass beads were found.

East Anglia, Figure 106b shows that there are very few individual locations where glass beads have been found when compared to Southwest England (Figure 106a). In contrast, Figure 106d shows that many stray glass bead finds in Northeast Scotland have been outside of the areas that have been excavated.

While the density maps show an overall density of excavations, Figure 107 shows the locations of each excavation and differentiates first between whether typed glass beads were present (shape), and second by the type of excavation (colour), and spatially represents the data presented in Figures 104 and 105. For example, in East Anglia, it highlights just how many developer-led excavations took place without finding glass beads (green X) and the small number of research based excavations that also did not reveal typed glass beads (red X). Overall, this highlights the effects of both research-based (red) and developer-led (green) excavations in each region, and the proportion of sites where glass beads were found (circles), which were relatively few.

Both of these maps visually illustrate the distribution of excavations throughout the study regions. While on the one hand it is clear that the excavations are not evenly distributed across the study regions, and are thus perhaps

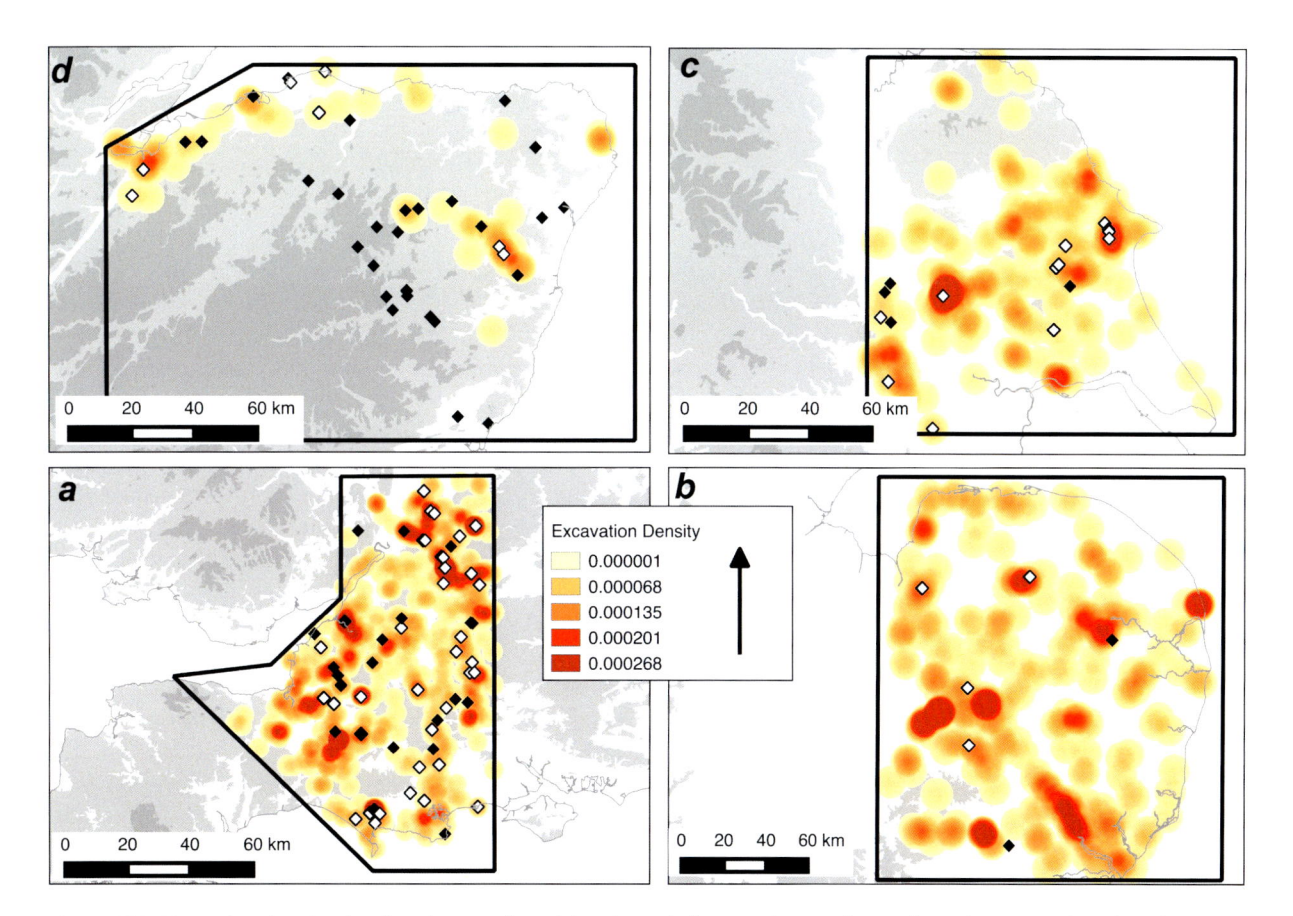

Figure 106: Maps showing the density of research and developer-led excavations within each study region. The white diamonds represent glass beads found through excavation, and the black diamonds represent other typed glass beads, usually found as stray finds. Yellow = low density of excavation, Red = high density of excavation. (a) Southwest England, (b) East Anglia, (c) East Yorkshire, (d) Northeast Scotland.

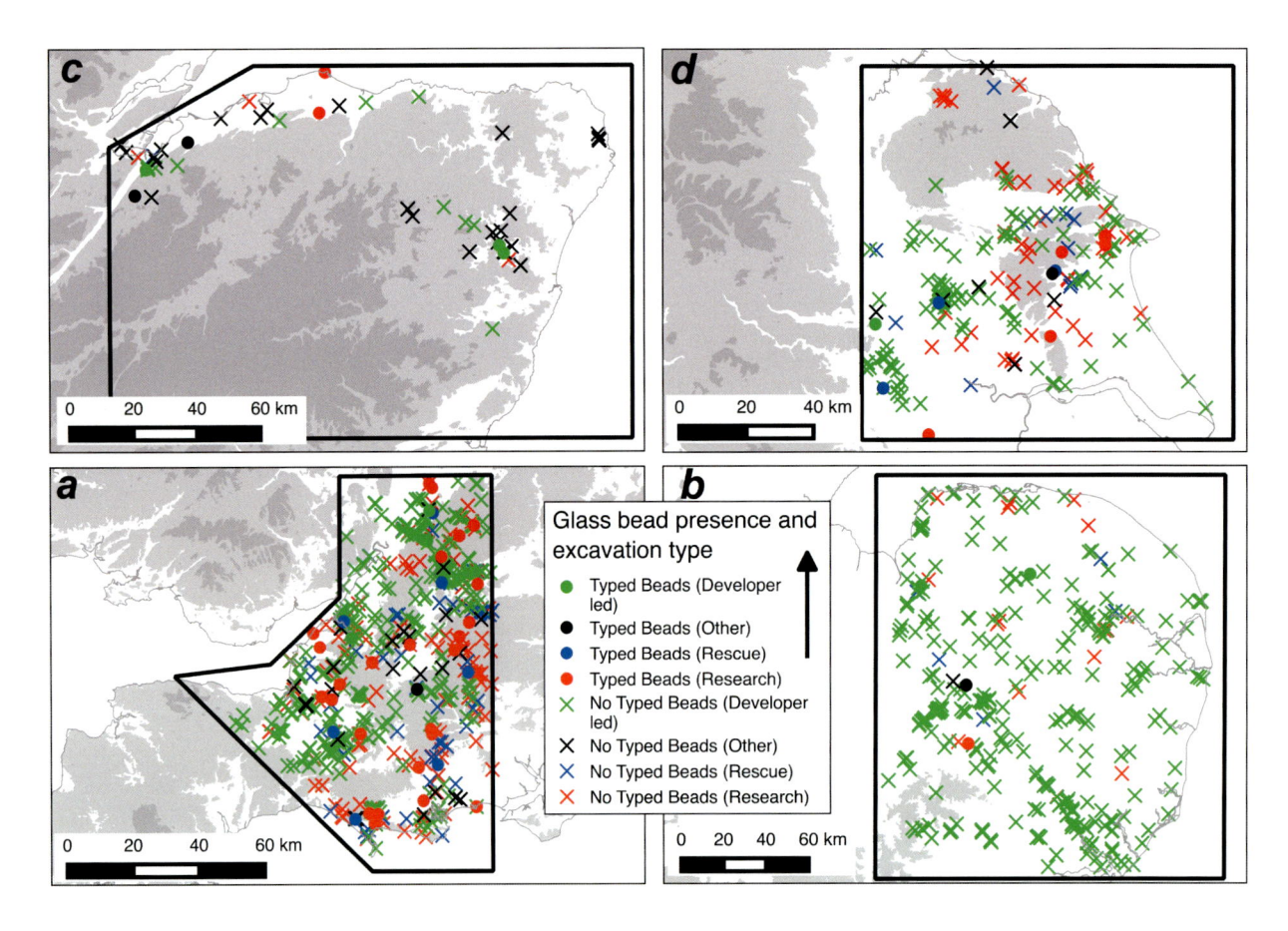

Figure 107: Maps showing locations of excavations. 'X' represents sites where no glass beads were found and circles represent were typed glass beads were found. Colour differentiates the type of excavation: Green=developer-led, Red=research, Blue=rescue, and black=other. (a) Southwest England, (b) East Anglia, (c) East Yorkshire, (d) Northeast Scotland.

not representative of a random sample, on the other hand it seems that more excavations may not necessarily result in more glass bead finds as shown in a comparison between Southwest England and East Anglia. Instead, it may be that real differences in material culture exist between different sites and between different regions. This idea will be revisited to in the site analysis section and in subsequent chapters.

Excavation Size and Methodology

In part, some of the patterns reflected in the density of finds and the locations where beads have been found could be due to the research methodology as outlined in Chapter 1; however, it may also be reflecting wider patterns in excavation methodology. Not all research and developer-led excavations are equal. One way that we can approach these differences is by examining differences in the size of the excavation. Some very small developer-funded excavations are limited to only a 1m^2 area, or less (often test pits). In these cases, it is sometimes difficult to put any material culture or features into context within the surrounding landscape, especially if the excavation is located within an urban environment. On the other hand, large-scale excavations benefit from the potential to put sites into a wider context.

One key difference in the methodology between research-based and developer-funded excavations is that the former has the flexibility to target specific areas of a site to answer specific research questions. For example, many of the early excavations of hillforts focused on the enclosing earthworks in order to understand the chronology of the site, as with Wheeler's excavations at Maiden Castle in Dorset (1943). This methodology introduces biases in the data, as the excavation of earthworks does not necessarily answer questions about domestic activities at sites, which are assumed to be located in the interior (cf. Cunliffe 1984a). Thus, material culture found in the context of earthworks is more ambiguous in terms of what practice is being reflected. In contrast, large-scale developer-funded excavations work within an affected area defined by a proposed development. From a review of the grey literature, there are three main methods of excavation within a large area:

- Randomly placed trenches to sample a percentage of the development site;

ARCHAEOLOGICAL CONTEXT

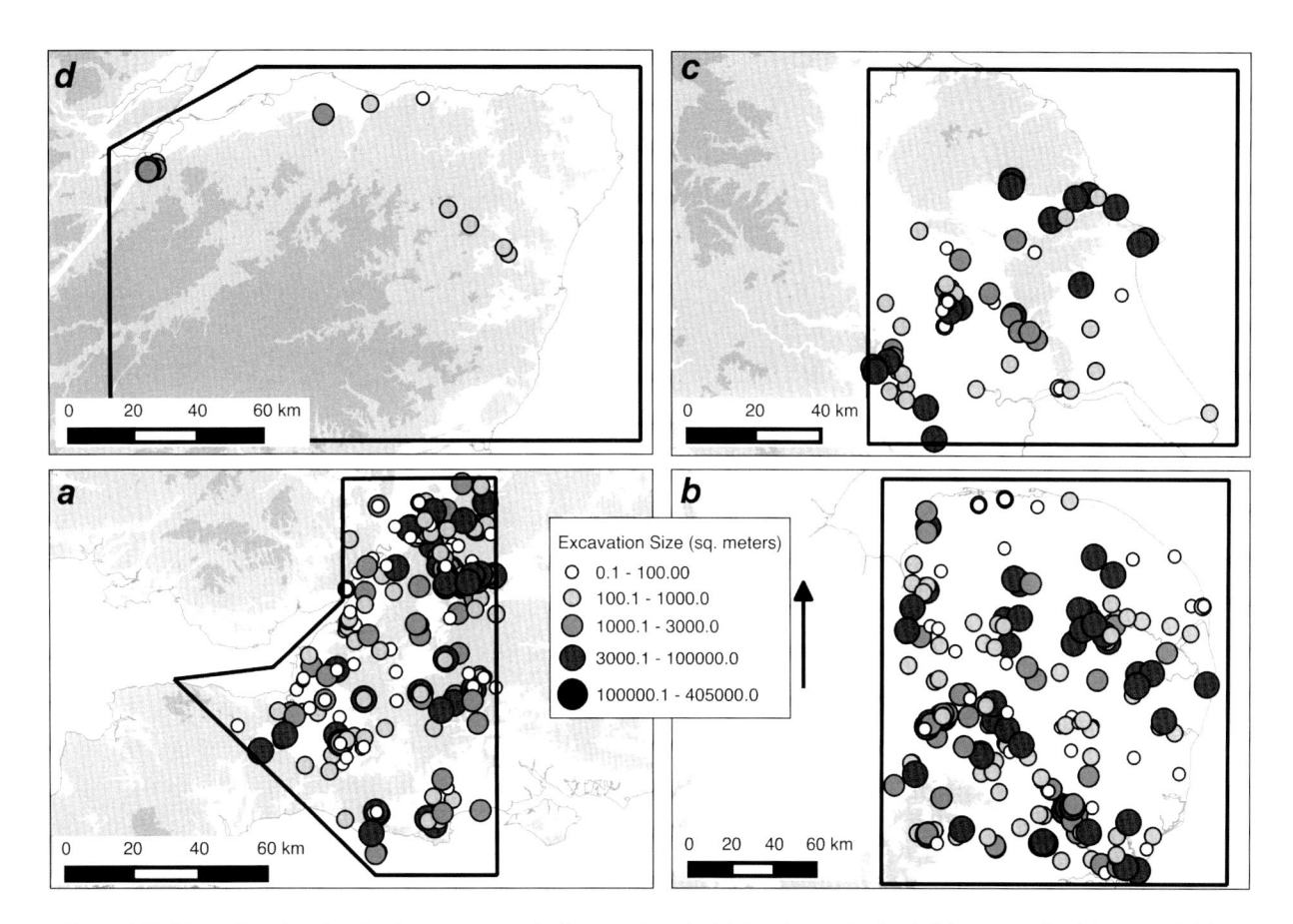

Figure 108: Maps showing the size (square meters) of excavations in (a) Southwest England, (b) East Anglia, (c) East Yorkshire, (d) Northeast Scotland.

- Trenches placed specifically to target features often located during geophysical survey, sometimes used in conjunction with randomly placed trenches;
- Total site strip and record, but only a pre-determined percentage of the features are excavated. Depending on the type of feature, some are completely excavated while others are half-sectioned.

All of these methods are utilised in developer-funded archaeology, but do not necessarily ensure that a site is dug in its entirety in terms of both surface size and depth.

In the study regions considered here, the size of the excavation was only explicitly stated for 41% of the excavation events, whereas for the remaining sites this information was not explicitly stated in the report. The available data on the size of the excavations shows a number of interesting trends. First, excavations within each region range from very small (0.1 m^2) to very large (405,000 m^2). Figure 108 shows the location of sites for which size data is known. Excavations that are under 5,000 m^2 in size make up the majority of excavations, while there are only a few sites in each region (except Northeast Scotland) where excavations were over 100,000 m^2 in size (Figure 109).

Typed glass beads have only been found at excavations where the size of the work was at least 1,000 m^2 (Figure 110). This may support the idea that glass beads are indeed very rare in the archaeological record. There are of course other factors that may be at work, such as the placement of the excavation and the sampling program employed as mentioned above; there are also other methodological issues. For instance, many of the recently found glass beads at Culduthel Farm and those from the 2001 chariot burial at Wetwang Slack were extremely small. The glass beads from the chariot burial were excavated under laboratory conditions. It is likely that because of the care and attention given to the excavation, these exceptionally small beads were recovered. At Culduthel Farm, the excavators undertook a number of environmental samples. Of the 25 glass beads that were found at the site, 52% were recovered due to the environmental sampling, and all of the glass beads found through sampling were exceptionally small. Other important finds from this site are the many glass fragments that suggest glass working occurred. These finds are incredibly rare and limited in nature. Up until these very small beads were found at these two sites, most Iron Age glass beads were at least 10mm in diameter and height. These new finds suggest that very small

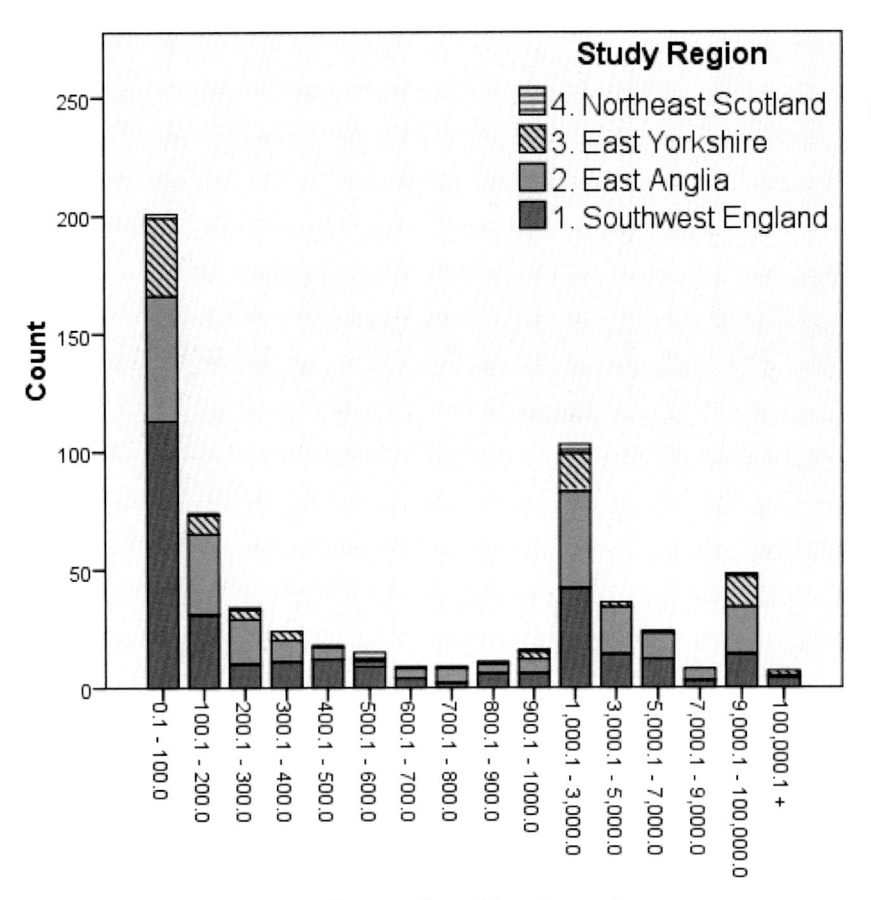

Figure 109: Chart showing the frequency of excavation size by study region.

Figure 110: Chart showing the frequency of excavation size and whether typed glass beads were present.

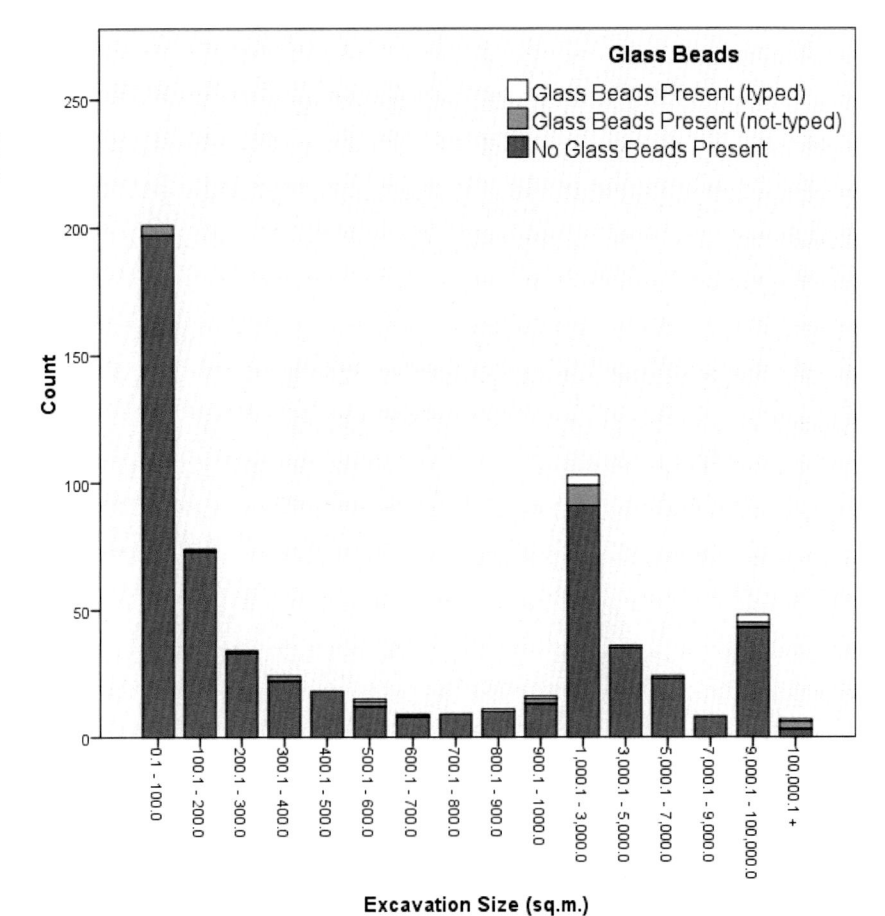

beads might have been more common than once thought and that their absence may be due to the excavation methodology and a limited sieving methodology.

Discussion

This section has aimed to provide some background analysis of the data to be discussed in the following section on site and feature types. It has done this through an analysis of different excavation methods in order to provide some understanding as to how excavation practice may introduce biases into the data. It has shown that despite the steadily increasing number of developer-funded excavations, this does not necessarily result in more glass bead finds. However, if this is reflecting real patterns in materiality, then by examining the negative evidence in this way, it is possible to put glass bead finds into a wider context of archaeological activity. That is to say that the number of known Iron Age sites has increased from the addition of developer-funded excavations, and because we do not see the same proportional increase in the number of Iron Age glass beads, it is possible to begin to demonstrate just how rare this type of artefact is.

Other contributing factors to the recovery of glass beads may be related to methodology. This includes the sites chosen for excavation, the placement of the trenches, and full excavation versus sampled feature excavation. In addition, this section has highlighted that the smallest glass beads have been recovered through laboratory excavation and environmental sampling. It may be that more of these miniscule examples have been overlooked due to their extremely small size and that they can only be recovered through systematic methods designed to retrieve things that might otherwise go un-noticed.

Site Types and Features

Artefact distribution, as shown above, takes finds out of their context and only examines them on a spatial level. By bringing together a detailed examination of artefacts, the type of site that they were recovered from, and the features in which they were found, it is possible to begin to develop a regional understanding of Iron Age practices.

Site Type

Considering the debates in Iron Age studies on the relationships between settlement form, social organisation, and value of objects, it is vital to examine not only the sites where glass beads were found, but also where they were not found. This section will consider both the positive and negative evidence for glass beads in order to place the sites with typed examples into a wider context of settlement in the Iron Age. The general patterns were highlighted in Chapter 4; however, this section analyses three aspects of site data. First, the site categories are discussed, and this is followed by a discussion of chronology. Finally, building on Henderson's (1992) work on decorated beads and site type, a comparison is undertaken of site type and glass bead complexity.

Categories

As Chapter 4 highlighted, the Iron Age archaeology in each of the study regions exhibit different characteristics. In order to make any analysis of the different types of sites comparable, it was necessary to develop terminology that could be applied throughout Britain. Out of necessity, the terms utilised for these comparisons needed to be simple. The reason for this is to be able to compare:

- Regional forms of activity sites;
- Sites that fluctuate over the Iron Age (i.e. from unenclosed, to enclosed, sometimes with intermittent periods of unenclosure);
- Different types of activity that frequently occur at the same location (settlement/domestic activity, inhumations, and 'ritual');
- Different chronological activity that frequently occurs at the same location ('Iron Age' settlement and Roman fort or villa on the same site).

With these issues in mind, seven terms have been utilised in this analysis. First, hillforts or 'hilltop enclosed settlements', as they are one of the most iconic settlements of this period. These sites were first distinguished from 'other enclosed settlements'. Any other settlement sites, including unenclosed settlements, and sites where it was unclear as to whether an enclosure was present due to the size/nature of the excavation, were categorized as 'other settlements'. These three types of settlement may have had evidence for a wide variety of activity, such as manufacturing and human/animal inhumations or other ritual activity. Where an inhumation exists on its own and not as a part of a settlement, the site is labelled as 'Inhumation/Cremation site only'.[11] 'Roman Villas' and 'Roman Military' sites without evidence for prior Iron Age activity have been labeled as their own categories. Finally, in cases where there are clear signs for late Prehistoric and/or Roman period activity, but the nature of it is unclear, an 'other activity' category was used.

One problem that presents itself when attempting to categorise sites, even generally, is that many of the excavations in East Yorkshire and East Anglia were not able to distinguish between Iron Age activity and Roman period activity. This stems from the difficulty introduced into interpretation when site reports try to categorise

---

[11] There have been no glass beads recovered from inhumations found actually within a settlement or within the boundaries of a settlement in the study regions. Where glass beads have been found with a skeleton, it has always been within a more 'formal' type of cemetery (e.g. East Yorkshire burials, cist burials, South Dorset style burials).

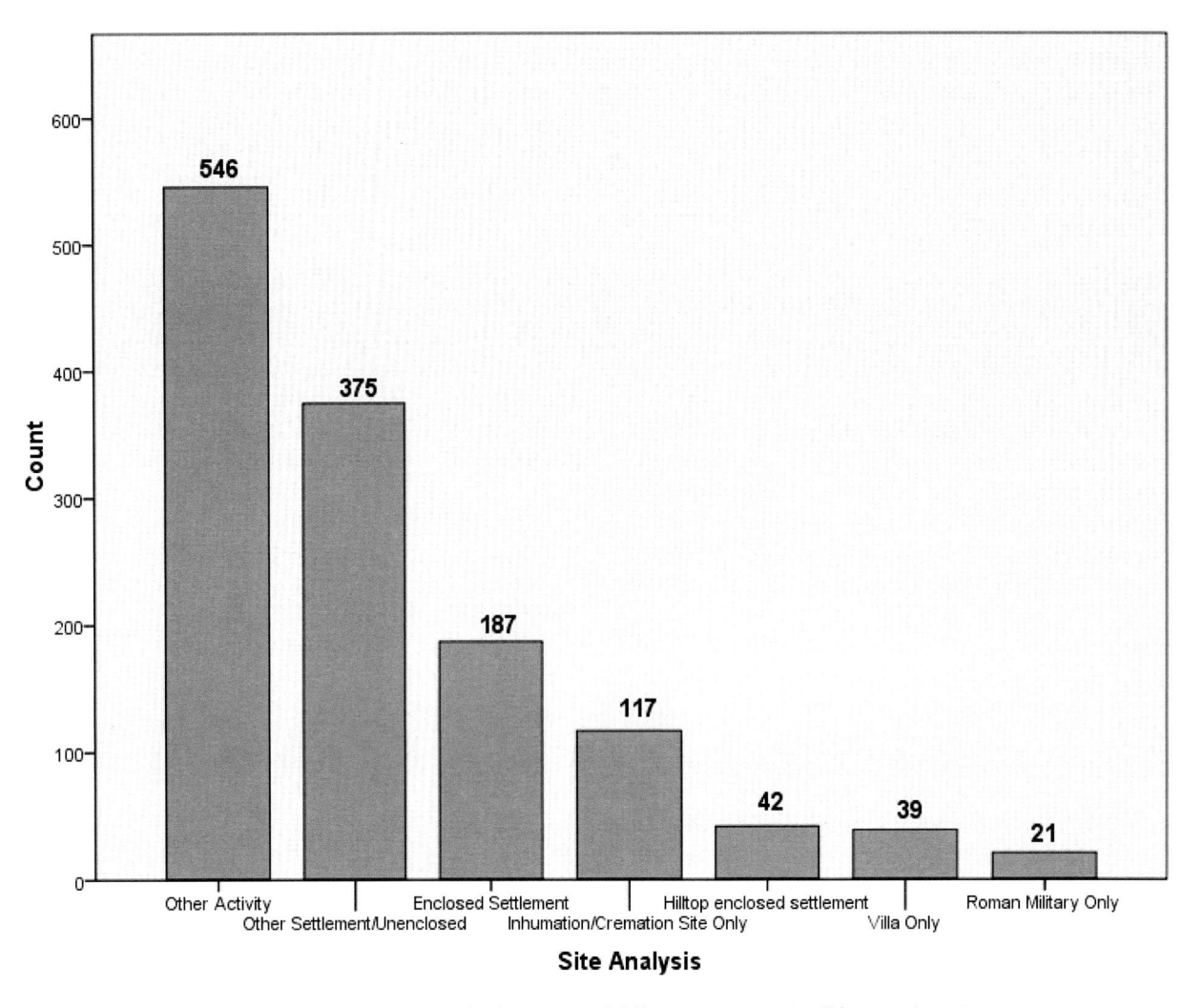

Figure 111: Bar-chart showing the frequency of different site types in all four study regions.

sites as 'pre-Roman', 'native style, but Roman period', 'Roman', and 'Romano-British'. Frequently, it is the material culture that is found on a site that is utilised to determine the period and level of 'Romanisation' or other Roman influence (Moore 2007a). Any Roman material culture found on a characteristically Iron Age (or, 'native') site is labeled as Roman period and taken to represent direct contact between 'natives' and Romans. In contrast, a lack of Roman artefacts on an Iron Age site is often labelled as 'native' or 'pre-Roman' in date. While the presence of such evidence can aid in dating at least some of the activity, it really does not demonstrate the extent to which the inhabitants had direct or even indirect contact with 'Romans'. Thus, for simplicity, this research has included all settlements that were not enclosed into the 'other settlement/unenclosed' category.

From these very general categories, most of the excavated sites in the study regions fall into the 'other activity' category (Figure 111). This is due to the small size of many of the excavations, as discussed in the previous section. Perhaps unsurprisingly, the 'other settlement/unenclosed' category is the second most frequent, followed by the 'enclosed settlement' category. These general trends are also seen even when taking a regional approach to the data (Figures 112). The raw frequency of the different site categories varies in each region, although the percentage chart demonstrates that proportionately similar occurrences of 'other activity' sites and 'other settlements/unenclosed' sites occurred across the different regions.

There are several patterns that emerge that emphasise the differences in the archaeology of each region. First, the number of excavated 'hilltop enclosed settlements' is largest for Southwest England compared to all other regions. Second, inhumation/cremation sites in both Southwest England and East Yorkshire are also more numerous than in East Anglia and Northeast Scotland. It is worth noting here that the scale of the inhumations differ between regions. In East Yorkshire, inhumations in the cemeteries at Wetwang/Garton Slack and at Rudston number in the hundreds. In contrast, those in Southwest England tend to be more isolated and smaller

ARCHAEOLOGICAL CONTEXT

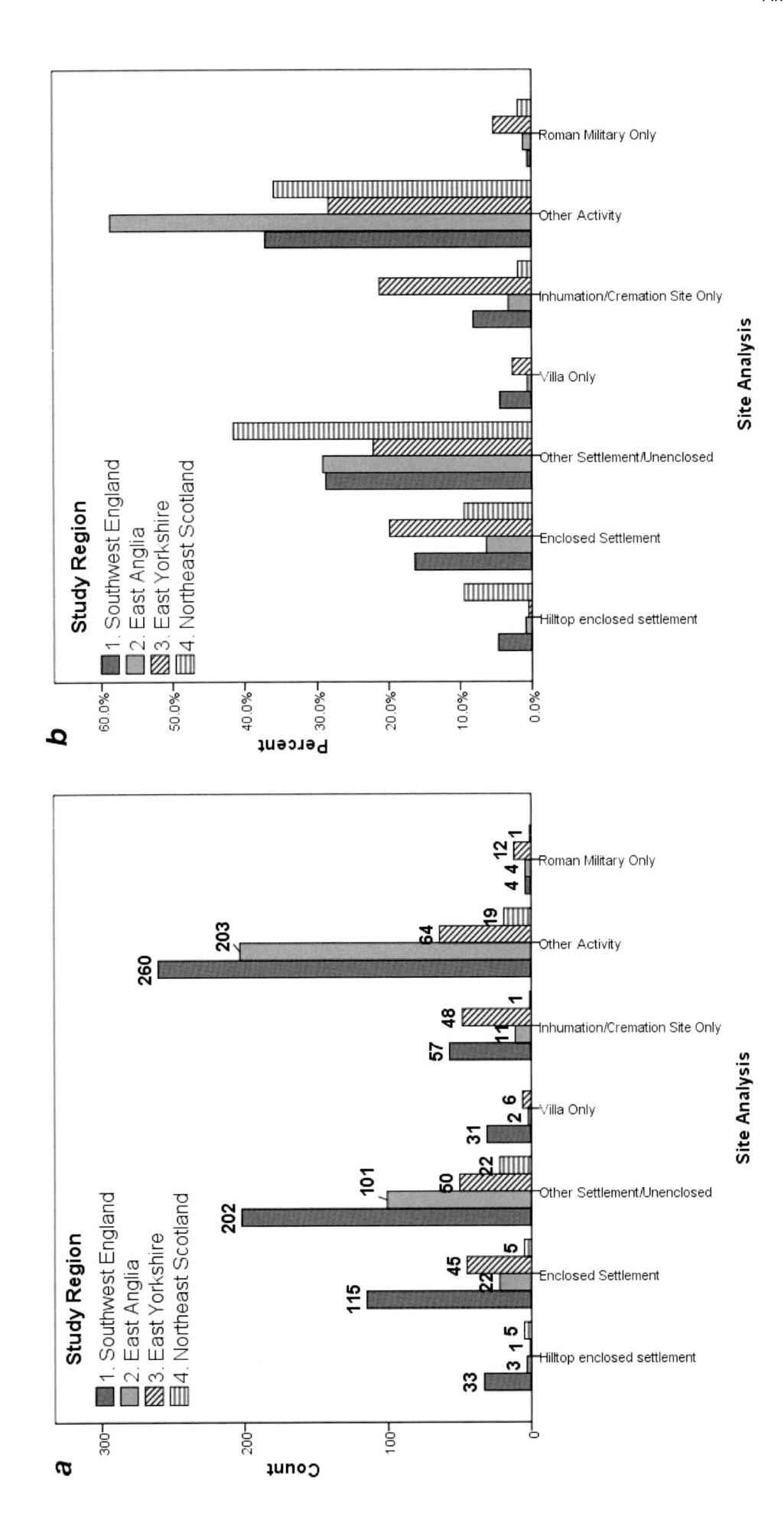

Figure 112: Bar-chart showing the (a) frequency, and (b) relative proportion of site types between study regions.

in scale, such as the mirror burial found at Birdlip in Gloucestershire, and the two mirror burials in Dorset (Chesil and Portesham). These patterns reflect the differing regional nature of the archaeology.

Turning now to the sites with typed glass beads, out of the 1,329 sites, they were only found at 4.5% of sites (Figure 113). The overall frequency of different site categories highlighted the large number of sites classified as 'other activity'; however, typed glass beads were often not found at these sites. Instead, they were found primarily at 'other settlements/unenclosed' sites (n=19) and 'enclosed sites' (n=16). Typed glass beads were also found at a number of 'hilltop enclosed settlements' (n=9) and in inhumation/cremations (n=8). Interestingly, typed 'Iron Age' glass beads were also found at two 'Roman villa only' sites, but not at 'Roman military only' sites.[12] A chi-square test suggests that there is strong evidence for an association between the type of site and the presence of typed glass beads (Figure 114, X^2=37.881, df=1, p<0.01). In this case, there may be reason to believe that typed glass beads are more likely to be present on specific types of sites rather than others. While in the past this has been connected with status (Guido 1978a; Henderson 1982; 1992), this need not be the case.

Taking the data for glass bead finds as a whole, they were mostly at settlement sites, although more specifically at sites with 'other' settlement activity (Figure 115). A regional approach assists in highlighting differing local practices (Figures 116). Glass beads in Southwest England are found at the greatest range of different sites, while other regions are more limited. Specific patterns are limited by the archaeology of the region, for example, glass beads were only found at hillforts in Southwest England, because there is a greater number of excavated sites there.

Chronology[13]

Just as it was difficult to characterise sites by the type of activity that occurred at them, it is also problematic to characterise sites by the point in time at which they were actively in use. Some sites exhibited activity specific to one period or possible crossover with another period, such as the Middle Iron Age or Middle Iron Age/Late Iron Age. Other sites were much more complex, sometimes with activity from the Late Bronze Age/Early Iron Age through to the Roman period, although this does not necessarily indicate continuous occupation throughout the year or from generation to generation. There were several other difficulties with this approach:

Site Type	Glass Beads Not Present	Glass Beads Present (not-typed)	Glass Beads Present (typed)	TOTAL
Hilltop Enclosed Dettlement	30	4	9	43
Enclosed Settlement	152	19	16	187
Other Settlement/Unenclosed	322	35	19	376
Villa Only	31	6	2	39
Inhumation/Cremation Site Only	99	10	8	117
Other Activity	525	15	6	546
Roman Military	16	5	0	21
TOTAL	1175	94	60	1329

Figure 113: List of the number of different types of sites and whether glass beads were present.

Site Type	No Typed Glass Beads	Typed Glass Beads Present	TOTAL
Enclosed Settlement	205	25	230
Other Settlement/Unenclosed	415	21	436
Inhumation/Cremation Site Only	109	8	117
Other Activity	540	6	546
TOTAL	1269	60	1329

Figure 114: Chi-square data for type of site and presence of glass beads. Note that some categories from Figure 113 have been condensed in order to create valid results in the chi-square test.

- Sites or periods described as combined or transitional periods (e.g. Late Bronze Age/Early Iron Age), especially for sites at the very end of the Iron Age and early conquest period;
- The term 'Romano-British' is used as a blanket term for anything post-conquest and pre-Medieval;
- Use of non-specific terminology, such as 'Late Prehistoric', 'Iron Age', 'Iron Age/Romano-British', 'earlier' meaning Iron Age versus 'later' meaning Romano-British;
- Early twentieth century publications that used the Hallstatt or La Téne chronologies, or the Hawkes (1958) Iron Age A, B, and C system.

Where possible, the different chronologies needed to be reconciled into one of the currently accepted models of periodisation used, namely Hill's (1995a) Early (c 700 - 450 BC), Middle (c 450 - 100 BC) and Late Iron Age (c 100 BC – AD 43) (although as noted in Chapter 4

---

[12] Some of the glass beads from Castleford were found at the civilian settlement, rather than within the fort.
[13] This section is approaching chronology from the depositional perspective, while the discussion in Chapter 5 discussed chronology in a broader typological perspective.

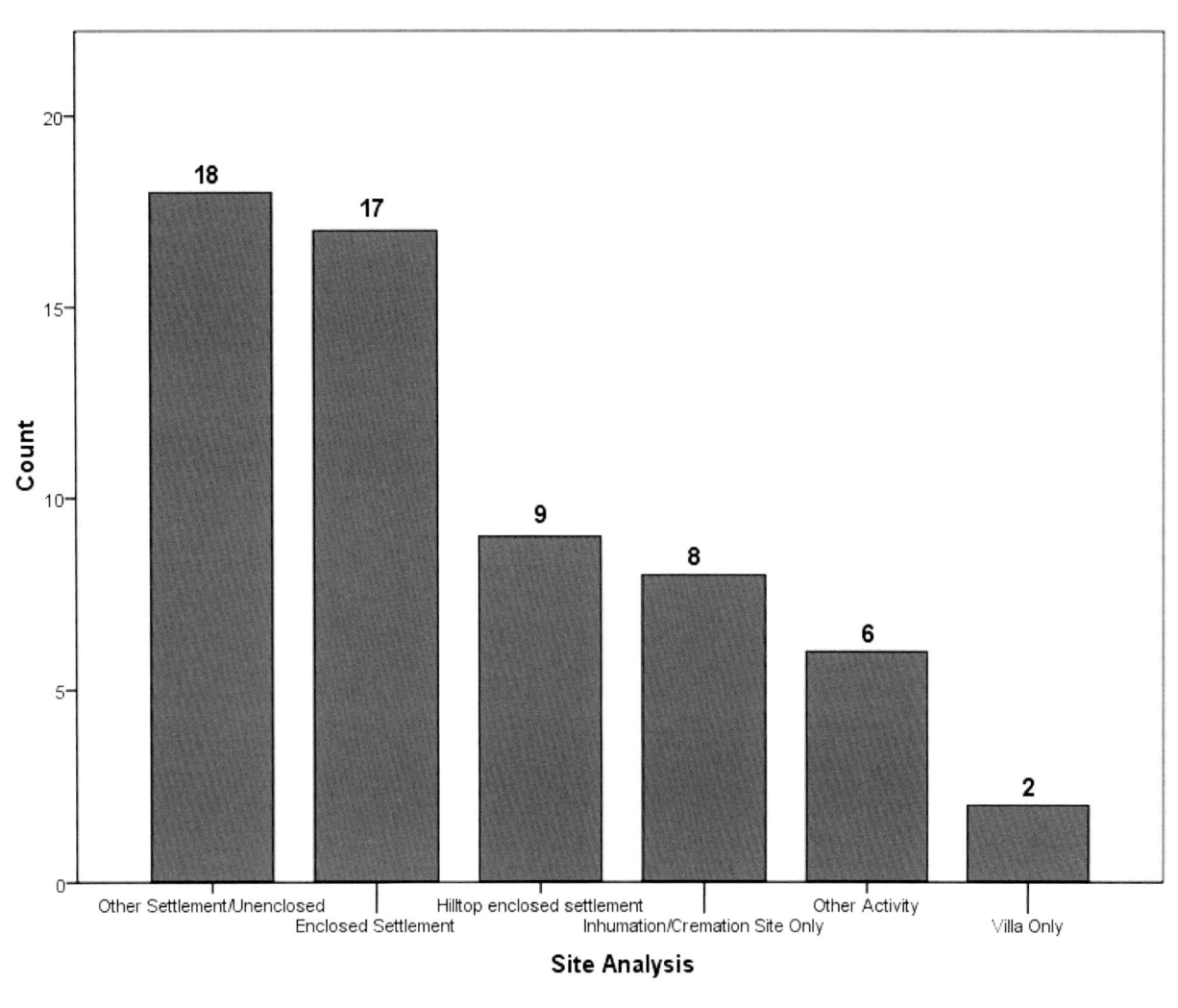

Figure 115: Bar-chart showing the frequency of sites where typed glass beads were found.

there are issues with using this periodisation to address all regions together). The second half of the first century AD and the beginning of the second century AD is considered as the Early Roman period. The Romano-British period follows. In some cases, there is not a distinction between the Romano-British period and the end of the Roman period, but where there is, the late fourth century AD and early fifth century AD are considered Late Roman. In Scottish Iron Age studies the Roman conquest of southern Britain is not recognised as a major chronological point of change, as the Iron Age in this region is described as having lasted longer into the first millennium AD (Harding 2004); however, I am simply using these terms in their chronological sense rather than in a cultural change sense. Romans did venture north of Hadrian's Wall and there was short-lived occupation along the Antonine Wall. In addition, there is a growing awareness of the impact of Roman material in non-conquered Scotland (Hunter 2001c; 2007a; b; Ingemark 2003; Macinnes 1989). Even if the presence of Roman artefacts north of Hadrian's Wall was not the result of direct contact, it is clear that there were changes in material culture (e.g. massive armlets). Despite these issues, it is possible to use the available data to give a general character of all the sites included in this study to some extent. This section first examines the date of all sites included in the study, and then will specifically examine the date of sites where typed glass beads were recovered through excavation.

A very raw count of the frequency of the activity from all sites included in this study demonstrates that the majority (by far) of the activity dates to the Romano-British period[14] (Figure 117). A regional view of the general chronology follows the main trend seen above. In terms of the frequency, in Southwest England, the number of sites through time steadily increases (Figure 118a). This trend can be seen in most regions, especially in the

---

[14] This raw count totals every period of activity from each site. Thus, a site with activity dating to the Middle Iron Age and the Romano-British period will count in two instances to each of the respective periods in the chart.

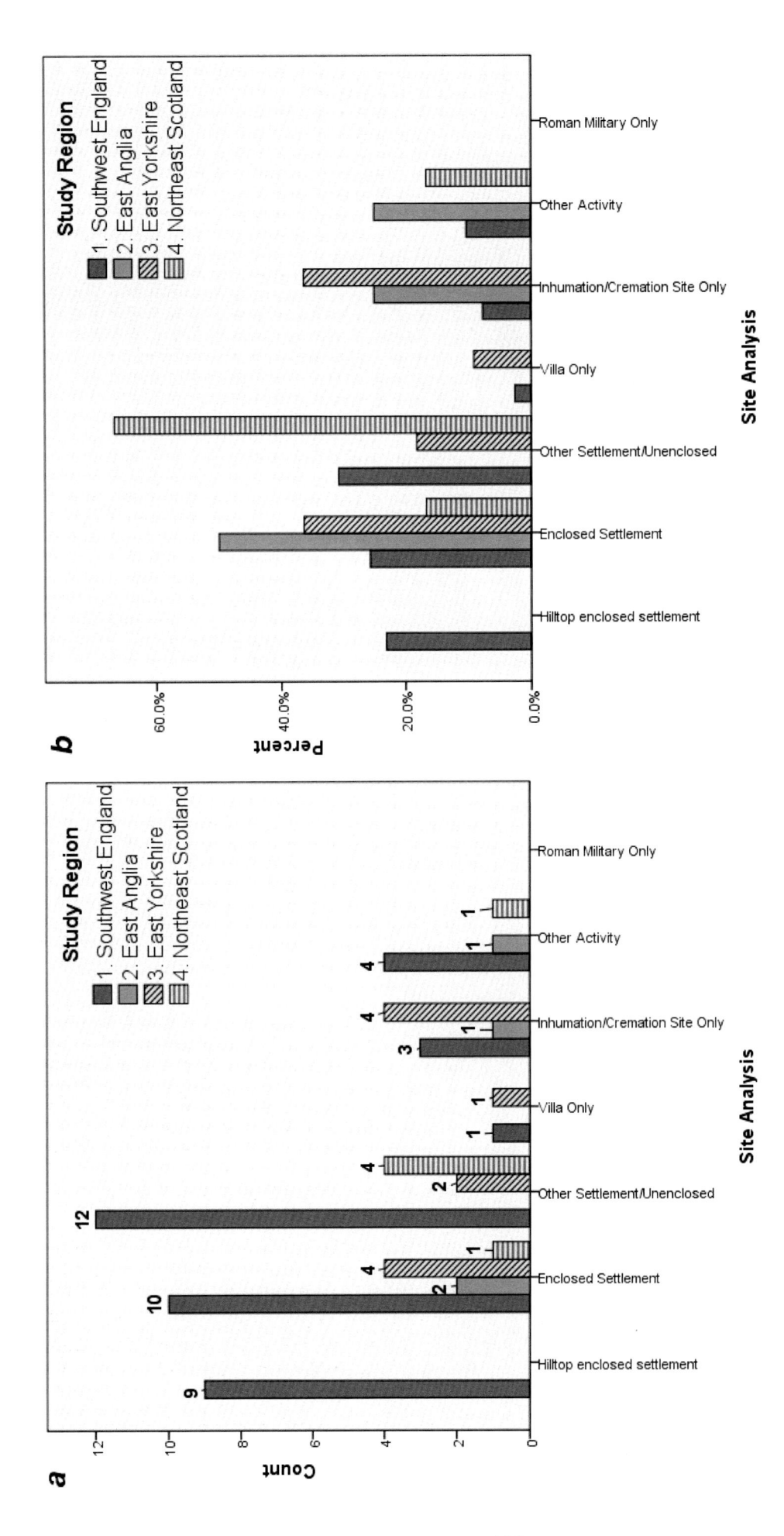

Figure 116: Bar-chart showing the (a) frequency, and (b) proportion of site types where typed glass beads were found by study region.

ARCHAEOLOGICAL CONTEXT

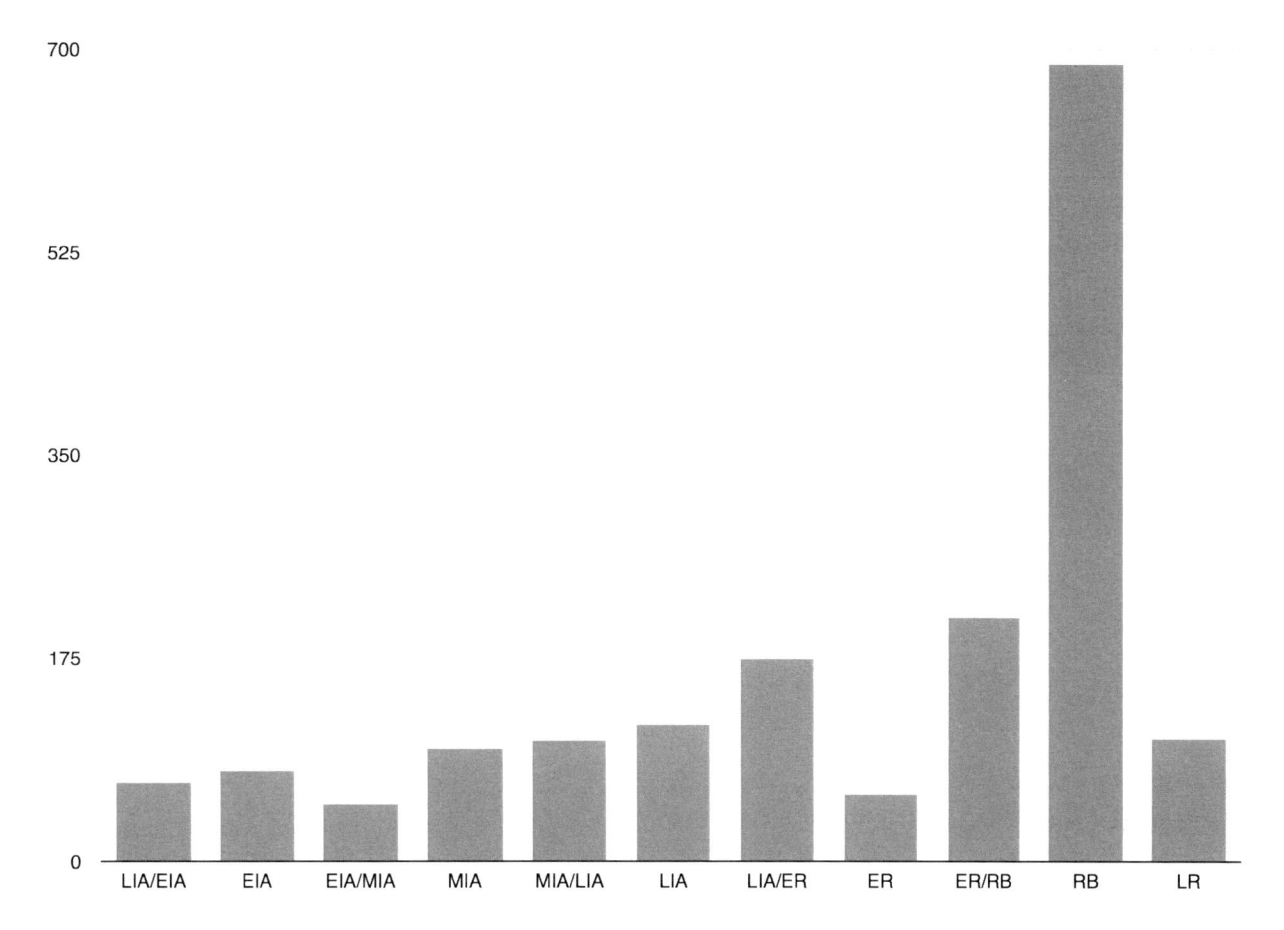

Figure 117: Bar-chart showing the frequency of the occurrence of activity from different periods for all study regions.

percentage chart in Figure 118b. Although the transition periods often demonstrate a decrease in frequency, this is probably a difficulty with the use of periodisation. Generally, we can say that from the available data, there is an increase in the frequency of activity over time in all study regions, resulting in an explosion of activity in the Romano-British period. However, this does not take into account the longevity of the activity as it only counts the frequency of period activity.

Before specifically examining the chronology of sites where typed glass beads were found, it is useful to explore in a general sense the periods of activity where typed glass beads were not found by site type, and where they were found during excavation (Figures 119). For the sake of simplicity, the chronological aspects of these charts have been simply divided into 'Iron Age Only', 'Iron Age and Roman/Romano-British' and 'Roman/Romano-British' evidence. Sites that have not produced glass beads span all periods and all site types. Sites that do have typed glass beads associated with them most frequently have evidence of both Iron Age and Roman/Romano-British period activity, although Iron Age only sites also occur. Typed glass beads are found less frequently from sites that only have evidence for Roman or Romano-British period activity, but they do occur at different types of sites and those where the activity is more ambiguous. This only gives a general picture of the types of sites where glass beads occur and do not occur and the periods that they date to. The following section will explicitly examine sites and site phases where typed glass beads were found. Although, here it is worth noting that these beads have been found primarily in enclosed settlement contexts, which were typical for the period.

Late Bronze Age/Early Iron Age

Twelve glass beads can be attributed to Late Bronze Age or Early Iron Age phases at six sites. All of these sites are in Southwest England (Figure 120) Of these sites, one is a hillfort, three are enclosed settlements, and one is a midden site. The types of beads that occur at these sites are very limited, as out of the thirteen glass beads from this period, only four different types are represented. All but one of these beads are a part of Class 1 simple monochrome beads, and the colours are limited to blue, green and yellow. Only one polychrome bead can be attributed to this period, which is from Swallowcliffe Down in Wiltshire (DB 4953). Perhaps one of the earliest beads is that from East Chisenbury in Wiltshire (DB 8736), where a bead was found stratified in the midden deposits with Late Bronze Age/Early Iron Age pottery (McOmish, Field *et al.* 2010). Another potentially early example of this type comes from Maiden Castle in Dorset

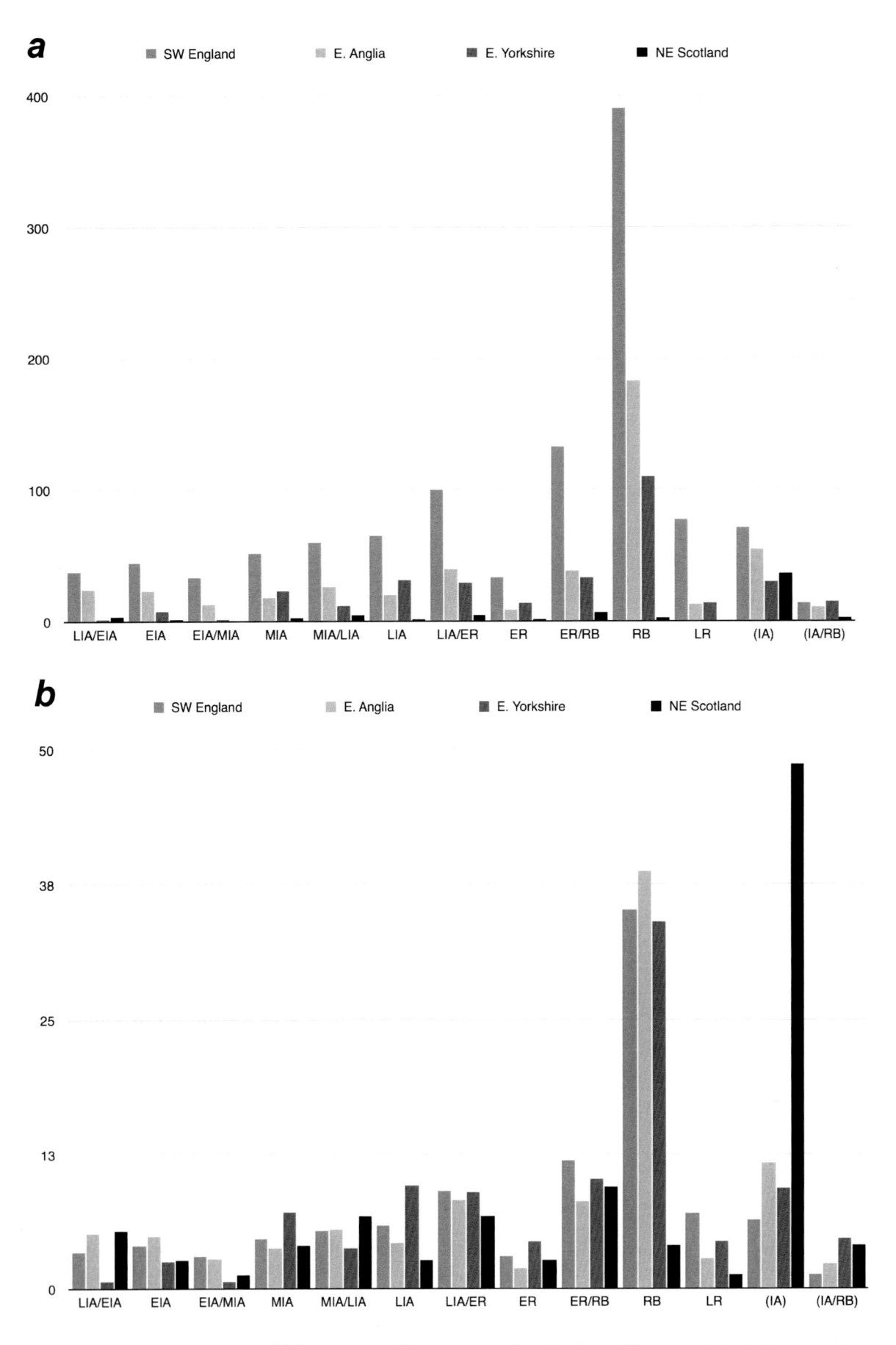

Figure 118: Bar-chart showing the (a) frequency, and (b) percentage of activity from different periods within each region.

Archaeological Context

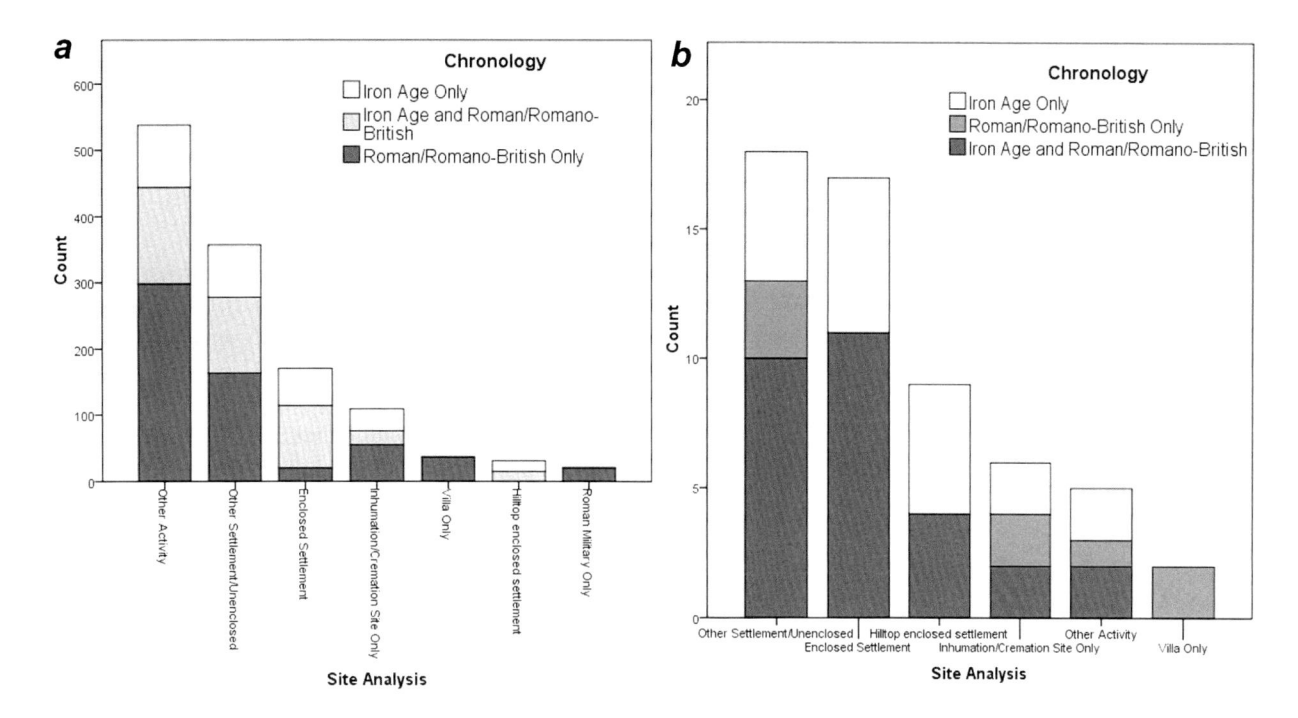

Figure 119: Bar-chart showing the frequency of sites and general period where typed glass beads were (a) not found at, and (b) present.

(DB 4176), where a bead was found in the earlier phases of the site. This group of early glass beads is extremely significant as many bear similarities to beads deposited in later contexts.

Middle Iron Age/Late Iron Age

In contrast to the Late Bronze Age/Early Iron Age period, over 1,000 glass beads from all regions (except Northeast Scotland) can be attributed to the Middle Iron Age/Late Iron Age period. The majority of these beads were found in Southwest England and East Yorkshire, while only one was found in East Anglia. The key difference between the glass beads found in Southwest England and East Yorkshire during this period is that in the former region the sites are all habitation sites, while in the latter most sites are inhumations, although a small minority are from settlements. This reflects the different nature of the archaeological records of these areas and is the result of differing depositional practices.

Not only were the glass beads diverse in Southwest England during this period, but also the same could be said of the sites where they were found (Figure 121a). Three sites can be categorised as general settlements, while three were 'lake villages'. Glass beads were also found during enclosed settlement phases at two sites, and a small number were found at hillforts. Out of the 357 glass beads from this region, 88% of the beads were found at both the east and west locations at Meare Lake Village, which also included the largest range of types. Small

Site	Site Type	Qty. Glass Beads	Type
East Chisenbury	Midden	1	Class 1: Type 110
Gussage All Saints	Enclosed Settlement	3	Class 1: Type 102, 106
Pimperne Down	Enclosed Settlement	1	Class 1: Type 102
Swallowcliffe Down	Enclosed Settlement	5	Class 1: Type 102
			Class 4: Type 427
Maiden Castle	Hillfort	2	Class 1: Type 102, 110

Figure 120: Sites in Southwest England with activity dating to the Late Bronze Age/Early Iron Age with glass beads.

numbers of beads were found at the remaining sites in this region. Slightly more unusual are the six beads from a hillfort at Conderton Camp in Worcestershire and the three beads from the nearby hillfort at Bredon's Norton. These are unusual due to the quantity when compared to the other sites, where single finds are more common (except for the lake villages). As is shown in the next section, their presence may be the result of intentional depositional behaviour.

In contrast to Southwest England, the glass beads from East Yorkshire are found at very different sites (Figure 121c). The majority of beads were from cemeteries, or in the case of Wetwang Slack, a cemetery connected to a settlement. It may be that the other sites, such as the complex of barrows at Arras and Cowlam, were also located near to settlements; however, this has not been investigated. Interestingly, at Wetwang and Garton Slack, the only glass beads that were found in the settlement area were found with other inhumations rather than being found in domestic contexts. Most of the glass beads from East Yorkshire burials were found in large numbers in each inhumation, although within some inhumations, such as at Burton Fleming, these were single finds. In addition to the beads from inhumations, two other beads have been found within the Middle Iron Age phase at Sutton Common. One of these was within the ritual enclosure, while the other was in a settlement context.

It is during this period that we can attribute a small group of glass beads from East Anglia. From Grandcourt Quarry sixteen examples were found; some of which are well-known, while others were previously unknown types (Figure 121b). One bead may have been manufactured in Britain, while the remaining beads may have come from continental Europe. The site as a whole is still awaiting final publication; however, it is clear that some unknown activity occurred as the main deposit was a pottery rich layer from which the majority of the beads were found. It may be that the site represents some aspect of ritual feasting; however, the large number of insular Middle/Late Iron Age brooches is unusual.

One other bead was found from a Middle Iron Age/Late Iron Age site in East Anglia. This enclosed settlement probably dates to this period, although it is difficult to distinguish from later early historic activity. The bead is a monochrome Class 1 Type 102 bead, thus it lacks decorative features that could be used to date the bead visually and is potentially the earliest glass bead from this region. The scarcity of glass beads in East Anglia, and the absence of glass beads from Northeast Scotland at this time suggest that this object did not play a large role in the material culture of these regions, or that the deposition practices were different from Southwest England and East Yorkshire.

Late Iron Age/Early Roman

By the Late Iron Age/Early Roman period, the trend of glass beads that was established in the previous period largely continued in Southwest England, but changed in all other regions (Figure 122a). The number of beads deposited at any one site during this period significantly decreased. In Southwest England, glass beads are found in at a variety of site types; the only difference from the previous period is that they are now found in inhumation features as well. It may be significant that these thirty-seven beads are thirteen types of polychrome decorated beads, and only five types of monochrome beads.

During this period a number of beads occur from excavations in Northeast Scotland (Figure 122b). As the majority of glass beads from this region were stray finds, these sites are important for dating all glass beads in this region. Here, forty-six beads have been found through excavation at three sites, and each of these sites has evidence for settlement in the form of roundhouses, although the question of enclosure is unclear. At Birnie, a search for evidence of an enclosure of the settlement yielded negative results, which considering the scale of excavation suggests that the settlement may have been unenclosed (Hunter 2002b). Interestingly, although the numbers of sites in this region are limited, the quantity of glass beads found at Culduthel and Birnie is larger than the majority of settlement sites found in Southwest England. In part, this may be due to the evidence for glass-working at Culduthel, such as the glass flakes and fragments of bi-coloured twisted rods. Yet, if these twenty-one glass beads were made at the site, then it is unclear why they were deposited as none of the examples were broken.

Early Roman/Romano-British

By the Early Roman/Romano-British period, Iron Age beads are found in even more limited numbers in deposits dating to this period. In Southwest England, the ten beads found in this region were found at settlement sites (Figure 123a). Most of these beads are the more complex Class 11 beads with meandering cables on the surface. There are very few beads of simple design, such as the Class 4 eye bead from Atworth villa, or the compound eye bead from Cirencester. Only one simple monochrome bead was found to date to this period, and this is a Class 1 Type 110 bead from Seamills near Bristol.

In East Anglia, the situation is little different (Figure 123b). Four glass beads were found at two sites. Three of these beads were found in a mixed hoard within a settlement at Billingford in Norfolk, while another bead was found in an early twentieth century hoard discovery at Santon Downham in Suffolk. It is unknown as to whether this second hoard was near to a settlement, or simply placed randomly in the landscape. Nonetheless, the bead was also amongst a number of objects, primarily metalwork, although there may have been a glass bangle fragment. The discovery of glass beads in hoard features is unusual, but will be explored further in the next section.

Finally, although no glass beads were found in East Yorkshire in the Late Iron Age/Early Roman period contexts, fifteen glass beads occurred in contexts dating to the Early Roman/Romano-British period (Figure 123c). These beads appear to be Iron Age types, but their context suggests that they were in use for far longer than many similar examples. For instance, amongst the beads from Castleford were a number of Class 1 plain

Archaeological Context

Site	Site Type	Qty. Glass Beads	Type
21 Church Road, Bishop's Cleeve	Settlement	1	**Class 6**: Type 901
Cannards Grave, Shepton Mallet	Settlement	1	**Class 1**: Type 110
Hengistbury Head	Settlement	1	**Class 1**: Type 104
Glastonbury Lake Village	'Lake village'	27	**Class 1**: Type 101, 102, 104, 105, 106 **Class 6**: Type 902, 1405, 1407 **Class 8**: Type 1606, 1610
Meare Lake Village (east)	'Lake village'	149	**Class 1**: Type 102, 104, 105, 106, 110 **Class 3**: Type 305, 306 **Class 6**: Type 801, 903, 906, 1000, 1001, 1003, 1400, 1407, 1416, 1417, 1419, 1420
Meare Lake Village (west)	'Lake village'	164	**Class 1**: type 102, 103, 106, 107, 108, 109, 110 **Class 2**: Type 203 **Class 4**: Type 422, 429 **Class 5**: Type 701 **Class 6**: 901, 906, 909, 1000, 1001, 1002, 1003, 1101, 1301, 1400, 1406, 1407, 1417, 1418, 1430 **Class 8**: Type 1602 **Class 11**: Type 3012
A417 Birdlip Bypass	Enclosed Settlement	1	**Class 6**: Type 1431
Totterdown Lane, Horcott	Enclosed Settlement	1	**Class 2**: Type 201
Bredon's Norton	Hillfort	3	**Class 1**: Type 102, 107
Conderton Camp	Hillfort	6	**Class 1**: Type 102, 110 **Class 4**: Type 426
Chalbury Camp, Bincombe	Hillfort	1	**Class 1**: Type 102
Lidbury Camp, Enford	Hillfort	1	**Class 2**: Type 204
Salmonsbury	Hillfort	1	**Class 1**: Type 102

Site	Site Type	Qty. Glass Beads	Type
West Stow	Enclosed Settlement	1	**Class 1**: Type 102
Grandcourt Quarry	Other Activity	16	**Class 1**: Type 102, 106, 107 **Class 2**: Type 201 **Class 4**: Type 502 **Class 5**: Type 701, 702 **Class 6**: Type 801, 1001, 1407 **Class 10**: Type 1801 **Class 11**: Type 2302, 2303, 2304

Site	Site Type	Qty. Glass Beads	Type
Queen's Barrow, Arras	Inhumation	71	**Class 4**: Type 411, 421, 424, 425, 426, 428 **Class 6**: Type 901, 905, 907
Burton Fleming	Inhumations	4	**Class 1**: Type 102 **Class 6**: Type 900
Burton Fleming: opposite Argam Lane	Inhumation	1	**Class 6**: Type 900
Barrow L, Cowlam	Inhumation	64	**Class 4**: Type 425 **Class 6**: 900, 901
Wetwang Slack	Inhumations	678	**Class 1**: Type 102 **Class 2**: Type 202 **Class 4**: Type 420, 423, 417, 418, 421, 410, 413, 414, 501, 503 **Class 6**: Type 901, 1001, 14107, 1417 **Class 11**: Type 2301
Garton Slack	Inhumation/ Settlement	35	**Class 1**: Type 102
Dalton Parlours	Enclosed Settlement	1	**Class 1**: Type 102
Sutton Common	Ritual Site/Enclosed Settlement	2	**Class 1**: Type 102

Figure 121: Sites with activity dating to the Middle Iron Age/Late Iron Age with glass beads (a) Southwest England, (b) East Anglia, (c) East Yorkshire.

Site	Site Type	Qty. Glass Beads	Type
Hengistbury Head	Settlement	2	**Class 10**: Type 1802
			Class 11: type 3016
Neigh Bridge, Somerford Keynes	Settlement	1	**Class 1**: Type 101
North Down Farm, Winterborne Kingston	Settlement	1	**Class 4**: Type 412
West Overton Down	Settlement	1	**Class 6**: Type 1201
Bagendon	Enclosed Settlement	5	**Class 1**: Type 102
			Class 11: type 3002, 3014, 3015
Claydon Pike: Warrens field	Enclosed Settlement	1	**Class 11**: Type 3003
Maiden Castle	Hillfort	3	**Class 1**: Type 102, 107, 110
Bulbury Camp	Hillfort hoard	8	**Class 1**: Type 107
Langton Herring	Inhumation	5	**Class 1**: Type 108
			Class 5: Type 701
			Class 8: Type 1604
			Class 9: Type 1704
			Class 11: Type 2801
Whitcombe, Dorset	Inhumation	10	**Class 1**: Type 107, 110
			Class 6: Type 901

Site	Site Type	Qty. Glass Beads	Type
Birnie	Settlement	24	**Class 1**: Type 110
			Class 3: Type 303
			Class 6: Type 1400, 1403, 1411, 1418, 1419
Culduthel Farm, Inverness	Settlement	21	**Class 1**: Type 102, 110
			Class 6: Type 1417, 1418
			Class 11: Type 2501
Thainstone, Kintore	Settlement	1	**Class 6**: Type 1419

Figure 122: Sites with activity dating to the Late Iron Age/Early Roman period with glass beads (a) Southwest England, (b) Northeast Scotland.

monochrome beads, including Type 110. The example of a Class 6 Type 1407 bead from the Roman villa at Rudston (DB 11630) is unusual as it was broken and re-purposed as a pendant. Finally, a very unusual bead was found in an inhumation at Trentholm Drive in York (DB 5704). The grey-scale illustration clearly places it in Guido's Group 1/Haevernick's Gruppe 24 beads found in Europe. The occurrence in a Roman period inhumation may further attest not only to beads as heirlooms, but perhaps also the movement of people, possibly over long distances, at this time (Eckardt 2010).

Post-Roman/Anglo-Saxon

Finally, there are a limited number of potential Iron Age beads found in post-Roman/Anglo-Saxon period contexts. These beads may indicate that such objects sometimes stayed in circulation for long periods of time. This probably should not be considered to be too unusual, as there have been two examples of fragmented Class 6 Type 1407 beads found set into metal jewellery pieces forming pendants, found in Anglo-Saxon burials. Examples are known from Cow Low, Derbyshire (Ozanne 1962, Figure 11e) and Street House, Redcar and Cleveland (Sherlock 2012). In Southwest England (Figure 124a), there are two possible Class 1 Type 110 beads found in an Anglo-Saxon inhumation at Burn Ground, Hampnett. There is a fragment of a bead that closely resembles Iron Age eye beads (Class 4) in a post-Roman context at Cadbury Congresbury. In Northeast Scotland (Figure 124b), there were two beads found in a structure that has been termed a 'Pict house' at Coldstone, which were nineteenth century discoveries. Nonetheless, despite the lack of contextual information for most stray finds in Northeast Scotland, in this case these two beads have some degree of context. Whether it was a 'Pict house' is debatable; nonetheless it seems likely that it dated to a later period.

ARCHAEOLOGICAL CONTEXT

Site	Site Type	Qty. Glass Beads	Type
A419/A417: Birdlip Quarry	Settlement	1	Class 11: Type 3012
Camerton	Settlement	1	Class 11: Type 3003
Catsgore	Settlement	2	Class 11: Type 3001, 3010
Cirencester	Settlement	3	Class 4: Type 601
			Class 5: Type 701
			Class 11: Type 3000
Haymes, Cleeve Hill	Settlement	1	Class 11: Type 3003
Seamills	Settlement	1	Class 1: Type 110
Atworth	Villa	1	Class 4: Type 410

Site	Site Type	Qty. Glass Beads	Type
Coldstone	Structure	2	Class 6: Type 1415, 1419

Site	Site Type	Qty. Glass Beads	Type
Castleford	Roman military/ settlement	12	Class 1: Type 101, 102, 103, 110
			Class 6: Type 901
Rudston	Villa	1	Class 6: Type 1407
Trentholme Drive, York	Inhumation	1	Class 10: Type 1800
Dalton Parlours	Settlement	1	Class 11: Type 3008

figure 123: Sites with activity dating to the Early Roman/Romano-British period with glass beads (a) Southwest England, (b) East Anglia, (c) East Yorkshire.

Site	Site Type	Qty. Glass Beads	Type
Burn Ground, Hampnett	Inhumation	2	Class 1: Type 110
Cadbury Congresbury	Hill-fort	1	Class 4: Type 410

Site	Site Type	Qty. Glass Beads	Type
Coldstone	Structure	2	Class 6: Type 1415, 1419

Figure 124: Sites with activity dating to the post-Roman/Anglo-Saxon period with glass beads (a) Southwest England, (b) Northeast Scotland.

Glass Bead Complexity

As discussed in Chapter 6, glass beads that date to the Iron Age exhibit a range of complexity. Henderson's (1992) analysis examined the number of decorated beads by site type, in order to understand site status. A critique of this analysis has already been presented; however, this analysis follows up his work by examining bead complexity in terms of colour and then decorative motif. Rather than seeing this complexity as a reflection of status, instead it aims to find patterns in deposition.

Colour Complexity

Manipulation of glass at various stages in the glass working procedure can affect the colour and opacity through the addition of oxides and minerals, and by manipulating the atmosphere of the furnace. As suggested by Henderson (1992), some oxides or minerals may have been more difficult to obtain, rendering some colours or degree of opacity rare. In addition, manipulating the atmosphere to change the colour may have been restricted specialist knowledge. Both of these types of complexity relate to the raw glass manufacturing process, or subsequent pigmentation of raw glass. By the time the bead itself comes to be formed, depending on available resources, the glass worker may have a choice about the simplicity or complexity of the bead that is created. In terms of colour, the simplest beads are monochrome, while beads that are more complex have two or more colours. The previous chapter established that within the study regions, there were no examples of beads with more than four colours, and even these were rare.

Colour complexity and the number of different types of sites are greatest in Southwest England (Figure 125). Here, monochrome beads are proportionally more frequent at hillforts, "lake villages", enclosed settlements, and inhumations. It is at the 'other settlements' where proportionately more polychrome beads are found. Despite the large numbers of glass beads at the lake village excavations, the majority of beads are either monochrome, or bi-chrome, with only a small minority being tri-chrome. The four-colour beads were found at a hillfort and other enclosed settlement sites, and some other miscellaneous sites.

Owing to the small number of glass beads from East Anglia, there were only a few glass beads and fewer site types. In this region, tri-chrome beads found in hoard features and 'other activity' sites are most complex (Figure 126). Similar to Southwest England, the enclosed sites primarily have monochrome beads, and settlement sites have a very limited number of monochrome and bi-chrome beads. It seems that special activity such as the hoard and the 'other activity' at Grandcourt Quarry account for the beads with the largest number of colours in this region.

Despite the large number of glass beads from East Yorkshire (Figure 127), their complexity is also limited. In this region, the overwhelming majority of beads were found in inhumations; however, over 60% of these beads were monochrome in colour. Only a select few were bi-chrome, and even fewer were tri-chrome. The prevalence for the use of monochrome beads is a trend followed at other site types in this region as most beads fall into this category. Despite the proportion of tri-coloured beads at enclosed settlements, in terms of the actual frequency, this is relatively rare.

Finally, in Northeast Scotland, the majority of the small numbers of beads from excavations are limited to either monochrome or bi-chrome appearances (Figure 128). As with Southwest England, a small number of tri-chrome beads were also found at hillforts in this region. However, this is extremely rare. Most beads in this region are monochrome in colour, although proportionately there is also a strong presence of bi-chrome beads.

Motif Complexity

Another form of complexity comes from the design on the bead. As in the colour discussion above, monochrome beads are the simplest beads as they do not exhibit a motif at all. A select few do have designs worked into the monochrome glass itself, but this is a very rare occurrence. Other beads without a motif are polychrome, but in these cases they do not utilise the colours in such a way as to create a design. In some cases they are simply layered together, or it may be that a secondary colour contaminated the overall colour. Simple motif beads are those that exhibit only one method of design, such as eye beads or beads with linear motifs. More complex designs are created in part by the combination of multiple types of simple motifs. This may be a somewhat arbitrary method of classifying beads by the level of complexity; however the reason for exploring the data in this way is that the manifestation of different types of techniques on the beads are taken into account. In addition, complex beads are rare, which may suggest that it was not something that was habitual, always technologically possible, or always desirable.

In Southwest England, the most complex beads are found proportionately more frequently at hillforts and sites classed as 'settlements' (Figure 129). However, these beads make up the minority of beads at these sites. Beads with no motif account for the substantial majority of beads at all sites, except at 'settlements' where simple motif beads are in the highest proportion. Beads in East Anglia are a mix of primarily no motif and simple motif beads (Figure 130). While both occurred at settlements, the bead at the enclosed settlement lacked a motif, while the bead found in the hoard had a simple motif. The beads from the 'other activity' at Grandcourt Quarry are a mix of no motif, simple motif, and complex motif, although the simple motifs are in the highest proportion.

In contrast, in East Yorkshire, the majority of beads at all site types have no motif (Figure 131) as a high proportion of these beads in inhumations features were very plain. Simple motif beads are found at enclosed settlements, and Roman military sites; however, their actual frequency is very low. The single bead from the Roman villa and a few examples from inhumations account for the only complex motif beads. In comparison with the previous three study regions, the beads found through excavation in Northeast Scotland are very different in their complexity (Figure 132). The majority of these beads were found at settlement sites, and display a mix of beads with no motif, simple motifs, and complex motifs. The beads without a motif by far make up the highest proportion of beads at these sites. However, at the hillforts, and other sites, beads have either simple motifs, or more rarely complex motifs. This is a significantly different pattern than in the other three regions.

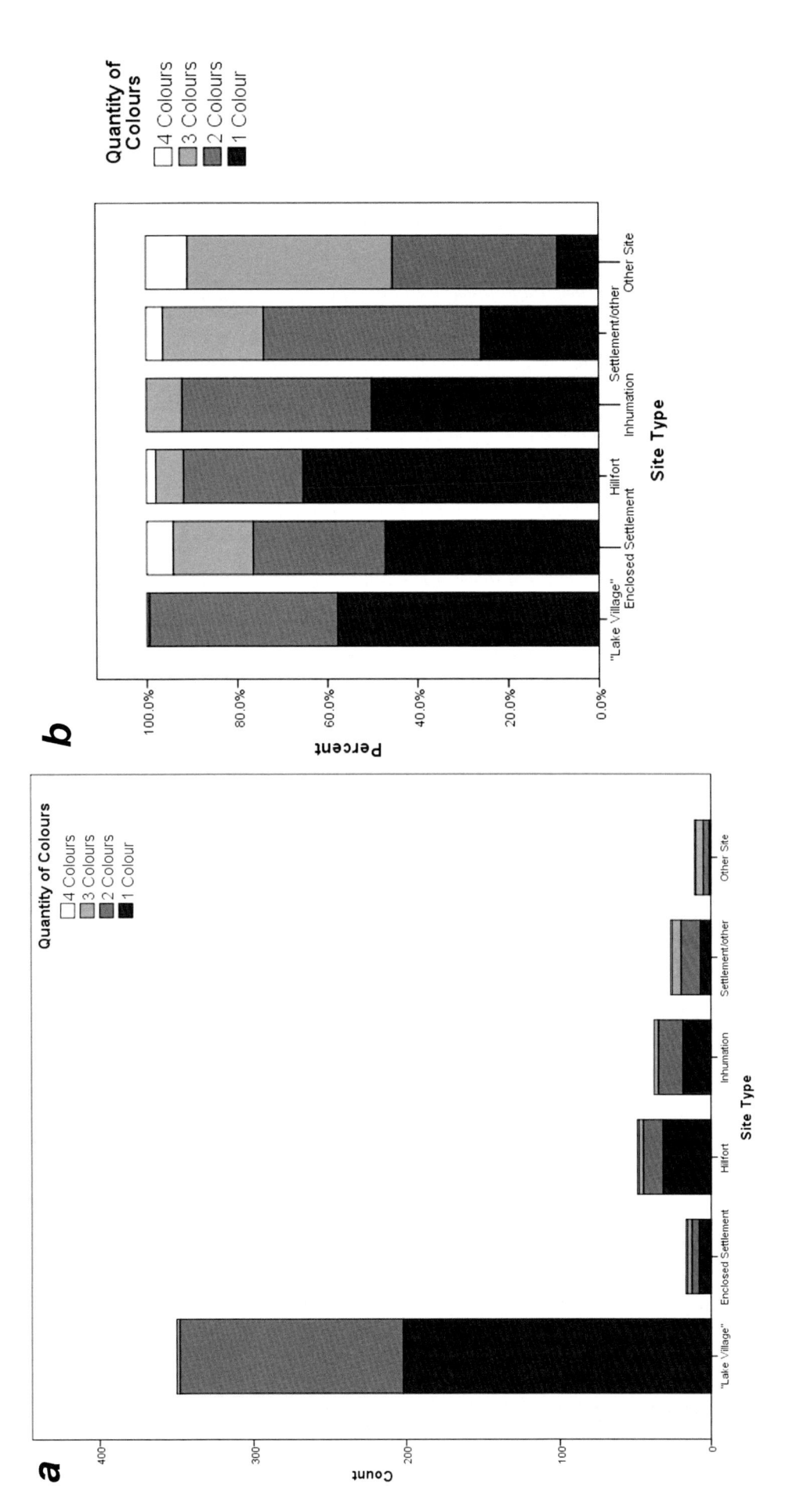

Figure 125: Bar-chart showing the number of colours of glass on each bead in Southwest England (a) frequency, (b) percentage.

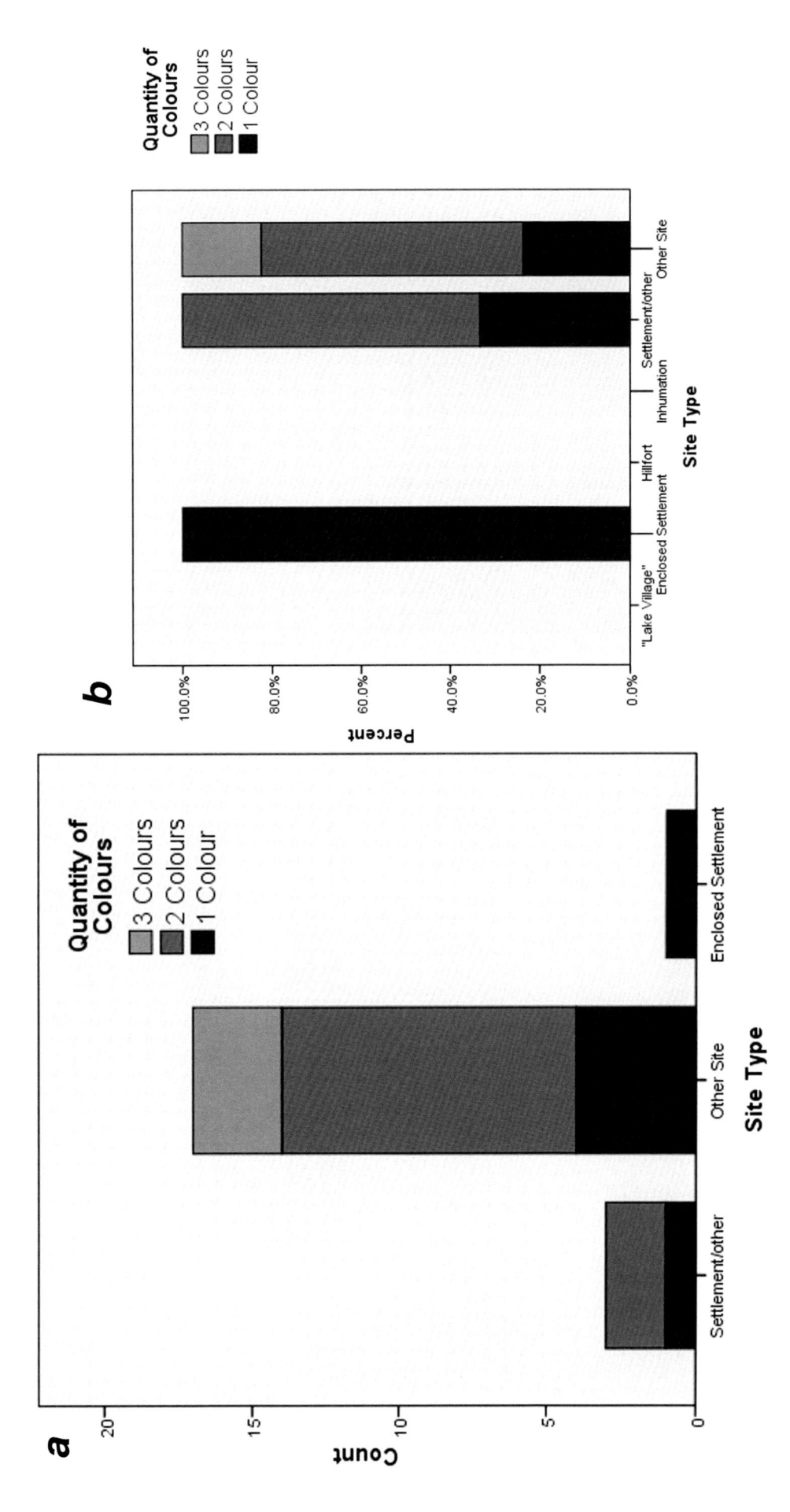

Figure 126: Bar-chart showing the number of colours of glass on each bead in East Anglia (a) frequency, (b) percentage.

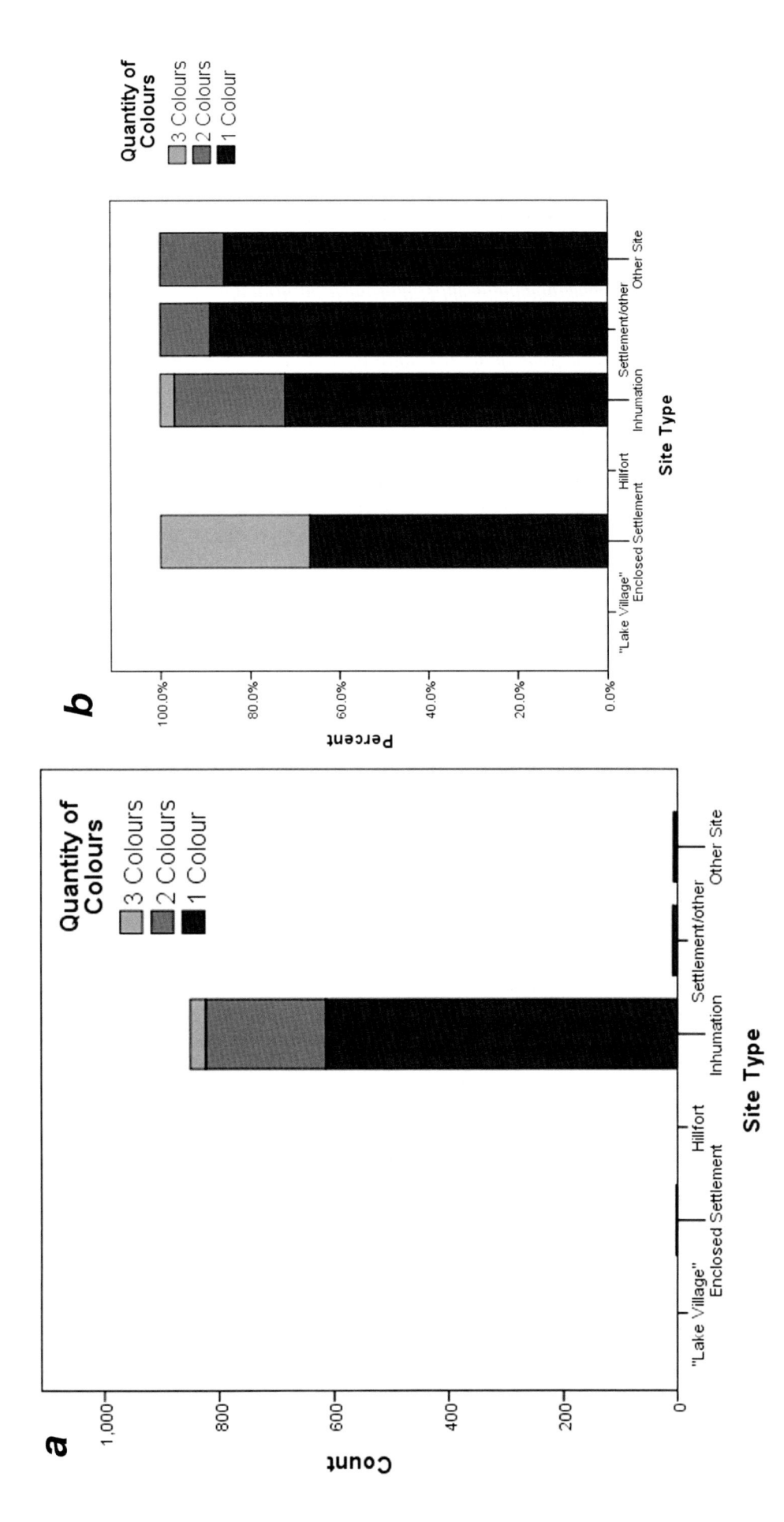

Figure 127: Bar-chart showing the number of colours of glass on each bead in East Yorkshire (a) frequency, (b) percentage.

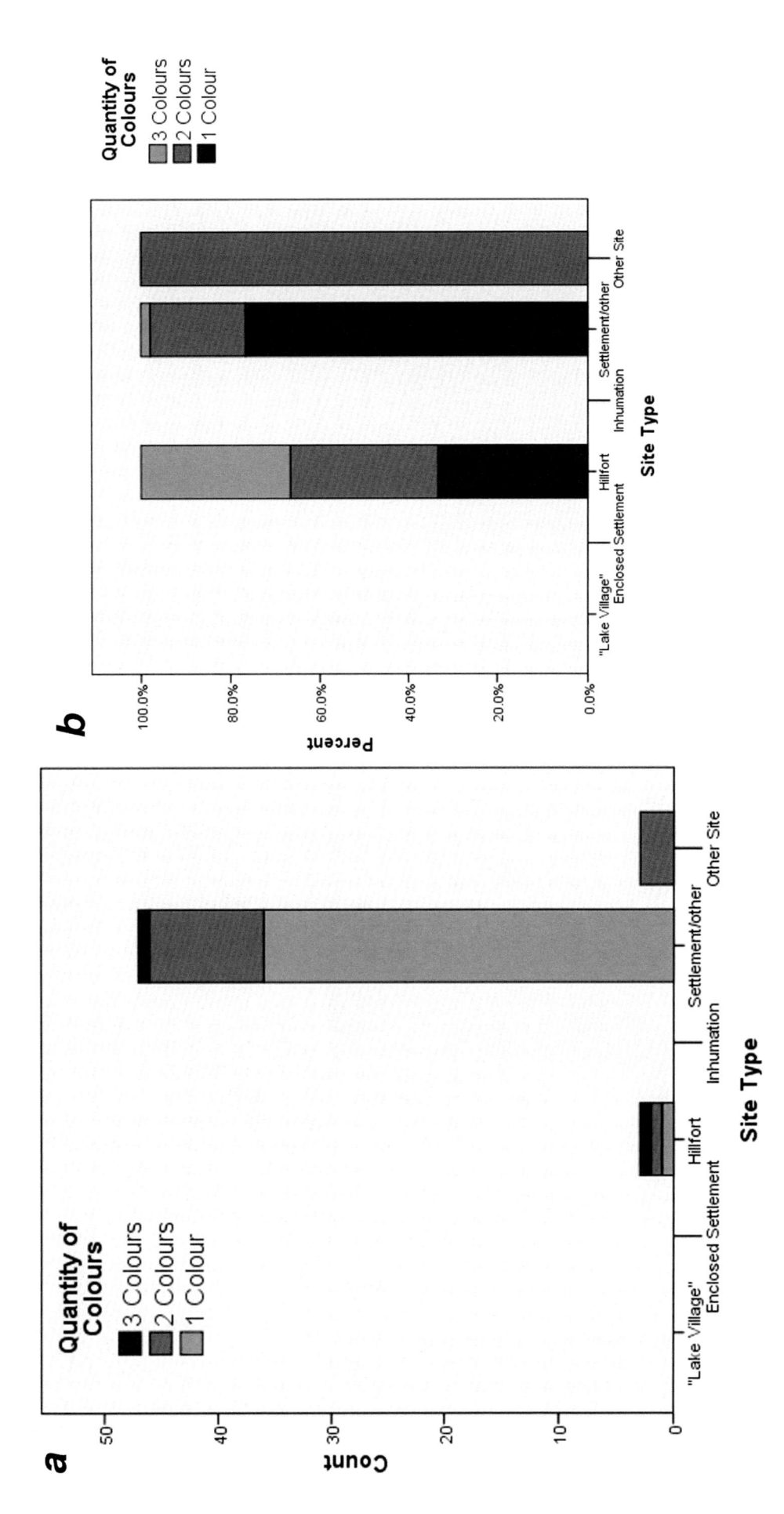

Figure 128: Bar-chart showing the number of colours of glass on each bead in Northeast Scotland (a) frequency, (b) percentage.

Discussion

As might be expected, simple beads in terms of both colour and decoration are more frequent, while complex beads are smaller in number. It might be expected that the more complex the bead, the more valuable it was, and thus it may indicate higher status or value. Taking the evidence for Southwest England as an example, it is clear that not only are beads from hillforts limited in number, but that they are proportionally some of the least complex examples. Although perhaps not informative about status, glass bead complexity is nonetheless essential for understanding patterns of glass bead use between the regions and at different types of sites (Figure 133). Here, two patterns emerge. First, that the unusual nature of the glass beads from East Anglia are highlighted as they peak at a rank of three instead of one, which suggests that the beads found here are unusual compared to the other study regions under consideration. Disregarding East Anglia, each study region is fairly similar in the different levels of bead complexity. Second, that there is a common pattern of complexity found at all site types, which suggests that the range of beads found at each type of site have a similar proportion of both simple and complex beads. This is significant because from both a region wide and site type perspective, there is a common pattern, which suggests that glass beads did not have an inherent status based on physical appearance alone. Instead, it may be derived from a combination of these aspects in addition to the biography of the object. The treatment of glass beads from depositional features will be explored in greater detail in the next section.

Feature Type

As with the site type analysis in the previous section, glass bead deposition practices vary between regions. However, just as many settlements change in their characterisation throughout the Iron Age, so too do depositional practices change within each region. The data for glass bead context at the feature level is extremely limited, and while it is known for 73% of the data, the large numbers from East Yorkshire inhumations and the beads from the lake villages skew this figure. Of these, 134 beads were found during excavation, but their context is unclear due to the nature of the final report, and a further 342 beads are simply known as 'stray' finds (usually found during the nineteenth century). This section will compare the different features in which glass beads were found for each study region. This will help to explore differences in depositional practices between regions.

Regional perspectives

Southwest England

Feature data is known for 517 glass beads in Southwest England (Figure 134a). The majority of beads were found in 'mound' features from the lake villages. Finds from inhumations and pits were also substantial, but there were also fewer numbers of finds from hoards, roundhouses, and ditches. Comparing the finds from features with site types suggest that most features were a part of hillforts, whether as hoards, pits, roundhouses, or found within the enclosure entrance (Figure 134b). Pit finds figure prominently not only at hillforts, but also in enclosed settlements, and other settlement sites.

Beads found in inhumation features that were not associated with a wider settlement context, are instead isolated sites. Chronologically, pit and roundhouse finds seem to be a practice from the Early Iron Age through to the Late Iron Age (Figure 134c). The finds from the lake villages distort the pattern of glass bead deposition, but leaving this aside, the remaining evidence suggests that there was a gradual increase in the number of glass beads deposited from the Early Iron Age to the Middle Iron Age. It is in the Late Iron Age that depositional practices began to change drastically. However, taking the lake village finds into consideration, the peak of glass bead deposition occurs between the Middle and Late Iron Age. The greatest variety of glass bead types was found at both inhumations and lake village mounds (eight different classes; Figure 134d). Class 1 beads are the most numerous and are found in the greatest variety of features. This might not be surprising, given the number of Class 1 beads discussed in the previous section. Mounds and inhumations, however, exhibit the greatest amount of variability in terms of the number of different classes found within one feature type.

East Anglia

Despite the small number of glass beads from East Anglia, the feature context is known for 69% of the twenty-six examples found during excavations (Figure 135a). The majority of the beads were found in the presumed special pottery dense deposit at Grandcourt Quarry. Of the remaining four beads from East Anglia, one was from a predominately metalwork hoard, and three were from a votive deposit in a pit (Figure 135b). Unfortunately, there is little else to say regarding these finds, as the final interpretation of Grandcourt Quarry is still awaiting completion and the exact nature of the activity is uncertain.

Other sites include the metalwork hoard, but it was not associated with a settlement. The votive pit on the other hand was found within a settlement and amongst the other objects deposited was a torc fragment and a ring-key. The author interpreted the collection of objects as something to do with circularity, as all the objects were round (Wallis 2011, 65). Chronologically, the special deposit was earliest, the hoard is likely to be Early Roman, while the votive pit seems to have been Romano-British in date (Figure 135c). The large number of beads from the special deposit is also reflected in

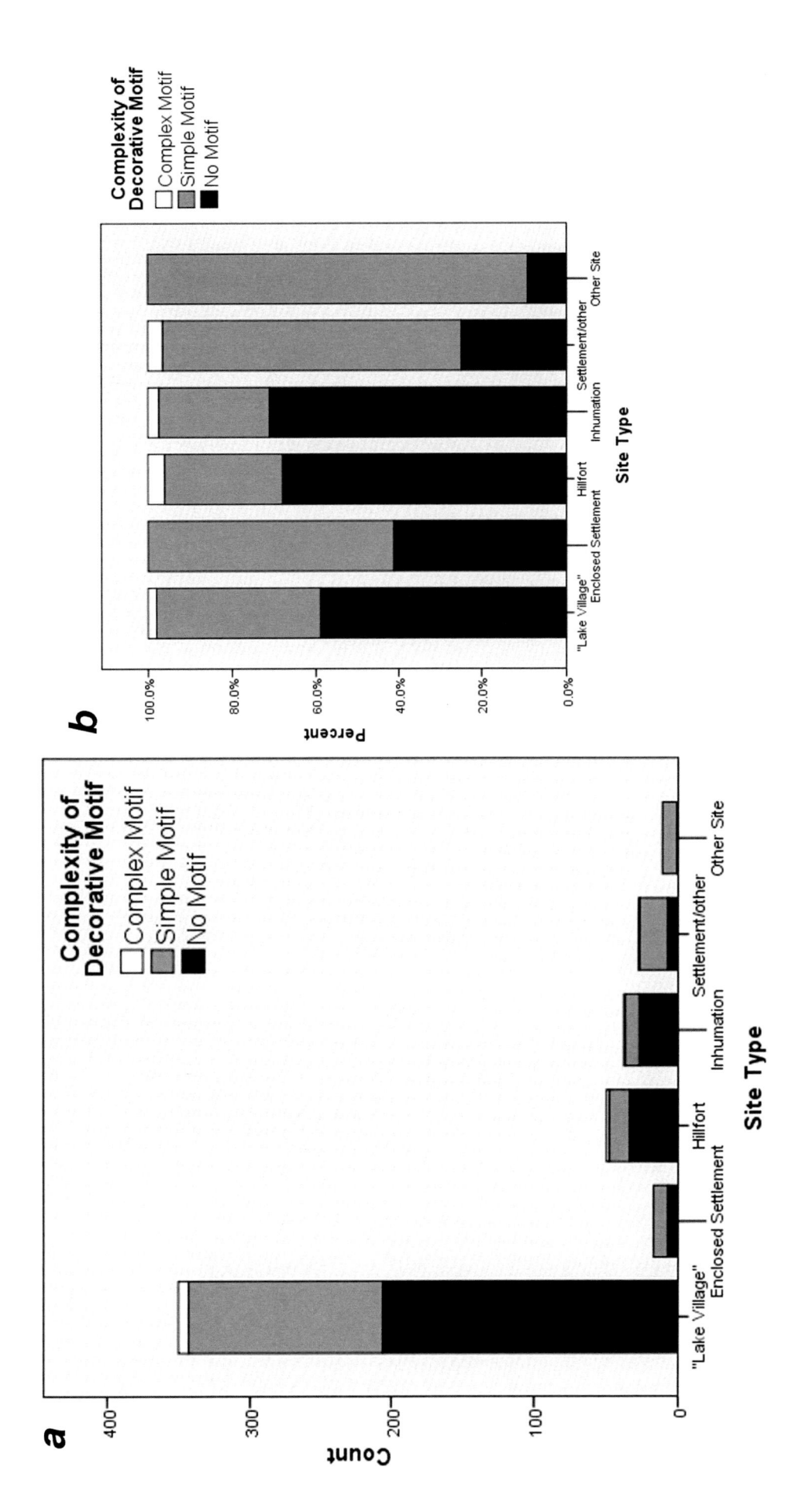

Figure 129: Bar-chart showing the frequency of glass beads at different site types in Southwest England (a) frequency, (b) percentage.

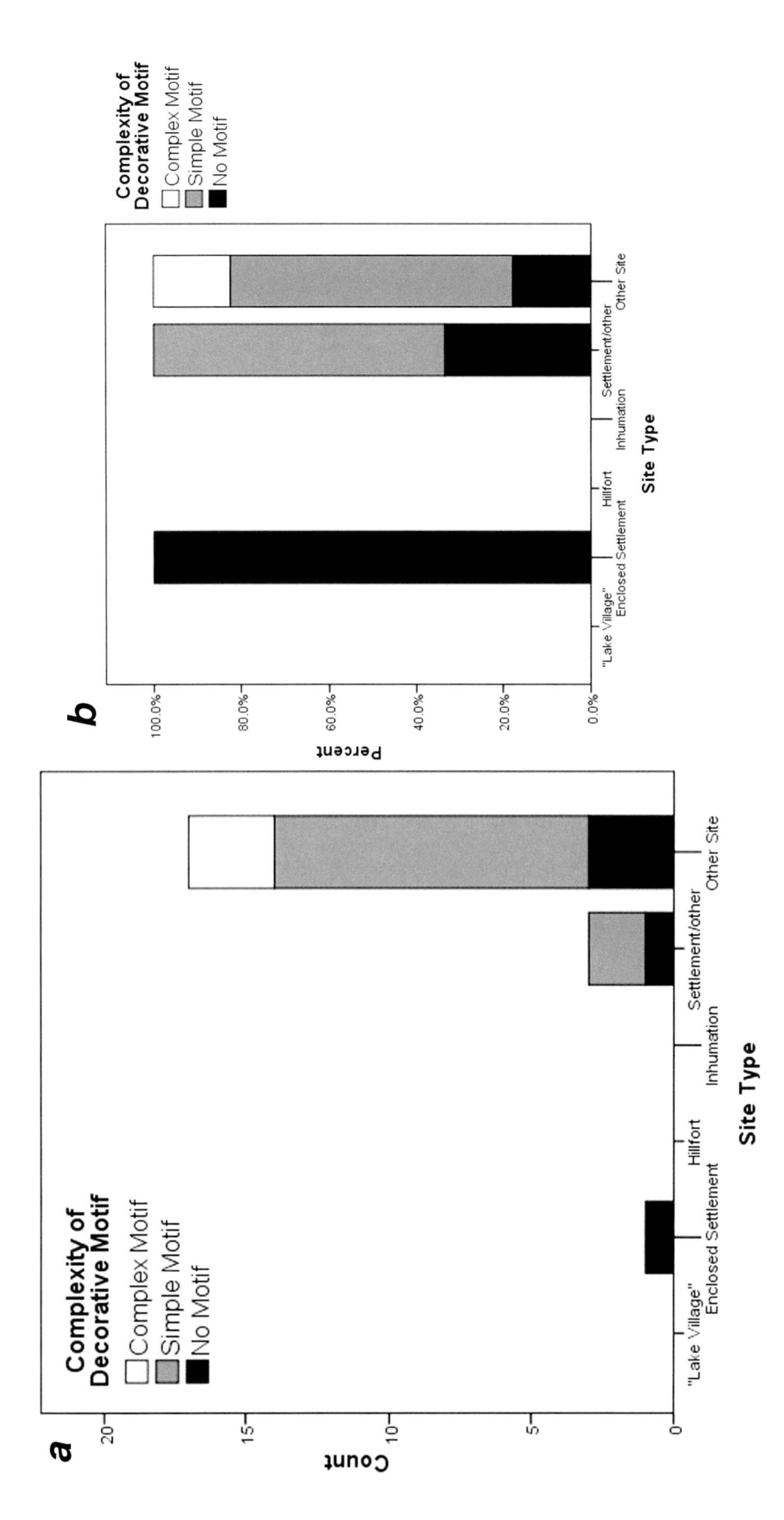

Figure 130: Bar-chart showing the frequency of glass beads at different site types in East Anglia (a) frequency, (b) percentage.

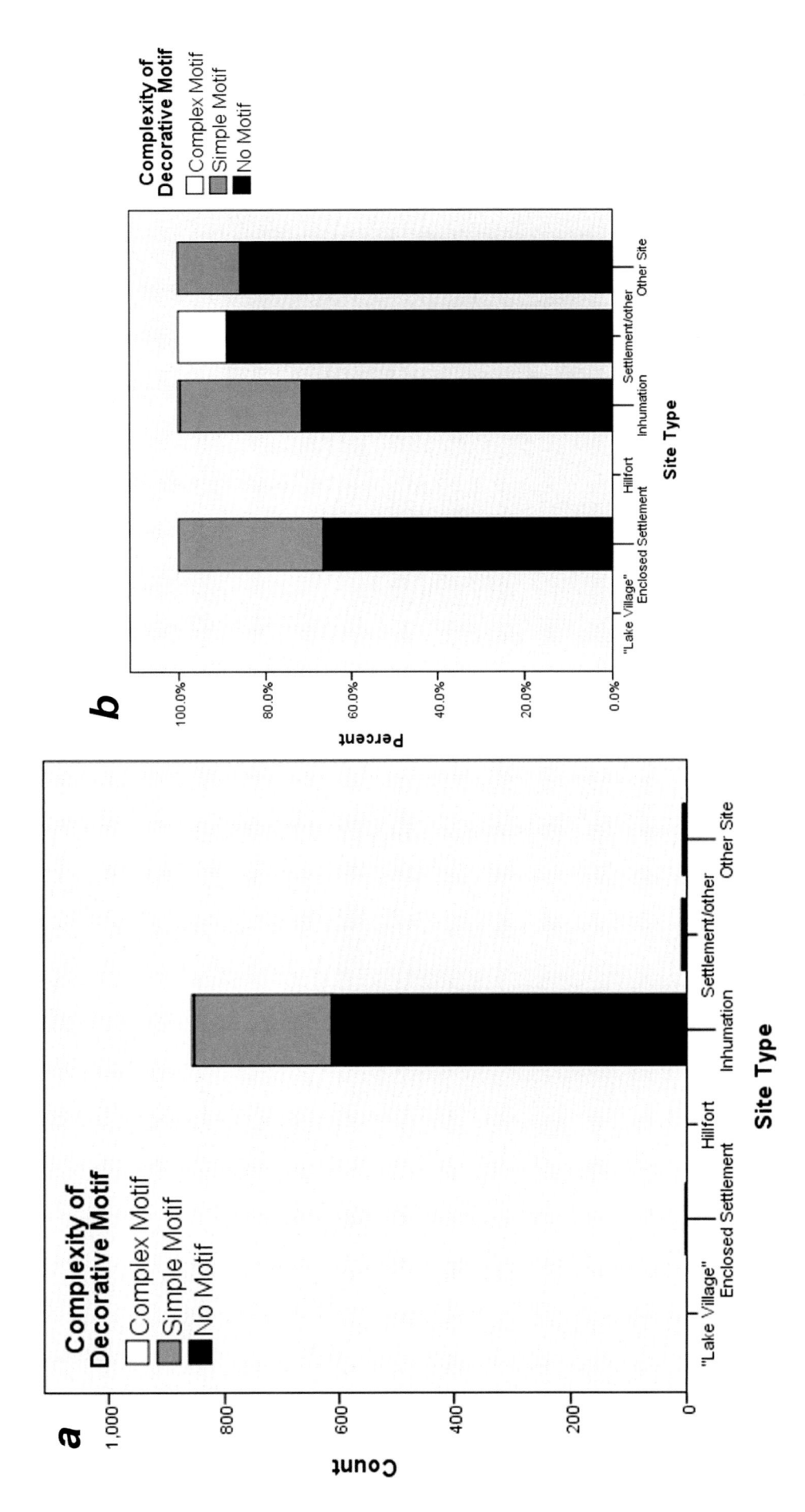

Figure 131: Bar-chart showing the frequency of glass beads at different site types in East Yorkshire (a) frequency, (b) percentage.

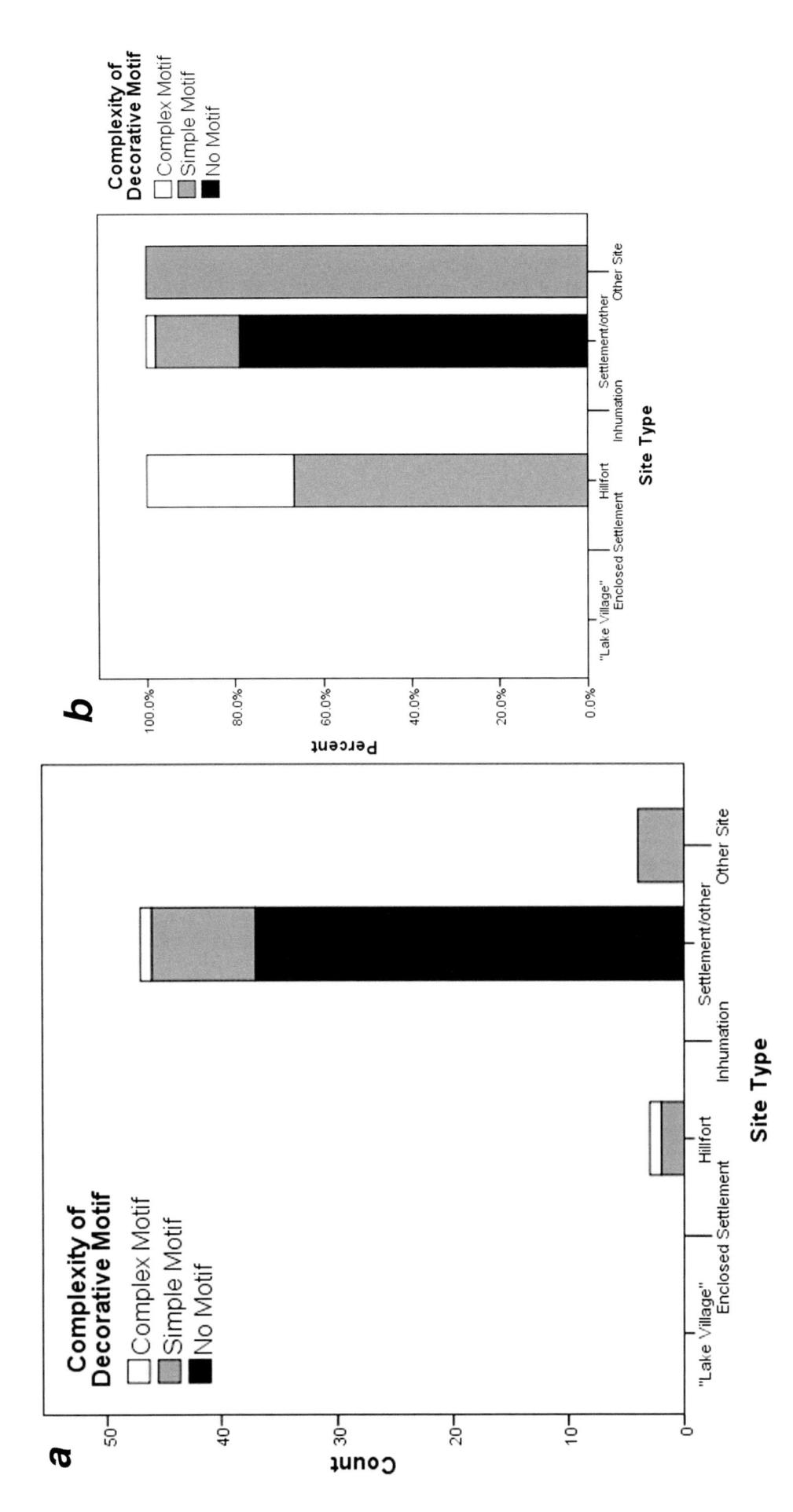

Figure 132: Bar-chart showing the frequency of glass beads at different site types in Northeast Scotland (a) frequency, (b) percentage.

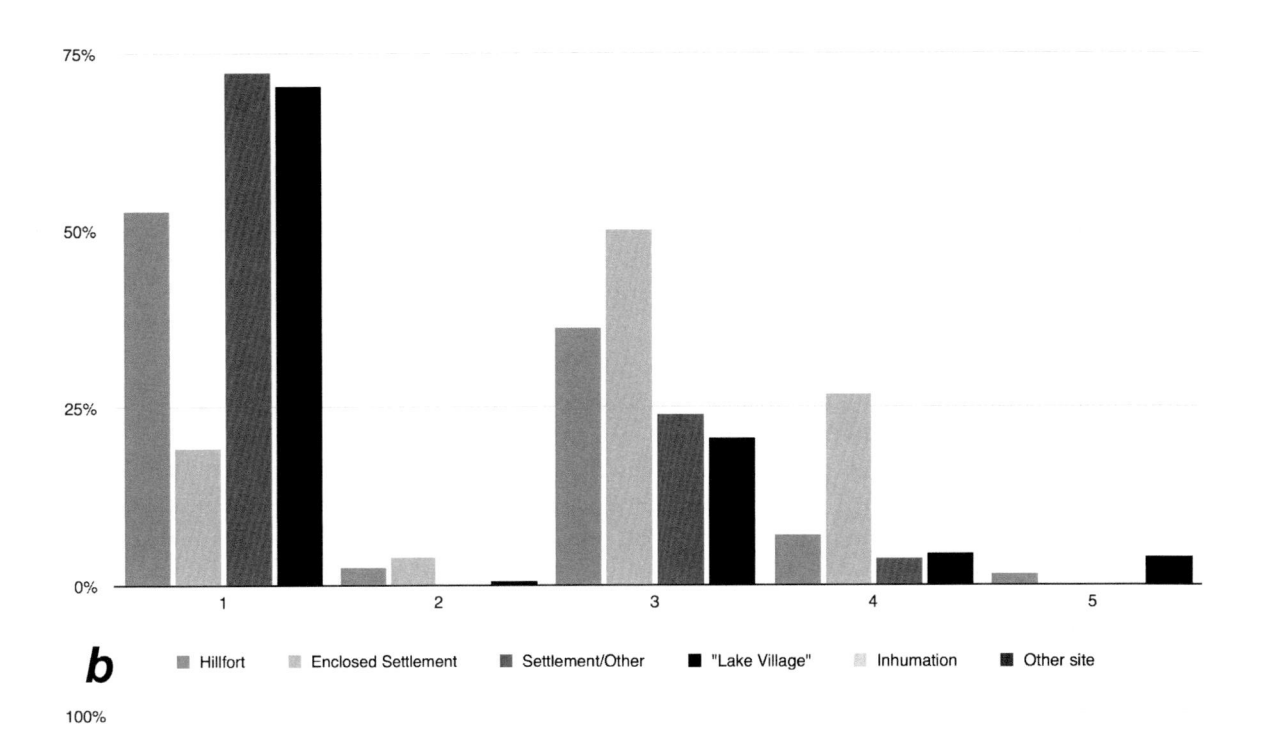

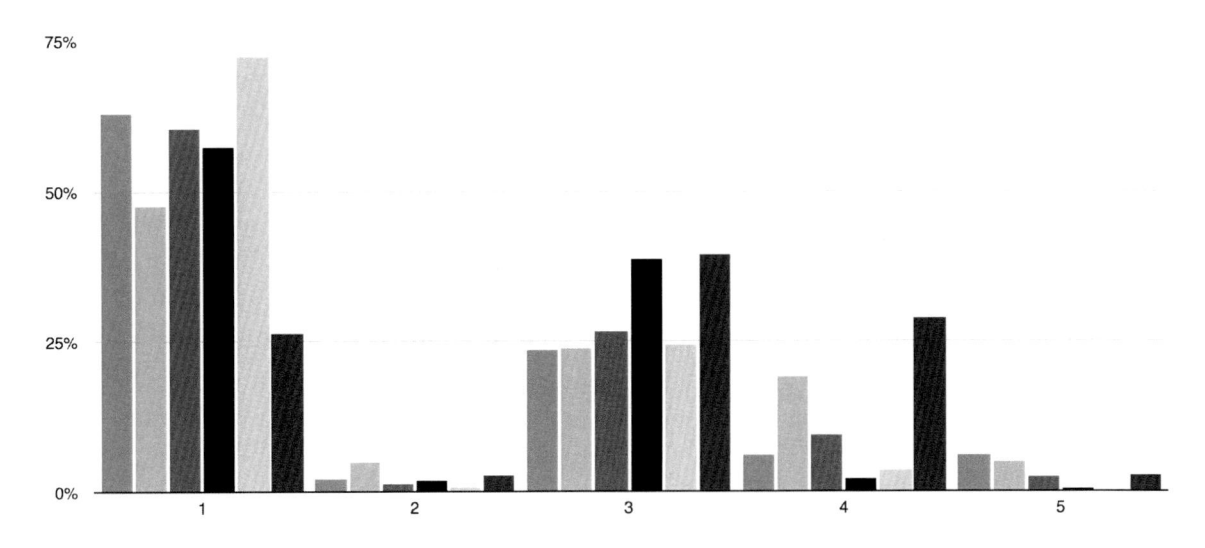

Figure 133: Chart showing the proportion of glass bead complexity rank (combining colour and decorative motif) by (a) study regions, (b) site type. Rank is from most simple (1) to most complex (5).

Archaeological Context

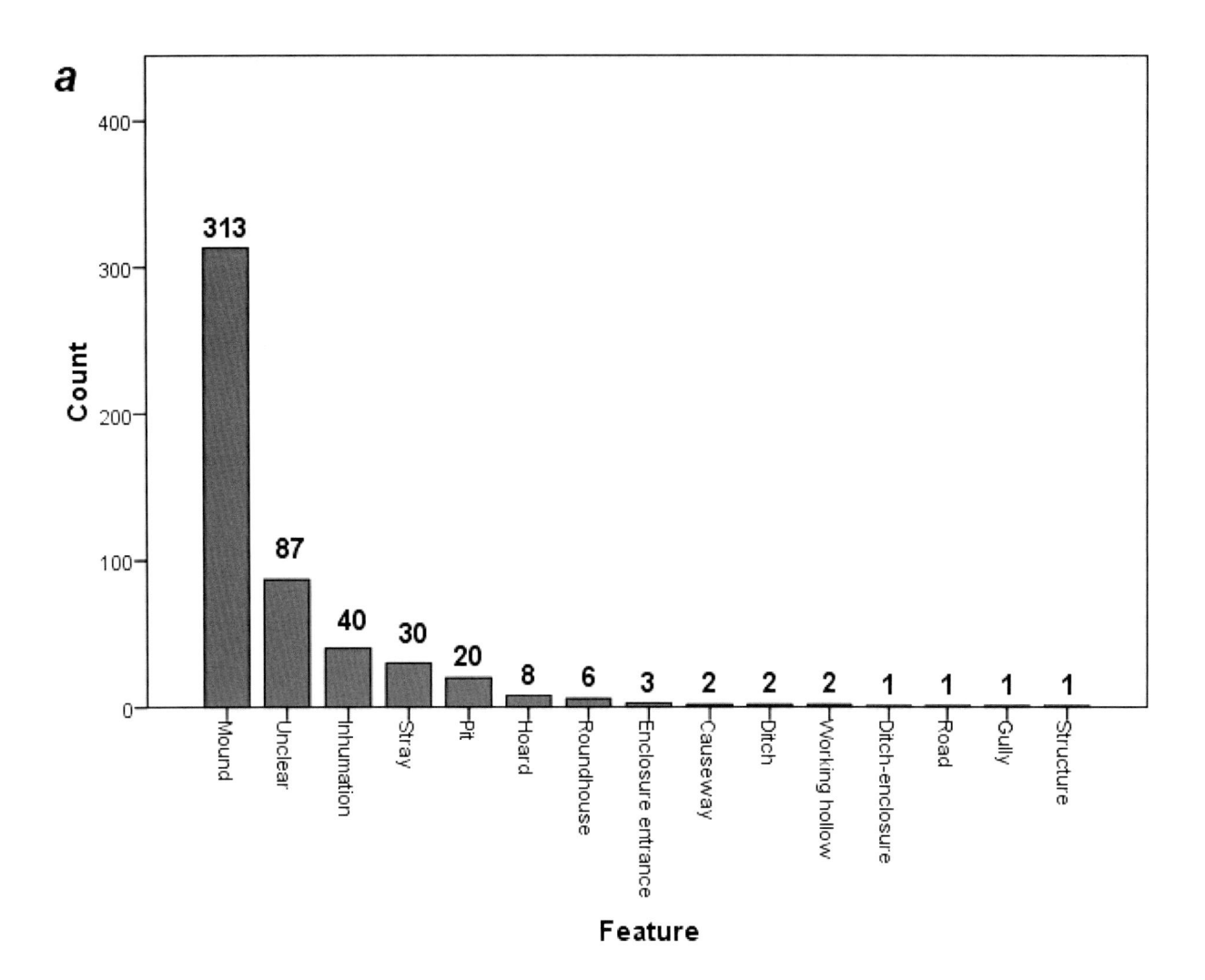

a

Bar chart – Glass bead frequency by feature:

Feature	Count
Mound	313
Unclear	87
Inhumation	40
Stray	30
Pit	20
Hoard	8
Roundhouse	6
Enclosure entrance	3
Causeway	2
Ditch	2
Working hollow	2
Ditch-enclosure	1
Road	1
Gully	1
Structure	1

b

	'Lake Village'	Enclosed Settlement	Hillfort	Inhumation	Settlement	TOTAL
Inhumation	-	-	-	15	-	15
Mound	313	-	-	-	-	313
Ditch	-	-	-	-	1	1
Ditch-enclosure	-	1	-	-	-	1
Enclosure entrance	-	-	3	-	-	3
Hoard	-	-	8	-	-	8
Pit	-	6	8	-	4	18
Road	-	-	1	-	-	1
Roundhouse	-	1	4	-	1	6
Structure	-	-	-	-	1	1
Working Hollow	-	-	2	-	-	2
TOTAL	313	8	26	15	7	369

c

	EIA	MIA	MIA/LIA	LIA	LIA/ER	RB	TOTAL
Inhumation	-	-	-	10	5	-	15
Mound	-	-	313	-	-	-	313
Ditch	-	-	-	-	1	-	1
Ditch-enclosure	-	-	3	-	-	-	3
Hoard	-	-	-	-	8	-	8
Pit	5	3	2	6	2	-	18
Road	-	-	-	-	1	-	1
Roundhouse	1	3	1	1	-	-	6
Structure	-	-	-	-	-	1	1
Working Hollow	-	2	-	-	-	-	2
TOTAL	6	9	319	18	16	1	369

Figure 134: Glass bead feature analysis for Southwest England (a) bar-chart of glass bead frequency by feature, (b) comparison of site type and feature type, (c) comparison of feature and period of activity.

DRESS AND IDENTITY IN IRON AGE BRITAIN

	Inhumation	Fort Road	Gully	Hearth	Hoard	Latrine	Mortuary Ring	Pit	Pit-Structure	Pit-Votive	Road	Mound	Roundhouse	Roundhouse-Posthole	Roundhouse-Ringditch	Slot	Souterraine	Special Deposit	Structure	Vicus Structure	Well	Working Hollow	Causeway	Cave	Ditch	Ditch-Enclosure	Enclosure Entrance	TOTAL
Class 1	19	-	1	-	8	-	-	8	-	-	-	179	4	-	-	-	-	-	-	-	-	2	1	-	1	-	3	226
Class 2	-	-	-	-	-	-	-	1	-	-	-	1	-	-	-	-	-	-	-	-	-	-	-	-	-	1	-	3
Class 3	8	-	-	-	-	-	-	-	-	-	-	2	-	-	-	-	-	-	-	-	-	-	-	-	-	-	-	10
Class 4	2	-	-	-	-	-	-	2	-	-	-	2	1	-	-	-	-	-	-	-	-	-	-	-	-	-	-	7
Class 5	1	-	-	-	-	-	-	-	-	-	-	2	-	-	-	-	-	-	-	-	-	-	-	-	-	-	-	3
Class 6	7	-	-	-	-	-	-	7	-	-	-	117	-	-	-	-	-	-	-	-	-	-	1	-	-	-	-	132
Class 7	-	-	-	-	-	-	-	-	-	-	-	-	-	-	-	-	-	-	-	-	-	-	-	-	-	-	-	0
Class 8	1	-	-	-	-	-	-	-	-	-	-	3	-	-	-	-	-	-	-	-	-	-	-	-	-	-	-	4
Class 9	1	-	-	-	-	-	-	-	-	-	-	-	-	-	-	-	-	-	-	-	-	-	-	-	-	-	-	1
Class 10	-	-	-	-	-	-	-	-	-	-	-	-	-	-	-	-	-	-	-	-	-	-	-	-	-	-	-	0
Class 11	1	-	-	-	-	-	-	2	-	-	-	5	-	-	-	1	-	-	1	-	-	-	-	-	1	-	-	10
TOTAL	40	0	1	0	8	0	0	20	0	0	0	311	5	0	0	0	0	0	1	0	0	2	2	0	2	1	3	396

Figure 134: Glass bead feature analysis for Southwest England. (d) Comparison of Classes and features.

the wide variety of bead types found at the site (Figure 135d). There is a limited degree of type overlap with the other sites at a more general class level. The votive pit contained both Class 1 and Class 6 beads, while the earlier hoard deposit contained a more complex Class 11 bead. Despite the differences in depositional date, it is interesting that within this region, all glass beads from an excavated context are from unusual or 'ritual' practices.

East Yorkshire

The feature level context of glass beads from East Yorkshire is known for 98% of the beads from this region. Unsurprisingly, most of these beads are from inhumations (Figure 136a), but a number were also discovered in other contexts as the site type analysis suggested. A number of beads were found in various contexts within the Roman fort at Castleford, including a road, latrine, hearth, pit, and a slot. In addition, seven beads were from the civilian settlement at Castleford (no further details). It seems unusual that so many of these Iron Age beads are found in these Roman contexts, and may suggested continued local practices into the Romano-British period (Figure 136b), when there are so few beads deposited in the Early Roman/Romano-British period at other contemporary sites. In part, this could be the result of excavation practice and the selection of sites chosen for study. Further beads were found in several other contexts including a mortuary ring and a pit that was part of a structure. In addition, two other beads come from a Roman villa structure and another from a well. However, the majority of the beads were deposited in Middle/Late Iron Age contexts (Figure 136c). These include both inhumations and several other contexts. Inhumations accounted for the highest variety of types found in any one context, while Class 1 beads are found in the largest number of feature types (Figure 136d). There is some overlap between features and the general class of bead found. For example, Class 6 beads were found in inhumations and a pit, and both Class 4 and Class 1 beads were found in mortuary ring contexts. Again, Class 1 beads are by far the most numerous, but they are also found in the widest variety of depositional features.

Northeast Scotland

Finally, in Northeast Scotland, where the majority of beads were stray or unclear in terms of their context, clear features is only known for 5% of the beads from this region (Figure 137a). Most were found in roundhouse ditch features, while another example was found in a roundhouse posthole. Unfortunately, the wider context of the site is unknown for most of these beads (Figure 137b). The available data shows that four beads were found in settlement contexts and that these date to the Late Iron Age/Early Roman period (Figure 137c). Class 6 beads are by far the most represented class (Figure

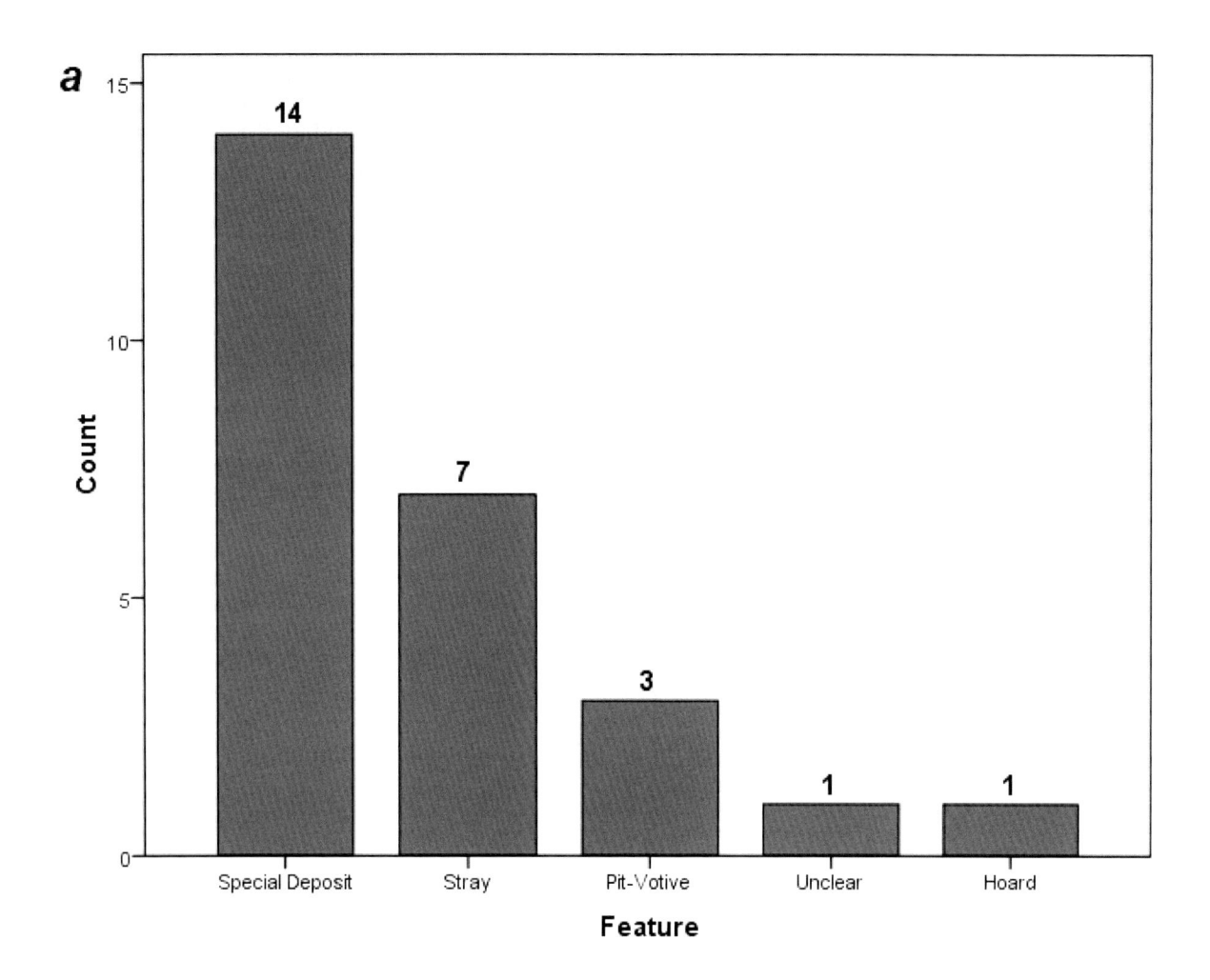

a

[Bar chart showing glass bead frequency by feature:
- Special Deposit: 14
- Stray: 7
- Pit-Votive: 3
- Unclear: 1
- Hoard: 1
Y-axis: Count; X-axis: Feature]

b

	Hoard	Settlement	Other Activity	TOTAL
Hoard	1	-	-	1
Pit-Votive	-	3	-	3
Special Deposit	-	-	14	14
TOTAL	**1**	**3**	**14**	**18**

c

	MIA/LIA	ER/RB	RB	TOTAL
Hoard	-	1	-	1
Pit-Votive	-	-	3	3
Special Deposit	14	-	-	14
TOTAL	**14**	**1**	**3**	**18**

Figure 135: Glass bead feature analysis for East Anglia (a) bar-chart of glass bead frequency by feature, (b) comparison of site type and feature type, (c) comparison of feature and period of activity.

137d). There are only a few examples of other classes in this data. It is hoped that as the final reports for both Birnie and Culduthel Farm are produced, this data will become clear.

Depositional Practices

The above analysis suggests that not only are beads found in different depositional contexts, but also this varies regionally. For example, in East Yorkshire the emphasis is on inhumation depositions, while in Southwest England, more beads are found in a variety of settlement contexts such as ditches, roundhouses, pits, or post-holes. However, by examining a specific feature type and exploring this cross-regionally, it should be possible to understand some general trends. This section will explore two of the most prolific feature types: pits and inhumations. But, first, it will explore bead deposition and the number of beads per deposition context.

Group vs. Single Depositions

One aspect that skews some of the general frequency data for glass bead finds is the occurrence of more than one bead per depositional feature. In these cases, there seems reason to consider that their existence in the archaeological record could be due to deliberate deposition, rather than casual loss. Of course this does not mean that all single finds were due to chance or accidental loss, as when the context is known, they seem to come from clear features as discussed above. In a general sense, out of the 1,788 glass beads included in this study, 46% were found as single finds (including stray finds), meaning that just over half were found in features with at least one other typed glass bead. In this study, there were contexts with fewer than twenty beads (a minimum of two), and at the other extreme was a single feature with 120 glass beads (although to this we could also add the 250 Class 1 Type 110 (Guido Class 8) beads from Culbin Sands, however the nature of the discovery is unclear). Figure 138 demonstrates the range of features with varying numbers of glass beads. Inhumations by far account for the largest concentrations of glass beads in any one context, while other context types account for very few numbers of glass beads.

Glass Beads in Pits

Glass beads have been found in twenty-two individual pits across the study regions in Southwest England, which reflects the nature of the archaeology of this region, and at fourteen different sites (Figure 139). Multiple pits at individual sites with glass beads are restricted to Maiden Castle in Dorset and Swallowcliffe Down in Wiltshire, where there were six pits at the former and four pits at the latter. Only single pits with glass beads were found at the remaining sites, which also ranged in date as shown in the table.

Unfortunately, the excavation reports are often unclear as to the full contents of the pits, and any relationship between different layers within the pits is sometimes lost. There are a few exceptions, such as at Conderton Camp. Although it is not explicit, it is possible to put together data from the report and determine that Pit C had eight layers. The dating at this site was established through a series of radiocarbon dates used to explore the chronology of the pottery sequence established for the site. This particular pit is of indeterminate date as the ceramic sherds were not abundant. Generally though, it was probably Middle Iron Age.

The Romano-British 'votive' pit from Billingford was relatively shallow at 0.21 meters. Fragmentary (possibly oak) wood chips were recovered from the surface and upper fill of the pit (Wallis 2011, 61). The interpretation of this pit as already mentioned; focusing on circularity it may have been a devotional offering to a deity, perhaps

Figure 135: Glass bead feature analysis for East Yorkshire. (d) Comparison of Classes and features.

	Class 1	Class 2	Class 4	Class 5	Class 6	Class 7	Class 8	Class 9	Class 10	Class 11	TOTAL
Inhumation	-	-	-	-	-	-	-	-	-	-	0
Fort Road	-	-	-	-	-	-	-	-	-	-	0
Gully	-	-	-	-	-	-	-	-	-	-	0
Hearth	-	-	-	-	-	-	-	-	-	-	0
Hoard	-	-	-	-	-	-	-	-	-	1	1
Latrine	-	-	-	-	-	-	-	-	-	-	0
Mortuary Ring	-	-	-	-	-	-	-	-	-	-	0
Pit	-	-	-	-	-	-	-	-	-	-	0
Pit-Structure	-	-	-	-	-	-	-	-	-	-	0
Pit-Votive	1	-	-	-	2	-	-	-	-	-	3
Road	-	-	-	-	-	-	-	-	-	-	0
Mound	-	-	-	-	-	-	-	-	-	-	0
Roundhouse	-	-	-	-	-	-	-	-	-	-	0
Roundhouse-Posthole	-	-	-	-	-	-	-	-	-	-	0
Roundhouse-Ringditch	-	-	-	-	-	-	-	-	-	-	0
Slot	-	-	-	-	-	-	-	-	-	-	0
Souterraine	-	-	-	-	-	-	-	-	-	-	0
Special Deposit	2	1	1	3	4	-	-	-	1	2	14
Structure	-	-	-	-	-	-	-	-	-	-	0
Vicus Structure	-	-	-	-	-	-	-	-	-	-	0
Well	-	-	-	-	-	-	-	-	-	-	0
Working Hollow	-	-	-	-	-	-	-	-	-	-	0
Causeway	-	-	-	-	-	-	-	-	-	-	0
Cave	-	-	-	-	-	-	-	-	-	-	0
Ditch	-	-	-	-	-	-	-	-	-	-	0
Ditch-Enclosure	-	-	-	-	-	-	-	-	-	-	0
Enclosure Entrance	-	-	-	-	-	-	-	-	-	-	0
TOTAL	3	1	1	3	6	0	0	0	1	3	18

a

[Bar chart showing glass bead counts by feature:]
- Inhumation: 857
- Unclear: 10
- Stray: 4
- Mortuary Ring: 2
- Fort Road: 2
- Hearth: 1
- Latrine: 1
- Pit-structure: 1
- Slot: 1
- Structure: 1
- Pit: 1
- Well: 1

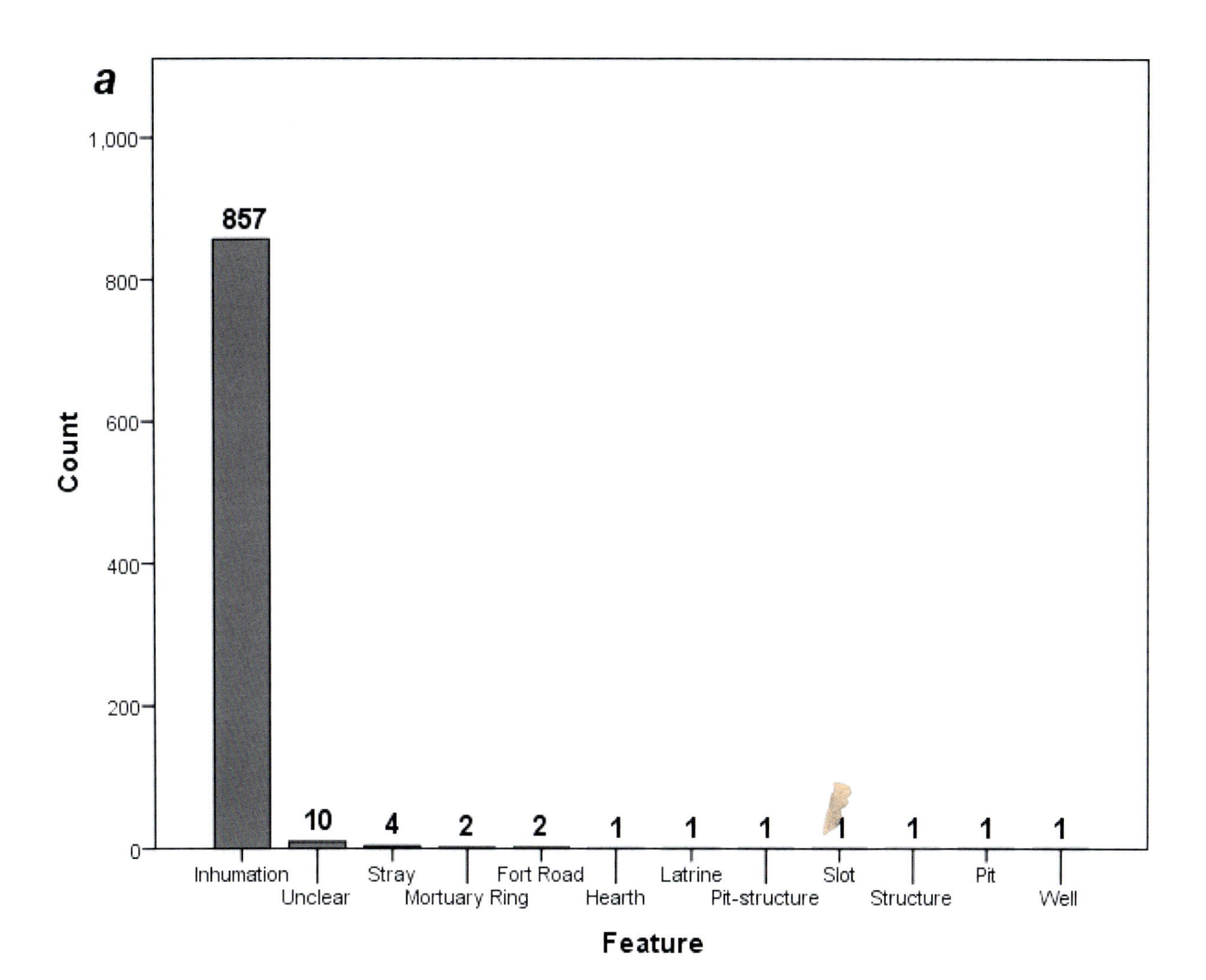

b

	Inhumation	Ritual Site	Roman Military	Settlement	Roman Villa	TOTAL
Inhumation	857	-	-	-	-	857
Fort Road	-	-	2	-	-	2
Hearth	-	-	1	-	-	1
Latrine	-	-	1	-	-	1
Mortuary Ring	-	1	-	-	-	1
Pit	-	-	1	-	-	1
Pit-Structure	-	-	-	1	-	1
Slot	-	-	1	-	-	1
Structure	-	-	-	-	1	1
Vicus Structure	-	-	-	7	-	7
Well	-	-	-	-	1	1
TOTAL	857	1	6	8	2	874

c

	MIA	ER	ER/RB	RB	TOTAL
Inhumation	856	-	1	-	857
Fort Road	-	2	-	-	2
Hearth	-	1	-	-	1
Latrine	-	1	-	-	1
Mortuary Ring	1	-	-	-	1
Pit	-	1	-	-	1
Pit-Structure	1	-	-	-	1
Slot	-	1	-	-	1
Structure	-	-	-	1	1
Vicus Structure	-	-	-	7	7
Well	-	-	-	1	1
TOTAL	858	6	1	9	874

Figure 136: Glass bead feature analysis for East Yorkshire (a) bar-chart of glass bead frequency by feature, (b) comparison of site type and feature type, (c) comparison of feature and period of activity.

Dress and Identity in Iron Age Britain

sun or sky related (Wallis 2011). One of the interesting aspects about the pit is the order in which the objects were found and their relative positions. They were not found clustered together at the top or the bottom of the pit, rather they were spread out from the bottom to nearly the top. In addition, both the stone ring and the torc seem to have been placed so that they were standing upright, while the others were placed on their sides. Could this be due to casual placement within the pit such as haphazardly dropping the objects? Or were they carefully arranged in this way?

For the remaining depositions, clear contents are known for 13 pits. The contents of these pits were variable and some contain many objects and some have very few objects (Figure 140). In depositions where glass beads were found with one other type of object, they occur with pottery, stone, worked bone/antler, or textile tools. More complex depositions contain a myriad of different artefact/ecofact types such as worked stone, tools, ferrous materials, and clay bits. The most frequently found materials are worked bone or antler, but also stone artefacts. Glass beads in pits are primarily found in the Southwest England region, and less so in other regions. While this could in part be reflecting differences in the number and types of sites that have been excavated in each region, it may also be reflecting regional practices. In Southwest England in particular, it seems that glass beads were an appropriate material for deposition within pits, although this seems to have occurred very rarely.

Glass Beads in Inhumations

In the study regions, glass beads were found in a total of 19 inhumations in all regions studied, except East Anglia. Where the details about the inhumation are known, all of these burials were single inhumation features, except for the inhumation at Garton Slack (burial 8 and 10 in grave 2) where there were two individuals, although the report specifies that all of the glass beads were clearly associated with only one skeleton (Brewster 1980, 257). Glass beads were found in these burial features both singly and as part of small and larger assemblages of glass beads. In addition, many of the inhumations contained further artefacts, interpreted as grave goods, many of which appear to be personal items. Where the skeletal material has been analysed for biological traits indicating sex, it is always female or possible female. In many of the antiquarian excavations, individuals in burials with glass beads have been assumed to be female as with the Clevedon cist burial, the Queen's Barrow, Arras, and at Barrow L, Cowlam. There have been no inhumations with Iron Age glass beads in any of the study regions where the sex is possibly or definitely male.

Two major inhumation trends are reflected in the regional data. First, in Southwest England (Figure 141), the inhumations primarily date to the Late Iron

Figure 136: Glass bead feature analysis for East Yorkshire. (d) Comparison of Classes and features.

	Inhumation	Fort Road	Gully	Hearth	Hoard	Latrine	Mortuary Ring	Pit	Pit-Structure	Pit-Votive	Road	Mound	Roundhouse	Roundhouse-Posthole	Roundhouse-Ringditch	Slot	Souterraine	Special Deposit	Structure	Vicus Structure	Well	Working Hollow	Causeway	Cave	Ditch	Ditch-enclosure	Enclosure Entrance	TOTAL
Class 1	597	2	-	1	-	1	1	-	1	-	-	-	-	-	-	1	-	-	1	7	-	-	-	-	-	-	-	612
Class 2	16	-	-	-	-	-	-	-	-	-	-	-	-	-	-	-	-	-	-	-	-	-	-	-	-	-	-	16
Class 3	-	-	-	-	-	-	-	-	-	-	-	-	-	-	-	-	-	-	-	-	-	-	-	-	-	-	-	0
Class 4	99	-	-	-	-	-	1	-	-	-	-	-	-	-	-	-	-	-	-	-	-	-	-	-	-	-	-	100
Class 5	-	-	-	-	-	-	-	-	-	-	-	-	-	-	-	-	-	-	-	-	-	-	-	-	-	-	-	0
Class 6	142	-	-	-	-	-	-	1	-	-	-	-	-	-	-	-	-	-	-	-	-	-	-	-	-	-	-	143
Class 7	-	-	-	-	-	-	-	-	-	-	-	-	-	-	-	-	-	-	-	-	-	-	-	-	-	-	-	0
Class 8	-	-	-	-	-	-	-	-	-	-	-	-	-	-	-	-	-	-	-	-	-	-	-	-	-	-	-	0
Class 9	-	-	-	-	-	-	-	-	-	-	-	-	-	-	-	-	-	-	-	-	-	-	-	-	-	-	-	0
Class 10	1	-	-	-	-	-	-	-	-	-	-	-	-	-	-	-	-	-	-	-	-	-	-	-	-	-	-	1
Class 11	1	-	-	-	-	-	-	-	-	-	-	-	-	-	-	-	-	-	-	-	1	-	-	-	-	-	-	2
TOTAL	856	2	0	1	0	1	2	1	1	0	0	0	0	0	0	1	0	0	1	7	1	0	0	0	0	0	0	874

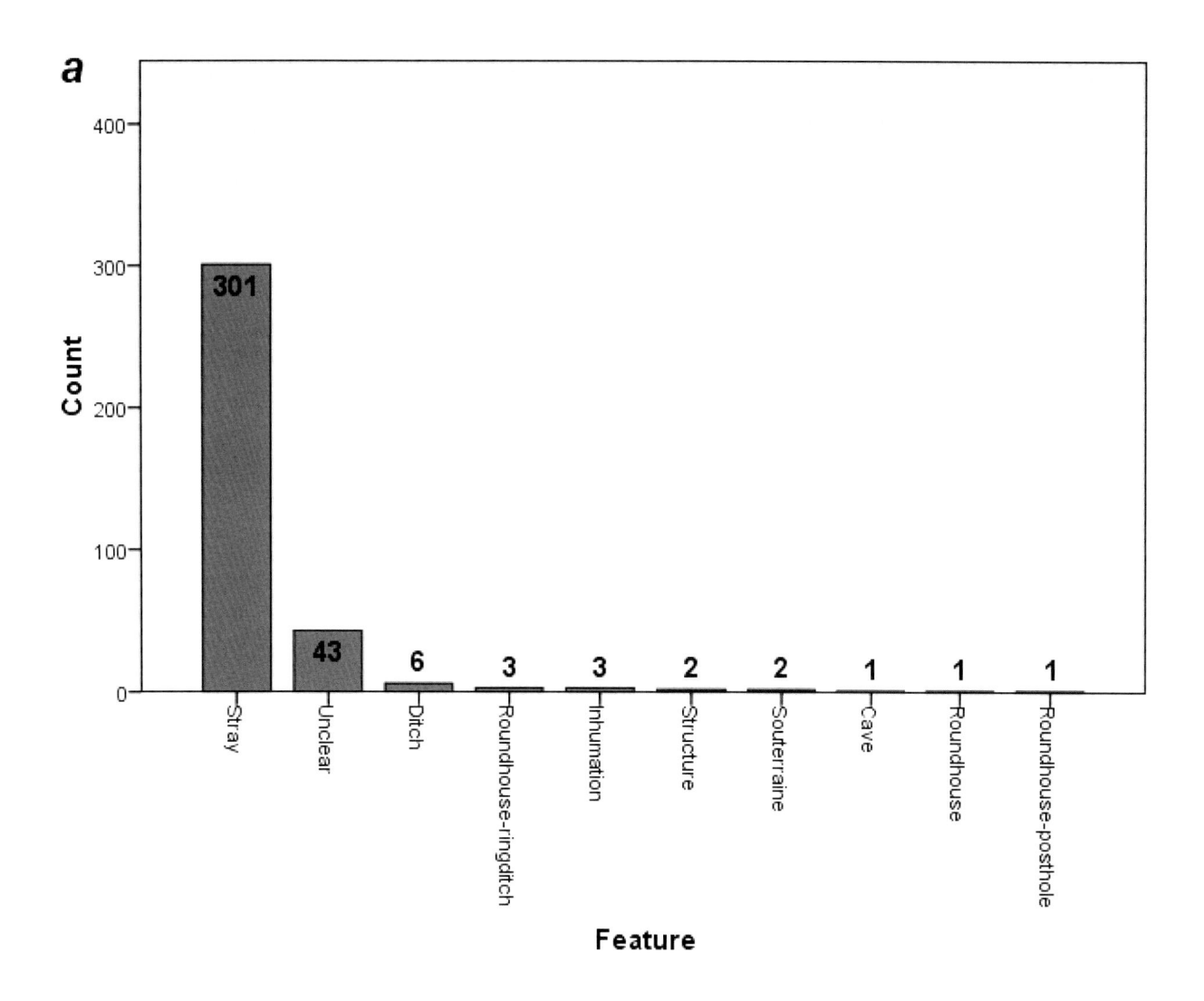

a

[Bar chart showing glass bead frequency by feature: Stray 301, Unclear 43, Ditch 6, Roundhouse-ringditch 3, Inhumation 3, Structure 2, Souterraine 2, Cave 1, Roundhouse 1, Roundhouse-posthole 1]

b

	Settlement	TOTAL
Roundhouse-Posthole	1	1
Roundhouse-Ringditch	3	3
TOTAL	4	4

c

	LIA/ER	TOTAL
Roundhouse-Posthole	1	1
Roundhouse-Ringditch	3	3
TOTAL	4	4

Figure 137: Glass bead feature analysis for Northeast Scotland (a) bar-chart of glass bead frequency by feature, (b) comparison of site type and feature type, (c) comparison of feature and period of activity.

Age/Early and Roman/Romano-British periods where this information is clearly known. Unfortunately for the inhumations at Battlesbury Camp, Chedworth, and Teffont Evias a date other than probably 'Iron Age' is impossible to determine from the literature.[15] The three Dorset burials fall within the Late Iron Age/Early Roman ('Durotrigian') tradition. Whitcombe burial 3 only had one glass bead and the only other items in the grave were animal remains (pig and possibly horse), while burial 8 on the other hand, contained both local and imported pottery, and a number of beads that possibly formed a necklace, although the record is not clear. Both inhumations were female, but the richer burial (no. 8) is thought to be the remains of a younger individual than the other (no. 3). This may suggest that age alone does not determine identity, but that it may be dependent on lineage or some other unknown factor.

---

[15] Attempts to locate the skeletal material from Teffont Evias have thus far been unsuccessful, and it appears that they may have been lost during World War II.

	Inhumation	Fort Road	Gully	Hearth	Hoard	Latrine	Mortuary Ring	Pit	Pit-Structure	Pit-Votive	Road	Mound	Roundhouse	Roundhouse-Posthole	Roundhouse-Ringditch	Slot	Souterraine	Special Deposit	Structure	Vicus Structure	Well	Working Hollow	Causeway	Cave	Ditch	Ditch-Enclosure	Enclosure Entrance	TOTAL
Class 1	-	-	-	-	-	-	-	-	-	-	-	-	-	-	1	-	-	-	-	-	-	-	-	-	-	-	-	1
Class 2	-	-	-	-	-	-	-	-	-	-	-	-	-	-	-	-	-	-	-	-	-	-	-	-	-	-	-	0
Class 3	-	-	-	-	-	-	-	-	-	-	-	-	-	-	-	-	-	-	-	-	-	-	-	-	-	-	-	0
Class 4	-	-	-	-	-	-	-	-	-	-	-	-	-	-	-	-	-	-	-	-	-	-	-	-	-	-	-	0
Class 5	-	-	-	-	-	-	-	-	-	-	-	-	-	-	-	-	-	-	-	-	-	-	-	-	-	-	-	0
Class 6	1	-	-	-	-	-	-	-	-	-	-	-	1	1	2	-	1	-	2	-	-	-	1	-	4	-	-	13
Class 7	1	-	-	-	-	-	-	-	-	-	-	-	-	-	-	-	-	-	-	-	-	-	-	-	-	-	-	1
Class 8	-	-	-	-	-	-	-	-	-	-	-	-	-	-	-	-	-	-	-	-	-	-	-	-	-	-	-	0
Class 9	-	-	-	-	-	-	-	-	-	-	-	-	-	-	-	-	-	-	-	-	-	-	-	-	-	-	-	0
Class 10	-	-	-	-	-	-	-	-	-	-	-	-	-	-	-	-	-	-	-	-	-	-	-	-	-	-	-	0
Class 11	-	-	-	-	-	-	-	-	-	-	-	-	-	-	-	-	-	-	-	-	-	-	-	-	2	-	-	2
TOTAL	2	0	0	0	0	0	0	0	0	0	0	0	1	1	3	0	1	0	2	0	0	0	1	0	6	0	0	17

Figure 137: Glass bead feature analysis for Northeast Scotland. (d) Comparison of Classes and features.

While the two Whitcombe burials contained objects consistent within this tradition, the Chesil mirror burial contained some unusual artefacts including: a decorated mirror, several stone beads, two brooches, a perforated Roman coin, tweezers, and an armlet or bracelet. Another inhumation accompanied by a mirror was found nearby at Portesham (Fitzpatrick 1997a). It was also likely female, but possibly older as her estimated age was between 26 and 45 years old (Fitzpatrick 1997a, 54). Bearing some similarity, the Chesil mirror burial was possibly female and between 18 and 20 years old (Craig-Atkins, Evans et al. 2013, 37). It is unfortunate that the context of the find was destroyed during its discovery, and it is unclear how the artefacts were placed in the grave in relation to the body. This may have been especially informative in terms of the glass beads and the perforated Roman coin. Nonetheless, it is clear that the five glass beads from this inhumation were unusual. Four of the beads are large and decorated, while the smallest one is a plain monochrome bead. All of the beads have larger perforation holes, and despite being found in a single features, there is little to indicate how these beads were used. Larger perforations suggest that they were perhaps threaded onto something with a large diameter, or perhaps an organic string (discussed further in Chapter 8).

The final inhumation in Southwest England with glass beads for which reliable data is available is a cist burial from Clevedon in Somerset. Despite being an early twentieth century find, and the bones being destroyed prior to an osteological examination, this inhumation is very unusual. Although the inhumation was contained in a cist, Whimster (1981, 74) did not see this particular cist, or other more northern examples, as an extension of the tradition centred around Scilly and Cornwall. Instead, he saw it, and others (such as at Birdlip), as a regional independent development. This particular inhumation, although not explicitly stated, was presumably assumed to be female due to the presence of 18 glass beads (Gray 1942). There were no metal artefacts that accompanied the burial, and the only other possible grave goods were a pebble and a few encrinites. The only hint to the period of the inhumation is that a number of the beads are paralleled at Meare Lake Village. However, several of the beads are very unusual and no other glass beads like these have been discovered as the use of opaque red glass in Iron Age Britain is extremely rare (DB 3252 - 3259).

The second major tradition is the inhumations in East Yorkshire, where they primarily date to the end of the Middle Iron Age - from about the third century BC to the early second century BC (Jay, Haselgrove et al. 2012) - and it seems reasonable at present to extend this date more broadly across the known East Yorkshire burial tradition, in the absence of other absolute dates. There are a total of 24 known inhumations in East Yorkshire that contained glass beads (Figure 142). Of these, 75% are located within the Garton/Wetwang Slack settlement

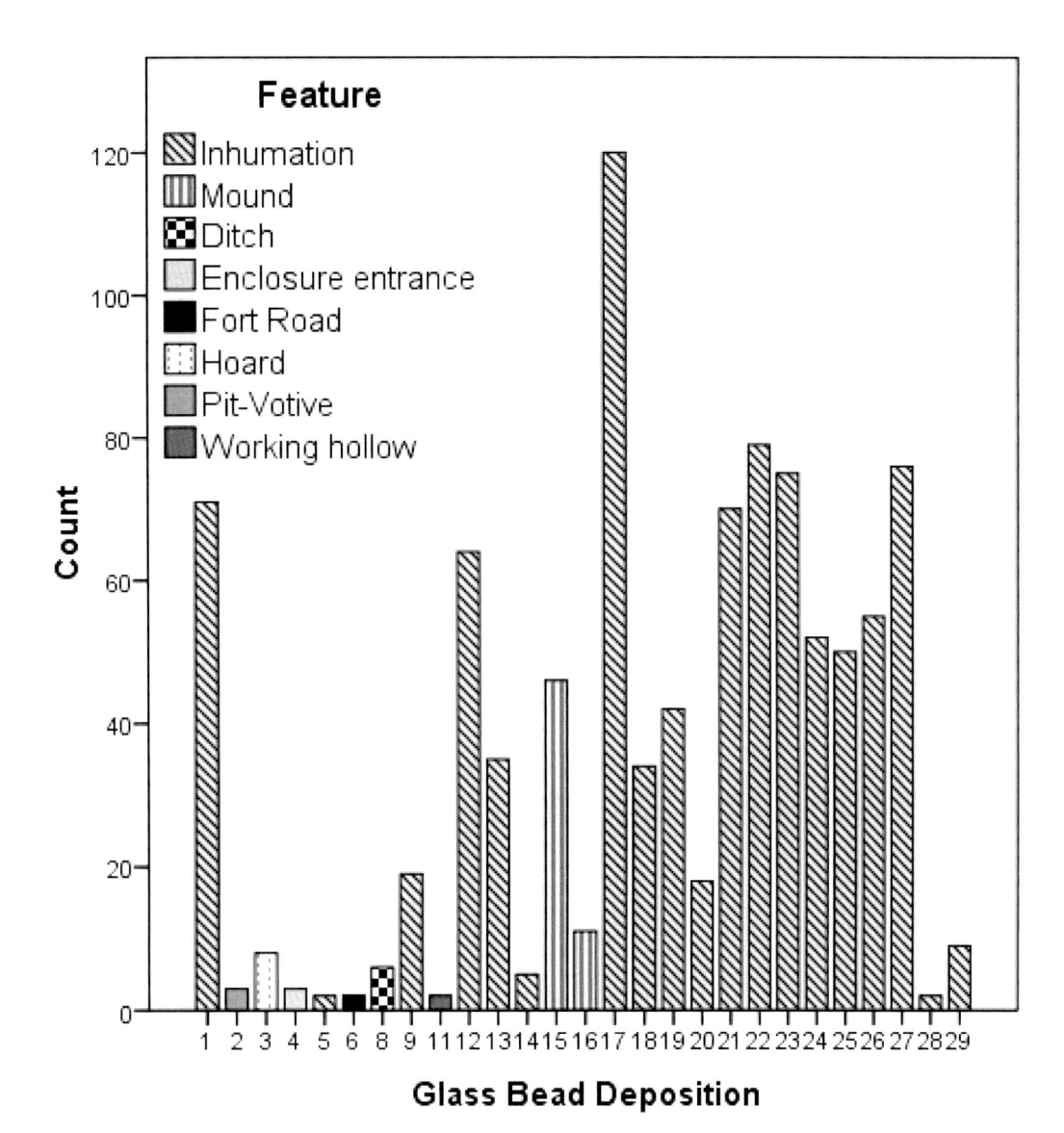

Figure 138: Bar-chart showing the number of beads found within single contexts.
(1) Queen's Barrow, Arras, (2) Billingford votive deposit, (3) Bulbury Camp Hoard, (4) Bredon's hill-fort, (5) Burn Ground Grave 7, (6) Castleford fort road, (7) Castleford vicus, (8) Cawdor Castle Ditch, (9) Clevedon cist burial, (11) Conderton Camp working hollow, (12) Barrow L, Cowlam, (13) Garton Slack 8 and10 Grave 2 burial 1, (14) Langton Herring Mirror burial, (15) Meare Lake Village 'necklace' G68, (16) Meare Lake Village 'necklace' G69, (17) 2001 Wetwang Slack chariot burial 'tassel', (18) Wetwag Slack burial 139, (19) Wetwang Slack burial 155, (20) Wetwang Slack burial 209, (21) Wetwang Slack burial 210, (22) Wetwang Slack burial 236, (23) Wetwang Slack burial 249, (24) Wetwang Slack burial 257, (25) Wetwang Slack burial 274, (26) Wetwang Slack burial 284, (27) Wewang Slack burial 376, (28) Wetwang Slack burial 64, (29) Whitcombe burial 8.

and cemetery site. Five of the inhumations contained only one glass bead (burials 17, 102, 268, 270, 277) and another had two glass beads (burial 64). The remaining inhumations had between 18 and 79 glass beads each, while 120 glass beads are known from the 2001 chariot burial. Only five of these inhumations had no other grave goods. The remaining 13 inhumations had a mix of different grave goods accompanying the body. Some were limited to just a pot and a sheep bone, while others had objects accompanying them. Stead's excavations at Rudston and Burton Fleming clearly show where the beads were found in relation to the body, although each

of the four inhumations with glass beads only contained a single example. In each case it seems that a glass bead was placed on or near the head of the individual, although the only broken example of a bead was found under pot sherds located near the head of burial BF19 (Stead 1991a, 292 and figure 119).

The Queen's Barrow from Arras, and Barrow L at Cowlam were both antiquarian finds from the nineteenth century (Stead 1979). Methods utilised to determine sex of both inhumations are unclear, thus attribution of a female gender was probably due to the accompanying

Site	Region	Date	Glass Bead	Pit Contents
21 Church Road, Bishop's Cleeve	SW England	MIA	Class 6 Type 901	MIA pottery
A417 Birdlip Bypass	SW England	MIA	Class 6 Type 1431	MIA pottery, dog skeleton
Cadbury Castle	SW England	-	Class 6 Type 1417	Decorated Glastonbury Ware
Claydon Pike: Warrens Field	SW England	LIA/ER	Class 11 Type 3003	Unknown details
Conderton Camp	SW England	MIA	Class 1 Type 102	Pit with pottery sherds at the bottom, middle layer with a bone pin fragment and an ovate pebble, below the modern turf was a glass bead, iron fragment and iron strip. The pit also contained animal bones and fired clay, but it is not clear which layer they were a part of.
Lidbury Camp	SW England	MIA/LIA	Class 2 Type 204	Bone needle (and frags.), sling stones, burnt clay, rubber fragment, hammer-stone, fossil echinus, pottery frags
Maiden Castle	SW England	LIA	Class 1 Type 110	Utilised pebble, iron blade
Maiden Castle	SW England	LIA	Class 1 Type 107	No other finds
Maiden Castle	SW England	LIA	Class 11 Type 2202	Chalk disc
Maiden Castle	SW England	LIA	Class 6 Type 1417	Unclear other than with Bii pottery
Maiden Castle	SW England	LIA	Class 6 Type 1407	Unclear other than with Bii pottery
Maiden Castle	SW England	LIA	Class 1 Type 106	Unclear other than with Bii pottery
Salmonsbury	SW England	MIA	Class 1 Type 102	Check
South Cadbury	SW England	-	Class 6 Type 1400	Glastonbury Ware
Swallowcliffe	SW England	EIA	Class 4 Type 427	Cu alloy awl, 2 bone gouges
Swallowcliffe	SW England	EIA	Class 1 Type 102	Chalk spindle whorl
Swallowcliffe	SW England	EIA	Class 1 Type 102	Weaving comb, 3 bone gouges, bone awl, sling bullet, chalk spindle whorl
Swallowcliffe	SW England	EIA	Class 1 Type 102	Animal bone, charcoal, pottery, loomweights, bone gouge, antler ferrule, sling stones, 2 iron knives, miniature pottery vessel
West Overton Down	SW England	LIA	Class 6 Type 1201	"occupation material", worn bone point
Billingford	East Anglia	Romano-British	Class 1 Type 106, 2 Class 6 Type 901	Cu alloy key, stone ring, Cu alloy torc, 2 cu alloy rings
Castleford	E Yorkshire	ER/RB	Class 6 Type 901	Trumpet brooch and colourless glass vessel fragment
Garton Slack 14	E Yorkshire	MIA	Class 1 Type 102	Jet ring, fragments of jet, animal rib spatula

Figure 139: List of sites where glass beads were found in pit contexts.

objects rather than through an osteological examination. Both inhumations included a single brooch, and the dates of these brooches have been used previously to date the inhumations. Although brooches are commonly used for dating, the unusual nature of both brooches adds confusion to the interpretations of both inhumations. For now, it may be best to think of these inhumations as late Middle Iron Age as well. Descriptions of the other objects of dress found in these inhumations are discussed in Chapter 8.

East Yorkshire is well known for the Iron Age inhumation practice and in some cases for the lavish grave goods that accompany the inhumations. In general, some of the most spectacular inhumations have been the Kirkburn sword burial (Stead 1991a, K3), the various chariot burials, and many of the female burials. However, despite our understanding of this region as one where inhumation was commonly practiced in the Middle Iron Age, the grave goods that accompanied the individuals were not standardised. In fact, out of the 753 possible individuals represented at Wetwang Slack and from Stead's excavations at Rudston, Burton Fleming, Garton Slack, and Kirkburn, only 34% had surviving grave goods (Figure 143). This ranged from a sherd or two of pottery and/or possibly a pig or sheep bone, to more elaborate burials with brooches, bracelets, finger-rings, and of course glass beads. Only twenty of these inhumations (3%) contained glass beads in any number (excluding antiquarian finds and the 2001 chariot burial). Thus, if these cemeteries are in any way representative of the Middle Iron Age population, then it again hints at the rarity of glass beads. The variety of different types of objects found within the graves may suggest that an inhumation 'package' or standardised set of objects did not exist at this time. Instead, it may be that the objects

ARCHAEOLOGICAL CONTEXT

Site	Pottery	Animal Remains	Stone	Worked Bone/Antler	Textile Production Tool	Iron	Clay	Fossil	Tool	Brooch	Glass Vessel Fragment	Torc	Key	Cu alloy Object
21 Church Road, Bishop's Cleeve	X													
Cadbury Castle	X													
South Cadbury	X													
A417 Birdlip Bypass	X	X												
Swallowcliffe	X	X	X	X	X	X								
Conderton Camp	X	X	X	X		X	X							
Lidbury Camp	X		X	X			X	X	X					
Swallowcliffe 22			X						X					
Swallowcliffe 36			X	X	X									
Garton Slack 14			X	X										
Maiden Castle			X											
West Overton				X										
Swallowcliffe 29					X									
Castleford										X	X			
Billingford		X										X	X	X

Figure 140: Table comparing the different types of objects found in pits with glass beads.

Site	Qty. Glass Beads	Glass Bead Type	Date
Battlesbury Camp	1	Class 1: Type 110	IA
Chedworth	1	Class 4: Type 410	?
Teffont Evias	1	Class 1: Type 102	Iron Age?
Whitcombe (3)	1	Class 1: Type 107	1st century AD
Whitcombe (8)	9	Class 1: Type 107, 110	1st century AD
		Class 6: Type 901	
Wookey Hole	1	Class 1: Type 410	LIA/RB
Burn Ground Grave 7	2	Class 1: Type 110	Anglo-Saxon
Clevedon	18	Class 1 Type 110	IA
		Class 3 Type 301, 302	
		Class 6 Type 1003	
Langton Herring	5	Class 1 Type 108	LIA/ER
		Class 5 Type 701	
		Class 8 Type 1604	
		Class 9 Type 1704	
		Class 11 Type 2801	

Figure 141: List of sites where glass beads were found in inhumations in Southwest England.

placed in the graves actually reflect the items used or worn by that person in everyday life.

There was one bead (Class 6 Type 1420, unknown date) from Northeast Scotland that reportedly was found in a burial cist at Inglismaldie House. As Chapter 4 demonstrated that there is very little evidence for inhumation in this region at this time, it may be a burial that is much later in date. However, the written description of the bead clearly indicates that it similar to the other triangular spiral beads from this region.

Summary

This section has examined the positive, and in some cases the negative, evidence for where glass beads have been found at the macro- (site) and micro- (feature) scale. The pattern of glass bead deposition is different in each

Site	Qty. Glass Beads	Glass Bead Type	Date
Trentholme Drive, York	1	Class 10 Type 1800	RB
Burton Fleming BF 19	1	Class 6 Type 900	MIA
Makeshift burial R16	1	Class 1 Type 102	MIA
Makeshift burial R 193	1	Class 1 Type 102	MIA
Makeshift burial R2	1	Class 1 Type 102	MIA
Queen's Barrow, Arras	71	Class 4 Type 411, 421, 424, 425, 426, 428; Class 6 Type 901, 905, 907	MIA
Barrow L, Cowlam	75	Class 4 Type 425; Class 9 Type 900, 901	MIA
Garton Slack 8 and 10 Grave 2 burial 1	35	Class 1 Type 201; Class 4 Type 410	MIA
Wetwang Slack Chariot Burial	120	Class 1 Type 102	MIA
Wetwang Slack 17	1	Class 6 Type 1407	MIA
Wetwang Slack 64	2	Class 2 Type 102	MIA
Wetwang Slack 102	1	Class 6 Type 1001	MIA
Wetwang Slack 139	34	Class 1 Type 102	MIA
Wetwang Slack 155	42	Class 1 Type 102	MIA
Wetwang Slack 209	18	Class 2 Type 202; Class 6 Type 901	MIA
Wetwang Slack 210	70	Class 1 Type 102	MIA
Wetwang Slack 236	79	Class 1 Type 102; Class 4 Type 420, 423	MIA
Wetwang Slack 249	75	Class 1 Type 102; Class 4 Type 417, 418, 421	MIA
Wetwang Slack 257	52	Class 1 Type 102	MIA
Wetwang Slack 268	1	Class 6 Type 1417	MIA
Wetwang Slack 270	1	Class 1 Type 102	MIA
Wetwang Slack 274	50	Class 4 Type 410, 417; Class 6 Type 901; Class 11 Type 2301	MIA
Wetwang Slack 277	1	Class 1 Type 102	MIA
Wetwang Slack 284	55	Class 1 Type 102; Class 4 Type 413, 414, 417; Class 6 Type 901	MIA
Wetwang Slack 376	76	Class 1 Type 102; Class 4 Type 501, 503	MIA

Figure 142: List of sites where glass beads were found in inhumations in East Yorkshire.

of these regions, depending on the local practice, which also changes throughout the Iron Age. In general, glass beads are often found within settlements (enclosed and unenclosed), and often within domestic features, such as near roundhouses or within pits. They are also found in inhumations with grave goods, and it may be that they belonged to the deceased. In either case, the number of sites where they have been found compared to the number of sites discussed here where they have not been found suggests that this object may have been extremely rare. This assumes that the number of glass beads found in the archaeological record is representative of the number of glass beads in circulation at the time. In the case of pottery, it has been suggested that the pottery in the archaeological record represents only a very small proportion of the objects actually in use at the time (Hill 1995b; Willis 1997).

Chronologically, there are very few identified glass beads from Early Iron Age contexts, but the majority of glass beads were found in deposits of the third and second century BC, primarily in Somerset and East Yorkshire. Whether the beads themselves were manufactured in Europe and deposited in Britain, or were made in Britain from European/Mediterranean glass sources, this significant episode of deposition in two different locations (i.e. Southwest England and East Yorkshire) points to a higher degree of continental

Site	Indiv. (n)	Female	?Female	Male	?Male	Unknown	Inhumations with artefacts
Wetwang Slack	446	209	8	142	17	68	96
Rudston (Makeshift cemetery)	200	41	29	34	20	63	104
Rudston (Argam Lane)	19	4	3	5	4	3	9
Burton Fleming	22	3	6	4	3	6	19
Burton Fleming (Bell Slack)	46	6	9	11	4	12	18
Garton Slack	9	4	-	5	-	-	5
Kirkburn	11	4	-	4	-	2	6
TOTAL	753	271	55	205	48	154	257
		326		253			

Figure 143: Frequency of inhumations in East Yorkshire.

contact that occurred in the Middle Iron Age. Although, such activity is usually attributed to the end of the first millennia BC (Hill 1995a). However, in the case of glass beads, it seems that this pattern ends abruptly just before or around the first century BC, and does not continue in significant numbers into the first century BC/AD. Although the degree to which Britain was isolated throughout prehistory, including the Early and Middle Iron Age has long been a topic of debate (e.g. Cunliffe 2007; Hill 1995a), there is growing evidence to support that Britain was not completely cut off from Europe, and may even have had significant contact with communities across the channel (Cunliffe and de Jersey 1997; Henderson 2008). Water features, such as the Bristol Channel and Humber Estuary potentially played an important role in cross-channel trade (Moore 2003).

Discussion

There are many ways that glass beads could be explored spatially. This chapter began by examining some of the broad patterns through typology distribution, which has shown that by using a more precise typology there are patterns in the deposition of beads when regions are compared. It then investigated the nature of the data in order to understand the impact of developer-funded excavations on the number of Iron Age beads known. This has shown that despite the large number of excavations there has not been a parallel increase in the number of beads discovered. The reasons behind this are numerous; however, there are two recent developer-funded excavations where glass beads have been found in large numbers that are of national importance (forthcoming, but see: Malone 2010; Murray 2007a). Although final publication is forthcoming for both sites, the finds and context could radically alter our perceptions of these object.

The site and feature analysis compared where glass beads were present and absent. While the discovery of glass beads could be an effect of the size and placement of trenches, this analysis has shown that there is evidence to suggest that glass beads were rare and that patterns of deposition follow regional practices. Finally, analyses of chronology in all sections, and some discussions from Chapter 5, shows that there are several examples of glass beads in Late Bronze Age/Early Iron Age contexts, but that there were major depositional episodes in two study regions between the third and second century BC. Even when the beads from the lake villages and East Yorkshire burials are excluded, this trend is still visible. This is significant given the increase in brooch deposition in the Late Iron Age, and is discussed further in Chapter 8 (Haselgrove 1997; Jundi and Hill 1997).

This chapter has shown that there are patterns in the spatial deposition of glass beads in Britain. It is essential to recognise that these analyses only reflect the end of the life history of the beads, and do not represent the changing meaning or changing practices during the active use period of the bead. Therefore, by examining the site type and feature type, we can only consider practices that relate to the individual acts connected with bead deposition.

In terms of bead deposition, the data suggests that there were multiple practices occurring simultaneously. First, beads were included with human remains at the time of burial. This ranges from a single bead, to several, to just over fifty. The second practice is the occurrence of what is often a single bead within domestic contexts: within roundhouse features, pits, or enclosure ditches. It is this group of finds that is most troubling. How and why did they enter the archaeological record? Is this practice an accurate reflection of the beads that were in circulation during the Iron Age? It is clear that at least some of these beads were not simply discarded; many are unbroken, complete examples. So, if they were not all discarded as rubbish, some may have been accidental losses or even intentional deposits. If this is the case, then it would be difficult to sustain an argument that these beads are representative of all of Iron Age beads, as Hill (1995b) has argued. Although, beads found in these contexts do not demonstrate how the bead was used in connection with dress, it does demonstrate that as an object of dress a bead was sometimes suitable for inclusion within these circumstances.

The finds from the so-called lake villages at Meare and Glastonbury in Somerset present a different problem. The 300+ glass beads found during these excavations are out of proportion compared to the finds from other features. Most of these finds were attributed to different mounds, which were thought to be the locations of various habitation structures. Overall, the finds from this site are generally acknowledged as remarkable due to the quantity and preservation, but do they represent an accurate reflection of past activity? Or are these objects wrapped up with the same issues of depositional intentionality as at other sites, despite the level of preservation? This relates back to the processes that created the archaeological record. It is unclear how daily life would have been radically different on the lake villages compared to other non-wetland occupational sites, especially given that they were not communities isolated from the rest of the southwest as demonstrated by the shared artefact types. For glass beads, the large numbers and consistent use of colourless and opaque yellow glass have been used as a basis for the suggestion that manufacturing occurred here (Guido 1978a; Henderson 1982; 1989). Very few examples of these beads were broken, suggesting that they did not enter the archaeological record as rubbish. So, why would so many glass beads be found throughout the site, and why would they enter the archaeological record at the same site where they were manufactured? Perhaps they too were a part of an intentional, possibly ritual, deposit. Similarly, at Culduthel Farm near Inverness, although the site does have evidence for both glass beads and glass working, why are the beads deposited in presumably the same place that they were manufactured?

Aside from glass beads found in inhumations and domestic contexts or other occupations, they generally were not found in any other circumstances, for example: in hoards or in watery features. The only major exceptions to this pattern are the pit depositions at Billingford in Norfolk and at Santon Downham in Suffolk. Although later in date, it is interesting that these hoards occur in the same region as the torc depositions at Snettisham. Other than the beads from the lake villages, they are not otherwise found in contexts related to water. Perhaps glass beads were unsuitable for inclusion in most hoards.

Given that the circumstances of the bead depositions (in domestic and inhumation features) suggest a deliberate act, rather than a straightforward reflection of the refuse of daily domestic life, the argument that glass beads were inherently a high-status object or conversely that the status of a site is reflected in the number of so-called prestige objects, is untenable. In the case of glass beads at domestic sites, the presence or absence of glass beads within site features is more a reflection of a particular act at a particular time with the 'correct' material for deposition on hand (Fontijn 2012; Kopytoff 1986). However, as it is this deliberately deposited material and surviving refuse that is available, in some cases it can still demonstrate the interconnectivity between communities, albeit with only the end node of the network known. For instance, beads with the 'Meare' style design and use of colour are found at other sites in the southwest, with two extreme examples considered here in East Yorkshire and East Anglia. The East Yorkshire examples were the only glass beads found in Burials 102 and 268. It is unclear if these possible female burials were from outside the local community as samples from these inhumations were not subject to isotopic study (Jay and Richards 2006). Assuming that these two individuals were local, perhaps these particular beads were valuable or treasured because the items passed through a long network of communities before being acquired by the community that lived at Wetwang/Garton Slack. Or perhaps because the colours were so different from the other beads found in this region, their uniqueness amongst the community created a feeling of value. Long distance trade networks and the value of particular materials, despite the distance from the source, have been demonstrated for quern stones, which existed alongside the local regional trade of pottery (Moore 2003).

For understanding how dress was created in Iron Age Britain, it is the beads from inhumation features that really provide the context for understanding how they were worn on the body. It is through these studies of features that it has been possible to bring together analyses of spatial distribution and the links between different types of beads that will be explored in the following chapter.

Chapter 8
Regional Bodily Adornment

Glass beads are simultaneously both a part and a whole (for fragmentation in archaeology, see: Chapman 2000; Chapman and Gaydarska 2007; Fowler 2004). Strands of individual glass beads can be used to create a necklace, or bracelet, but can also be used together in a myriad of other ways, such as hair ornaments, sewn onto textiles or other garments, attached to other objects, or they could be carried as a curio or trinket. However, multiple beads are not necessary for use, as single beads can be treated in the same way, although with a different effect. The best evidence for how glass beads were used is derived from burial evidence, where beads placed on or around the body may indicate the method in which they were worn. Despite the scarcity of inhumation burials and their geographic and chronological limitations, combined with the potential that such burials were reserved for certain individuals or circumstances (e.g. the Clevedon cist burial), it is from this data that we can begin to posit a wider understanding of dress during the Iron Age.

While previous chapters have considered glass beads individually in terms of their overall visual characteristics (Chapter 5 and 6), and the context of their deposition (Chapter 7), this chapter will specifically examine the way they were used in connection with the body. By drawing on inhumation evidence, this chapter will first demonstrate how glass beads formed a part of dress and will then put them into the wider context of other objects through an examination of other artefacts included in inhumations. Evidence from settlements that might explain the way in which glass beads were used on the body is rare, but a short examination of the evidence from Meare Lake Village will be given. Following these analyses, regional data for dress, particularly from brooches, pins, torcs, bracelets (including objects described as armlets, anklets, and arm-rings), and finger/toe-rings will be examined to determine patterns of regional dress. Finally, this data will be put into a wider context by a comparison to object distributions using Portable Antiquities Scheme data. It is from these analyses that it will be possible to begin to see regional patterns of material culture related to dress, and different regional identities.

Glass Bead Use

Evidence for the way in which glass beads were used is best derived from the context of the finds. Multiple beads found together may indicate that they were worn together. While this may be true to some extent for groups of beads found together in settlement contexts, their placement may not accurately reflect past practice. However, the presence of multiple beads is unusual and may therefore represent a larger object made from several glass beads. In contrast, beads found in burials, especially those instances with multiple beads, may indicate where on the body they were worn and in what manner, such as the arrangement of beads if strung or sewn to a garment. Unfortunately, this level of clarity is not always expressed in the excavation report, but the location of the beads in relation to the body is more likely to be recorded. Drawing on information from inhumations and settlement contexts, this section examines the evidence for the way in which the beads were used and in the case of inhumation features, it also places glass beads into the wider context of dress by comparing the different types of accompanying material culture that may have been a part of the individual's daily dress.

Inhumations

The inhumations under consideration are very few in number. Those of Iron Age date found within the Southwest England and East Yorkshire study regions have only been considered here (the two possible cist burials from Northeast Scotland are unverified), and although many of the beads from Grandcourt Quarry in Norfolk were found in the same rich pottery spread, it is unlikely that they were worn together (Foulds Forthcoming-b). This is partly due to the scattered nature of their finds spots at the site, but also because of the range of types and sizes. Even within the large numbers of inhumation burials in East Yorkshire, where this seems to have been a normative practice for a short period of time, the number of inhumations where glass beads occur are extremely rare. As shown in Chapter 7, inhumations with glass beads account for less than 3% of the known individual inhumations in this region. In Southwest England, the burial practice is inconsistent and scattered, suggesting that this was never a standard practice (Carr and Knüsel 1997; Moore 2006b), except perhaps for the Late Iron Age burials in Dorset.

One of the difficulties with interpreting the objects found within these inhumations is it may be that there were specific reasons for individuals in both regions to have been chosen for inhumation and that they may not be representative of the population. Another problem is that the artefacts accompanying the body may not have necessarily been worn by that individual in life. Although this may be a problem and a potential bias in an interpretation of the practices of dress, this issue can be addressed by putting such an analysis into a wider context through a study of other objects related to dress from outside inhumation features. This section will examine in detail the beads found in inhumations, evidence for how they were used, and finally discuss the wider evidence for dress through the other material culture included in the inhumations.

East Yorkshire Inhumations

Necklace Length

As demonstrated in previous chapters, the inclusion of glass beads within inhumations was not only rare, but the number and types of beads also varied considerably. If strung together as a single strand, the glass beads from each of these inhumations would have formed a necklace of different lengths (placement in grave that supports that these glass beads formed necklaces is presented below). Necklaces of different lengths would have had different impacts on both the viewer and the wearer (Figure 144). A shorter necklace (approximately 355mm), when worn around the neck, is very snug and potentially could inhibit breathing if worn too tight. A very long necklace (approximately 838mm) hangs below the chest and is more likely to swing around during body movement, and potentially bump into other objects and possibly cause damage to the beads. The number of beads needed to make a smaller or longer strand is dependent on the size of the beads themselves, as well as the consistency in size. Different sizes of beads would also affect the weight of the overall strung object, but in general a shorter necklace will be lighter than a longer necklace.

In East Yorkshire inhumations where more than one glass bead was found accompanying the body, only nine out of thirteen inhumations had enough glass beads to form a strand long enough to go around a neck (approx. 355.0mm, Figure 145). Glass beads from Wetwang Slack burials 284, 210, and 257, would have formed a very short necklace or choker that sits right around the neck. Glass beads from Wetwang Slack burials 236, 376, 249, and 274, would have created a necklace of medium length that would sit just below the collarbone. And finally, the Cowlam L necklace and Arras Queeen's barrow would have formed the longest necklaces with the former hanging as low as the mid-sternum, and the latter at the bottom of the sternum.

Today, jewellery companies make necklaces a minimum of approximately 356mm in length, which is just long enough to go around most adult necks. The glass beads from the remaining four burials (Wetwang Slack burials 155, 209, 139, and the 2001 chariot burial) would not form a necklace long enough to go around an adult sized neck, based on this minimum length. This assumes that they were used on their own and without any other

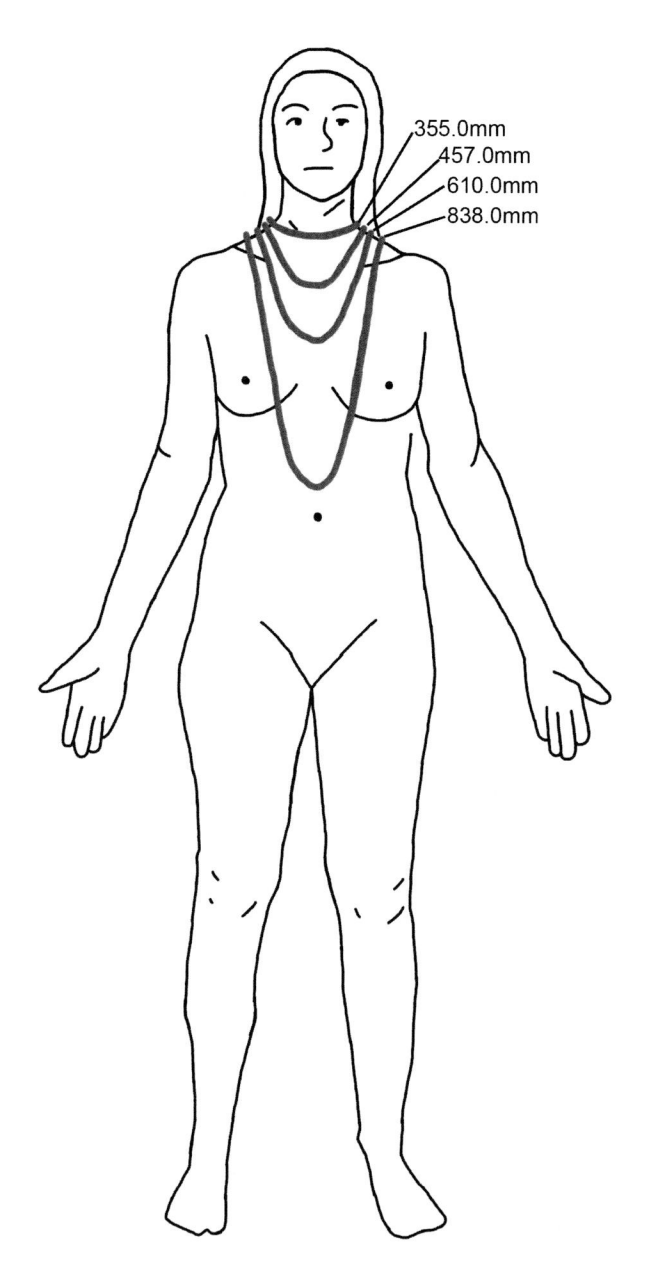

Figure 144: Illustration showing four different lengths of necklaces to demonstrate the different effects of differing lengths of strands of glass beads.

beads. Although it is entirely likely that in the Iron Age the average adult's neck circumference was smaller than today, the largest of this group of beads would have made a strand approximately 207.4mm long. It seems very unlikely that the beads were used in this way. The beads from Wetwang Slack burials 139 and 155 were, however, found next to the individual's neck. John Dent (1984, 171) has suggested that the remaining length of these necklaces would have been made up of beads of organic material that has not survived. Another possibility is that they were simply strung onto a material such as a cord or leather thong that was of the necessary length to go around the individual's neck. The result would be a necklace with loose beads that could easily shift around

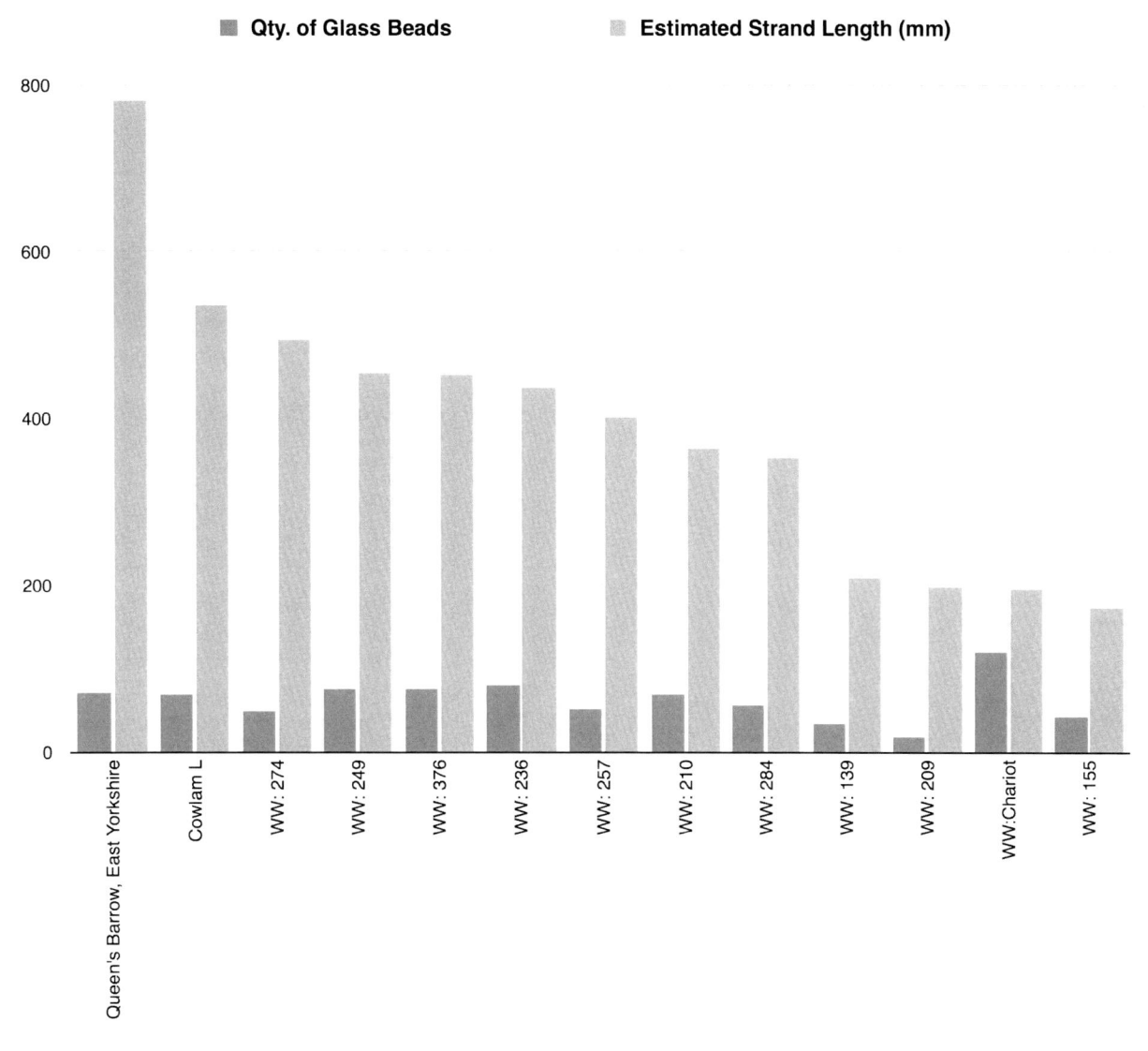

Figure 145: Bar chart comparing the number of glass beads in each possible necklace with the estimated length of each strand of beads in East Yorkshire.

on the threading material possibly creating noise as the beads clacked against each other. Another possibility is that they were not strung, and may have been worn in the hair or sewn onto a garment in the neck or shoulder region.

In contrast, the beads from Wetwang Slack burial 209 and the 2001 chariot burial were not found around or near the individual's neck. The unusual beads from burial 209 (Class 2 Type 202) were found scattered over the body and it has been suggested that this individual's death and burial were not closely contemporary and the body may even have been mummified (John Dent, pers. comm.). Therefore, it is unclear how these beads were worn, especially given that these large beads probably would not have formed a strand long enough to go around a neck. However, it is possible that some of the beads were lost between death and burial.

The beads from the 2001 chariot burial form another unusual case. This is the only instance in which 120 miniscule glass beads have been found and they were in association with a mirror. It has been suggested that these beads formed part of a tassel that was hung from the mirror or a bag enclosing the mirror (Hill 2001). It is also possible that they were sewn onto a textile or leather bag, as there may not have been enough beads to form such a tassel.

Overall, the necklace length data suggests that most of the glass beads found together would have formed a full strand that would have been relatively short, some just around the neck, others slightly longer. As necklaces, they would have drawn attention to the neck and upper chest region. It is really only the Cowlam L and Queen's Barrow necklaces that are exceptionally long if worn as a single strand, making these two individuals stand out

Dress and Identity in Iron Age Britain

Necklace/Burial Context	102	106	202	410	411	413	414	417	418	420	421	423	424	425	426	428	501	503	900	901	905	907	2301	Total
Queen's Barrow	-	-	-	-	19	-	-	-	-	-	4	-	14	1	1	1	-	-	-	10	1	13	-	64
Cowlam Barrow L	-	-	-	-	-	-	-	-	-	-	-	-	-	1	-	-	-	-	4	59	-	-	-	64
Garton Slack, G2B1	28	-	-	7	-	-	-	-	-	-	-	-	-	-	-	-	-	-	-	-	-	-	-	35
WWS Chariot Burial	120	-	-	-	-	-	-	-	-	-	-	-	-	-	-	-	-	-	-	-	-	-	-	120
Wetwang Burial 139	34	-	-	-	-	-	-	-	-	-	-	-	-	-	-	-	-	-	-	-	-	-	-	34
Wetwang Burial 155	42	-	-	-	-	-	-	-	-	-	-	-	-	-	-	-	-	-	-	-	-	-	-	42
Wetwang Burial 209	-	-	16	-	-	-	-	-	-	-	-	-	-	-	-	-	-	-	-	2	-	-	-	18
Wetwang Burial 210	70	-	-	-	-	-	-	-	-	-	-	-	-	-	-	-	-	-	-	-	-	-	-	70
Wetwang Burial 236	63	-	-	-	-	-	-	-	-	12	-	4	-	-	-	-	-	-	-	-	-	-	-	79
Wetwang Burial 249	59	-	-	-	-	-	-	11	1	-	4	-	-	-	-	-	-	-	-	-	-	-	-	75
Wetwang Burial 257	52	-	-	-	-	-	-	-	-	-	-	-	-	-	-	-	-	-	-	-	-	-	-	52
Wetwang Burial 274	-	-	-	1	-	-	-	1	-	-	-	-	-	-	-	-	-	-	-	47	-	-	1	50
Wetwang Burial 284	46	1	-	-	-	4	2	1	-	-	-	-	-	-	-	-	-	-	-	1	-	-	-	54
Wetwang Burial 376	72	-	-	-	-	-	-	-	-	-	-	-	-	-	-	-	2	1	-	-	-	-	-	76
Wetwang Burial 64	2	-	-	-	-	-	-	-	-	-	-	-	-	-	-	-	-	-	-	-	-	-	-	2
TOTAL	588	1	16	8	19	4	2	13	1	12	8	4	14	2	1	1	2	1	4	119	1	13	1	835

Figure 146: Comparison of East Yorkshire burials and bead types. Dark grey highlight indicates bead types that are repeated across necklaces, light grey highlight indicates bead types that only occur singly on one necklace and are not found elsewhere.

from the rest. These would have drawn attention to a larger area of the upper torso.

Bead Types

When comparing the different types of beads used on these necklaces, it is interesting that there is some overlap and others that remain unique (Figure 146). The Queen's Barrow necklace is exceptional because it is made up of the largest range of bead types compared to all other necklaces. Out of the nine types found on this necklace, three types are shared with other necklaces. It is also interesting that the widely occurring Type 102 plain blue beads were not found on the Queen's Barrow necklace, but are found on nearly every other East Yorkshire necklace. Figure 146 also highlights that there are five types of glass beads that are shared between necklaces (highlighted in dark grey, Type 410 is a dummy type for beads where details are unclear). This includes the plain blue Type 102 beads, Type 417 blue beads with three green and white eyes, Type 421 blue beads with nine blue and white eyes, Type 425 blue beads with twelve blue and white eyes, and Type 901 blue beads with white zig-zag/wave design. There are also fifteen bead types that only occur on single necklaces where there is no cross-over (highlighted in light grey).

Bead Dimensions

Similarity between beads on necklaces within each inhumation can be seen by comparing the dimensions of the beads. This was introduced briefly in Chapter 6; however, this section will take a more detailed approach. Figure 147 compares all known bead dimensions from those forming necklaces under discussion in this section. Some discernible groupings can be seen, such as those from Cowlam Barrow L and Wetwang burial 274, but in general, there is a large amount of overlap particularly around 10mm Diameter/Width and 5mm Height measurements. By singling out specific types, it is possible to search for patterns of bead size between each of the necklaces. For example, the most numerous type of bead is Type 102 plain blue beads. When the dimensions of these beads are plotted, there is much overlap (Figure 148a) even though visually some of these beads appear to be very different. This demonstrates that these individual plain beads fall in a similar same size range and there is not a clear definition of bead size that is apparent between the necklaces. It may be that many of these beads were interchangeable, or that there was little differentiation between these plain beads. In essence, they would have been considered to be 'the same'. There are some differences in size, such as the example from Wetwang burial 284 (Type 417), which is clearly smaller in diameter compared to those from burials 236 and 274. However, this could be an effect of the small sample size.

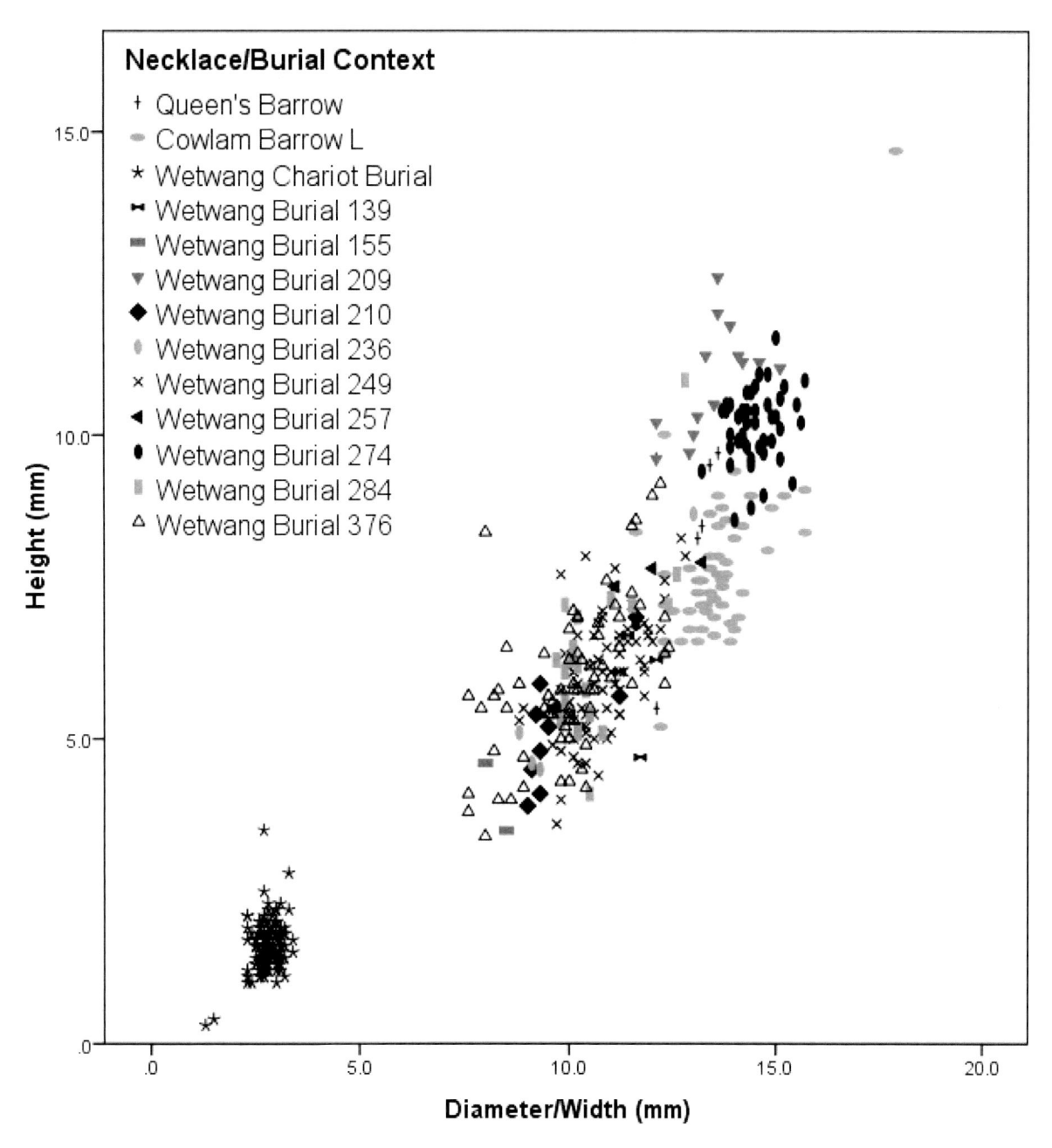

Figure 147: Scatter-graph comparing the size of all East Yorkshire glass beads from burials.

In comparison, Type 901 shows a very different pattern (Figure 148d). Most examples of this type are found in the Cowlam Barrow L and the Wetwang burial 274 forming two distinct size-based clusters with some overlap. Visual comparison of these beads shows that the burial 274 examples are much more weathered, but could in fact be the same as the Cowlam Barrow L beads.[16] Based on dimensions and decorative motif, however, the beads for each necklace were specifically chosen based on size, with the burial 274 beads being slightly but consistently larger. The overlap may suggest that either they were made in the same place and same time, but were part of different batches, or that there may have been some trade or interaction between groups of people. Perhaps they were all a part of one large necklace that was later split into two. The similarity in size between the burial 274, 209, and Queen's Barrow Type 901 beads further suggests interaction between people.

Within the Wetwang necklaces, given that all of the inhumations were from a single site that is connected with a nearby settlement, it probably is not unusual for there to be cross-over in different types. However, the

---

[16] It may be that different soil conditions have caused the beads from these two burials to weather differently. This needs to be investigated further.

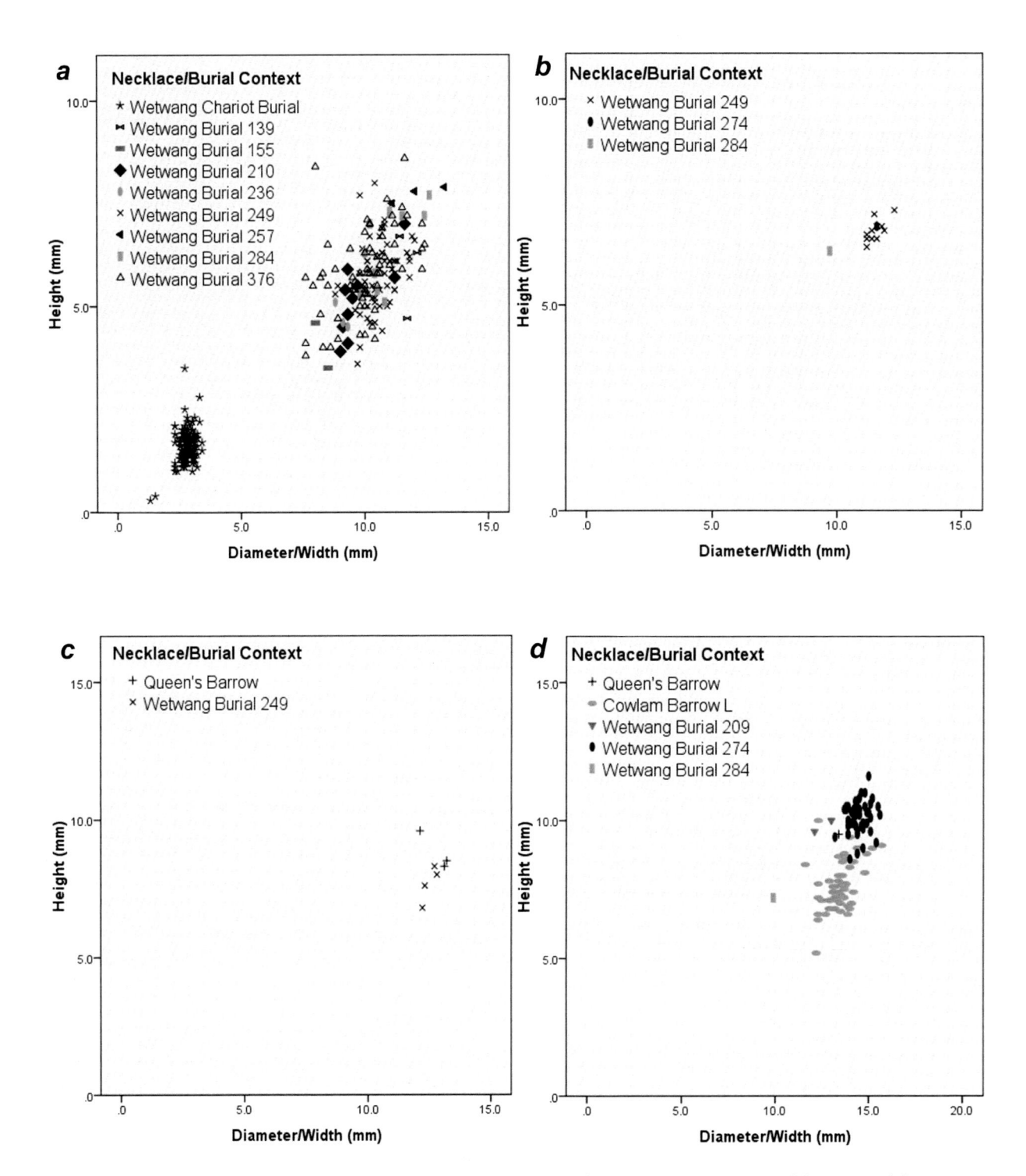

Figure 148: Scatter-graph comparing the size of four different bead types from East Yorkshire burials: (a) Type 102, (b) Type 417, (c) Type 421, (d) Type 901.

		Motif Type							
		Plain Blue	Plain Green	Melon	Simple Eye	Complex Eye	Wave/zig-zag	Double Wave/zig-zag	TOTAL
Necklace/Burial Context	Queen's Barrow	-	-	-	40	-	24	-	64
	Cowlam Barrow L	-	-	-	1	-	63	-	64
	Garton Slack, Grave 2 Barrow 1	28	-	-	7	-	-	-	35
	Wetwang Chariot Burial	120	-	-	-	-	-	-	120
	Wetwang Burial 139	34	-	-	-	-	-	-	34
	Wetwang Burial 155	42	-	-	-	-	-	-	42
	Wetwang Burial 209	-	-	16	-	-	2	-	18
	Wetwang Burial 210	70	-	-	-	-	-	-	70
	Wetwang Burial 236	63	-	-	16	-	-	-	79
	Wetwang Burial 249	59	-	-	.	-	-	-	75
	Wetwang Burial 257	52	-	-	-	-	-	-	52
	Wetwang Burial 274	-	-	-	1	-	47	1	50
	Wetwang Burial 284	46	-	-	7	-	1	-	54
	Wetwang Burial 376	72	1	-	-	3	-	-	76
	Wetwang Burial 64	2	-	-	-	-	-	-	2
	Total	588	1	16	88	3	137	1	835

Figure 149: Comparison of different motifs found on East Yorkshire necklaces.

more distant connection with the Arras and Cowlam necklaces suggests a wider network of communication and interaction. Within and between these sites, why do the same bead types occur on different necklaces? And, why are there bead types for which there are no comparisons? Do these connections between necklaces indicate both local connections and regional networks of people that perhaps exchanged beads either through gifting or other forms of exchange? Would beads that are seemingly unique amongst the necklaces have been consistently recognised and possibly indicate some wider network of communication? This is a question that is returned to in Chapter 9.

Pattern and Repetition

While much of this analysis has focused on individual bead characteristics and bead types, these objects were probably worn together as part of a larger object, whether as a necklace or other decorative element. One observable pattern is repetition of bead types and in some cases pattern (Figure 149). Beads from Wetwang burials 139, 155, 210, 257, and 64 were only plain annular or globular beads. All other necklaces had beads with patterns in their entirety or made up a component of the necklace. For example, the Queen's Barrow necklace is made entirely out of beads with simple eyes and beads with wave/zig-zag motifs, the beads from burial 209 are all melon beads, and the necklaces from burials 236 and 249 incorporate both plain and beads with simple eyes in approximately the same proportion. Unusual motifs are the complex eye from burial 376 and the double wave/zig-zag from burial 274.

Although it is tempting to study beads on an individual basis, it is important to consider how they may have been used. Through repetition and alternation with other types of beads, an overall pattern is created. Partial reconstructions of necklaces are shown in Figure 150, which tries to reveal the overall effect of decorated beads used together. Although these are idealised reconstructions, they nonetheless provide an aid in illustrating the dominant trend in their appearance. The unusual melon beads from burial 209 would have created a striking pattern of beads simple in colour, but complex in form when compared to the simple plain blue beads. The thinner sections of each of the lobes may have allowed for a greater opportunity for light to be transmitted through the glass and thus increasing their 'blueness'. The necklace from burial 274 is made almost entirely out of single wave/zig-zag annular/globular beads, which when strung together gives the illusion of a multi-component chevron repeating design throughout the necklace. Three beads, however, are different. These include a bead with a double wave/zig-zag, and a bead with three eyes made from white and green glass and another eye bead of unknown description. Perhaps the two eye beads represented the eyes of a face amid the confusion of the moving zig-zagging lines. Beads from burial 249 are primarily plain blue beads, but there are also two different types of eye beads. Most are plain blue beads with three eyes made from white and what appears

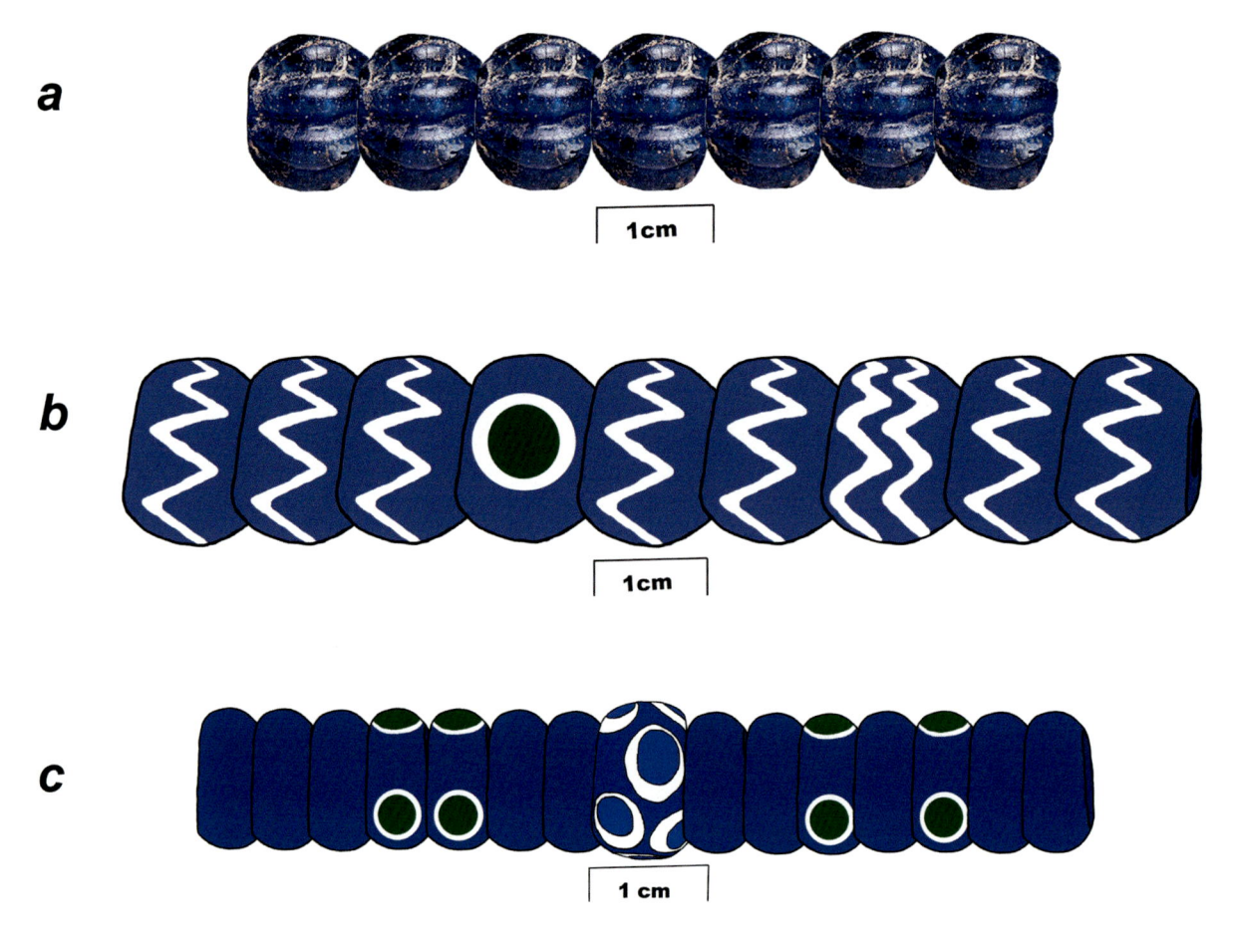

Figure 150: Hypothetical reconstruction of glass beads from Wetwang Slack:
(a) Burial 209, (b) Burial 274, (c) Burial 249.

to be green glass, but there is also one cylindrical blue bead with twelve eyes made from white and blue glass. The repetition of the eye motif gives the necklace an overall 'spotty' appearance. The repetition in the overall pattern suggests that different motifs were deliberately brought together to form a consistent pattern throughout.

In contrast, although not interpreted as having been a necklace or other object worn on the body, we return to the 120 tiny glass beads from the 2001 Wetwang Slack Chariot burial. As it has been suggested that the beads formed a tassel (Hill 2001), two experimental reconstructions with similarly sized beads were undertaken utilising two different methods.[17] First, the strands of the tassel were created where each was made entirely of beads (Figure 151a). As there were only 120 beads, four strands with thirty beads each made a very small tassel (only approximately 55mm long). With the given number of beads, additional strands would render the overall tassel even shorter. The second method used to make the tassel required more strands, but fewer beads on each strand (Figure 151b). Using this method, forty strands were used with three beads on each strand. Here the length of the tassel is not determined by the number of beads, but by the length of the material utilised to string the beads. While the resulting tassel is interesting, and fuller in shape, it is very easily tangled. It is very difficult to interpret these beads as no other beads from this period are as small. However, it seems unlikely that given their size and the small number that they were used in this way.

Hill's current interpretation is that the beads formed the drawstring of the bag that held the mirror, or were directly attached to the mirror's handle (pers. comm.), yet this also seems unlikely (Figure 151c shows the beads as a continuous loop). These delicate beads have such a tiny perforation, that only material such as horsehair or individual flax fibers could be passed through. It is unlikely that these beads formed a part of an object that would be put under stress, as it would take very little pressure to snap the fiber and render the beads lost. Even as a tassel, these beads may have been under the same stress. It seems most likely that these beads were sewn directly onto a textile or leather object.

---

[17] Using modern glass beads of approximately the same size: Average Diameter: 2.085mm, Average Height: 1.36mm, from a sample statistically representative of all beads used (n=20) (Agresti and Finlay 2009)

REGIONAL BODILY ADORNMENT

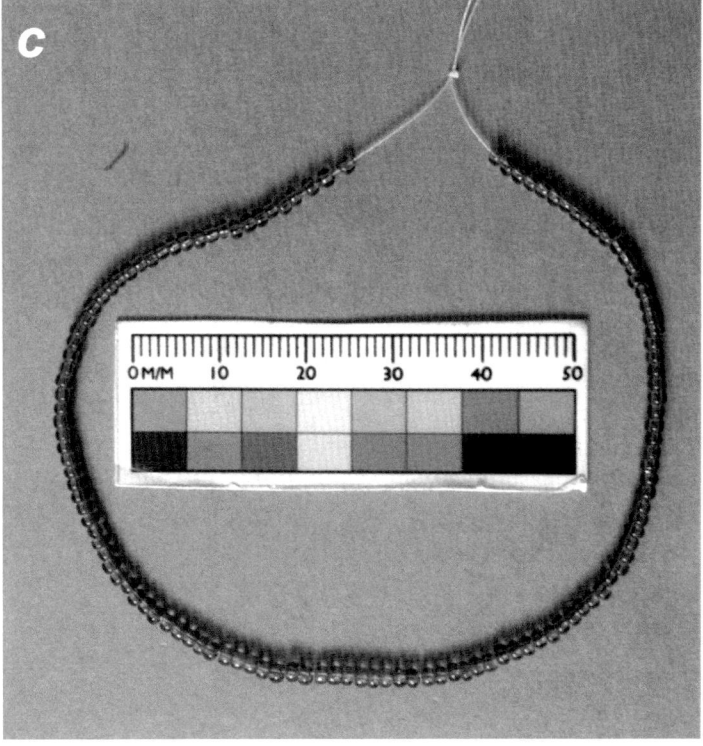

Figure 151: Hypothetical reconstructions using 120 glass beads. (a) 4-strand tassel, (b) 40-strand tassel with three beads per strand, (c) continuous loop of beads.

Placement on the Body

The glass beads from the East Yorkshire burials stand out compared to other glass beads found throughout Britain. It is a rare situation that allows interpretations of how they were used and where they were placed on the body. It has already been mentioned that the number of inhumations in East Yorkshire where glass beads do occur is very limited compared to the hundreds of inhumations. However, glass beads are only one type of object that was included within the inhumations. In most of these, other objects are found alongside the glass beads including pottery and brooches (Figure 152). Where gender has been determined through osteoarchaeological methods, inhumations with glass beads have been determined to be female, possibly female, or gender undetermined, suggesting that they were worn predominantly or exclusively by females.

Within the East Yorkshire burials, the location of the object included in the grave hints at how it was used, or at least in what form it was placed within the burial (Figure 153). For glass beads, it has been suggested that they were worn as necklaces, because of their location next to the individual. In most cases, they were found next to the head or neck, with the exception of seven cases. In four inhumations, the beads were found next to the shoulder: Wetwang burials 268, 270 and 277 (single beads), and Wetwang burial 274 (forty-nine beads); two cases where the beads were not in direct association with the body: Burton Fleming burial 19 (single bead under a pot), and the 2001 chariot burial (120 beads associated with a mirror); and finally, Wetwang burial 209 where the beads were found scattered over the human remains (not included in Figure 153). In these cases it may be that the beads were not worn by the individual at the time of inhumation, because they did not constitute everyday wear, or because although the beads were strongly associated with the individual, they were not worn at the time of death. Alternatively, they may have been added to the inhumation by the community in commemoration of the deceased individual.

Other artefacts included within the inhumations include other types of beads made from amber, copper alloy, and jet, as well as brooches, pins, bracelets, and finger- or toe-rings. Out of 127 inhumations with artefacts of dress, approximately 78% contained only a single object (Figure 154). The 'richest' burial in terms of the number of objects related to dress is the Queen's Barrow, which included eight individual objects and again highlights the unusual nature of this inhumation. By far, the most frequent type of artefact was the brooch (Figure 155), and in contexts where only one type of dress object occurs, it is most often a brooch. Necklaces made from beads were relatively rare, with bracelets and brooches occurring more frequently. Object types that occurred even less frequently include pendants, finger-rings, toe-rings, the possible torc, and anklets. So, while comparing the number of inhumations with glass beads to the overall number of known excavated inhumations (400+), it suggests that while glass bead necklaces are extremely rare, there are other objects that occur even less frequently. If the objects included in these inhumations reflect who was using them, then this suggests that very few people wore any of these objects, although brooches may have been an object that was more widespread, but only marginally so.

So far, this section has only hinted at the location of objects in relation to the body, such as for the reasoning behind describing some groups of glass beads as necklaces. For other types of objects, their location within inhumations confirms their use. For example, large rings are most often found on wrists and forearms, and small rings have been found on fingers and toes. Objects, such as brooches, have been found in a variety of locations on the body (see Figure 156 for definition of body region terminology). They are mostly associated with the upper body, including the head and arms, but there are six instances where they have been found in association with the lower body. The moving mechanism of the brooch allows for things to become attached on a semi-permanent basis; however, the type of garments that were attached is unclear. It is assumed that they attached textile, or other organic materials, as they are not usually found attached to other objects. Traces of textiles have been preserved in brooch corrosion, which supports the idea that they attached textile garments (eg Stead 1991a). The range of possible locations that brooches have been found on bodies makes it unclear as to whether this is reflecting the manner in which garments were attached during life, or perhaps how the body was prepared at the time of burial in a specific way relating to death (i.e. a shroud).

Objects found in these inhumations can be broadly defined as being placed in five major zones on the body (Figure 157). Most objects are found in the head and neck region, followed by the upper body/shoulder, and arm region. Objects are found in the fewest numbers around the lower body and leg/foot region. The implications for this patterning is that people were deliberately wearing objects in places that are more likely to be at eye level, or that could be moved into eye level (such as arm/wrist/hand). These objects might have been important indicators giving information about a person's status, family, connections, or other role within the community. If these objects were only worn at the time of death, then they would still have had some important meaning for the community audience or the interred individual.

Southwest England Inhumations

Inhumations in Southwest England with glass beads are few in number. As discussed in Chapter 7, five out

Regional Bodily Adornment

Site	Qty. Glass Beads	Glass Bead Type	Date	Details
Burton Fleming BF 19	1	Class 6 Type 900	MIA	?sex, 35-45 years old, with large pottery sherds, iron brooch, iron ring on neck, glass bead and iron fragment under pot, sheep bone with pot.
Makeshift burial R16	1	Class 1 Type 102	MIA	?female, age 25-35, in coffin with a pot in front of face, glass bead under skull near ear, also sheep bone in pot
Makeshift burial R 193	1	Class 1 Type 102	MIA	?female, age 25-45, cu alloy ring on neck, glass bead on face, iron fragment near right elbow
Makeshift burial R2	1	Class 1 Type 102	MIA	?sex, age 17-25, pot over ankles, iron brooch in front of face, glass bead between right shoulder and skull, shale bracelet on left forearm, sheep bone beneath skull
Queen's Barrow, Arras	71	Class 4 Type 411, 421, 424, 425, 426, 428 Class 6 Type 901, 905, 907	MIA	Assumed female, with: fibula, pendant, 2 Cu alloy bracelets, gold ring, toilet set, amber ring, Cu ring
Barrow L, Cowlam	75	Class 4 Type 425 Class 9 Type 900, 901	MIA	Assumed female, with: bracelet, brooch, shale bracelet fragment
Garton Slack 8 and 10 Grave 2 burial 1	35	Class 1 Type 201 Class 4 Type 410	MIA	Female, aged 25-30, supine, trussed, beads along chest and behind neck, with: bone ring
Wetwang Slack Chariot Burial	120	Class 1 Type 102	MIA	Female, aged 35-45, Burial with vehicle, horse objects, iron mirror, involute brooch. Beads found in area around mirror, suggested to be a tassel
Wetwang Slack 17	1	Class 6 Type 1407	MIA	?sex, ?adult, crouched, left side. Bronze pin found against skull, glass bead on chest.
Wetwang Slack 64	2	Class 2 Type 102	MIA	Female, 20-25 years, Cu alloy ring with the two glass beads and one amber bead threaded on, plus a pair of tweezers.
Wetwang Slack 102	1	Class 6 Type 1001	MIA	Female, 25-35 years, with jet or shale bead.
Wetwang Slack 139	34	Class 1 Type 102	MIA	Female, 25-35 years old.
Wetwang Slack 155	42	Class 1 Type 102	MIA	Female, 25-35 years old, with: 2 Cu alloy bracelets, possible earring, brooch with possible coral inlay.
Wetwang Slack 209	18	Class 2 Type 202 Class 6 Type 901	MIA	Female, 30-35 years old.
Wetwang Slack 210	70	Class 1 Type 102	MIA	Female, 35-35 years old, with: Cu alloy bracelet and Cu alloy ring with tweezers and 1 bead
Wetwang Slack 236	79	Class 1 Type 102 Class 4 Type 420, 423	MIA	Female, 35-45 years old, with S-brooch and Cu alloy bracelet
Wetwang Slack 249	75	Class 1 Type 102 Class 4 Type 417, 418, 421	MIA	Female, 35-45 years old
Wetwang Slack 257	52	Class 1 Type 102	MIA	Female, 20-25 years old, with: Cu alloy ring
Wetwang Slack 268	1	Class 6 Type 1417	MIA	Female, 25-35 years old, with iron brooch
Wetwang Slack 270	1	Class 1 Type 102	MIA	Female, 35-45 years old, with La Tène I brooch, 3 iron staples
Wetwang Slack 274	50	Class 4 Type 410, 417 Class 6 Type 901 Class 11 Type 2301	MIA	Female, 35-45 years old, Cu alloy brooch
Wetwang Slack 277	1	Class 1 Type 102	MIA	Female, 35-45 years old, with pot and sheep bone
Wetwang Slack 284	55	Class 1 Type 102 Class 4 Type 413, 414, 417 Class 6 Type 901	MIA	Female, 35-45 years old
Wetwang Slack 376	76	Class 1 Type 102 Class 4 Type 501, 503	MIA	Female 25-35 years old

Figure 152: List of sites where glass beads were found in inhumations in East Yorkshire.

Object	Head	Neck	Arm	Elbow	Forearm	Wrist	Hand	Finger	Knee	Ankle	Feet	Toe	Shoulder	Upper Body	Lower Body	Body	Total
Amber bead		1															1
Cu-alloy bead	2												1				3
Cu-alloy Bead/Ring	1																1
Cu-alloy Ring w/ 3 Glass Beads	1																1
Glass Bead	2	12											4			2	20
Stone Bead/Ring	2									1							3
Jet Bead	1	2															3
Cu-alloy Pendant		1															1
Amber ring						1											1
Bone ring						1											1
Toe-Ring												1					1
Cu-alloy Toe-Ring												1					1
Anklet										1							1
Cu-alloy Bracelet				4	4									1			9
Jet Bracelet				1													1
Stone Bracelet				2													2
Brooch	1																1
Cu-alloy Brooch	2	1											1	1		1	6
Iron Brooch	19	13	2	3	1	1	3		1				7	6	5		61
Iron Pin	2	1									1						4
Cu-alloy Earring	1																1
Iron Ring		1															1
Cu-alloy Ring		2															2
TOTAL	34	34	2	3	8	5	3	2	1	1	2	2	13	8	5	3	126

Figure 153: Comparison of different artefact types and their location on the body where known from East Yorkshire.

of nine inhumations only contained a single bead and are not well documented, while another was probably Anglo-Saxon in date, but which incorporated some possible Iron Age beads (Figure 158). This leaves a total of three inhumations with glass beads likely to have been worn as a necklace (Figure 159). On their own, none of these probable necklaces would have made a strand long enough to be fitted around a modern adult neck, as the largest is only 132mm in length (Whitcombe 8). As with the shorter strands of glass beads from East Yorkshire, it may be that they were worn on a strand of fibre or leather that was long enough to encircle a neck, or that other organic components also made up the necklace, but did not survive, or that they were worn or used in a different way.

Hypothetical reconstructions of all three possible necklaces further demonstrate some issues with interpretation. The Chesil mirror burial beads (Figure 160a) are almost all very large, and do not form a coherent pattern. The short length formed by the beads strung together and awkward juxtapositions suggest that this may not be how these beads were used (Foulds Forthcoming-a). Whereas the frequency of the different bead types in the Clevedon cist burial and Whitcombe 8 burial suggest that they could have formed symmetrical strands of beads (Figure 160b-c). Unfortunately, it is only with the Whitcombe burial we have an idea as to where the beads were located in connection with the body. The site report notes that these were found in a cluster next to the left shoulder (Aitken and Aitken 1990, 64). For the other two inhumations, these details have not been preserved.

The beads from the Clevedon cist burial and the Whitcombe 8 burial can be used to create a symmetrical necklace, which suggests that they may have been purposely used in this way. As a strand, the Chesil mirror burial beads are perplexing given the sizes, colours, decoration, number of beads, and possible continental connections (and the other objects contained within the inhumation described below). Perhaps these beads were combined and used for some other purpose. These beads may be the embodiment of different relationships or networks coming together and manifesting in one conglomerate object. If this was the case, the realisation

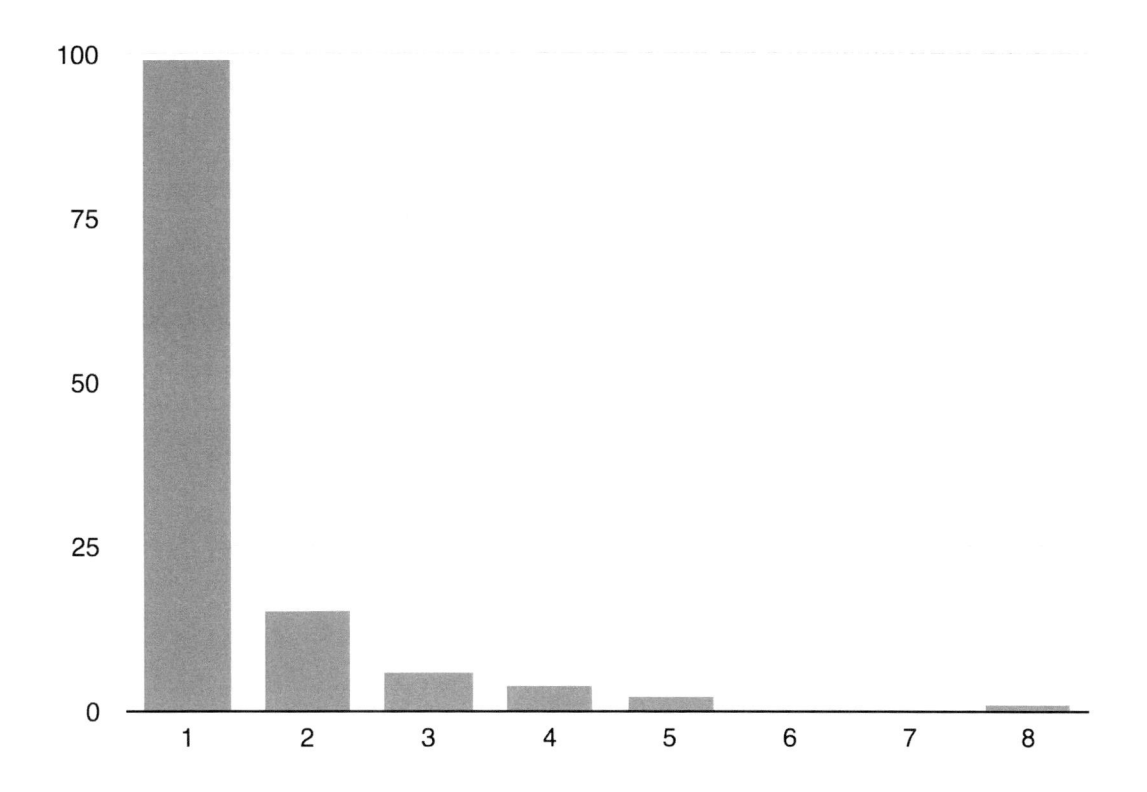

Figure 154: Bar-chart showing the frequency of dress objects within 127 inhumations in East Yorkshire (groups of beads that likely formed a necklace or other object are counted once).

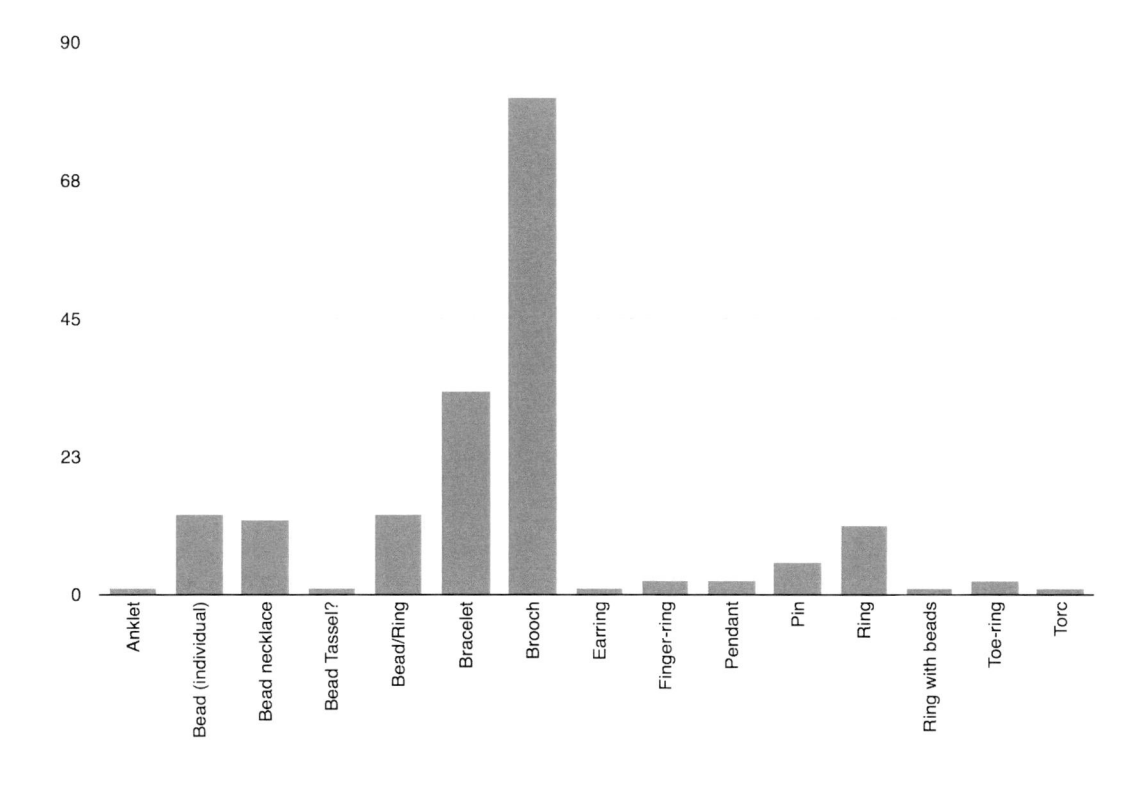

Figure 155: Bar-chart showing the frequency of different dress objects within 127 inhumations in East Yorkshire.

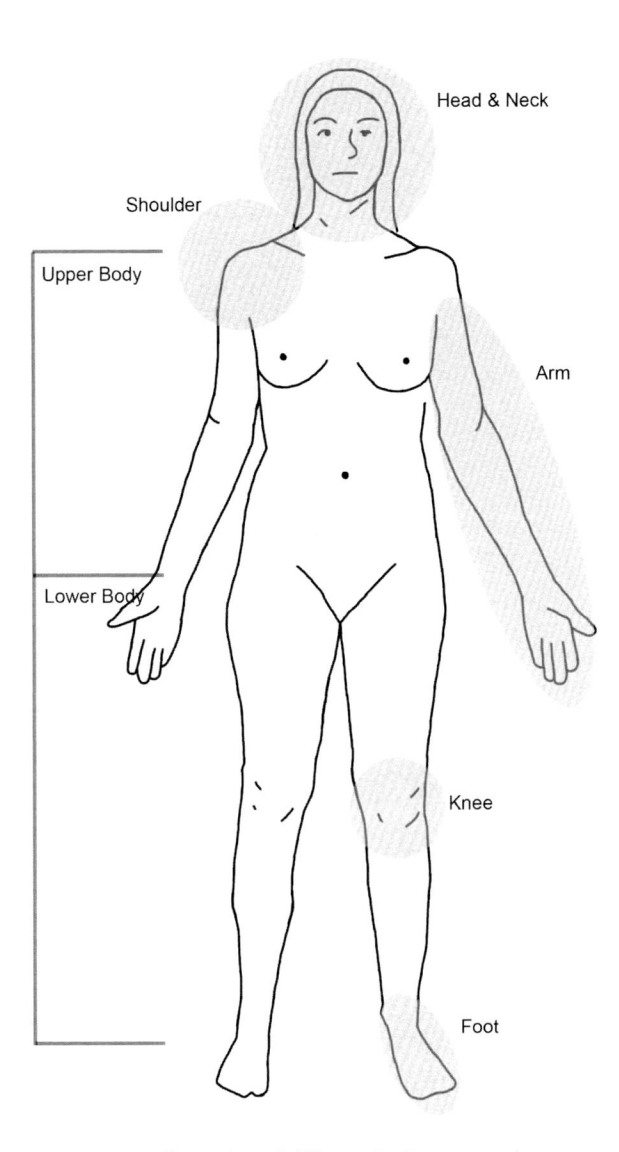

Figure 156: Illustration of different body zones and terms.

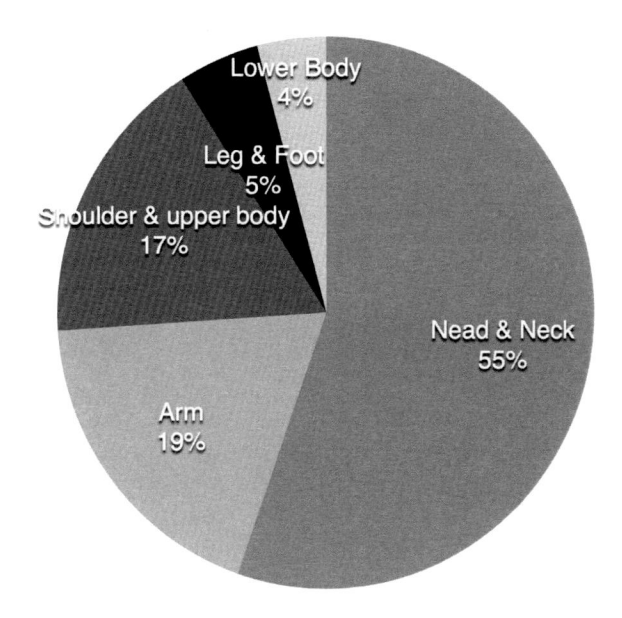

Figure 157: Pie-chart showing the proportions of artefacts and the body zones that they were found in association with (beaded necklaces are only counted as one instance).

of these relationships in material form may have been more important than symmetry or repetition of pattern.

Additional objects of dress were only found in the Chesil mirror burial as the only other remains included in the Whitcombe 8 burial were parts of a pig, a bird, and some pottery ('Durotrigian' ware and Samian), and the Clevedon cist burial contained a pebble end encrinites. The Chesil mirror burial, however, included a range of object: two brooches, a perforated Roman coin, an armlet or bracelet, three stone beads (the stone beads are included in Figure 160a), and other objects possibly related to appearance: tweezers and a mirror.

Other inhumations with objects of dress are limited to a small number, most of which are Later Iron Age in date, such as the Birdlip mirror burial in Gloucestershire, the Portesham mirror burial in Dorset, and probably a number of skeletons from Maiden Castle in Dorset. Five inhumations from Dibble's Farm in Somerset may be Early Iron Age in date due to the presence of a La Tène I brooch within Burial 47c. As with the East Yorkshire burials, the majority of inhumations contained only single objects, usually brooches (Figures 161-2). The Chesil mirror burial had five objects of dress, which is more than any other burial. However the Birdlip mirror burial contained a larger range of objects, including a copper alloy vessel and a knife. The placement of objects of dress within the inhumation, where known, focuses generally on the upper body, especially the shoulder and arms, with the lower body playing a minor role (Figure 163). Not only are there a limited number of inhumations for this region, but the range of objects included with the inhumations is also limited.

Non-Inhumations

The frequency of glass beads found in clusters in the same feature outside of inhumations is very limited. Groups of beads with close associations mainly come from the mound features at Glastonbury and Meare Lake Villages. However, there are two problems with the interpretation of these bead clusters. First, at Glastonbury Lake Village, a fragment of a Type 1405 is described as originating from Mound 59. During examination of the beads, it was discovered that this fragment connects to G1, which was found at Mound 62. These two mounds are very close to each other, and unfortunately, there are no further details as to where on the mounds these fragments were found. However, this does highlight one of the problems with the recording method used during

Site	Qty. Glass Beads	Glass Bead Type	Date	Details
Battlesbury Camp	1	Class 1 Type 110	IA	19th century find. Cremation burial with two later inhumations later placed next to it. Single bead found on chest of one skeleton.
Chedworth	1	Class 4 Type 410	?	Found in barrow
Teffont Evias	1	Class 1 Type 102	Iron Age?	With inhumation
Whitcombe (3)	1	Class 1 Type 107	1st century AD	Female, 25-30 years old, flexed, with part of pig skull and possible horse jaw
Whitcombe (8)	9	Class 1 Type 107, 110; Class 6 Type 901	1st century AD	Female, 15-17 years old, flexed, with Durotrigian and Samian ware, 19 glass beads, 2 wooden beads, 1 faience bead, fragment of pig jaw and leg bone of domestic fowl.
Wookey Hole	1	Class 1 Type 410	LIA/RB	With possible female skeleton
Burn Ground Grave 7	2	Class 1 Type 110	Anglo-Saxon	At least 138 other beads (amber and glass), small knife
Clevedon	18	Class 1 Type 110; Class 3 Type 301, 302; Class 6 Type 1003	IA	Assumed female, cist burial, with pebble and encrinites
Langton Herring	5	Class 1 Type 108; Class 5 Type 701; Class 8 Type 1604; Class 9 Type 1704; Class 11 Type 2801	LIA/ER	?female burial, 18-23 years old, with 2 brooches, 1 perforated Roman coin, tweezers, armlet/bracelet, 3 stone beads, and a mirror

Figure 158: List of sites where glass beads were found in inhumations in Southwest England.

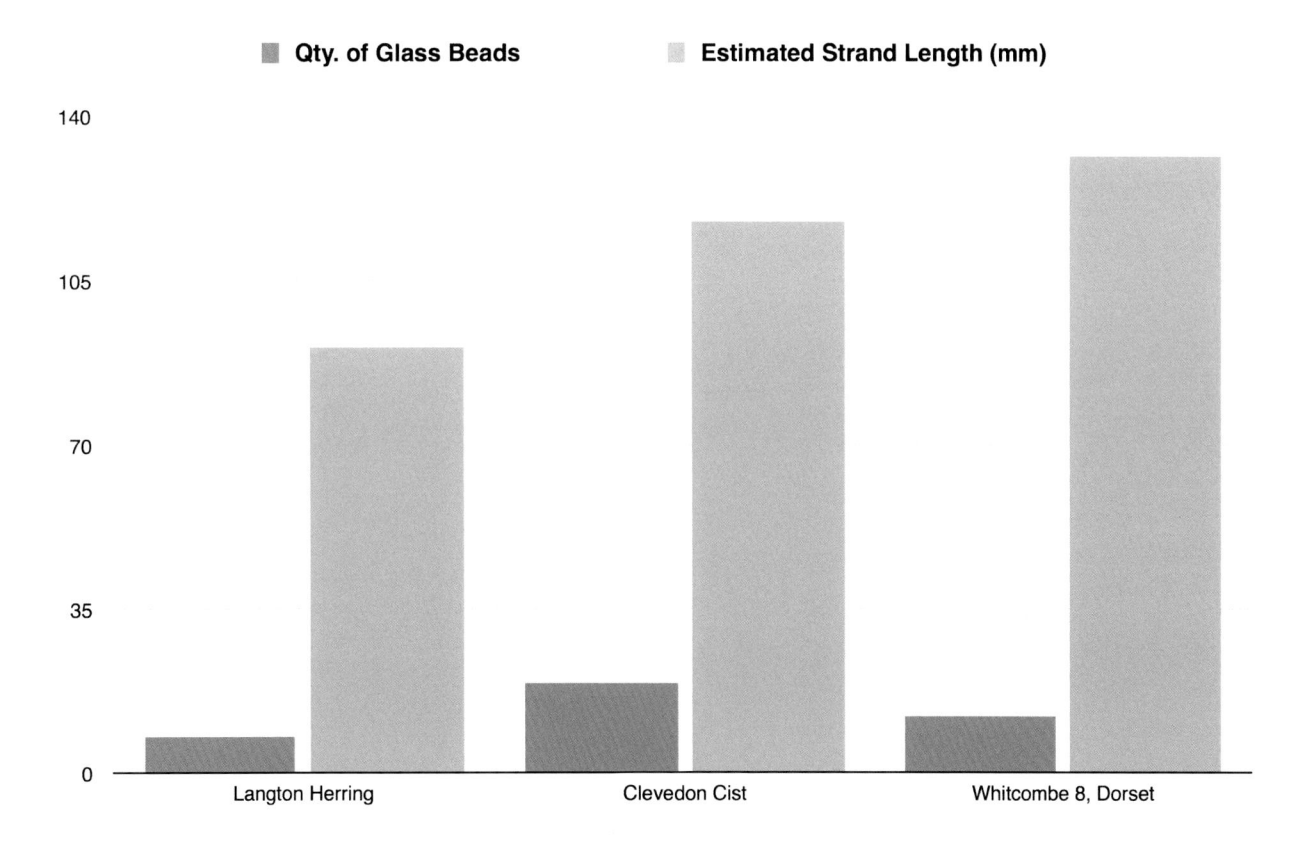

Figure 159: Bar-chart comparing the number of glass beads and length of glass bead strand for each possible strand of glass beads in Southwest England.

Figure 160: Hypothetical reconstruction of glass beads from Southwest England: (a) glass and stone beads from Chesil mirror burial, Dorset, (b) glass beads from the Cleveland Cist burial, Somerset, (c) glass, faience, and wood(?) beads from Burial 8 Whitcombe, Dorset.

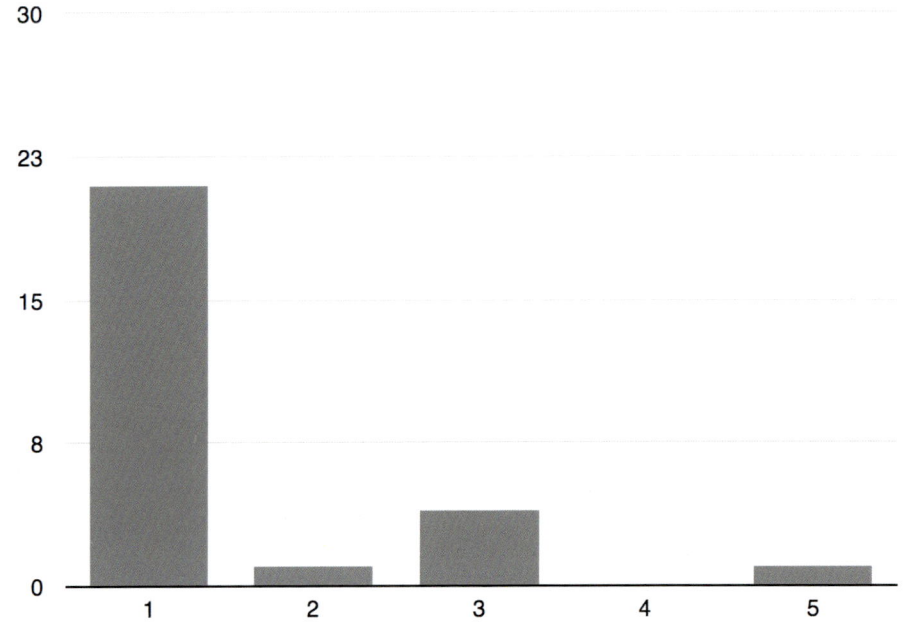

Figure 161: Bar chart showing the frequency of the number of objects of dress within each Southwest England inhumation (27 inhumations, 40 objects).

Object	Shoulder	Arm	Wrist	Finger	Toe	Not with Body	Total
Stone Armlet		1					1
Iron Bracelet			2				2
Cu-Alloy Bracelets		3					3
Cu-Alloy Toe-ring					3	1	4
Iron Finger-ring				1			1
Cu-Alloy Brooch	3					3	6
Beads	11						11
TOTAL	14	4	2	1	3	4	28

Figure 162: Comparison of different object types and their location on the body in Southwest England.

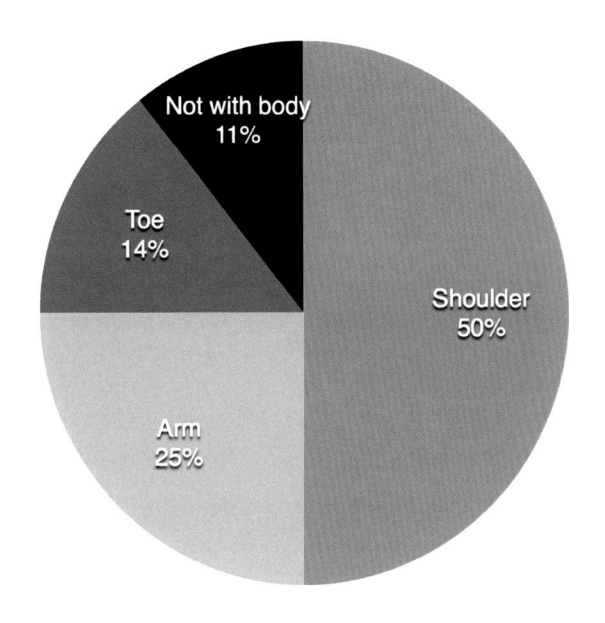

Figure 163: Pie-chart comparing the location of 28 objects in connection with the body in Southwest England.

these excavations, as associated beads could be assigned to different mounds. Or, it may be that the context of the finds does not accurately reflect a domestic settlement and there may be other depositional practices occurring, as with structured deposits within pits.

The second major issue with interpreting these finds is also related to recording practices. Plain beads, such as Type 102 beads, are only given a mound number, while decorated beads are given mound numbers plus an additional descriptor, such as 'near hearth', or level number. So, while all beads can be ascribed to a mound, not all can be plotted with the information given in the report. Both of these issues present problems when it comes to interpreting the beads as clusters and the practices that they represent. While these problems cannot be overcome immediately, through a detailed analysis of the types of beads, colours, and lengths of strands, it may be possible to suggest whether or not the beads form a coherent group.

From the excavations at Meare Lake Village East, two clusters of beads have been described as necklaces. Catalogue number G68 is a cluster of forty-six glass beads found at Mound 22, and G69 is a cluster of eleven beads found at Mound 47. Neither would have formed a strand long enough alone to go around a modern adult neck (Figure 164), and as with other possible strands they may not have been worn as a necklace, or were simply strung onto string of the appropriate length. As a necklace, G68 could have been symmetrical and incorporated four different bead types: Types 110, 1416, 1417, and 2201. The Type 2201 (DB 4289) bead is the most unusual, as it is a sub-triangular green bead with opaque yellow double wave with a yellow dot in-between each of the swags, and is at present unique. The reconstruction published in the excavation report (Coles 1987, 85 figure 3.22) and displayed in the Somerset Museum in Taunton (Figure 165) shows it being strung in a symmetrical design, but it is unclear if this reflects information at the time of the find or creative interpretation. In comparison, G69 was interpreted as simply a strand of Type 110 beads.

In both cases, these were not the only beads found at their respective mounds. At Mound 22, there were a total of seventy-one beads (mostly glass, but some amber, jet, and stone), plus other objects, such as fragments of shale armlets, and at Mound 47, there was an additional glass bead and a possible amber bead found outside of the cluster suggested to be a necklace. It is not clear how G68 and G69 relate to the other beads from the mounds, and it may be that they were all a part of a single object.

Other potentially significant clusters of beads found at individual mounds include Mounds 7, 33, and 34 at Meare Lake Village West. By comparing the dimensions of necklaces G68 and G69 with the other bead clusters, some interesting patterns emerge (Figure 166). The beads from G68 and G69 both tightly cluster, which may be indicative of their use together as they would have formed a consistent strand of beads. Beads from

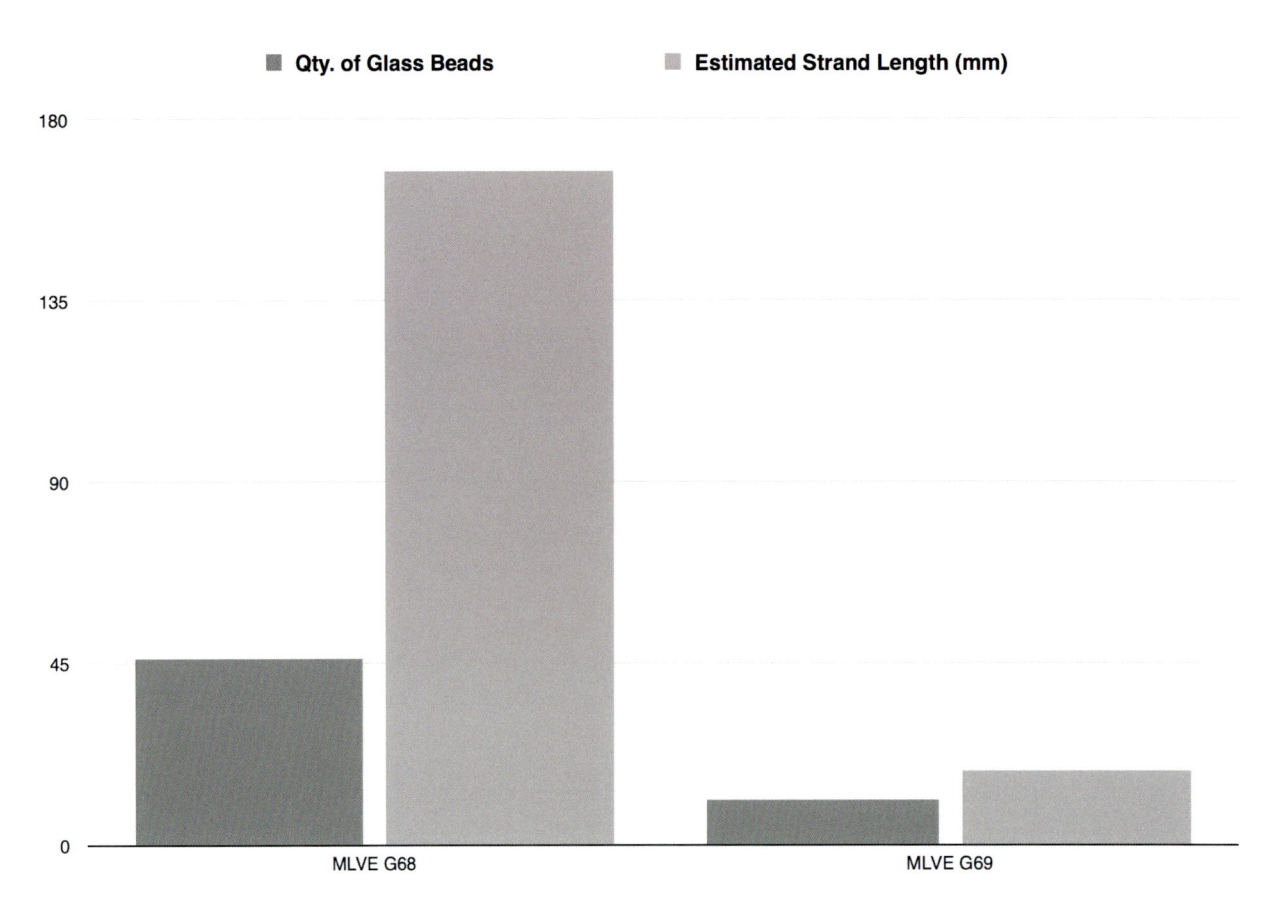

Figure 164: Bar-chart showing the number of glass beads and the length of a strand of beads if strung together.

Figure 165: Hypothetical reconstruction of possible necklace (G68, Somerset Museum) from Meare Lake Village East in Somerset.

both Mounds 33 and 34 may have formed strands as there is some clustering, but also because the clusters are diagonal suggesting gradation of size. However, the beads from Mound 7 do not appear to tightly cluster. It may be that these beads were not worn together, or that they were, but did not form a consistent strand of beads, although it is still unclear how beads were worn together.

Glass Beads in an Artefactual Context

Glass beads were not the only artefact worn on the body, as there is extant evidence for a range of different types of objects that were used during the Iron Age. While the above section discussed the different artefacts found in inhumations, this section will begin to put the grave

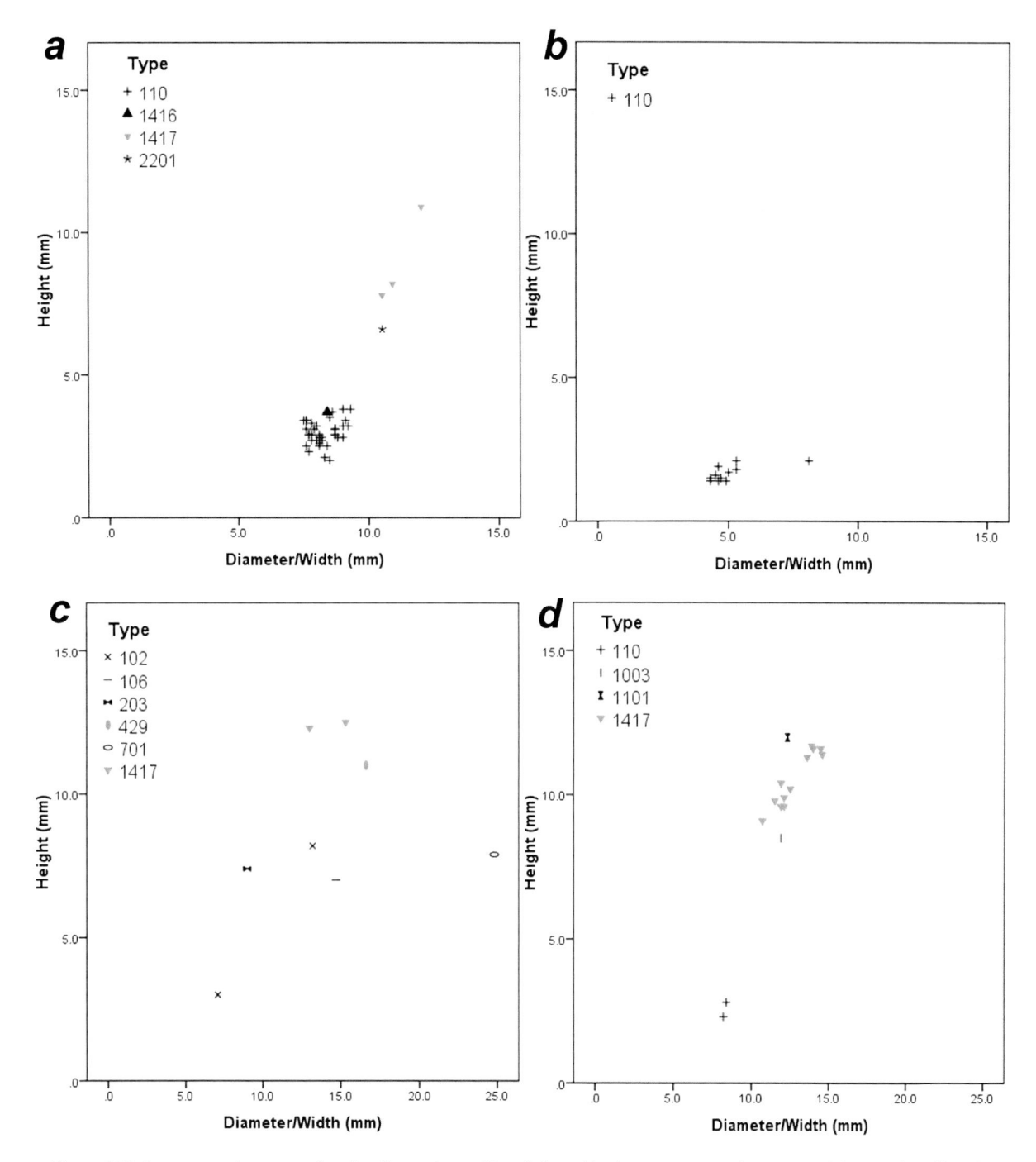

Figure 166: Scatter-graphs comparing the dimensions of beads found in the same mound context at Meare Lake Village in Somerset. (a) Necklace G68 from MLVE Mound 22; (b) Necklace G69 from MLVE Mound 47; (c) MLVW Mound 7; (d) MLVW Mound 33.

goods into a wider context by examining those from outside inhumations in order to begin to understand the changing and diverse nature of dress. The first section will specifically address objects of dress found primarily during excavation and recorded in the database, and will then examine data from the Portable Antiquities Scheme database.

Objects of Dress

Within the literature review of Iron Age, Roman, and Romano-British excavated sites, over twenty different types of objects were encountered. In part, this large number of object types is due to inconsistent terminology used in reports, as well as unclear identification of objects. For example circular objects could be described

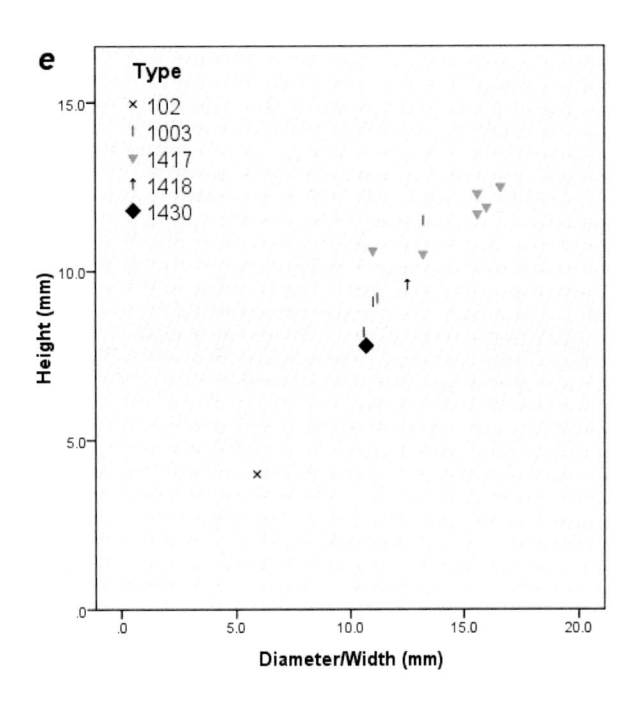

Figure 166: Scatter-graphs comparing the dimensions of beads found in the same mound context at Meare Lake Village in Somerset. (e) MLVW Mound 34.

as beads, rings, finger-rings, toe-rings, bracelets, bangles, armlets, and anklets without an indication of how these objects were similar or dissimilar.[18] Finger-rings and toe-rings are implied to be smaller than other rings that were presumably worn on either the ankle, wrist, or arm, however there were some 'rings' that seem to fit neither of these categories and it may be that they were not worn on the body, but instead had a utilitarian purpose. Because of this inconsistency and the abundance of object types, five types of objects were chosen for the focus of this analysis: brooches, pins, finger/toe-rings, wrist/ankle/arm rings, and torcs. These object types are used in the analyses that follow.

These five object types form a good foundation for the assessment of dress because they are numerous, some have been the subject of previous study, and because they vary over time or have specific periods in which they flourish in Iron Age Britain. However, although brooches have long been the subject of examination due to their periodic changes in appearance throughout the Iron Age (e.g. Haselgrove 1997; Hull and Hawkes 1987; Mackreth 2011), others have only been the subject of limited or no study. For example, Dunning's (1934b) work remains the primary study on Iron Age pins, although Romano-British pins have been studied more recently (Cool 1990; Crummy 1979). Rings have not been

the subject of extensive Britain-wide study, but instead have been discussed in a more localised scope (Calkin 1953; Dent 1984; Mansel-Pleydell 1896; Sydenham 1844), or in the case of copper alloy bracelets and arm-rings they have been included within wider studies of Celtic Art (e.g. Jope 2000; MacGregor 1976). Torcs also have been studied under the heading of Celtic Art, and a basic typology for the earlier examples was proposed by Stead (1991b) in his report on the Snettisham finds. Later collars and so-called 'beaded' torcs have not been the subject of consistent study outside of the realms of Celtic Art. Finger-rings and toe-rings have never been the subject of study on either regional or national levels, despite their frequent presence.

Due to the nature of the background of the study of each of the five artefact categories, a basic typology has been proposed with the aim of providing a consistent terminology to be used in this study. These have been derived largely on stylistic grounds and future analysis really needs to examine these objects in greater detail. For example, the diameters of larger rings presumably worn on the wrist, ankle, or arm, as well as smaller rings worn on the fingers and toes would help to characterise more ambiguous objects. One of the problems with developing even an interim typology is that objects from each of these artefact types have been made from different materials. For brooches and torcs, these objects are limited to metals, especially copper alloy and iron, but in the case of torcs, this also includes gold, silver, and electrum. Pins, larger rings and smaller rings have also been made out of bone, stone (primarily shale and jet), and in some cases: glass. It is possible that non-extant examples of pins were made from wood, and other arm or ankle decoration was made from twisted fiber, or animal fur as evidenced for Lindow Man (Stead, Bourke et al. 1986), but these cannot be considered further here. The typologies developed are defined in Figure 167. In the case of brooches, they are simply referred to by their general Iron Age sub-period, such as Middle Iron Age or Early Iron Age. Later Iron Age or Early Roman period brooches (including Birdip, Nauheim and Colchester) have been grouped together under the same heading, while brooches that date from around AD 100 are considered to be Early Roman or Early Roman/Romano-British for the sake of simplicity. These typologies are not meant to be very precise, but to give a very general overview of the different types of objects that were in use.

Although five artefact types were chosen for study in this section, they were not present within each of the study regions in equal number (Figure 168). For example, arm/wrist/ankle rings and toe/finger rings were found in their largest numbers in Southwest England, while torcs were more frequent in East Anglia. Each region is skewed by a different site: Southwest England by Meare Lake Village, East Anglia by Ken Hill at Snettisham, and Wetwang/

---

[18] Unfortunately, it was not within the scope of the present research to undertake such analysis, as it would have required systematic measuring of a large number of objects as the diameter of these types of artefacts are not consistently recorded in the literature.

a

Type	Description
1	Swan-neck
2.A.1.	Ring-headed made from wire with a straight pin
2.A.2.	Cast ring-headed pin with a straight pin
2.B.1.	Ring-headed made from wire with a bent neck
2.B.2.	Plain cast ring-headed pin with a bent neck
2.B.3.	Fancy cast ring-headed pin with a bent neck
2.C.1.	Ring-headed pin made from wire with an involuted shank
3	Plate headed pin
4	Spiral headed pin
5	Stick pin
6	Miscellaneous

b

Type	Description
Metal 1	Annular or penannular ring
Metal 2	Overlapping terminal ring
Metal 3	Spiralled ring
Metal 4	Ring with hook closure
Metal 5	Ring with mortise and tenon closure
Glass 1	Continental Type
Glass 2	British Type
Stone 1	Round-ish profile
Stone 2	Plano-convex profile
Stone 3	Triangular profile
Stone 4	Rectangular profile
Stone 5	Circumferential Lines
Stone 6	Inscribed Decoration
Stone 7	Notched ribbed design
Stone 8	Notched and inscribed design
Stone 9	Other fancy types

c

Type	Description
1.A.	Plain annular/nearly annular/slight overlap ring
1.B.	Linear bands on an annular/nearly annular/slight overlap ring
1.C.	Notched decoration on an annular/nearly annular/slight overlap ring
2.A.1.	Plain spiralled wire band
2.A.2.	Decorated spiralled wire band
2.B.1.	Plain spiralled strip band
2.B.2.	Simple decoration on a spiralled strip band
2.B.3.	Decorated expanded mid-section of a spiralled strip band
2.B.4.	Ring/dot decoration on a spiralled strip band
2.B.5.	Miscellaneous decoration on a spiralled strip band
3	Double ring
4	Bezel ring
5	Miscellaneous

d

Type	Description
1	Beaded Torc
2	Loop Terminal
3	Ring Terminal
4	Buffer Terminal
5	Collar
6	Tubular
7	Twisted ribbon

Figure 167: Proposed typologies: (a) Pins, (b) Wrist/Arm/Ankle Rings, (c) Finger- and Toe-rings, (d) Torcs.

Garton Slack continues to contribute a large number of other objects related to dress in East Yorkshire. In comparison, very few of these types of objects have been found in Northeast Scotland, the most numerous objects being the massive style armlets found throughout the area (Hunter 2006c; MacGregor 1976) along with a number of later period cast pins from Sculptor's Cave in Morayshire (Benton 1931b). This has implications for understanding dress and deposition. By examining the variation within each of the study regions, it will be possible to further highlight regional patterns.

Brooches

Besides torcs, one of the most iconic objects of the British Iron Age is the brooch. These objects have been described as the 'safety pin' of the Iron Age due to their articulated pin mechanism (spring or hinge), which permitted the user to attach garments together or objects to garments. These artefacts are frequently used for dating archaeological features, especially prior to the advent of scientific dating methods, as their morphology changed throughout the Iron Age (Haselgrove 1997; Hull and Hawkes 1987). Quantification of the frequency of brooch deposition has suggests that the proportion of brooches deposited in different contexts changed throughout the Iron Age (Haselgrove 1997). By the Late Iron Age, not only had the contexts of deposition changed, but also the number of brooches that were deposited into the archaeological record had vastly increased. One explanation could be that the use of brooches as a part of dress became more popular; however, it may also be that the behaviour associated with object deposition changed during this period (Haselgrove 1997).

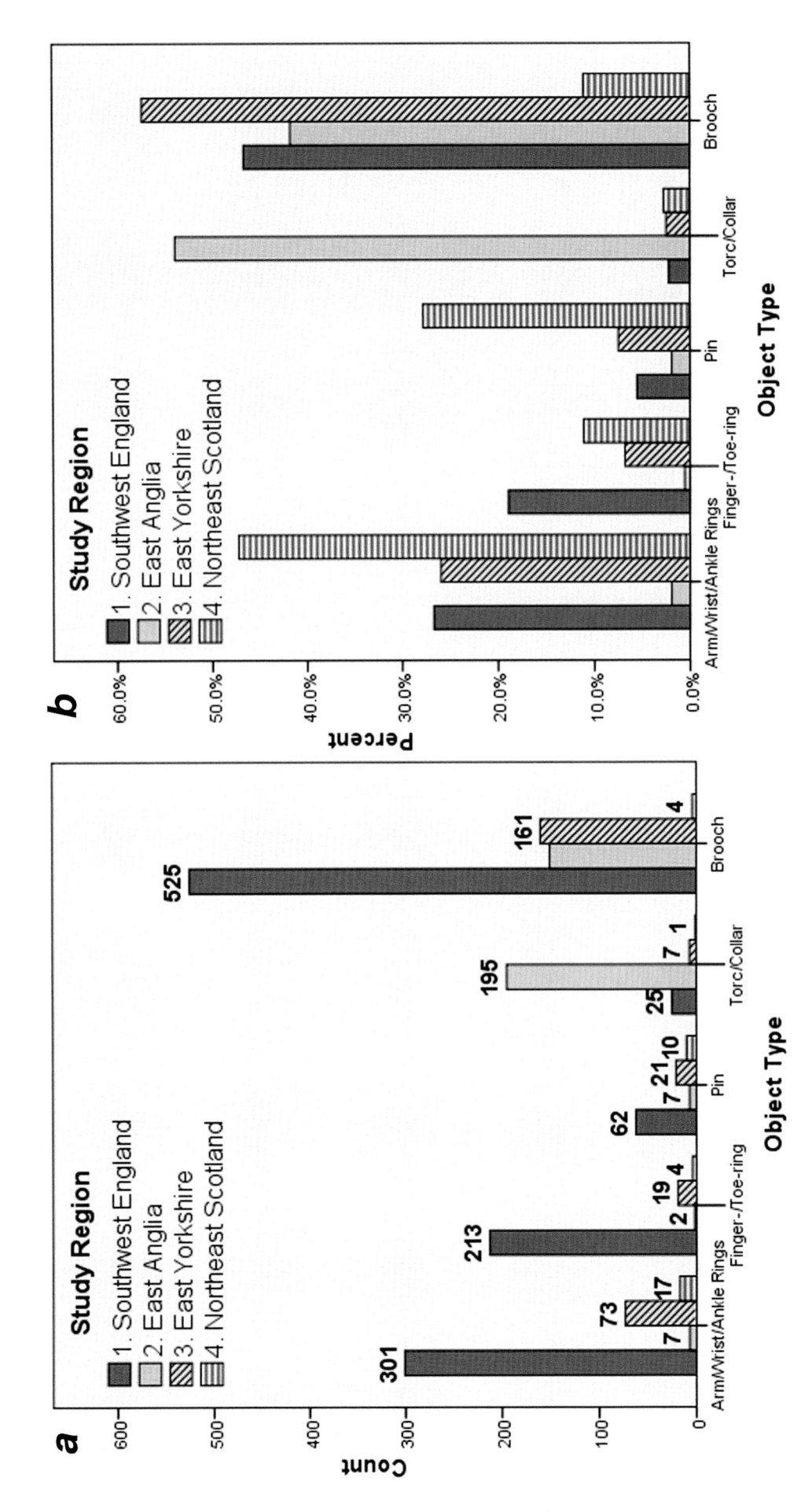

Figure 168: Bar-charts comparing the frequency of different types of artefacts in each study region: (a) Frequency, (b) Percentage.

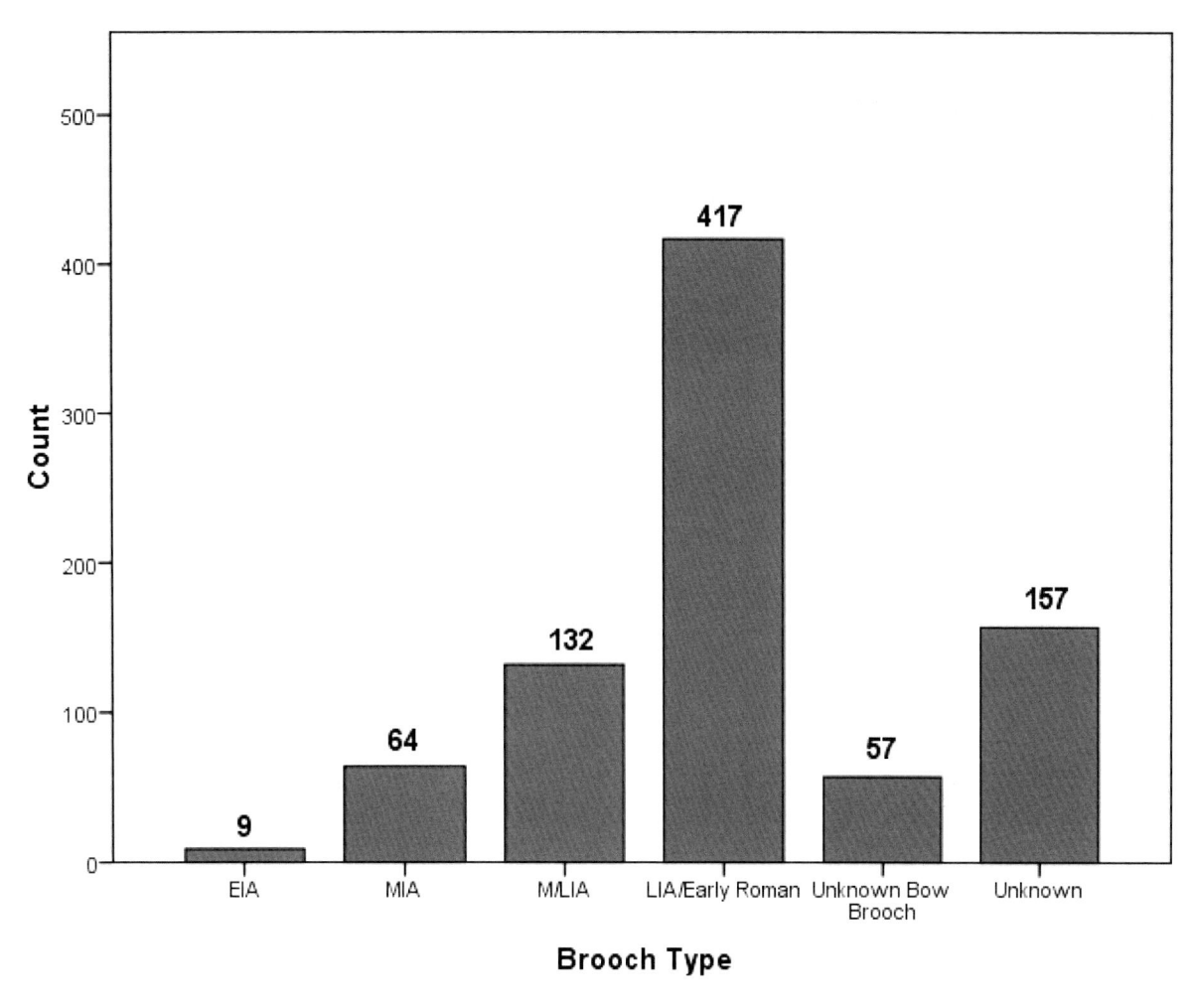

Figure 169: General frequency of brooches throughout the Iron Age using data from all study regions.

Within the regions studied here, the nature of the brooches and their deposition are variable. For example, in Southwest England, brooches have been found in settlement contexts that date throughout the Iron Age, possibly suggesting that they were used throughout the period. However, in Northeast Scotland they were confined to the period after the Roman invasion in southern Britain. Interestingly, some of the examples, such as at Birnie in Morayshire, are particularly exceptional (Hunter 2007b). In contrast, in East Yorkshire they have been found primarily within the Middle/Late Iron Age square barrow inhumations, where they have added to the long-standing question as to whether the inhumations represent a local population, or whether they were immigrants from continental Europe. The interpretation of these brooches becomes particularly confusing as they can exhibit similarities with continental examples, yet with insular design (Stead 1965; 1979).

As brooches have been primarily considered in terms of their chronological and morphological traits, there has been little consideration on the regional use of brooches for dress. With other types of artefacts, this is partly due to the relative absence of brooches in some regions, which may relate to the recovery of artefacts through antiquarian and archaeological investigations, but is also related to depositional practices and the types of materials that entered the record. However, beyond the idea that brooches were used to attach elements of dress, there is no real understanding as to how they were used.

In terms of chronology and frequency, the brooches from the four study regions follow the identified pattern of brooch frequency and deposition (Hill 1995a; b; 1997; Jundi and Hill 1997), where there are considerably fewer Early Iron Age brooches compared to Later Iron Age and Early Roman brooches (Figure 169). However, by taking a regional approach, it is clear that this trend is not found in all study regions (Figure 170). In particular, the brooches from East Yorkshire are probably Middle or early Late Iron Age, while regions such as Southwest England and East Anglia follow the general trend more closely. These differences in frequency may be related to different depositional practices, as Jundi and Hill have suggested that differences in depositional practices may account for the overall pattern (Jundi and Hill 1997, 127), however other possibilities will be explored below.

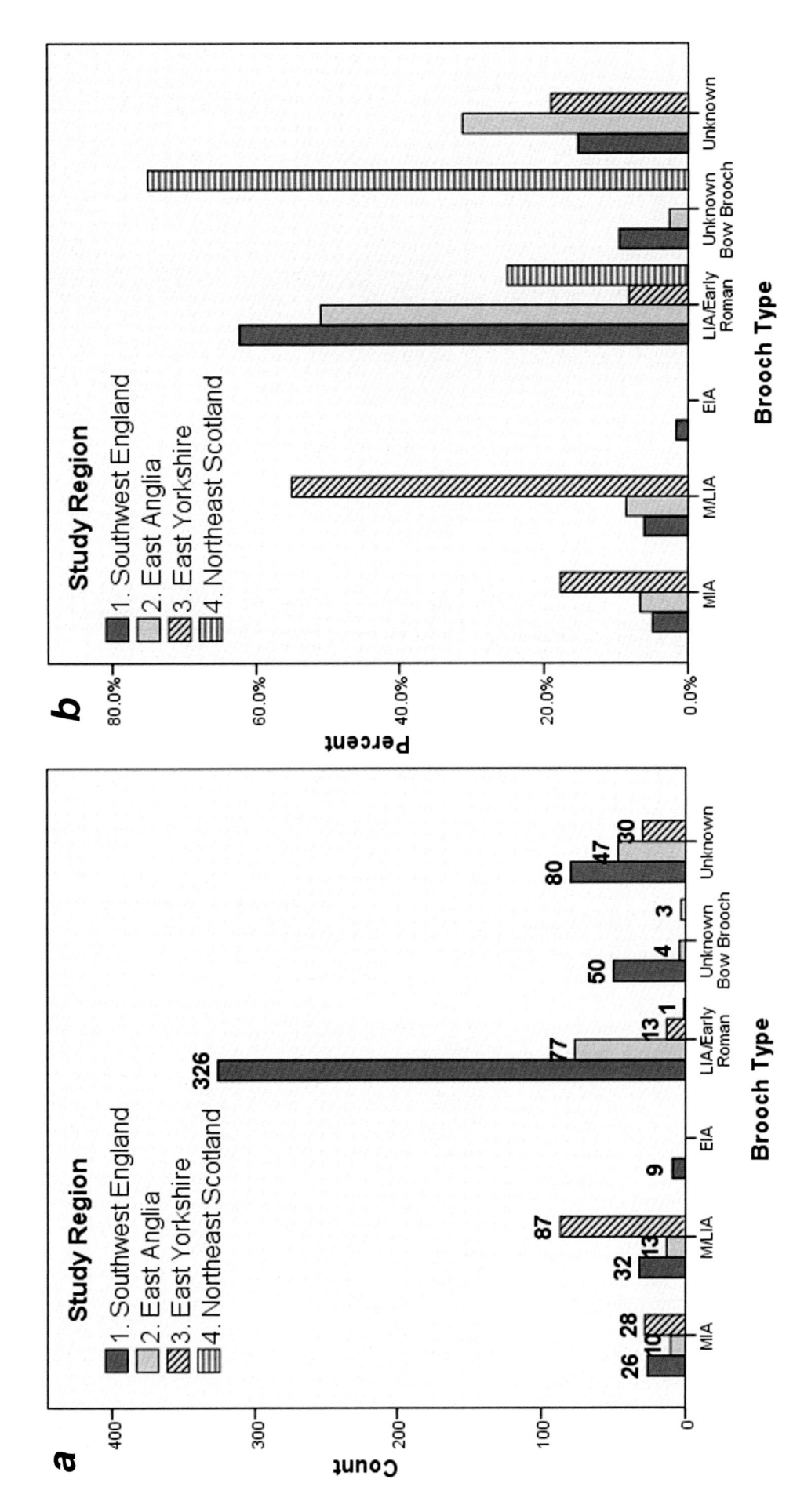

Figure 170: Bar-charts comparing the frequency of brooches by date: (a) Frequency; (b) Percentage.

Torcs

One of the most enigmatic objects of the British and European Iron Age, which has been found in perplexing numbers in East Anglia, is the torc. More examples have been found at Snettisham than the rest of Britain. In the absence of other chronologically informative objects, such as brooches, the chronology of this object is dependent on other artefacts. Examples of Gallo-Belgic coins were found in the 'scrap' collections of metal in Snettisham Hoards B, C, and F, and a Gallo-Belgic D quarter stater was found in the terminal of the "Great Torc" from Hoard E. The original date for the deposition of torcs was given as the last quarter of the first century BC to early first century AD, as first proposed by Clark (1939). This date was challenged by Stead (1991b), who suggested that they were deposited in the first quarter of the first century BC. However, drawing on re-dated coin evidence, Hutcheson (2004, 23-4) has pushed the date back even farther by suggesting that they were deposited as early as the second century BC, but possibly as late as the mid-first century BC. Given the strong possibility for an earlier date of deposition, the implication is that it becomes unlikely that Boudiccea and other inhabitants of East Anglia wore this item at the time of the conquest and rebellion (Hutcheson 2004).

As an object type, torcs manifested in an earlier form as early as the late Bronze Age as part of what has been termed an 'ornament horizon' (Roberts 2007). However, the use of this earlier type ends before the beginning of the Iron Age, and neck-rings are not found in Britain again until the end of the Iron Age. During this intervening period in Britain, there are very few objects in use that were made from precious metals. The situation is different in continental Europe, where torcs made from bronze are found in fifth century BC female burials. This may suggest that women primarily wore them. However, from the fourth century BC, the gendered use of torcs becomes more complicated, as contemporary depictions show males wearing torcs, although they are not found in contemporary male graves (Eluère 1987).

The reasons for the deposition of the torcs at Snettisham have tended to focus on functional or logical explanations (e.g. Stead 1991b), but, as with coins and horse equipment, the discussion often turns to ideas of power or status. In Britain, these objects are often interpreted as an elite status object (e.g. Cunliffe 2005), due in part to the connections with the continental material, but also because many were made from precious materials (e.g. gold, silver) and some exhibit intricate and delicate decoration. In this interpretation of the torc as an elite status object, the status of the individual wearing the object is reflected to the audience or community through its use. In an alternative approach, Hill (2011, 256) has suggested that rather than reflecting the individuals' status, the torc was a symbol of the community's status.

Both glass beads and torcs have suffered from similar interpretive issues. Are these objects inherently high-status as suggested by Henderson (1992) due to the material that they were made from? Or, because some examples were decorated? One of the downfalls of this approach of interpreting objects is that it does not take the biography of individual objects into account. For example, the extensive repairs on the 'Grotesque torc' and the continued use of some glass beads despite their broken appearance, may suggest that these individual objects had some greater meaning within the society by the individuals that actively used them. In addition, the disappearance of the classic Iron Age torc, and the emergence of Late Iron Age and Early Roman beaded torcs and collars, suggests that the continued use of the neck and collar bone area may have been an important area for the display of status. This may also apply to the use of glass beads, although it is interesting that when considering the study regions examined here, both Southwest England and East Yorkshire have very few, if any, torcs, but glass beads were found in larger numbers. In contrast, in East Anglia there were more torcs, but considerably fewer glass beads. Finally, in Scotland, glass beads seem to occur alongside torcs or other collars, although in Northeast Scotland there are more of the former than the latter. These patterns may suggest that this area of the body may have been consistently used for more elite forms of dress, and so beads and torcs may have been an more important indicator of status than other object types.

Torcs, such as those occurring at Snettisham, occur in a wide variety of styles: loop terminal, buffer terminal, ring terminal, and tubular. Other types, such as the beaded torcs and other collar type neck ornaments are presumed to be later due to their style (Jope 2000, 148; MacGregor 1976, 93). Of these torc types, the most frequent is the loop terminal types (Figure 171), although even these can vary in their level of ornateness. For example, the Ipswich torcs have a simple loop terminal, but others have cast decoration on their terminals (Owles 1969). Others, such as the Spettisbury loop-terminal torc from Dorset (Hawkes 1940), has plain undecorated terminals. While the majority of torcs come from East Anglia, loop, ring and buffer terminal types are found in both this region and Southwest England where they occur in smaller numbers (Figure 172). Beaded torcs, on the other hand have been found in Southwest England and East Yorkshire, while collars are only known from the former. However, additional collars are known from other areas of Scotland, such as the example from Stichill in the Scottish Borders (MacGregor 1976, catalogue 210). The implication, however, is that the earlier types of torcs are primarily a regional occurrence, occurring mainly within Norfolk and Suffolk, and only very occasionally elsewhere in Southern Britain. Later types of torcs have a farther-reaching spread, but take on a new appearance.

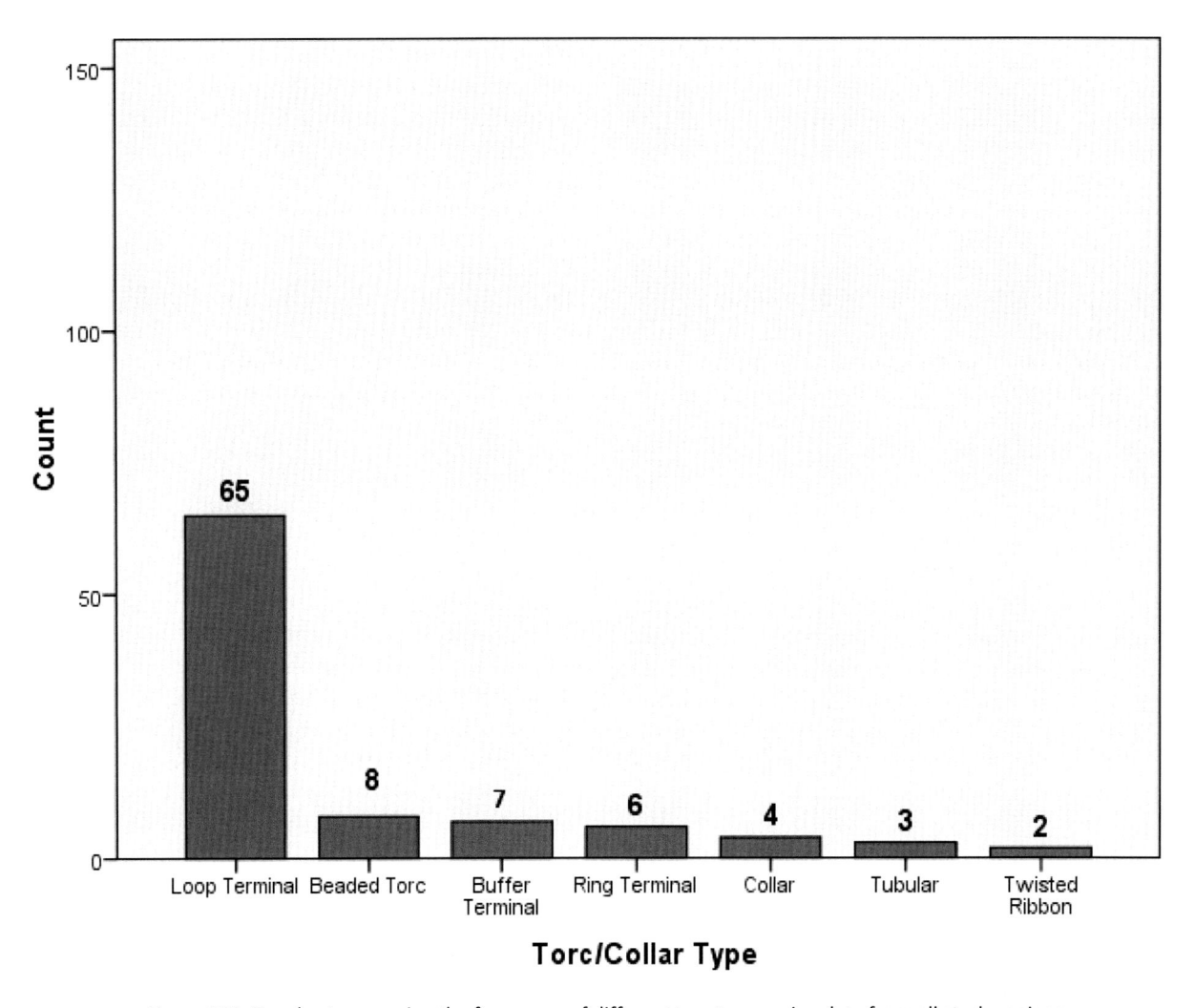

Figure 171: Bar-chart comparing the frequency of different torc types using data from all study regions.

Rings (Bracelets, Arm-rings, Bangles, Armlets, Finger-rings, and Toe-rings)

Except for in the cases of Kimmeridge shale rings (Calkin 1953; Mansel-Pleydell 1896; Sydenham 1844), later 'British' type glass bangles (Kilbride-Jones 1937; Price 1988; Stevenson 1956; 1976), and a regional discussions of bracelets from East Yorkshire (Dent 1984; Stead 1965; 1979), there has been very little study of both large rings and smaller rings.

Larger rings worn around the wrist, ankle, or arm, have been identified in three major types of material: metals (copper alloy, iron, gold), glass, and stones (shale and jet). Unlike the brooches and torcs, consistent analysis is lacking for this type of object and further research is needed in order to determine the validity of the terms and typology. Nonetheless, the typology presented here provides a starting point for discussing this type of object. Here, the typology has separated objects by broad material group as it is the material that dictates the form and any decoration. For example, while both metal and shale bracelets can be annular, a shale bracelet could not utilise a mortise and tenon closure. Of these types, it is the simplest annular/penannular and 'round-ish' types that are the most frequent (Figure 173), while more complex types are less frequent. However, even within the metal annular/penannular type, there is considerable variation in form, but this is something that will need to be investigated in greater detail at a later date. By examining the types by region, a number of trends emerge (Figure 174). The Southwest has the greatest variety of types, including most of the shale armlets, and proportionally the majority of these larger rings are made up of shale armlets from this region, while there is a smaller occurrence of glass and metal rings. Metal rings, however, are most frequent in East Yorkshire, especially annular/penannular, overlapping terminal, and mortise and tenon types. All glass rings of continental type are found in Southwest England, while British types are found in Southwest England and Northeast Scotland (other Romano-British types are found in East Yorkshire, but are not considered here). Without taking time into account, this shows that there are some general trends in

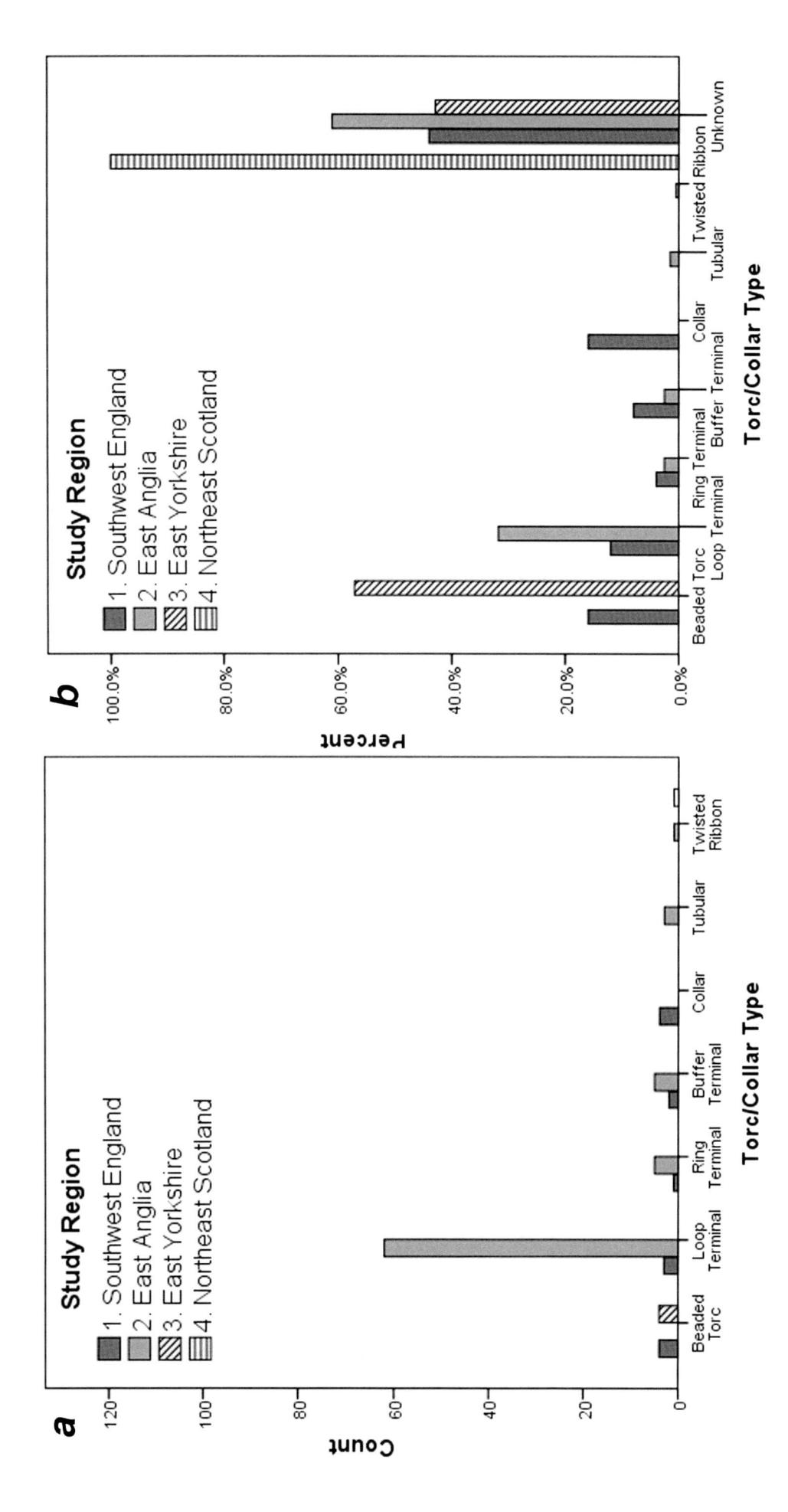

Figure 172: Bar-charts comparing the frequency of different torc types by study regions: (a) Frequency; (b) Percentage.

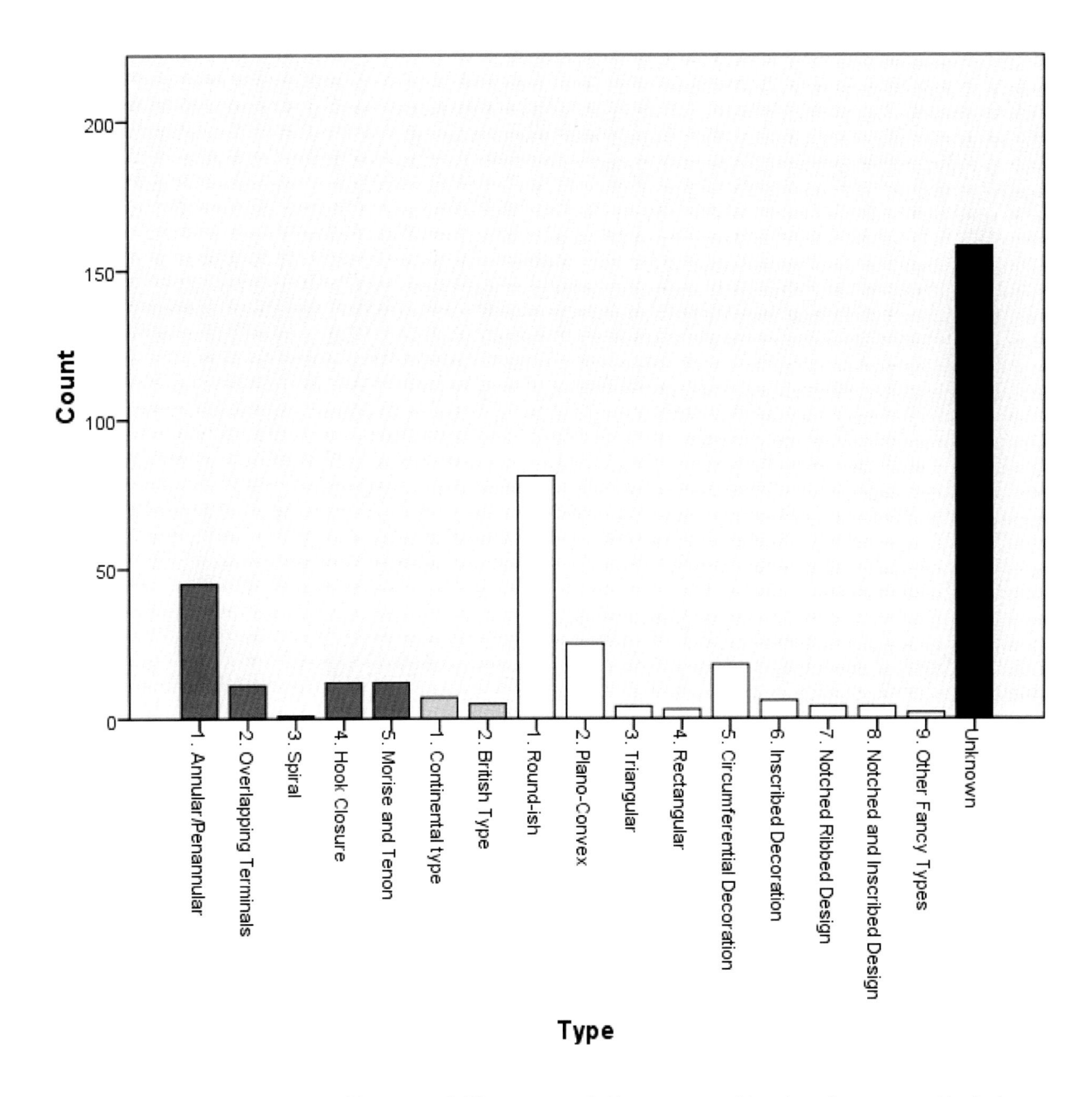

Figure 173: Bar-chart showing general frequency of different types of objects worn on either the wrist, arm, or ankle. Dark grey are types made mostly out of metal, usually iron or copper alloy, medium grey are two types of glass rings, and lightest grey are different types of objects made from stone, usually shale or jet.

the data as to which types are most frequent in different regions.

The trend of smaller rings worn on the fingers or toes is very similar to that of the larger rings, although despite some similarities in form, they vary considerably. The two most frequent types of finger-/toe-rings is (1) the annular or nearly annular, or sometimes with a slight overlap group (1.A.- 1.C.) and, (2) the spiral group (2.A.1 – 2.B.5) (Figure 175). These groupings have been further divided based on decoration and other characteristics of similarity. Within both groups, it is the plainer examples that occur most frequently. The majority of these rings and the greatest variety were found in Southwest England (Figure 176). Most other rings were found in East Yorkshire and there were very few from East Anglia and Northeast Scotland.

Pins

Finally, pins were also made from a variety of different types of material, but copper alloy is most common.

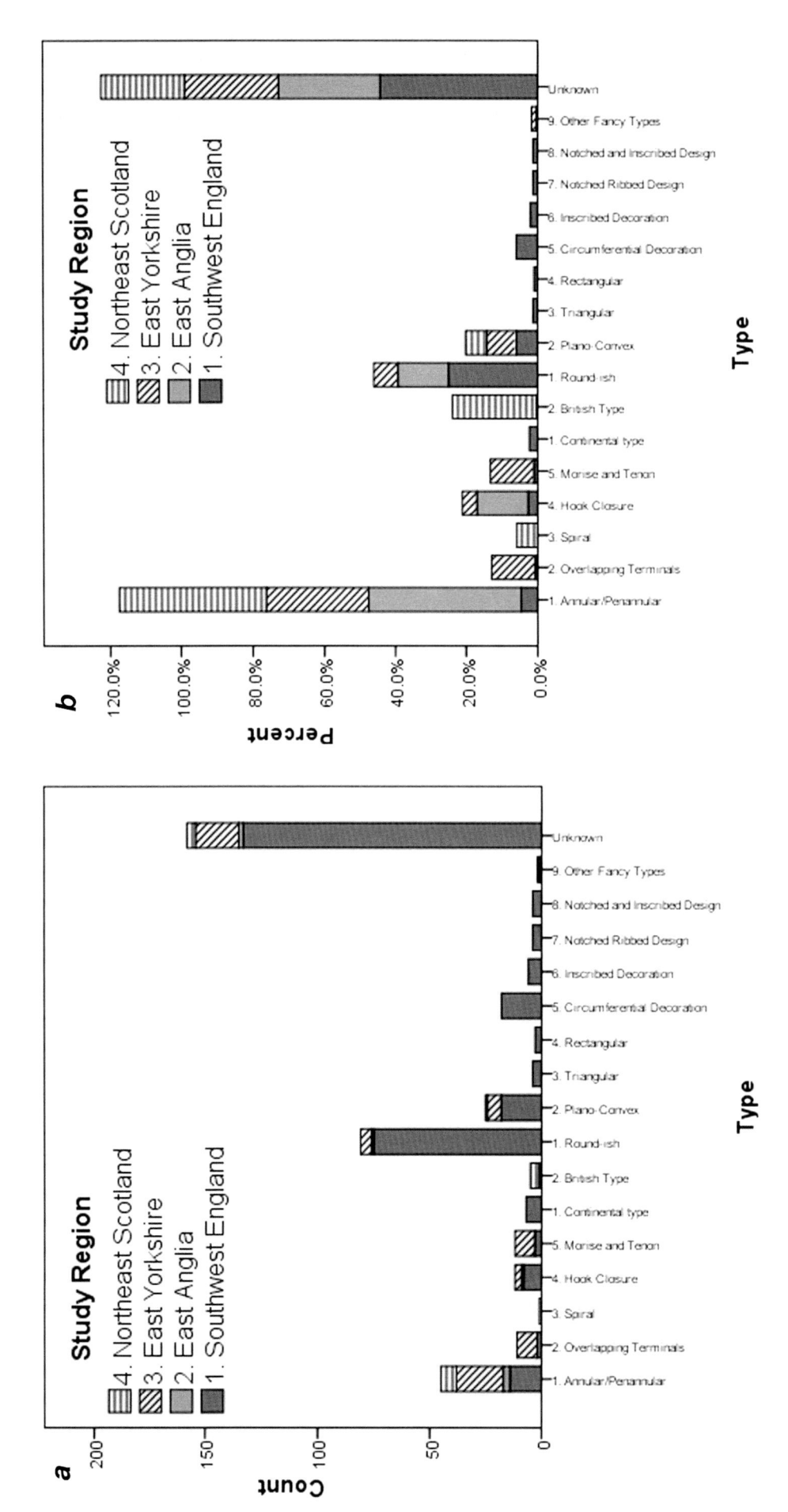

Figure 174: Bar-charts comparing the frequency of different types of rings worn on the wrist, arm, and ankle by study region: (a) Frequency, (b) Percentage.

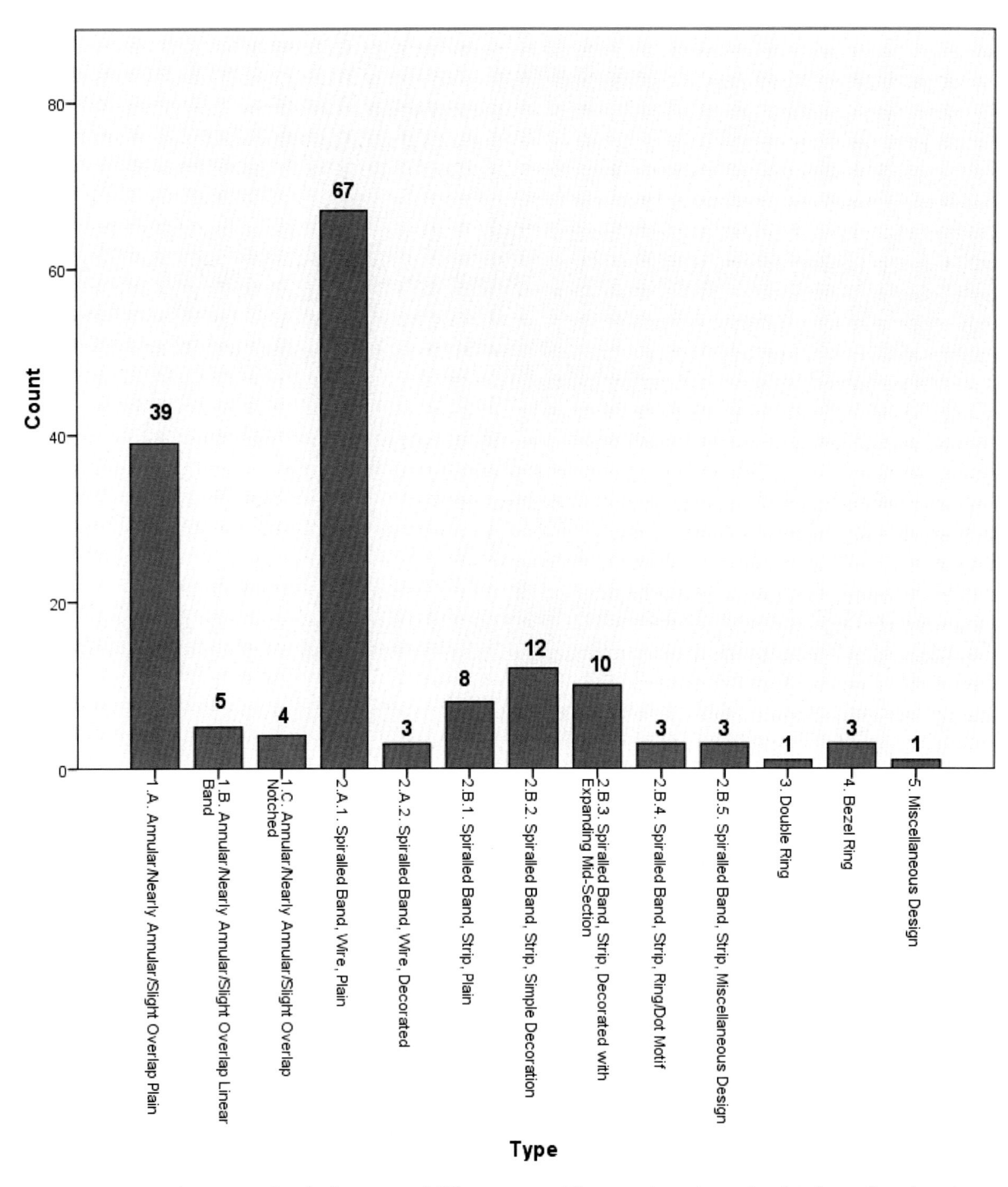

Figure 175: Bar-chart comparing the frequency of different types of finger- and toe-rings using data from all study regions.

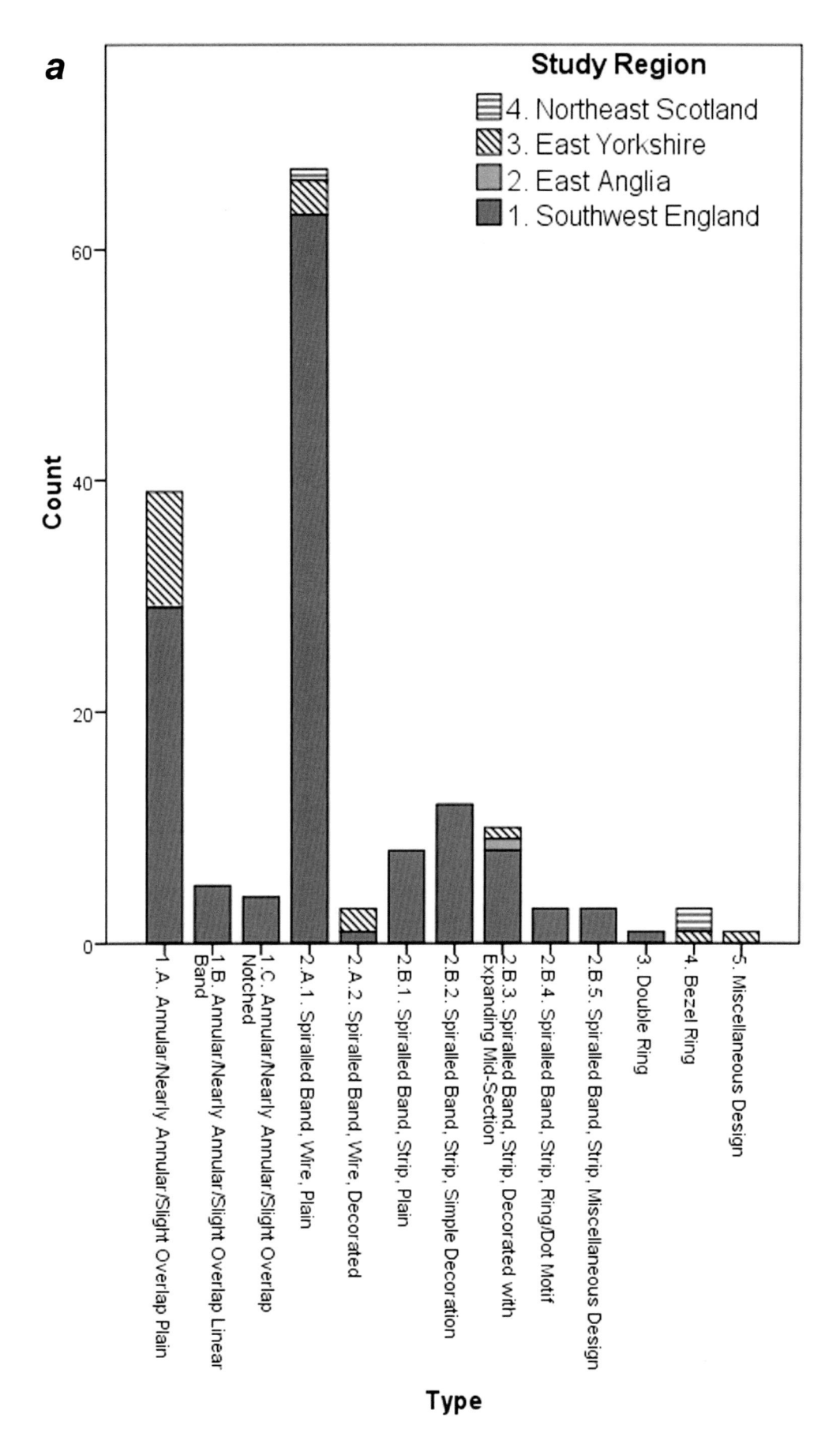

Figure 176: Bar-charts comparing the frequency of finger- and toe-rings in each of the study regions. (a) Frequency.

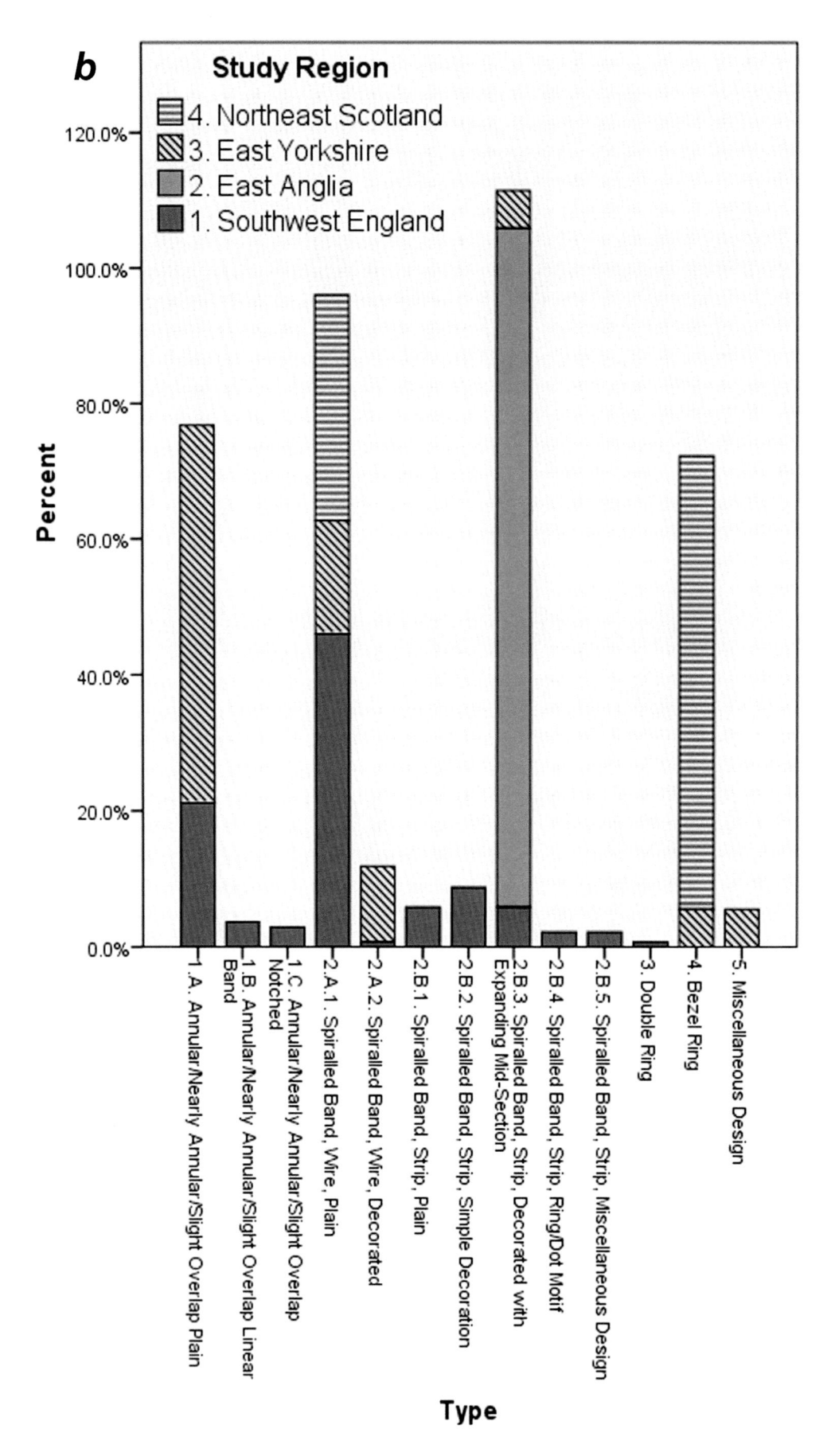

Figure 176: Bar-charts comparing the frequency of finger- and toe-rings in each of the study regions, (b) Percentage.

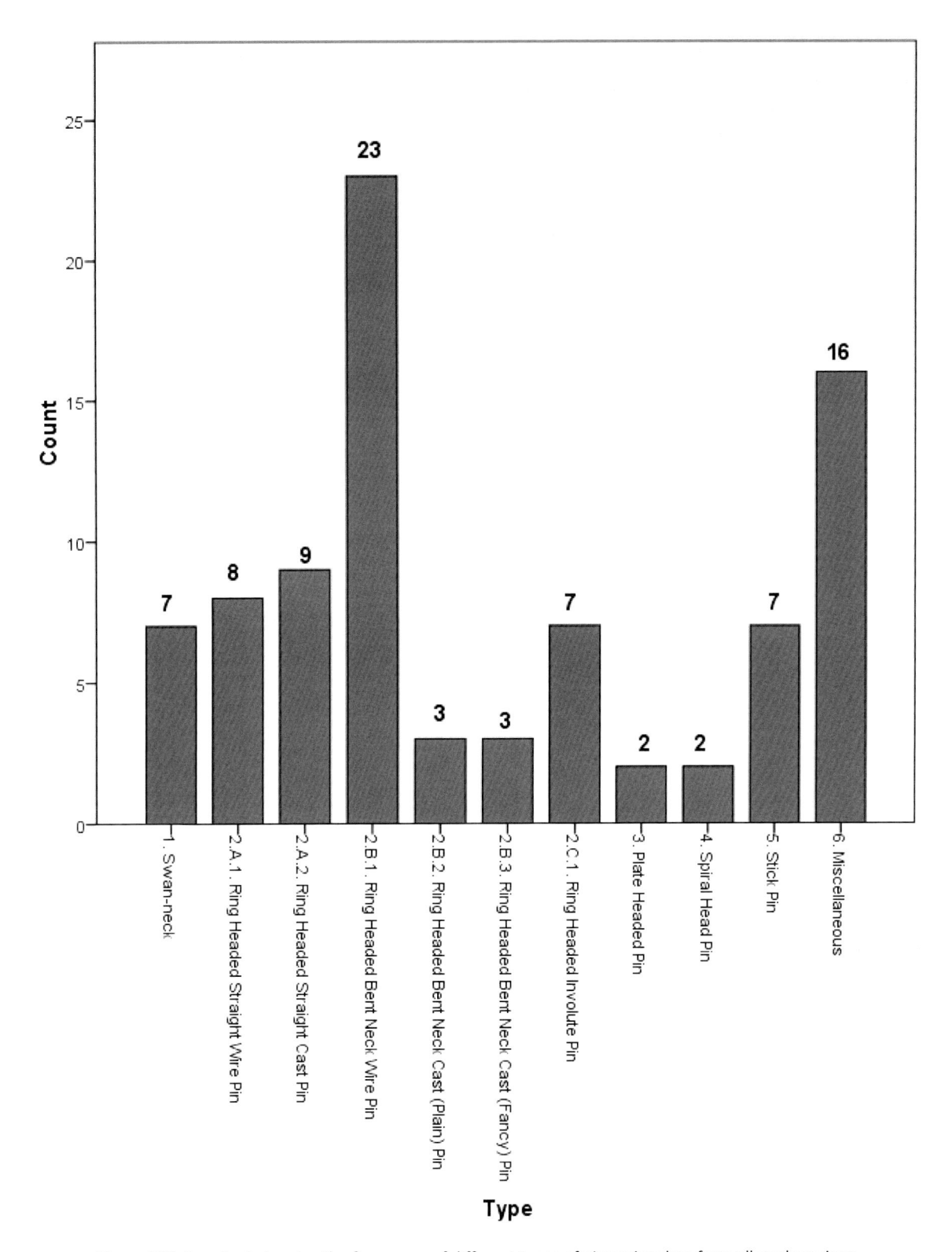

Figure 177: Bar-chart showing the frequency of different types of pins using data from all study regions.

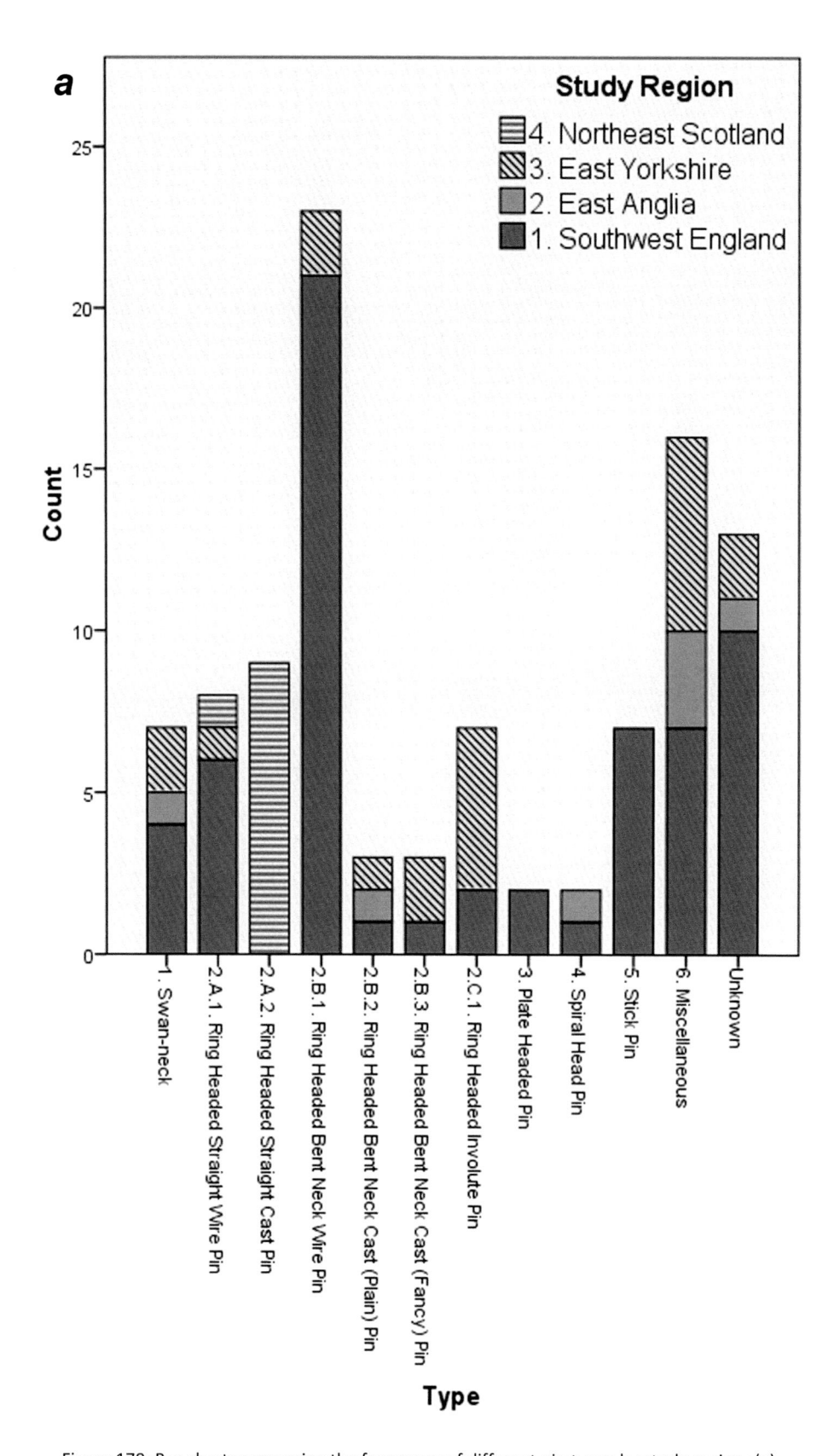

Figure 178: Bar-charts comparing the frequency of different pin types by study region: (a) Frequency.

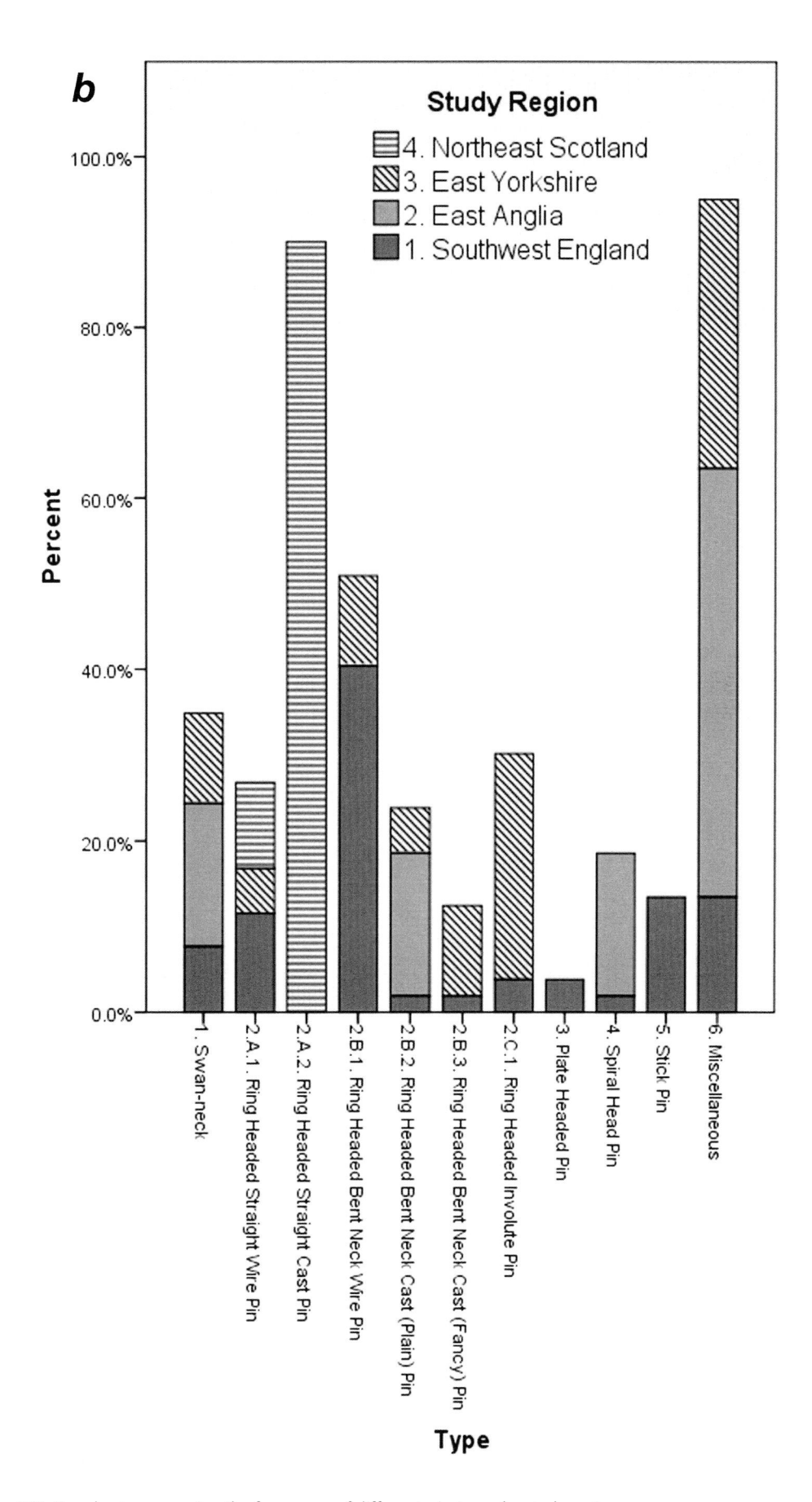

Figure 178: Bar-charts comparing the frequency of different pin types by study region: (b) Percentage.

While carved bone pins are often primarily Roman artefact (Allason-Jones 1989, 132; Croom 2000, 123; Crummy 1979) several were noted from Conderton Camp in Southwest England in an Iron Age context. However, these organic pins were in the extreme minority. Several swan-neck type pins were identified, but most pins were ring-headed. However, despite the similarity in the ring-head feature, they were noted to vary based on whether a bend at the neck was present or not, manufacture from either wire or cast, the bend in the pin-shaft, and the elaborateness of the pin (Figure 177). Pins were primarily from Southwest England, but many were also found in East Yorkshire (Figure 178). Very few pins were found in East Anglia, which were primarily swan-neck type and other miscellaneous unique types of pins. In Northeast Scotland, only one type was found: the cast ring-headed straight pin.

Interpretation

Despite differences in the frequency and the appearance of these objects in each study region, there are trends in the occurrence of these objects over time. The general pattern is that there was less material culture, such as brooches, in the Earlier Iron Age, but that there is a material culture explosion by the Late Iron Age (Hill 1995a). While this could be due to a number of factors including the use of organic materials that are not often archaeologically recognisable, depositional practices, and access to raw materials, this trend is seen in the overall pattern of all these objects presently under consideration (Figure 179a). A similar trend is seen with brooches (Figure 179f). However, for the remaining objects, this is not the case. Wrist/arm/ankle, finger/toe-rings, and pins all peak in their frequency earlier than the peak for brooches. Instead they peak around the Middle Iron Age and earliest Late Iron Age. This is also true of the earlier torcs (not the beaded torcs or collars), which are thought to date to a period prior to the Roman invasion (Garrow and Gosden 2012, 134; Hutcheson 2004). The implications of this pattern will be discussed below.

Wider Artefact Context

Finally, the last area of comparison is to examine how glass beads are distributed throughout Britain compared to other types of objects. In this instance, a density map of glass beads was created using the corrected and modified version of the Guido catalogue during the initial review of all her sources, and the additions made by the present research in the four study regions. Although the remaining region's data is not yet up-to-date, no other map can be produced at this stage in the research and there is not currently a database that would allow such a map to be created. The current known density of glass beads is shown in Figure 180. It highlights the areas where glass beads are densest and omits areas where only occasional examples have been found. Interestingly, it shows that within one area in East Yorkshire (namely Wetwang/Garton Slack) the density is at the maximum range, while in Southwest England the dense areas are spread out over the region, with two 'hot- spots'. In Northeast Scotland, the single area with the densest area of finds remains around Culbin Sands, and despite a few isolated finds in East Anglia that may have been of Iron Age date, it is now possible to fill in some of the blank areas.

Comparative data was drawn from the Portable Antiquities Scheme database from four main categories of finds: brooches, coins, body maintenance, and horse equipment (Figure 181). In all cases, it can be shown that the data is skewed primarily towards eastern Britain, especially around East Anglia, although for brooches there is another dense area in Hampshire, and coins have dense find areas in southern Dorset and also in Hampshire. It may be that the preponderance of finds in East Anglia is due to higher levels of metal-detectorist activity and recording practices; however, these objects are all types that become more numerous by the end of the Iron Age and are absent or are only present in very small numbers prior to this period.

Discussion

This chapter opened by stating that glass beads were both a part and a whole. A single bead is an object on its own, and these are found in settlement contexts, possibly as a part of ritual deposition, and in inhumations. These singly occurring beads might indicate that they were used as single objects. Groups of beads can be brought together to form larger, more complex objects. In burial features, these have been suggested to form strands that were worn around the neck due to their proximity to the head and neck. In both cases, it is possible that the single or bead groups might not have been worn by the individual in life, but could have been gifts or tokens of memory deposited by the living with the deceased individual. Thus, although preserved as a single object, they were taken out of the multi-bead context for deposition.

Assuming that the groups of beads did form a neck ornament, estimates have suggested that there were differences in the overall lengths. One potential necklace in particular stands out compared to all other potential necklaces: the Queen's Barrow necklace from East Yorkshire. This particular necklace combines numerous different types, some of which are shared with other East Yorkshire necklaces, and some of which were unique among them. It is also the only necklace in East Yorkshire to combine both predominantly blue and green beads. This unusual combination of colours for this region, the long length of the necklace (or at least the large number of beads), along with the other objects in the inhumation, suggests that this individual may have

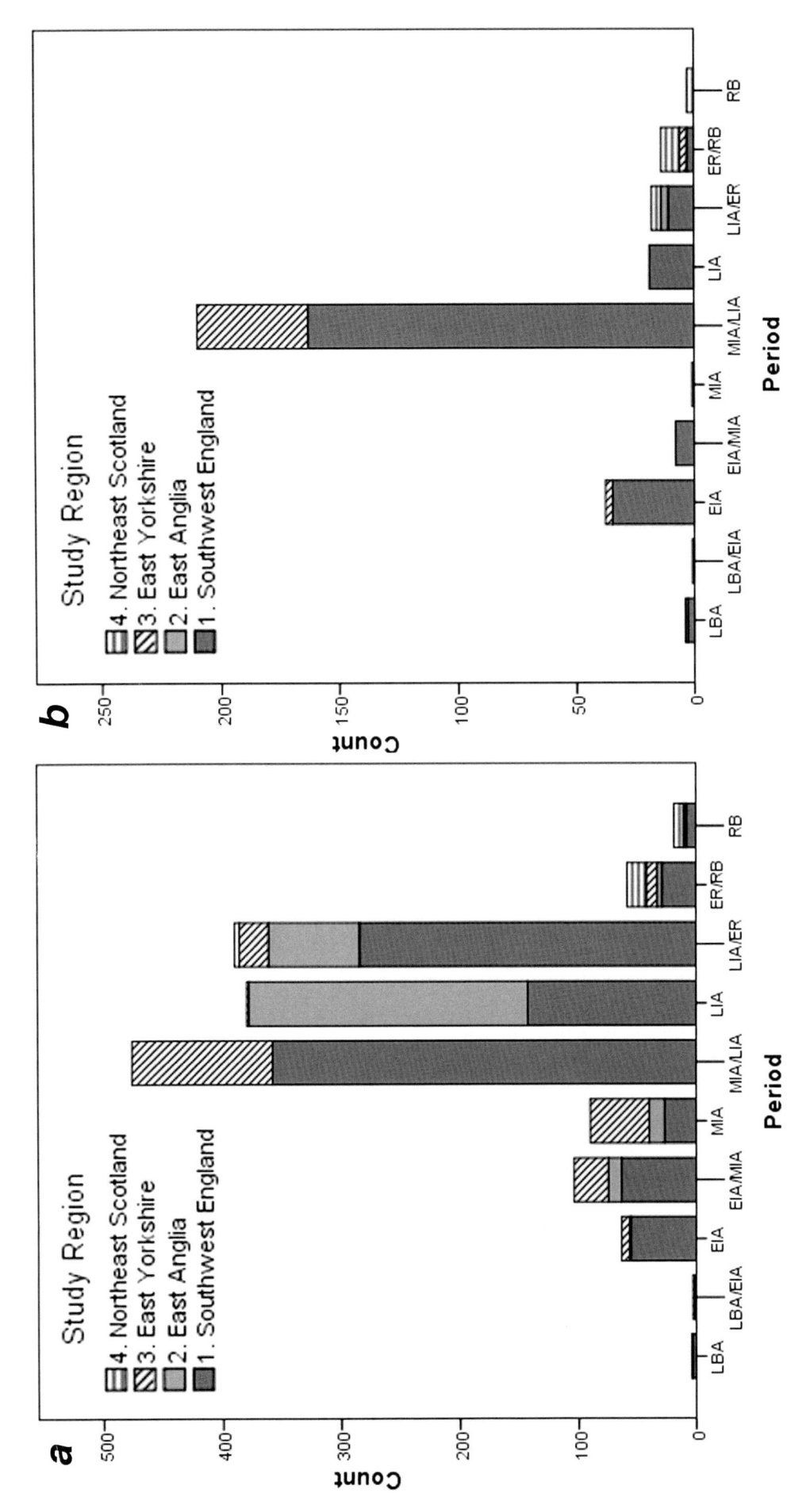

Figure 179: Bar-charts showing the frequency of objects in study regions over time: (a) All Objects, (b) Arm/Wrist/Ankle rings.

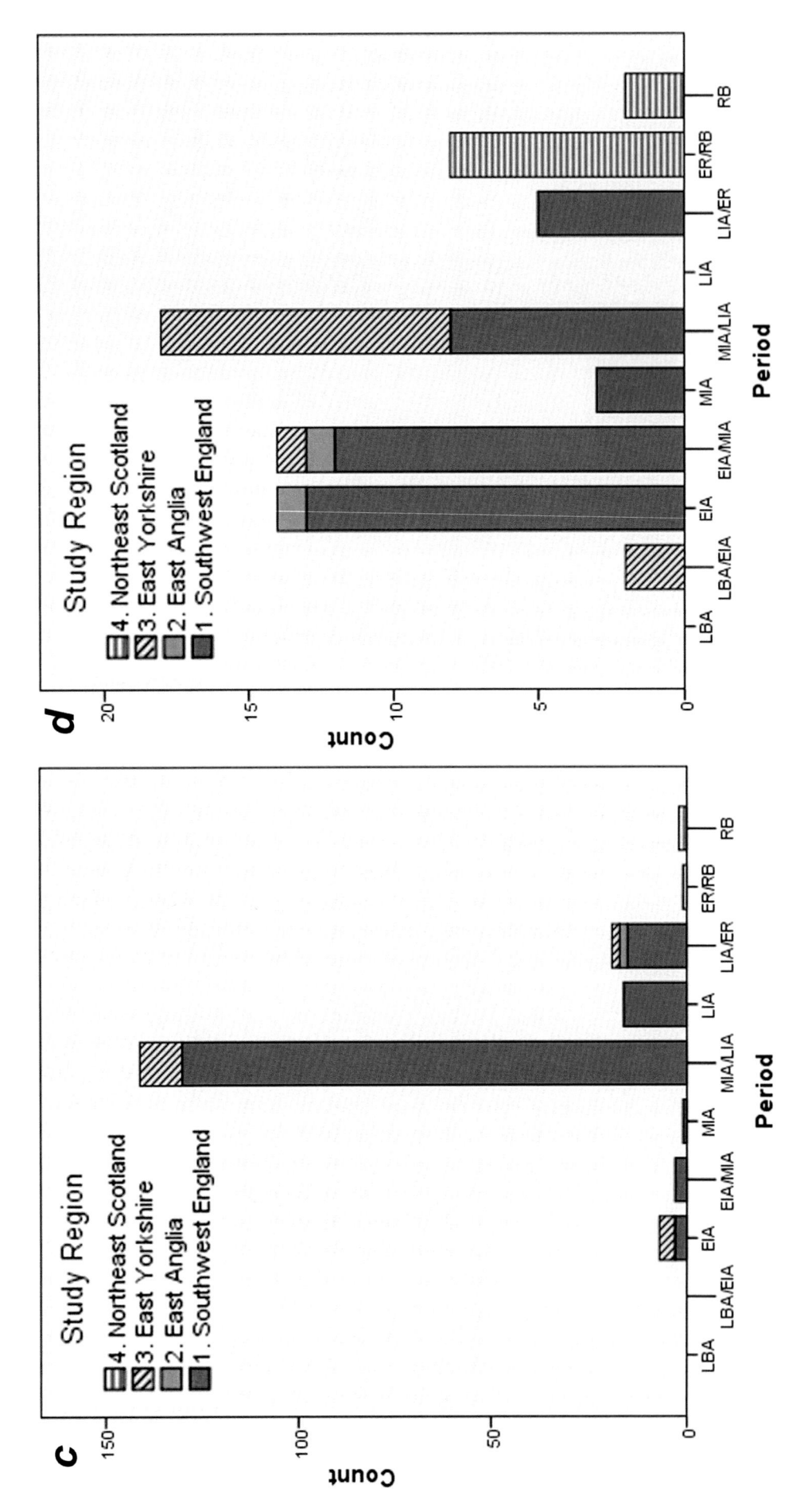

Figure 179: Bar-charts showing the frequency of objects in study regions over time: (c) Finger-/Toe-rings, (d) Pins.

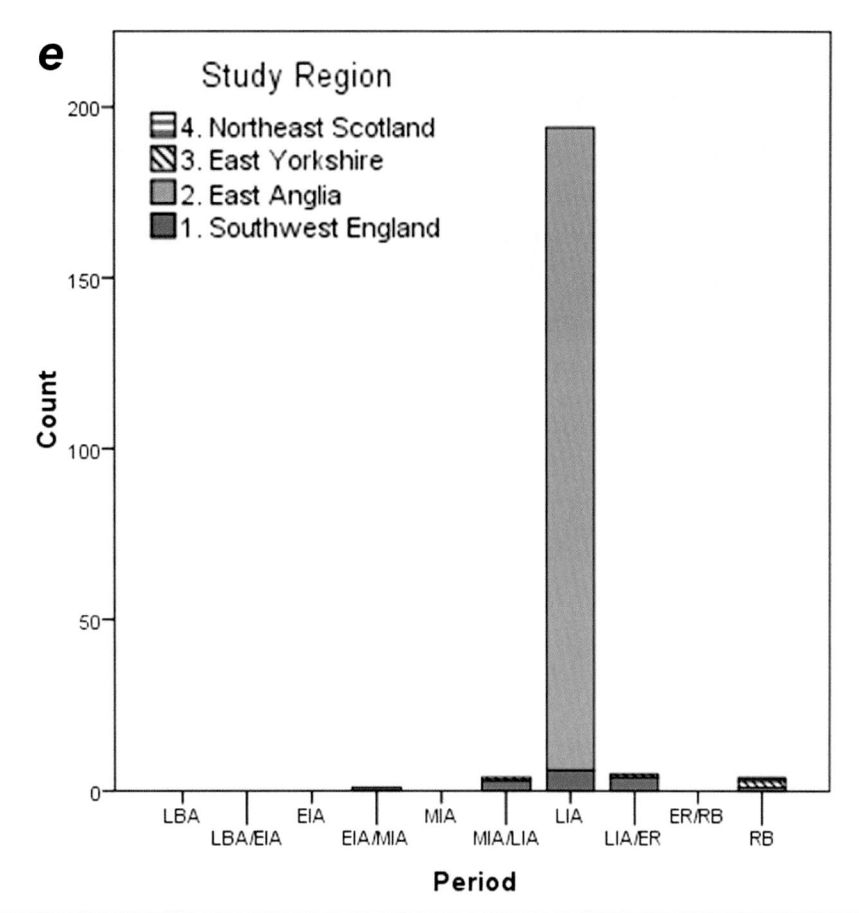

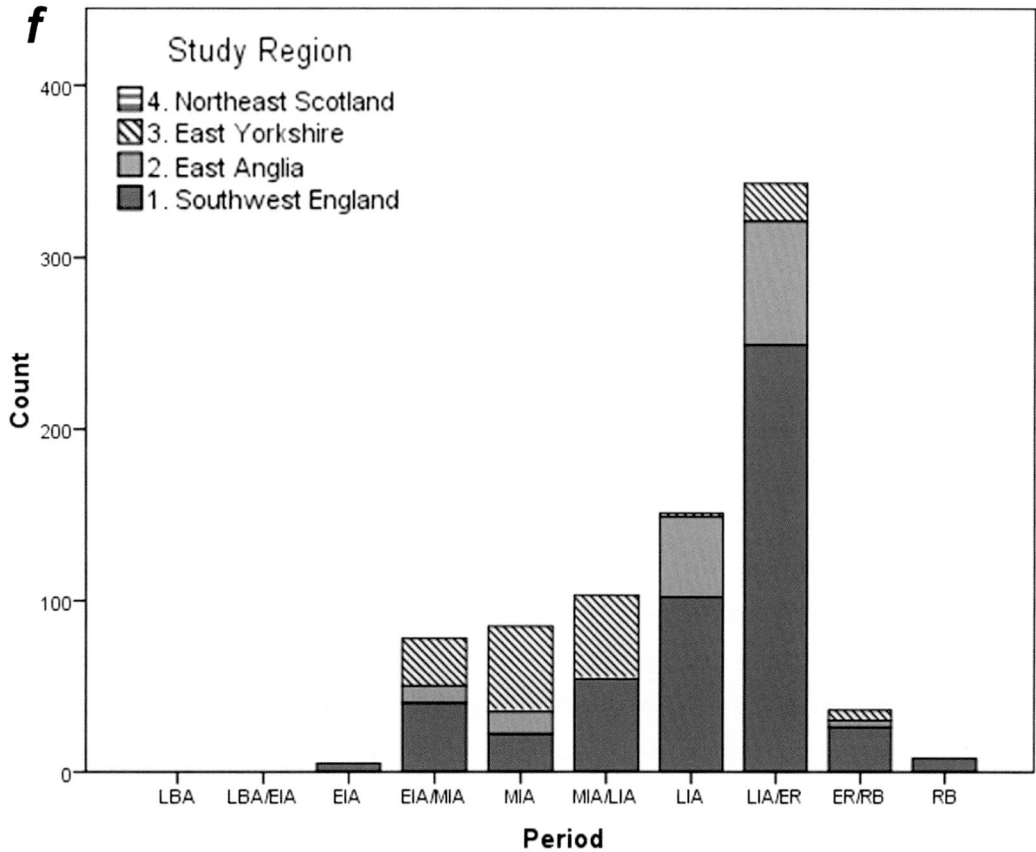

Figure 179: Bar-charts showing the frequency of objects in study regions over time: (e) Torcs, (f) Brooches.

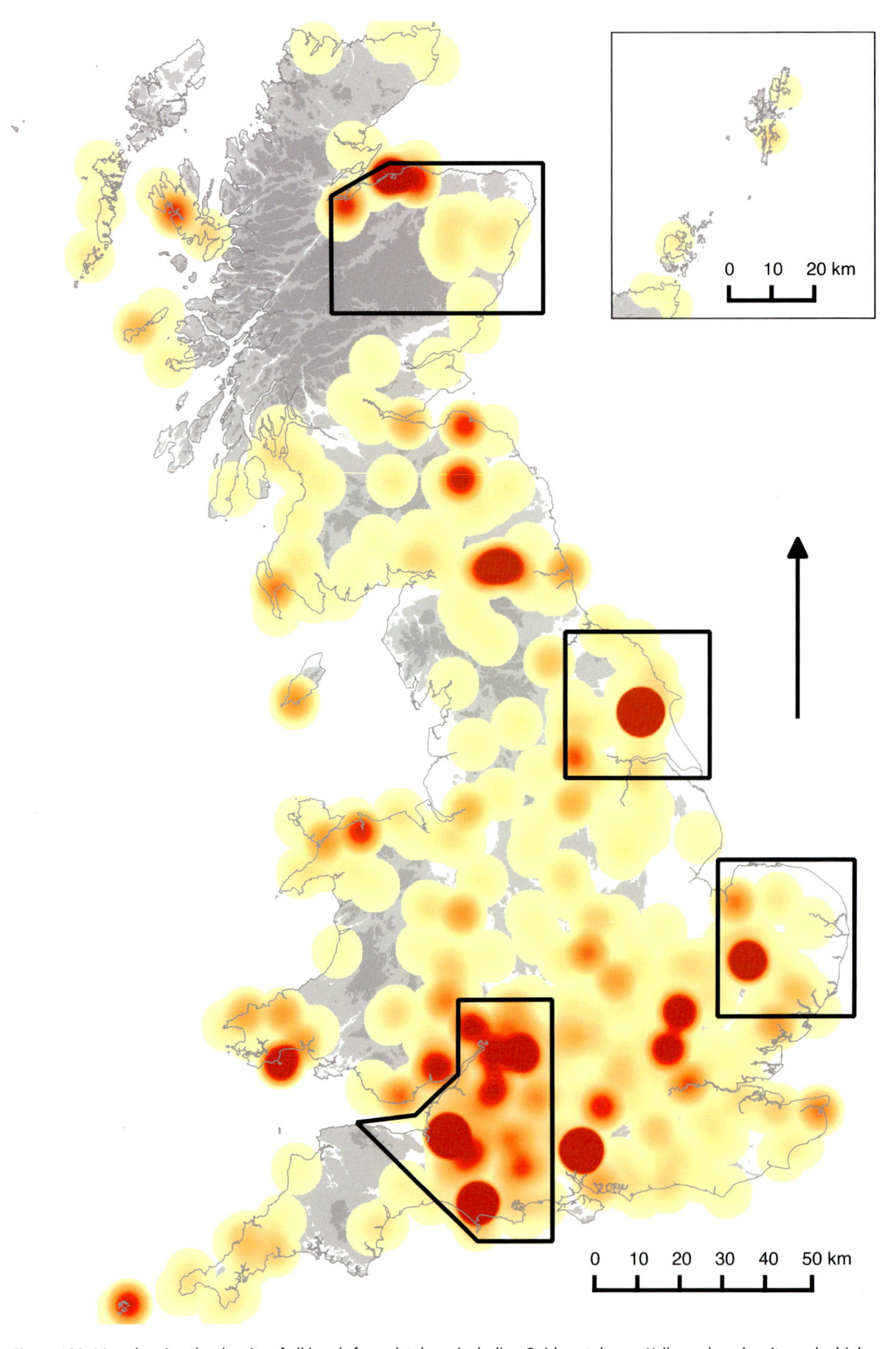

Figure 180: Map showing the density of all beads from database including Guido catalogue. Yellow = low density, red = high density.

REGIONAL BODILY ADORNMENT

Figure 181: Comparison of the distribution of different Iron Age artefacts from Portable Antiquity Scheme data. (a) Brooches, (b) Coins. Yellow = low density, red = high density.

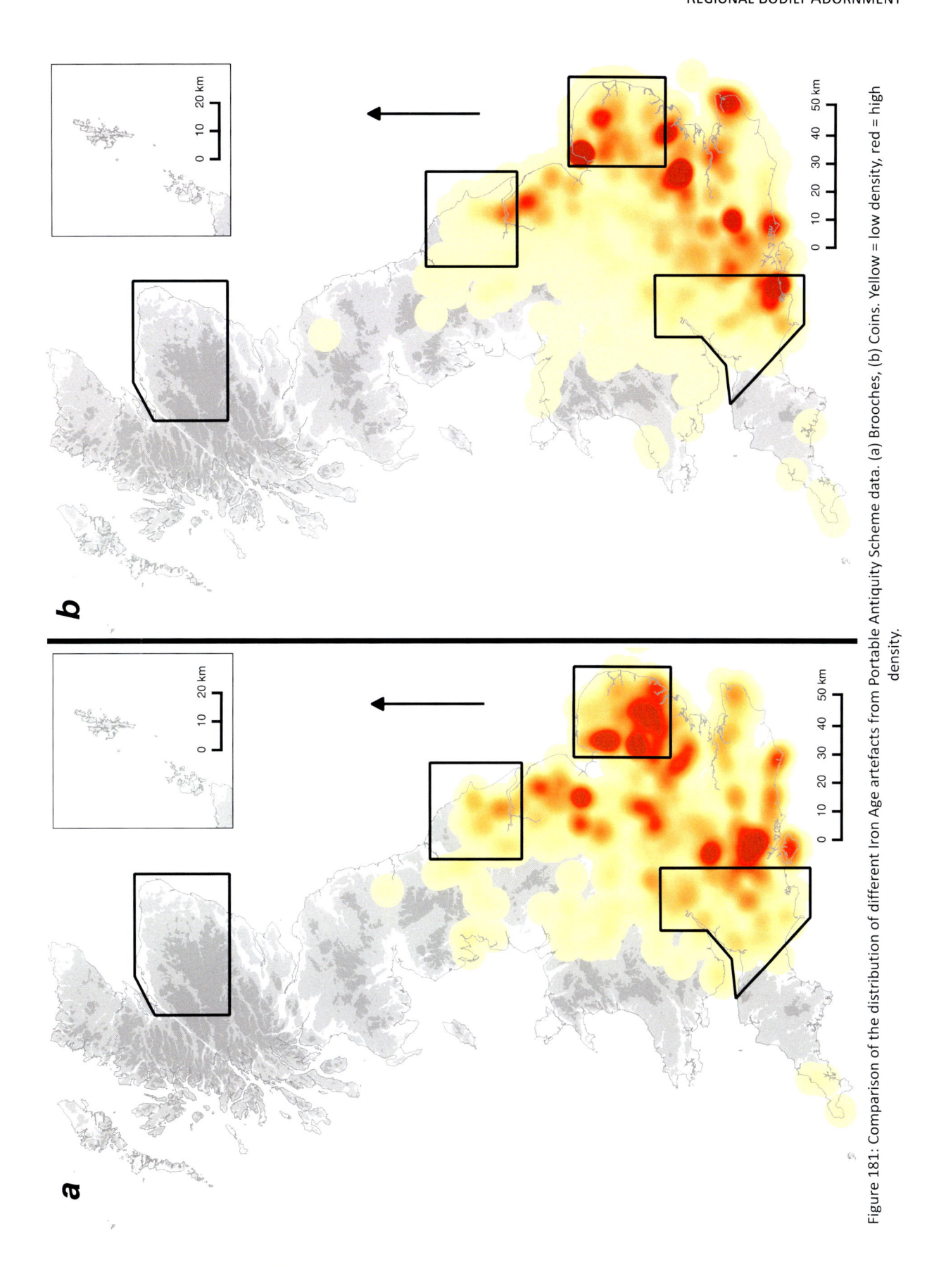

Dress and Identity in Iron Age Britain

Figure 181: Comparison of the distribution of different Iron Age artefacts from Portable Antiquity Scheme data. (c) Cosmetic Objects, (d) Horse related gear. Yellow = low density, red = high density.

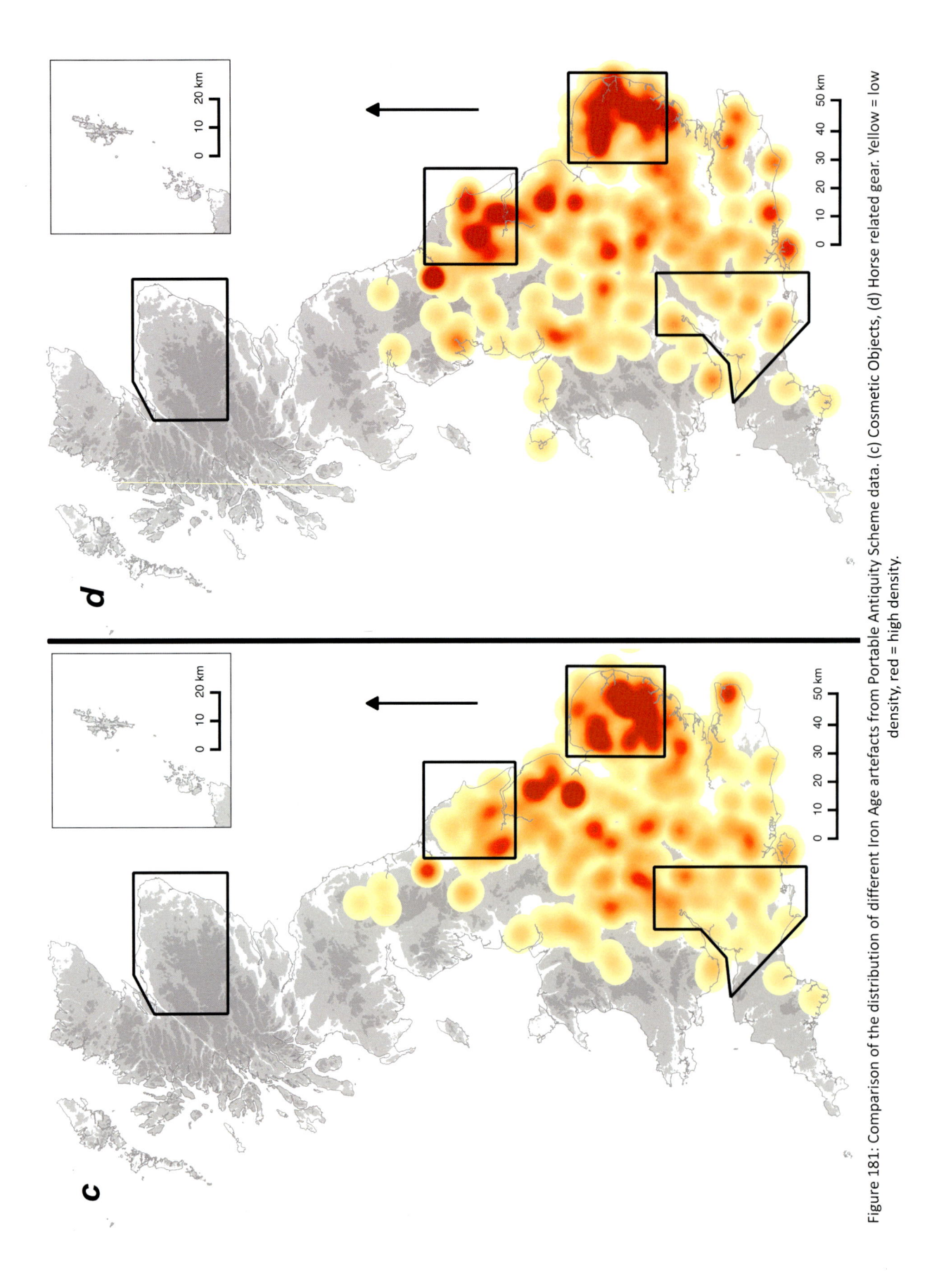

stood out in life just as they did in death. Beads from other inhumations strung as necklaces display patterns of repetition in decorative motif, and in some cases they may have combined beads into a symmetrical pattern of bead shape, colour, and motif.

Just as a bead is simultaneously a part and a whole, they are also only one part of a larger range of objects that constituted dress. As with beads, these objects varied in appearance, geographically, in frequency, and over time. With some of these objects, the way they were worn is clear, such as bracelets on wrists, finger-rings on fingers, and toe-rings on toes. For others, the purpose continues to be less clear. For example, there is little understanding of the types of garments that brooches pinned together, or if they were visible or hidden when worn. Although pins in the Roman period are associated with hair-styles (Allason-Jones 1989), they may have been used in the same way in the Iron Age, or perhaps in a similar way to a brooch. Rings remain particularly ambiguous, as some are too large to stay on fingers or toes, but too small to slip over the wrist. Perhaps they were worn by children, or in some other presently unknown way. It is, however, worth speculating to a point about how they were used, but at the same time question why they did not feature extensively within inhumations. Perhaps they were not always suitable for burial, or the limited burial tradition provided only a small opportunity for objects to become associated with individuals.

Different objects would have emphasised or drawn the viewer's eye to different areas of the body. Two areas of the body have been shown to be most important. First, the area around the head and the neck, where glass beads and presumably torcs, were worn. This area, being near the head and thus eye contact, may have been important in terms of the display of objects of dress, and perhaps even other dress practices, such as tattooing. This upper-body area is also the region where many brooches have been found, suggesting that this was an area where garments were attached. It may be that this is an area where other organic elements featured, such as textile decoration, furs, pendants or talismans, and cords or other braids.

The second area of display that seems to have been important is the arm, where bracelets were worn on wrists, finger-rings on fingers, and potentially armbands or arm-rings around the upper arm or forearm. These objects imply that these areas of the body would have been exposed in some manner so that the objects could be seen, although in the case of the largest arm-rings, such as the massive armlets from Scotland, they may have been worn over arm coverings. Items, such as finger-rings and bracelets, would have been even more noticeable through gesticulation. Some of these objects may have encumbered movement during physical tasks and may even have made audible noises when bracelets clanked or bumped into other tools, such as quern stones.

The other less prominent and less frequent region of the body where objects of dress have been found associated with is the lower body. Anklets have been found around the ankle, while small rings have been found on toe-bones of some individuals. When standing, these objects would have been less visible in part because they were not near eye contact, but also because they potentially could be obscured from view due to long garments or foot coverings. The presence of rings on toes suggests that total foot enclosures were not worn, and either these individuals went barefoot or that semi-enclosed footwear where the upper surface of the foot was not enclosed was worn. Another explanation might be that this individual died during the summer months when foot coverings were not necessary for warmth. By wearing these objects, the individual's movement may also have been encumbered in walking, running, and performing tasks of physical labour. Some tasks may also have posed a damage threat to these objects. In contrast, other postures, such as sitting on the floor or other furniture, may have rendered these objects more visible.

Dress, then, seems to have varied throughout the Iron Age, and the data hints that someone from East Yorkshire would have dressed differently from someone from Southwest England, or even East Anglia. Although some of these apparent differences could be attributed to differences in excavation practice or even differences in depositional practice, none-the-less, the objects that have been recovered from each of these regions vary rather than suggesting that there was a homogeneous form of Iron Age dress. On one level, these differences in dress may have been connected with regional or local group identity. A member would be recognised by what they wore, while an outsider may have worn different objects, or in a different way, or these objects may have been completely absent.

Identity at both a local and wider level is related to what a person wore. However, even in the East Yorkshire region, for which we have some of the best burial data that may represent a single population around the Middle to Late Iron Age at Wetwang Slack, very few inhumations included these objects of dress, whether brooches, glass beads, or other items. The rare occurrence of even the most ubiquitous Iron Age artefact within the burials, the brooch, suggests that these might not be objects worn by everyone if this evidence can be taken to be a true reflection of access to such objects. It is tempting to see this differentiation as indicators of different levels of status. Alternatively, perhaps the garments worn by different individuals varied and brooches were not a required closure or attaching mechanism that was needed by every individual. Instead, other objects may have been used that have not have survived. Likewise, perhaps more individuals wore beads made from organic materials, but only those made from glass, jet, and copper alloy survived.

The occurrence of glass beads in female inhumations (where this has been analysed scientifically) in the East Yorkshire burials have led some to suggest that these beads may have indicated a more specific identity, such as age and gender. Giles (2008a, 72) has suggested that there may a connection between the use of these blue glass beads with maturity and femininity. This may be true, as the data suggests, but these glass beads only occur in a very small minority of inhumations and could not be said to form a wider pattern (it is also unclear to what extent the Queen's Barrow and Cowlam L barrow were identified as female as they were excavated in the nineteenth century). Instead, the majority of the individuals interred at Wetwang Slack lack these glass beads. Therefore, their use as a symbol of maturity and femininity may have been limited.

Instead, I wish to emphasise two key ideas: first, that there is overlap in types between some of the necklaces in East Yorkshire. This may indicate some interrelated network of individuals on a wider, but still regional scale. Second, although the East Yorkshire practices are often seen as an isolated occurrence and Jay's work on population isotopes (Jay and Richards 2006) and the radiocarbon dating (Jay, Haselgrove et al. 2012) suggest that this population were neither immigrants nor were they emulating a contemporary burial practice from the continent, a wide-ranging network is supported by the glass beads that extends from southwest England and to continental Europe. Links between East Yorkshire and the continent may be further supported by the similarities in horse gear found in this region and in the near Continent (Anthoons 2012). In terms of the beads, this is supported by the presence of two beads in the Wetwang burials that can be attributed to the Meare style beads of Somerset (in Burial 102 and 268) and the wider similarity between the East Yorkshire beads and the continent (Venclová 1990). Further research that compares British glass beads with continental examples is essential here in order to assess the similarity more fully.

Finally, the last topic to be addressed here is situation. On the one hand, artefacts from inhumations may reflect daily dress, or burial costume reserved only for this occasion. Alternatively, these objects may have been donations from the community, and may in no way represent the objects worn in life by the individual interred. In addition, we can speculate about the range of objects that may have been worn as dress, but for which we have little direct evidence: fur armbands and textiles to name a few. It does not follow that these extant objects were high-status simply because they survive, because they are made of precious or exotic materials, nor because many of them are beautiful.

The torc makes a good example. This object, with parallels from continental European Iron Age, in the past has been connected with ideas of wealth, power, and status (Champion 1995, 413; Creighton 2000, 31; Davies 1996, 73; Eluère 1987, 23; MacGregor 1976, 93), whether worn by an individual or as a symbol of community status (Hill 2011, 256). While many are made from precious metals, others are made from copper alloy, and there is a whole range of different types of designs especially around the terminals. The massive armlets from northern Scotland are similar in this respect, although they are made out of copper alloys and some also had glass enameling. When feature information is known, torcs come from pit deposits and other domestic features. In either case, their presence in the archaeological record could be due to ritual activity, or in the case of finds amid domestic features they could be the result of accidental loss, especially in the case of fragments. It may be that these objects were chosen for deposition in some cases due to their inherent high-status value.

Due to the physical properties of torcs (e.g. precious metal, highly decorated), they are probably one of the most controversial categories of objects for interpretation. While many torcs outside of Ken Hill at Snettisham are isolated finds, it is the unusual deposition at this site (including possible layering by metal content (Stead 1991b)) where ideas of status and hierarchy come to the fore. However, it is the exceedingly large numbers of torcs at Ken Hill (approximately 168) that suggests that these were objects that were worn by many people. Given that objects, such as torcs, are often seen as being used in the context of a hierarchical society, if all of the torcs at Snettisham were being worn at the time just before deposition, then it argues against the hypothesis for both a hierarchical society and the torc as an object of status. Instead, we are seeing a regional form of dress that is not necessarily differentiated by status through the wearing of a certain type of object, as the whole population cannot be made up of high-status individuals. Therefore, the torc, and perhaps even other collars or impressively large armlets, were objects of everyday dress rather than specifically a status object.

Conclusion

From the available evidence, differences in dress on the regional level can be defined: in Southwest England, in addition to the use of glass beads, there are bracelets or other larger rings as well as rings for the toes or fingers especially by the end of the Middle Iron Age, and possibly the earlier part of the Late Iron Age. This includes a mix of different raw materials, with shale figuring prominently in the material for the larger rings. In East Anglia, the data suggests that for most of the Iron Age, objects related to dress were rare, except for a limited number of pins, rings and brooches. By the Later Iron Age, the torc plays a prominent role as a neck ornament. In East Yorkshire, in addition to the glass beads, larger rings for arms or wrists as well as pins were most frequent from the end of the Middle Iron Age through the early part of the Late Iron Age. A range of brooches over a wider period of time can also be attributed to this region, but the heirloom effect is unclear, which may lead to a distorted chronology. Finally, in Northeast Scotland, the available evidence suggests that on the one hand these objects did not play a large role in the creation of dress in this region, but also that a specific type of pin and armlet have been found in multiple locations across this region. Perhaps in earlier periods, the role of dress was fulfilled primarily through non-surviving materials, such as furs or other textiles.

This chapter has explored the specific glass beads that have been found in inhumations, other objects found in inhumations, the wider patterns of dress found through excavation, as well as more widespread patterns in other artefact data from the PAS database. It has explored the ways in which dress may have conveyed different identities, from the community to the individual, as a way of understanding the meaning behind dress in Iron Age Britain. While the resolution of dress data is unclear in many respects, it is apparent that dress varied on a regional level, but that on an individual level there may have been more at play. For example: the amount of physical labour undertaken, the situation or occasion for wearing these particular items of dress, and finally the posture or other gestures used by individuals, may all have effected the choices and decisions associated with dress. This chapter has built on the data presented in the previous two analysis chapters, and this data will be brought together for discussion in the next and final chapter.

Chapter 9
Glass Beads in their Social Context

This research set out to examine the archaeological evidence for dress in Iron Age Britain. It has shown that by drawing on multiple lines of evidence, it is possible to begin to develop a narrative of dress. In general, studies of material culture from Iron Age Britain often focus on the increasing visibility of materiality that was especially expressed in later Iron Age depositions (Hill 1995a). Growing and strengthening contacts with continental Europe are often cited as the key explanation for change in material culture in the Late Iron Age (Fitzpatrick 1990; Haselgrove 1982). Although the cause and effect relationship for this change has already been critically questioned (Hill 2007), it has become clear that this is not the pattern seen with all material. It has been possible to show that the frequency of glass beads peaked earlier than that seen with brooches (e.g. Haselgrove 1997), which along with pottery have been taken to be reflective of material culture patterns. This suggests that materiality may not have been linear, which has implications for understanding a number of artefacts in circulation during this period, as so many of the examples were found in intentional deposits, such as those in East Yorkshire.

The aims of this research focused on three key areas. First, to systematically and critically evaluate the appearance, chronology, and deposition of glass beads; second, to investigate glass beads within a wider context of other objects associated with dress in the Iron Age; and finally, to use the archaeological record to begin to develop a narrative of dress in Iron Age Britain. The following sections will summarise the key themes and expand on the significance for understanding dress and identity during this period, and it will highlight areas where future research could begin to address the questions that remain.

Glass Beads in Iron Age Britain

Through both a typological approach and systematic analysis of four key physical characteristics, this study has demonstrated that Iron Age glass beads from Britain were extremely diverse. This realisation was not something that was easily apparent from the Guido classification, which in effect obscured the level of variability. No doubt this could simply be the result of different approaches to classification, and the differences produced by 'lumpers' and 'splitters' (Adams 1988, 45). However, I have tried to be as clear as possible as to how the typology was created, and the ways in which it was intended to be used. My interest here was in understanding how aspects, such as shape, colour, and decorative motif, were used and manipulated to create the desired bead.

Beyond typology, the analyses have shown that clear regional patterns are visible in the use of colour and decorative motif. Some regions had a greater range of colours and combinations of colours, while others were more restricted. The colour blue and its combination with white for decorated beads are especially characteristic of East Yorkshire, while colourless and yellow glass beads were found in large numbers in Southwest England. Beads from Northeast Scotland on the other hand, were made from a large variety of colours, but they were consistently decorated with yellow glass. Here, blue and white glasses were used very infrequently. The regional patterns of colour suggest that, if glass beads were manufactured in Britain, then there was limited, if any, exchange of raw material. The use of these colours and combination of colours may have held regional significance, perhaps identifying local inhabitants, versus non-local visitors.

Patterns of decorative motif showed that the applied-spiral and different types of eye beads were characteristic of this period. The spiral was found on large numbers of glass beads from Southwest England and Northeast Scotland, but was not found in the same numbers in East Yorkshire. Instead, in this region, it is eye beads that were predominately found. However, it is unclear why the spiral should manifest itself so distinctly in both Southwest England and Northeast Scotland, and why the eye bead, which is found throughout much of southern Britain, is not a motif found in Northeast Scotland. As with colour, these different motifs may have been reflecting a strong sense of regional identity. Some of the beads probably originated from continental Europe, given some of the visual affinities between these beads. However, the meaning and identity portrayed when worn is unclear. For example, it is unclear if they were imported in the strict commodity sense, or whether they were brought to Britain through movements of people and subsequently became a part of the social interactions through exchange or deposition. In either case, it may be that these beads were recognised as exotic or foreign and may have indicated a message about the wearer.

In all respects, the glass beads from East Anglia are the most anomalous. These beads, although extremely few in number, exhibit one of the highest levels of variability within the study regions. Several of the beads are unparalleled, even when taking Britain as a whole into consideration (based on Guido's catalogue). This has been shown to be true for their appearance, but also for the ways in which they were deposited. Although the evidence is limited in this region, glass beads from secure find contexts have all been found in circumstances that suggest either ritual or otherwise intentional deposition behaviour, which could be reflecting the wider regional practice of metalwork deposition. The earliest example is the beads from Grandcourt Quarry in the Middle/Late Iron Age. Given the evidence for other intentionally deposited artefacts in this region, especially at Ken Hill near Snettisham, perhaps this should not be considered to be too unusual.

From the feature data, we can see three broad regional patterns. Although not every artefact followed this pattern, glass beads were found in hoard, votive pits, or other special deposits in East Anglia, with inhumations in East Yorkshire, in pits and a limited number of inhumations in Southwest England, and in other settlement features in both Southwest England and in Northeast Scotland. These differing patterns of deposition suggest that Iron Age people were doing different things with glass beads. This patterned deposition occurred at different times in the Iron Age, which reflects both regional and chronological practices. Due to these differing practices, it is possible to suggest that the artefact biography of each of these objects would have been different and it is not possible to interpret the meaning of all glass beads in the same way.

Differences in artefact biography add to some of the difficulty of establishing a chronology of glass beads. There is little evidence to suggest that glass bead types or other characteristics followed a linear pattern of development. Instead, each bead would be a part of the habitus of the community, which may have resulted in deposition. This depositional date does not indicate the length of time that a bead was in use, or the time of manufacture. The depositional practice suggests that most beads were deposited in the Middle Iron Age, but the length of time that the beads were cycling through different communities prior to this event is not clear. Although possible, it is unclear if older beads were melted down to create new beads, thus hampering studies of frequencies, chronology, and type.

As three of the four study regions were chosen due to the high frequency of glass beads from several key sites, there is the danger that this study contains an inherent bias. Hundreds of beads have been found at sites, such as Wetwang/Garton Slack in East Yorkshire, Culbin Sands in Morayshire, and Meare Lake Village in Somerset. In contrast, only a few Iron Age glass beads were initially known from East Anglia, some of which were from dubious contexts. Recently excavated sites (within the last ten years) have found large numbers of finds from these regions, which has significantly added to our understanding (i.e. Chesil mirror burial in Dorset, Grandcourt Quarry in Norfolk, and Culduthel Farm near Inverness).

It may be that outside of these regions, the beads differ in form and date. This study has not considered the Late Iron Age activity from the Southeast, such as at Kent or Essex. However, a cursory examination of the evidence from sites, such as King Harry's Lane (Stead and Rigby 1989), and Stanway (Crummy 2007) has revealed that glass beads were either absent, or not found in large numbers at these sites. The examples found at King Harry's Lane were plain beads with no decoration (Stead and Rigby 1989). A possible exception being the two fragments of glass beads from the burial in Welwyn Garden City in Hertfordshire (DB 5053, DB 5054). However, the context of these finds suggest that they were used as games pieces rather than worn on the body (Stead 1967). It is possible, given a wider geographic area of study, that the pattern established in this study will remain as the dominant Britain-wide pattern.

The best evidence for the way in which these glass beads were used is derived from their inclusion in burials. Inhumations covered by this study where the placement of the beads has been recorded include most of the inhumations with glass beads from Wetwang Slack in East Yorkshire, and Whitcombe burial 8 in Dorset. Where recorded, glass beads were often found around the neck region of the individual suggesting that they were probably worn as a necklace. It is likely that beads found with the Cleveland cist burial in Somerset, Barrow L at Cowlam, and the Queen's Barrow at Arras also formed necklaces, although their position was not recorded. While the beads from all of these burials are generally similar in size (approximately 10mm in diameter and height), the Chesil mirror burial beads from Dorset are very unusual. As it was not possible to record the placement of the beads, it is unclear how they related to the body, and thus interpretations of their use are very difficult. Four of the five beads are very large and they do not form a consistent pattern, as with the other necklaces. It remains a possibility that they were worn around the neck, but equally they could have been used as charms or talismans suspended from the mirror, or used as spindle whorls.

The glass beads from burial features give us the best associations between artefacts and individuals. Giles (2012) has already noted the preponderance of blue glass beads associated with mature women at Wetwang Slack, and has suggested that there may be some connection between the beads and mature female identity. However, the inhumations with glass beads accounted for less than 5% of the population at the cemetery. It is not clear if these women were contemporaries, or whether they lived over the course of the use of the cemetery. However, they are representative of such a small section of the population that it seems unlikely that the beads represented femininity or maturity alone, as there were 200 other adult women buried at the site. Instead, I have suggested here that the beads may be representative of a network of connections between different communities, as several of the types found at the Queen's Barrow at Arras have been found on the necklaces at Wetwang. The two 'Meare style' beads found at Wetwang Slack may represent further contacts, while the unusual melon beads may indicate connections with continental communities.

The blue melon beads are an enigma, as no other examples have been found in Britain. It may be that they are another type that was manufactured in Europe. Alternatively, it may be that these beads were manufactured locally at an as yet unidentified location. In this case, these beads may have represented a sense of belonging to the community, perhaps with ties to nearby communities, such as at Rudston and Burton Fleming. With so many of the bead types isolated to this region, and the small number of individuals that wore them, perhaps they were meaningful to the people of this region and not considered appropriate to trade or exchange outside of the area.

In contrast to the burial evidence, there were the glass beads from settlements and other special deposits. Although they were not closely associated with human remains, they nonetheless are informative about wider discussions of regionality. This research has shown that there are strong regional patterns in the use of colours, decorative motifs, and the deposition of glass beads, suggesting that their use indicated a regional identity. However, it is intriguing that there was limited overlap for some physical characteristics, such as the spiral motif occurring in all regions, but with the largest number in Southwest England and Northeast Scotland. Guido (1978a, 76) suggested that this was due to a migration of glass workers from Meare to the area around Culbin Sands, although she thought that there was at least several hundred years between the two production centres. Surprisingly, the radiocarbon dates for the glass beads at Culduthel Farm near Inverness suggest that the glass beads, or perhaps glass working, at this site could have been contemporary with the Meare Lake Village activity at the earliest (Headland Archaeology, pers. comm.). Why the spiral motif was so important for both of these communities is unclear, however, it is interesting that the colour used on the bodies of these beads contrast both light (Southwest England) and dark (Northeast Scotland), but beads from both regions utilised yellow for the decoration extensively.

The implications for this study is that glass beads in the different regions follow different patterns, which may reflect wider patterns of dress and identity. The frequency of these objects suggests that glass beads were an important part of dress in all regions, with the exception of East Anglia. However, the glass beads from the inhumations in East Yorkshire is a reminder that large numbers of beads does not necessarily mean that many people were wearing them. Thus, the hundreds of glass beads from Meare Lake Village may only have constituted a handful of necklaces when strung together. It is this idea of rarity that I now wish to discuss.

This research has shown that despite the growing number of excavations through developer-led projects that this object type has not similarly increased in numbers. In some cases, this may be due to the size or the location of the excavation in relation to the rest of the site. It could also be down to the type of site that was excavated. Even at the Wetwang excavations, the proportion of any burial with a single or many glass beads in minuscule. Therefore, glass beads seem to be quite a rare artefact. This brings us to a number of issues:

- Is rarity simply an effect of excavation location and methodology, including the lack of sieving, and the bias towards the recovery of metalwork during metal-detecting?
- Is this rarity a reflection of depositional and survival factors and we are seeing a reduced number of glass beads that were in use in the Iron Age?
- Is this rarity proportionally reflecting the real numbers of glass beads in use in the Iron Age?

Research history and excavation factors probably play some role in the material culture found, but it will never be possible to excavate everywhere or recover every shred of evidence. However, it may be that the material culture that has been recovered is the result of specific practices in the past. Willis (1997) and Hill (1995b) have both shown that there is a significant differences between the number of pottery vessels found and the estimated number of pottery vessels in use at any given time. Could glass beads be comparatively similar? Again, this returns to the biography of the artefacts and the inherent partibility of beads and how artefacts should be counted. Pots are quite different in this respect, as we can tell whether a vessel is whole or fragmented. Beads, on the other hand, are simultaneously a part and a whole. If each single bead deposition in a given area actually made up a single object (i.e. a strand of beads), some beads may not have been deposited and remain missing, and others may never be recovered. In any case, it would be impossible to determine whether the beads from different contexts were worn together. However, if they did, then hypothetically, there would be even fewer people wearing glass beads.

Finally, assuming that the glass beads were rare in the Iron Age, what does this mean for how they were treated, or how the people that wore them were treated? Others have suggested that glass beads were 'exotic' and a 'luxury' due to their valuable nature (Guido 1978a;

Henderson 1992). As they were high-status objects, they were worn by high-status individuals. Glass beads certainly would have had a value in the Iron Age, but does value necessarily equate to high-status? Perhaps status was expressed in more ways than simply by wearing more objects, and was reflected by a person's place in the community and relationships outside of the community, than simply through material culture. For example, Lindow Man was not found with any other associated artefacts that he might have been wearing, other than the fox fur armband and the possible necklace (or possible garrotte) around his neck (Stead, Bourke *et al.* 1986, 38). However, it was the delicate treatment of his fingernails that suggested that he did not engage in manual labour, as they were finely kept (Stead, Bourke *et al.* 1986, 66). Therefore, an individual wearing glass beads may have stood out, but this does not mean that they were higher in status. Glass beads are perhaps best explained as a potentially valuable object, worn by some, that may have reflected regional identities rather than status or other individual identities.

Dress in Iron Age Britain

Glass beads did not exist outside of a world of other dress artefacts. A general comparison of the changing materiality from the Bronze Age to the Iron Age suggests that concern, display, and manipulation of appearances fluctuated throughout this period (Hill 1997; Jundi and Hill 1997; Roberts 2007). The material record suggests that in the Late Bronze Age and Early Iron Age, there was generally less material related to bodily adornment or dress. This period is frequently considered to be one of social change (Hill 1995a). By the Later Iron Age, artefacts worn on the body and those that assist with the care and maintenance of the body become more numerous, such as brooches (Haselgrove 1997; Jundi and Hill 1997), tattooing (Carr 2005) and toilet instruments (Eckardt 2008; Hill 1997). The implications are that there was a changing attitude towards the body, in terms of how the body should by styled, groomed, or dressed.

Glass beads fit in differently with the available evidence. Instead of a major increase in the materiality of the Late Iron Age, this study has shown that for the study regions researched, artefacts were more numerous in the Middle Iron Age, and fewer finds date to the Late Iron Age. Although not one of the object types chosen for the present study, it is interesting that beads made from other types of material (i.e. jet, amber, clay) are not used extensively during this period either. There are a few amber beads from the East Yorkshire burials (Stead 1979), but in general, the use of amber during this period is very restricted (Beck 1991, 105). Grandcourt Quarry is an exception to this pattern as sixty-two amber beads were recovered mostly from the pottery-rich zone during the excavation (Malone 2010) as well as the large amber beads from the Birdlip burial in Gloucestershire (Bellows 1881). In general though, there is not a pre-existing tradition for the use of other types of beads that was subsequently replaced by glass beads, which was then replaced by Roman beads. Instead, the available evidence indicates the development of the use of glass beads emerges independently of a previous thriving tradition.

This study sought to bring together multiple lines of evidence to compare dress in multiple regions. This has shown that even by taking the largest assemblage of artefacts (brooches) into account, most objects appear to have been deposited in the Middle-Late Iron transition, rather than firmly in the Late Iron Age period. Interestingly, there is evidence for objects of dress being worn in the Early Iron Age, such as pins and bracelets (or other arm-rings). While there clearly was a jump in the number of objects deposited between the Early-Middle Iron Age versus the Middle-Late Iron Age, this early period was not devoid of such objects. On the one hand it could be argued that this represents an even earlier increase in continental contact; however, the decline in the use of glass beads and change in material culture by the Late Iron Age further supports that this was a period of fluctuation and redefinition of identities. It may be that brooches came to replace the use of glass beads by the Late Iron Age.

The organisation and display of individuals is a challenging topic for this period due to the lack of burial evidence. However, by examining the wider patterns of materiality, it is clear that there were regional patterns of dress. The evidence for both East Yorkshire and Southwest England suggests that a wide variety of brooches, pins, and bracelets were worn. In East Anglia on the other hand, many of these types of artefacts were rare, or at least overshadowed by the large number of pre-conquest torcs. Other examples were rarely found outside of Norfolk and Suffolk, while in contrast the post-conquest collars were found in all other study regions. There is little evidence for dress artefacts prior to the first few centuries AD (except perhaps some glass beads if the radiocarbon dates from Culduthel are more widely applicable) in Northeast Scotland. It is at this period that we can attributed many of the massive style armlets, which as with the emergence of glass beads, there is little evidence to show that these objects replaced an earlier tradition (unless made from organic material). Overall, the evidence points to a strongly regional character of dress, whether it incorporated a highly material component or not.

Entwistle (2000) emphasised the situational and experiential aspects of dress. While this is difficult to assess for Iron Age Britain, it seems that some tasks would have been challenging when wearing some of the heavier items, such as torcs and collars, bracelets, anklets, and necklaces of glass beads. These individuals may have either removed these objects while undertaking tasks or labour, or they may have been worn for special occasions. On the other hand, if this was a society with different social ranks (not necessarily to the extreme of the hierarchical triangle), then perhaps some individuals did not participate in labour intensive tasks or other activities that may have damaged the objects. In the future, it would be useful to closely examine bracelets and finger-rings to determine whether there is any indication that they were worn while engaging in activities.

Areas for Future Research and Conclusion

Building on the results and interpretations of this research, there are several key areas that need to be studied in order to advance our understanding of prehistoric glass, dress, identity, and society during the Iron Age. First, as this research examined in detail four study regions, further analysis would benefit from a wider geographic scope. In particular, a study of the remainder of southern Britain would enable a better understanding of material culture and differing practices especially in the Later Iron Age. Other key areas for further comparison include the East Midlands, Wales, and the Western Isles of Scotland. Ideally, a review of all the evidence for Britain would be beneficial, and could allow wide-scale comparisons of patterns.

Second, as archaeological evidence already suggests that glass beads and other objects either originated or were inspired by continental traditions, it would be beneficial if a systematic comparison between the British and European material was made. Much of the previous work that has been published compares British objects of dress with continental examples, but only consider single artefact types (e.g. Dunning 1934b), artefacts within a small geographic area, and are greatly out of date (e.g. Stead 1965; 1979). In addition, there is often a preference for the comparison of metalwork, rather than objects of other materials (i.e glass). By undertaking a comparison of a variety of groups of material culture related to dress and display that builds on the present research, cross-channel comparisons of dress and identity will be enabled. This will provide insight into the changing dynamic of Iron Age society in Britain and in continental Europe.

A third area of future research is further scientific investigation of prehistoric glass. The work pioneered by Bertini (2012) through the use of LA-ICP-MS, and other techniques on Scottish beads, has already demonstrated the valuable nature of such analyses. One problem that such analyses would be able to assist in answering is in the effects of weathering on glass. The surface of a glass object can be both chemically and mechanically weathered (Newton and Davison 1989). If two beads that were made from the same glass batch were left to be weathered under different conditions, then today they may appear to be more different than they were initially. Chemical analysis may be able to determine the extent of the similarity or differences between glass compositions, despite differing appearances.

Coupled with the scientific investigation is the need for experimental work, which forms a fourth area for future research. Through experimentation, from the creation of raw glass and the manufacture of beads, it would be possible to better understand the tools, techniques, skill, and scope of glass manufacture and working. Through such work, it would also be possible to observe the types of debitage, scrap, or other detritus that may or may not accumulate. These clues may help us to identify such activity in the archaeological record.

Although not so much an area of research, this work has highlighted the absolute need for systematic environmental sampling at the very least for identifying otherwise unnoticed small glass objects in the archaeological record. Both the finds from Culduthel Farm and the 2001 Wetwang Slack chariot burial attest to the extremely small size of some examples. These are unlikely to be found in settlement contexts without the aid of sieving.

Supplementing the study of glass beads is the need for comparative studies of other artefacts related to dress. This book could only lightly delve into this topic, due to the vastness of the evidence. It has proposed a very basic way of comparing several other types of artefacts. In some cases, typologies already existed that could be used for analysis. However, in most cases this was not possible and a typology needed to be proposed in order to identify Iron Age examples and aid in comparisons. Further studies of this material are needed, and this research has highlighted not only this need, but the amount of material that is available for analysis.

Finally, a glass bead is not just an object and neither is it simply a dot on a map. They are, instead, the result of a complex mesh of cultural reasoning and practices that do not offer a straightforward explanation. However, practices do emerge from the data as we can see clear patterns that suggest that they were culturally constituted in use and in deposition. From this analysis of four study regions, this suggests that their use not only varied through time, but also regionally.

Appendix A
Terminology and Guide to Recording Glass Beads

The quality of the descriptions of glass beads varies between archaeology reports and the typologies designed by Guido (1978a), Stead (1979), Dent (1984), and Gray (Bulleid and Gray 1966). Therefore, for comparability, consistency and clarification it became necessary to define a number of terms. The necessary terminology concerns the description of the physical appearance of the beads, namely: size, shape, colour, and decoration.

Glass beads dating to the Iron Age are often very simple in their nature compared to other time periods and cultures, but they do require a specialised and standardised vocabulary for describing them. Iron Age beads could exhibit an unlimited number of characteristics; however, their one key aspect is that they have a single central perforation that allows the object to be strung. Although similar types of objects with multiple perforations (i.e. 'spacer beads') existed in previous periods, such as on Bronze Age jet necklaces, there is no evidence for their use in the Iron Age. If they were used, then they were likely made from organic material that has not preserved. Beads with off-centre perforations are considered to be pendants and to date have also not been found in Iron Age contexts. Caution is also needed when classifying an object as a bead, as beads and spindle whorls can sometimes be confused (Liu 1978). Both of these objects can be very small and have a centrally located perforation and it can serve as both a bead and spindle whorl at different times. Context of deposition would be the ideal method for distinguishing between whorls and beads, but as has been shown in this research, unless the deposition was made in an inhumation, the feature gives very little indication as to how the object was used.

Dimensions and Shape

Description of the size of glass beads is based on three primary measurements (Figure 182). As the majority of glass beads from the Iron Age were round when viewed from the perforated end, **Diameter** is used to describe the line that passes through the perforation. In some examples, beads are not perfectly round or they may have had intentional decorative protrusions. In these cases, the maximum diameter was recorded. For beads that were not round when viewed from the perforation end, Length and Width measurements were taken through the perforation. In order to make this measurement comparable throughout the study, the larger of length and width was compared with bead diameters.

The second measurement, **Height**, refers to the length from one end of the perforation to the other end. Together, diameter and height express the overall size of each bead. Just as the overall size of each bead varied, so too did the size of the perforation. This reflects both the size of the mandrel that the bead was formed on, and the maximum size of the material that could be used to string each bead onto. This measurement is referred to as **Perforation Diameter**.

Closely related to dimensional data is bead shape. The terminology used here largely follows the terms used by Guido, although she did not explicitly define them. It is essential to define them here, as they are used throughout (Figure 183). Others (especially Beck 1928), have used shape in conjunction with a Diameter:Height ratio of bead measurements. For example, a perfect sphere would have a 1:1 ratio. A modern 1 pence coin would have a 20.35:1.67 ratio or could be described as 12.19, meaning that the diameter is much larger than the height and is therefore disc shaped. What this describes is the relative diameter compared to the height. Thus all round beads with a value of 1 would be perfectly spherical, while a round bead with a ratio value of 2 would be roughly disc shaped. Beck (1928) used these ratios in his universal approach to classifying bead shape. This comprehensive guide divided beads into Long, Standard, Short, and Disc beads according to their Diameter:Height ratio.

This differentiation in shape for round beads is largely followed throughout the analyses, but with some modification (Figure 184). Round bead shape terms are termed **barrel, globular,** and **annular.** This approach has been especially useful as beads between about 1.4 and 1.7 are often difficult to differentiate between globular and annular beads with these proportions. However, it is recognised that these definitions are completely arbitrary and may not reflect the shape types used by the Iron Age glassworker (see Figure 21 and Figure 51). One might expect that there would be clear distinctions between beads of more spherical shape and those that are more disc-like in shape. However, as the analyses showed in Chapter 6, this is not the case. Instead, beads described as globular and annular form a continuous spread between the boundaries of both descriptions. This suggests that the rules for creating bead shapes were not clearly defined. Instead of thinking of these shape terms as permanent and unbending, especially for globular, annular, and barrel beads, it is better to think of them as towards one end of the spectrum or another.

The majority of linear measurements were taken first-hand using a set of plastic digital calipers. On some fragmented beads, particularly those where less than 50%

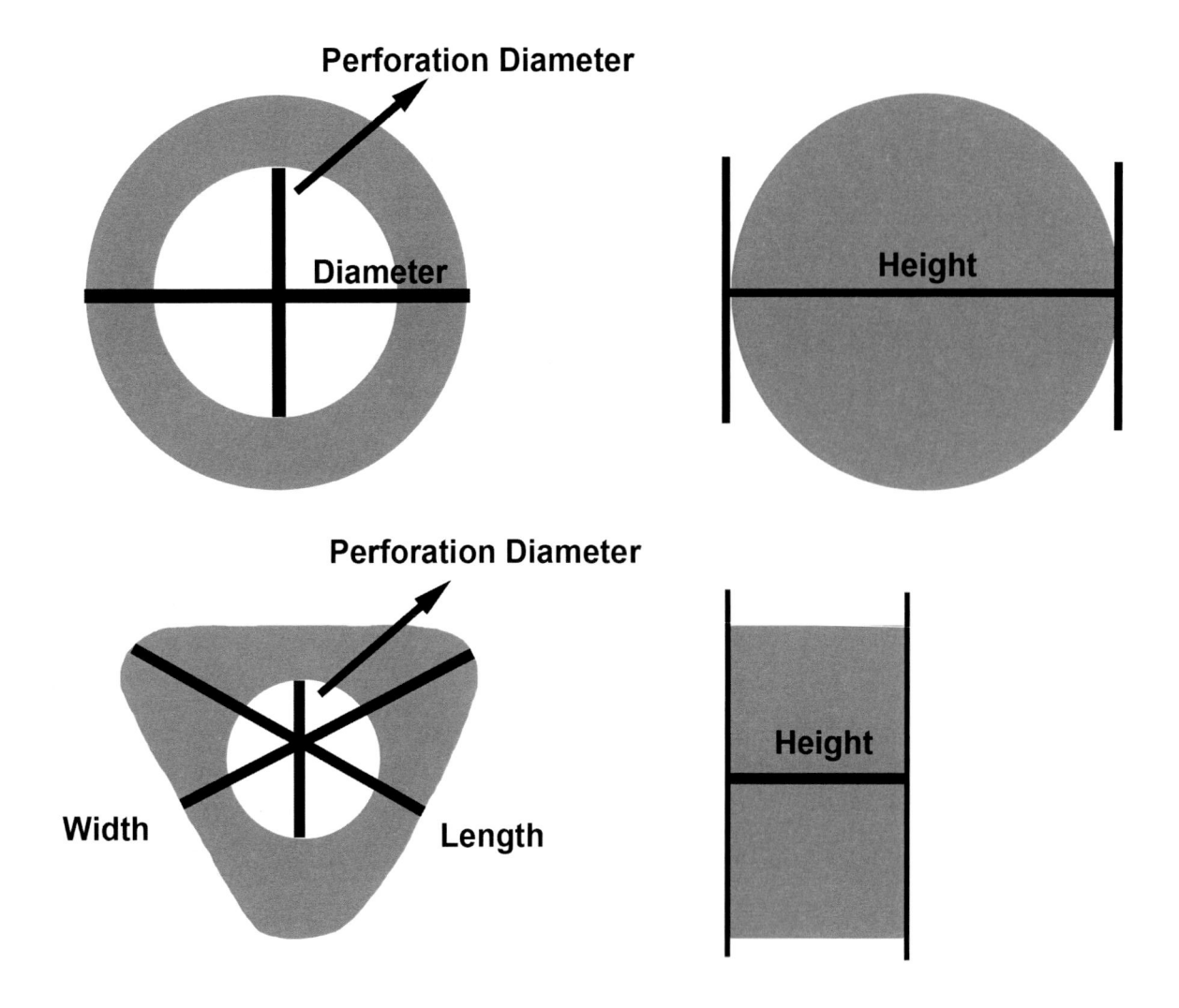

Figure 182: Bead measurements of round and non-round beads.

remained, the diameter could be estimated. As a digital photograph of each bead was taken with a scale bar at the time of analysis, measurements of fragmented beads could be estimated with the aid of computer software. ImageJ (available for free: http://imagej.nih.gov/ij/) was used for this purpose and tests that were conducted have shown that this is a fairly accurate method for measuring glass beads.

In addition to bead dimensions, the weight of each bead was recorded where possible (i.e. when not mounted permanently onto a display board, or strung together for display). This was accomplished with a standard digital pocket scale.

Colour and Decorative Motif

Providing a description of colour was perhaps one of the most challenging aspects of discussing glass beads. Such a description is made up in part by the hue, but can be affected by the degree of translucency. For example, shining light through a very translucent piece

Figure 183: Illustration of different bead shapes.

Shape	Description
Globular	A roughly spherical bead that should have a Diameter:Height ratio between 1.0 and 1.5.
Annular	A round bead that should have a Diamater:Height ratio of at least 1.5, or larger. A cross-section of the ring should be roughly D-shaped, and profile view should be rounded.
Cylindrical	A bead with a round circumference and a Diameter:Height ratio less than 1.0. The profile view should be square, rather than rounded as with annular beads.
Barrel	A round bead that has a longer height than diameter and has a Diameter:Height ratio of 0.9 or less. This bead is not to be confused with the cylindrical type as it does not have any edges and does not have a rectangular cross-section.
Sub-triangular	These beads are roughly triangular in shape, although instead of having pointed ends, they are much softer and rounded.
Truncated-triangle	These beads are roughly hexagonal and appears as though the limbs of a sub-triangular bead were removed.
Melon	This shape is named after the Roman melon beads that are most frequently made from faience, although some glass versions are known. However, this shape is also found in Iron Age contexts. It is composed of a more or less globular shaped bead, and indents are impressed into the surface of the bead and creating valleys and ridges.

Figure 184: Bead shapes as determined by ratio used throughout book.

of glass can affect the perception of its colour. In glass, both colour and opacity are manipulated through the addition of minerals or metal-oxides. Natural glass, or glass that has not been altered, will often appear as a pale translucent green due to iron impurities in the silica (Henderson 2000, 27). It is sometimes referred to as bottle-glass, although this should not be confused with colourless glass that has been decolourised through the use of additives.

In other literature about glass, discussions regarding colour are often restricted to their chemical composition obtained through the use of analytical techniques, such as XRF or SEM (e.g. Arletti, Vezzalini *et al.* 2008; Foster and Jackson 2009; Henderson 1982; Linden, Cosyns *et al.* 2009). However, chemical analysis was not a goal of this research project, as it does not describe the way in which a colour was used in combination with other colours. Nor does it aid in our exploration as to how the glass was used or provide data on the wider archaeological context. Colour can also be measured through the use of equipment, such as a spectrophotometer. The pilot study phase of this project tested the applicability of such equipment with glass beads. Unfortunately, this method was deemed unsuitable for this purpose, because the application of colour on these beads often occurs as very thin threads or small dots, which were too small for analysis. This made it impossible to apply this type of approach to all types of Iron Age glass beads, thus making it difficult to gather data for a statistically representative sample.

Due to the difficulties of describing colour in a non-subjective manner, this study relied on the observations made by the author during first-hand analysis. In many cases this allowed the published descriptions to be confirmed or elaborated where necessary. As a record of observations, the digital photographs were taken with a colour scale bar to help ensure that the photographs were taken under similar lighting conditions, and thus not distorted by lighting. It also allows for material held in different museums to be compared later, as for example the beads from the Queen's Barrow from Arras, East Yorkshire are split between the Yorkshire Museum and the British Museum. In cases where glass beads could not be viewed for the thesis, written descriptions had to be relied upon.

Each description of a colour found on an Iron Age glass bead should include the hue, whether it is translucent or opaque, and in what sense it was used on the bead. For example DB 16364 (Figure 189m) would be described as: translucent green. As a second example, DB 4316 (Figure 189x) bead would be described as: opaque yellow. Both of these examples are monochrome, so the colour refers to the body of the bead.

Guido identified 16 different motifs in her discussion of glass bead appearances (Figure 3). However, her descriptions and accompanying images left out a number of motifs and do not correctly demonstrate how the motifs are used on glass beads. As one of the attributes of physical appearance that was analysed during the research, it is necessary to define the different motifs that were found on the beads (Figure 185).

For the majority of these beads, a decorated bead was created by applying decorative elements to a monochrome bead with a contrasting colour of glass (Figure 186). This decoration is seen on beads with eye motifs, and linear designs, such as circumferential lines or zig-zags/wave motifs. For other motifs, the design is actually integral to the bead form, such as the wrapped or whirl beads (as in Figure 185). Some of the decorative motifs are continuous, such as the waves and whirls that completely encircle the bead. Others beads are made up of multiple instances of each motif. For example, motifs

⊙	Simple Eye	/////////	Cable
⊙	Complex Eye	~~~	Cable wave
⊛	Compound Eye	⊙ ◯	Perforation Colour
☰	Circumferential Lines	◐ ◐	Wrapped Beads
∿	Wave/zig-zag	✺ ❘	Ray
▦	Criss-cross	✹	Whirl
▨	Diagonal Criss-cross		
∧∧	Chevrons		Whirl with Cable
◎	Spiral		
≪≪	Pinnate		

Figure 185: Identified decorative motifs.

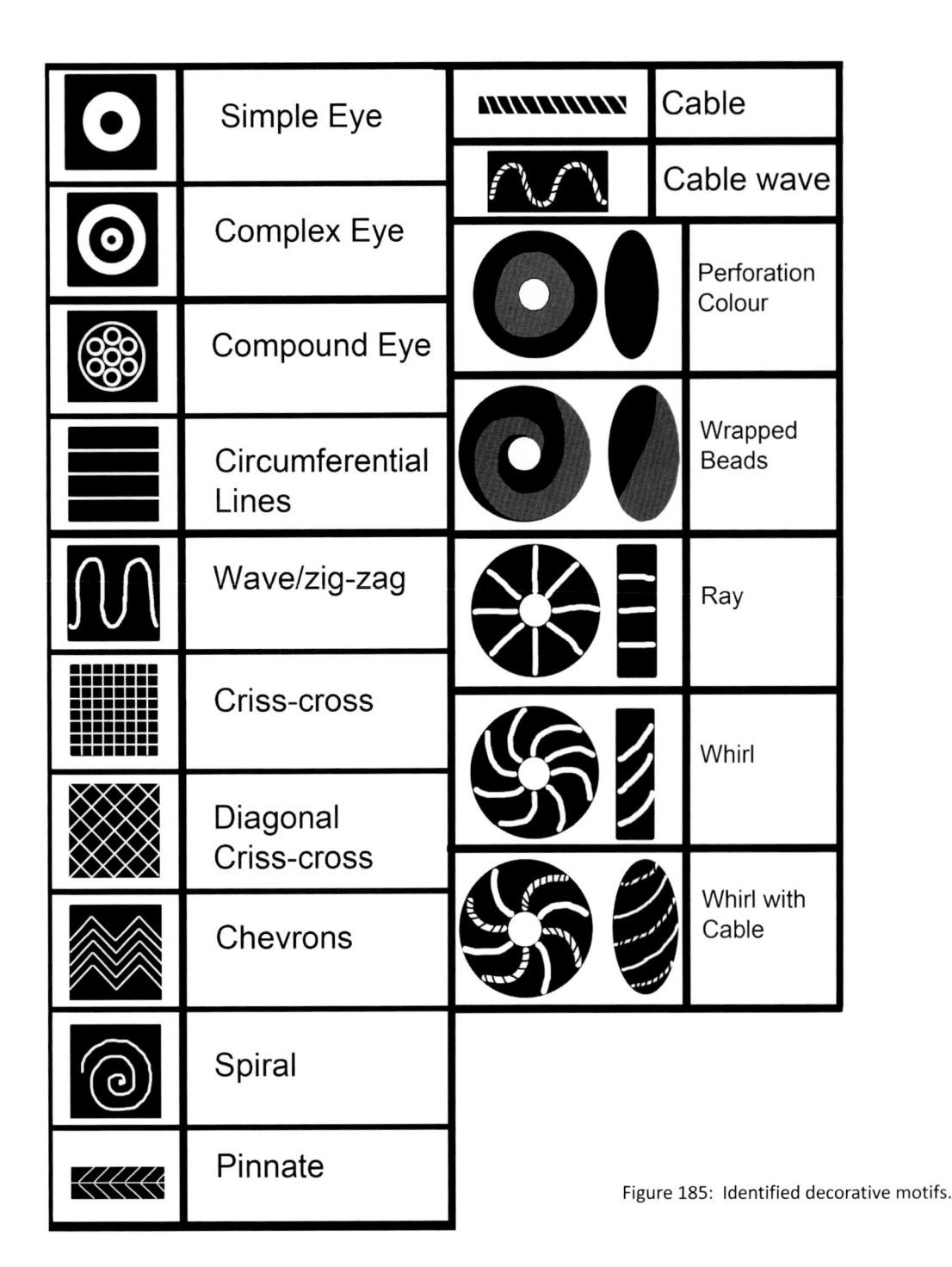

such as eyes and spirals always occur at least three times on the surface of the bead. The placement on the surface of the bead usually follows three main patterns (Figure 187). A full description of each motif can be found in Figure 188.

Other Aspects

There are a few other characteristics of glass beads that are worth recording and reporting on. In addition to measuring the perforation size, as mentioned above, the shape of the perforation should be recorded. Not all perforations are circular, as some are oval and even square. Perforations can also be described as 'tapering', where one is larger than the other, or they can be described a 'straight', where they are equal in size. This most likely relates to the shape of the mandrel used to make the bead on. Glass beads made on a mandrel are not likely to be 'hourglass' shaped, like some stone beads, due to the methods of manufacture.

The current state of the bead should also be recorded. For example, an approximation of the percent present, the degree of weathering, and whether any secondary modifications are present. It is not unusual for Iron Age glass beads to be found whole, as much of the glass of

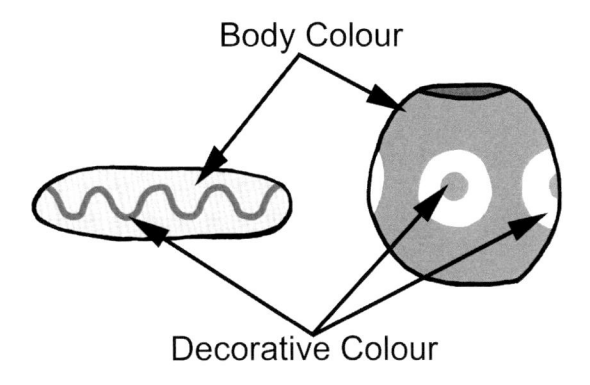

Figure 186: Example of bead colour terminology on polychrome beads with dot and linear decorative motifs.

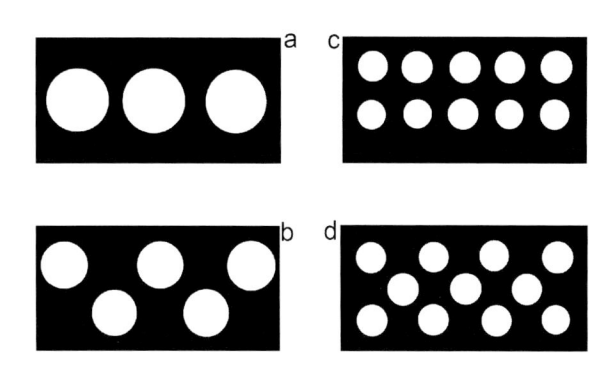

Figure 187: Diagram of motif placement on the beads. (a) single circumferential, (b) single alternating, (c) paired circumferential, (d) pairs and single circumferential.

this period appears to be very long lasting and unbroken. When they are broken, it is usually half a bead that remains although smaller pieces are also sometimes found. A few examples exhibit evidence of secondary modification (e.g. DB 11630 in Figure 191v), which should be recorded. Finally, the degree of weathering that is visible on the surface should be assessed. Brill (1999) provides a good method of assessment of weathering stages.

Photographing Glass Beads

High quality photographs are essential, not only for recording the condition and appearance of glass beads, but also to be transparent about the terminology used and to be able to make comparisons based on photographs alone. A good photograph should be well composed, lit, and there should be consistency in the way beads are presented. Ideally, the camera should be affixed to a tri-pod and shutter release cable to ensure that the user does not cause blurriness to the photograph. A spirit level should be used to ensure that the camera is square with the table. This is especially important, as it ensures that if the images are used for analytical purposes, that any measurements will be accurate.

The background and composure of a picture should be as consistent as possible. As Iron Age glass beads can be both very lightly coloured and very dark, I used a light gray photographic background to photograph them on. A black background is heavily advised against, as many of the beads are very dark. I did not use any special lighting when photographing beads, as facilities and study space at museums were variable. Instead, I used the light that was available. Ideally, the bead should be evenly lit, so details are not obscured. I used a scale bar with a colour scale to ensure that when the digital photographs were processed, images could be corrected were necessary.

Assuming the bead is complete, photographs should be taken of both perforation ends, as well as a profile view. In many cases, as beads can be irregularly shaped and decoration can extend to the non-viewable side, many photographs should be taken of the profile as the bead is rotated. This means that the entire pattern is captured. In addition to these photos, further photos may be needed to capture specific details, such as interesting or unusual features, breakage, evidence of wear, or secondary modificiation. This may include photos where the bead is positioned so that it is oblique, especially for details of the perforation hole. For consistency, fragmented beads should be photographed in the same manner for comparison with complete beads.

Due to the round and/or odd-shaped nature of glass beads (or in the case of broken beads), at least one of these views may be difficult without the bead rolling around. I took a small plastic box of white sand with me, which was used as the sand helps prop up the object when taking photographs. The box I used was also large enough for a photographic scale to be included. If at least part of one perforation end remains, it is important to take a picture of the bead squarely set into the sand box (with scale bar), so that software can be used to estimate the original diameter. I experimented with the use of a light box for illuminating transparent glass beads, which had mixed success. Often, the light was not strong enough to pass through some of the deepest glass. I found that a powerful LED torch had better success.

Chronology Terminology

One of the difficulties in comparing evidence for different areas of Britain during the Iron Age is in the terminology used to discuss chronology. As change through time is tracked by changes in settlement, artefacts, and practices for the treatment of the dead, this can be very

Motif	Description
Simple Eye	This motif was probably created by alternating two different colours of glass. The technique gives the illusion that a ring of contrasting colour is suspended within the body of the glass. An alternative method of producing this type of decoration may have been to take a small ring of the contrasting glass, and to suspend it within the main body of the bead. This alternative method is suggested by some examples where the contrasting glass has weathered out of the bead and leaves a channel and a 'mushroom' of the body glass in the centre.
Complex Eye	This motif is very similar to the simple eye, and was probably made in the same way as the two methods described above, however it is made with four layers of glass rather than two.
Compound Eye	This motif uses the same technique used for the simple eye, but in a different way. First a large simple eye is made, and then smaller eyes are placed on top of the first large eye.
Circumferential Lines	These linear lines are placed around the circumference of a bead and are more or less straight. They usually appear in groups, or combined with other motifs, rather than singly.
Wave/Zig-zag	This motif is a strand of contrasting glass that is applied in a wave or zig-zag pattern usually around the circumference of the bead. It can appear very regular or other examples show inconsistent waves. Usually, they are used singly, but there are some beads where a two-strand wave is used, sometimes in conjunction with other motifs.
Chevron	Multiple zig-zags make up chevron designs that can cover a bead's body. While zig-zags were probably formed by trailing decorative glass in this pattern, many of the chevron beads indicate a different method of decorative process. These beads appear to have been wrapped by one continuous strand of decorative glass, sometimes 10 times around the body of the bead, from one perforation end to the other. Then, a sharp instrument was lightly inserted into the surface of the bead and dragged across. This pulls the body and decorative glass in the direction pulled forming peaks.
Criss-Cross	This design is a combination of both circumferential and vertical lines (from perforation to perforation). The lines form right angles.
Diagonal Criss-cross/Lattice	This is a criss-cross design that has been applied at a 45 degree angle.
Spiral	This design appears to have been made by trailing melted glass on the surface of the bead and then heated until made flush with the surface.
Pinnate	This is called a chevron by Guido, but here it has been re-termed to avoid confusion with the zig-zag/chevron motif. The single example of this has a circumferential line with short strands branching off towards the perforation.
Cable	This is a rod formed by a twist of at least two very thin rods of glass. It is then applied to the bead.
Cable Wave	This is similar to the wave/zig-zag design, but instead it is created using a cable made by at least two colours of glass.
Perforation Colour	This is the application of a glass colour around the perforation of the bead. It extends through the perforation and lines the perforation surface. It is often irregular.
Ray	These are lines of glass in a contrasting colour that extend from the perforation and wrap around the circumference edge and back to the perforation on the other side. The lines end up more or less where they started. The inside of the perforation appears messy from the contrasting glass colour.
Whirl	This is very similar to the ray, but instead of being straight lines, they bend around the bead. On the perforation side they form a whirl design, but the circumference view has slanted lines.
Whirl and Cable	This is a more complex whirl design that alternates a cable with a solid line.
Wrapped	Beads that fall under this category are unique. They are mixture of at least two different colours and appear as though they were made from one rod of glass that was wrapped around a mandrel. More complex examples also have a cable incorporated into the rod.
Mottled/Irregular Colour	In some cases, beads exhibit polychromatism; however, there is no formal linear or other applied design. Sometimes, this is deliberate, and creates a mottled design, such as several of the Guido Group 1 beads. However, most examples are completely irregular.
All Over Bumps	These beads are monochrome in colour and are large annular or cylindrical beads with raised bumps covering the surface.

Figure 188: Description of bead decoration terminology.

regional (e.g. Harding 2004; Moore 2006b). Therefore, a common terminology is needed in order to discuss periods throughout Britain. Here, I have borrowed from Hill's (1995a) periodisation from his overview of the Iron Age in Britain:

- Early Iron Age: c. 800 – 450 BC
- Middle Iron Age: c. 450 – 100 BC
- Late Iron Age: c. 100 BC – AD 43
- Early Roman: c. 1st century AD
- Romano-British: c. end 1st century AD+

In term of the transition to the Roman period, I have used 'Early Roman' and 'Romano-British' purely as a short hand method for referring to a date range, rather than the effect of romanisation or level of interaction with the Romans. As it can be particularly difficult to separate out Late Iron Age and Early Roman period activity and these periods overlap, depending on the archaeological evidence for dating, in some cases these periods are combined and in other cases they are left separate.

Appendix B
Guido Iron Age Glass Bead Types

The Guido (1978a) typology of Iron Age glass beads has been the most significant and most used method for classifying and interpreting this object. As a supplement to the main text, for the ease of following the discussions in Chapter 5 this appendix provides descriptions of each of Guido's types, and additional details, such as their distribution and date where possible.

Class 1

The first bead in Guido's typology is the Class 1 'Arras' bead, which was named after the finds from Grave L at Cowlam and the Queen's Barrow in East Yorkshire. Guido distinguishes between two sub-types and characterised them as:

> …both [are] normally about 12mm in diameter and 10mm height. They are invariably dark blue, decorated with white rings round blue eyes…Type I [have] fewer and larger eyes…[and the] white rings have often fallen out and leave only the circular groove around the eye which is part of the ground of the bead…Type II [have] many more eyes… (1978a, 46)

The dimensions given are very vague and she does not clearly define their shape, but the dimensions suggest a globular, but not perfectly spherical shape.

Although this type of bead, especially Type II, has been found throughout England, it is especially concentrated in East Yorkshire, but also in the Severn Valley. Guido suggests that parallels between the finds from the Cowlam burial and Queen's Barrow in East Yorkshire and artefacts from Switzerland may indicate a fifth century BC date, while other examples date between the third and first centuries BC. However, she also suggests that they may originate from much further afield: in eight or seventh century BC Phoenicia, although some may have been copied in Europe.

Class 2

The Class 2 beads, also called 'Welwyn Garden City' type beads are very similar to the Class 1 beads in terms of colour and design motif. Guido defined them as:

> …rather big, globular beads made out of dark blue glass into which two registers of eyes enclosed by two irregular white circles…These 'eyes' are both very much larger and more irregular than those on the Arras Type beads just discussed (1978a, 48).

The difference between these beads and the Class 1 beads is the larger size and structure of the eye, and the arrangement of the eyes on the surface of the bead. The eyes on these beads are much more complex, whereas the Class 1 bead eyes are made from a layer of opaque white and translucent blue over the translucent blue bead base. The Class 2 bead eyes were made by layering opaque white and translucent blue twice, which created a more complex eye. The arrangement of the eyes on the beads are different from the Class 1 examples, as the illustration shows that they were placed in pairs rather than alternating pair and single eyes. However, at the time of publication, there were only two examples of this type of bead, none of which were complete examples. Therefore, it is unclear if Guido's description is an accurate reflection of this type of bead.

One of the two examples of Class 2 beads was found in the village of Wiggonholt near Pulborough in Sussex in a pit with second century AD Romano-British pottery (Evans 1974). The other example comes from a late La Tène III burial in Welwyn Garden City, Hertfordshire thought to date to the first century BC (Stead 1967). However, the location where these beads were manufactured remains unknown. Guido suggests that they may have come from northern Italy or the head of the Adriatic (Guido 1978a, 48-9). In general, she dates them to the first century BC, although as she pointed out, they could be much older.

Class 3

The Class 3 'South Harting' type is the third type of bead where eyes were used for the decorative motif. Guido described them as:

> … fairly large annular beads with a diameter of approximately 20-30mm and a height of about 15-20mm. Almost invariably they are made of dark blue glass, and they generally have three equidistant eyes…often of different coloured glass but are always surrounded with an opaque white ring. Occasionally there are only two eyes, and related specimens may have two or more registers of eyes (1978a, 49).

Guido suggested that, although there were similar beads found in France, they have yellow rings of glass instead of white ones. However, in contrast to many of her other Continental types of beads, she suggested that they may have been manufactured in Britain and then exported to the continent (1978a, 50). This explanation was supported by the larger numbers of these beads found in Britain compared to the continent. These beads are primarily found at early Romano-British sites, although Guido was adamant that they were not affiliated with Roman culture.

Class 4

The Class 4 'Findon' type were the last of the beads with an eye motif decoration. These were very different from the first three classes, as they are described as: 'opaque yellow beads with two superimposed rows of blue and white eyes' (Guido 1978a, 50). Unfortunately, Guido did not give average dimensions or an indication of the shape of these beads. However, she did state that they are a well-known type of bead on the continent, but that the blue-green versions have not been found in Britain (1978a, 50).

There is much uncertainty about the date of these beads, but Guido suggested a fourth or third century BC date (1978a, 51). However, for the continental examples she gives dates as early as the fifth century BC for examples from Villeneuve Renneville near Épernay, while other examples date from the fourth to second centuries BC. She suggested that they were probably manufactured in the Mediterranean region possibly in the sixth century BC and only survive as heirlooms in the first century BC.

Class 5

These Class 5 'Hanging Langford' beads are very different from many of the types that Guido distinguishes. They were described as:

> …annular beads…generally about 20mm in diameter and about 6mm in height; the straight perforation measures about 10mm across. Around the perforation on the inner side of the bead, an irregular and discontinuous band of opaque yellow glass has been applied in such a way that it glows through the clear colourless glass… (Guido 1978a, 51)

This description is unusual compared to Guido's other descriptions, as she was very specific by providing a general diameter, height, peroration shape and size. Two other classes in Guido's classification are also made out of colourless and opaque yellow glasses only: Class 10 and 11 beads. Both of these other classes (described in full below) were thought to have been manufactured in Britain. However, despite being made from the same colours of glass, the Class 5 beads distribution does not follow the distribution pattern seen for the Class 10 and 11 beads, thus she proposed that they are their own class. This is supported by similar finds from Continental Europe, which suggested that Class 5 beads must have been imported into Britain. In addition, some examples of bangles that existed in both Europe and Britain exhibited a very similar method of decoration. By combining this data with the continental evidence and finds in Britain, Guido suggested that these date from the second century BC to the first century AD.

Class 6

This bead type, like the Class 5 beads, is also very large, and the first of the types with an applied spiral motif. Guido described the 'Oldbury' type beads as:

> …roughly 25-30mm in diameter and rather more annular than globular, about 15-20mm in height. The perforation…is approximately 10mm wide. The glass is dark, almost opaque, blue, appearing to be nearly black sometimes unless held to the light. The ornament generally consists of three, more rarely two, registers of trailed and marvered spirals, carefully made in opaque white, or less commonly yellow glass round the circumference of the bead often on small bosses…A variant of the Oldbury Class is here called the Colchester Class (B). It is distinguished by having opaque yellow glass double swags running between the spirals (1978a, 53-4)

Thus, the sub-class B is exactly the same as the main sub-type (A), except that they have a double yellow swag placed between the spirals.

Guido pointed to continental parallels for this bead type, as similar examples have been found in Europe. In general, she suggested a date from about 150 BC until the Roman conquest. From the distribution map, she suggested that they were imported into two primary areas: southeast England and in the Bristol Channel where the beads then spread out through Britain. Some examples have been found as far north as Kilmany in Fife and one was found on the Isle of Coll in western Scotland. However, she did not speculate on the significance of these northern specimens.

Class 7

Guido had termed the Class 7 beads 'Celtic whirl' or 'ray' beads because they are:

> …large annular glass beads with whirls or rays in a contrasting colour…applied…on a blue or purple, brown, or light yellow ground and they may have a straight or rounded hour-glass perforation. The whirls or rays emerge from the perforation. In addition some of the beads have circumferential bands of a contrasting colour, usually underlying the whirls (1978a, 57).

The class was sub-divided into three types depending on the main colour of the bead. Thus, sub-type a has either a blue or purple ground, sub-type b beads are made with a brown or yellowish-brown colour, and finally, sub-type c is for all other colours, but mostly consists of green, white, or colourless.

Guido suggested that the type a beads dated from 150 BC to AD 50 and are found especially around the Bristol Channel area. There are, for example, the specimens from Meare and Glastonbury Lake Villages, but also at Danebury, Hampshire and at Wick Wood in Wiltshire. Type b was dated to the first century BC as examples come from Hengistbury Head in Dorset, Welwyn Garden City in Hertfordshire, and Glastonbury Lake Village in Somerset. Guido was unable to attribute a date to the type c examples, but they were mostly found in Ireland. Continental examples of whirl or ray beads are always large and annular and have been found in a variety of colours.

Class 8

As with the Class 5 beads, the Class 8 beads lacked decoration. Guido described them as:

> …small opaque yellow annular beads…sometimes extremely fine and thin…they seldom exceed 12mm in diameter…[with] flattened upper and lower surfaces often present around the perforation… (1978a, 73)

These beads were found throughout Britain, although notable concentrations have been found at Meare Lake Village in Somerset, and at Culbin Sands in Morayshire. However, they were notably absent from the eastern half of Britain below the modern Scottish border. Assuming that they were all made at Meare Lake Village, Guido suggested that they originated in the third to second century BC, and that the people who possessed the knowledge for glasswork moved to Scotland and continued making these beads there until Agricola ended their manufacturing. Therefore, the northern examples may date to the same time as the Meare Lake Village examples or may date to a later period: first century BC to early first century AD.

Class 9

Guido described this class as:

> …annular beads decorated with two-colour twisted cables…sub-divided according to the group colour, as follows: (A) natural glass [translucent green]; (B) cobalt blue or purple; (C) brown or golden brown. All these cable decorated beads are annular in shape, and vary usually between 20 to 30mm in diameter, and 10 to 15mm in height… (Guido 1978a, 77)

From Guido's description, the key aspect that sets these beads apart from other beads is the use of the cable as the primary decorative motif. However, some of Guido's Class 14 beads, which are discussed below, also include the use of the cable, it is the way in which it was applied that distinguishes these two classes apart. The three sub-types suggest that the colour choice for this class is limited to translucent green, blue, purple, and browns.

Although Guido discussed the date of these beads individually by sub-type, in general these beads are dated to the first century BC and she suggested that they 'died out' by the first century AD (Guido 1978a, 77). She suggested that they were made somewhere in the south, again possibly around Meare Lake Village, as they are found especially in the Bristol Valley. These glass bead makers moved to Scotland around 50 BC, and continued to make glass beads with cables (Class 14), but they were only poor imitations of the Class 9 beads (Guido 1978a, 79). She also saw a connection between both cable beads (Class 9 and 14) and the manufacture of some glass armlets (Guido 1978a, 78-9).

Class 10

These are perhaps one of the best known of all Iron Age glass beads from Britain. Guido described these beads as:

> …translucent and colourless, usually globular in shape, but some of the spirals were slightly flattened by marvering into a sub-triangular shape. The dimensions of these beads vary from about 9 to 14mm in height, and 11 to 18mm in diameter. The perforations are small and neatly made. The decoration consists of three carefully wound spirals in opaque yellow glass, occupying almost the whole surface of the bead (Guido 1978a, 79).

This description and the illustrations of the Class 10 beads suggested a fairly homogeneous assemblage.

The date of these beads is largely dependent on the dates of the finds at Meare Lake Village in Somerset, as it is at this site that they are found in their largest numbers. Guido suggested that these beads flourished between 250 BC and AD 50, although their use may have ended earlier due to the influx of the Belgae (Guido 1978a, 81).

Class 11

These are beads that Guido has termed 'Meare variant beads', meaning that they were variations on the Class 10 spiral bead. She described them as:

> …colourless glass beads decorated with opaque yellow designs. Although the decoration of these 'Meare variant' beads is dissimilar, it is clear that they are all closely related among themselves, and were in all probability produced in the same workshop (Guido 1978a, 81).

She identified 11 different 'variants' according to their decorative motif. The most common sub-type is 'a', which is decorated with multiple chevrons along the circumference of the bead. For many of the other sub-types, there has so far been only one example of each.

As there are so few examples of most of the sub-types, very few dates or date ranges were given. However, on the advice of Michael Avery, Guido suggested that the class a beads were contemporary with the Class 10 spiral beads, so this puts them around the mid-third century to the first century BC (Guido 1978a, 82). Again, with the type g wave beads, Avery puts these at the first centuries BC/AD (Guido 1978a, 83).

Class 12

These beads are unusual in their shape, as they appear to be a larger annular bead attached to a smaller one. Guido describes them as: '…two elements, one larger than the other like a modern collar stud' (Guido 1978a, 84). Of the two known examples, one is made completely out of opaque yellow glass, while the other one is made from colourless glass with opaque yellow zig-zags. This class is entirely based on shape as the former more closely resembles the Class 8 annular beads, although it was found at Lidbury camp in Wiltshire, and the latter resembles several of the Class 11 variants and was found at Meare Lake Village in Somerset.

Despite there being so few examples in this class, Guido suggested a third or second to - first century BC date for this type of bead. Again, as there were no other known examples from the continent, Guido regards these as having been manufactured in Britain (Guido 1978a, 84).

Class 13

These 'North Scottish spiral-decorated beads' are another bead to utilise the applied spiral motif. Guido described them as:

> …similar in size (11-22mm in diameter and 10-18mm in height), shape, and pattern to the Class 10 [beads]…, but they differ in two main aspects: they more generally show a slightly angular shape …and the bead is never colourless, but … greenish, brown, dark blue or some other dark colour. The spirals are invariably yellow and the perforations small (Guido 1978a, 85).

From her description of Class 13 beads, it is implied that they exactly parallel the Class 10 beads, except that they are more angular, and never colourless.

Although Guido saw a possible connection between the Class 13 beads and their southern inspiration, the Class 10 bead, Guido discounted the possibility that these beads were somehow related to continental examples. The continental versions were descried by Guido as '…more triangular in shape and nearly always on a blue ground' and as only 'superficially similar' to the Scottish versions (1978a, 85). Instead, as with the Class 8 and Class 14 beads, the Class 13 beads were made by glassworkers who migrated from Meare Lake Village in Somerset and began to make 'inferior' beads in northeast Scotland (1978a, 81). She suggested that they began to migrate in the first century BC and that the Class 14 beads date to as late as about the first century AD or perhaps as late as the late second century AD, but that the Agricolan conquest probably put an end to the production of glass beads (Guido 1978a, 81, 87).

Class 14

Guido's final class is the Class 14: 'North Scottish decorated annular beads'. She described them as:

> …no two beads are identical, and it is only by a certain generic resemblance which they share that they can be isolated as a class…The colours are nearly always opaque and include mostly blues, mauves, and browns; an opaque yellow element is present in almost every example. In size they vary from over 30mm in diameter to a few mm…A closer look at the patterns with which they are decorated shows that these are derived from two elements: whirls or rays as in the Celtic beads of Class 7, and the ladder patterns which are in effect imitation cables (1978a, 87).

Despite differences in colour and decorative motifs, she did not sub-divide these beads into sub-types. She offers little else in the way of description, and as will be shown in the new typology, there is a considerable amount of variability and difference within the Class.

Group 1

Guido (1978a) borrowed this type from Haevernick's (1960) Group 24, which is described as: '…usually blue…spattered with white or yellow dots of varying sizes,…varying from 22-45mm in diameter and 9 to 19mm in height…' (Guido 1978a, 59-60). Haevernick (1960) catalogues several from Europe, although their main concentration is in the Czech Republic, where Guido (1978a, 60) suggested that they may have been manufactured in the first century BC. In Britain, however, she dates them to around 50 BC to AD 50 (Guido 1978a, 60).

Group 2

These beads were described as 'Miscellaneous spiral-decorated beads' by Guido (1978a, 60). She gives very little information about these beads, as they do not seem to form a homogeneous group, rather, as the name suggests, they are quite varied. The one unifying characteristic is the applied spiral motif, but they are also united by their difference in appearance to Classes 6, 10, and 13.

Group 3

As with the Group 2 beads, this type is a mix of 'Miscellaneous horned beads, some with eyes or spirals' (Guido 1978a, 60). Therefore, they do not form a coherent group, nor is it possible to attribute the entire type to a period. Instead, each individual bead needs to be considered by their own evidence.

Group 4

These beads are extremely rare in Britain, but are more common on the continent. They are called 'Garrow Tor' types after a find from Bodmin Moor, Cornwall (Guido 1978a, 62). They were decorated with eye motifs, but are very different from the motifs found on Classes 1 to 4. Guido (1978a, 61) described them as:

> …generally slightly more annular than globular and about 15mm in diameter. The classic ground colour is turquoise, but more rarely dark blue and into this ground three fairly large mustard-coloured roundels are inset, surrounded by white rings, and…regularly arranged blue eyes ring with white. These eyes are stratified as in Arras Type II beads.

There are several examples of this type of bead from Britain, and a number from Ireland. However, Guido (1978a, 62) has suggested that the Irish examples do not date to the same period as the British examples as although they use the same motif, they appear to be different. She suggests that they were later copies, although there is nothing to support this later date. The British examples on the other hand, are likened to the examples from the Reinheim princess burial. These beads were thought to date to the fourth century BC, and although larger, were considered to be 'ancestral' to the British examples (Guido 1978a, 62).

Group 5

These beads have a plain coloured body and were decorated with an often contrasting colour forming a wave motif. They were subdivided into nine main types by the colours used, although sub-type d was further divided into four additional types.

Group 6 and 7

These two groups of beads are not decorated and are primarily made from single colours of glass. Group 6 beads are annular, while Group 7 beads are globular in shape. They have been sub-divided by colour and size. Group 6 sizes were defined as: Large – over 30mm in diameter, Medium – between 15 and 30mm in diameter, and small – under 15mm (Guido 1978a, 65). These size groupings are not the same as those used for Group 7 beads. Here, Large – over 15mm in diameter, Medium and Small are under 15mm in diameter (Guido 1978a, 69).

Group 8

This is the last and final group in Guido's (1978a) typology of glass beads. She called this group 'exotic beads of Iron Age date', but it seems best to describe these beads as otherwise unique as they do not fit in with any of the other type descriptions. As with several of the other Guido Groups, each of these beads included in this type need to be carefully considered on their own merits. Guido suggested that eventually parallels may be found either in Britain or the continent. This is the case for at least one such bead. Her illustration of one of these beads (her Figure 23 no. 7), a bead from Boxford in Berkshire now has a parallel that was found recently at the excavations at Totterdown Lane (Pine and Preston 2002).

Appendix C
List of All New Types

Class 1: Simple monochrome beads

A. Simple shapes

101: Annular, globular, barrel, cylinder shapes; black body colour (Figure 189a)
102: Annular, globular, barrel, cylinder shapes; blue body colour (Figure 189b-f)
103: Annular, globular, barrel, cylinder shapes; blue-green body colour (Figure 189g)
104: Annular, globular, barrel, cylinder shapes; brown body colour (Figure 189h, i)
105: Annular, globular, barrel, cylinder shapes; colourless body colour (Figure 189j, k)
106: Annular, globular, barrel, cylinder shapes; green body colour (Figure 189l-o)
107: Annular, globular, barrel, cylinder shapes; orange body colour (Figure 189p)
108: Annular, globular, barrel, cylinder shapes; purple body colour (Figure 189q, r)
109: Annular, globular, barrel, cylinder shapes; red body colour (Figure 189s, t)
110: Annular, globular, barrel, cylinder shapes; yellow body colour (Figure 189u-ab)

Class 2: Monochrome beads

A. Complex shapes

201: All over bumps; blue body colour (Figure 189ac)
202: Melon shaped; blue body colour (Figure 189ad)
203: Segmented shape; yellow body colour (Figure 189ae)
204: Stud shaped; yellow body colour

Class 3: Polychrome beads, no design motif

301: Barrel shape; body colour is colourless and red (Figure 189af)
302: Barrel shape; body colour is colourless, red, and yellow (Figure 189ag)
303: Sub-triangular shape; body colour is colourless and yellow
304: Annular shape; body colour is green, white, and yellow (Figure 189ah)
305: Annular shape; body colour is red and yellow (Figure 189ai)
306: Annular shape; body colour is red and white (Figure 189aj)

Class 4: Beads with eyes

A. Simple Eyes

410: Missing details
411: 3 eyes placed around the circumference of the bead; blue body colour, decoration is in blue and white, globular shape (Figure 190a, b)
412: 3 eyes placed around the circumference of the bead; blue body colour, decoration is blue and white, cylindrical shape (Figure 190c)
413: 3 eyes placed around the circumference of the bead; blue body colour, decoration is blue and white, annular shape (Figure 190d, e)
414: 3 eyes placed around the circumference of the bead; blue body colour, decoration is blue and white, sub-triangular shape (Figure 190f, g)
415: 3 eyes placed around the circumference of the bead; blue body colour, decoration is brown, white, and green, globular shape
416: 3 eyes placed around the circumference of the bead; blue body colour, decoration is green, orange, and white, annular shape (Figure 190h)
417: 3 eyes placed around the circumference of the bead; blue body colour, decoration is green and white, annular shape (Figure 190i-k)
418: 3 eyes placed around the circumference of the bead; blue body colour, decoration is green and white, globular shape (Figure 190l)
419: 3 eyes placed around the circumference of the bead; blue body colour, decoration is red and white, unknown shape
420: 3 eyes placed around the circumference of the bead; brown body colour, decoration is blue and white, globular shape (but some shapes are unknown) (Figure 190m)
421: 9 eyes placed around the circumference of the bead in a 2-1-2 pattern, blue body colour, decoration is blue and white; cylindrical shape (Figure 190n-o)
422: 9 eyes placed around the circumference of the bead in a 2-1-2 pattern, blue body colour, decoration is blue and white; globular shape (Figure 190p-q)
423: 9 eyes placed around the circumference of the bead in a 2-1-2 pattern, blue body colour, decoration is blue and white; unknown shape
424: 12 eyes placed around the circumference of the bead in a 2-1-2 pattern, blue body colour, decoration is blue and white; cylindrical shape (Figure 190r)
425: 12 eyes placed around the circumference of the bead in a 2-1-2 pattern, blue body colour, decoration is blue and white; globular shape (Figure 190s-t)

426: 15 eyes placed around the circumference of the bead in a 2-1-2 pattern, blue body colour, decoration is blue and white; annular shape

427: 15 eyes placed around the circumference of the bead in a 2-1-2 pattern, blue body colour, decoration is blue and white; cylindrical shape (Figure 190u)

428: 17 eyes placed around the circumference of the bead in a 2-1-2 pattern, blue body colour, decoration is blue and white; globular shape (Figure 190v)

429: 21 eyes placed around the circumference of the bead in a 2-1-2 pattern, blue body colour, decoration is blue and white; cylindrical shape (Figure 190w)

B. Complex Eyes

500: Complex eye decoration, but details are missing

501: 3 eyes placed around the circumference of the bead, blue body colour, decoration is blue and white, sub-triangular shape (Figure 190x-y)

502: Unknown number of eyes, blue body colour, decoration is blue and white, barrel shape (Figure 190z)

503: 3 eyes placed around the circumference of the bead, blue body colour, decoration is blue, green, and white, sub-triangular shape (Figure 190aa)

C. Compound Eyes

600: Compound eye decoration, but details are missing

601: 3 compound eyes placed around the circumference of the bead, blue body colour, decoration is blue and white, globular shape (Figure 190ab)

Class 5: Beads with perforation colour

700: Not enough details

A. With yellow

701: Colourless annular bead with yellow on the inside of the perforation (Figure 190ac, ad)

B. With blue

702: Colourless annular bead with blue on the inside of the perforation (Figure 190ae)

Class 6: Beads with linear design

A. Multiple circumferential lines

800: Circumferential line decoration, but full details are missing

801: Motif is not clear, but the body colour is blue and the decoration is made with white and yellow glass, annular shape

802: 7 circumferential lines, colourless body colour, decoration is yellow, annular shape (Figure 191a)

B. Single wave/zig-zag

900: Single wave decoration, but full details are missing

901: Single wave/zig-zag decoration, blue body colour, decoration is white, globular or annular shape (Figure 191b, c)

902: Single wave/zig-zag decoration, blue body colour, decoration is blue, annular shape (Figure 191d)

903: Single wave/zig-zag decoration, blue body colour, decoration is yellow, annular shape (Figure 191e)

904: Single wave/zig-zag decoration, blue and white body colour, decoration is blue, annular shape (Figure 191f)

905: Single wave/zig-zag decoration, blue-green body colour, decoration is yellow, annular shape (Figure 191g)

906: Single wave/zig-zag decoration, colourless body colour, decoration is yellow, annular shape (Figure 191h, i)

907: Single wave/zig-zag decoration, green body colour, decoration is white, globular or annular shape

908: Single wave/zig-zag decoration, green body colour, decoration is yellow, cylindrical shape

909: Single wave/zig-zag decoration, yellow body colour, decoration is blue, annular shape (Figure 191j)

910: Single wave/zig-zag decoration, yellow body colour, decoration is brown, annular shape

C. Chevrons

1000: Multiple chevron decoration around the circumference of the bead, but missing details

1001: Multiple chevron decoration around the circumference of the bead, colourless body colour, decoration is yellow, annular shape (Figure 191k)

1002: Multiple chevron decoration around the circumference of the bead, colourless body colour, decoration is yellow, barrel shape (Figure 191l)

1003: Multiple chevron decoration around the circumference of the bead, colourless body colour, decoration is yellow, globular shape (Figure 191m)

D. Criss-cross

1100: Criss-cross decoration over the surface of the bead, but missing details

1101: Criss-cross decoration over the surface of the bead, colourless body colour, decoration is yellow, shape is barrel or globular (Figure 191n)

E. Diagonal criss-cross

1200: Diagonal criss-cross decoration over the surface of the bead, but missing details

1201: Diagonal criss-cross decoration over the surface of the bead, green body colour, decoration is yellow, unknown shape

F. Pinnate

1300: Pinnate decoration over the surface of the bead, but missing details

1301: Pinnate decoration over the surface of the bead, colourless body colour, decoration is yellow, unknown shape (Figure 191o)

G. Spirals

1400: Spiral decoration over the surface of the bead, but missing details

1401: Single row of 3 spirals on the surface of the bead, black body colour, decoration is yellow, annular shape

1402: Single row of 3 spirals on the surface of the bead, black body colour, decoration is yellow, sub-triangular shape

1403: Single row of 3 spirals on the surface of the bead, black body colour, decoration is yellow, truncated triangle shape

1404: Single row of 3 spirals on the surface of the bead, blue body colour, decoration is green and red, unknown shape

1405: Single row of 3 spirals on the surface of the bead, blue body colour, decoration is white, annular or globular shape (Figure 191p-q)

1406: Single row of 3 spirals on the surface of the bead, blue body colour, decoration is white, globular shape (Figure 191r)

1407: Spirals in a 2-1-2 pattern around the circumference of the bead, blue body colour, decoration is white, shape varies from annular to globular (Figure 191s-v)

1408: Single row of 2 spirals on the surface of the bead, blue body colour, decoration is yellow, globular shape (Figure 191w)

1409: Single row of 3 spirals on the surface of the bead, blue body colour, decoration is yellow, globular shape (Figure 191x)

1410: Single row of 3 spirals on the surface of the bead, blue body colour, decoration is yellow, sub-triangular shape (Figure 191y)

1411: Single row of 3 spirals on the surface of the bead, blue body colour, decoration is yellow, truncated triangle shape (Figure 191z)

1412: Single row of 3 spirals on the surface of the bead, blue-green body colour, decoration is yellow, globular shape (Figure 191aa)

1413: Single row of 3 spirals on the surface of the bead, blue-green body colour, decoration is yellow, truncated triangle shape (Figure 191ab)

1414: Single row of 3 spirals on the surface of the bead, blue and brown body colour, decoration is black, unknown shape

1415: Single row of 3 spirals on the surface of the bead, brown body colour, decoration is yellow, subtriangular shape (Figure 191ac)

1416: Single row of 3 spirals on the surface of the bead, colourless body colour, decoration is yellow, annular shape (Figure 191ad)

1417: Single row of 3 spirals on the surface of the bead, colourless body colour, decoration is yellow, globular shape (Figure 191ae, af)

1418: Single row of 3 spirals on the surface of the bead, colourless body colour, decoration is yellow, sub-triangular shape (Figure 191ag, ah)

1419: Single row of 3 spirals on the surface of the bead, colourless body colour, decoration is yellow, truncated triangle shape (Figure 191ai)

1420: Single row of 3 spirals on the surface of the bead, colourless and red body colour, decoration is yellow, unknown shape (Figure 191aj)

1421: Single row of 3 spirals on the surface of the bead, green body colour, decoration is red and yellow, unknown shape (Figure 191ak)

1422: Single row of 3 spirals on the surface of the bead, green body colour, decoration is yellow, sub-triangular shape (Figure 191al)

1423: Single row of 3 spirals on the surface of the bead, green body colour, decoration is yellow, truncated triangle shape (Figure 191am)

1424: Single row of 3 spirals on the surface of the bead, green and orange body colour, decoration is yellow, annular shape (Figure 191an)

1425: Single row of 3 spirals on the surface of the bead, orange body colour, decoration is yellow, sub-triangular shape (Figure 191ao)

1426: Single row of 3 spirals on the surface of the bead, orange and red body colour, decoration is yellow, sub-triangular shape (Figure 191ap)

1427: Single row of 3 spirals on the surface of the bead, purple body colour, decoration is yellow, truncated triangle shape (Figure 191aq)

1428: Single row of 3 spirals on the surface of the bead, blue and colourless mottled body colour, decoration is yellow, sub-triangular shape (Figure 191ar)

1429: Single row of 3 spirals on the surface of the bead, blue and red mottled body colour, decoration is yellow, sub-triangular shape (Figure 191as)

1430: Single row of 3 spirals on the surface of the bead, colourless mottled body colour, decoration is white and yellow, globular shape (Figure 191at)

1431: Single whirl on the surface of the bead, blue body colour, decoration is blue and yellow, annular shape

Class 7: Wrapped beads

A. Simple wrapped

1501: Multiple and varied colours forming the body of an annular bead (Figure 192b, c, h)

Class 8: Whirl beads

A. Simple whirl

1601: Annular bead with a whirl pattern made from black and yellow (Figure 192a)
1602: Annular bead with a whirl pattern made from blue and white (Figure 192e)
1603: Annular bead with a whirl pattern made from blue, white, and yellow (Figure 192g)
1604: Annular bead with a whirl pattern made from blue and yellow (Figure 192n)
1605: Annular bead with a whirl pattern made from brown, white, and yellow
1606: Annular bead with a whirl pattern made from brown and yellow
1607: Annular bead with a whirl pattern made from green, white, and yellow (Figure 192f)
1608: Annular bead with a whirl pattern made from green and yellow (Figure 192i)
1609: Annular bead with a whirl pattern made from orange and yellow (Figure 192j)
1610: Annular bead with a whirl pattern made from purple and white
1611: Annular bead with a whirl pattern made from white and blue-green (Figure 192k)

Class 9: Ray beads

A. Simple ray

1702: Annular bead with a ray pattern made from blue and yellow (Figure 192l)
1703: Annular bead with a ray pattern made from colourless and yellow
1704: Annular bead with a ray pattern made from green, brown, and white (Figure 192m)

Class 10: Beads with spots

A. Bead with spots

1800: Bead with spots or mottled surface, but full details are missing
1801: Annular bead with mottled spots made from blue, white, and yellow (Figure 192d)
1802: Annular bead with mottled spots made from blue and white

Class 11: Complex motifs

2101: Annular bead with white and yellow body and purple circumferential line.
2201: Sub-triangular bead with green body and yellow wave and dot decoration (Figure 193a)
2202: Globular bead with colourless and blue body and blue and white dot and wave decoration

2301: Globular bead blue body and white double line zig-zag decoration (Figure 193b)
2302: Annular bead with blue body and white and yellow double line zig-zag (Figure 193c)
2303: Annular bead with colourless body and yellow double line zig-zag (Figure 193d)
2304: Annular bead with white body and yellow double line zig-zag (Figure 193e)
2306: Annular bead with yellow body and green and yellow double line wave (Figure 193f)
2307: Stud shaped colourless bead with multiple yellow zig-zags (Figure 193g)
2401: Globular colourless bead with yellow chevrons and a circumferential line (Figure 193h)
2501: Truncated triangle bead in colourless glass with a green and yellow cabled spiral (Figure 193i)
2502: Sub-triangular shaped green bead with a spiral and dot design made from red, white and yellow (Figure 193j)
2503: Truncated triangle bead in green and red with yellow spirals and perforation colour
2504: Globular red-purple bead with a white perforation with yellow spirals (Figure 193k)
2505: Truncated triangle red-purple bead with a white perforation with yellow spirals (Figure 193l)
2506: Truncated triangle blue bead with indented yellow spirals (Figure 193m)
2507: Truncated triangle brown bead with indented yellow spirals (Figure 193n)
2601: Annular wrapped bead in black and yellow with a black and white cable (Figure 193o)
2602: Annular wrapped bead in black and yellow with a black and yellow cable (Figure 193p)
2603: Annular wrapped bead in brown and yellow with a brown and white cable (Figure 193q)
2604: Annular wrapped bead in colourless and yellow with a blue and white cable (Figure 193r)
2605: Annular wrapped bead in colourless and yellow with a brown and white cable (Figure 193s)
2701: Annular black bead with yellow, and blue and white cable
2702: Annular blue bead with blue and white cable
2703: Annular blue bead with a green and white cable (Figure 193t)
2704: Annular brown bead with a blue and white cable (Figure 193u)
2705: Annular green bead with a blue and white cable (Figure 194a)
2706: Annular orange bead with a orange and yellow cable (Figure 194b)
2801: Annular purple bead with whirl and circumferential lines in purple and white (Figure 194c)
2802: Annular blue bead with a whirl and mottled colour in white and yellow
2901: Annular blue bead with white rays and circumferential line
3000: Cable-wave decorated bead, but missing details

List of All New Types

3001: Annular black bead with a blue and white cable wave
3002: Annular blue bead with a colourless and yellow cable wave (Figure 194d)
3003: Annular blue bead with a blue and white cable wave (Figure 194e)
3004: Annular blue bead with a blue and yellow cable wave
3005: Annular blue bead with a green and yellow cable wave (Figure 194f)
3006: Annular bead made from blue, colourless, purple, and yellow with a cable wave made from blue and yellow (Figure 194g)
3008: Annular blue-green bead with a brown and white cable wave
3009: Annular blue-green bead with a green and yellow cable wave (Figure 194h)
3010: Annular brown bead with a blue and white cable wave
3011: Annular colourless and green bead with a blue and white cable wave (Figure 194i)
3012: Annular green bead with a black and yellow cable wave (Figure 194j)
3013: Annular green bead with a blue cable wave
3014: Annular green bead with a bleu and white cable wave
3015: Annular green bead with a blue and yellow cable wave
3016: Annular green bead with a purple and yellow cable wave
3017: Annular orange bead with a blue and white cable wave
3018: Annular purple bead and with a purple and white cable wave (Figure 194k)
3019: Annular yellow bead with a blue and white cable wave (Figure 194l)

Guide to the Illustrated Glass Beads

Figures 189 – 194 contain examples of Iron Age beads mentioned in the text and examples of the majority of the different types. The 'DB no' will allow you to look up additional information about each bead in the accompanying data download.

a b c d e f g

h i j k l

m n o p q

r s t u v w x y z

aa ab ac ad ae

af ag ah ai aj

1 cm

Guide to the Illustrated Glass Beads

Figure	Class	Type	Site	DB no	Acknowledgement	Accession no
a	1	101	Glastonbury Lake Village	7580	Courtesy of the Glastonbury Antiquarian Society	G25
b	1	102	Grandcourt Quarry	9975	Archaeology Project Services	SF 89
c	1	102	Wetwang Slack Chariot	9741-9860	© The Trustees of the British Museum	2001, 0401.22
d	1	102	Wetwang Slack Burial 284	16082	Courtesy of Hull and East Riding Museums:Hull Museums	KINCM: 2010.7.245
e	1	102	Meare Lake Village (west)	7546	Courtesy of The Museum of Somerset	G39
f	1	102	Wetwang Slack Buial 249	16085	Courtesy of Hull and East Riding Museums:Hull Museums	KINCM: 2010.7.310 Bead 2
g	1	103	Meare Lake Village	13614	Courtesy of The Museum of Somerset	82-AA-128/3
h	1	104	Glastonbury Lake Village	3930	Courtesy of the Glastonbury Antiquarian Society	G4
i	1	104	Meare Lake Village (east)	4299	Courtesy of The Museum of Somerset	G6
j	1	105	Glastonbury Lake Village	7579	Courtesy of the Glastonbury Antiquarian Society	G24
k	1	105	Meare Lake Village (east)	13921	Courtesy of The Museum of Somerset	G66.47
l	1	106	Grandcourt Quarry	9977	Archaeology Project Services	SF 156
m	1	106	Glastonbury Lake Village	16364	Courtesy of the Glastonbury Antiquarian Society	G19
n	1	106	Meare Lake Village	7541	Courtesy of The Museum of Somerset	G11
o	1	106	Glastonbury Lake Village	3926	Courtesy of the Glastonbury Antiquarian Society	G8
p	1	107	Claydon Pike	12710	© Cotswold District Council	1998/21/3735
q	1	108	Chesil Mirror Burial	9989	© Bournemouth University	SF8
r	1	108	Meare Lake Village	7556	Courtesy of The Museum of Somerset	G56
s	1	109	Meare Lake Village (west)	16363	Courtesy of The Museum of Somerset	G5
t	1	109	Meare Lake Village (west)	7552	Courtesy of The Museum of Somerset	G133
u	1	110	Culduthel Farm	3771	Headland Archaeology	-
v	1	110	Clevedon Cist Burial	3260	Courtesy of The Museum of Somerset	OS.AA-5/2
w	1	110	Meare Lake Village (west)	4327	Courtesy of The Museum of Somerset	G12
x	1	110	Meare Lake Village (west)	4316	Courtesy of The Museum of Somerset	G13
y	1	110	Meare Lake Village (west)	4334	Courtesy of The Museum of Somerset	G16
z	1	110	Meare Lake Village (east)	13738	Courtesy of The Museum of Somerset	G17
aa	1	110	Meare Lake Village (east)	13742	Courtesy of The Museum of Somerset	G21
ab	1	110	Culbin Sands	3463, 3467, 3476, 3504-3688	Courtesy of the National Museum of Scotland	BIB5
ac	2	201	Grandcourt Quarry	9972	Archaeology Project Services	SF 48
ad	2	202	Wetwang Slack Burial 209	15863	Courtesy of Hull and East Riding Museums:Hull Museums	KINCM:2010.7.307
ae	2	203	Meare Lake Village (west)	7540	Courtesy of The Museum of Somerset	G35
af	3	301	Clevedon Cist Burial	3253	Courtesy of The Museum of Somerset	OS.AA-5/17
ag	3	302	Clevedon Cist Burial	3258	Courtesy of The Museum of Somerset	OS.AA-5/18
ah	3	304	Culbin Sands	3418	Published with kind permission of the Elgin Museum	ELGNM:1967.48
ai	3	305	Meare Lake Village (east)	13759	Courtesy of The Museum of Somerset	G38
aj	3	306	Meare Lake Village (east)	4293	Courtesy of The Museum of Somerset	G73

Figure 189: Examples of Class 1, 2, and 3 beads.

DRESS AND IDENTITY IN IRON AGE BRITAIN

a b c d e f
g h i j k
l m n o p
q r s t u v
w x y z aa ab

ac ad ae

1 cm

Guide to the Illustrated Glass Beads

Figure	Class	Type	Site	DB no	Acknowledgement	Accession no
a	4	411	Queen's Barrow, Arras	5391	© The Trustees of the British Museum	1873,1219.177
b	4	411	Queen's Barrow, Arras	5396	Courtesy of the York Museums Trust	YORKM:1948.913.1
c	4	412	North Down Farm, Dorset	15044	© Bournemouth University	SF25
d	4	413	Wetwang Slack Burial 284	16131	Courtesy of Hull and East Riding Museums:Hull Museums	KINCM:2010.7.245
e	4	413	Wetwang Slack Burial 284	16133	Courtesy of Hull and East Riding Museums:Hull Museums	KINCM:2010.7.245
f	4	414	Wetwang Slack Burial 284	16130	Courtesy of Hull and East Riding Museums:Hull Museums	KINCM:2010.7.245
g	4	414	Wetwang Slack Burial 284	16132	Courtesy of Hull and East Riding Museums:Hull Museums	KINCM:2010.7.245
h	4	416	Gussage Down, Dorset	3999	Courtesy of the Dorset County Museum	1889.1.21
i	4	417	Wetwang Slack Burial 274	16080	Courtesy of Hull and East Riding Museums:Hull Museums	KINCM:2010.7.312
j	4	417	Wetwang Slack Burial 284	16136	Courtesy of Hull and East Riding Museums:Hull Museums	KINCM:2010.7.245
k	4	417	Wetwang Slack Burial 249	16431	Courtesy of Hull and East Riding Museums:Hull Museums	KINCM:2010.7.310
l	4	418	Wetwang Slack Burial 249	16435	Courtesy of Hull and East Riding Museums:Hull Museums	KINCM:2010.7.310
m	4	420	Wetwang Slack Burial 236	16013	Courtesy of Hull and East Riding Museums:Hull Museums	KINCM:2010.7.236
n	4	421	Queen's Barrow, Arras	5377	Courtesy of the York Museums Trust	YORKM:1943.911.2
o	4	421	Wetwang Slack Burial 249	16423-16426	Courtesy of Hull and East Riding Museums:Hull Museums	KINCM:2010.7.310
p	4	422	Meare Lake Village	4397	Courtesy of The Museum of Somerset	G65
q	4	422	10 Eastgate Street	17280	© Gloucester Museums Service	GLRCM:1969.79
r	4	424	Queen's Barrow, Arras	2817	© The Trustees of the British Museum	1873,1219.178
s	4	425	Cowlam Barrow L	3345	© The Trustees of the British Museum	1873,1219.536
t	4	425	Queen's Barrow, Arras	5398	Courtesy of the York Museums Trust	YORKM:1948.917.2
u	4	427	Swallowcliffe Down	4953	Reproduced courtesy of the Wiltshire Museum, Devizes	DZSWS:2006.29.56
v	4	428	Queen's Barrow, Arras	5407	Courtesy of the York Museums Trust	YORKM:1948.917.11
w	4	429	Meare Lake Village (west)	4398	Courtesy of The Museum of Somerset	G8
x	4	501	Wetwang Slack Burial 376	16210	Courtesy of Hull and East Riding Museums:Hull Museums	KINCM:2010.7.309
y	4	501	Wetwang Slack Burial 376	16211	Courtesy of Hull and East Riding Museums:Hull Museums	KINCM:2010.7.309
z	4	502	Grandcourt Quarry	9965	Archaeology Project Services	SF11
aa	4	503	Wetwang Slack Burial 376	16212	Courtesy of Hull and East Riding Museums:Hull Museums	KINCM:2010.7.309
ab	4	601	Cirencester	3217	© Cotswold District Council	A273
ac	5	701	Cirencester	3212	© Cotswold District Council	C908
ad	5	701	Grandcourt Quarry	9974	Archaeology Project Services	SF75
ae	5	702	Grandcourt Quarry	9973	Archaeology Project Services	SF71

Figure 190: Examples of Class 4 and 5 beads.

DRESS AND IDENTITY IN IRON AGE BRITAIN

a b c d e f g h i j
k l m n o p q r
s t u v w x
y z aa ab ac ad ae af
ag ah ai aj ak al am
an ao ap aq ar as at

1 cm

Guide to the Illustrated Glass Beads

Figure	Class	Type	Site	DB no	Acknowledgement	Accession no
a	6	802	Meare Lake Village	4294	Courtesy of The Museum of Somerset	G29
b	6	901	Meare Lake Village (west)	4392	Courtesy of The Museum of Somerset	G38
c	6	901	Queen's Barrow, Arras	2782	© The Trustees of the British Museum	1880,0802.144
d	6	902	Glastonbury Lake Village	3925	Courtesy of the Glastonbury Antiquarian Society	G18
e	6	903	Meare Lake Village	13725	Courtesy of The Museum of Somerset	G2
f	6	904	Cadbury Castle	7933	Courtesy of The Museum of Somerset	76-AA-165/7877
g	6	905	Queen's Barrow, Arras	5351	© The Trustees of the British Museum	1873,1219.179
h	6	906	Meare Lake Village	4389	Courtesy of The Museum of Somerset	G33
i	6	906	Meare Lake Village	13915	Courtesy of The Museum of Somerset	G52
j	6	909	Meare Lake Village	4305	Courtesy of The Museum of Somerset	G135
k	6	1001	Meare Lake Village	4365	Courtesy of The Museum of Somerset	G48
l	6	1002	Meare Lake Village	17410	Courtesy of The Museum of Somerset	G1968/23/2000/5
m	6	1003	Meare Lake Village	4367	Courtesy of The Museum of Somerset	G68
n	6	1101	Meare Lake Village	4306	Courtesy of The Museum of Somerset	G69
o	6	1301	Meare Lake Village	4390	Courtesy of The Museum of Somerset	G14
p	6	1405	Glastonbury Lake Village	3935	Courtesy of the Glastonbury Antiquarian Society	G12
q	6	1405	Glastonbury Lake Village	3936	Courtesy of the Glastonbury Antiquarian Society	G1
r	6	1406	Meare Lake Village	4288	Courtesy of The Museum of Somerset	G15
s	6	1407	Marnhull Dorset	4283	Courtesy of the Gillingham Museum, Dorset	1974.23.9.29
t	6	1407	Swanage, Bristol City	4957	Courtesy of the Bristol Museum and Art Gallery	BCM F710
u	6	1407	Stoke Holy Cross, Norfolk	10013	Courtesy of Norfolk Museum Service	NM:2010.190.1
v	6	1407	Rudston Roman villa	11630	Courtesy of Hull and East Riding Museums:Hull Museums	KINCM: 1986.1826.158 SF40
w	6	1408	Meare Lake Village	4287	Courtesy of The Museum of Somerset	G46
x	6	1409	Cawdor Castle	3165	Courtesy of the National Museum of Scotland	FJ 4
y	6	1410	Bedlam?	2891	Courtesy of the National Museum of Scotland	FJ 14
z	6	1411	Burghead	3009	Courtesy of the National Museum of Scotland	FJ 6
aa	6	1412	Cawdor Castle	3162	Courtesy of the National Museum of Scotland	FJ 2
ab	6	1413	Culbin Sands	3733	Courtesy of The Hunterian, University of Glasgow	GLAHM B1951.971.3
ac	6	1415	Coldstone	3301	Courtesy of the National Museum of Scotland	FJ 7
ad	6	1416	Meare Lake Village (east)	13890	Courtesy of The Museum of Somerset	G 78EV
ae	6	1417	Meare Lake Village (west)	6932	Courtesy of The Museum of Somerset	G44
af	6	1417	Meare Lake Village (east)	13729	Courtesy of The Museum of Somerset	G8
ag	6	1418	Meare Lake Village (west)	6940	Courtesy of The Museum of Somerset	G98
ah	6	1418	Meare Lake Village (west)	7539	Courtesy of The Museum of Somerset	G142
ai	6	1419	Meare Lake Village (east)	13901	Courtesy of The Museum of Somerset	G89
aj	6	1420	Meare Lake Village (east)	17406	Courtesy of The Museum of Somerset	G75EV
ak	6	1421	Orton	4530	Published with kind permission of the Elgin Museum	ELGNM: 1970.13
al	6	1422	Aberdeenshire?	2761	© University of Aberdeen	ABDUA:15545
am	6	1423	Tap o'Noth	4960	© University of Aberdeen	ABDUA:15590
an	6	1424	Culbin Sands	3751	Courtesy of The Hunterian, University of Glasgow	GLAHM: B1951.971.11
ao	6	1425	Mill of Gellan, Tarland, Aberdeenshire	4414	© University of Aberdeen	ABDUA:15544
ap	6	1426	Aberdeenshire	17566	© University of Aberdeen	ABDUA:15543
aq	6	1427	Culbin Sands	17564	© University of Aberdeen	ABDUA:15514
ar	6	1428	Culbin Sands	3469	Courtesy of the National Museum of Scotland	BIB 19
as	6	1429	Tough Parish	4983	Courtesy of the National Museum of Scotland	FJ 65
at	6	1430	Meare Lake Village (west)	6935	Courtesy of The Museum of Somerset	G81

Figure 191: Examples of Class 6 beads.

DRESS AND IDENTITY IN IRON AGE BRITAIN

a b c
d e f
g h i
j k l
m n

1 cm

Figure	Class	Type	Site	DB no	Acknowledgement	Accession no
a	8	1601	Chapel of Garloch	3172	© University of Aberdeen	ABDUA: 15530
b	7	1501	'Aberdeenshire'	2758	© University of Aberdeen	ABDUA: 15539
c	7	1501	Mains of Concraig	4278	© University of Aberdeen	ABDUA: 17438
d	10	1801	Grandcourt Quarry	9966	Archaeology Project Services	SF16
e	8	1602	Meare Lake Village (west)	4301	Courtesy of The Museum of Somerset	G73
f	8	1607	Culbin sands	3391	Courtesy of the National Museum of Scotland	BIB16
g	8	1603	Aberdeenshire?	2687	Courtesy of the National Museum of Scotland	FJ71
h	7	1501	Aberdeenshire?	2685	Courtesy of the National Museum of Scotland	FJ70
i	8	1608	Bagendon	17441	© Cotswold District Council	
j	8	1609	Aberdeenshire?	2688	Courtesy of the National Museum of Scotland	FJ73
k	8	1611	Cloisterseat	3265	Courtesy of the National Museum of Scotland	FJ19
l	9	1702	Unknown	10014	Courtesy of Norfolk Museum Service	NM:1950.179.16.4
m	9	1704	Chesil Mirror Burial	9994	© Bournemouth University	SF12
n	8	1604	Chesil Mirror Burial	9987	© Bournemouth University	SF6

Figure 192: Examples of Class 7, 8, 9, and 10 beads.

DRESS AND IDENTITY IN IRON AGE BRITAIN

a b c d e f

g h i j

k l m n

o p q

r s t u

1 cm

Figure	Class	Type	Site	DB no	Acknowledgement	Accession no
a	11	2201	Meare Lake Village (east)	4289	Courtesy of The Museum of Somerset	G68EV
b	11	2301	Wetwang Slack Burial 274	16078	Courtesy of Hull and East Riding Museums:Hull Museums	KINCM:2010.7.312
c	11	2302	Grandcourt Quarry	9980	Archaeology Project Services	SF184
d	11	2303	Grandcourt Quarry	9971	Archaeology Project Services	SF24
e	11	2304	Grandcourt Quarry	9976	Archaeology Project Services	SF92
f	11	2306	Meare Lake Village (east)	13760	Courtesy of The Museum of Somerset	G39
g	11	2307	Meare Lake Village (east)	4296	Courtesy of The Museum of Somerset	G4
h	11	2401	Meare Lake Village (east)	13772	Courtesy of The Museum of Somerset	G54
i	11	2501	Culduthel Farm	3789	Headland archaeology	SF846
j	11	2502	'Aberdeenshire'	2759	© University of Aberdeen	ABDUA:15542
k	11	2504	Culbin Sands	3473	Courtesy of the National Museum of Scotland	BIB11
l	11	2505	Morayshire?	2752	Published with kind permission of the Moray Council Museum's Service	1981.6
m	11	2506	Culbin Sands	3745	Courtesy of The Hunterian, University of Glasgow	GLAHM:B1951971.2
n	11	2507	Culbin Sands	3421	Courtesy of the National Museum of Scotland	BIB10
o	11	2601	Aberdeenshire?	2686	Courtesy of the National Museum of Scotland	FJ72
p	11	2602	Lickleyhead	4227	Courtesy of the National Museum of Scotland	FJ139
q	11	2603	Aberdeenshire?	2747	Courtesy of the National Museum of Scotland	FJ117
r	11	2604	Culbin Sands	3749	Courtesy of The Hunterian, University of Glasgow	GLAHM:B1951.971.7
s	11	2605	Smithston	4855	Courtesy of the National Museum of Scotland	L1961.9
t	11	2703	Culbin Sands	3461	Courtesy of the National Museum of Scotland	BIB17
u	11	2704	Cawdor Castle	3166	Courtesy of the National Museum of Scotland	FJ17

Figure 193: Examples of Class 11 beads.

Dress and Identity in Iron Age Britain

a   b   c

d   e   f   g   h   i

j   k   l   m   n   o

p   q

1 cm

Guide to the Illustrated Glass Beads

Figure	Class	Type	Site	DB no	Acknoweldgement	Accession no
a	11	2705	Cawdor Castle	3168	Courtesy of the National Museum of Scotland	FJ18
b	11	2706	Culbin Sands	3753	Courtesy of The Hunterian, University of Glasgow	GLAHM: B1951.971.10
c	11	2801	Chesil Mirror Burial	9985	© Bournemouth University	SF4
d	11	3002	Bagendon	2844	© Cotswold District Council	CIRN:A342.5.18
e	11	3003	Camerton	3085	Courtesy of the Bristol Museum and Art Gallery	BCM:Fb7012
f	11	3005	Charterhouse-on-Mendip	3174	Courtesy of the Bristol Museum and Art Gallery	BCM:F2085
g	11	3006	Bagendon	2841	© Cotswold District Council	CIRN:A342.5.20
h	11	3009	Cadbury Castle	7931	Courtesy of The Museum of Somerset	76-AA-165/7887/CAD
i	11	3011	Charterhouse-on-Mendip	3173	Courtesy of the Bristol Museum and Art Gallery	BCM:F2084
j	11	3012	Meare Lake Village (west)	4303	Courtesy of The Museum of Somerset	G78
k	11	3018	Frocester Court	11258	© Gloucester Museums Service	Y22
l	11	3019	Chester Street	17222	© Cotswold District Council	CIRN:1980.137.81
m			Charterhouse-on-Mendip	3175	Courtesy of the Bristol Museum and Art Gallery	BCM:F2083
n			Welwyn Garden City burial	5053	© The Trustees of the British Museum	1967,0202.66
o			Welwyn Garden City burial	5054	© The Trustees of the British Museum	1967,0202.67
p			Haughley	4022	© Ashmolean Museum, University of Oxford	ASH:1909.417
q			Ducklington	6460	© Ashmolean Museum, University of Oxford	ASH:1836.236

Figure 194: Examples of Class 11 and un-typed beads.

Bibliography

Abbott, C., 1996. *County Farm, Chilton, Archaeological Evaluation,* Unpublished Report, Suffolk County Council 96/63, Suffolk HER CHT 009.

Abbott, C., 1997. *Stratford St. Mary - East Bergholt Pipeline, Archaeological Monitoring and Excavation,* Unpublished Report, Suffolk County Council 97/48, Suffolk HER SSM 001.

Abbott, C. and K. Forrest, 1996. *Excavations at Darmsden, Suffolk, 1994,* Unpublished Report, Suffolk County Council 96/26, Suffolk HER BRK 020.

Abbott, C. and T. Loader, 1997a. *Goddard Road, Ipswich, Archaeological Evaluation and Monitoring,* Unpublished Report, Suffolk County Council 97/59, Suffolk HER IPS 282.

Abbott, C. and T. Loader, 1997b. *Lovetofts Drive, Ipswich, Archaeological Evaluation,* Unpublished Report, Suffolk County Council 97/57, Suffolk HER IPS 283.

Abramson, P., 1996. Excavations Along the Caythorpe Gas Pipeline, North Humberside. *Yorkshire Archaeological Journal,* 68, 1-88.

Adam, N., 2001. *Construction of a New Water Main at Chilton Polden, Somerset,* Unpublished Report, AC Archaeology Report no. 4401/2/0, Somerset HER 18033.

Adams, D., 2002. *Report on an Archaeological Evaluation at Langham Point, Langham, Norfolk,* Unpublished Report, Norfolk Archaeological Unit 683, Norfolk HER 36872.

Adams, M., K. Doyle and A. Grassam, 2008. *Bridge House Diaries, Worlington Road, Mildenhall, Suffolk, Archaeological Evaluation and Watching Brief,* Unpublished Report, Archaeological Solutions Ltd. 3026, Suffolk HER BTM 040.

Adams, N. J., 2006. *Land at Leckhamton, Cheltenham, Gloucestershire, Archaeological Evaluation,* Unpublished Report, Cotswold Archaeology Report no. 06140, Gloucestershire SMR 28802.

Adams, W. Y., 1988. Archaeological Classification: Theory Versus Practice. *Antiquity,* 62(234), 40-56.

Adams, W. Y. and E. W. Adams, 1991. *Archaeological Typology and Practical Reality,* Cambridge: Cambridge University Press.

Adkins, L. and R. Adkins, 1988. *Northover House, Ilchester, Somerset, Archaeological Evaluation Archive Report,* Unpublished Report, Somerset SMR 57133.

Adkins, L. and R. Adkins, 1991. Excavations at Ham Hill, 1991. *Somerset Archaeology and Natural History Society,* 135, 89-94.

Adkins, L. and R. Adkins, 1995. *Excavations at Ham Hill Montacute, Somerset 1994,* Unpublished Report, Wessex Archaeology 37602c, Somerset SMR 56900.

Agresti, A. and B. Finlay, 2009. *Statistical Methods for the Social Sciences,* New Jersey: Pearson Prentice Hall.

Aitken, G. and N. Aitken, 1982. Excavations on the Library Site, Colliton Park, Dorchester, 1961-3. *Dorset Natural History and Archaeological Society,* 104, 93-126.

Aitken, G. M. and G. N. Aitken, 1990. Excavations at Whitcombe, 1965-1967. *Proceedings of the Dorset Natural History and Archaeological Society,* 112, 57-94.

Aitken, G. N., 1958. *Excavations at West Coker Villa Site, in Parish of West Coker, Somerset,* Unpublished Report Somerset SMR 15105.

Akerman, J. Y., 1852. Vi. Remarks on a Coloured Drawing of Some Ancient Beads, Executed by Benjamin Nightingale, Esq., from Specimens in His Possession. *Archaeologia,* 34, 46-52.

Albone, J., 2001. *Archaeological Evaluation at Land South of Norwich Road, Caister-on-Sea, Norfolk,* Unpublished Report, Archaeological Project Services 031/01, Norfolk HER 35843.

Albone, J., 2003. *Archaeological Evaluation at the Old Hall Hotel, Caister on Sea, Norfolk,* Unpublished Report, Archaeological Project Services 232/02, Norfolk HER 37421.

Albone, J., 2006. *Archaeological Excavation on Land Off Norwich Road, Caister-on-Sea, Norfolk,* Unpublished Report, Archaeological Project Services 108/03, Norfolk HER 37421.

Alcock, L., 1967. A Reconnaissance Excavation at South Cadbury Castle, Somerset, 1966. *Antiquaries Journal,* 47, 70-76.

Alcock, L., 1969. Excavations at South Cadbury Castle, 1968, a Summary Report. *Antiquaries Journal,* 49, 30-40.

Aldhouse-Green, M., 2001. *Dying for the Gods: Human Sacrifice in Iron Age and Roman Europe,* Stroud: Tempus.

Aldhouse-Green, M., 2004. Crowning Glories: Languages of Hair in Later Prehistoric Europe. *Proceedings of the Prehistoric Society,* 70, 299-325.

Alexander, D., 1996a. *A96 - Kintore Bypass, Archaeological Evaluation,* Unpublished Report, Centre for Field Archaeology no. 274, RCAHMS MS 1081/66.

Alexander, D., 1996b. *A96 - Kntore Bypass, Deer's Den and Tavelty Excavations,* Unpublished Report,

Centre for Field Archaeology no. 311, RCAHMS MS 1081/66.

Alexander, D., 2000. Excavations of Neolithic Pits, Later Prehistoric Structures and a Roman Temporary Camp Along the Line of the A96 Kintore and Blackburn Bypass, Aberdeenshire. *Proceedings of the Society of Antiquaries of Scotland,* 130, 11-75.

Allason-Jones, L., 1989. *Women in Roman Britain,* London: British Museum Publications.

Allen, D., 1958. Belgic Coins as Illustrations of Life in the Late Pre-Roman Iron Age of Britain. *Proceedings of the Prehistoric Society,* 24, 43-63.

Allen, M. and C. Clay, 2007. *Archaeological Strip, Map and Record: Exploration Wellsite at Willows a, Reighton, North Yorkshire,* Unpublished Report, Allen Archaeological Associates, Humber Archaeology Partnership.

Allen, T., T. Darvill, S. Green and M. Jones, 1993. *Excavations at Roughground Farm, Lechlade, Gloucestershire: A Prehistoric and Roman Landscape,* Oxford: The Oxford University Committee for Archaeology.

Allum, C., C. Place and R. McConnell, 2009. *D9301: Spaxton Water Main Replacement, Spaxton, Somerset: Geophysical Survey and Archaeological Field Evaluation,* Unpublished Report, Context One, Somerset HER 18161.

Ames, J., 2004. *An Interim Report on an Archaeological Evaluation at A11 Fiveways to Thetford Road Improvements Scheme,* Unpublished Report, Norfolk Archaeological Unit no 1027.

Ames, J., 2005a. *An Archaeological Evaluation at Browick Road, Wymondham, Norfolk,* Unpublished Report, Norfolk Archaeological Unit 1050, Norfolk HER 41125.

Ames, J., 2005b. *An Archaeological Evaluation at the Rectory, Scole, Norfolk,* Unpublished Report, Norfolk Archaeological Unit 1067, Norfolk HER 41282.

Ames, J., 2005c. *An Archaeological Evaluation Feltwell Road, Southery, Norfolk,* Unpublished Report, Norfolk Archaeological Unit 1039, Norfolk HER 41028.

Ames, J., 2006. *Archaeological Field Survey and Trial Trench Evaluation at Stanfield Quarry, Stanfield and Beetley, Norfolk, Interim Report,* Unpublished Report, NAU Archaeology 1221, Norfolk HER 30660.

Ames, J., 2010. *An Archaeological Evaluation at Middleton Main Replacement, Grandcourt Farm Scheme, East Winch, Norfolk,* Unpublished Report, NAU Archaeology 2344, Norfolk HER 50836.

Anderson, J., 1883. *Scotland in Pagan Times, the Iron Age,* Edinburgh: David Douglas.

Anderson, J., 1902. Notices of Cists Discovered in a Cairn at Cairnhill, Parish of Monquhitter, Aberdeenshire, and at Doune, Perthshire. *Proceedings of the Society of Antiquaries of Scotland,* 36, 675-88.

Anderson, J. and G. F. Black, 1888. Reports on Local Museums in Scotland, Obtained through Dr R.H. Gunning's Jubilee Gift to the Society. *Proceedings of the Society of Antiquaries of Scotland,* 22, 331-422.

Anderson, S., 1997. *Ixworth Pipeline, Archaeological Monitoring Report and Excavation,* Unpublished Report, Suffolk County Council 97/35, Suffolk HER IXT 031, IXW 043 and OXW 044.

Anderson, S., 2002. *Smye's Corner, Shrublands Quarry, Coddenham, Suffolk, Assessment and Updated Project Design,* Unpublished Report, Suffolk County Council 2002/81, Suffolk HER CDD 050.

Anderson, S. and J. Caruth, 1998. *Tarmac Ingham Quarry, Archaeological Excavation Report,* Unpublished Report, Suffolk County Council 98/91, Suffolk HER FSG 013 and 015.

Andrews, P., 1999a. *Excavations at Guildhall Street, 1989, Site 25296,* Dereham, Norfolk: East Anglian Archaeology Report no. 87.

Andrews, P., 1999b. *Excavations at St Nicholas' Street, 1990, Site 1134,* Dereham, Norfolk: East Anglian Archaeology Report no. 87.

Andrews, P., 2009. The Discovery, Excavation and Preservation of a Detached Roman Bath-House at Truckle Hill, North Wraxall. *Wiltshire Archaeology and Natural History Society,* 102, 129-49.

Annable, F. K., 1966. A Late First-Century Well at Cvnetio. *Wiltshire Archaeology and Natural History Society,* 61, 9-24.

Anon., *Archaeology on the A19 Easingwold by-Pass: Assessment Report and Updated Project Design,* Unpublished Report, York Archaeological Trust, North Yorkshire HER S8100.

Anon., 1864. Donations to the Museum. *Proceedings of the Society of Antiquaries of Scotland,* 5, 300.

Anon., 1868. Donations to the Library and Museum. *Proceedings of the Society of Antiquaries of Scotland,* 7, 320.

Anon., 1870. Donations to and Purchases for the Museum and Library, and Exhibits in the Museum. *Proceedings of the Society of Antiquaries of Scotland,* 7, 265-67, 313-3121, 357-360, 396-398, 459-462, 477-480.

Anon., 1873. Donations to and Purchases for the Museum. *Proceedings of the Society of Antiquaries of Scotland,* 9, 356-67, 80-84, 443-46, 60-64, 504-06, 32-40.

Anon., 1874. Donations to the Museum. *Proceedings of the Society of Antiquaries of Scotland,* 10, 699.

Anon., 1890. Donations to the Museum. *Proceedings of the Society of Antiquaries of Scotland,* 24, 379.

Anon., 1893. Donations to and Purchases for the Museum and Library. *Proceedings of the Society of Antiquaries of Scotland*, 27, 12.

Anon., 1894. Donations to the Museum. *Proceedings of the Society of Antiquaries of Scotland,* 28, 62.

Anon., 1919-1920. Donations to the Museum. *Proceedings of the Society of Antiquaries of Scotland*, 54, 15.

Anon., 1938. Lillyhorn Villa, Bisley. *Transactions of the Bristol and Gloucestershire Archaeological Society*, 60, 351-52.

Anon., 1971. *Bush Marsh, Bawdrip, Somerset, M5*, Unpublished Report, Somerset SMR 44743.

Anon., 1975. *Discovery and Excavation in Scotland*, 26.

Anon., 1985. *Discovery and Excavation in Scotland*, 27.

Anon., 1989. *Discovery and Excavation in Scotland*, 30.

Anon., 1990. Brackla. *Discovery and Excavation in Scotland*, 24.

Anon., 1991a. *Proposed Quarry Development, Ham Hill, Somerset, Archaeological Assessment*, Unpublished Report, Somerset SMR 56906.

Anon., 1991b. *Report on an Archaeological Evaluation at 14-20 Blossom Street, York*, Unpublished Report, York Archaeological Trust, CYC 16.

Anon., 1991c. *Report on an Archaeological Evaluation at 89 the Mount, York*, Unpublished Report, York Archaeological Trust, CYC 10.

Anon., 1991d. *Report on an Archaeological Evaluation at Adams Hydraulics, York, Phase 3*, Unpublished Report, York Archaeological Trust, CYC 12.

Anon., 1991e. *Report on an Archaeological Evaluation at the Ideal Laundry, Trinity Lane, York*, Unpublished Report, York Archaeological Trust, CYC 11.

Anon., 1992a. *50 Piccadilly, York, a Report on an Archaeological Evaluation*, Unpublished Report, York Archaeological Trust, Evaluation Report 1992/14, CYC 34.

Anon., 1992b. *A Concise Report on an Archaeological Evaluation at 41 Piccadilly, York*, Unpublished Report, York Archaeological Report 1992/16, CYC 39.

Anon., 1992c. *Ilchester to Odcombe Water Pipeline, Somerset: Archaeological Evaluation and Watching Brief*, Unpublished Report, Wessex Archaeology Report no. W451, Somerset HER 28839.

Anon., 1992d. *Simpson's Yard, 38 Piccadilly, York, a Report on an Archaeological Evaluation*, Unpublished Report, York Archaeological Trust Evaluation Report 1992/13, CYC 33.

Anon., 1993a. *A303 - Sparkford to Ilchester Road Improvement: Archaeological Evaluation*, Unpublished Report, Wessex Archaeology W530.02 on OASIS.

Anon., 1993b. *Ilchester, Free Street*, Unpublished Report, Somerset SMR 55937.

Anon., 1994. *Free Street Ilchester, Master Yard, Phase 2, Archaeological Watching Brief*, Unpublished Report, Somerset SMR 55940.

Anon., 1995a. *Discovery and Excavation in Scotland*, 44.

Anon., 1995b. *52 Monkgate, York, Archaeological Evaluation*, Unpublished Report, MAP Archaeological Consultancy Ltd., CYC 56.

Anon., 1995c. *Ilchester, Great Yard, Archaeological Excavations 1995*, Unpublished Report, Somerset SMR 56902.

Anon., 1996a. *Germany Beck - Fulford, Archaeological Sample Excavations, Interim Report*, Unpublished Report, MAP Archaeological Consultancy Ltd., CYC 71.

Anon., 1996b. *Land at Horcott, Gloucestershire, Sitecode: Horc 96, an Archaeological Evaluation Report*, Unpublished Report, Oxford Archaeological Unit, Gloucestershire HER 15370.

Anon., 1996c. *Rievaulx Bank, North Yorkshire, Archaeolgoical Watching Brief*, Unpublished Report, MAP Archaeological Consultancy Ltd.

Anon., 1996d. *The Starting Gate, Tadcaster Road, Dringhouses, York*, Unpublished Report, York Archaeological Trust, Evaluation Report no. 9, CYC 95.

Anon., 1996e. *The Warrener, Thetford, Norfolk, Archaeological Evaluation 1996*, Unpublished Report, Wessex Archaeology 41400, Norfolk HER 31897.

Anon., 1996f. *Yorkshire Water Pipeline Moor Monkton to Elvington Archaeological Assessment Report*, Unpublished Report, York Archaeological Trust Field Report no. 30, CYC 72.

Anon., 1997a. *Archaeological Evaluation of Filwood Playing Fields, Knowle, West, Bristol*, Unpublished Report, BaRAS BA/F345, Bristol City HER 20254.

Anon., 1997b. *Archaeological Watching Brief on the Construction of 132 and 33kv Overhead Electricity Lines to Seabank Power Station, Hallen, Bristol*, Unpublished Report, BaRAS Report 263/1997, Bristol City HER 20233.

Anon., 1997c. *The Fox Public House, 60 Tadcaster Road, Dringhouses, York, Report on an Archaeological Investigation*, Unpublished Report, York Archaeological Trust Field Report no. 18, CYC 79.

Anon., 1997d. *Land at Hilly Fields, Upper Hollway, Taunton, Archaeological Field Evaluation*, Unpublished Report, Wessex Archaeology 43878, Somerset HER 57171.

Anon., 1997e. *Land at Millend Lane, Blakeney, Gloucestershire, Archaeological Evaluation*, Unpublished Report, Cotswold Archaeological Trust Report no. 97449, Gloucestershire HER 17988.

Anon., 1997f. *Regency Mews, Tadcaster Road, Dringhouses, York, Report on an Archaeological Excavation*, Unpublished Report, York Archaeological Trust Field Report no. 30, CYC 116.

Anon., 1997g. *Report on an Archaeological Evaluation, Water Lane, Clifton, York*, Unpublished Report, York Archaeological Trust Field Report no. 20, CYC 104.

Anon., 1998a. *Bhs Store, Feasegate, York, Report on an Archaeological Excavation and Watching Brief*, Unpublished Report, York Archaeological Trust Field Report no. 30, CYC 148.

Anon., 1998b. *Excavations at Ham Hill, Montacute, Somerset, Interim Report,* Unpublished Report, Wessex Archaeology Report 37604a, Somerset HER 56993.

Anon., 1998c. *Multi-Agg Quarry Extension, Kempsford, Gloucestershire, Archaeological Evaluation Report,* Unpublished Report, Oxford Archaeological Unit, Gloucestershire HER 7621.

Anon., 1999a. *Aldham Mill Hill Storage Depot, Hadleight, Archaeological Evaluation Archive Report,* Unpublished Report, Suffolk County Council 99/53, Suffolk HER HAD 059.

Anon., 1999b. *Crossgates Farm - Phases II and III, Seamer, North Yorkshire, Interim Report,* Unpublished Report, MAP Archaeological Consultancy, North Yorkshire HER S7651.

Anon., 1999c. *Evaluation Excavation at Land Off Bury Road, Ipswich,* Unpublished Report, John Samuels Archaeological Consultants, JSAC 461/99/03, Suffolk HER IPS 387.

Anon., 1999d. *Harton to Hildenley Water Pipeline, Site Narrative and Post-Excavation Assessment,* Unpublished Report, Northern Archaeological Associates, NAA 99/44, North Yorkshire HER S11191.

Anon., 1999e. *Lechlade Manor, Lechlade-on-Thames, Archaeological Evaluation,* Unpublished Report, Cotswold Archaeological Trust Report no. 991049, Gloucestershire HER 20519.

Anon., 1999f. *Ncp Car Park, 64-74 Skeldergate, York, Report on an Archaeological Watching Brief,* Unpublished Report, York Archaeological Trust Field Report no. 44, CYC 176.

Anon., 1999g. *The Thatched Cottage, Wortley, Gloucestershire: An Archaeological Field Evaluation,* Unpublished Report, Gloucestershire SMR 2867.

Anon., 1999h. *Whitewall, Norton, North Yorkshire, Archaeological Evaluation,* Unpublished Report, MAP Archaeological Consultancy Ltd., North Yorkshire HER S7993.

Anon., 2000a. *28-40 Blossom Street, York, Archaeological Report,* Unpublished Report, MAP Archaeological Consultancy Ltd. 03-04-00, CYC 248.

Anon., 2000b. *52-54 Ashcroft Road, Cirencester, Gloucestershire, Archaeological Watching Brief,* Unpublished Report, Cotswold Archaeological Trust Report no. 1200, Gloucestershire HER 21143.

Anon., 2000c. *Brockworth Msa Gloucestershre, Archaeoogical Evaluation,* Unpublished Report, Cotswold Archaeological Trust Report no. 001214, Gloucestershire HER 20087.

Anon., 2000d. *Lower Mill Farm, Somerford Keynes, Gloucestershire,* Unpublished Report, Cotswold Archaeological Trust Report no. 001240, Gloucestershire HER 20901.

Anon., 2000e. *A Report on an Archaeological Watching Brief at Land Off Bury Road, Ipswich,* Unpublished Report, John Samuels Archaeological Consultants, JSAC 461/00/05, Suffolk HER IPS 387.

Anon., 2000f. *Teeside to Saltend Ethylene Pipeline, Sites 719 and 720, Skeugh Farm, Stillington, North Yorkshire, Post-Excavation Assessment Report,* Unpublished Report, Northern Archaeological Associates, NAA 00/76 North Yorks HER S553.

Anon., 2001a. *8 Pirnhow Street, Ditchingham, an Archaeological Evaluation, Final,* Unpublished Report, RPS Consultants, Norfolk HER 36221.

Anon., 2001b. *Balk Field, Pocklington, East Yorkshire, Archaeological Watching Brief,* Unpublished Report, Northern Archaeological Associates, NAA 01/21 UHU 792.

Anon., 2001c. *The Corner House, Prospect Place, Victoria Road, Cirencester, Gloucestershire, Archaeological Watching Brief,* Unpublished Report, Cotswold Archaeological Trust Report no. 01028, Gloucestershire HER 22037.

Anon., 2001d. *Crossgates Farm - Phases III, Seamer, North Yorkshire, Archaeological Excavations,* Unpublished Report, MAP Archaeological Consultancy, North Yorkshire HER S8186.

Anon., 2001e. *Hengistbury Head Outdoor Education and Field Studies Centre, Results of a Geophysical Survey and an Archaeological Evaluation,* Unpublished Report, Wessex Archaeology 50092.2, Dorset HER.

Anon., 2001f. *Shapwick Road, Hamworthy Poole, Interim Report on Archaeological Excavations and Observations During Phase 2 Drainage Works,* Unpublished Report, Terrain Archaeology, 5050.4, Dorset HER.

Anon., 2001g. *Teeside to Saltend Ethylene Pipeline, Sites 718 and 721, Sike Spa, Crayke, North Yorkshire, Post-Excavation Assessment Report,* Unpublished Report, Northern Archaeological Associates, NAA 00/75, North Yorkshire HER 2034.

Anon., 2002a. *7 City Bank View: Archaeological Watching Brief,* Unpublished Report, Foundations Archaeology, Available on OASIS.

Anon., 2002b. *A303 Stonehenge, Archaeological Surveys, Archaeological Evaluation Report, Areas L and O,* Unpublished Report, Wessex Archaeology, 5042.1a.

Anon., 2002c. *Archaeological Watching Brief at the Mappleton Waste Water Treatment Plant and Flow Transfer Pipeline,* Unpublished Report, Humber Field Archaeology Report no. 524, EHU 859.

Anon., 2002d. *Blue Bridge Lane and Fishergate House, Archaeological Excavation, Preliminary Statement,* Unpublished Report, Field Archaeology Specialists, CYC 430.

Anon., 2003a. *1 Cripps Road, Cirencester: Archaeological Evaluation,* Unpublished Report, Foundations Archaeology, Available on OASIS.

Anon., 2003b. *A303 Stonehenge, Archaeological Surveys, Archaeological Evaluation Report, Areas 1,*

2, 3, and 4, Unpublished Report, Wessex Archaeology S2524.1.

Anon., 2003c. *An Archaeological Watching Brief at Lone Farm, Kilham, Watching Brief Report,* Unpublished Report, Humber Field Archaeology Report no. 642, EHU 1051.

Anon., 2003d. *Castle Hill, Ipswich, Suffolk, Archaeological Evaluation and an Assessment of the Results,* Unpublished Report, Wessex Archaeology 52568.02, Suffolk HER IPS 421.

Anon., 2003e. *Ham Hill Quarry, Hamdon Hill, Montacute, Somerset, Archaeological Excavation 2002: Post-Excavation Assessment Report,* Unpublished Report, Wessex Archaeology Report no. 51679, Somerset HER 28624.

Anon., 2003f. *Interim Report on a Gradiometer Survey and Excavations at Englands, Charlton Horethorne,* Unpublished Report, Somerset HER 22956.

Anon., 2003g. *Results of an Archaeological Trial Evaluation: On Land at 82 School Road, Foulden, Norfolk,* Unpublished Report, M and M Archaeological Services, Norfolk HER 37611.

Anon., 2003h. *Yorkshire Derwent Aquaduct Duplication Main, Elivington to Riccall, Post-Excavation Assessment Report,* Unpublished Report, Northern Archaeological Associates, NAA 03/68, North Yorkshire HER S9144.

Anon., 2003i. *Yorkshire Derwent Aqueduct Duplication Main, Elvington to Riccall, Post-Excavation Assessment Report,* Unpublished Report, Northern Archaeological Associates NAA 03/68, CYC 512.

Anon., 2004a. *An Archaeological Watching Brief at Land West of Glen Garth, Hayton,* Unpublished Report, Humber Field Archaeology Report no 703, EHU 1058.

Anon., 2004b. *An Archaeological Watching Brief at Mires Beck Nursery, Low Mill Lane, North Cave,* Unpublished Report, Humber Field Archaeology Report no. 662, Humber HER.

Anon., 2004c. *Whitestaunton Manor House, Whitestaunton, Somerset,* Unpublished Report, Wessex Archaeology 52568, Somerset HER 17068.

Anon., 2005a. *5 Prospect Place, Cirencester, Gloucestershire, Archaeological Watching Brief,* Unpublished Report, Archaeology and Planning Solutions, Gloucestershire HER 27950.

Anon., 2005b. *141 Gloucester Street, Cirencester, Archaeological Watching Brief,* Unpublished Report, Archaeology and Planning Solutions, Gloucestershire HER 27950.

Anon., 2005c. *Archaeological Evaluation Report, Windrush View, Lansdown, Bourton on the Water, Gloucestershire,* Unpublished Report, CgMs Limited and 110 Archaeology, Gloucestershire HER 28023.

Anon., 2005d. *Archaeological Observation Investigation and Recording at 23 Welton Road, Brough,* Unpublished Report, Humber Field Archaeology Report no. 755, EHU 1159.

Anon., 2005e. *Archaeological Recording at 86, Watermoor Road, Cirencester,* Unpublished Report, 110 Archaeology, Gloucestershire HER 28153.

Anon., 2005f. *Henbury Secondary School, Bristol: Post-Excavation Assessment and Updated Project Design,* Unpublished Report, Cotswold Archaeology 04157.

Anon., 2005g. *Land North of Worston Road, Highbridge, Somerset,* Unpublished Report, BaRAS Report no. 1481/2005, Somerset HER 18740.

Anon., 2005h. *Land Off Brandon Road, Swaffham, Norfolk, Archaeological Field Evaluation,* Unpublished Report, Albion Archaeology 2005/62, Norfolk HER 41938.

Anon., 2005i. *Low Farm, Kirby Grindalythe, North Yorkshire, Archaeological Excavation,* Unpublished Report, MAP Archaeological Consultancy, North Yorkshire HER S16251.

Anon., 2005j. *New Road Garage, 26-27 New Road, Driffield, Archaeological Watching Brief Report,* Unpublished Report, MAP Archaeological Consultancy Ltd., EHU 1128.

Anon., 2005k. *Prehistoric Occupation at Coxford Abbey Quarry, East Rudham, Norfolk,* Unpublished Report, Archaeological Solutions, Norfolk HER 41273.

Anon., 2005l. *Report on an Archaeological Evaluation, Flatiron Field, Dunnington,* Unpublished Report, On Site Archaeology Ltd., OSA Report no. OSA04EV08 CYC 668.

Anon., 2005m. *Stamford Bridge Water Pipeline, Archaeological Watching Brief and Excavation, Post-Excavation Assessment Report,* Unpublished Report, EHU no reference number.

Anon., 2006a. *Archaeological Recording at Camp House, Station Road, Bourton-on-the-Water,* Unpublished Report, 110 Archaeology, Gloucestershire HER 28437.

Anon., 2006b. *Archaeological Watching Brief at No. 31 Hadrian Close, Sea Mills, Bristol,* Unpublished Report, BaRAS 1671/2006, Bristol City HER 22413.

Anon., 2006c. *Gainsborough Building, Bath, Archaeological Evaluation Report,* Unpublished Report, Oxford Archaeology 2947, Available on OASIS.

Anon., 2006d. *Land at the Rear of Dorchester Police Station, Archaeological Watching Brief Report,* Unpublished Report, Wessex Archaeology 61010.01, Dorset HER EDO 4826.

Anon., 2006e. *Land Off Brandon Road, Swaffham, Norfolk, Archaeological Investigation,* Unpublished Report, Albion Archaeology 2006/35, Norfolk HER 41938.

Anon., 2006f. *St. Monical Trust, Very Sheltered Housing (Vsh) Site, West Street, Bedminster, Bristol, Archaeological Evaluation, Excavation and Monitoring Exercise, Assessment Report and Updated Project Design,* Unpublished Report, Bristol City HER 22135.

Anon., 2007a. *A14 Haughley Bends Improvements, Archaeological Evaluation and Watching Brief,* Unpublished Report, Wessex Archaeology, 60951.02, Available on OASIS.

Anon., 2007b. *Archaeological Evaluation Report, Land to the Rear of 56-70 Greet Road, Winchcombe, Cheltenham, Gloucestershire,* Unpublished Report, Gloucestershire HER 29076.

Anon., 2007c. *Buttington Terrace, Sedbury, Cheptstow, an Archaeological Evaluation,* Unpublished Report, Monmouth Archaeology MA51.06, Gloucestershire HER 32524.

Anon., 2007d. *No. 80 Roman Way, Sneyd Park, Bristol, Archaeological Watching Brief Project,* Unpublished Report, Avon Archaeological Unit Ltd., Bristol City HER 24546.

Anon., 2008a. *An Archaeological Evaluation on Land at Lavender House, Welton Road, Brough, East Riding of Yorkshire,* Unpublished Report, Humber Field Archaeology Field Archaeology Report no. 294, EHU 1558.

Anon., 2008b. *Land to the North of 25 and 27 Welton Road, Brough, East Yorkshire, Archaeological Observation, Investigations and Recording Brief Report,* Unpublished Report, MAP Archaeological Consultancy, EHU 1530.

Anon., 2009a. *An Iron Age Settlement at Shropham, Norfolk, Draft Publication Report,* Unpublished Report, NAU Archaeology, Norfolk HER 36218.

Anon., 2009b. *Lyde Road, Yeovil, Somerset: Archaeological Field Evaluation Report,* Unpublished Report, Wessex Archaeology 57110.02, Gloucestershire HER 27039.

Anon., 2010. *Gale Common - Ash Disposal Site Phase III, Womersley, North Yorkshire, Archaeological Works: Full Analysis Report,* Unpublished Report, Archaeological Services Durham University Report no. 2167, North Yorkshire HER S16356.

Anon., 2011. *4 Purley Avenue, Cirencester, Gloucestershire, Archaeological Evaluation,* Unpublished Report, Foundations Archaeology Report no. 727, Gloucestershire HER 38975.

Anthony, S., 2005. *Site 10a, Viscount Way, South Marston Park, Swindon, an Archaeological Evaluation Report,* Unpublished Report, Museum of London Archaeology Service.

Anthoons, G., 2012. It's a Small World…Closer Contacts in the Early Third Century BC, in *In Search of the Iron Age: Proceedings of the Iron Age Research Student Seminar 2008, University of Leicester*, eds. M. Sterry, A. Tullett and N. Ray, Leceister: School of Archaeology and Ancient History, University of Leicester, Leicester University Monograph 18, 127-43.

Antoni, B., M. Johnson and J. M. McComish, 2009. *Heslington East, York, Assessment Report,* Unpublished Report, York Archaeological Trust Report no. 2009/48, CYC 1034, 1035, 1036.

Appadurai, A., 1986. Commodities and the Politics of Value, in *The Social Life of Things: Commodities in Cultural Perspective*, ed. A. Appadurai, Cambridge: Cambridge University Press, 3-63.

ApSimon, A. M., 1965. The Roman Temple on Brean Down, Somerset. *Proceedings of the University of Bristol Spelaeological Society,* 10, 195-258.

ApSimon, A. M., P. A. Rahtz and L. G. Harris, 1958. The Iron Age a Ditch and Pottery at Pagan's Hill, Chew Stoke. *Proceedings of the University of Bristol Spelaeological Society,* 8(2), 97-105.

Arletti, R., G. Vezzalini, S. Quartieri, D. Ferrari, M. Merlini and M. Cotte, 2008. Polychrome Glass from Etruscan Sites: First Non-Destructive Characterization with Synchrotron M-XRF, M-Xanes and Xrpd. *Applied Physics A: Material Science and Processing,* 92, 127-35.

Armit, I., 1991. The Atlantic Scottish Iron Age: Five Levels of Chronology. *Proceedings of the Society of Antiquaries of Scotland,* 121, 181-214.

Armit, I., 1997. *Celtic Scotland,* London: Batsford.

Armit, I., 1999. Life after Hownam: The Iron Age in South-East Scotland, in *Northern Exposure: Interpretative Devolution and the Iron Ages in Britain*, ed. B. Bevan, Leicester: Leicester Archaeology Monograph no. 4, 65-79.

Armit, I., 2007. Hillforts at War: From Maiden Castle to Taniwaha Pā. *Proceedings of the Prehistoric Society,* 73, 25-37.

Armit, I., 2012. *Headhunting and the Body in Iron Age Europe,* Cambridge: Cambridge University Press.

Armit, I. and J. McKenzie, 2013. *An Inherited Place: Broxmouth Hillfort and the South East Scottish Iron Age,* Edinburgh: Society of Antiquaries of Scotland.

Ashwin, T., 1996a. Excavations of an Iron Age Site at Silfield, Wymondham, Norfolk, 1992-3. *Norfolk Archaeology,* 42(3), 241-82.

Ashwin, T., 1996b. *Norfolk and Norwich Hospital 2000, Colney, Report on Archaeological Evaluation, July-August 1996,* Unpublished Report, Norfolk Archaeological Unit 182, Norfolk HER 31871.

Atfield, R., 2007. *Land at Culford School, Culford, Archaeological Evaluation Report,* Unpublished Report, Suffolk County Council 2007/49, Suffolk HER CUL 045.

Atkins, R. and A. Connor, 2010. *Farmers and Ironsmiths: Prehistoric, Roman and Anglo-Saxon Settlement Beside Brandon Road, Thetford, Norfolk,* Dereham, Norfolk: East Anglian Archaeology Report no. 134.

Atkinson, D., 1997. *Trial Excavations on Land Off Main Street, Beeford, November 1996,* Unpublished Report, Humber Archaeology Partnership Report no. 14, EHU 511.

Atkinson, D., 1999. *Watching Brief at Queen Street South, Withersea 1998,* Unpublished Report, Humber Archaeology Report no. 282, Humber HER.

Avery, M., 1968. Excavations at Meare East, 1966. *Somerset Archaeology and Natural History*, 112, 21-39.

Avery, M., N.D. *The Meare Lake Village Excavations of 1966*, Unpublished Report provided by M. Avery April 2012.

Baddeley, W., 1930. The Romano-British Temple, Chedworth. *Transactions of the Bristol and Gloucestershire Archaeological Society*, 52, 255-64.

Bailey, C. J., 1963. An Early Iron Age 'B' Hearth Site Indicating Salt Working on the North Shore of the Fleet at Wyke Regis. *Dorset Natural History and Archaeological Society*, 84, 132-36.

Bailey, C. J., 1968. An Early Iron Age/Romano-British Site at Pins Knoll, Litton Cheney. *Dorset Natural History and Archaeological Society*, 89, 147-59.

Bailey, C. J., 1976. Two Romano-British Cist Burials at Portesham, Dorset. *Dorset Natural History and Archaeological Society*, 97, 51.

Bailey, C. J., 1985. The Romano-British Site at Walls, Puncknowle, Dorset. *Dorset Natural History and Archaeological Society*, 107, 55-86.

Bain, S. and I. Cullen, 1996. *Discovery and Excavation in Scotland*, 65.

Balch, H. E., 1911. A Late-Celtic and Romano-British Cave-Dwelling at Wookey-Hole, near Wells, Somerset. *Archaeologia*, 62, 565-92.

Balch, H. E., 1913. Further Excavations at the Late-Celtic and Romano-British Cave-Dwelling at Wookey Hole, Somerset. *Archaeologia*, 64, 337-46.

Balch, H. E., 1928. Excavations at Wookey Hole and Other Mendip Caves, 1926-7. *Antiquaries Journal*, 8, 193-210.

Bales, E., 1999. *Orion Business Park, Blackacre Hill, Great Blakenham, Archaeological Evaluation*, Unpublished Report, Suffolk County Council 99/39, Suffolk HER BLG017.

Bales, E., C. Good and J. Meredith, 2006. *Ravenswood (Former Ipswich Airport), a Report on the Archaeological Evaluations and Excavations, 1999-2000*, Unpublished Report, Suffolk County Council 2006/229, Suffolk HER.

Barber, A., 1996. *Former Unitarian Chapel, Gosditch Street, Cirencester, Gloucestershire, Archaeological Evaluation*, Unpublished Report, Cotswold Archaeology Trust Report no. 96375, Gloucestershire HER 28899.

Barber, A., 1999. *8 Church Street, Cirencester, Gloucestershire, Archaeological Evaluation*, Unpublished Report, Cotswold Archaeology Trust Report no. 99988, Gloucestershire HER 20355.

Barber, A., 2003. *Cotswold School Swimming Pool, Bourton-on-the-Water, Gloucestershire*, Unpublished Report, Cotswold Archaeology 03099, Gloucestershire HER 22358.

Barber, A., 2009a. *Chedworth Roman Villa, Gloucestershire, Archaeological Evaluation*, Unpublished Report, Cotswold Archaeology Report no. 09158, Available on OASIS.

Barber, A., 2009b. *Land Adjacent to 29-32 Lavender Lane, Trinity Road, Cirencester, Gloucestershire, Archaeological Evaluation*, Unpublished Report, Cotswold Archaeology Report 09121, Gloucestershire HER 33715.

Barber, A., 2009c. *Land at the Down Ampney Estate, Gloucestershire and Wiltshire, Archaeological Evaluation*, Unpublished Report, Cotswold Archaeology Report 09069, Available on OASIS.

Barber, A., 2009d. *Land East of Lydney Site a (South), Lydney, Gloucestershire, Archaeological Evaluation*, Unpublished Report, Cotswold Archaeology Report no. 10214, Available on OASIS.

Barber, A., 2010. *Land at Bristol Road Weston-Super-Mare, North Somerset, Archaeological Evaluation*, Unpublished Report, Cotswold Archaeology Report 10214, Available on OASIS.

Barber, A. and N. Holbrook, 1997. *A Roman Iron Smelting Site at Blakeney, Gloucestershire, Excavations at Mill End Lane 1997*, Unpublished Report, Cotswold Archaeological Trust, Report no. 991012, Gloucestershire HER 17988.

Barber, A. J. and N. Holbrook, 2000. A Roman Iron-Smelting Site at Blakeney, Gloucestershire: Excavations at Millend Late 1997. *Transactions of the Bristol and Gloucestershire Archaeological Society*, 118, 33-60.

Barber, A. J. and G. T. Walker, 1998. Home Farm, Bishop's Cleeve: Excavations of a Romano-British Occupation Site 1993-4. *Transactions of the Bristol and Gloucestershire Archaeological Society*, 116, 117-39.

Barclay, G. J., 1993. The Excavation of Pit Circles at Romancamp Gate, Fochabers, Moray. *Proceedings of the Society of Antiquaries of Scotland*, 123, 255-68.

Barclay, G. J. and M. Tolan, 1990. *Romancamp Gate, Fochabers, Moray, 1990: Interim Report*, Unpublished Report, RCAHMS MS 656/2.

Barker, W. R., 1900. Remains of a Roman Villa Discovered at Brislington, December 1899. *Transactions of the Bristol and Gloucestershire Archaeological Society*, 23, 289-308.

Barker, W. R., 1901. Remains of a Roman Villa Discovered at Brislington. *Transactions of the Bristol and Gloucestershire Archaeological Society*, 24, 283-92.

Barnes, R. and J. B. Eicher (eds.), 1993. *Dress and Gender: Making and Meaning in Cultural Contexts*, Oxford: Berg.

Barrett, J. C., 1981. Aspects of the Iron Age in Atlantic Scotland. A Case Study in Problems of Archaeological Interpretation. *Proceedings of the Society of Antiquaries of Scotland*, 111, 205-19.

Barrett, J. C., P. W. M. Freeman and A. Woodward, 2000. *Cadbury Castle, Somerset: The Later Prehistoric and Early Historic Archaeology,* London: English Heritage Archaeological Report 20.

Barrett, J. H. and G. C. Boon, 1972. A Roman Counterfeiter's Den, Part 1., White Woman's Hole, near Leighton, Mendip Hills, Somerset. *Proceedings of the University of Bristol Spelaeological Society,* 13(1), 61-69.

Barrett, R., 2001. *An Archaeological Watching Brief at 98-100 Evesham Road, Cheltenham, Gloucestershire,* Unpublished Report, Gloucestershire County Council, Gloucestershire HER 20900.

Barrett, R., 2002. *A Watching Brief at 52 Ebrington, Ebrington, Gloucestershire,* Unpublished Report, Gloucestershire County Council, Gloucestershire HER 21342.

Barrett, R., 2003. *An Archaeological Evaluation of Land Opposite 2-14 Station Street, Cheltenham, Gloucestershire,* Unpublished Report, Gloucestershire County Council, Gloucestershire HER 22102.

Barrett, R., 2005a. *An Archaeological Evaluation at Larch House, Bourton-on-the-Water, Gloucestershire,* Unpublished Report, Gloucestershire County Council, Gloucestershire HER 27761.

Barrett, R., 2005b. *Archaeological Excavation, the High School for Girls, Denmark Road, Gloucester,* Unpublished Report, Gloucestershire County Council, Gloucestershire HER 26815.

Barrett, R. M., 2006. *An Archaeological Evaluation of Land at Hazleton, Whiteshoots Hill, Cold Aston, Gloucestershire,* Unpublished Report, Gloucestershire County Council, Gloucestershire HER 28206.

Barrett, R. M., 2007a. *An Archaeological Evaluation at Tewkesbury Road, Ucklington, Gloucestershire,* Unpublished Report, Gloucestershire County Council, Gloucestershire HER 29096.

Barrett, R. M., 2007b. *An Archaeological Evaluation of Land at Rectory Meadows, Church Lane, Rudford, Gloucestershire,* Unpublished Report, Gloucestershire County Council, Gloucestershire HER 29658.

Bartlett, J. E. and R. W. Mackey, 1972. Excavations on Walkington Wold, 1967-1969. *East Riding Archaeologist,* 1(2), 1-100.

Barton, K. J., 1964. Star Roman Villa, Shipham, Somerset. *Somerset Archaeology and Natural History Society,* 108, 45-98.

Bashford, L., 1999. *An Archaeological Evaluation on Land at Glebelands, Slimbridge, Gloucestershire,* Unpublished Report, Gloucestershire County Council, Gloucestershire HER 20591.

Bashford, L., 2000a. *Archaeological Evaluation at 98-100 Evesham Road, Cheltenham, Gloucestershire,* Unpublished Report, Gloucestershire County Council, Gloucestershire HER 20900.

Bashford, L., 2000b. *An Archaeological Watching Brief at 41, Ashcroft Gardens, Cirencester, Gloucestershire,* Unpublished Report, Gloucestershire County Council, Gloucestershire HER 20706.

Bashford, R., 2006. *Kingshill North, Cirencester, Gloucestershire, Archaeological Evaluation Report,* Unpublished Report, Oxford Archaeological Unit 3048, Gloucestershire HER 28654.

Bateman, C., 1998. *Gloucester Business Park Link Road, Brockworth, Gloucester, Archaeological Evaluation,* Unpublished Report, Cotswold Archaeological Trust Report no. 98920, Gloucestershire HER 20087.

Bateman, C., 2000. Excavations Along the Littleton Drew to Chippenham Gas Pipeline. *Wiltshire Archaeology and Natural History Society,* 93, 90-104.

Bateman, C., 2004. *3 Corinium Gate, Cirencester, Gloucestershire, Archaeological Evaluation,* Unpublished Report, Cotswold Archaeological Trust Report no. 04037, Gloucestershire HER 26573.

Bateman, C. and D. Enright, 2000. Excavations of Bronze Age and Romano-British Sites Along the Chippenham Western Bypass A4 to A350 Link. *Wiltshire Archaeology and Natural History Society,* 93, 233-54.

Bateman, C., D. Enright and N. Oakey, 2003. Prehistoric and Anglo-Saxon Settlements to the Rear of Sherborne House, Lechlade, Excavations in 1997. *Transactions of the Bristol and Gloucestershire Archaeological Society,* 121, 23-96.

Bates, S., 1996. *Heath Farm, Postwick,* Unpublished Report, Norfolk Archaeological Unit 162, Norfolk HER 31109.

Bates, S., 2000. Excavations at Quidney Farm, Saham Toney, Norfolk 1995. *Britannia,* 31, 201-38.

Bates, S., 2001. *Report on an Archaeological Evaluation in Rear Garden of No. 2 Church Street Diss,* Unpublished Report, Norfolk Archaeological Unit 587, Norfolk HER 35981.

Bates, S., 2002. *Report on an Archaeological Evaluation at Short Drove, Downham Market,* Unpublished Report, Norfolk Archaeological Unit 699, Norfolk HER 37093.

Bates, S., 2003. *Assessment Report and Updated Project Design for Archaeological Excavations and Watching Brief on the North Pickenham to West Bradenham Supply Mains,* Unpublished Report, Norfolk Archaeological Unit 825, Norfolk HER 27097-37106.

Bates, S., 2006. *An Archaeological Strip and Record Excavation at Longdell Hills, Easton, Norfolk,* Unpublished Report, NAU Archaeology 1187, Norfolk HER 36414.

Bates, S., 2008a. *An Archaeological Evaluation at Crimplesham Replacement Quarry, Norfolk,* Unpublished Report, NAU Archaeology 1754, Norfolk HER 50596.

Bates, S., 2008b. *An Archaeological Strip, Map, and Sample Excavation at East Bilney Quarry, Norfolk. An Interim Report,* Unpublished Report, NAU Archaeology 1686, Norfolk HER 39348.

Bates, S. and A. Shelley, 2004. *8-12 Red Lion Street, Aylsham, Norfolk, Post-Fieldwork Assessment of Potential for Analaysis and Updated Project Design,* Unpublished Report, Norfolk Archaeological Unit 824, Norfolk HER 37376.

Bates, S. and A. Shelley, 2005. Excavations on Red Lion Street, Aylsham, 2003. *Norfolk Archaeology,* 44(4), 617-43.

Beadsmoore, E., 2005. *Frimstone Carrstone Quarry, Snettisham, Norfolk: An Archaeological Evaluation,* Unpublished Report, Cambridge Archaeological Unit 707, Norfolk HER 41936.

Beadsmoore, E., 2007a. *Frimstone Carrstone Quarry, Snettisham, Norfolk: A 'Strip, Map and Record' Excavation,* Unpublished Report, Cambridge Archaeological Unit 771, Norfolk HER 41936.

Beadsmoore, E., 2007b. *Mayton Wood, Buxton with Lammas, Norfolk, a 'Strip, Map and Record' Excavation,* Unpublished Report, Cambridge Archaeological Unity 765, Norfolk 39833.

Beavis, J., 1975. Excavations at Abbotsbury Castle, Hill-Fort, 1974. *Dorset Natural History and Archaeological Society,* 96, 56-58.

Beck, C. W., 1991. *Amber in Prehistoric Britain,* Oxford: Oxbow.

Beck, H. C., 1928. Classification and Nomenclature of Beads and Pendants. *Archaeologia,* 77, 1-76.

Bell, M., 1991. *Brean Down Chalets: Archaeological Assessment, September 1991,* Unpublished Report, St Davids University College, Lampeter, Somerset HER 11343.

Bellamy, P., 2001. *Prrox Roofing Supplies, Rigler Road, Hamworthy, Poole, Archaeological Observations, September 2001,* Unpublished Report, Terrain Archaeology 5085.1, Dorset HER.

Bellamy, P., 2005. *Beaulieu Road, Amesbury, Wiltshire, Archaeological Evaluation,* Unpublished Report, Terrain Archaeology Report no. 53203/2/1.

Bellamy, P. and A. Graham, 2004. *Mill House, Lopen, South Somerset, Archaeological Evaluation, October-November 2001,* Unpublished Report, Terrain Archaeology Report no. 5092.1, Somerset SMR 15590.

Bellamy, P. S., 1991. Observations at Merchant's Garage, High West Street, Dorchester, 1983. *Dorset Natural History and Archaeological Society,* 113, 41-54.

Bellamy, P. S., 2004. Roman Defences at Dorford Baptist Church, Bridport Road, Dorchester. *Dorset Natural History and Archaeological Society,* 126, 166-70.

Bellows, J., 1881. On Some Bronze and Other Articles Found near Birdlip. *Transactions of the Bristol and Gloucestershire Archaeological Society,* 5, 137-40.

Bellows, J., 1882. Remarks on Skeletons Found at Gloucester in 1881. *Transactions of the Bristol and Gloucestershire Archaeological Society,* 6, 345-48.

Bennett, J. and N. Wright, 2008. *Larks Rise, Old Gloucester Road, Bourton-on-the-Water, Gloucestershire, Archaeological Watching Brief,* Unpublished Report, Cotswold Archaeology 08010, Gloucestershire SMR 33151.

Benton, S., 1931a. The Excavation of the Sculptor's Cave, Covesea, Morayshire. *Proceedings of the Society of Antiquairies of Scotland,* 65, 177-216.

Benton, S., 1931b. The Excavations of the Sculptor's Cave, Covesea, Morayshire. *Proceedings of the Society of Antiquaries of Scotland,* 65, 177-216.

Berlin, B. and P. Kay, 1999. *Basic Color Terms: Their Universality and Evolution,* Stanford: CSLI.

Bertini, M., 2012. *Novel Application of Micro- and Non-Destructive Analytical Techniques for the Analysis of Iron Age Glass Beads from North-Eastern Scotland,* Unpublished Ph.D. Thesis, University of Aberdeen.

Bertini, M., A. Shortland, K. Milek and E. M. Krupp, 2011. Investigation of Iron Age North-Eastern Scottish Glass Beads Using Element Analysis with LA-ICP-MS. *Journal of Archaeological Science,* 38(10), 2750-66.

Beswick, P., M. R. Megaw, J. V. S. Megaw and P. Northover, 1990. A Decorated Late Iron Age Torc from Dinnington, South Yorkshire. *Antiquaries Journal,* 70, 16-33.

Bevan, B., 1997. Bounding the Landscape: Place and Identity During the Yorkshire Wolds Iron Age, in *Reconstructing Iron Age Societies: New Approaches to the British Iron Age*, eds. A. Gwilt and C. Haselgrove, Oxford: Oxbow Monograph 71, 181-91.

Bevan, B., 1999. Land~Life~Death~Regeneration: Interpreting a Middle Iron Age Landscape in Eastern Yorkshire, in *Northern Exposure: Interpretative Devolution and the Iron Ages in Britain*, ed. B. Bevan, Leicester: Leicester University Archaeology Monograph no. 4, 123-48.

Birbeck, V., 2002. Excavations on Iron Age and Romano-British Settlements at Cannards Grave, Shetpon Mallet. *Somerset Archaeology and Natural History Society,* 144, 41-116.

Birbeck, V., 2006. Excavations on the Old Ditch Linear Earthwork, Breach Hill, Tilshead. *Wiltshire Archaeology and Natural History Society,* 99, 79-103.

Birks, C., 2001. *Report on an Archaeological Evaluation at A11 Roudham to Attleborough Improvement Scheme,* Unpublished Report, Norfolk Archaeological Unit 567, Norfolk HER 35776.

Birks, C., 2003a. *An Archaeological Evaluation Associated with the A11 Attleborough Bypass Scheme,* Unpublished Report, Norfolk Archaeological Unit 868, Norfolk HER 39690.

Birks, C., 2003b. *An Archaeological Evaluation at Cringleford Park and Ride,* Unpublished Report, Norfolk Archaeological Unit 890, Norfolk HER 39823.

Birks, C., 2005. *Report on an Archaeological Evaluation at Land at Front Street, Worstead Norfolk,* Unpublished Report, Chris Birks CB007R, Norfolk HER 41157.

Birks, C. and D. Robertson, 2004. *A Mid to Late Iron Age Settlement at Stanford: Excavations at Lynford Quarry, 2000-2001,* Unpublished Report, Norfolk Archaeological Unit 919, Norfolk HER 35165.

Birks, C. and D. Robertson, 2005. Prehistoric Settlement at Stanford: Excavations at Lynford Quarry, Norfolk 2000-2001. *Norfolk Archaeology,* 44(4), 676-701.

Bishop, B., 2005. *Mayton Wood, Buxton with Lammas, Norfolk, a 'Strip, Map and Sample' Excavation, Phase 2,* Unpublished Report, Cambridge Archaeological Unit 693, Norfolk HER 39833.

Bishop, M. C., 1997. *A New Flavian Military Site at Roecliffe, Excavation Report,* Unpublished Report, Northern Archaeological Associates, NAA 97/53.

Bishop, M. C., 1999. An Iron Age and Romano-British 'Ladder' Settlement at Melton, East Yorkshire. *Yorkshire Archaeological Journal,* 71, 23-63.

Black, G. F., 1891. Report on the Archaeological Examination of the Culbin Sands, Elginshire, Obtained under the Victoria Jubilee Gift of His Excellency Dr R. H. Gunning. *Proceedings of the Society of Antiquaries of Scotland,* 25, 484-511.

Blagg, T., J. Plouviez and A. Tester, 2004. *Excavations at a Large Romano-British Settlement at Hatcheston, Suffolk in 1973-4,* Dereham, Norfolk: East Anglian Archaeological Report no. 106.

Boon, G. C., 1945. The Roman Site at Sea Mills, 1945-46. *Transactions of the Bristol and Gloucestershire Archaeological Society,* 66, 258-95.

Boon, G. C., 1961. Notes: A Late-Roman Bronze Buckle-Plate from Sea Mills. *Antiquaries Journal,* 41, 87-89.

Boore, E., 1999. A Romano-British Site at Lawrence Weston, Bristol, 1995. *Bristol and Avon Archaeology,* 16, 1-47.

Booth, P. and D. Stansbie, 2003. *Kempsford Quarry, Gloucestershire, Report on Excavations 2000-2001,* Unpublished Report, Oxford Archaeology, Gloucestershire HER 3156.

Borić, D. and J. Robb, 2008. Body Theory in Archaeology, in *Past Bodies: Body Centred Research in Archaeology,* eds. D. Borić and J. Robb, Oxford: Oxbow, 1-7.

Boulter, S., 1993a. *A.A.C. Wattisham, Excavation Report,* Unpublished Report, Suffolk County Council 93/26, Suffolk HER BCG 005.

Boulter, S., 1993b. *RAF Wattisham, Great Bricett, Archaeological Evaluation,* Unpublished Report, Suffolk County Council 93/25, Suffolk HER.

Boulter, S., 1994. *Tuddenham-Playford, Rising Main, Record of Monitoring and Excavation,* Unpublished Report, Suffolk County Council 94/33, Suffolk HER TDM 007, 015, 016.

Boulter, S., 1995. *Coast Protection Scheme, Brackenbury Phase II, an Archaeological Evaluation,* Unpublished Report, Suffolk County Council, Suffolk HER FEX 008.

Boulter, S., 1996a. *The Albany, Excavation Report,* Unpublished Report, Suffolk County Council 96/22, Suffolk HER IPS 240.

Boulter, S., 1996b. *Bloodmoor Hill, Carlton Collville, Evaluation Report,* Unpublished Report, Suffolk County Council 96/4, Suffolk HER CAC 014.

Boulter, S., 1996c. *Shrubland Park Estate, Coddenham, Evaluation Report,* Unpublished Report, Suffolk County Council 96/85, Suffolk HER CDD 050.

Boulter, S., 1997a. *Debenham Community Woodland, Debenham, Record of an Archaeological Evaluation,* Unpublished Report, Suffolk County Council 97/64, Suffolk HER DBN 090.

Boulter, S., 1997b. *Former Firmin Site, Handford Road, Ipswich, Record of an Archaeolgical Evaluation,* Unpublished Report, Suffolk County Council 97/25, Suffolk HER IPS 280.

Boulter, S., 1997c. *Grundisburgh, the Old School, Excavation Report,* Unpublished Report, Suffolk County Council 94/22, Suffolk HER GRU 037.

Boulter, S., 1998. *Trimley St Martin, Record of an Archaeological Excavation and Monitoring,* Unpublished Report, Suffolk County Council 98/4, Suffolk HER TYN 029.

Boulter, S., 1999a. *Archaeological Monitoring of Groundworks Associated with the Land-Plots Previously Occupied by Everard and Donrovin, High Street, Oxford,* Unpublished Report, Suffolk County Council 99/37, Suffolk HER ORF 028.

Boulter, S., 1999b. *Risbridge Home, Kredlington, Record of an Archaeological Excavation,* Unpublished Report, Suffolk County Council 98/9, Suffolk HER KDG 019.

Boulter, S., 2002. *A Record of an Archaeological Evaluation of Land at Gallows Hill, Barking Suffolk,* Unpublished Report, Suffolk County Council 2002/53, Suffolk HER BRK 104.

Boulter, S., 2005. *Handford Road, Ipswich, Archaeological Assessment Report,* Unpublished Report, Suffolk County Council 2004/87, Suffolk HER IPS 280.

Boulter, S., 2006. *Highfield Nursery, Ipswich, a Record of Archaeological Monitoring,* Unpublished Report, Suffolk County Council Archaeological Service Report 2006/53, Available on OASIS.

Boulter, S., 2008. *An Assessment of the Archaeology Recorded in New Phases 5, 6, 7 (a and B), 9, 11 and 12 of Flixton Park Quarry,* Unpublished Report, Suffolk County Council 2006/54, Suffolk HER.

Boulter, S., 2010. *Rear of 4 Highfield Approach, Ipswich, Archaeological Evaluation Report,* Unpublished Report, Suffolk County Council 2010/024, Suffolk HER IPS 618.

Boulter, S. and K. Sparkes, 1997. *Flixton Park, Flixton, Preliminary Record of Archaeological Deposits Recorded During Soil Stripping in Area 5,* Unpublished Report, Suffolk County Council 97/46, Suffolk HER FLN 053.

Bourdieu, P., 1984. *Distinction: A Social Critique of the Judgement of Taste*, London: Routledge.

Bourdieu, P., 1990. *The Logic of Practice,* Stanford: Stanford University Press.

Bowden, W., 2008. A New Roman Site near Caistor St. Edmund, *The Annual, The Bulletin of the Norfolk Archaeological and Historical Research Group*, 17, 9-18.

Boyle, A., M. Gocher, G. Hey and G. Laws, 1998. *Shorncote Quarry, Somerford Keynes, Gloucestershire, Eastern Extension, Areas 18 and 2, Post Excavation Assessment and Research Design,* Unpublished Report, Oxford Archaeological Unit, Gloucestershire HER 15477.

Boyle, M., 2004. *An Archaeological Strip and Record Excavation at Longdell Hills, Easton, Norfolk, Interim Report,* Unpublished Report, Norfolk Archaeological Unit 859, Norfolk HER 36414.

Boyle, M. J., 2006. *An Archaeological Strip and Record Excavation at Longdell Hills, Easton, Norfolk,* Unpublished Report, NAU Archaeology 1126, Norfolk HER 36414.

Bradley, R., 1975. Maumbury Rings, Dorchester: The Excavations of 1908-1913. *Archaeologia,* 105, 1-97.

Bradley, R., 2007. *The Prehistory of Britain and Ireland,* Cambridge: Cambridge University Press.

Bradley-Lovekin, T., 2007. *Archaeological Watching Brief on Land at Tranquility, Marsh Lane, Brancaster, Norfolk,* Unpublished Report, Archaeological Project Services 082/07, Norfolk HER 50282.

Bradley-Lovekin, T., 2008. *Archaeological Evaluation of Land to the Rear of 10-12 Common Road, Snettisham, Norfolk,* Unpublished Report, Archaeological Project Services 65/08, Norfolk HER 51519.

Bradley-Lovekin, T., 2009a. *Archaeological Evaluation on Land at 17 Roman Way, Caister on Sea, Norfolk,* Unpublished Report, Archaeological Project Services 001/09, Norfolk HER 52560.

Bradley-Lovekin, T., 2009b. *Archaeological Watching Brief on Land at 17 Roman Way, Caister on Sea, Norfolk,* Unpublished Report, Archaeological Project Services 45/09, Norfolk HER 52560.

Brakspear, H., 1904. The Roman Villa at Box. *Wiltshire Archaeology and Natural History Society,* 33, 236-62.

Bray, L. S., 2006. *The Archaeology of Iron Production: Romano-British Evidence from the Exemoor Region, Volume 1 of 2,* Unpublished PhD Thesis, University of Exeter, Somerset HER 29720.

Brennard, M., 1999. *Report on an Archaeological Evaluation at Brandon Road, Thetford,* Unpublished Report, Norfolk Archaeological Unit 382, Norfolk HER 33812.

Brennard, M., 2000. *Report on an Archaeological Evaluation at the Football Training Ground, Trowse Newton, Nowich,* Unpublished Report, Norfolk Archaeological Unit 475, Norfolk HER 25709.

Brett, M., 2004. *Land to the East of Federal Mogul, Lydney, Gloucestershire, Archaeological Evaluation,* Unpublished Report, Cotswold Archaeology 04157, Gloucestershire HER 27570.

Brett, M. and A. Hancocks, 2008. Excavations at Lower Mill Farm, Somerford Keynes, Gloucestershire, 2001. *Transactions of the Bristol and Gloucestershire Archaeological Society,* 126, 107-11.

Brett, M., A. Hancocks and E. McSloy, 2003. *Lower Mill Estate Somerford Keynes, Gloucestershire, Post-Excavation Assessment and Updated Project Design,* Unpublished Report, Cotswold Archaeological Trust Report no. 03131, Gloucestershire HER 20901.

Brett, M. and E. R. McSloy, 2011. Prehistoric Pits and Roman Enclosures on the A419 Blunsdon Bypass, Blunsdon St Andrew, Excavations 2006-7. *Wiltshire Archaeology and Natural History Society,* 104, 95-114.

Brett, M. and M. Watts, 2008. *Excavations at Stepstair Lane, 2002-3,* Cirencester: Cotswold Archaeology.

Brewster, T. C. M., 1957. Excavations at Newham's Pit, Staxton, 1947-48. *Yorkshire Archaeological Journal,* 39, 193-223.

Brewster, T. C. M., 1963. *The Excavations at Staple Howe,* Wintringham: The East Riding Archaeological Research Committee.

Brewster, T. C. M., 1980. *The Excavation of Garton and Wetwang Slacks,* Malton, Yorks.: East Riding Archaeological Research Committee.

Bride, A.-S., 2005. Le Mobilier De Verre Des Fouilles Anciennes Et Récentes De Bibracte, in *Études Sur Bibracte, 1*Glux-en-Glenne: Bibracte - Centre Archéologique Européen, 81-161.

Brigers, J. L., 2010. *An Archaeological Watching Brief to the North and West of 23, Southview Road, Westonzoyland,* Unpublished Report, Prospect Archaeology, Somerset HER 28548.

Brill, R. H., 1999. *Chemical Analysis of Early Glass,* Corning, N.Y.: The Corning Museum of Glass.

Brinklow, D., 1997. *A19/A64 Interchange, Fulford, Road Improvement Scheme, Report on an Archaeological Watching Brief,* York Archaeological Trust.

Brogan, G. and S. Unger, 2007. *The Spread Eagle Public House, Barton Bendish, Norfolk, an Archaeological Evaluation,* Unpublished Report, Archaeological Solutions 295, Norfolk HER 51026.

Brooks, R., 2008. *Maples, the Spinney, Long Melford, Archaeological Monitoring Report,* Unpublished Report, Suffolk County Council 2008/024, Suffolk HER LMD 174.

Brooks, R., 2010a. *Base Perimeter Road, Mildenhall, Archaeological Excavation Report,* Unpublished Report, Suffolk County Council 2010/030, Suffolk HER MNL 600.

Brooks, R., 2010b. *Former CES Building, RAF Mildenhall, Archaeological Excavation Report,* Unpublished Report, Suffolk County Council 2010/048, Suffolk HER MNL 610.

Broomhead, R. A., 1998a. *Castle Hill Quarry, Cannington, an Archaeological Watching Brief for the Castle Hill Quarry Co. Ltd.*, Unpublished Report, Somerset HER 28899.

Broomhead, R. A., 1998b. *Sycamore Lodge East Brent, an Archaeological Evaluation for Mr. D.J. Cornish*, Unpublished Report, Somerset HER 12974.

Broomhead, R. A., 1999a. *Kings of Wessex Community School Archaeological Observations on Behalf of Somerset County Council*, Unpublished Report, Somerset HER 12891.

Broomhead, R. A., 1999b. *Sycamore Lodge, East Brench, Archaeological Observations on Behalf of Mr. D.J. Cornish*, Unpublished Report, Somerset HER 12976.

Broomhead, R. A., 2002. *Rossholme School, East Brent, an Archaeological Evaluation for Mrs. S.J. Webb*, Unpublished Report, Somerset HER 15968.

Broomhead, R. A., 2004. *4 Lister Close, Ilchester, an Archaeological Evaluation on Behalf of Mr and Mrs N. Pamplin*, Unpublished Report, Somerset HER 28264.

Broomhead, R. A., 2005. *8 High Street, Ilchester, Archaeological Observations on Behalf of Mrs B Gunn*, Unpublished Report, Somerset HER 28248.

Broomhead, R. A., 2006. *Amulet Way, Shepton Mallet, an Archaeological Evaluation on Behalf of Tamarind Development Ltd.*, Unpublished Report, Somerset HER 14258.

Brossler, A., M. Gocher, G. Laws and M. Roberts, 2002. Shorncote Quarry: Excavations of a Late Prehistoric Landscape in the Upper Thames Valley, 1997 and 1998. *Transactions of the Bristol and Gloucestershire Archaeological Society*, 120, 37-87.

Brown, F., C. Howard-Davis, M. Brennard, A. Boyle, T. Evants, S. O'Connor, A. Spence, R. Heawood and A. Lupton, 2007. *The Archaeology of the A1 (M) Darrington to Dishforth DBFO Road Scheme*, Lancaster: Oxford Archaeology North.

Brown, J. C., 1965. A Romano-British Site at St. Mary's Lane, Portishead, Somerset. *Proceedings of the University of Bristol Spelaeological Society*, 10, 259-71.

Brown, L., M. Corney and P. J. Woodward, 1995. An Iron Age and Romano-British Settlement on Oakley Down, Wimborne St. Giles, Dorset. *Dorset Natural History and Archaeological Society*, 117, 67-79.

Brown, P. D. C. and A. D. McWhirr, 1969. Cirencester, 1967-68, Eighth Interim Report. *Antiquaries Journal*, 44, 222-43.

Bruce, G., 2003. *St. Oswald's School, Fulford, York., Report on an Archaeological Evaluation*, Unpublished Report, On Site Archaeology Ltd., Report no: OSA02EV14 CYC 473.

Brugmann, B., 2004. *Glass Beads from Early Anglo-Saxon Graves: A Study of the Provenance and Chronology of Glass Beads Form Early Anglo-Saxon Graves, Based on Visual Examination*, Oxford: Oxbow.

Buchanan, S., 2005. Discovery and Excavation in Scotland. 94.

Budge, A. R., J. R. Russel and G. C. Boon, 1974. Excavations and Fieldwork at Charterhouse-on-Mendip, 1960-67. *Proceedings of the University of Bristol Spelaeological Society*, 13(3), 327-47.

Bulleid, A. and H. Gray, 1917. *The Glastonbury Lake Village: A Full Description of the Excavations and the Relics Discovered 1892-1907*, Glastonbury: Glastonbury Antiquarian Society.

Bulleid, A. and H. Gray, 1948a. *The Meare Lake Village, Volume 1*, Taunton: Taunton Castle.

Bulleid, A. and H. Gray, 1948b. *The Meare Lake Village, Volume 2*, Taunton: Taunton Castle.

Bulleid, A. and H. Gray, 1966. *The Meare Lake Village, Volume 3*, Taunton: Taunton Castle.

Burchill, R., 1996. Survey and Re-Excavation at Kingston Roman Villa. *Bristol and Avon Archaeology*, 13, 47-51.

Burne, A. H., 1944. Discovery of a Roman Coffin at Corsham, October 1942. *Wiltshire Archaeology and Natural History Society*, 50, 371-72.

Burroughes, G., 2008. *Excavation Report of the Roman Road at Great Hallows, Stoke Ash, Suffolk*, Unpublished Report, Suffolk Archaeological Group, Suffolk HER SAS 017.

Burrow, E. J., W. H. Knowles, A. E. W. Paine and J. W. Gray, 1925. Excavations on Leckhampton Hill, Cheltenham, During the Summer of 1925. *Transactions of the Bristol and Gloucestershire Archaeological Society*, 47, 81-112.

Burrow, I., 1981. *Wadeford Roman Villa, Combe St Nicholas, Watching Brief - 12-13th February 1981*, Unpublished Report, Somerset HER 27185.

Burrow, I. C. G., 1976. Brean Down Hillfort, Somerset, 1974. *Proceedings of the University of Bristol Spelaeological Society*, 14(2), 141-54.

Bushe-Fox, J. P., 1915. *Excavations at Hengistbury Head, Hampshire in 1911-12*, Society of Antiquaries of London Research report no. 3.

Butterworth, C., 2003. Multi-Period Finds from Quarleston Farm, Winterborne Stickland, 1994-5. *Dorset Natural History and Archaeological Society*, 125, 147-50.

Butterworth, C. A., 1992. Excavations at Norton Bavant Borrow Pit, Wiltshire, 1987. *Wiltshire Archaeology and Natural History Society*, 85, 1-26.

Butterworth, C. A. and R. S. Smith, 1997. Excavations at the Hermitage, Old Town, Swindon. *Wiltshire Archaeology and Natural History Society*, 90, 55-76.

Caine, C., 2010. *A Proposed Development on Land to the North of Aginghill's Farm, Monkton Heathfield, Somerset, Results of an Archaeological Trench Evaluation*, Unpublished Report, AC Archaeology no. ACD208/2/0, Somerset HER 30240.

Calkin, J. B., 1935. An Early Romano-British Kiln at Corfe Mullen, Dorset. *Antiquaries Journal*, 15, 42-55.

Calkin, J. B., 1947. Two Romano-British Burials at Kimmeridge. *Dorset Natural History and Archaeological Society*, 69, 33-41.

Calkin, J. B., 1953. 'Kimmeridge Coal-Money'. The Romano-British Shale Industry. *Proceedings of the Dorset Natural History and Archaeological Society*, 75, 45-71.

Calkin, J. B., 1964. Some Early Iron Age Sites in the Bournemouth Area. *Dorset Natural History and Archaeological Society*, 86, 120-30.

Callander, J. G., 1916. Notice of a Jet Necklace Found in a Cist in a Bronze Age Cemetery, Discovered on Burgie Lodge Farm, Morayshire, with Notes on Scottish Prehistoric Jet Ornaments. *Proceedings of the Society of Antiquaries of Scotland*, 50, 201-40.

Callender, M. and N. Thomas, 1953. Roman House at Kingshall Farm, Cricklade. *Wiltshire Archaeology and Natural History Society*, 555, 34-39.

Cameron, K., 1997. *Archaeological Excavation at Candle Stane Recumbent Stone Circle, Insch, Aberdeenshire,* Unpublished Report, Centre for Field Archaeology Report no. 322, RCAHMS MS 726/109.

Cameron, K., 1999. Excavation of an Iron Age Timber Structure Beside the Candle Stane Recumbent Stone Circle, Aberdeenshire. *Proceedings of the Society of Antiquaries of Scotland*, 129, 359-72.

Cameron, K. and M. Cressey, 1996. *Archaeological Excavation at Candle Stane Recumbant Stone Circle, Insch, Aberdeenshire,* Unpublished Report, Centre for Field Archaeology Report no. 301, RCAHMS MS 726/131.

Cardwell, P., 1989. Excavations at Cat Babbleton Farm, Ganton, North Yorkshire, 1986. *Yorkshire Archaeological Journal*, 61, 15-27.

Carr, G., 2003. Creolisation, Pidginisation and the Interpretation of Unique Artefacts in Early Roman Britain, in *TRAC 2002: Proceedings of the Twelfth Theoretical Roman Archaeology Conference, Kent 2002*, eds. G. Carr, E. Swift and J. Weekes, Oxford: Oxbow, 113-25.

Carr, G., 2005. Woad, Tattooing and Identity in Later Iron Age and Early Roman Britain. *Oxford Journal of Archaeology*, 24(3), 273-92.

Carr, G., 2006. *Creolised Bodies and Hybrid Identities: Examining the Early Roman Period in Essex and Hertfordshire,* Oxford: BAR British Series no. 418.

Carr, G. and C. J. Knüsel, 1997. The Ritual Framework of Excarnation by Exposure as the Mortuary Practice of the Early and Middle Iron Ages of Central Southern Britain, in *Reconstructing Iron Age Societies: New Approaches to the British Iron Age*, eds. A. Gwilt and C. Haselgrove, Oxford: Oxbow Monograph 71, 167-73.

Carr, J., 1985. Excavations on the Mound, Glastonbury, Somerset, 1971. *Somerset Archaeology and Natural History Society*, 129, 37-62.

Carter, S., 1991. *Tulloch Wood, Forres, Structures Report,* Unpublished Report, Scottish Development Department RCAHMS MS 2732/2/1.

Carter, S., 1993. Tulloch Wood, Forres, Moray: The Survey and Dating of a Fragment of Prehistoric Landscape. *Proceedings of the Society of Antiquaries of Scotland*, 123, 215-33.

Carter, S., 2002. Contract Archaeology in Scotland. *Antiquity*, 76, 869-73.

Carter, S. and F. Hunter, 2003. An Iron Age Chariot Burial from Scotland. *Antiquity*, 77, 531-35.

Caruth, J., 1993. *The 'Pightle' Needham Market, Archaeological Excavation Report,* Unpublished Report, Suffolk County Council, Suffolk HER LMD 082.

Caruth, J., 1994. *Roman Way, Long Melford, Archaeolgoical Evaulation Report,* Unpublished Report, Suffolk County Council 94/25, Suffolk HER LMD 082.

Caruth, J., 1995. *Euston to Cambridge Water Mains Pipeline, a Report on the Archaeological Monitoring and Excavations,* Unpublished Report, Suffolk Archaeological Unit 96/5, Suffolk HER.

Caruth, J., 1996. *Mildenhall Psi 2, Archaeological Evaluation Report,* Unpublished Report, Suffolk County Council 96/64, Suffolk HER MNL 491.

Caruth, J., 1997a. *Archaeological Evaluation Report, Newmarket Isolation Hospital, Fordham Road Exning,* Unpublished Report, Suffolk County Council 97/40, Suffolk HER EXG 074.

Caruth, J., 1997b. *Roman Way, Long Melford, Archaeological Monitoring Report,* Unpublished Report, Suffolk County Council 97/10, Suffolk HER LMD 082.

Caruth, J., 1997c. *Two Storage Buildings, Cambridge Road, Lakenheath, Archaeological Evaluation Report,* Unpubished Report, Suffolk County Council 97/8, Suffolk HER LKH 194.

Caruth, J., 2000. *Hospital Zone Maintenance, RAF Lakenheath, Archaeological Excavation and Monitoring Report,* Unpublished Report, Suffolk County Council 2000/13, Suffolk HER LKH 207.

Caruth, J., 2001a. *RAF Lakenheath Intermediate School Extension, Archaeological Monitoring Report,* Unpublished Report, Suffolk County Council 2001/77, Suffolk HER ERL 118.

Caruth, J., 2001b. *RAF Lakenheath, Extension to Building 1155, Archaeological Excavation Report,* Unpublished Report, Suffolk County Council 2001/3, Suffolk HER LKH 210.

Caruth, J., 2001c. *RAF Lakenheath, New Perimeter Road, Archaeological Monitoring Report,* Unpublished Report, Suffolk County Council 2001/71, Suffolk HER LKH 211.

Caruth, J., 2002a. *Improve Military Family Housing RAF Lakenheath, Archaeologial Monitoring Report,* Unpublished Report, Suffolk County Council 2002/68, Suffolk HER ERL 11 and ERL 112.

Caruth, J., 2002b. *New Tennis Courts, RAF Lakenheath, Archaeological Monitoring Report,* Unpublished Report, Suffolk County Council 2002/14, Suffolk HER ERL 117.

Caruth, J., 2003a. *Child Development Centre, RAF Lakenheath, a Report on the Archaeological Excavations, 2001,* Unpublished Report, Suffolk County Council 2003/100, Suffolk HER ERL 089.

Caruth, J., 2003b. *Dormitory 937, RAF Lakenheath, Archaeological Excavation Report and Assessment of Potential for Analysis, 1999,* Unpublished Report, Suffolk County Council 2003/11, Suffolk HER ERL 107.

Caruth, J., 2003c. *Old Dalgety Granary Site, Stoke Road Clare, Archaeological Watching Brief Report,* Unpublished Report, Suffolk County Council 2003/5, Suffolk HER CLA 029.

Caruth, J., 2004. *Trial Hole for New Pipeline at Wixoe, Wix 017, Archaeological Monitoring Report,* Unpublished Report, Suffolk County Council Archaeological Services, Available on OASIS.

Caruth, J., 2005a. *Archaeological Monitoring Report, RAF Lakenheath, Electric Trench between Buildings 1106 and 1108, Lkh 247, a Report on on the Archaeological Monitoring, 2005,* Unpublished Report, Suffolk County Council 2005/124, Available on OASIS.

Caruth, J., 2005b. *Archaeological Monitoring Report, RAF Lakenheath, Tanker Access Road, Erl 133,* Unpublished Report, Suffolk County Council Archaeological Service 2005/95, Available on OASIS.

Caruth, J., 2006a. *7, The Highlands, Exning, Archaeological Evaluation Report, 2006,* Unpublished Report, Suffolk County Council 2006/036, Suffolk HER EXG 082.

Caruth, J., 2006b. *RAF Lakenheath, Waste Water Treatment Works, Archaeological Monitoring Report,* Unpublished Report, Suffolk County Council 2006/086, Suffolk HER ERL 152.

Caruth, J., 2007a. *New Roundabout and Car Park at Norwich Road, RAF Lakenheath, Archaeological Monitoring Report,* Unpublished Report, Suffolk County Council 2007/138, Suffolk HER LKH 302.

Caruth, J., 2007b. *Street Sweeper Dump Site, RAF Lakenheath,* Unpublished Report, Suffolk County Council 2007/008, Suffolk HER ERL 160.

Caruth, J., 2009a. *Blackdyke Close Excavation, RAF Feltwell, Norfolk, Archaeological Excavation Report,* Unpublished Report, Suffolk County Council 2009/305, Norfolk HER 52795.

Caruth, J., 2009b. *Norwich Road and Exeter Crescent Road Realignment, RAF Lakenheath, Archaeological Excavation Report,* Unpublished Report, Suffolk County Council 2009/125, Suffolk HER ERL 161.

Casey, P. J. and B. Hoffman, 1999. Excavations at the Roman Temple in Lydney Park, Gloucestershire in 1980 and 1981. *Antiquaries Journal,* 79, 81-143.

Cass, S., 2009a. *Clare Primary School. Clare, Archaeological Evaluation Report,* Unpublished Report, Suffolk County Council 2009/214, Suffolk HER CLA 059.

Cass, S., 2009b. *New Car Park, Suffolk Punch Trust, Visitor Centre, Hollesley Bay Colony, Archaeological Evaluation Report,* Unpublished Report, Suffolk County Council 2009/290, Suffolk HER HLY 110.

Cass, S., 2010a. *Clare Primary School, Clare, Archaeological Excavation Report,* Unpublished Report, Suffolk County Council 2010285, Suffolk HER CLA 059.

Cass, S., 2010b. *Museums of East Anglian Life, Stowmarket, Archaeological Evaluation Report,* Unpublished Report, Suffolk County Council 2010/170, Suffolk HER SKT 056.

Cass, S., 2010c. *New Visitor Centre, Suffolk Punch Trust, Hollesley Bay, Archaeological Monitoring Report,* Unpublished Report, Suffolk County Council 2010/098, Suffolk HER HLY 110.

Cass, S., 2010d. *Orwell High School, Felixstowe, Archaeological Evaluation Report,* Unpublished Report, 2010/058, Suffolk HER FEX 281.

Cass, S., 2010e. *Past Garden, Church Green House, Low Street, Badingham,* Unpublished Report, Suffolk County Council Archaeological Service Report no. 2010/124, Suffolk HER BDG 051.

Cass, S., 2010f. *St Felix RC Primary School, Haverhill, Archaeological Monitoring Report,* Unpublished Report, Suffolk County Council 2010/001, Suffolk HER HVH 071.

Cass, S., 2011. *Chilton Development Main, Reinforcement Pipeline Scheme, Chilton, Archaeological Project Report,* Unpublished Report, Suffolk County Council Archaeological Service Report no. 2009/186, Suffolk HER CHT 019.

Casson, L., J. Drummond-Murray and A. Frances, 2014. *Romano-British Round Houses to Medieval Parish: Excavations at 10 Gresham Street, City of London, 1999-2002,* MOLA Monograph 67.

Catchpole, T., 2002. Excavations at West Drive, Cheltenham, Gloucestershire 1997-9. *Transactions of the Bristol and Gloucestershire Archaeological Society,* 120, 89-101.

Catchpole, T., 2007. Excavations at the Sewage Treatment Works, Dymock, Gloucestershire, 1995. *Transactions of the Bristol and Gloucestershire Archaeological Society,* 125, 137-219.

Cavers, G., 2008. The Later Prehistory of 'Black Holes': Regionality and the South-West Scottish Iron Age. *Proceedings of the Society of Antiquaries of Scotland,* 138, 13-26.

Chadwick, S. E. and M. W. Thompson, 1956. Note on an Iron Age Habitation Site near Battlesbury Camp, Warminster. *Wiltshire Archaeology and Natural History Society,* 56, 262-64.

Champion, S., 1976. *Leckhampton Hill, Gloucestershire, 1925 and 1970,* London: Academic Press.

Champion, S., 1995. Jewellery and Adornment, in *The Celtic World*, ed. M. J. Green, London: Routledge, 411-19.

Chapman, J., 2000. *Fragmentation in Archaeology: People, Places and Broken Objects in the Prehistory of South Eastern Europe*, London: Routledge.

Chapman, J. (ed.) 2002. *Colourful Prehistories: The Problem with the Berlin and Kay Colour Paradigm*, Oxford: Berg.

Chapman, J. and B. Gaydarska, 2007. *Parts and Wholes: Fragmentation in Prehistoric Context*, Oxford: Oxbow.

Childe, V. G., 1929. *The Danube in Prehistory*, Oxford: Clarendon Press.

Childe, V. G., 1933. Excavations at Castlelaw Fort, Midlothian. *Proceedings of the Society of Antiquaries of Scotland*, 67, 362-88.

Childe, V. G., 1935. *The Prehistory of Scotland*, London: Kegan Paul, Trench, Trubner and Co.

Childe, V. G., 1940. *Prehistoric Communities of the British Isles*, London: W and R Chambers.

Childe, V. G., 1946. *Scotland before the Scots*, London: Methuen.

Childe, V. G. and C. D. Forde, 1932. Excavations in Two Iron Age Forts at Earn's Heugh, near Coldingham. *Proceedings of the Society of Antiquaries of Scotland*, 66, 152-83.

Christison, D., 1898. *Early Fortifications in Scotland*, Edinburgh: William Blackwood.

Clark, G., 1966. The Invasion Hypothesis in British Archaeology. *Antiquity*, 40(159), 172-89.

Clarke, C., 2010. *St. Bede's Catholic School, Long Cross, Bristol, an Archaeological Post-Excavation Assessment Report*, Unpublished Report, AOC Archaeology 30501, Bristol City HER.

Clarke, R., 1937. The Roman Villages at Brettenham and Needham and the Contemporary Road System. *Norfolk Archaeology*, 26(2), 123-63.

Clarke, R., 1938. An Iron Age Hut at Postwick and an Earthwork on East Wretham Heath, Norfolk. *Norfolk Archaeology*, 26(3), 271-80.

Clarke, R. and H. Apling, 1935. An Iron Age Tumulus on Warborough Hill, Stiffkey. *Norfolk Archaeology*, 25(3), 408-28.

Clarke, R. R., 1939. The Iron Age in Norfolk and Suffolk. *Archaeological Journal*, 96, 1-113.

Clay, R. C. C., 1924. An Early Iron Age Site on Fifield Bavant Down. *Wiltshire Archaeology and Natural History Society*, 42, 457-96.

Clay, R. C. C., 1925. An Inhabited Site of La Tene I Date, on Swallowcliffe Down. *Wiltshire Archaeology and Natural History Society*, 43, 59-93.

Clay, R. C. C., 1927. Supplementary Report on the Early Iron Age Village on Swallowcliffe Down. *Wiltshire Archaeology and Natural History Society*, 43, 540-47.

Clements, C. F., 1974. *An Exploratory Trench on the Line of the Proposed A30 West Coker by-Pass near Chessels Roman Villa in 1974*, Unpublished Report, Somerset HER 15610.

Clifford, E. M., 1930. A Prehistoric and Roman Site at Barnwood near Gloucester. *Transactions of the Bristol and Gloucestershire Archaeological Society*, 55, 201-54.

Clifford, E. M., 1933. The Roman Villa, Hucclecote. *Transactions of the Bristol and Gloucestershire Archaeological Society*, 55, 323-76.

Clifford, E. M., 1934. An Early Iron Age Site at Barnwood, Gloucestershire. *Transactions of the Bristol and Gloucestershire Archaeological Society*, 56, 227-30.

Clifford, E. M., 1937. The Earthworks at Rodborough, Amberley, and Minchinhampton, Gloucestershire. *Transactions of the Bristol and Gloucestershire Archaeological Society*, 59, 287-307.

Clifford, E. M., 1961. *Bagendon: A Belgic Oppidum, a Record of the Excavations of 1954-56*, Cambridge: Heffer.

Close, R. S., 1972. Excavations of Iron Age Hut Circles at Percy Rigg, Kildale. *Yorkshire Archaeological Journal*, 44, 23-31.

Close, R. S., R. H. Hayes and D. A. Spratt, 1975. Romano-British Settlements at Crag Bank and Lounsdale, near Kildale, North Riding. *Yorkshire Archaeological Journal*, 47, 61-68.

Coleman, L., 1997. *The Cotswold School, Bourton-on-the-Water, Gloucestershire, Archaeological Evaluation*, Unpublished Report, Cotswold Archaeological Trust Report no 97854, Gloucestershire HER 19899.

Coleman, L., 1999a. *10 Chester Street, Cirencester, Gloucestershire*, Unpublished Report, Cotswold Archaeological Trust Report no. 99991, Gloucestershire HER 20356.

Coleman, L., 1999b. *Grange Hill Quarry, Naunton, Gloucestershire, Archaeological Evaluation*, Unpublished Report, Cotswold Archaeological Trust Report no. 99984, Gloucestershire HER 20358.

Coleman, L., K. Cullen and D. Kenyon, 2001. *The Royal Agricultural College, Cirencester, Gloucestershire, Archaeological Evaluation*, Unpublished Report, Cotswold Archaeological Trust Report no. 001221, Gloucestershire HER 20665.

Coleman, L. and M. Leah, 1998. *Prehistoric Occupation at the Cotswold School, Bourton-on-the-Water, Gloucestershire, Archaeological Excavations 1998*, Unpublished Report, Cotswold Archaeological Trust Report no. 98918, Gloucestershire HER 19899.

Coles, B. J., S. E. Rouillard and C. Backway, 1986. *The 1984 Excavations at Meare*: Somerset Levels Papers no. 12.

Coles, J., 1970. Discovery and Excavation in Scotland. 33.

Coles, J. M., 1987. *Meare Village East, the Excavations of A. Bulleid and H. St. George Gray, 1932-1956*, Somerset Levels Papers no. 13.

Coles, J. M., B. J. Coles and R. A. Morgan, 1988. *Excavations at the Glastonbury Lake Village,* Somerset Levels Papers no. 14.

Coles, J. M. and S. Minnitt, 1995. *Industrious and Fairly Civilized: The Glastonbury Lake Village,* Taunton: Somerset Levels Project and Somerset County Council Museums Service.

Coles, J. M. and J. J. Taylor, 1970. The Excavations of a Midden in the Culbin Sands, Morayshire. *Proceedings of the Society of Antiquaries of Scotland,* 87-99.

Coles, S. and J. Pine, 2009. Excavations of an Iron Age and Roman Settlement and Salt Production Site at Shapwick Road, Hamworthy, Poole, Dorset, 2005-6. *Dorset Natural History and Archaeological Society,* 130, 63-98.

Collard, M. and T. Havard, 2011. The Prehistoric and Medieval Defences of Malmesbury: Archaeological Investigations at Holloway, 2005-2006. *Wiltshire Archaeology and Natural History Society,* 104, 79-94.

Collis, J., 1994. The Iron Age, in *Building on the Past,* ed. B. Vyner, London: Royal Archaeological Institute, 123-48.

Collis, J., 2003. *The Celts: Origins, Myths and Inventions,* Stroud: Tempus.

Collis, J., 2008. Constructing Chronologies: Lessons from the Iron Age, in *Construire Le Temps: Histoire Et Méthodes Des Chronologies Et Calendriers Des Derniers Millénaires Avant Notre Ère En Europe Occidentale. Actes Du Xxxe Colloque International De Halma-Ipel, UMR 8164 (CNRS, Lille 3, MCC) 7-9 Décembre 2006, Lille,* ed. A. Lehoërff, Glux-en-Glenne: Bibracte, 85-104.

Collis, J., 2011. 'Reconstructing Iron Age Society' Revisited, in *Atlantic Europe in the First Millennium BC: Crossing the Divide* Oxford: Oxford University Press, 223-41.

Colls, K., 2004. *77 Victoria Road, Cirencester, Gloucestershire, Archaeological Evaluation,* Unpublished Report, Cotswold Archaeological Trust Report no. 04026, Gloucestershire HER 26532.

Colls, K. and K. Krawiec, 2005. *Dean Farm Bishop's Cleeve, Gloucestershire, Fieldwork Summary 2005,* Unpublished Report, Birmingham University Archaeology Project no. 1312, Gloucestershire HER 20562.

Connor, A. and L. Muldowney, 2006. *Romano-British and Anglo-Saxon Buildings at the Old School, Feltwell, Norfolk,* Unpublished Report, Cambridge Archaeological Field Unit 925, Norfolk HER 40913.

Cook, M., 2008a. *Discovery and Excavation in Scotland,* 123.

Cook, M., 2008b. Rituals, Roundhouses and Romans: Excavations at Kintore, Aberdeenshire, 2000-2006, in *Scottish Trust for Archaeological Research* Scottish Trust for Archaeological Research.

Cook, M. and L. Dunbar, 2008. *Rituals, Roundhouses and Romans, Excavations at Kintore, Aberdeenshire 2000-2006,* Edinburgh: Scottish Trust for Archaeological Research.

Cook, M., L. Dunbar and R. Engl, 2008. *Discovery and Excavation in Scotland,* 23.

Cook, M. and R. Engl, 2005. *Discovery and Excavation in Scotland,* 16.

Cook, M. and R. Engl, 2006. *Discovery and Excavation in Scotland,* 19.

Cook, M., R. Engl, L. Dunbar, H. Dkolska and S. Sagrott, 2008. *Hillforts of Strathdon Phase 2: Data Structure Report,* Unpublished Report, AOC Archaeology Group.

Cool, H. E. M., 1990. Roman Metal Hair Pins from Southern Britain. *Archaeometry,* 147, 148-82.

Cool, H. E. M., G. Lloyd-Morgan and A. D. Hooley, 1995. *Finds from the Fortress, the Archaeology of York, Volume 17: The Small Finds,* York: York Archaeological Trust for Excavation and Research.

Cool, H. E. M. and C. Philo, 1998. *Roman Castleford, Excavations 1974-85, Volume 1, the Small Finds*: Yorkshire Archaeology no. 4.

Cooper, A., 2003. *Myrtle Road, Hethersett, Norfolk, Archaeolgoical Trial Trenching,* Unpublished Report, Cambridge Archaeological Unit 534, Norfolk HER 37645.

Cooper, O., 2008. *Skirlaugh Sewage Pumping Station and Rising Main, near Beverley, East Riding of Yorkshire,* Unpublished Report, Northern Archaeological Associates 08/23 EHU 1526.

Cope-Faulkner, P., 2006. *Archaeological Watching Brief at the Old Hall Hotel, Caister-on-Sea, Norfolk,* Unpublished Report, Archaeological Project Services 109/03 Norfolk HER 37421.

Cope-Faulkner, P. and A. Failes, 2010. *Assessment of the Archaeological Remains and an Updated Project Design for Excavation at Holt House Farm, Wicken, Norfolk,* Unpublished Report, Archaeological Project Services 19/10, Norfolk HER 38183.

Corder, P., 1935. A Roman Site near Cawood. *Yorkshire Archaeological Journal,* 32, 333-38.

Corder, P. and J. Kirk, 1932. *A Roman Villa at Langton, near Malton, E. Yorkshire*, The Yorkshire Archaeological Society, Roman Malton and District Report no. 4.

Corney, M. and S. Robinson, 2007. Shillingstone Roman Villa (St 8295 1065): Summary Account and Interpretation. *Dorset Natural History and Archaeological Society,* 128, 110-17.

Cottrell, T. and S. Robinson, 2002. *An Archaeological Evaluation for a Proposed Development at the Anglo Trading Estate, Shepton Mallett, Somerset,* Unpublished Report, AC Archaeology Report no. 0102/1/0, Somerset HER 16198.

Cowgill, G. L., 1990. Artifact Classification and Archaeological Purposes, in *Mathematics and Information Science in Archaeology: A Flexible Framework,* ed. A. Voorrips, Bonn: Studies in Modern Archaeology volume 3, 61-78.

Cox, P. and C. M. Hearne, 1991. *Redeemed from the Heath, the Archaeology of the Wytch Farm Oilfield (1987-90)*, Dorset Natural History and Archaeological Society Monograph 9.

Cox, P. W., 1988. Excavations and Survey on Furzey Island, Poole Harbour, Dorset, 1985. *Dorset Natural History and Archaeological Society*, 110, 49-72.

Cox, S., 1997. Further Evidence of a Romano-British Agricultural Settlement at Filwood Park, Bristol, 1998. *Bristol and Avon Archaeology*, 14, 59-73.

Cox, S. and J. Samuel, 2001. *Excavations at Nerrol's Farm, Cheddon Fitzpaine, Somerset, 1992-2000*, Unpublished Report, Bristol and Region Archaeological Services, Somerset HER 11686.

Craig-Atkins, E., D. Evans, H. Manley and M. Russel, 2013. The Chesil Mirror and Other Effects of a Young Celtic Woman. *British Archaeology*, 132, 36-41.

Crank, N. A. and J. Grant, 2003. *Land Adjacent to 13 Station New Road, Brundall, Norfolk, an Archaeological Evaluation by Trial Trenching*, Unpublished Report, Archaeological Solutions 1482, Norfolk HER 39832.

Craven, J. A., 2004a. *Darmsden Hall Farm Quarry, Barking, Archaeological Excavation Report 2003*, Unpublished Report, Suffolk County Council 2004/120, Suffolk HER BRK 020.

Craven, J. A., 2004b. *Extension to Ingram Quarry, Fornham St Genevieve, Archaeological Evaluation Report, 2004*, Unpublished Report, Suffolk County Council 2004/122, Suffolk HER FSG 017.

Craven, J. A., 2005a. *'The Island', Marston's Pit, Cavenham Heath Quarry, Archaeological Report, 2005*, Unpublished Report, Suffolk County Council 2005/28, Suffolk HER CAM 043.

Craven, J. A., 2005b. *New Access Control, Gate 2, RAF Lakenheath, Erl 120, a Report on the Archaeological Excavations, 2002*, Unpublished Report, Suffolk County Council Archaeological Service 2005/27, Available on OASIS.

Craven, J. A., 2005c. *Thunderbrid Way, RAF Lakenheath, Eriswell, Archaeological Monitoring Report, 2005*, Unpublished Report, Suffolk County Council 2005/86, Suffolk HER ERL 142.

Craven, J. A., 2006a. *Archaeological Monitoring Report, Refueler Facility, RAF Lakenheath, Lakenheath, Lkh 267*, Unpublished Report, Suffolk County Council Archaeological Service Report 2006/74, Available on OASIS.

Craven, J. A., 2006b. *Archaeological Watching Brief Report, Land at Wyken Hall, Wyken Road, Stanton, Snt 046*, Unpublished Report, Suffolk County Council Archaeological Service Report 2006/75, Avaialble on OASIS.

Craven, J. A., 2006c. *Elveden Estate Coin Hoard, Archaeological Excavation Report, 2005*, Unpublished Report, Suffolk County Council 2006/32, Suffolk HER ELV 065.

Craven, J. A., 2006d. *Fitness Centre, RAF Lakenheath, Archaeological Excavation Report 2004*, Unpublished Report, Suffolk County Council 2006/027, Suffolk HER ERL 130.

Craven, J. A., 2006e. *Land North of Apple Acre Road, Hanchet End, Haverhill, a Report on the Archaeological Evaluation, 2006*, Unpublished Report, Suffolk County council 2006/78, Suffolk HER HVH 058.

Craven, J. A., 2006f. *Land Off Chalkstone Way, Haverhill, a Report on the Archaeological Evaluation 2006*, Unpublished Report, Suffolk County Council 2006/67, Suffolk HER HVH 059.

Craven, J. A., 2006g. *PIK Housing, Washington Street, Beck Row, Mildenahall, Archaeological Evaluation Report*, Unpublished Report, Suffolk County Council 2006/187, Suffolk HER MNL 570.

Craven, J. A., 2006h. *St John's House Hospital, Lion Road, Palgrave, Archaeological Evaluation Report*, Unpublished Report, Suffolk County Council 2006/026, Suffolk HER PAL 024.

Craven, J. A., 2006i. *Stormwater Drainage Adjacent Rochester Road, RAF Lakenheath, Archaeological Monitoring Report, 2004*, Unpublished Report, Suffolk County Council 2005/103, Suffolk HER ERL 141.

Craven, J. A., 2007. *The Gables, Hall Street, Long Melford, Archaeological Monitoring Report*, Unpublished Report, Suffolk County Council 2007/28, Suffolk HER LMD 154.

Craven, J. A., 2008a. *Land Adjoining Smoke House Inn and Skelton's Drove, Beck Row, Mildenhall, Archaeological Evaluation Report*, Unpublished Report, Suffolk County Council 2008/07, Suffolk HER MNL 598.

Craven, J. A., 2008b. *Land at Rear of 'Almacks', Long Melford, Archaeological Monitoring Report*, Unpublished Report, Suffolk County Council 2008/99, Suffolk HER LMD 137 and LMD 157.

Craven, J. A., 2008c. *Land Off Chalkstone Way, Haverhill, Archaeological Excavation Report, 2006*, Unpublished Report, Suffolk County Council 2007/87, Suffolk HER HVH 059.

Craven, J. A., 2008d. *St John's House Hospital, Lion Road, Palgrave, Archaeological Evaluation Report*, Unpublished Report, Suffolk County Council 2008/22, Suffolk HER PAL 024.

Craven, J. A., 2009a. *Former Smoke House Inn, Beck Row, Mildenhall, Archaeological Evaluation Report*, Unpublished Report, Suffolk County Council Archaeological Report no. 2009/240, Suffolk HER MNL 618.

Craven, J. A., 2009b. *Land Adjacent to Park Grove, Eurston Estate, Sapiston, Archaeological Evaluation Report*, Unpublished Report, Suffolk County Council 2008/213, Suffolk HER SAP 012.

Craven, J. A., 2009c. *Land Adjacent to the Street and Homsey, Green Road Beck Row, Mildenhall,*

Archaeological Evaluation Report, Unpublished Report, Suffolk County Council Archaeological Report no 2009/240, Suffolk HER MNL 619.

Craven, J. A., 2009d. *Phase V, Liberty Village, RAF Lakenheath, Eriwell, Archaeological Evaluation Report,* Unpublished Report, Report 2009/150, Suffolk HER ERL 203.

Craven, J. A., 2010a. *New Executive Villas, Center Parcs, Elveden, Archaeological Excavation Report,* Unpublished Report, Suffolk County Council 2010/102, Suffolk HER ELV 067.

Craven, J. A., 2010b. *Phase 2, Rear of Smoke House Inn, Beck Row, Mildenhall, Archaeological Excavation Report,* Unpublished Report, Suffolk County Council 2010/206, Suffolk HER MNL 536.

Craven, J. A., 2010c. *Thunderbird Way, Erl 211 and Nato Place/Kennedy Street, Erl 212, RAF Lakenheath, Eriswell, Suffolk, Archaeoogical Monitoring Report,* Unpublished Report, Suffolk County Council Archaeological Service Report no. 2010/189, Suffolk HER ERL 211.

Craven, J. A., 2010d. *West Row Primary School, Beeches Road, Mildenhall, Archaeological Evaluation Report,* Unpublished Report, Suffolk County Council Report 2010/157, Suffolk HER MNL 637.

Crawley, P., 2009a. *An Archaeological Evaluation at Church Farm, Mautby Lane, Filby, Norfolk,* Unpublished Report, NAU Archaeology 2109, Norfolk HER 52702.

Crawley, P., 2009b. *An Archaeological Excavation and Watching Brief at Uplands, Caister-on-Sea, Norfolk, Assessment Report and Updated Project Design,* Unpublished Report, NAU Archaeology 1878a, Norfolk HER 45329.

Crawley, P., 2009c. *An Archaeological Strip, Map and Sample Excavation at St Michael's Hospital, Aylsham, Norfolk, Assessment Report and Updated Project Design,* Unpublished Report, NAU Archaeology 1442, Norfolk HER 40920.

Crawley, P. E., 2010. *An Archaeological Evaluation at Church Close, Hoxne, Suffolk, Amended,* Unpublished Report, NAU Archaeology 2332, Suffolk HER HXN 048.

Crawley, P. E., 2011. *An Archaeological Evaluation on the Anglian Water, Norse Avenue Off Site Scheme, Bradfield Combust, Suffolk,* Unpublished Report, NAU Archaeology 2494, Suffolk HER BRC 015.

Creighton, J., 2000. *Coins and Power in Late Iron Age Britain,* Cambridge: Cambridge University Press.

Cressey, M., B. Finlayson and J. Hamilton, 1998. Discovery and Excavation in Scotland, 52-54.

Cripps, W. J., 1898. Notes on the Roman Basilica at Cirencester, Lately Discovered. *Transactions of the Bristol and Gloucestershire Archaeological Society,* 21, 70-78.

Crockett, A., 1996. Archaeological Sites Along the Ilchester to Odcombe Pipeline. *Somerset Archaeology and Natural History Society,* 139, 59-88.

Crockett, A. and A. P. Fitzpatrick, 1998. Archaeological Mitigation in the Flavian Fort Annexe and Later Roman Settlement at Bradley Street, Castleford, West Yorkshire, 1991-93. *Yorkshire Archaeological Journal,* 70, 35-60.

Croft, B., 2000. Twenty-Five Years of Planning and Archaeology in Somerset, in *Somerset Archaeology: Papers to Mark 150 Years of the Somerset Archaeological and Natural History Society,* ed. C. J. Webster, Taunton: Somerset Archaeological and Natural History Society, 127-33.

Cromarty, A. M., M. R. Roberts and A. Smith, 2007. Archaeological Investigations at Stubbs Farm, Kempsford, Gloucestershire, 1991-1995, in *Iron Age and Roman Settlement in the Upper Thames Valley, Excavations at Claydon Pike and Other Sites within the Cotswold Water Park,* eds. D. Miles, S. Palmer, A. Smith and G. P. Jones, Oxford: Oxbow.

Crook, M., 1946-48. A Roman Coffin Found at Batheaston. *Proceedings of the Bristol Spelaeological Society,* 6(1), 55-56.

Croom, A., 2000. *Roman Clothing and Fashion,* Stroud: Amberley.

Crowson, A., 1997. *Evaluation Excavations of Allotment Gardens, Creake Road, Burnham Market,* Unpublished Report, Norfolk Archaeological Unit 284, Norfolk HER 32791.

Crummy, N., 1979. A Chronology of Romano-British Bone Pins. *Britannia,* 10, 157-63.

Crummy, P., 2007. *Stanway: An Élite Burial Site at Camulodunum,* London: Society for the Promotion of Roman Studies.

Cruse, G., 2005. *32 London Road, Gloucester, Gloucestershire, Archaeological Observation,* Unpublished Report, Border Archaeology BA0430MBLRG, Available on OASIS.

Cudlip, D., 2005. *31 Victoria Road, Cirencester, Gloucestershire, Archaeological Evaluation,* Unpublished Report, Cotswold Archaeology Report 04214, Gloucestershire HER 27846.

Cudlip, D., 2006. *21 Victoria Road, Cirencester, Gloucestershire, Archaeological Evaluation,* Unpublished Report, Cotswold Archaeology 06040, Gloucestershire HER 32641.

Cudlip, D., 2009. *Post Office Site, 12 Castle Street, Cirencester, Gloucestershire, Programme of Archaeological Works,* Unpublished Report, Cotswold Archaeology Report 09016, Available on OASIS.

Cudlip, D. and J. Hart, 2010. *New Sports Hall, Cotswold School, Bourton-on-the-Water, Gloucestershire, Archaeological Excavation,* Unpublished Report, Cotswold Archaeology Report 09113, Available on OASIS.

Cullen, I., 1994. *Berry Hill, Oyne,* Unpublished Report, GUARD Report no. 176, RCAHMS MS 725/71.

Cullen, I., 1996. *Allanfearn, Archaeological Assessment and Excavation,* Unpublished Report, GUARD Report no. 110.3 and 110.4, RCAHMS MS 725/124.

Cullen, K., 2002. *Mains Renewal - Mains Renewal - Mast Reservoir to Paywell Farm, Blagdon, Priddy, Somerset, Archaeological Watching Brief,* Unpublished Report, Somerset HER 27271.

Cullen, K., 2003. *Land to the Rear of the Rectory, Wellington Hill, Horfield, Bristol, Archaeological Evaluation,* Unpublished Report, Cotswold Archaeology 03005, Bristol HER 21565.

Cunliffe, B., 1966. Excavations at Gatcombe, Somerset, in 1965 and 1966. *Proceedings of the University of Bristol Spelaeological Society,* 11, 126-60.

Cunliffe, B., 1968. Excavations at Eldon's Seat, Encombe, Dorset, Parts I, II and Iv. *Proceedings of the Prehistoric Society,* 34, 191-237.

Cunliffe, B., 1984a. *Danebury: An Iron Age Hillfort in Hampshire, Volume 1: The Excavations 1969-1978, the Site,* York: CBA Research Report 52.

Cunliffe, B., 1984b. *Danebury: An Iron Age Hillfort in Hampshire. Volume 2: The Excavations, 1969-1978, the Finds,* London: CBA Research Report 52.

Cunliffe, B., 1984c. Gloucestershire and the Iron Age of Southern Britain. *Transactions of the Bristol and Gloucestershire Archaeological Society,* 102, 5-15.

Cunliffe, B., 1987. *Hengistbury Head, Dorset, Volume 1: The Prehistoric and Roman Settlement, 3500 BC - AD 500,* Oxford: Oxford University Committee for Archaeology Monograph no. 13.

Cunliffe, B., 1992. Pits, Preconceptions and Propitiation in the British Iron Age. *Oxford Journal of Archaeology,* 11(1), 69-83.

Cunliffe, B., 2005. *Iron Age Communities in Britain: An Account of England, Scotland and Wales from the Seventh Century BC until the Roman Conquest, Fourth Edition,* London: Routledge.

Cunliffe, B., 2007. Continent Cut Off by Fog: Just How Insular Is Britain? *Scottish Archaeological Journal,* 29(2), 99-112.

Cunliffe, B. and P. de Jersey, 1997. *Armorica and Britain: Cross-Channel Relationships in the Late First Millennium BC,* Oxford: Oxford University Committee for Archaeology, Monograph 45.

Cunnington, B. H. and M. E. Cunnington, 1913. Casterley Camp. *Wiltshire Archaeology and Natural History Society,* 38, 53-105.

Cunnington, E., 1885. On a Hoard of Bronze, Iron, and Other Objects Found in Belbury Camp, Dorset. *Archaeologia,* 48, 115-20.

Cunnington, H., 1886. Description of the Opening of a British Dwelling-Pit at Bechampton. *Wiltshire Archaeology and Natural History Society,* 23, 65-68.

Cunnington, M. E., 1908. Oliver's Camp, Devizes. *Wiltshire Archaeology and Natural History Society,* 35, 408-44.

Cunnington, M. E., 1911. Knap Hill Camp. *Wiltshire Archaeology and Natural History Society,* 37, 42-65.

Cunnington, M. E., 1912. A Late Celtic Inhabited Site at All Cannings Cross Farm. *Wiltshire Archaeology and Natural History Society,* 37, 526-38.

Cunnington, M. E., 1917. Lidbury Camp. *Wiltshire Archaeology and Natural History Society,* 40, 12-36.

Cunnington, M. E., 1923. *The Early Iron Age Inhabited Site at All Cannings Cross Farm, Wiltshire: A Description of the Excavations, and Objects Found by Mr and Mrs B.H. Cunnington, 1911-1922,* Devizes: George Simpson.

Cunnington, M. E., 1925. Fisbury Rings, an Account of Excavations in 1924. *Wiltshire Archaeology and Natural History Society,* 43, 48-58.

Cunnington, M. E., 1930. Romano-British Wiltshire. *Wiltshire Archaeology and Natural History Society,* 45, 166-216.

Cunnington, M. E., 1933. Excavations in the Yarnbury Castle Camp, 1932. *Wiltshire Archaeology and Natural History Society,* 46, 198-213.

Curle, A. O., 1914. Account of excavations on Traprain Law in the Parish of Prestonkirk, County of Haddington, in 1914. *Proceedings of the Society of Antiquaries of Scotland,* 49, 139-202.

Curle, A. O. and J. E. Cree, 1915. Account of excavations on Traprain Law in the Parish of Prestonkirk, County of Haddington, in 1915. With descriptions of the animal remains. *Proceedings of the Society of Antiquaries of Scotland,* 50, 64-144.

Currie, C. K., 1992. Excavations and Surveys at the Roman Kiln Site, Brinkworth, 1986. *Wiltshire Archaeology and Natural History Society,* 85, 27-50.

Cuttler, R. and J. Halsted, 1999. *Iron Age and Romano-British Activity at Arle Court, Cheltenham, Gloucestershire, 1999,* Unpublished Report, Birmingham Archaeology, Gloucestershire HER 32358.

Dallas, C., 1993. *Excavations in Thetford by B.K. Davison between 1964 and 1970,* Dereham, Norfolk: East Anglian Archaeology Report no. 62.

Damant, R., 2004. *Archaeological Watching Brief, 91 Abbey Road, Leiston,* Unpublished Report, Suffolk County Council Archaeological Service Report no. 2004/143, Available on OASIS.

Darling, M. J., 1993. *Caister-on-Sea Excavations by Charles Green, 1951-55,* Dereham, Norfolk: East Anglian Archaeology Report no. 60.

Darvill, T., R. Hingley, M. Jones and J. Timby, 1986. A Neolithic and Iron Age Site at the Loders, Lechlade, Gloucestershire. *Transactions of the Bristol and Gloucestershire Archaeological Society,* 104, 27-48.

Darvill, T. and J. Timby, 1986. Excavations at Saintbridge, Gloucester, 1981. *Transactions of the Bristol and Gloucestershire Archaeological Society,* 104, 49-60.

Darvill, T. and J. R. Timby, 1998. *Excavations by the Late W L Cox at Syreford Mill, 1973-1977,* Cirencester: Cotswold Archaeological Trust.

Davey, J. and G. Cooper, 2004. Romano-British Sites in the Parish of Sandford Orcas, Dorset. *Dorset Natural History and Archaeological Society*, 126, 43-62.

Davies, J., 1996. Where Eagles Dare: The Iron Age of Norfolk. *Proceedings of the Prehistoric Society*, 62, 63-92.

Davies, J., 1999. Patterns, Power and Political Progress in Iron Age Norfolk, in *Land of the Iceni: The Iron Age in Northern East Anglia*, eds. D. Davies and T. Williamson, Norwich: Centre of East Anglian Studies, 14-44.

Davies, J. (ed.) 2011. *The Iron Age in Northern East Anglia: New Work in the Land of the Iceni,* Oxford: BAR British Series no. 549.

Davies, J. and T. Williamson (eds.), 1999a. *Land of the Iceni: The Iron Age in Northern East Anglia,* Norwich: Centre of East Anglian Studies.

Davies, J. and T. Williamson, 1999b. Studying the Iron Age, in *Land of the Iceni: The Iron Age in Northern East Anglia*, eds. J. Davies and T. Williamson, Norwich: Centre of East Anglian Studies, 7-13.

Davies, J. A., 1991. *Excavations at Ford Place, 1985-6,* Dereham, Norfolk: East Anglian Archaeology Report no. 54.

Davies, J. A., 1992. Excavations at the North Wall, Casitor St. Edmund, 1987-89. *Norfolk Archaeology,* 41(3), 325-37.

Davies, J. A., 1993. Excavation of an Iron Age Pit Group at London Road, Thetford. *Norfolk Archaeology,* 41(4), 441-61.

Davies, J. A. and T. Gregory, 1991. *Excavations at Thetford Castle, 1962 and 1985-6,* Dereham, Norfolk: East Anglian Archaeology Report no. 54.

Davies, S. M. and D. Grieve, 1986. The Poundbury Pipe-Line: Archaeological Observations and Excavations. *Dorset Natural History and Archaeological Society,* 108, 81-88.

Davies, S. M., L. C. Stacey and P. J. Woodward, 1985. Excavations at Alington Avenue, Fordington, Dorchester 1984/85: Interim Report. *Dorset Natural History and Archaeological Society,* 107, 101-10.

Davis, C. E., 1884. The Excavations of Roman Baths at Bath. *Transactions of the Bristol and Gloucestershire Archaeological Society,* 8, 89-113.

Davis, M. and A. Gwilt, 2008. Material, Style and Identity in First Century AD Metalwork, with Particular Reference to the Seven Sisters Hoard, in *Rethinking Celtic Art,* eds. D. Garrow, C. Gosden and J. D. Hill, Oxford: Oxbow, 146-84.

Davison, S., 1999. *Ixworth Repeater Station, Mill Road, Pakenham, Archaeological Monitoring Report,* Unpublished Report, Suffolk County Council 99/11, Suffolk HER PKM 027.

Dent, J., 1983. A Summary of the Excavations Carried out in Garton Slack and Wetwang Slack 1964-1980. *East Riding Archaeologist,* 7, 1-14.

Dent, J., 1984. *Wetwang Slack: An Iron Age Cemetery on the Yorkshire Wolds,* Unpublished M.Phil Thesis, University of Sheffield.

Dent, J., 1999. The Yorkshire Wolds in Late Prehistory and the Emergence of an Iron Age Society, in *Further Light on the Parisi: Recent Discoveries in Iron Age and Roman East Yorkshire*, ed. P. Halkon, Hull: East Riding Archaeology Society, 4-11.

Dereham, K., 1999a. *An Archaeological Evaluation at the Cotswold Motor Museum, Bourton-on-the-Water, Gloucestershire,* Unpublished Report, Gloucestershire County Council, Gloucestershire HER 18631.

Dereham, K., 1999b. *An Archaeological Evaluation at the Cotswold School, Bourton-on-the-Water, Gloucestershire,* Unpublished Report, Gloucestershire County Council, Gloucestershire HER 19899.

Dereham, K., 2001a. *An Archaeological Evaluation at Greystones Farm, Greystones Lane, Bourton-on-the-Water, Gloucestershire,* Unpublished Report, Gloucestershire County Council, Gloucestershire HER 21791.

Dereham, K., 2001b. *An Archaeological Evaluation of the Proposed Car Park on Land Behind the Old Forge Garage, Dymock, Gloucestershire,* Unpublished Report, Gloucestershire County Council, Glocuestershire HER 21168.

DeRoche, D., 1997. Studying Iron Age Production, in *Reconstructing Iron Age Societies: New Approaches to the British Iron Age,* eds. A. Gwilt and C. Haselgrove, Oxford: Oxbow Monograph 71, 19-25.

DeRoche, D., 2012. England: Bronze and Iron Ages, in *Textiles and Textile Production in Europe: From Prehistory to AD 400,* eds. M. Gleba and U. Mannering, Oxford: Oxbow, 444-50.

Dewar, H. S. L., 1968. Report on Excavations at Somerleigh Court, Dorchester, 1966-67. *Dorset Natural History and Archaeological Society,* 89, 164-67.

Diamond, S. and S. Randell, 2000. *Archaeological Watching Brief at the A1237/B1363 Junction, Wingginton Road, Clifton Moor, York,* Unpublished Report, AOC Archaeology, CYC 213.

Díaz-Andreu, M. and S. Lucy, 2005. Introduction, in *The Archaeology of Identity: Approaches to Gender, Age, Status, Ethnicity and Religion,* eds. M. Díaz-Andreu, S. Lucy, S. Babić and D. N. Edwards, London: Routledge, 1-12.

Dickinson, C. and P. Wenham, 1957. Discoveries in the Roman Cemetery on the Mount, York. *Yorkshire Archaeological Journal,* 39, 283-323.

Dickson, A., 2006. *Report on an Archaeological Watching Brief, Land to the Rear of Fernlea, Hayton,* Unpublished Report, On-Site Archaeology OSA06WB37, EHU 1442.

Dieze, V. and C. King, 2004. *Monkton Heathfield, Taunton, Somerset, Archaeological Evaluation*

Report, Unpublished Report, Oxford Archaeology 2384, Available on OASIS.

Dixon, P., 1976. *Crickley Hill, 1969-1972,* London: Academic Press.

Dixon, P., 1994. *Crickley Hill, Volume 1, the Hillfort Defences,* University of Nottingham: Crickley Hill Trust and the Department of Archaeology.

Dobiat, C., H. Matthäus, B. Raftery and J. Henderson, 1987. *Glasperlen Der Vorrömischen Eisenzeit II Nach Unterlagen Von Th. E. Haevernick. Ringaugenperlen Und Verwandte Perlengruppen*, Marburger Studien zur vor- und Frühgeschichte Band 9.

Dobson, D. P., 1937. Excavations, Sea Mills, near Bristol. *Transactions of the Bristol and Gloucestershire Archaeological Society,* 61, 202-23.

Dobson, D. P., 1939. Excavations at Sea Mills, near Bristol, 1938. *Transactions of the Bristol and Gloucestershire Archaeological Society,* 61, 202-23.

Dockrill, S. J., 1981. A Late Iron Age and Romano-British Site at Wyke Regis, Dorset. *Dorset Natural History and Archaeological Society,* 103, 131-32.

Dockrill, S. J., Z. Outram and C. M. Batt, 2006. Time and Place: A New Chronology for the Origin of the Broch Based on the Scientific Dating Programme at the Old Scatness Broch, Shetland. *Proceedings of the Society of Antiquaries of Scotland,* 136, 89-110.

Donovan, H. E., 1933. Excavations at Bourton on the Water. *Transactions of the Bristol and Gloucestershire Archaeological Society,* 55, 377.

Donovan, H. E., 1934. Excavations of a Romano-British Building at Bourton on the Water, Gloucestershire, 1934. *Transactions of the Bristol and Gloucestershire Archaeological Society,* 56, 99-128.

Dowden, W. A., 1962. Little Solsbury Hill Camp. 1. Report on the Excavations of 1958. *Proceedings of the University of Bristol Spelaeological Society,* 9(3), 177-82.

Doyle, K., K. Nicholson, R. Rennell, J. Williams and P. Weston, 2005. *Land at Ditchingham, Norfolk, an Archaeological Evaluation,* Unpublished Report, Archaeological Solutions 1667, Norfolk HER 40213.

Doyle, K., L. O'Brien and J. Williams, 2005. *Land to the Rear of the Old School, the Beck, Feltwell, Norfolk, an Archaeological Evaluation,* Unpublished Report, Archaeological Solutions 1679, Norfolk HER 40913.

Doyle, K., S. Unger, A. A. S. Newton and C. George, 2008. *Beetley Quarry, Beetley, Norfolk, an Archaeological Excavation Interim Report,* Unpublished Report, Archaeological Solutions 3019, Norfolk HER 37159.

Draper, J. and C. Chaplin, 1982. *Dorchester Excavations Volume 1: Excavations at Wadham House 1968; Dorchester Prison 1970, 1975 and 1978; and Glyde Path Road 1966,* Dorset Natural History and Archaeological Society Monograph 2.

Dudley, D., 1961. Some Cist-Graves in Poynter's Garden, St Mary's, Isle of Scilly. *Proceedings of the West Cornwall Field Club,* 2(5), 221-31.

Duffy, J., 2003. *Building 1125, RAF Lakenheath, Archaeological Excavation Report,* Unpublished Report, Suffolk County Council 2003/41, Suffolk HER LKH 146.

Dunbar, L., 2002. *Discovery and Excavation in Scotland,* 10.

Dunbar, L., 2004. *Discovery and Excavation in Scotland,* 16-7.

Duncan, J. S., 1999. *Milton of Leys,* Unpublished Report, GUARD Report no. 660, RCAHMS MS 725/215.

Dundes, A. (ed.) 1992. *The Evil Eye: A Casebook,* Madison: University of Wisconsin.

Dungworth, D. B., 1996. The Production of Copper Alloys in Iron Age Britain. *Proceedings of the Prehistoric Society,* 62, 399-421.

Dunnell, R. C., 1978. Style and Function: A Fundamental Dichotomy. *American Antiquity,* 43(2), 192-202.

Dunnell, R. C., 1986. Methodological Issues in Americanist Artifact Classification. *Advances in Archaeological Method and Theory,* 9, 149-207.

Dunnell, R. C., 2002. *Systematics in Prehistory,* Caldwell, N.J.: The Blackburn Press.

Dunning, G. C., 1933. Oxenton Hill Camp, with Drawings of Pottery. *Transactions of the Bristol and Gloucestershire Archaeological Society,* 55, 383-84.

Dunning, G. C., 1934a. A Roman Burial on Summerhill, above Naunton. *Transactions of the Bristol and Gloucestershire Archaeological Society,* 56, 129-31.

Dunning, G. C., 1934b. The Swan's-Neck and Ring-Headed Pins of the Early Iron Age in Britain. *Archaeological Journal,* 91, 269-87.

Dunning, G. C., 1976. Salmonsbury, Bourton-on-the-Water, Gloucestershire, in *Hillforts: Later Prehistoric Earthworks in Britain and Ireland,* ed. D. W. Harding, London: Academic Press.

Dutton, A., 2005. *Results of an Archaeological Evaluation at Upper Slackbuie, Inverness,* Unpublished Report, Headland Archaeology Ltd., RCAHMS MS 5565.

Eckardt, H., 2008. Technologies of the Body: Iron Age and Roman Grooming and Display, in *Rethinking Celtic Art*, eds. D. Garrow, C. Gosden and J. D. Hill, Oxford: Oxbow, 113-28.

Eckardt, H. (ed.) 2010. *Roman Diasporas: Archaeological Approaches to Mobility and Diversity in the Roman Empire,* Portsmouth, R.I.: Journal of Roman Archaeology.

Eckardt, H. and N. Crummy, 2008. *Styling the Body in Late Iron Age and Roman Britain: A Contextual Approach to Toilet Instruments*, Monographies Instrumentum no. 36.

Eddy, M. R., 1983. A Roman Settlement and Early Medieval Motte at Moot-Hill, Great Driffield, North Humberside. *East Riding Archaeologist,* 7, 40-51.

Eicher, J. B. (ed.) 1995. *Dress and Ethnicity: Change across Space and Time,* Oxford: Berg.

Eisen, G., 1916. The Characteristics of Eye Beads from the Earliest Times to the Present. *American Journal of Archaeology,* 20(1), 1-27.

Ellis, C. and A. B. Powell, 2008. *An Iron Age Settlement Outside Battlesbury Hillfort, Warminster, and Sites Along the Southern Range Road*, Wessex Archaeology Report 22.

Ellis, P., 1984. *Catsgore 1979, Further Excavations of the Romano-British Village*, Western Archaeological Trust.

Ellis, P., 1987a. *Brewery Lane, Shepton Mallet, Somerset, an Archaeological Evaluation October 1987*, Unpublished Report, Birmingham University Field Archaeology Unit, Somerset HER 11079.

Ellis, P., 1987b. Sea Mills, Bristol: The 1965-68 Excavations in the Roman Town of Abonae. *Transactions of the Bristol and Gloucestershire Archaeological Society*, 105, 15-108.

Ellis, P., 1989. Norton Fitzwarren Hillfort: A Report on the Excavations by Nancy and Philip Langmaid between 1968 and 1971. *Somerset Archaeology and Natural History Society*, 133, 1-74.

Ellis, P., 1994. *II.3: The North East Defences; a Watching Brief in Kingshams in 1980*, Sheffield Excavation Reports 2.

Ellis, P., 1995. Archaeological Investigations on the Proposed Line of the A46 North of Bath. *Bristol and Avon Archaeology*, 12, 56-67.

Ellis, P., 1998. *Hilly Fields, Upper Holway, Taunton, Archaeological Field Evaluation 1998*, Unpublished Report, Birmingham University Field Archaeology Unit, Project no. 533, Somerset HER 57172.

Ellis, P. and A. Ellison, 1994. *II.9: The Ilchester Bypass, an Archaeological Watching Brief 1975-1976*, Sheffield Excavation Reports 2.

Ellis, P. and P. Leach, 1996. *The Roman Small Town at Shepton Mallet, Somerset, the Tesco Excavation, 1996*, Unpublished Report, Birmingham University Field Archaeology Unit Project no. 499, Somerset HER 44801.

Ellis, P. and P. Leach, 1997. *Ilchester Archaeology: A Watching Brief and Salvage Excavats at Ivel House, 1997*, Unpublished Report, Somerset HER 35988.

Ellis, P. and P. Leach, 1998. Ilchester Archaeology: A Watching Brief and Salvage Excavations at Ivel House, 1997. *Somerset Archaeology and Natural History Society*, 141, 35-55.

Ellis, P. and R. McDonnell, 1986. *Salvage Excavations and Recording of Romano-British and Post-Roman Remains at the Town Hall, Ilchester, 1986*, Unpublished Report, Somerset HER 55925.

Ellis, P. and R. Scutchings, 1994. *II.7: Minor Excavations and Watching Briefs 1976-83*, Sheffield Excavation Reports 2.

Ellison, A. and T. Pearson, 1977. Ham Hill 1975: A Watching Brief. *Somerset Archaeology and Natural History*, 121, 97-100.

Ellison, J. A., 1966. Excavations at Caister-on-Sea, 1962-63. *Norfolk Archaeology*, 34(1), 45-73.

Ellison, P., 2000. *A Roman Villa Found at Stawell in August 2000*, Unpublished Report, Bridgewater and District Archaeological Society, Somerset HER 11082.

Ellison, P., 2001a. *A Romano-British 'Barn' at Ford Farm*, Unpublished Report, Somerset HER 15584.

Ellison, P., 2001b. *A Romano-British Villa Found at Stawell*, Unpublished Report, Bridgewater and District Archaeological Society, Somerset HER 15046.

Ellison, P., 2003. *A Report on a Roman Villa Found at Ford near Stawell*, Unpublished Report, Bridgewater and District Archaeological Society, Somerset HER 16919.

Elsden, M. A., 1999. *Archaeological Evaluation of Land Adjacent to Old Reepham Road, Bawdeswell, Norfolk*, Unpublished Report, Archaeological Project Services 29/99, Norfolk HER 34163.

Eluère, C., 1987. Celtic Gold Torcs. *Gold Bulletin*, 20, 22-37.

Emery, G., 2005. *Assessment Report and Updated Project Design for an Archaeological Excavation at Ford Place Nursing Home, Thetford*, Unpublished Report, Norfolk Archaeological Unit Report 1005, Available on OASIS.

Emery, G., 2008. *An Archaeological Excavation at Geltwell, Southery, Norfolk*, Unpublished Report, NAU Archaeology 1390, Norfolk HER 41028.

Emery, G., 2009. *An Archaeological Evaluation and Strip, Map and Sample Excavation at 93-101 Ber Street, Norwich*, Unpublished Report, NAU Archaeology 1293, Norfolk HER 45439.

Enright, D. and M. Watts, 2002. *A Romano-British and Medieval Settlement Site at Stoke Road, Bishop's Cleeve, Gloucestershire, Excavations in 1997*, Cotswold Archaeology, Bristol and Gloucestershire Archaeological Report no. 1.

Entwistle, J., 2000. *The Fashioned Body*, Cambridge: Polity.

Erskine, G. P. and P. Ellis, 2008. Excavations at Atworth Roman Villa, Wiltshire 1970-1975. *Wiltshire Archaeology and Natural History Society*, 101, 51-129.

Etheridge, D., 2002a. *79 Sea Mills Lane, Sea Mills, Bristol, Archaeological Watching Brief and Evaluation*, Unpublished Report, Avon Archaeological Unit, Bristol City HER 20976, 32077, 2002/60.

Etheridge, D., 2002b. *Avonleigh Nursing Home, Stoke Park Road South, Stoke Bishop, Bristol, Archaeological Watching Brief*, Unpublished Report, Avon Archaeological Unit, Bristol City HER 20939.

Etheridge, D., 2002c. *Imperial Park, Brislington, Bristol, Archaeological Monitoring and Recording*, Unpublished Report, Avon Archaeological Unit, Bristol City HER 20931.

Evans, D. and M. Alexander, 2009. A Late Iron Age and Romano-British Field System at Site 10a, South Marston Park, Wiltshire. *Wiltshire Archaeology and Natural History Society*, 102, 114-28.

Evans, D. and A. Hancocks, 2006. Romano-British, Late Saxon and Medieval Remains at the Old Showground, Chedder: Excavations in 2001. *Somerset Archaeology and Natural History Society,* 149, 107-22.

Evans, D., N. Holbrook and E. R. McSloy, 2006. *A Later Iron Age Cemetery and Roman Settlement at Henbury School, Bristol: Excavations in 2004,* Cotswold Archaeology, Bristol and Gloucestershire Archaeological Report no. 4.

Evans, K. J., 1974. Excavations on a Romano-British Site, Wiggonholt, 1964. *Sussex Archaeological Collections,* 112, 97-151.

Evans, P. and S. Robinson, 2006. *Alstone Lake Village, Alstone, Somerset,* Unpublished Report, AC Archaeology Report no. 5406/1/0, Somerset HER 30201.

Evans, R., 2005. *Archaeological Evaluation on Land at Browns Fen, Stoke Ferry, Norfolk,* Unpublished Report, Archaeological Project Services 60/05, Norfolk HER 40949.

Everett, L., 2000. *Managed Retreat, Trimley Marshes, Trimley St. Martin, Archaeological Evaluation, Monitoring and Excavation Archive Report,* Unpublished Report, Suffolk County Council 2000/97, Suffolk HER TYN 073.

Everett, L., 2008a. *Land between Lady Lane and Tower Mill Lane, Hadleigh, Archaeological Evaluation Report,* Unpublished Report, Suffolk County Council 2008/059, Suffolk HER HAD 085 and HAD 089.

Everett, L., 2008b. *Ullswater Road, Campsey Ash, Archaeological Monitoring Report,* Unpublished Report, Suffolk County Council 2006/06, Suffolk HER CAA 025.

Everett, L., 2010. *Irvine House, Main Road, Chelmondiston, Archaeological Evaluation Report,* Unpublished Report, Suffolk County Council 2010/113, Suffolk HER CHL 056.

Everett, L., S. Anderson, K. Powell and I. Riddler, 2003. *Vicarage Farm, Coddenham, Archaeological Evaluation Report, 2003,* Unpublished Report, Suffolk County Council 2003/66, Suffolk HER CDD 022.

Everett, L. and C. Tester, 2002. *Archaeological Excavation Report, Land Off Gardeners Walk, Elmswell,* Unpublished Report, Suffolk County Council 2001/106, Suffolk HER EWL 013.

Everett, L., C. Tester and S. W. Anderson, A., 2001. *Orion Business Park, Blackacre Hill, Great Blakenham, Archaeological Monitoring and Excavation Archive Report,* Unpublished Report, Suffolk County Council 99/78, Suffolk HER BLG 017.

Farnell, A. and J. Salvatore, 2010. *An Archaeological Trench Evaluation at Land at the Hatcheries, Bathpool, Taunton, Somerset,* Unpublished Report, Exeter Archaeology Report no. 10.48, Somerset HER 28203.

Farrar, R. A., 1966. Roman Inhumation Burials at Burton Bradstock and Chickerell, Dorset. *Dorset Natural History and Archaeological Society,* 87, 114-18.

Farrar, R. A. H., 1969. A Late Roman Black-Burnished Pottery Industry in Dorset and Its Affinities. *Dorset Natural History and Archaeological Society,* 90, 174-80.

Farrell, S., 2000. *Report of Archaeological Trial Trenching and Geophysical Survey, October - December 2000, Lochloy Highland,* Unpublished Report, RCAHMS MS 1131/11.

Farrell, S., 2001. *Report of Archaeological Excavation February 2001 - March 2001, Lochloy, Highland Phase 2,* Unpublished Report, RCAHMS MS 1131/18.

Farrell, S., 2005. *Discovery and Excavation in Scotland,* 94.

Farrell, S., 2006. *Discovery and Excavation in Scotland,* 98.

Farwell, D. E. and T. L. Molleson, 1993. *Excavations at Poundbury 1966-80, Volume II, The Cemeteries*: Dorset Natural History and Archaeological Society Monograph 11.

Fenton-Thomas, C., 2009. *A Place by the Sea: Excavations at Sewerby Cottage Farm Bridlington,* On-Site Archaeology Monograph no. 1.

Fern, C., 2006. *Report of the Archaeological Evaluation at Clark's Common Farm, Everingham (Ever 06), East Riding, North Yorkshire,* Unpublished Report, EHU 1271.

Fern, C., 2007. *Sutton Hoo Visitor's Centre, Tranmer House, Bromeswell, Sufolk, Assessement and Project Design,* Unpublished Report, Suffolk County Council 2007/116, Suffolk HER BML 018.

Fern, C., 2010. *Report on Archaeological Recording at Sherburn Church-of-England Primary School, St Hilda's Street, Sherburn, North Yorkshire,* Unpublished Report, Fern Archaeology, North Yorkshire HER.

Ferris, I. M. and L. Bevan, 1993. Excavations at Maidenbrook Farm, Cheddon Fitzpaine, 1990. *Somerset Archaeology and Natural History Society,* 137, 1-40.

Feugère, M. and M. Py, 1989. Les Bracelets En Verre De Nages (Gard) (Les Castels, Fouilles 1958-1981), in *Le Verre Préromain En Europe Occidentale,* ed. M. Feugère, Montagnac: Monique Mergoil, 153-67.

Field, N. H., 1966. Romano-British Settlement at Studland, Dorset, Final Report on the Excavation, 1952-58. *Dorset Natural History and Archaeological Society,* 87, 142-207.

Field, N. H., 1982. The Iron Age and Romano-British Settlement on Bradford Down, Pamphill, Dorset. *Dorset Natural History and Archaeological Society,* 104, 71-92.

Finney, A., 2009. *Land to the South of West Garth, Cayton, North Yorkshire, Archaeological Evaluation by Trial Trenching,* Unpublished Report, MAP

Archaeological Consultancy, North Yorks HER S12736.

Finney, A. E., 1989. *Crossgates Farm - Seamer, Archaeological Watching Brief Excavation, Area D,* Unpublished Report, ERARC North Yorks HER S8190.

Fitzpatrick, A. P., 1990. *Cross-Channel Contact in the British Later Iron Age with Particular Reference to the British Archaeological Evidence,* Unpublished Ph.D. Thesis, Durham University.

Fitzpatrick, A. P., 1992. The Snettisham, Norfolk, Hoards of Iron Age Torques: Sacred or Profane? *Antiquity,* 66, 395-98.

Fitzpatrick, A. P., 1997a. A 1st-Century AD 'Durotrigian' Inhumation Burial with a Decorated Iron Age Mirror from Portesham, Dorset. *Proceedings of the Dorset Natural History and Archaeological Society,* 118, 51-70.

Fitzpatrick, A. P., 1997b. Everyday Life in Iron Age Wessex, in *Reconstructing Iron Age Societies: New Approaches to the British Iron Age,* eds. A. Gwilt and C. Haselgrove, Oxford: Oxbow Monograph 71, 73-86.

Fitzpatrick, A. P., 2001. Cross-Channel Exchange, Hengistbury Head, and the End of Hillforts, in *Society and Settlement in Iron Age Europe,* ed. J. R. Collis, Sheffield: J.R. Collis, 82-94.

Fitzpatrick, A. P., 2005. Gifts for the Golden Gods: Iron Age Hoards of Torques and Coins, in *Iron Age Coinage and Ritual Practices,* eds. C. Haselgrove and D. Wigg-Wolf, Verlag Philipp Von Zabern: Mainz Am Rhein, 157-82.

Fitzpatrick, A. P., 2007. Later Bronze Age and Iron Age, in *The Archaeology of South West England: South West Archaeological Research Framework, Resource Assessment and Research Agenda,* ed. C. J. Webster, Taunton: Somerset County Council, 117-44.

Fitzpatrick, A. P. and A. D. Crockett, 1998. A Romano-British Settlement and Inhumation Cemetery at Eyewell Farm, Chilmark. *Wiltshire Archaeology and Natural History Society,* 91, 11-33.

Flack, S. and T. Gregory, 1988. Excavations at Brancaster, 1985. *Norfolk Archaeology,* 40(2), 164-71.

Fletcher, M. and G. R. Lock, 2005. *Digging Numbers: Elementary Statistics for Archaeologists (Second Edition),* Oxford: Oxford University School of Archaeology.

Flintcroft, M., 1992. *Evaluation Report, Park Farm, Silfield, Wymondham,* Unpublished Report, Norfolk Archaeological Unit, Norfolk HER 25881-25892.

Flintcroft, M., 2001. *Excavations of a Romano-British Settlement on the A149 Snettisham Bypass, 1989,* Dereham, Norfolk: East Anglian Archaeology Report no. 93.

Foll, H. E., 1925. Roman Remains, Bredon Hill. *Transactions of the Bristol and Gloucestershire Archaeological Society,* 47, 350-52.

Fontijin, D., 2012. Meaningful but Beyond Words? Interpreting Material Culture Patterning. *Archaeological Dialogues,* 19(2), 120-24.

Ford, J. A., 1954. The Type Concept Revisited. *American Anthropologist,* 56, 42-54.

Ford, J. A. and J. H. Steward, 1954. On the Concept of Types. *American Anthropologist,* 56(1), 42-57.

Ford, S., 1999. *Nursteed Farm, Brickley Lane, Devizes, Wiltshire, Archaeological Evaluation,* Unpublished Report, Thames Valley Archaeological Services, BLD99734.

Forrest, K., 1993. *Evaluation Report, Dunston Hall, Stoke Holy Cross, Norfolk,* Unpublished Report, Norfolk Archaeological Unit, Norfolk HER 29734-29736.

Forrest, K., 1995. *Hoxne Context Project,* Unpublished Report, Suffolk County Council, Suffolk HER HXN 019.

Fortner, B. and T. E. Meyer, 1997. *Number by Colours: A Guide to Using Colour to Understand Technical Data,* Santa Clara, California: Springer.

Foster, H. E. and C. M. Jackson, 2009. The Composition of 'Naturally Coloured' Late Roman Vessel Glass from Britain and the Implications for Models of Glass Production and Supply. *Journal of Archaeological Science,* 36(2), 189-204.

Foucault, M., 1979. *Discipline and Punish: The Birth of the Prison,* Harmondsworth: Penguin.

Foucault, M., 1980. Body/Power, in *Power/Knowledge: Selected Interviews and Other Writings 1972-1977,* ed. C. Gordon, Brighton: Pearson Education, 55-62.

Foulds, E. M., Forthcoming-a. Report on the Glass Beads in the Chesil Mirror Burial, Dorset.

Foulds, E. M., Forthcoming-b. Report on the Iron Age Glass Beads, in *Grandcourt Quarry, East Winch, Norfolk,* ed. S. Malone.

Fowler, C., 2004. *The Archaeology of Personhood: An Anthropological Approach,* London: Routledge.

Fowler, E., 1960. The Origins and Development of the Penannular Brooch in Europe. *Proceedings of the Prehistoric Society,* 26, 149-77.

Fowler, M. J., 1953. The Typology of Brooches of the Iron Age in Wessex. *Archaeological Journal,* 110, 88-105.

Fowler, P. J., 1962. A Note on Archaeological Finds from the A.E.A. Effluent Pipe-Line, Winfrith Heath to Arish Mell, 1959. *Dorset Natural History and Archaeological Society,* 84, 125-31.

Fowler, P. J., 1965. A Cross-Dyke on Buxbury Hill, Sutton Mandeville. *Wiltshire Archaeology and Natural History Society,* 60, 47-51.

Fowler, P. J., 1968. Excavations of a Romano-British Settlement at Row of Ashes Farm, Butcombe, North Somerset, Interim Report, 1966-1967. *Proceedings of the University of Bristol Spelaeological Society,* 11, 209-36.

Fowler, P. J., 2000. *Excavations within a Later Prehistoric Field System on Overton Down, West*

Overton, Wiltshire: Land-Use over 4,000 Years: FYFOD Working PAPER FWP63, Available Online at http://archaeologydatatservice.ac.uk.

Fowler, P. J., J. W. G. Musty and C. C. Taylor, 1965. Some Earthwork Enclosures in Wiltshire. *Wiltshire Archaeology and Natural History Society*, 60, 52-74.

Fowler, P. J. and B. Walters, 1981. Archaeology and the M4 Motorway, 1969-71. *Wiltshire Archaeology and Natural History Society*, 74/75, 69-130.

Fox, C., 1958. *Pattern and Purpose: A Survey of Early Celtic Art in Britain*, Cardiff: National Museum of Wales.

Frank, S., 1982. *Glass and Archaeology*, London: Academic Press.

Fraser, J., 2002. *An Archaeological Evaluation at Snuff Mill Lane, Cottingham, East Riding of Yorkshire, June 2002*, Unpublished Report, Humber Field Archaeology Report no. 111, Humberside HER DHE/2001/631.

Fraser, J. and T. Brigham, 2009. A Romano-British and Medieval Haven at Brough. *East Riding Archaeologist*, 12, 115-26.

Fraser, J. and T. Bringham, 2009. Excavations at Eastgate South, Driffield, 2001. *East Riding Archaeologist*, 12, 172-207.

Frere, S. and R. Clarke, 1945. The Romano-British Village at Needham, Norfolk. *Norfolk Archaeology*, 28(4), 187-216.

Frey, O.-H., H. Matthäus and C. Braun, 1983. *Glasperlen Der Vorrömischen Eisenzeit I Nach Unterlagen Von Th. E. Haevernick*, Marburger Studien zur vor- und Frühgeschichte Band 5.

Fulford, M. G., A. B. Powell, R. Entwistle and F. Raymond, 2006. *Iron Age and Romano-British Settlements and Landscapes of Salisbury Plain*, Wessex Archaeology Report 20.

Fyles, C., 2007. *Archaeological Excavation at Slackbuie Inverness*, Unpublished Report, SUAT Ltd.

Gale, J., P. Cheetham and J. Laver, 2004. Excavations at High Lea Farm, Hinton Martell, Dorset: An Interim Report on Fieldwork Undertaken During 2002-3. *Dorset Natural History and Archaeological Society*, 126, 160-66.

Gallagher, B., 2005a. *Butleigh, County Somerset, an Archaeological Test Pit Evaluation, 10-11 December 2005, Assessment Report*, Unpublished Report, Somerset HER 28508.

Gallagher, B., 2005b. *Dinnington Somerset: An Interim Report on the Archaeological Evaluation by Time Team (8-10 May 2002)*, Unpublished Report, Somerset HER 15453.

Gardener, R. and S. Boulter, 2003. *Land Off Low Road, Debenham, Archaeological Excavation Report, 2003*, Unpublished Report, Suffolk County Council 2003/35, Suffolk HER DBN 104.

Gardiner, J., M. J. Allen, S. Hamilton-Dyer, M. Laidlaw and R. G. Scaife, 2002. Making the Most of It: Late Prehistoric Pastoralism in the Avon Levels, Severn Estuary. *Proceedings of the Prehistoric Society*, 68, 1-39.

Gardner, K. S., 1998. Abbot's Leigh - a 1st/2nd Century Romano-British Site. *Bristol and Avon Archaeology*, 15, 27-31.

Gardner, R., 2004. *Nethergate Street Garage, Clare, Archaeological Evaluation Report, 2004*, Unpublished Report, Suffolk County Council 2004/152, Suffolk HER CLA 043.

Gardner, R. and M. Sutherland, 2001. *Barham Quarry: Wiltding Aggregates, Ltd. Suffolk, an Archaeological Evaluation, Phase 1*, Unpublished Report, Hertfordshire Archaeological Trust 1002, Suffolk HER BRH 043.

Gardner, R. V., 2003. *Land to the Rear of 'Wrights', St Catherines Road, Little St Marys, Long Melford, Archaeological Evaluation Report*, Unpublished Report, Suffolk County Council 2002/139, Suffolk HER LMD 136.

Garner-Lahire, J., 2000. *Archaeological Excavation and Survey, York Minster Library*, Unpublished Report, Field Archaeology Specialists, CYC 557.

Garrett, C. S., 1938. Chesters Roman Villa, Woolaston, Gloucestershire. *Archaeological Cambrensis*, 43, 93-125.

Garrow, D., 2000. *An Archaeological Evaluation by Trial Trenching at Norwich Road, Kilverstone, Norfolk*, Unpublished Report, Cambridge Archaeological Unit 397, Norfolk HER 34489.

Garrow, D., 2002. *Archaeological Excavations at Norwich Road, Kilverstone, Norfolk*, Unpublished Report, Cambridge Archaeological unit 463, Norfolk HER 34489.

Garrow, D., 2003. *Excavations at Kilverstone, Broom Covert, Area E*, Unpublished Report, Cambridge Archaeological Unit 518, Norfolk HER 37349.

Garrow, D., 2008. The Space and Time of Celtic Art: Interrogating the 'Technologies of Enchantment' Database, in *Rethinking Celtic Art*, eds. D. Garrow, C. Gosden and J. D. Hill, Oxford: Oxbow, 15-39.

Garrow, D. and C. Gosden, 2012. *Technologies of Enchantment?: Exploring Celtic Art: 400 BC to AD 100*, Oxford: Oxford University Press.

Garrow, D., C. Gosden and J. D. Hill (eds.), 2008. *Rethinking Celtic Art*, Oxford: Oxbow.

Gebhard, R., 1989a. *Der Glasschmuck Aus Dem Oppidum Von Manching*, Wiesbaden: Steiner.

Gebhard, R., 1989b. Le Verre À Manching: Données Chronologiques Et Apport Des Analyses, in *Le Verre Préromain En Europe Occidentale*, ed. M. Feugère, Montagnac: Monique Mergoil, 99-106.

Gebhard, R., 1989c. Pour Une Nouvelle Typologie Des Bracelets Celtiques En Verre, in *Le Verre Préromain En Europe Occidentale*, ed. M. Feugère, Montagnac: Monique Mergoil, 73-83.

Gell, A., 1988. Technology and Magic. *Anthropology Today*, 4(2), 6-9.

Gell, A., 1998. *Art and Agency: An Anthropological Theory,* Oxford: Claredon.

Gelling, P. S., 1977. Excavations on Pilsdon Pen, Dorset, 1964-71. *Proceedings of the Prehistoric Society,* 43, 263-86.

Gentles, D., Harden, G., 1986. *Discovery and Excavation in Scotland,* 17.

Gerrard, C., 2007. *The Shapwick Project, Somerset, a Rural Landscape Explored,* London: English Heritage and the Society for Medieval Archaeology Monograph no. 25.

Gibson, A., 2002. *Prehistoric Pottery in Britain and Ireland,* Stroud: Tempus.

Gilbert, D., 2008. *An Archaeological Evaluation at Glenda Spooner Farm, Brincil Hill Lane, Kingsdon, Somerset,* Unpublished Report, John Moor Heritage Services, Available on OASIS.

Giles, M., 2007a. Good Fences Make Good Neighbours? Exploring the Ladder Enclosures of Late Iron Age East Yorkshire, in *The Later Iron Age in Britain and Beyond,* eds. C. Haselgrove and T. Moore, Oxford: Oxbow, 235-49.

Giles, M., 2007b. Refiguring Rights in the Early Iron Age Landscapes of East Yorkshire, in *The Earlier Iron Age in Britain and the near Continent,* eds. C. Haselgrove and T. Moore, Oxford: Oxbow, 103-18.

Giles, M., 2008a. Seeing Red: The Aesthetics of Material Object in the British and Irish Iron Age, in *Rethinking Celtic Art*, eds. D. Garrow, C. Gosden and J. D. Hill, Oxford: Oxbow, 59-77.

Giles, M., 2008b. The Use of Colour in Iron Age Art: A Case Study from East Yorkshire. *Yorkshire Archaeological Society Prehistory Research Section Bulletin,* 45, 71-73.

Giles, M., 2012. *A Forged Glamour: Landscape, Identity and Material Culture in the Iron Age,* Oxford: Windgather Press.

Gill, D., 1996a. *Archaeological Evaluation Report, Ingham Quarry, Fornham St. Genevieve,* Unpublished Report, Suffolk County Council 96/74, Suffolk HER FSG 012.

Gill, D., 1996b. *Eldo House Farm, Bury St. Edmunds, Archaeological Evaluation Report,* Unpublished Report, Suffolk County Council 1996/083, Suffolk HER BSE 131.

Gill, D., 1997. *Little St. Marys, Long Melford, Archaeological Evaluation Report,* Unpublished Report, Suffolk County Council 97/7, Suffolk HER LMD 115.

Gill, D., 1999. *RAF Mildenhall, New and Repaired Parking Lots, Archaeological Excavation Report,* Unpublished Report, Suffolk County Council 2000/11, Suffolk HER MNL 491.

Gill, D., 2000. *Aafes Gas Station/Shopette/Snack Bar, Douglas Avenue, RAF Lakenheath, Archaeological Excavation Report,* Unpublished Report, Suffolk County Council 2002/87, Suffolk HER LKH 214.

Gill, D., 2001. *Land Adjacent to the Old Police House, Beeches Road, West Row, Mildenhall, Archaeological Evaluation Report,* Unpublished Report, Suffolk County Council 2001/70, Suffolk HER MNL 193.

Gingell, C., 1982. Excavations of an Iron Age Enclosure at Groundwell Farm, Blunsdon St Andrew, 1976-7. *Wiltshire Archaeology and Natural History Society,* 76, 33-75.

Gleba, M., C. Munkholt and M.-L. Nosch (eds.), 2008. *Dressing the Past,* Oxford: Oxbow.

Gomez de Soto, J., 2003. Oiseaux, Chevaux, Hommes Et Autres Images. Les <<Singes>> Sur Céramique En Gaule Du Ha A2/B1 Au Ha D. Genèse, Apogée, Décadence Et Postérite, in *Décors, Images Et Signes De L'âge Du Fer Européen. Actes Du Xxvi Colloque De L'association Française Pour L'etude De L'age Du Fer. Paris Et Saint-Denis 9-12 Mai 2002,* eds. O. Buchsenschutz, A. Bulard, M.-B. Chardenoux and N. Ginous, Tours: FERACF, 11-26.

Gondek, M. and G. Noble, 2005. *Discovery and Excavation in Scotland*, 19.

Gosden, C., 1985. Gifts and Kin in Early Iron Age Europe. *Man, New series,* 20(3), 475-93.

Gosden, C., 2005. What Do Objects Want? *Journal of Archaeological Method and Theory,* 12(3), 193-211.

Gosden, C. and Y. Marshall, 1999. The Cultural Biography of Objects. *World Archaeology,* 31(2), 169-78.

Goult, D., 2004. *An Archaeological Watching Brief in 2002 at the King's Head, Church Road, Bishop's Cleeve, Gloucestershire,* Unpublished Report, Gloucestershire County Council, Gloucestershire HER 20200.

Grace, P. and N. Holbrook, 2008. *The Probable Theatre and Surrounding Area: Observations in 1969,* Cirencester: Cotswold Archaeology.

Gracie, H. S., 1963. St. Peter's Church, Frocester. *Transactions of the Bristol and Gloucestershire Archaeological Society,* 82, 148-67.

Gracie, H. S., 1970. Frocester Court Roman Villa, Gloucestershire: First Report, 1961-67. Building A. *Transactions of the Bristol and Gloucestershire Archaeological Society,* 89, 15-86.

Graham, A., 1997. *Archaeological Observations at the Waggon House, West Street, Ilchester, Somerset,* Unpublished Report, Somerset HER 55986.

Graham, A., 2005. *Archaeological Observations on the Site of a New Skateboard Facility, Ilchester, Somerset,* Unpublished Report, Somerset HER 18608.

Graham, A. and C. Newman, 1993. Recent Excavations of Iron Age and Romano-British Enclosures in the Avon Valley, Wiltshire. *Wiltshire Archaeology and Natural History Society*, 86, 8-57.

Graham, A. H. and S. M. Davies, 1993. *Excavations in the Town Centre of Trowbridge, Wiltshire, 1977 and 1986-1988,* Wessex Archaeology Report 2.

Graham, A. H. and J. M. Mills, 1996. A Romano-British Building at Crimbleford Knap, Seavington St Mary.

Somerset Archaeology and Natural History Society, 139, 119-34.

Grant, J. and M. Sutherland, 2003. *Lodge Farm, Costessey, Norfolk, an Archaeological Evaluation (Trial Trenching)*, Unpublished Report, Archaeological Solutions 1455, Norfolk HER 37646.

Grassam, A., 2007. *Pheasant's Walk, Earsham Quarry, Norfolk, Post Excavation Assessment and Updated Project Design*, Unpublished Report, Archaeological Solutions 2897, Norfolk HER 44609.

Grassam, A. and P. Weston, 2004. *Land at East Bilney Quarry, Beetley, Norfolk, an Archaeological Evaluation*, Unpublished Report, Archaeological Solutions 1583, Norfolk HER 39348.

Gray, H., 1904. Excavations at Small Down Camp, near Evercreech. *Somerset Archaeology and Natural History Society*, 50, 32-49.

Gray, H., 1908. Excavations at Norton Camp, near Tuanton, 1908. *Somerset Archaeology and Natural History Society*, 54, 131-43.

Gray, H., 1909. Excavations at the 'Amphitheatre', Charterhouse-on-Medip, 1909. *Somerset Archaeology and Natural History Society*, 55, 118-37.

Gray, H., 1913. Trial-Excavations at Cadbury Castle, S. Somerset, 1913. *Somerset Archaeology and Natural History Society*, 59, 1-24.

Gray, H., 1923. Archaeological Remains, Ham Hill, South Somerset. *Somerset Archaeology and Natural History Society*, 69, 49-53.

Gray, H., 1924a. Excavations at Ham Hill, South Somerset. *Somerset Archaeology and Natural History Society*, 70, 104-16.

Gray, H., 1924b. Part of a Hoard of Roman Coins Found on Sandford Hill, Somerset. *Somerset Archaeology and Natural History Society*, 70, 86-96.

Gray, H., 1925. Excavations at Ham Hill, South Somerset. *Somerset Archaeology and Natural History Society*, 71, 57-76.

Gray, H., 1930. Excavations at Kingsdown Camp, Mells, Somerset, 1927-9. *Archaeologia*, 80, 58-98.

Gray, H., 1933. Roman Coffins at Ilchester. *Somerset Archaeology and Natural History Society*, 79, 101-08.

Gray, H., 1937. A Second Hoard of Late Roman Coins from Shapwick Heath, Somerset. *Somerset Archaeology and Natural History Society*, 83, 148-52.

Gray, H., 1942. Glass Beads Found in a Cist-Burial at Clevedon. *Somerset Archaeology and Natural History Society*, 88, 73-79.

Gray, H., 1947. The Excavations at Iwerne, 1897. *Archaeological Journal*, 104, 50-62.

Green, C., 1949. The Birdlip Early Iron Age Burials, a Review. *Proceedings of the Prehistoric Society*, 15, 188-90.

Green, C., 1977. *Excavations in the Roman Kiln Field at Brampton, 1973-4*, Dereham, Norfolk: East Anglian Archaeology no. 5.

Green, C. S., 1987. *Excavations at Poundbury, Dorchester, Dorset 1966-1982, Volume I: The Settlements*, Dorset Natural History and Archaeological Society Monograph no. 7.

Green, F. M. L., 2004. *An Archaeological Evaluation at Three Score, Bowthorpe, Norwich*, Unpublished Report, Norfolk Archaeological Unit 1010, Norfolk HER 40711.

Green, F. M. L., 2006. *An Archaeological Strip, Map and Sample Excavation at Land Next to Rushford Church, Brettenham, Norfolk*, Unpublished Report, NAU Archaeology 1106, Norfolk HER 40919.

Green, F. M. L., 2010. *An Archaeological Excavation at Three Score Community Residential Development, Bowthorpe, Norwich*, Unpublished Report, NAU Archaeology 1417, Norfolk HER 40711.

Green, H. S., 1971. Wansdyke, Excavations 1966 to 1970. *Wiltshire Archaeology and Natural History Society*, 66, 129-46.

Green, J. P., 1979. Citizen House, 1970, in *Excavations in Bath 1950-1975*, ed. B. Cunliffe, Bristol: Committee for Rescue Archaeology in Avon, Gloucestershire and Somerset.

Green, J. P., 1993. Excavations at Dorchester Hospital (Site C), Dorchester, Dorset. *Dorset Natural History and Archaeological Society*, 115, 71-100.

Green, M., 2007. *Monkton-up-Wimborne Later Bronze Age to Early Iron Age Enclosure*, Cambridge: McDonald Institute Monograph.

Greenwell, W., 1872. *British Barrows: A Record of the Examination of Sepulchral Mounds in Various Parts of England*, Oxford: Clarendon Press.

Greenwell, W., 1906. Early Iron Age Burials in Yorkshire. *Archaeologia*, 60, 251-324.

Gregory, R., 2001. Excavations by the Late G D B Jones and C M Daniels Along the Moray Firth Littoral. *Proceedings of the Society of Antiquaries of Scotland*, 131, 177-222.

Gregory, T., 1976. A Hoard of Late Roman Metalwork from Weeting, Norfolk. *Norfolk Archaeology*, 36(3), 265-72.

Gregory, T., 1977. *The Enclosure at Ashill*, Dereham, Norfolk: East Anglia Archaeology Report no. 5.

Gregory, T., 1979. Early Romano-British Pottery Production at Thorpe St. Andrew, Norwich. *Norfolk Archaeology*, 37, 202-07.

Gregory, T., 1986. *An Enclosure of the First Century AD at Thronham*, Dereham, Norfolk: East Anglian Archaeology Report no. 30.

Gregory, T., 1991. *Excavations in Thetford, 1980-1982, Fison Way, Volume I*, Dereham, Norfolk: East Anglian Archaeology Report no. 53.

Greig, M., 1996. *Discovery and Excavation in Scotland*, 9.

Grimes, W. F., 1960. *Excavations on Defence Sites, 1939-1945: I. Mainly Neolithic-Bronze Age,* London: Minishtry of Works Archaeological Reports no. 3.

Guido, M., 1978a. *The Glass Beads of the Prehistoric and Roman Periods in Britain and Ireland,* London: The Society of Antiquaries of London Report no. 35.

Guido, M., 1978b. An Iron Age Burial from Battlesbury. *Wiltshire Archaeology and Natural History Society,* 72/73, 177-78.

Guido, M., 1999. *The Glass Beads of Anglo-Saxon England C. AD 400-700: A Preliminary Visual Classification of the More Definitive and Diagnostic Types,* London: Reports of the Research Committee of the Society of Antiquarians of London, No. 58.

Guido, M., J. Henderson, M. Cable, J. Bayley and L. Biek, 1984. A Bronze Age Glass Bead from Wilsford, Wiltshire: Barrow G42 in the Lake Group. *Proceedings of the Prehistoric Society,* 50, 245-54.

Guillard, M.-C., 1989. La Verrerie Protohistorique De Mandeure (Doubs), in *Le Verre Préromain En Europe Occidentale,* ed. M. Feugère, Montagnac: Monique Mergoil, 145-52.

Gurney, D., 1990. A Romano-British Pottery Kiln at Blackborough End, Middleton. *Norfolk Archaeology,* 41(1), 83-92.

Gurney, D., 1991. *An Iron Age Structure on the North Tuddenham Bypass,* Unpublished Report, Norfolk Landscape Archaeology, Norfolk HER 28341.

Gustaven, L., 2003. *2-4 Driffield Terrace, The Mount, York, Archaeological Evaluation,* Unpublished Report, Field Archaeology Specialists, DYD 518.

Gwilt, A., J. Joy and F. Hunter, August 2010. *Celtic Art Database,* http://www.britishmuseum.org/research/projects/technologies_of_enchantment/the_celtic_art_database.aspx.

Haddington, M., 2001. *An Archaeological Evaluation at Northover Manor Hotel, Northover, Ilchester, October 2001,* Unpublished Report, Charles and Nancy Hollinrake no. 247, Somerset HER 15131.

Haevernick, T. E., 1960. *Die Glasarmringe Und Ringperlen Der Mittel- Und Spätlatènezeit Auf Dem Europäischen Festland,* Bonn: Rudolf Habelt Verlag.

Haldane, J. W., 1975. The Excavations at Stokeleigh Camp, Avon, (St 559733). *Proceedings of the University of Bristol Spelaeological Society,* 14(1), 29-63.

Hale, A. G. C., 1994. Discovery and Excavation in Scotland, 35-6, 39.

Hale, A. G. C., 1995. Discovery and Excavation in Scotland, 40.

Hale, A. G. C., 1996. Discovery and Excavation in Scotland, 65-6.

Halkon, P. and M. Millett, 1999. *Rural Settlement and Industry: Studies in the Iron Age and Roman Archaeology of Lowland East Yorkshire,* Yorkshire Archaeological Report no. 4.

Hall, J. J., A. Little and M. Locock, 1996. Excavations at Attlebridge, 1989. *Norfolk Archaeology,* 42(3), 296-320.

Hall, R. V., 2005. *Archaeological Monitoring at Caister Old Hall, Caister-on-Sea, Norfolk,* Unpublished Report, Archaeological Project Services 06/05, Norfolk HER 40651.

Halliday, S., 2007. The Later Prehistoric Landscape, in *In the Shadow of Bennachie: A Field Archaeology of Donside, Aberdeenshire,* ed. RCAHMS, Edinburgh: Society of Antiquaries of Scotland, 79-114.

Hamilton, J. and C. McGill, 1997a. *A96-Kintore and Blackburn Bypass, Archaeological Watching Brief,* Unpublished Report, Centre for Field Archaeology Report no. 360, RCAHMS MS 1081/67.

Hamilton, J. and C. McGill, 1997b. *Discovery and Excavation in Scotland,* 10.

Hamilton, S., 2002. Between Ritual and Routine: Interpreting British Prehistoric Pottery Production and Distribution, in *Prehistoric Britain: The Ceramic Basis,* eds. A. Woodward and J. D. Hill, Oxford: Oxbow, 38-53.

Hammond, S., D. Gilbert and D. Heale, 2009. *An Archaeological Evaluation at Land Off Greet Road, Winchcombe, Gloucestershire,* Unpublished Report, John Moore Heritage Services, Available on OASIS.

Hancocks, A., M. Watts and N. Holrook, 2005. *Excavation at Watching Brief at Cotswold District Council Offices, Trinity Road, Cirencester, 2001-2002,* Unpublished Report, Cotswold Archaeology Trust Report no. 05044, Gloucestershire HER 27760.

Harden, J., 1986. *Craig Phadrig,* Unpublished Manuscript, RCAHMS MS 583/1.

Harding, D. W., 2004. *The Iron Age in Northern Britain: Celts and Romans, Natives and Invaders,* London: Routledge.

Harding, D. W., 2007. *The Archaeology of Celtic Art,* London: Routledge.

Harding, D. W., I. M. Blake and P. J. Reynolds, 1993. *An Iron Age Settlement in Dorset: Excavation and Reconstruction,* University of Edinburgh, Department of Archaeology, Monograph no. 1.

Harding, P. A. and C. Lewis, 1997. Archaeological Investigations at Tockenham, 1994. *Wiltshire Archaeology and Natural History Society,* 90, 26-41.

Harlow, M. (ed.) 2012. *Dress and Identity,* Oxford: BAR International Series no. 2356.

Harrison, S., 2003. *An Archaeological Watching Brief at Pexton Road (Western Extension), Kelleythorpe Industrial Estate, Driffield, East Riding of Yorkshire, January - September 2003,* Unpublished Report, Stephen Harrison Archaeological and Historical Research Services, EHU 1009.

Hart, J., 1999. *Watermoore House, Cirencester, Archaeological Evaluation,* Unpublished Report, Cotswold Archaeology Trust Report no. 991120, Gloucestershire HER 30463.

Hart, J., 2005. *31 Hadrian Close, Sea Mills, Bristol, Archaeological Evaluation,* Unpublished Report, Cotswold Archaeology 05116, Bristol City HER.

Hart, J., 2008. *Land at Charfield Road, Kingswood, Gloucestershire, Archaeological Excavation,* Unpublished Report, Cotswold Archaeology Report no. 08225, Available on OASIS.

Hart, J., 2009a. *Honeybourne to Wormington Natural Gas Pipeline, Worcestershire and Gloucestershire, Post-Excavation Assessment and Updated Project Design,* Unpublished Report, Cotswold Archaeology Report no. 08197, Gloucestershire HER 33900.

Hart, J., 2009b. *Land at Mendip Avenue, Shepton Mallet, Somerset,* Unpublished Report, Cotswold Archaeology 2765, Somerset HER 298373.

Hart, J., 2011. *10 Corinium Gate, Cirencester, Gloucestershire, Archaeological Evaluation,* Unpublished Report, Cotswold Archaeology Report 11001, Available on OASIS.

Hart, J. and M. Alexander, 2007. *Prehistoric, Romano-British and Medieval Remains at Blenheim Farm, Moreton-in-Marsh, Gloucestershire, Excavations in 2003.* Cotstwold Archaeology, Bristol and Gloucestershire Archaeological report no. 5.

Hart, J., M. Alexander and E. McSloy, 2004. *Blenheim Farm, Moreton-in-Marsh, Gloucestershire, Post-Excavation Assessment and Updated Project Design,* Unpublished Report, Cotswold Archaeology Trust Report no. 04107, Gloucestershire HER 27448.

Hart, J., M. Collard and N. Holbrook, 2005. A New Roman Villa near Malmesbury. *Wiltshire Archaeology and Natural History Society,* 98, 297-306.

Hartley, B. R., 1976. *Excavations at Lease Rigg, 1976,* Unpublished Report, NYMNP HER 4052.

Hartley, B. R., 1978. *Interim Report on Excavation at Lease Rigg, 1978,* Unpublished Report, NYMNP HER 4052.

Harvard, T., 2000. *The Thatched Cottage, Wortley, Gloucestershire, Archaeological Watching Brief,* Unpublished Report, Cotswold Archaeological Trust Report no. 001135, Gloucestershire HER 5655.

Harvard, T., 2003. *Land at Poulton Gorse, Poulton, Gloucestershire, Archaeological Evaluation,* Unpublished Report, Cotswold Archaeological Trust Report no. 03034, Gloucestershire HER 22105.

Harvard, T., 2005. *St. George's Place, Cheltenham, Gloucestershire, Archaeological Evaluation,* Unpublished Report, Cotswold Archaeology Trust Report no. 05169, Gloucestershire HER 28144.

Harvard, T., 2010a. *Berkeley Vale Wind Park, Stinchcombe, Gloucestershire, Archaeological Evaluation,* Unpublished Report, Cotswold Archaeology report 10229, Available on OASIS.

Harvard, T., 2010b. *Deerhurst Flood Alleviation Scheme, Gloucestershire, Archaeological Evaluation and Watching Brief,* Unpublished Report, Cotswold Archaeology Report 10002, Available on OASIS.

Harvard, T., K. Cullen and M. Watts, 2008. *Evaluation and Watching Brief between School Lane and Stepstair Lane, 2003-5,* Cirencester: Cotswold Archaeology.

Harvard, T. and M. Watts, 2008. *Bingham Hall, Kings Street, 2002,* Cirencester: Cotswold Archaeology.

Haselgrove, C., 1982. Wealth, Prestige and Power: The Dynamics of Late Iron Age Political Centralization in South-East England, in *Ranking, Resource and Exchange,* eds. C. Renfrew and S. Shennan, Cambridge: Cambridge University Press, 79-88.

Haselgrove, C., 1997. Iron Age Brooch Deposition and Chronology, in *Reconstructing Iron Age Societies: New Approaches to the British Iron Age,* eds. A. Gwilt and C. Haselgrove, Oxford: Oxbow Monograph 71, 51-72.

Haselgrove, C., 2009. *The Traprain Law Environs Project: fieldwork and excavations 2000-2004,* Edinburgh: Society of Antiquaries of Scotland.

Haselgrove, C., I. Armit, T. Champion, J. Creighton, A. Gwilt, J. D. Hill, F. Hunter and A. Woodward, 2001. *Understanding the British Iron Age: An Agenda for Action. A Report for the Iron Age Research Seminar and the Council of the Prehistoric Society,* Salisbury: Trust for Wessex Archaeology.

Hastie, M., 2004. *Report of an Archaeological Evaluation at Culduthel Mains Farm Phase 1 and 4, Inverness,* Unpublished Report, Headland Archaeology Ltd., RCAHMS MS 5562.

Hatherley, C., 2004. *Discovery and Excavation in Scotland,* 16.

Hattatt, R., 1985. *Iron Age and Roman Brooches: A Second Selection of Brooches from the Author's Collection,* Oxford: Oxbow.

Hattatt, R., 1989. *Ancient Brooches and Other Artefacts: A Fourth Selection of Brooches Together with Some Other Antiquities from the Author's Collection,* Oxford: Oxbow.

Haverfield, F., 1915. *The Romanization of Roman Britain,* Oxford: Clarendon Press.

Hawkes, C., 1931. Hill-Forts. *Antiquity,* 5(17), 60-97.

Hawkes, C. F. C., 1940. An Iron Torc from Spettisbury Rings, Dorset. *Archaeological Journal,* 97, 112-14.

Hawkes, C. F. C., 1958. The A.B.C. Of the British Iron Age, in *Problems of the Iron Age in Southern Britain,* ed. S. Frere, London: University of London Institute of Archaeology Occasional Paper no. 11, 1-17.

Hawkes, C. F. C., 1959. The A.B.C. Of the British Iron Age. *Antiquity,* 33(131), 1-13.

Hawkes, C. J., J. M. Rogers and E. K. Tratman, 1978. Romano-British Cemetery in the Fourth Chamber of Wookey Hole Cave, Somerset. *Proceedings of the University of Bristol Spelaeological Society,* 15(1), 23-52.

Hawkes, J., 1992. *Archaeological Evaluation at the Proposed Extension to Cheddar Sewage Works, Somerset, January 1992,* Unpublished Report, AC Archaeology, Somerset HER 35982.

Hayes, R. H., 1966. A Romano-British Site at Pale End Kildale. *Yorkshire Archaeological Journal,* 41, 687-700.

Hayward, L. C., 1952. The Roman Villa at Lufton, near Yeovil. *Somerset Archaeology and Natural History Society,* 97, 91-112.

Heard, K., 2007. *Archaeological Evaluation Report, Home Farm, Woolverstone, Wlv 047,* Unpublished Report, Suffolk County Council Archaeological Services 2007/228, Available on OASIS.

Heard, K., 2010a. *Post-Excavation Assessment Report, Household Waste and Recycling Centre, South Lowestoft Industrial Estate, Hadenham Road, Gisleham, Suffolk,* Unpublished Report, Suffolk County Council 2009/297, Suffolk HER CAC 035.

Heard, K., 2010b. *Westfield Replacement/Samuel Ward Extension, Chalkstone Way, Haverhill, Suffolk, Archaeological Evaluation Report,* Unpublished Report, Suffolk County Council 2010/049, Suffolk HER HVH 072.

Heard, K., 2011. *Cedars Park, Stowmarket to Baylham Pumping Station, Anglian Water Pipeline (Phase 2), Post-Excavation Assessment Report,* Unpublished Report, Suffolk County Council Archaeology Service Report no. 2009/269, Suffolk HER BAY 037.

Heaton, R., 2004. *An Archaeological Watching Brief at Lansdowne House, High Street, Lansdaown, Bourton-on-the-Water,* Unpublished Report, Gloucestershire County Council, Gloucestershire HER 27129.

Heaton, R., 2005. *An Archaeological Watching Brief at Gloucester Music Library, Greyfriars, Gloucester,* Unpublished Report, Gloucestershire County Council, Gloucestershire HER 27688.

Hencken, T. C., 1938. The Excavation of the Iron Age Camp on Bredon Hill, Gloucestershire, 1935-1937. *Archaeological Journal,* 95, 1-111.

Henderson, J., 1978. Glass, and the Manufacture of Prehistoric and Other Early Glass Beads. Part I: Technical Background and Theory. *Irish Archaeological Research Forum,* 5, 55-62.

Henderson, J., 1980. Some New Evidence for Iron Age Glass-Working in Britain. *Antiquity,* 54(210), 60-61.

Henderson, J., 1981. A Report on the Glass Excavated from Meare Village West 1979, in *Meare Village West 1979,* ed. J. M. Coles, Taunton: Somerset Levels Papers 7, 55-60.

Henderson, J., 1982. *X-Ray Fluorescence Analysis of Iron Age Glass,* Unpublished Ph.D. Thesis, University of Bradford.

Henderson, J., 1985. The Raw Materials of Early Glass Production. *Oxford Journal of Archaeology,* 4(3), 267-91.

Henderson, J., 1987. The Archaeology and Technology of Glass from Meare Village East, in *Meare Village East,* ed. J. M. Coles, Taunton: Somerset Levels Papers no. 13, 170-82.

Henderson, J., 1989. The Evidence for Regional Production of Iron Age Glass in Britain, in *Le Verre Préromain En Europe Occidental,* Montagnac: Mergoil, 63-72.

Henderson, J., 1992. Industrial Specialization in Late Iron Age Britain and Europe. *Archaeological Journal,* 148, 104-48.

Henderson, J., 1995. A Response to R. Lierke's Paper, in *Glass Beads - Cultural History, Technology, Experiment and Analogy,* eds. M. Rasmussen, U. L. Hansen and U. Näsman, Lejre, Denmark: Historical Archaeological Experimental Centre, 121.

Henderson, J., 2000. *The Science and Archaeology of Materials, an Investigation of Inorganic Materials,* London: Routledge.

Henderson, J. C., 2008. *The Atlantic Iron Age: Settlement and Identity in the First Millennium BC,* London: Routledge.

Herne, C. M. and R. J. C. Smith, 1991. A Late Iron Age Settlement and Black-Burnished Ware (Bb1) Production Site at Worgret, near Wareham, Dorset (1986-7). *Dorset Natural History and Archaeological Society,* 113, 55-105.

Herodian, *Roman History*.

Herring, E., 2003. Body Art and the Daunian Stelae, in *Inhabiting Symbols: Symbol and Image in the Ancient Mediterranean,* eds. J. B. Wilkins and E. Herring, London: Accordia Research Institute on the Mediterranean Volume 5, University of London, 121-36.

Heslop, M. and M. Langdon, 1993. *Excavation at 38 Alstone Road, West Huntspill, Somerset, St 313467. March/April,* Unpublished Report, Bridgewater and District Archaeological Society, Somerset HER 12258.

Heslop, M. and M. Langdon, 1996. Excavation at West Huntspill, 1993. *Somerset Archaeology and Natural History Society,* 139, 89-97.

Hey, G., 2000. *Cotswold Community at Ashton Keynes,* Unpublished Oxford Archaeology Unit Report.

Hey, G., 2007. Unravelling the Iron Age Landscape of the Upper Thames Valley, in *The Later Iron Age in Britain and Beyond,* eds. C. Haselgrove and T. Moore, Oxford: Oxbow, 156-72.

Hickling, S., 2007. *An Archaeological Excavation on Land to the South and West of the Gloucester Businness Park, Brockworth, Gloucestershire,* Unpublished Report, Gloucestershire County Council, Gloucestershire HER 28394.

Hickling, S., 2009. *An Archaeological Excavation and Watching Brief at Priory Road, Great Cressingham, Norfolk,* Unpublished Report, NAU Archaeology 1720, Norfolk HER 37409.

Hicks, J. D. and J. A. Wilson, 1975. Romano-British Kilns at Hasholme. *East Riding Archaeologist,* 2, 49-70.

Hill, J. D., 1995a. The Pre-Roman Iron Age in Britain and Ireland (Ca. 800 B.C. To A.D. 100): An Overview. *Journal of World Prehistory,* 9(1), 47-98.

Hill, J. D., 1995b. *Ritual and Rubbish in the Iron Age of Wessex: A Study of the Formation of a Specific Archaeological Record,* Oxford: BAR British Series no. 242.

Hill, J. D., 1996. Hill-Forts and the Iron Age of Wessex, in *The Iron Age in Britain and Ireland: Recent Trends,* eds. T. C. Champion and J. R. Collis, Sheffield: J.R. Collis Publications, 95-116.

Hill, J. D., 1997. 'The End of One Kind of Body and the Beginning of Another Kind of Body'? Toilet Instruments and 'Romanization' in Southern England During the First Century AD in *Reconstructing Iron Age Societies: New Approaches to the British Iron Age,* eds. A. Gwilt and C. Haselgrove, Oxford: Oxbow Monograph 71, 96-107.

Hill, J. D., 2001. A New Cart/Chariot Burial from Wetwang, East Yorkshire. *Past,* 38, 2-3.

Hill, J. D., 2007. The Dynamics of Social Change in Later Iron Age Eastern and South-Eastern England C. 300 BC - AD 43, in *The Later Iron Age in Britain and Beyond,* eds. C. Haselgrove and T. Moore, Oxford: Oxbow, 16-40.

Hill, J. D., 2011. How Did British Middle and Late Pre-Roman Iron Age Societies Work (If They Did)?, in *Atlantic Europe in the First Millennium BC: Crossing the Divide,* eds. T. Moore and X.-L. Armada, Oxford: Oxford University Press, 242-63.

Hill, J. N. and R. K. Evans, 1972. A Model for Classification and Typology, in *Models in Archaeology,* ed. D. L. Clarke, London: Methuen, 231-73.

Hinchliffe, J., 1985. *Excavations at Brancaster 1974 and 1977,* Gressenhall: Norfolk Archaeological Unit.

Hingley, R., 1992. Society in Scotland from 700 BC to AD 200. *Proceedings of the Society of Antiquaries of Scotland,* 122, 7-53.

Hingley, R., 1996. The 'Legacy' of Rome: The Rise, Decline, and Fall of the Theory of Romanization, in *Roman Imperialsim: Post-Colonial Perspectives,* eds. J. Webster and N. J. Cooper, Leicester: School of Archaeological Studies, University of Leicester, 35-48.

Hingley, R., 2005. *Globalizing Roman Culture: Unity, Diversity and Empire,* London: Routledge.

Hingley, R., 2006. The Deposition of Iron Objects in Britain During the Later Prehistoric and Roman Periods: Contextual Analysis and the Significance of Iron. *Britannia,* 37, 213-57.

Hingley, R., 2009. Esoteric Knowledge? Ancient Bronze Artefacts from Iron Age Contexts. *Proceedings of the Prehistoric Society,* 75, 143-65.

Hingley, R., 2011. Iron Age Knowledge: Pre-Roman Peoples and Myths of Origin, in *Atlantic Europe in the First Millennium BC: Crossing the Divide,* eds. T. Moore and X.-L. Armada, Oxford: Oxford University Press.

Hipgrave, J. A., T. Pearson and R. Scutchings, 1976. *Excavations at Bos House, Ilchester - Interim Report*: Ilkly and District Archaeological Society Annual Report, Somerset HER 53038.

Hoad, S., 2004. *RAF Fairford Airfield Development, Gloucestershire, a Report on the Excavation,* Unpublished Report, Museum of London Archaeology Service, Gloucestershire HER 27494.

Hoad, S., 2006. RAF Fairford: Archaeological Evaluation and Excavations Conducted between 1999 and 2001. *Transactions of the Bristol and Gloucestershire Archaeological Society,* 124, 37-54.

Hobbs, B., 2001. *Report on an Archaeological Watching Brief at Ellingham Hall Estate, Ellingham, Norfolk,* Unpublished Report, Norfolk Archaeological Unit 617, Norfolk HER 36050.

Hobbs, B., 2004. *An Archaeological Evaluation on Land to the Rear of 95 Lynne Road, Downham Market, Norfolk,* Unpublished Report, Norfolk Archaeological Unit 977, Norfolk HER 40378.

Hobbs, B., 2008. *An Archaeological Watching Brief at 9 Beacon Hill, Burnham Market, Norfolk,* Unpublished Report, NAU Archaeology 1323, Norfolk HER 49125.

Hobbs, B., 2009a. *An Archaeological Evaluation and Watching Brief at Caister First School, Caister-on-Sea, Norfolk,* Unpublished Report, NAU Archaeology 1991, Norfolk HER 51819.

Hobbs, B., 2009b. *An Archaeological Watching Brief at Queen Anne House, Caistor Lane, Caister St. Edmund, Norwich,* Unpublished Report, NAU Archaeology Report 1863, Norfolk HER 51654.

Hodder, I., 1982. *Symbols in Action: Ethnoarchaeological Studies in Material Culture,* Cambridge: Cambridge University Press.

Hodges, L. and S. Westall, 2010. *An Archaeological Evaluation at Land Off Church Avenue, Halvergate, Norfolk,* Unpublished Report, NAU Archaeology Report 2248, Norfolk HER 53090.

Hogan, S., 2011. *Morland Road, Ipswich, Post-Excavation Assessment,* Unpublished Report, Cambridge Archaeological Unit 996, Suffolk HER.

Holbroock, N., E. R. McSloy and D. Evans, 2008. *Excavations and Watching Brief Along Old Tetbury Road, 2004-6,* Cirencester: Cotswold Archaeology.

Holbrook, N., 2008. *Observations at Stratton Watermeadows,* Cirencester: Cotswold Archaeology.

Holbrook, N. and C. Bateman, 2008. The South Gate Cemetery of Roman Gloucester: Excavations at Parliament Street, 2001. *Transactions of the Bristol and Gloucestershire Archaeological Society,* 126, 91-106.

Holbrook, N. and K. Hirst, 2008. *Investigations by the Time Team in Insula IX, 1999,* Cirencester: Cotswold Archaeology.

Holbrook, N. and A. Thomas, 2008. *Excavations in Insula II at Cotswold Mill, 1998-9,* Cirencester: Cotswold Archaeology.

Hollinrake, C. and N. Hollinrake, 1991a. *An Archaeological Watching Brief at 'the Paddocks',*

West Street, Ilchester, 1991, Interim Report, Unpublished Report, Somerset HER 56932.
Hollinrake, C. and N. Hollinrake, 1991b. *Persimmons Homes, Shepton Mallet, November 1991*, Unpublished Report, Somerset HER 25561.
Hollinrake, C. and N. Hollinrake, 1992. *Somerton, St. Cleer's 1992 Archaeological Impact Assessment*, Unpublished Report, Somerset HER 35957.
Hollinrake, C. and N. Hollinrake, 1994a. *An Archaeological Watching Brief in the Churchyard of Holy Trinity Parish Church, Street*, Unpublished Report, Report no. 53, Somerset HER 11587.
Hollinrake, C. and N. Hollinrake, 1994b. *Archaeology on the Polden Villages Pipeline, Excavations at Edington Clover Close, Interim Report*, Unpublished Report, Report no. 65, Somerset HER 30391.
Hollinrake, C. and N. Hollinrake, 1994c. *Polden Villages Pipeline Project, Edington Eastfield*, Unpublished Report, Report no. 77, Somerset HER 30393.
Hollinrake, C. and N. Hollinrake, 1994d. *Polden Villages Pipeline Project, Edington, Jear's Croft*, Unpublished Report, Report no. 68, Somerset HER 30395.
Hollinrake, C. and N. Hollinrake, 1994e. *Polden Villages Pipeline Projects, Edington Holy Well*, Unpublished Report, Report no. 71, Somerset HER 30394.
Hollinrake, C. and N. Hollinrake, 1996. [Untitled], Unpublished Report, Somerset HER 56932.
Hollinrake, C. and N. Hollinrake, 1997a. *An Archaeological Evaluation at Perrott Hill School, North Perrott*, Unpublished Report, Report no. 104, Somerset HER 56919.
Hollinrake, C. and N. Hollinrake, 1997b. *An Archaeological Evaluation at the Crooked Chimney*, Unpublished Report, Report no. 93, Somerset HER 44990.
Hollinrake, C. and N. Hollinrake, 1997c. *An Archaeological Excavation at Perrott Hill Schoool, North Perrott, Fieldwork Report, Nps 97*, Unpublished Report, Report no. 221, Somerset HER 11314.
Hollinrake, C. and N. Hollinrake, 1997d. *An Archaeological Excavation of a Water Pipe Trench on Dundon Hillfort, Compton Dundon, Somerset, Interim Report*, Unpublished Report, Report no. 100, Somerset HER 28557.
Hollinrake, C. and N. Hollinrake, 1999. *An Archaeological Watching Brief on a New Sports Pavilion and Service Trenches in Towsend Close, Ilchester*, Unpublished Report, no. 176, Somerset HER 57059.
Hollinrake, C. and N. Hollinrake, 2000. *An Archaeological Evaluation at Kings of Wessex School, Cheddar*, Unpublished Report, Report no. 206, Somerset HER 44966.
Hollinrake, C. and N. Hollinrake, 2001a. *An Archaeological Evaluation at Perrott Hill School, North Perrott, March 2001*, Unpublished Report, Report no. 227, Somerset HER 11678.

Hollinrake, C. and N. Hollinrake, 2001b. *An Archaeological Watching Brief at Perrott Hill Schoool, North Perrott, July 2001*, Unpublished Report, Report no. 241, Somerset HER 15141.
Hollinrake, C. and N. Hollinrake, 2005a. *An Archaeological Watching Brief at the Grove Farm Quarry Extension, Pitcombe*, Unpublished Report, no. 357, Somerset HER 28253.
Hollinrake, C. and N. Hollinrake, 2005b. *An Archaeological Watching Brief Behind Northover Manor Hotel, Ilchester*, Unpublished Report, Hollinrake Report no. 365, Somerset HER 14354.
Hollinrake, C. and N. Hollinrake, 2009. *Archaeological Excavations in the Southern Extension to the Dimmer Landfill Site, Alford near Castle Cary*, Unpublished Report, Hollinrake Report no. 441, Somerset HER 28467.
Hollinrake, C. and N. Hollinrake, 2010. *An Archaeological Excavation at Doltons Farm, Front Street, Chedzoy, Area 6*, Unpublished Report no. 444, Somerset HER 28418.
Hollinrake, N., 1991. *Archaeological Recording of House Plot Foundations at the Persimmon Homes Development Site, Fosse Lane, Shepton Mallet*, Unpublished Report, Somerset HER 15104.
Holloway, B. and H. Brooks, 2011. *Report on an Archaeological Trial Trenching Evaluation: Land to South of Railway Line, Westerfield Road, Ipswich, Suffolk, November 2009/February 2010, October/November 2010*, Unpublished Report, Colchester Archaeological Trust 545, Suffolk HER IPS 616.
Holmes, M., 2006. *Archaeological Trial Excavation at Norton Subcourse Quarry, Norfolk*, Unpublished Report, Northamptonshire Archaeology 06/002, Norfolk HER 40918.
Holt, R., 2010. *Land West of Bath, Newton St Loe, Bath and North East Somerset, Archaeological Evaluation*, Unpublished Report, Cotswold Archaeology Report 10224, Available on OASIS.
Hood, A., 2009a. *Land at 'Rossilyn', Church Lane, Alvington, Gloucestershire, Archaeological Excavation and Recording; Post-Excavation Assessment*, Unpublished Report, Foundations Archaeology Report no. 633, Available on OASIS.
Hood, A., 2009b. *Land at Mill Lane, Swindon, Wiltshire, Archaeological Excavation and Associated Watching Briefs (Phase 3): Post-Excavation Assessment*, Unpublished Report, Foundation Archaeology Report no. 646.
Hood, A., 2009c. *Land West of Elm Grove, Ebrington, Gloucestershire, Archaeological Evaluation*, Unpublished Report, Foundations Archaeology Report no. 640, Gloucestershire HER 33594.
Hood, A., 2010a. *34 Watermoor Road, Cirencester, Gloucestershire, Archaeological Evaluation*, Unpublished Report, Foundations Archaeology, Available on OASIS.

Hood, A., 2010b. *Land at 38 Rissington Road, Bourton-on-the-Water, Gloucestershire, Archaeological Excavation and Recording; Post-Excavation Assessment,* Unpublished Report, Foundations Archaeology Report no. 717, Gloucestershire HER 38278.

Hopkinson, G., 1998. *Fetter Lane Electricity Sub-Station, York, an Archaeological Evaluation,* Unpublished Report, On-Site Archaeology 99EV07 (interim), CYC 158.

Hopkinson, G., 2000. *An Archaeological Evaluation and Excavation Assessment Report,* Unpublished Report, On Site Archaeology 99EV02/99EX03, North Yorks HER S472.

Horne, P., 1937. The Early Iron Age Site at Camerton, Somerset. *Somerset Archaeology and Natural History Society,* 83, 155-65.

Hornsby, W. and J. D. Laverick, 1933. The Roman Signal-Station at Goldsborough, near Whitby, Yorks. *Archaeological Journal,* 89, 203-19.

Hoskins, J., 1998. *Biographical Objects: How Things Tell the Stories of People's Lives,* London: Routledge.

Hoskins, J., 2006. Agency, Biography and Objects, in *Handbook of Material Culture,* eds. C. Tilley, W. Keane, S. Kuechler-Fogden, M. Rowlands and P. Spyer, London: Sage Publications, 74-84.

Hounsell, D., 2006. *Bittering Quarry Extension, Longham, Norfolk, an Archaeological Evaluation,* Unpublished Report, Cambridge Archaeological Field Unit 848, Norfolk HER 41949.

Howard, S., 1988. Rescue Excavations of a Roman Enclosure and Field at West Moors, Dorset, 1988. *Dorset Natural History and Archaeological Society,* 110, 99-115.

Howlett, D. R., 1960. A Roman Pottery Kiln at Upper Sheringham, Norfolk. *Norfolk Archaeology,* 32(3), 211-19.

Hughes, E. G., 1990. *Excavations at Stoke Lane, Wincaton, Somerset, 1990: Interim Statement,* Unpublished Report, Birmingham University Field Archaeology Unit, Somerset HER 15155.

Hughes, S. and E. Firth, 2010a. *Area 1 and Area 6, Phase 2, Stockmoore Village, Brigewater, Somerset, Results of an Archaeological Trench Evaluation,* Unpublished Report, AC Archaeology ACD192/2/0, Available on OASIS.

Hughes, S. and E. Firth, 2010b. *Land at Siddington Road, Cirencester, Gloucestershire, Results of an Archaeological Trench Evaluation,* Unpublished Report, AC Archaeology ACD166/2/0, Available on OASIS.

Hulka, K., 1998. *Archaeological Evaluation Report, Glebe Allotments, Church Knapp, Wyke Road, Wyke Regis, Weymouth, Dorset,* Unpublished Report, AOC Archaeology, GAW98, Dorset HER.

Hull, M. R. and C. F. C. Hawkes, 1987. *Corpus of Ancient Brooches in Britain: Pre-Roman Bow Brooches,* Oxford: BAR British Series no. 168.

Hume, L., 2006. *Archaeological Excavations on the Former Mail Marketing International Site, West Street, Bedminster, Bristol, Assessment Report and Updated Project Design,* Unpublished Report, Avon Archaeological Unit, Bristol City HER 24797.

Hunter, F., 1994a. *Discovery and Excavation in Scotland,* 23-4.

Hunter, F., 1994b. *Excavations at Leitchestown, Deskford, Banffshire 1994,* Edinburgh: Unpublished Report, National Museums of Scotland, RCAHMS MS 735/23.

Hunter, F., 1995a. *Discovery and Excavation in Scotland,* 29-30.

Hunter, F., 1995b. *Excavations at Leitchestown, Deskford, Banffshire 1995,* Edinburgh: Unpublished Report, National Museums of Scotland, RCAHMS MS 735/21.

Hunter, F., 1996a. *Discovery and Excavation in Scotland,* 74-6.

Hunter, F., 1996b. *Excavations at Leitchestown, Deskford, Banffshire 1996,* Edinburgh: Unpublished Report, National Museums of Scotland, RCAHMS MS 735/22.

Hunter, F., 1997. Iron Age Hoarding in Scotland and Northern England, in *Reconstructing Iron Age Societies: New Approaches to the British Iron Age,* eds. A. Gwilt and C. Haselgrove, Oxford: Oxbow Monograph 71, 108-33.

Hunter, F., 1999. *Fieldwork at Birnie, Moray, 1998,* Edinburgh: Department of Archaeology, National Museums Scotland.

Hunter, F., 2000. *Excavations at Birnie, Moray, 1999,* Edinburgh: Department of Archaeology, National Museums Scotland.

Hunter, F., 2001a. The Carnyx in Iron Age Europe. *Antiquaries Journal,* 81, 77-108.

Hunter, F., 2001b. *Excavations at Birnie, Moray, 2000,* Edinburgh: Department of Archaeology, National Museums Scotland.

Hunter, F., 2001c. Roman and Native in Scotland: New Approaches. *Journal of Roman Archaeology,* 14, 289-309.

Hunter, F., 2002a. Birnie: Buying a Peace on the Northern Frontier. *Current Archaeology,* 181, 12-16.

Hunter, F., 2002b. *Excavations at Birnie, Moray, 2001,* Edinburgh: Department of Archaeology, National Museums Scotland.

Hunter, F., 2003. *Excavations at Birnie, Moray, 2002,* Edinburgh: Department of Archaeology, National Museums Scotland.

Hunter, F., 2004. *Excavations at Birnie, Moray, 2003,* Edinburgh: Department of Archaeology, National Museums Scotland.

Hunter, F., 2005. *Excavations at Birnie, Moray, 2004,* Edinburgh: Department of Archaeology, National Museums Scotland.

Hunter, F., 2006a. *Discovery and Excavation in Scotland,* 110.

Hunter, F., 2006b. *Excavations at Birnie, Moray, 2005,* Edinburgh: Department of Archaeology, National Museums Scotland.

Hunter, F., 2006c. New Light on Iron Age Massive Armlets. *Proceedings of the Society of Antiquaries of Scotland,* 136, 135-60.

Hunter, F., 2007a. Artefacts, Regions, and Identities in the Northern British Iron Age, in *The Later Iron Age in Britain and Beyond,* eds. C. Haselgrove and T. Moore, Oxford: Oxbow, 286-96.

Hunter, F., 2007b. *Beyond the Edge of the Empire - Caledonians, Picts and Romans,* Rosemarkie, Ross-shire: Groam House Museum.

Hunter, F., 2007c. *Excavations at Birnie, Moray, 2006,* Edinburgh: Department of Archaeology, National Museums Scotland.

Hunter, F., 2008a. *Excavations at Birnie, Moray, 2007,* Edinburgh: Department of Archaeology, National Museums Scotland.

Hunter, F., 2008b. Glass, in *Rituals, Roundhouses and Romans, Excavations at Kintore, Aberdeenshire 2000-2006,* eds. M. Cook and L. Dunbar, Edinburgh: Scottish Trust for Archaeological Research.

Hunter, F., 2009. *Excavations at Birnie, Moray, 2008,* Edinburgh: Department of Archaeology, National Museums Scotland.

Hunter, K. and T. E. Haevernick, 1995. *Glasperlen Der Vorrömischen Eisenzeit Iv Schichtaugenperlen,* Marburger Studien zur vor- und Frühgeschichte Band 18.

Hunter-Mann, K., 1999. Excavations at Vespasian's Camp Iron Age Hillfort, 1987. *Wiltshire Archaeology and Natural History Society,* 92, 39-52.

Hurst, H., 1972. Excavations at Gloucester, 1968-1971: First Interim Report. *Antiquaries Journal,* 52, 24-69.

Hurst, H., 1974. Excavations at Gloucester, 1971-1973: Second Interim Report. *Antiquaries Journal,* 54, 8-52.

Hurst, H., 1975. Excavations at Gloucester, Third Interim Report: Kingsholm 1967-75. *Antiquaries Journal,* 55, 267-94.

Hurst, H. R., 1986. *Gloucester, the Roman and Later Defences, Excavations on the East Defences and a Reassessment of the Defensive Sequence,* Gloucester Archaeological Reports, Volume 2.

Hurst, H. R., 1987. Excavations at Box Roman Villa, 1967-8. *Wiltshire Archaeology and Natural History Society,* 81, 19-51.

Hurst, J. D. and J. S. Wacher, 1986. A Multi-Period Site at Poxwell, Dorset. *Dorset Natural History and Archaeological Society,* 108, 63-80.

Hutcheson, N., 2004. *Later Iron Age Norfolk: Metalwork, Landscape and Society,* Oxford: BAR British Series no. 361.

Hutcheson, N., 2011. Excavations at Snettisham, Norfolk, 2004: Re-Investigating the Past, in *The Iron Age in Northern East Anglia: New Work in the Land of the Iceni,* ed. C. Davies, Oxford: BAR British Series no. 549, 41-48.

Ingemark, D., 2003. *Glass, Alcohol and Power in Roman Iron Age Scotland. A Study of the Roman Vessel Glass from Non-Roman/Native Sites in North Northumberland and Scotland,* Unpublished Ph.D. Thesis, Lund University.

Ingram, R., 2005. *Faience and Glass Beads from the Late Bronze Age Shipwreck at Uluburun,* Unpublished MA Thesis, Texas A and M University.

Inman, R., D. R. Brown, R. E. Goddard and D. E. Spratt, 1985. Roxby Iron Age Settlement and the Iron Age in North-East Yorkshire. *Proceedings of the Prehistoric Society,* 51, 181-213.

Jackson, R., 2000. Archaeological Excavations at Upper Maudlin Street, Bristol in 1973, 1976 and 1999. *Bristol and Avon Archaeology,* 17, 29-110.

Jackson, R., 2007. *A Roman Settlement and Medieval Manor House in South Bristol, Excavations at Inns Court,* Unpublished Report, Bristol and Region Archaeological Services.

Jacobsthal, P., 1969. *Early Celtic Art,* Oxford: Claredon Press.

James, S., 1999. *The Atlantic Celts: Ancient People or Modern Invention?,* Madison: University of Wisconsin Press.

James, S., 2001. Soldiers and Civilians: Identity and Interaction in Roman Britain, in *Britons and Romans: Advancing an Archaeological Agenda,* eds. S. James and M. Millett, York: CBA Research Report 125, 77-89.

James, S., 2007. A Bloodless Past: The Pacification of Early Iron Age Britain, in *The Earlier Iron Age in Britain and the near Continent,* eds. C. Haselgrove and R. Pope, Oxford: Oxbow, 160-73.

Jarvis, K., 1992. An Inter-Tidal Zone Romano-British Site on Brownsea Island. *Dorset Natural History and Archaeological Society,* 114, 89-95.

Jarvis, K., 1993. Excavations at Hamworthy in 1974. *Dorset Natural History and Archaeological Society,* 115, 101-09.

Jarvis, K. S., 1982. Three Cist Burials at Herston, Swanage. *Dorset Natural History and Archaeological Society,* 104, 192-94.

Jarvis, K. S., 1984. A Late Iron Age Site with a Currency-Bar Hoard at Bearwood, Poole, Dorset. *Dorset Natural History and Archaeological Society,* 106, 138-42.

Jay, M., B. T. Fuller, M. P. Richards, C. Knüsel and S. S. King, 2008. Iron Age Breastfeeding Practices in Britain: Isotopic Evidence from Wetwang Slack, East Yorkshire. *American Journal of Physical Anthropology,* 136, 1-11.

Jay, M., C. Haselgrove, D. Hamilton, J. D. Hill and J. Dent, 2012. Chariots and Context: New Radiocarbon Dates from Wetwang and the Chronology of Iron Age Burials and Brooches in East Yorkshire. *Oxford Journal of Archaeology,* 31(2), 161-89.

Jay, M. and M. P. Richards, 2006. Diet in the Iron Age Cemetery Population at Wetwang Slack, East Yorkshire, UK: Carbon and Nitrogen Stable Isotope Evidence. *Journal of Archaeological Science,* 33(5), 653-62.

Jefferies, F. W., 1950. Roman Burial and Other Remains at Wickhouse Farm, Saltford, Keynsham Manor Estate. *Somerset Archaeology and Natural History Society,* 95, 106-11.

Jennings, D., J. Muir, S. Palemer and A. Smith, 2004. *Thornhill Farm, Fairford, Gloucestershire, an Iron Age and Roman Pastoral Site in the Upper Thames Valley,* Oxford: Oxford Archaeology, Thames Valley Landscapes Monograph no. 23.

Johns, C., 2006. An Iron Age Sword and Mirror Cist Burial from Bryher, Isles of Scilly. *Cornwall Archaeological Society,* 41-42, 1-79.

Johnson, M., 1993. Investigations of a Multi-Period Landscape, Potter Brompton, North Yorkshire. *Yorkshire Archaeological Journal,* 65, 1-9.

Johnson, M., 2004a. *An Assessment Report on an Archaeological Excavation, Huntington South Moor, York,* Unpublished Report, York Archaeological Trust Report no. 2004/16, CYC 560.

Johnson, M., 2004b. *The Mount School, Dalton Terrace, York, a Report on an Archaeological Excavation,* Unpublished Report, York Archaeological Trust Report no. 2004/65, CYC 612.

Johnson, P. and B. Walters, 1988. Exploratory Excavations of Roman Buildings at Cherhill and Manningford Bruce. *Wiltshire Archaeology and Natural History Society,* 82, 77-91.

Johnson, S., 1983. *Burgh Castle, Excavations by Charles Green 1958-61,* Dereham, Norfolk: East Anglian Archaeology Report no. 20.

Jones, A. E., 1991. *Northover, Ilchester, an Archaeological Evaluation 1991,* Unpublished Report, Birmingham University Field Archaeology Unit Report no. 184, Somerset HER 15794.

Jones, B., *Moray Excavation Archive Catalogue,* Unpublished Report, RCAHMS 5154.

Jones, B., 1990. *Home Rose (Cawdor, Easter Galcantray) Excavation Archive,* Unpublished Report, RCAHMS MS 5146/5-12.

Jones, B., I. Keillar and K. Maude, 1993. The Moray Aerial Survey: Discovering the Prehistoric and Proto-Historic Landscape, in *Moray: Province and People,* ed. W. D. H. Seller, Edinburgh: The Scottish Society for Northern Studies, 47-74.

Jones, G. D. B. and I. Keiller, 1980. *Discovery and Excavation in Scotland,* 18.

Jones, L., 2001. *An Archaeological Evaluation of Land Adjoining the Former Brockworth Airfield, Brockworth, Gloucestershire,* Unpublished Report, Birmingham University Field Archaeology Unit Project no. 803, Gloucestershire Her 20733.

Jones, M. U., 1971. Aldborough, West Riding, 1964: Excavations at the South Gate and Bastion and at Extra-Mural Sites. *Yorkshire Archaeological Journal,* 43, 39-78.

Jope, E. M., 2000. *Early Celtic Art in the British Isles,* Oxford: Claredon.

Joy, J., 2007. *Reflections on the Iron Age: Biographies of Mirrors,* Unpublished Ph.D. Thesis, University of Southampton.

Joy, J., 2011a. Exploring Status and Identity in Later Iron Age Britain: Reinterpreting Mirror Burials, in *Atlantic Europe in the First Millennium BC: Crossing the Divide,* eds. T. Moore and X.-L. Armada, Oxford: Oxford University Press, 468-87.

Joy, J., 2011b. 'Fancy Objects' in the British Iron Age: Why Decorate? *Proceedings of the Prehistoric Society,* 77, 205-30.

Joyce, S., 2010. *Cleevelands, Bishop's Cleeve, Gloucestershire, Archaeological Evaluation,* Unpublished Report, Cotswold Archaeology Report 10041, Available on OASIS.

Julius Caesar, *The Gallic War*.

Jundi, S. and J. D. Hill, 1997. Brooches and Identities in First Century AD Britain: More Than Meets the Eye?, in *TRAC 97: Proceedings of the Seventh Annual Theoretical Roman Archaeology Conference, Which Formed Part of the Second International Roman Archaeology Conference, University of Nottingham, April 1997,* eds. C. Forcey, J. Hawthorne and R. Witcher, Oxford: Oxbow, 125-37.

Kaenel, G. and F. Müller, 1989. A Propos De Certains Types De Bracelets En Verre Du Plateau Suisse, in *Le Verre Préromain En Europe Occidentale,* ed. M. Feugère, Montagnac: Monique Mergoil, 121-27.

Karl, R., 2004. Celtoscepticism: A Convenient Excuse for Ignoring Non-Archaeological Evidence?, in *Archaeology and Ancient History, Breaking Down the Boundaries* London: Routledge, 185-99.

Karl, R., 2008. Random Coincidences, Or: The Return of the Celtic to Iron Age Britain. *Proceedings of the Prehistoric Society,* 74, 69-78.

Keiller, A., 1965. *Windmill Hill and Avebury: Excavations by Alexander Keiller 1925-1939,* Oxford: Clarendon Press.

Kendall, G. A., 1999. *Report on an Archaeological Evaluation at the Oaks, Harvey Lane, Thorpe St Andrew,* Unpublished Report, Norfolk Archaeological Unit 433, Norfolk HER 34516.

Kenney, J., 2008. *Recent Excavations at Llandygai, near Bangor, North Wales*: Gynedd Archaeological Trust.

Kent, B. J. W., 1934. A Roman Settlement at Wetherby. *Yorkshire Archaeological Journal,* 31, 171-94.

Kenyon, D., 1997. *Church Farm, Icomb, Gloucestershire, Archaeological Evaluation,* Unpublished Report, Cotswold Archaeology Trust Report no. 97512, Gloucestershire HER 19846.

Kenyon, R. C., 1980. *Excavations at Rillington, North Yorkshire, 10 October 1980,* Unpublished Report, North Yorkshire Archaeological Rescue Advisory Panel, North Yorks HER S7062.

Kidd, K. E. and M. A. Kidd, 1970. A Classification System for Glass Beads for the Use of Field Archaeologists. *Canadian Historic Sites,* 1, 46-89.

Kilbride-Jones, H. E., 1935. An Aberdeenshire Iron Age Miscellany: (1) Stone Circle at Foularton; (2) Bronze Terret from Rhynie, and Distribution of the Type. *Proceedings of the Society of Antiquaries of Scotland,* 69, 445-54.

Kilbride-Jones, H. E., 1937. Glass Armlets in Britain. *Proceedings of the Society of Antiquaries of Scotland,* 72, 366-95.

King, D. G., 1963a. Bury Wood Camp, Report on Excavations, 1959. *Wiltshire Archaeology and Natural History Society,* 58, 40-47.

King, D. G., 1963b. Bury Wood Camp, Report on Excavations, 1960. *Wiltshire Archaeology and Natural History Society,* 58, 185-208.

King, D. G., 1967. Bury Wood Camp, Excavations in the Area of the Southwest Opening. *Wiltshire Archaeology and Natural History Society,* 62, 1-15.

King, D. G., 1969. Bury Wood Camp, Excavations in the North-East and North-West Areas. *Wiltshire Archaeology and Natural History Society,* 64, 21-50.

King, R., 2002. *35 Ashcroft Road, Cirencester, Gloucestershire, Archaeological Watching Brief,* Unpublished Report, Foundations Archaeology Report no. 209, Gloucestershire HER 21315.

King, R., 2005. *50-52 Lewis Lane, Cirencester, Gloucestershire, Archaeological Evaluation,* Unpublished Report, Foundations Archaeology Report no. 413, Gloucestershire HER 27962.

King, R., 2008. *Rossilyn, Knapp Lane, Alvington, Gloucestershire, Archaeological Evaluation,* Unpublished Report, Foundations Archaeology Report no. 603, Available on OASIS.

King, R., A. Barber and J. Timby, 1996. Excavations at West Lane, Kemble: An Iron-Age, Roman and Saxon Burial Site and a Medieval Building. *Transactions of the Bristol and Gloucestershire Archaeological Society,* 114, 15-54.

Klejn, L. S., 1982. *Archaeological Typology (Translated by Penelope Dole),* Oxford: BAR International Series no. 153.

Knappett, C., 2011. *An Archaeology of Interaction: Network Perspectives on Material Culture and Society,* Oxford: Oxford University Press.

Knocker, G. M., 1967. Excavations at Red Castle, Thetford. *Norfolk Archaeology,* 34(2), 119-86.

Knowles, W. H., 1925. The Roman Baths at Bath, with an Account of the Excavations Conducted During 1923. *Archaeologia,* 75, 1-18.

Kopytoff, I., 1986. The Cultural Biography of Things: Commoditization as Process, in *The Social Life of Things: Commodities in Cultural Perspective*, ed. A. Appadurai, Cambridge: Cambridge University Press, 3-63.

Ladle, L., 1994. *Bestwall Quarry, Archaeology Project, Phase 3,* Unpublished Report, Wareham and District Archaeology and Local History Society, Dorset HER.

Ladle, L., 1995. *Bestwall Quarry, Archaeological Project, Phase 4,* Unpublished Report, Wareham and District Archaeology and Local History Society, Dorset HER.

Ladle, L., 1996. *Bestwall Quarry, Archaeological Project, Phase 5,* Unpublished Report, Wareham and District Archaeology and Local History Society, Dorset HER.

Ladle, L., 1997. *Bestwall Quarry, Archaeological Project, Phase 6,* Unpublished Report, Wareham and District Archaeology and Local History Society, Dorset HER.

Ladle, L., 1998. *Beswall Quarry, Archaeological Project, Phase 7,* Unpublished Report, Wareham and District Archaeology and Local History Society, Dorset HER.

Ladle, L., 1999. *Bestwall Quarry, Archaeological Project, Phase 8,* Unpublished Report, Wareham and District Archaeology and Local History Society, Dorset HER.

Ladle, L., 2001. *Bestwall Quarry, Archaeological Project, Phase 10,* Unpublished Report, Wareham and District Archaeology and Local History Society, Dorset HER.

Ladle, L., 2002. *Bestwall Quarry, Archaeology Project Phase 11,* Unpublished Report, Wareham and District Archaeology and Local History Society, Dorset HER.

Lally, M. and K. Nicholson, N.D. *A Romano-British Industrial Site and Associated Ritual Activity at East Winch, Norfolk,* Unpublished Report, Norfolk HER 37413.

Lambdin, C. and R. Holley, 2011. *St. Algar's Roman Villa, an Interim Report on the August 2010 Evaluation Trenches,* Bath and Camerton Archaeological Society, Unpublished Report, Somerset HER 28572.

Lamdin-Whymark, H., K. Brady and A. Smith, 2009. Excavation of a Neolithic to Roman Landscape at Horcott Pit, near Fairford, Gloucestershire, in 2002 and 2003. *Transactions of the Bristol and Gloucestershire Archaeological Society,* 127, 45-131.

Lancley, J., 1992. Late Iron Age and Romano-British Sites Located on the Chalbury to Osmington Water Main. *Dorset Natural History and Archaeological Society,* 114, 254-58.

Langmaid, N., 1971. Norton Fitzwarren. *Current Archaeology,* 28, 116-20.

Langton, B., 2002. *3 Peters Road, Cirencester, Gloucestershire, Archaeological Evaluation,* Unpublished Report, Foundations Archaeology Report no. 242, Gloucestershire HER 21750.

Lankstead, D., 2007. Archaeological Excavations at Heath House and Highwood House, Stapleton, Bristol, 2004-2005. *Bristol and Avon Archaeology,* 22, 115-33.

Last, J., 2000. *An Archaeological Assessment and Updated Project Design for the Publication of Excavations at Game Farm, Brandon, Suffolk, 1999*, Unpublished Report, Hertfordshire Archaeological Trust 671, Suffolk HER BRD 154.

Lawton, I. G., 1993. Apple Tree Farm 1987-1992, an Ebor Ware Kiln Site. *Yorkshire Archaeological Society Bulletin*, 10, 4-8.

Lawton, I. G., 1999. *Derventio - Roman Stamford Bridge Update*, Unpublished Report, CYC 246.

Leach, P., 1980. *Westlands Roman Villa, Yeovil, Trial Excavations - November 1980: Interim Report*: Committee for Rescue Archaeology in Avon, Gloucestershire and Somerset, Somerset HER 15677.

Leach, P., 1982a. *Ilchester, Volume 1, Excavations 1974-1975*, Western Archaeological Trust Excavation Monograph no. 3.

Leach, P., 1982b. *Northover, the Late Roman Cemetery, Ilchester, Somerset, Interim Assessment*, Unpublished Report, Somerset HER 55910.

Leach, P., 1985. Westland, an Evaluation of the Romano-British Settlement, 1980. *Somerset Archaeology and Natural History Society*, 129, 63-67.

Leach, P., 1987a. *Ilchester Great Yard 1987, an Archaeological Evaluation*, Unpublished Report, Birmingham University Field Archaeology Unit, Somerset HER 55872.

Leach, P., 1987b. *Lyster Close, Ilchester: An Archaeological Evaluation 1987*, Unpublished Report, Somerset HER 55929.

Leach, P., 1988. *The Chessels, West Coker, Somerset, an Archaeological Evaluation 1988*, Unpublished Report, Birmingham University Field Archaeology Unit, Somerset HER 15494.

Leach, P., 1989. *The Paddocks, West Street, Ilchester: An Archaeological Evaluation, February 1989*, Unpublished Report, Birmingham University Field Archaeology Unit, Somerset HER 55938.

Leach, P., 1991. *An Archaeological Evaluation at Bullimore Farm, Shepton Mallet, Somerset 1991*, Unpublished Report, Birmingham University Field Archaeology Unit, Somerset HER 25616.

Leach, P., 1992a. *An Archaeological Evaluation of Development Land at Fosse Lane, Shepton Mallet, Somerset, 1992*, Unpublished Report, Birmingham University Field Archaeology Unit Report no. 217, Somerset HER 30241.

Leach, P., 1992b. *Mendip Business Park, Shepton Mallet, a Further Archaeological Assessment 1992*, Unpublished Report, Birmingham University Field Archaeology Unit Report no. 216, Somerset HER 35940.

Leach, P. (ed.) 1994a. *Ilchester Volume 2: Archaeology, Excavations and Fieldwork to 1984*, Sheffield Excavations Reports 2.

Leach, P., 1994b. *Mendip Business Park, Shepton Mallet, Site a, Archaeological Excavations in Advance of Development*, Unpublished Report, Birmingham University Field Archaeology Unit Report no. 298, Somerset HER 35939.

Leach, P., 1994c. *Northover; an Evaluation of the Late Roman Cemetery, 1982*, Sheffield Excavation Report 2.

Leach, P., 1994d. *The Southeast Defences; Excavations at Limington Road 1981*, Sheffield Excavation Report 2.

Leach, P., 1994e. *The West Rampart; Excavations Behind No. 16 High Street (Priory Road), 1970*, Sheffield Excavation Report 2.

Leach, P., 1995. *Frog Lane, Shepton Mallet: An Archaeological Evaluation 1995*, Unpublished Report, Birmingham University Field Archaeology Unit Project no. 352, Somerset HER 25615.

Leach, P., 1999. *An Archaeological Evaluation at Coate's Barn, Greinton, December 1999*, Unpublished Report, Somerset HER 44865.

Leach, P., 2000. *Coates Barn, Greinton, an Archaeological Watching Brief, July 2000*, Unpublished Report, Somerset HER 44865.

Leach, P., 2002. *An Archaeological Excavation at the Northover Manor Hotel, Northover, Ilchester*, Unpublished Report, Hollinrake Report no. 263, Somerset HER 15459.

Leach, P., 2003. *11 West Street, Ilchester, an Archaeological Evaluation, April 2003*, Unpublished Report, Somerset HER 16331.

Leach, P., 2004. *An Interim Report on Excavations at the Wolf Development Site, Fosse Lane, Shepton Mallet, Somerset, Summer 2004*, Unpublished Report, Somerset HER 17303.

Leach, P., 2005. *23 Limington Road, Ilchester, Archaeological Watching Brief, 2005*, Unpublished Report, Somerset HER 17898.

Leach, P., 2007a. *The Old School House, Ilchester, an Archaeological Watching Brief, July 2007*, Unpublished Report, Somerset HER 26094.

Leach, P., 2007b. *Saxon Place, Cheddar, Archaeological Evaluation, December 2007*, Unpublished Report, Somerset HER 22522.

Leach, P., 2009. Prehistoric Ritual Landscape and Other Remains at Field Farm, Shepton Mallet. *Somerset Archaeology and Natural History Society*, 152, 11-68.

Leach, P. and J. Casey, 1986. *Ilchester Dolphin Lane 1986, an Archaeological Assessment*, Unpublished Report, Birmingham University Field Archaeology Unit, Somerset HER 55926.

Leach, P. and P. Ellis, 1991. Ilchester Archaeology: Excavation on the Western Defences and Suburbs, 1985. *Somerset Archaeology and Natural History Society*, 135, 11-84.

Leach, P. and P. Ellis, 1994a. *Almshouse Lane and Church Street, Excavation and Watching Briefs in the Grounds of Manor Farm House 1977, 1980, 1983 and 1984*, Sheffield Excavation Report 2.

Leach, P. and P. Ellis, 1994b. *A Prehistoric Enclosure in the South Meadows, Ilchester*, Sheffield Excavation Report 2.

Leach, P. and P. Ellis, 2004. Roman and Medieval Remains at Manor Farm, Castle Cary. *Somerset Archaeology and Natural History Society,* 147, 81-128.

Leach, P. and A. Jones, 1988. *Ilchester: Archaeological Training Excavation 1988, an Interim Report,* Unpublished Report, Birmingham University Field Archaeology Unit, Somerset HER 55935.

Leach, P. and N. Thew, 1985. *A Late Iron Age 'Oppidum' at Ilchester, Somerset, an Interim Assessment 1984,* Unpublished Report, Western Archaeological Trust, Somerset HER 56930.

Leach, S., H. Eckardt, C. Chenery, G. Müldner and M. Lewis, 2010. A Lady of York: Migration, Ethnicity and Identity in Roman Britain. *Antiquity,* 84, 131-45.

Lee, J., 1997. The Knapton Generating Station and Gas Pipeline Excavations. *Yorkshire Archaeological Journal,* 69, 21-38.

Leech, R., 1976. Romano-British and Medieval Settlement at Wearne, Huish Episcopi. *Somerset Archaeology and Natural History Society,* 120, 45-50.

Leech, R., 1977. Late Iron Age and Romano-British Briquetage Sites at Quarrylands Lane, Badgworth. *Somerset Archaeology and Natural History Society,* 121, 89-96.

Leech, R., 1982. *Excavations at Catsgore 1970-1973,* Western Archaeological Trust Excavation Monograph no. 2.

Leins, I., 2008. What Can Be Inferred from Regional Stylistic Diversity on Iron Age Coinage?, in *Rethinking Celtic Art*, eds. D. Garrow, C. Gosden and J. D. Hill, Oxford: Oxbow, 100-12.

Leivers, M., C. Chisham, S. Knight and C. Stevens, 2007. Excavations at Ham Hill Quarry, Hamdon Hill, Montacute, 2002. *Somerset Archaeology and Natural History Society,* 150, 39-62.

Lemonnier, P., 1992. *Elements for an Anthropology of Technology,* Ann Arbor: The University of Michgan Anthropological Papers no. 88.

Lewis-Williams, J. D., 1997. Agency, Art and Altered Consciousness: A Motif in French (Quercy) Upper Palaeolithic Parietal Art. *Antiquity,* 71(274), 810-30.

Lewis-Williams, J. D., T. A. Dowson, P. G. Bahn, H. G. Bandi, R. G. Bednarik, J. Clegg, M. Consens, W. Davis, B. Delluc, G. Delluc, P. Faulstich, J. Halverson, R. Layton, C. Martindale, V. Mirimanov, C. G. Turner, J. M. Vastokas, M. Winkelman and A. Wylie, 1988. The Signs of All Times: Entoptic Phenomena in Upper Palaeolithic Art. *Current Anthropology,* 29, 201-45.

Lewis-Williams, J. D. and D. Pearce, 2005. *Inside the Neolithic Mind: Consciousness, Cosmos and the Realm of the Gods,* London: Thames and Hudson.

Liddell, T., 2008. *Archaeological Evaluation of Land Off Muston Road, Filey, North Yorkshire,* Unpublished Report, North Pennines Archaeology Ltd.; CP, 658/08, North Yorks. HER.

Lierke, R., 1990. Early History of Lampwork - Some Facts, Findings and Theories. Part 1. Kunckle's Description of Lampworking in the "Ars Vitraria Experimentalis". *Glastechnische Berichte,* 63(12), 363-69.

Lierke, R., 1992. Early History of Lampwork - Some Facts, Findings and Theories Part 2. *Glastechnische Berichte,* 65(12), 341-48.

Lierke, R., 1995. *Commentary to Lierke/Birkhill/Molnar 1995, Experimental Reproduction of Spiral Beads,* http://www.rosemarie-lierke.de/Publikationen/Comment_LBM/comment_lbm.html.

Lierke, R., F. Birkhill and P. Molnar, 1995. Experimental Reproduction of Spiral Beads, in *Glass Beads - Cultural History, Technology, Experiment and Analogy*, eds. M. Rasmussen, U. L. Hanesen and U. Näsman, Lejre, Denmark: Historical-Archaeological Experimental Centre, 117-19.

Linden, V., P. Cosyns, O. Schalm, S. Cagno, K. Nys, K. Jassens, A. Nowak, B. Wagner and E. Bulska, 2009. Deeply Coloured and Black Glass in the Northern Provinces of the Roman Empire: Differences and Similarities in Chemical Composition before and after AD 150. *Archaeometry,* 51(5), 822-44.

Linton, H., 1876. Notice of a Collection of Flint Arrow-Heads and Bronze and Iron Relics from the Site of an Ancient Settlement Recently Discovered in the Culbin Sands, near Findhorn, Morayshire. *Proceedings of the Society of Antiquaries of Scotland*, 11, 543-46.

Liu, R. K., 1978. Spindle Whorls: Pt. I. Some Comments and Speculations. *Bead Journal,* 3, 87-103.

Lloyd, G. D., 1968. A Roman Pottery Kiln in the Parish of Lockington. *East Riding Archaeologist,* 1(1), 28-38.

Lockyear, K., 2007. Where Do We Go from Here? Recording and Analysing Roman Coins from Archaeological Excavations. *Britannia,* 38, 211-24.

Lockyear, K., 2012. Dating Coins, Dating with Coins. *Oxford Journal of Archaeology,* 31(2), 191-211.

Longman, T., 2000. *Archaeological Assessment of Lechlade Manor, Lechlade-on-Thames, Gloucestershire,* Unpublished Report, Bristol and Region Archaeological Services no. 644/2000, Gloucestershire HER 20519.

Longman, T., 2006. Iron Age and Later Defences at Malmesbury: Excavations 1998-2000. *Wiltshire Archaeology and Natural History Society,* 99, 104-64.

Lovell, J., 1999. Further Investigations of an Iron Age and Romano-British Farmstead on Cockey Down, near Salisbury. *Wiltshire Archaeology and Natural History Society,* 92, 33-38.

Lovell, J., 2006. Excavations of a Romano-British Farmstead at RNAS Yeovilton. *Somerset Archaeoogy and Natural History Society,* 149, 7-70.

Lovell, J., G. Wakeham, J. Timby and M. J. Allen, 2007. Iron-Age to Saxon Farming Settlement at Bishop's Cleeve, Gloucestershire: Excavations South of Church Road, 1998 and 2004. *Transactions of the Bristol and Gloucestershire Archaeological Society,* 125, 95-129.

Lucas, G., 2005. *The Archaeology of Time,* London: Routledge.

Lucas, R. N., 1993. *The Romano-British Villa at Halstock, Dorset, Excavations 1967-1985,* Dorset Natural History and Archaeological Society Monograph no. 13.

Luckett, L., 2000. Investigations of a Roman Villa Site at Euridge Manor Farm, Colerne. *Wiltshire Archaeology and Natural History Society,* 93, 218-32.

Lyne, M., 2002. The Late Iron Age and Romano-British Pottery Production Sites at Redcliff, Arne and Stoborough. *Dorset Natural History and Archaeological Society,* 124, 45-99.

Lyons, A., 2002. *Archaeological Investigations at Strickland Avenue and Station Road, Snettisham, 1991, 1994, 1998 and 2000, Draft Report,* Unpublished Report, Norfolk HER 28450.

MacGregor, A., 1978. *Roman Finds from Skeldergate and Bishophill, the Archaeology of York Volume 17: The Small Finds,* York: York Archaeological Trust for Excavation and Research.

MacGregor, M., 1976. *Early Celtic Art in North Britain: A Study of Decorative Metalwork from the Third Century B.C. To the Third Century A.D.,* Leicester: Leicester University Press.

Macinnes, L., 1989. Baubles, Bangles and Beads: Trade and Exchange in Roman Scotland, in *Barbarians and Romans in North-West Europe: From the Later Republic to Late Antiquity,* eds. J. C. Barrett, A. P. Fitzpatrick and L. Macinnes, Oxford: BAR International Series no. 471, 108-16.

Mackey, R., 1997. *12 Cave Road, Brough-on-Humber, East Yorkshire, Archaeological Watching Brief Report,* Unpublished Report, Northern Archaeological Associates, NAA 97/81, EHU 679.

MacKie, E., 1965a. Brochs in the Hebridean Iron Age. *Antiquity,* 39(156), 266-78.

MacKie, E., 1965b. The Origin and Development of the Broch and Wheelhouse Building Cultures of the Scottish Iron Age. *Proceedings of the Prehistoric Society,* 31, 93-146.

MacKie, E., 1969. Radiocarbon Dates and the Scottish Iron Age. *Antiquity,* 43, 15-26.

MacKie, E., 1974. *Dun Mor Vaul: An Iron Age Broch on Tiree,* Glasgow: University of Glasgow Press.

MacKie, E., 2008. The Broch Cultures of Atlantic Scotland: Origins, High Noon and Decline. Part 1: Early Iron Age Beginnings C.700 - 200 BC. *Oxford Journal of Archaeology,* 27(3), 261-79.

MacKie, E., 2010. The Broch Cultures of Atlantic Scotland. Part 2. The Middle Iron Age: High Noon and Decline C. 200 BC - AD 550. *Oxford Journal of Archaeology,* 29(1), 89-117.

Mackreth, D. F., 2011. *Brooches in Late Iron Age and Roman Britain,* Oxford: Oxbow.

Maclean, J., 1888. Manor of Tockington, and the Roman Villa. *Transactions of the Bristol and Gloucestershire Archaeological Society,* 12, 123-69.

Maclean, J., 1889. The Roman Villa, Tockington (Second Notice). *Transactions of the Bristol and Gloucestershire Archaeological Society,* 13, 196-202.

MacNab, N., 1996. *Elworthy Barrows, Brompton Ralph, Somerset, Archaeological Evaluation,* Unpublished Report, Oxford Archaeological unit, Somerset HER 15609.

MacNab, N., 2004. *Heslington East, Heslington, York, a Report on an Archaeological Evaluation,* Unpublished Report, York Archaeological Trust Report no. 2004/23, CYC 584.

Maddock, S. and P. Mahon, 2006. A Romano-British Prone Burial from Bratton, Wiltshire. *Wiltshire Archaeology and Natural History Society,* 99, 190-203.

Mallet Vatcher, F. d., 1963. The Excavation of the Roman Earthworks at Winterslow, Wits. *Antiquaries Journal,* 43, 197-213.

Malone, S., 2010. *Assessment of the Archaeological Remains and an Updated Project Design for Excavations at Grandcourt Quarry, East Winch, Norfolk,* Unpublished Report, Archaeological Project Services.

Mannering, U., M. Gleba and M. B. Hansen, 2012. Denmark, in *Textiles and Textile Production in Europe: From Prehistory to AD 400,* eds. M. Gleba and U. Mannering, Oxford: Oxbow, 444-50.

Manning, W. H., 1972. Ironwork Hoards in Iron Age and Roman Britain. *Britannia,* 3, 224-50.

Mansel-Pleydell, J. C., 1896. Kimmeridge Coal-Money and Other Manufactured Articles from the Kimmeridge Shale. *Dorset Natural History and Antiquarian Field Club Proceedings,* 13, 177-90.

Marcus, M. I., 1993. Incorporating the Body: Adornment, Gender, and Social Identity in Ancient Iran. *Cambridge Archaeological Journal,* 3(2), 157-78.

Marquess of Lansdown, 1927. A Roman Villa at Nuthills, near Bowood. *Wiltshire Archaeology and Natural History Society,* 44, 49-59.

Marshall, A., 2004. *Farmstead and Stronghold: Development of an Iron Age and Roman Settlement Complex at the Park-Bowsings, near Guiting Power, Gloucestershire,* Cotswold Archaeological Research Group.

Marshall, A., 2007. *Royal Naval Air Station (RNAS) Yeovilton, Somerset: Archaeological Watching Brief*

Report, Unpublished Report, Oxford Archaeology, Somerset HER 22530.

Marshall, A., S. Palmer and A. Smith, 2007. Archaeological Investigations at Whelford Bowmoor, Gloucestershire, 1983, 1985 and 1988, in *Iron Age and Roman Settlement in the Upper Thames Valley, Excavations at Claydon Pike and Other Sites within the Cotswold Water Park,* eds. D. Miles, S. Palmer, A. Smith and G. P. Jones, Oxford: Oxbow.

Martin, A. T., 1923. Excavations at Sea Mills. *Transactions of the Bristol and Gloucestershire Archaeological Society,* 45, 193-201.

Martin, E., 1988. *Burgh: The Iron Age and Roman Enclosure,* Dereham, Norfolk: East Anglian Archaeology Report no. 40.

Martin, E., 1993. *Settlements on Hill-Tops: Seven Prehistoric Sites in Suffolk,* Dereham, Norfolk: East Anglian Archaeology Report no. 65.

Martin, E., 1999. Suffolk in the Iron Age, in *Land of the Iceni: The Iron Age in Northern East Anglia,* eds. J. Davies and T. Williamson, Norwich: Centre of East Anglian Studies, 45-99.

Martin, P. and S. Driscoll, 2009. *Excavations of a Romano-British Site, Butleigh, Somerset, Season One 2009,* Unpublished Report, Absolute Archaeology, Somerset HER 28184.

Marwood, R., 1997a. *Report on an Archaeological Watching Brief of a Sewer Repair Adjacent to 59 Low Petergate, York,* Unpublished Report, York Archaeological Trust, CYC 139.

Marwood, R., 1997b. *Report on an Archaeological Watching Brief of a Sewer Repair Adjacent to 70 Low Petergate,* Unpublished Report, York Archaeological Trust, CYC 140.

Marwood, R., 1997c. *Report on an Archaeological Watching Brief of a Sewer Repair Adjacent to 81 Low Petergate,* Unpublished Report, York Archaeological Trust, CYC 142.

Marwood, R., 1997d. *Report on an Archaeological Watching Brief of a Sewer Repair Adjacent to 93 Low Petergate, York,* Unpublished Report, York Archaeological Trust, CYC 143.

Marwood, R., 1998. *Report on an Archaeological Watching Brief of a Sewer Repair Adjacent to 72 Low Petergate, York,* Unpublished Report, York Archaeological Trust, CYC 141.

Maskelyne, N. S., 1887. Barbury Castle. *Wiltshire Archaeology and Natural History Society,* 23, 180-94.

Mason, C. and T. Hawtin, 2009. *Longrun Flood Compensation Scheme, Taunton, Somerset, an Archaeological Watching Brief and Excavation Assessment Report,* Unpublished Report, Context One, Somerset HER 28209.

Mason, E. J., 1953. Romano-British Lead Smelting Site at Priddy, Somerset. *Belfry Bulletin, Bristol Exploration Club,* 70, 1-4.

Masser, P., J. Jones and B. McGill, 2005. Romano-British Settlement and Land Use on the Avonmouth Levels: The Evidence of the Pucklechurch to Seabank Pipeline Project. *Transactions of the Bristol and Gloucestershire Archaeological Society,* 123, 55-86.

Masser, P. and B. McGill, 2004. Excavations of Romano-British Sites at Tockington Park Farm and Westerleigh, South Gloucestershire, in 1997. *Transactions of the Bristol and Gloucestershire Archaeological Society,* 122, 95-116.

Mathewson, A., 1878. Notes of the Age of the Settlement on the Sands of Culbin. *Proceedings of the Society of Antiquaries of Scotland,* 12, 302-05.

Mattingly, D. J. (ed.) 1997a. *Dialogues in Roman Imperialism: Power, Discourse, and Discrepant Experience in the Roman Empire,* Portsmouth, R.I.: Journal of Roman Studies Supplementary Studies no 23.

Mattingly, D. J., 1997b. Dialogues of Power and Experience in the Roman Empire, in *Dialogues in Roman Imperialism: Power, Discourse, and Discrepant Experience in the Roman Empire,* ed. D. J. Mattingly, Portsmouth, R.I.: Journal of Roman Studies Supplementary Studies no 23, 7-26.

Mauss, M., 1990 (1950). *The Gift* London: Routledge (translated by Cohen and West).

Mayer, D. and R. Kind, 2002. *50 Watermoor Road, Cirencester, Gloucestershire, Archaeological Evaluation,* Unpublished Report, Foundations Archaeology Report 253, Gloucestershire HER 21916.

Mayes, A., 2002. *The Cinema Site, Lewis Lane, Cirencester, Gloucestershire, Archaeological Evaluation, Test Pits, 11, 12, 13 and 14,* Unpublished Report, Oxford Archaeology no. 1426, Available on OASIS.

Maynard, D., 1988. Excavations on a Pipeline near the River Frome, Worgret, Dorset. *Dorset Natural History and Archaeological Society,* 110, 77-98.

McCall, W., T. Schofield, C. Davies and P. Tompson, 2010. *Breydon Water Holiday Park, Yare Village, Butt Lane, Burgh Castle, Norfolk Nr31 9qb,* Unpublished Report, Archaeological Solutions 3464, Norfolk HER 49204.

McComish, J., 2001. *Platform 1, York Railway Station, York, Report on the Archaeological Excavation of a Human Burial,* Unpublished Report, York Archaeological Trust Field Report no. 3, CYC 311.

McConnell, R., T. Urch and K. Mathews, 2005. *Kings of Wessex Community School, Station Road, Cheddar, Somerset, an Archaeological Field Evaluation,* Unpublished Report, Context One Archaeological Services, Somerset HER 17793.

McCrone, P., 1990. *Wincanton by-Pass, Stoke Lane Evaluation 1990,* Unpublished Report, Somerset HER 15156.

McDonald, T., 1999. *Site a, Phase II, Cedars Park, Stowmarket, Archaeological Excavation Interim*

Report, Unpublished Report, Hertfordshire Archaeological Trust 617, Suffolk HER.

McDonald, T. and G. Seddon, 2000. *Phases 2b and 2c Cedars Park, Stowmarket, an Archaeological Evaluation,* Unpublished Report, Hertfordshire Archaeological Trust, Suffolk HER.

McDonnel, R. and P. Leach, 1994a. *Church Street Car Park 1968, Excavations by D.M. Evans,* Sheffield Excavation Report 2.

McDonnel, R. and P. Leach, 1994b. *The South Gate; Excavations in the Rectory Gardens, 1969,* Sheffield Excavation Report 2.

McDonnell, R. R. J., 1990. *Report on the Archaeological Evaluation at Maidenbrook Farm, Cheddon Fitzpaine,* Unpublished Report, Somerset HER 44702.

McKinley, J. I., 1999a. Excavations at Ham Hill, Montacute, Somerset 1994 and 1998. *Somerset Archaeology and Natural History Society,* 142, 77-137.

McKinley, J. I., 1999b. Further Excavations of an Iron Age and Romano-British Enclosed Settlement at Figheldean, near Netheravon. *Wiltshire Archaeology and Natural History Society,* 92, 7-32.

McKinley, J. I., 2009. Deviant' Burials from a Late Romano-British Cemetery at Little Keep, Dorchester. *Dorset Natural History and Archaeological Society,* 130, 43-61.

McNicoll-Norbury, J., 2009. *Byways, Cleve and Linden, Bathwick Street, Bath, an Archaeological Evaluation for Princegate Estates,* Unpublished Report, Thames Valley Archaeological Services, BSB 07/138, Available on OASIS.

McOmish, D., D. Field and G. Brown, 2010. The Late Bronze Age and Early Iron Age Midden Site at East Chisenbury, Wiltshire. *Wiltshire Archaeology and Natural History Society,* 103, 35-101.

McWhirr, A., L. Viner and C. Wells, 1982. *Romano-British Cemeteries at Cirencester, Cirencester Excavations II,* Cirencester: Corinium Museum.

Meara, H., 2008. *Britzen Farm, Shurdington, Gloucestershire, Archaeological Evaluation Report,* Unpublished Report, Oxford Archaeology Job 4118, Available on OASIS.

Meara, H., 2010. *Archaeological Excavation of Land at Saltmarsh Drive, Lawrence Weston, Bristol,* Unpublished Report, Bristol and Region Archaeological Services 2284B/2010, Available on OASIS.

Medlycott, M. (ed.) 2011. *Research and Archaeology Revisited: A Revised Framework for the East of England,* East Anglian Archaeology Occasional Paper no. 24.

Megaw, J. S., 1970. *Art of the European Iron Age: A Study of the Elusive Image,* Bath: Adams and Dart.

Megaw, J. V. S. and M. R. Megaw, 1998. 'The Mechanism of (Celtic) Dreams?': A Partial Response to Our Critics. *Antiquity,* 72(276), 432-35.

Mellor, A. S. and R. Goodchilde, 1940. The Roman Villa at Atworth, Wilts. *Wiltshire Archaeology and Natural History Society,* 49, 46-95.

Mellor, V., 2005. *Archaeological Evaluation on Land West of Mill View Court, Station Road, Snettisham, Norfolk,* Unpublished Report, Archaeological Project Services 44/05, Norfolk HER 41123.

Meredith, J., 2000a. *Haughley Crauford's CEVC Primary School Archaeological Excavations November 1999,* Unpublished Report, Suffolk County Council 2000/08, Suffolk HER HGH 015.

Meredith, J., 2000b. *Lady Lane Industrial Estate, Hadleigh, Archaeological Evaluation Report,* Unpublished Report, Suffolk County Council 2000/66, Suffolk HER HAD 061.

Meredith, J., 2000c. *Stow Park, Bungay, Archaeological Evaluation Archive Report,* Unpublished Report, Suffolk County Council 2000/25, Suffolk HER BUN 041 and BUN 042.

Meredith, J., 2001. *Church Farm, Halesworth, a Report on an Archaeological Excavation and Monitoring,* Unpublished Report, Suffolk County Council 2000/09, Suffolk HER HWT 019.

Meredith, J., 2006. *Archaeological Evaluation Report, the Driftway, Capel St. Mary,* Unpublished Report, Suffolk County Council 2006/014, Suffolk HER CSM 027.

Meredith, J., 2007a. *Barber's Point, First, Report on the Excavations in 2004 and 2006,* Unpublished Report, Suffolk County Council 2007/185, Suffolk HER FRS 001.

Meredith, J., 2007b. *Carlton Hall, Church Lane, Carlton Colville, Archaeological Evaluation Report, 2007,* Unpublished Report, Suffolk County Council 2007/229, Suffolk HER CAC 043.

Meredith, J., 2007c. *Red Hill Road, Hadleigh, a Report on the Archaeological Excavations 2001,* Unpublished Report, Suffolk County Council 2004, 104, Suffolk HER HAD 061.

Meredith, J., 2009. *Archaeological Monitoring Report, the Driftway, the Street, Chapel St. Mary,* Unpublished Report, Suffolk County Council 2009/206, Suffolk HER CSM 027.

Michaels, T., 2004. *Millstone Cottage, Bourton-on-the-Water, Gloucestershire, Archaeological Watching Brief,* Unpublished Report, Foundations Archaeology Report no. 385, Gloucestershire HER 27618.

Michelman, S. O. and T. V. Erekosima, 1993. Kalabari Dress in Nigeria, in *Dress and Gender: Making and Meaning in Cultural Contexts,* eds. R. Barnes and J. B. Eicher, Oxford: Berg, 164-82.

Miles, D., S. Palmer, A. Smith and G. P. Jones, 2007. *Iron Age and Roman Settlement in the Upper Thames Valley, Excavations at Claydon Pike and Other Sites within the Cotswold Water Park,* Oxford: Oxford Archaeology, Thames Valley Landscapes Monograph no. 26.

Miles, H. and T. J. Miles, 1969. Settlement Sites of the Late Pre-Roman Iron Age in the Somerset Levels. *Somerset Archaeology and Natural History Society,* 113, 17-55.

Millbank, D. and J. Pine, 2009. *Dryleaze Farm Quarry (Northern Extension), Siddington, Gloucestershire, an Archaeological Evaluation,* Unpublished Report, Thames Valley Archaeological Services DFG09/123, Available on OASIS.

Miller, D., 2004. *Archaeological Watching Brief at 40/41 High Street, Tewkesbury, Archaeological Service,* Unpublished Report, Worcestershire County Council 929, Gloucestershire HER 22252.

Miller, D., 2010. *Stuff,* Cambridge: Polity.

Millett, M. (ed.) 2006. *Shiptonthorpe, East Yorkshire: Archaeological Studies of the Romano-British Roadside Settlement,* Yorkshire Archaeological Report no. 5.

Millett, M., 1990. *The Romanization of Britain: An Essay in Archaeological Interpretation,* Cambridge: Cambridge University Press.

Milstead, I. D., 2011. *Sewage Attenuation Tanks, 28-40 Blossom Street, York, Excavation Analysis Report,* Unpublished Report, York Archaeological Trust Report no. 2011/11, CYC 1090.

Minnitt, S., 2000. The Iron Age Wetlands of Central Somerset, in *Somerset Archaeology: Papers to Mark 150 Years of the Somerset Archaeological and Natural History Society,* ed. C. J. Webster, Taunton: Somerset Archaeological and Natural History Society, 73-8.

Mitchelson, N., 1963. Roman Malton: The Civilian Settlement, Excavations in Orchard Field, 1949-1952. *Yorkshire Archaeological Journal,* 41, 209-61.

Monaghan, J. M., 1991. A Roman Marching Camp and Native Settlement Site at Newton Kyme, Tadcaster. *Yorkshire Archaeological Journal,* 63, 51-58.

Moore, T., 2003. *Iron Age Societies in the Severn-Cotswolds: Developing Narratives of Social and Landscape Change,* Unpublished Ph.D. Thesis, Durham University.

Moore, T., 2006a. *Following the Digger: The Impact of Developer-Funded Archaeology on Academic and Public Perceptions of Cultural Landscapes,* http://conferences.ncl.ac.uk/unescolandscapes/files/MOOREtom.pdf.

Moore, T., 2006b. The Iron Age, in *Twenty-Five Years of Archaeology in Gloucestershire: A Review of New Discoveries and New Thinking in Gloucestershire, South Gloucestershire and Bristol, 1979-2004,* eds. N. Holbrook and J. Jurica, Cotswold Archaeology, Bristol and Gloucestershire Archaeological Report no. 3, 61-96.

Moore, T., 2007a. Life on the Edge? Exchange, Community, and Identity in the Later Iron Age of the Severn-Cotswolds, in *The Later Iron Age in Britain and Beyond,* eds. C. Haselgrove and T. Moore, Oxford: Oxbow, 41-61.

Moore, T., 2007b. Perceiving Communities: Exchange, Landscapes and Social Networks in the Later Iron Age of Western Britain. *Oxford Journal of Archaeology,* 26, 79-102.

Moore, T., 2011. Detribalizing the Later Prehistoric Past: Concepts of Tribes in Iron Age and Roman Studies. *Journal of Social Archaeology,* 11(3), 1-28.

Moore, T., 2012. Beyond the Oppida: Polyfocal Complexes and Late Iron Age Societies in Southern Britain. *Oxford Journal of Archaeology,* 31(4), 391-417.

Moore, W. F. and M. S. Ross, 1989. The Romano-British Settlement, Common Mead Lane, Gillingham, Dorset. *Dorset Natural History and Archaeological Society,* 111, 57-70.

Moorhead, S., 2009. Three Roman Coin Hoards from Wiltshire Terminating in Coins of Probus (AD 276-82). *Wiltshire Archaeology and Natural History Society,* 102, 150-59.

Morris, E. L., 1988. The Iron Age Occupation at Dibble's Farm, Christon. *Somerset Archaeology and Natural History Society,* 132, 23-81.

Morris, E. L. and A. B. Powell, 2011. Iron Age Pits and Decorated Pottery at Strawberry Hill, West Lavington. *Wiltshire Archaeology and Natural History Society,* 104, 62-78.

Morris, P., 1975. Early Iron Age and Roman Remains at Southill, Radipole Lane, Weymouth. *Dorset Natural History and Archaeological Society,* 96, 54-55.

Morris, T., 2004. *An Archaeological Evaluation at Watermoor, Church of England Primary School, Watermoor Road, Cirencester,* Unpublished Report, Gloucestershire County Council, Gloucestershire HER 27111.

Mortimer, J. R., 1905. *Forty Years' Researches in British and Saxon Burial Mounds in East Yorkshire: Including Romano-British Discoveries, and a Description of the Ancient Entrenchments of a Section of the Yorkshire Wolds,* Brown and sons, limited.

Morton, R., 194. *Powell's School Site, Cirencester, Stage 2 Archaeological Evaluation,* Unpublished Report, Cotswold Archaeology Trust Report no. 94192, Gloucestershire HER 28712.

Morton, R., 1996. *Boundary Wall, Watermoor House, Cirencester, Gloucestershire, Archaeological Evaluation,* Unpublished Report, Cotwold Archaeological Trust Report no. 96398, Gloucestershire HER 30462.

Mudd, A., 2002. *Excavations at Melford Meadows, Brettenham, 1994: Romano-British and Early Saxon Occupations,* Dereham, Norfolk: East Anglian Archaeology Report no. 99.

Mudd, A., R. J. Williams and A. Lupton, 1999. *Excavations Alongside Roman Ermin Street, Gloucestershire and Wiltshire, the Archaeology of the A419/A417 Swindon to Gloucester Road Scheme,* Oxford: Oxford Archaeological Unit.

Muldowney, M., 2008a. *Chapelside, 9 Chapel Green, Long Melford, Archaeological Monitoring Report,* Unpublished Report, Suffolk County Council 2008/210, Suffolk HER LMD 179.

Muldowney, M., 2008b. *Land Adjacent to Adastral Park, Martlesham, Ipswich, Mrm 140, Archaeological Evaluation Report,* Unpublished Report, Suffolk County Council Archaeological Service.

Muldowney, M., 2009a. *New Car Parks at High Lodge, Santon Downham, Stn 088, Archaeological Monitoring Report,* Unpublished Report, Suffolk County Council Archaeological Service 2009/109, Suffolk HER STN 088.

Muldowney, M., 2009b. *West Row Primary School, Rear Extension, Mnl 613, Archaeological Evaluation Report,* Unpublished Report, Suffolk County Council Archaeological Service 2009/020, Suffolk HER 613.

Muldowney, M., 2010a. *29, Swanfield, Long Melford, Archaeological Monitoring Report,* Unpublished Report, Suffolk County Council 2010/191, Suffolk HER LMD 187.

Muldowney, M., 2010b. *Archaeological Evaluation Report, Alexandra House, Hospital Road, Bury St. Edmunds,* Unpublished Report, Suffolk County Council 2010/059, Suffolk HER BSE 343.

Muldowney, M., 2010c. *Land Adjacent to Beech House, Hospital, Exning, Archaeological Excavation Report,* Unpublished Report, Suffolk County Council 2998, 214, Suffolk HER EXG 083.

Muldowney, M., 2010d. *Mulligan's Yard, Cowlinge, Archaeological Monitoring Report,* Unpublished Report, Suffolk County Council 2009/230, Suffolk HER COW 026.

Muldowney, M., 2010e. *West Row Primary School, West Row, Mildenhall, Archaeological Excavation Report,* Unpublished Report, Suffolk County Council 2009/120, Suffolk HER MNL 612.

Mullin, D., 2005. *An Archaeological Watching Brief at Storopack, Newent Business Park, Newent, Gloucestershire, September 2005,* Unpublished Report, Gloucestershire County Council, Gloucestershire HER 27754.

Mullin, D., 2009. *Kingshill, North, Cirencester, Gloucestershire, Post-Excavation Assessment,* Unpublished Report, Oxford Archaeology Unit no. JN 3048, Gloucestershire HER 33769.

Mumford, J. and C. Parry, 1995. *Proposed A417 Lechlade Bypass, Gloucestershire: Archaeological Field Evaluation, First Report: Geophysical Survey; Fieldwalking; Trial Excavation North of Hambridge Lane,* Unpublished Report, Gloucestershire County Council, Available on OASIS.

Murray, H., 1999. *Discovery and Excavation in Scotland,* 10.

Murray, H., 2002. Late Prehistoric Settlement, Berryhill, Aberdeenshire. *Proceedings of the Society of Antiquaries of Scotland,* 132, 213-217.

Murray, H. K. and J. C. Murray, 2006a. *Discovery and Excavation in Scotland,* 18.

Murray, H. K. and J. C. Murray, 2006b. *Thainstone Business Park, Inverurie, Aberdeenshire,* Scottish Archaeological Internet Report 21.

Murray, H. K. and J. C. Murray, 2007. *Discovery and Excavation in Scotland,* 23.

Murray, J. C., 2001. *Archaeological Watching Brief for North of Scotland Water Authority on New Water Pipeline, 28 February - 20 July 2001,* Unpublished Report, RCAHMS 2918.

Murray, R., 2006. *Discovery and Excavation in Scotland,* Glasgow, 94-5.

Murray, R., 2007a. *Culduthel Mains Farm, Inverness: Phase 5. Excavations of a Later Prehistoric Settlement: Assessment Report,* Unpublished Report, Headland Archaeology Ltd.

Murray, R., 2007b. *Discovery and Excavation in Scotland,* 114-5.

Murray, R., 2007c. Iron-Masters of the Caledonians. *Current Archaeology,* 212, 20-25.

Murrell, K., 2009. *Land Off Hardwick Roundabout, Kings Lynn, Norfolk, an Archaeological Evaluation,* Unpublished Report, Cambridge Archaeological Unit 876, Norfolk HER 52618.

Musty, J. W. G., 1959a. A Pipe-Line near Old Sarum: Prehistoric, Roman and Medieval Finds Including Two Twelfth Century Lime Kilns. *Wiltshire Archaeology and Natural History Society,* 57, 179-91.

Musty, J. W. G., 1959b. A Romano-British Building at Highpost, Middle Woodford. *Wiltshire Archaeology and Natural History Society,* 57, 173-75.

Nan Kivell, R. d. C., 1925. Objects Found During Excavations on the Romano-British Site at Cold Kitchen Hill, Brixton Deverill, 1924. *Wiltshire Archaeology and Natural History Society,* 43, 180-91.

Nan Kivell, R. d. C., 1926. Objects Found During Excavations on the Romano-British Site at Cold Kitchen Hill, Brixton Deverill, Witls. *Wiltshire Archaeology and Natural History Society,* 43, 327-32.

Nan Kivell, R. d. C., 1927a. Objects Found During Excavations on the Romano-British Site at Cold Kitchen Hill, Brixton Deverill, 1924. *Wiltshire Archaeology and Natural History Society,* 43, 180-91.

Nan Kivell, R. d. C., 1927b. Objects Found During Excavations on the Romano-British Site at Stockton Earthworks. *Wiltshire Archaeology and Natural History Society,* 43, 389-94.

Nan Kivell, R. d. C., 1928. Objects Found During Excavations on the Romano-British Site at Cold Kitchen Hill, Brixton Deverill, 1926. *Wiltshire Archaeology and Natural History Society,* 44, 138-42.

Newman, C. and E. L. Morris, 2001. Iron Age and Romano-British Sites Along the Bowden Reservoir Link Pipeline, South-East Somerset. *Somerset Archaeology and Natural History Society*, 143, 1-27.

Newman, J., 2010a. *CEVC Primary School, Church Field, Monks Eleigh, Suffolk, Archaeological Evaluation Report*, Unpublished Report, John Newman Archaeological Services, Available on OASIS.

Newman, J., 2010b. *Nelson Farm, Ashbocking Road, Witnesham, Suffolk, Archaeological Monitoring Report*, Unpublished Report, John Newman Archaeological Services, Available on OASIS.

Newman, J., 2011. *Part of Side Garden, Mill House, Mill Lane, Alderton, Suffolk, Archaeological Evaluation and Monitoring Report*, Unpublished Report, John Newman Archaeological Services, Available on OASIS.

Newton, R. and S. Davison, 1989. *Conservation of Glass*, London: Butterworths.

Nichols, P., 1998. *An Archaeological Watching Brief at 29 Church Street, Cirencester, Gloucestershire*, Unpublished Report, Gloucestershire County Council, Gloucestershire HER 20286.

Nichols, P., 1999. *An Archaeological Evaluation at Dean Farm, Bishop's Cleeve, Gloucestershire*, Unpublished Report, Gloucestershire County Council, Gloucestershire HER 20562.

Nichols, P., 2000. *An Archaeological Excavation at the Cotswold School, Bourton-on-the-Water, Gloucestershire*, Unpublished Report, Gloucestershire County Council, Gloucestershire HER 19899.

Nichols, P., 2001. *An Archaeological Evaluation in the Area of a Proposed Artificial Sports Pitch at the Cotswold School, Bourton-on-the-Water, Gloucestershire*, Unpublished Report, Gloucestershire County Council, Gloucestershire HER 19899.

Nichols, P., 2004a. *An Archaeological Evaluation at Cirencester Park Polo Club, Daglingworth, Gloucestershire*, Unpublished Report, Gloucestershire County Council, Gloucestershire HER 22292.

Nichols, P., 2004b. *Archaeological Evaluation at the Cotswold School, Station Road, Bourton-on-the-Water, Gloucestershire 2001 and 2002*, Unpublished Report, Gloucestershire County Council, Gloucestershire HER 19899.

Nichols, P., 2006. *An Archaeological Excavation at Bourton-on-the-Water Primary School, Gloucestershire, 2003*, Unpublished Report, Gloucestershire County Council, Gloucestershire HER 22183.

Noon, S., 2007. *Swilington Brick Works, Archaeological Trench Evaluation*, Unpublished Report, Network Archaeology Report no. 530.

Noort, R. v. d., H. Chapman and J. Collis, 2007. *Sutton Common: The Excavation of an Iron Age 'Marsh-Fort'*, York: CBA Research Report 154.

Norman, C., 2002. *Notes Based on Unpublished Records Relating to the Maylands (M5) Site, Wellington Without*, Unpublished Report, Somerset HER 16422.

Norton, A., 2006. *The Arkenside Hotel, Lewis Lane, Cirencester, Gloucestershire - Archaeological Evaluation Report*, Unpublished Report, Oxford Archaeology Unit 3033, Gloucestershire HER 28353.

Norton, A. and J. Hiller, 2002. *Horcott Pitt, Fairford, Gloucestershire: Phase 12 Gravel Extraction: Archaeological Report on Features Mapping*, Unpublished Report, Oxford Archaeological Unit, Gloucestershire HER 21783.

O'Neil, H. E., 1939. Reports on Roman Remains, Gloucestershire. *Wiltshire Archaeology and Natural History Society*, 61, 107-31.

Orme, B. J., J. M. Coles, A. E. Caseldine and G. N. Bailey, 1981. *Meare Village West 1979*, Somerset Levels Papers no. 7.

Orme, B. J., J. M. Coles and R. J. Silverston, 1983. *Meare Village East 1982*, Somerset Levels Papers no. 9.

Orme, B. J., J. M. Coles and C. R. Sturdy, 1979. *Meare Lake Village West: A Report on Recent Work*, Somerset levels Papers no. 5.

Oswald, A., 1997. A Doorway on the Past: Practical and Mystic Concerns in the Orientation of Roundhouse Doorways, in *Reconstructing Iron Age Societies: New Approaches to the British Iron Age*, eds. A. Gwilt and C. Haselgrove, Oxford: Oxbow Monograph 71, 87-95.

Oswin, J., 2007. *Peare Roman Villa, Bath and Camerton Archaeological Society*, Unpublished Report, Somerset HER 28024 and 28025.

Ottoway, P., 2005. *1-3 Driffield Terrace, York, Assessment Report on an Archaeological Excavation*, Unpublished Report, York Archaeological Trust Report no. 2005/27, CYC 705.

Outram, Z., C. M. Batt, E. J. Rhodes and S. J. Dockrill, 2010. The Integration of Chronological and Archaeological Information to Date Building Construction: An Example from Shetland, Scotland, UK. *Journal of Archaeological Science*, 37 (11), 2821-30.

Owen, M., 1979. *Walcot Street, 1971*, Bristol: Committee for Rescue Archaeology in Avon, Gloucestershire and Somerset.

Owles, E., 1969. The Ipswich Gold Torcs. *Antiquity*, 43(171), 208-12.

Ozanne, A., 1962. The Peak Dwellers. *Medieval Archaeology*, 6-7, 15-52.

Painter, K. S., 1964. Excavations of the Roman Villa at Hinton St. Mary, 1964. *Dorset Natural History and Archaeological Society*, 86, 150-54.

Palmer, S., 2009. *Excavations of an Enigmatic Multi-Period Site on the Isle of Portland, Dorset*, Oxford: BAR British Series no. 499.

Papworth, M., 2004. *Brent Knoll, Somerset, Report on the Excavation of Three Post-Holes for Easter Crosses*, Unpublished Report, National Trust, Somerset HER 17268.

Papworth, M., 2011. *The Search for the Durotriges: Dorset and the West Country in the Late Iron Age*, Stroud: The History Press.

Parfitt, K., 1995. *Iron Age Burials from Mill Hill, Deal*, London: British Museum Press.

Parker Pearson, M., 1996. Food, Fertility and Front Doors in the First Millennium BC, in *The Iron Age in Britain and Ireland: Recent Trends*, eds. T. C. Champion and J. Collis, Sheffield: University of Sheffield, 117-32.

Parker Pearson, M., N. Sharples and J. Mulville, 1996. Brochs and Iron Age Society: A Reappraisal. *Antiquity*, 70, 1-11.

Parker Pearson, M. and R. E. Sydes, 1997. The Iron Age Enclosures and Prehistoric Landscape of Sutton Common, South Yorkshire. *Proceedings of the Prehistoric Society*, 63, 221-59.

Parry, C., 1994. Symonds Yat Promontory Fort, English Bichnor, Gloucestershire: Excavations 1990-91. *Wiltshire Archaeology and Natural History Society*, 112, 59-72.

Parry, C., 1998. Excavations near Birdlip, Cowley, Gloucestershire, 1987-8. *Wiltshire Archaeology and Natural History Society*, 116, 25-92.

Parry, C., 1999. Iron-Age, Romano-British and Medieval Occupation at Bishop's Cleeve, Gloucestershire: Excavations at Gilder's Paddock 1989 and 1990-1. *Wiltshire Archaeology and Natural History Society*, 117, 89-118.

Parry, D., 2010. *Land at Shawswell Farm, Rendcomb, Gloucestershire, Archaeological Watching Brief*, Unpublished Report, Cotswold Archaeology Report 10160, Available on OASIS.

Passmore, A. D., 1899. Notes on a Roman Building and Interments Lately Discovered at Swindon. *Wiltshire Archaeology and Natural History Society*, 30, 217-21.

Patten, R., 2004. *Mayton Wood, Buxton and Lammas, Norfolk: A 'Strip, Map and Sample Excavation, Phase 1*, Unpublished Report, Cambridge Archaeological Unit 649, Norfolk HER 39833.

Payne, R., 2006. *Site Off Marissal Road, Henbury, Bristol*, Unpublished Report, Avon Archaeological Unit BR79, Bristol City HER 224.

Peacock, D. P. S., 1987. Iron Age and Roman Quern Production at Lodsworth, West Sussex. *Antiquaries Journal*, 67, 61-85.

Penn, K., 2009. *An Archaeological Watching Brief at Norwich Road, Caister-on-Sea, Norfolk*, Unpublished Report, NAU Archaeology 2014, Norfolk HER 51885.

Percival, J. and G. Trimble, 2008. Excavations at Crow Hall Park, London Road, Downham Market, 1999-2000. *Norfolk Archaeology*, 45, 293-336.

Percival, S., 1995. Iron Age Pottery from Two Pits at Fincham, Norfolk. *Norfolk Archaeology*, 42(2), 215-17.

Perry, C., 1996. *The Forum Centre, Lewis Lane, Cirencester: Archaeological Evaluation, 1996*, Unpublished Report, Gloucestershire HER 17630.

Phelps, A., 2009. *An Archaeological Evaluation at the Lodge, North Wootton, Norfolk*, Unpublished Report, NAU Archaeology Report BAU 2096, Norfolk HER 53908.

Phelps, A., 2010. *An Archaeological Evaluation at Land Opposite the Scole Inn, Scole, Norfolk*, Unpublished Report, NAU Archaeology Report 1817, Norfolk HER 54903.

Philips, B., 1981. Starveall Farm, Romano-British Villa. *Wiltshire Archaeology and Natural History Society*, 74/75, 40-55.

Philips, C., 2002. *Report on an Archaeological Evaluation at Thompson Hall Cottage, Thompson, Norfolk*, Unpublished Report, Norfolk Archaeological Unit 702, Norfolk HER 37135.

Philips, J. T., 1960. An Iron Age Site at Driffield, East Riding, Yorks. *Yorkshire Archaeological Journal*, 40, 183-91.

Phillips, A. D., 1995. *An Archaeolgoical Evaluation of the Site Proposed for the York Minster Library Extension*, Unpublished Report, CYC 65.

Phillips, T. and R. Bradley, 2004. Developer-Funded Fieldwork in Scotland, 1990-2003: An Overview of the Prehistoric Evidence. *Proceedings of the Society of Antiquaries of Scotland*, 134, 17-51.

Piggott, C. M., 1939. An Iron Age 'a' Site on Harnham Hill. *Wiltshire Archaeology and Natural History Society*, 48, 513-22.

Piggott, C. M., 1947-48. Excavation at Hownam Rings, Roxburghshire. *Proceedings of the Society of Antiquaries of Scotland*, 82, 193-225.

Piggott, C. M., 1948. The Iron Age Settlement at Hayhope Knowe, Roxburghshire. Excavations 1949. *Proceedings of the Society of Antiquaries of Scotland*, 83, 45-67.

Piggott, C. M., 1949. The Excavations at Bonchester Hill, 1950. *Proceedings of the Society of Antiquaries of Scotland*, 84, 113-37.

Piggott, C. M., 1953a. An Iron Age Barrow in the New Forest. *Antiquaries Journal*, 33, 14-21.

Piggott, C. M., 1953b. Milton Loch Crannog 1: A Native House of the 2nd Century AD in Kirkudbrightshire. *Proceedings of the Society of Antiquaries of Scotland*, 87, 124-52.

Piggott, S., 1947. The Excavations at Cairnpapple Hill, West Lothian, 1947-48. *Proceedings of the Society of Antiquaries of Scotland*, 82, 68-123.

Piggott, S., 1951. *A Picture Book of Ancient British Art*, Cambridge: Cambridge University Press.

Piggott, S., 1957. Excavations at Braidwood Fort, Midlothian and Craig's Quarry, Direleton, East

Lothian. *Proceedings of the Society of Antiquaries of Scotland,* 91, 61-77.

Piggott, S., 1966. A Scheme for the Scottish Iron Age, in *The Iron Age in Northern Britain,* ed. A. L. F. Rivet, Edinburgh: Edinburgh University Press, 1-15.

Piggott, S., 1970. *Early Celtic Art,* Edinburgh: Edinburgh University Press.

Pine, J., 2002. *Totterdown Lane, Norcott, near Fairford, Gloucestershire: Phase 2: A Post-Excavation Assessment,* Unpublished Report, Thames Valley Archaeological Services Ltd., Gloucestershire HER 21693.

Pine, J., 2009. *Wetstone Bridge Farm, Marston Meyse, Gloucestershire and Wiltshire: An Archaeological Evaluation,* Unpublished Report, Thames Valley Archaeological Services WMM09/07, Available on OASIS.

Pine, J. and S. Preston, 2002. *Totterdown Lane, Horcott, near Fairford, Gloucestershire,* Reading: Thames Valley Archaeological Services.

Pine, J. and S. Preston, 2004. *Iron Age and Roman Settlement and Landscape at Totterdown Lane, Horcott near Fairford, Gloucestershire,* Thames Valley Archaeological Services Monograph no. 6.

Pinnock, D., 2007. *Joseph Rowntree School, New Earswick, Report on an Archaeological Evaluation,* Unpublished Report, On Site Archaeology Ltd. Report no. OSA07EV09, CYC 857.

Pitt-Rivers, A. L.-F., 1887-1898. *Excavations in Cranborne Chase, near Rushmore, on the Borders of Dorset and Wilts.,* London: Harrison and Sons.

Pitts, M., 2010. Re-Thinking the Southern British Oppida: Networks, Kingdoms and Material Culture. *European Journal of Archaeology,* 13(1), 32-63.

Place, C., 2009. *B9871: Maundown Water Treatment Works, Wiveliscombe, Somerset, an Archaeological Watching Brief and Limited Excavation,* Unpublished Report, Context One Archaeological Services, Somerset HER 28436.

Plouviez, J., 1989. A Romano-British Pottery Kiln at Stowmarket. *Proceedings of the Suffolk Institute of Archaeology,* 37(1), 1-12.

Pollard, J., 2002. The Nature of Archaeological Deposits and Finds Assemblages, in *Prehistoric Britain: The Ceramic Basis,* eds. A. Woodward and J. D. Hill, Oxford: Oxbow, 22-33.

Poore, D., D. Thomason and A. Brossler, 2002. Iron Age Settlement and Roman Activity at Brickley Lane, Devizes, Wiltshire, 1999. *Wiltshire Archaeology and Natural History Society,* 95, 214-39.

Pope, R. and I. Ralston, 2011. Approaching Sex and Status in Iron Age Britain with Reference to the Nearer Continent, in *Atlantic Europe in the First Millennium BC: Crossing the Divide,* eds. T. Moore and X.-L. Armada, Oxford: Oxford University Press, 375-416.

Portable Antiquities Scheme, 2003. http://finds.org.uk/.

Powell, A., M. J. Allen, J. Chapman, R. Every, R. Gale, P. Harding, S. Knight, J. I. McKinley and C. Stevens, 2005. Excavations Along the Old Sarum Water Pipeline, North of Salisbury. *Wiltshire Archaeology and Natural History Society,* 98, 250-80.

Powell, A. B., 2004. Valley of the South Winterborne, near West Stafford. *Dorset Natural History and Archaeological Society,* 126, 157-60.

Powell, A. B., 2010. Prehistoric, Romano-British and Medieval Activity at Ridge Green, Shaw, Swindon. *Wiltshire Archaeology and Natural History Society,* 103, 130-41.

Powell, A. B., 2011. Investigations at Wanborough Roman Small Town, Along the A419 Covington Noise Barrier. *Wiltshire Archaeology and Natural History Society,* 104, 115-26.

Powell, A. B., G. P. Jones and L. Mepham, 2008. An Iron Age and Romano-British Settlement at Cleveland Farm, Ashton Keynes, Wiltshire. *Wiltshire Archaeology and Natural History Society,* 101, 18-50.

Powell, A. B., L. Mepham and C. J. Stevens, 2009. Investigations of Later Prehistoric and Romano-British Settlement at Huntworth, 2006. *Somerset Archaeology and Natural History Society,* 152, 69-81.

Powell, K., G. Laws and L. Brown, 2009. A Late Neolithic/Early Bronze Age Enclosure and Iron Age and Romano-British Settlement at Latton Lands, Wiltshire. *Wiltshire Archaeology and Natural History Society,* 102, 22-113.

Powell, K., A. Smith and G. Laws, 2010. *Evolution of a Farming Community in the Upper Thames Valley: Volume 1: Site Narrative and Overview,* Oxford: Oxford Archaeology Thames Valley Landscape Monograph no. 31.

Powlesland, D., 1986. Excavations at Heslerton, North Yorkshire 1978-82. *Archaeological Journal,* 143, 53-173.

Price, E., 2000. *Frocester: A Romano-British Settlement, Its Antecedents and Successors,* Gloucester and District Archaeological Research Group.

Price, J., 1988. Romano-British Glass Bangles from East Yorkshire, in *Recent Research in Roman Yorkshire. Studies in Honour of Mary Kitson Clark (Mrs Derwas Chitty),* eds. J. Price, P. R. Wilson, C. S. Briggs and S. J. Hardman, Oxford: BAR British Series no.193, 339-66.

Price, J. and S. Cottam, 1998. *Romano-British Glass Vessels: A Handbook,* York: Council for British Archaeology.

Price, R. and L. Watts, 1980. Rescue Excavations at Combe Hay, Somerset 1968-1973. *Somerset Archaeology and Natural History Society,* 124, 1-49.

Pulak, C., 1998. The Uluburun Shipwreck: An Overview. *The International Journal of Nautical Archaeology,* 27.3, 188-224.

Pullinger, J., 1991. Excavation Report - the Roman Villa at Boughspring with a New Assessment. *Dean Archaeology*, 3, 13-26.

Radford, C. A. R., 1951a. The Roman Site at Catsgore, Somerton. *Somerset Archaeology and Natural History Society*, 96, 41-77.

Radford, C. A. R., 1951b. *The Roman Villa at Littleton*, Unpublished Report, Somerset HER 28549.

Rahtz, P., 1951. The Roman Temple at Pagans Hill, Chew Stoke, N. Somerset. *Somerset Archaeology and Natural History Society*, 96, 112-42.

Rahtz, P., 1961. An Excavation on Bokerly Dyke, 1958. *Archaeological Journal*, 118, 65-99.

Rahtz, P., 1963. A Roman Villa at Downton. *Wiltshire Archaeology and Natural History Society*, 58, 303-41.

Rahtz, P., 1969. Cannington Hillfort 1963. *Somerset Archaeology and Natural History Society*, 113, 56-68.

Rahtz, P., 1990. Bower Chalke 1959: Excavations at Great Ditch Banks and Middle Chase Ditch. *Wiltshire Archaeology and Natural History Society*, 83, 1-49.

Rahtz, P. and J. Bateman, 1986. *Wharram Grange Roman Villa 1975-82*, York University Archaeological Publications 2.

Rahtz, P. and J. Brown, 1958-59. Blaise Castle Hill, Bristol, 1957. *Proceedings of the University of Bristol Spelaeological Society*, 8, 147-71.

Rahtz, P. and E. Greenfield, 1977. *Excavations at Chew Valley Lake Somerset*, Department of the Environment Archaeological Reports no. 8.

Rahtz, P., S. Hirst and S. M. Wright, 2000. *Cannington Cemetery, Excavations 1962-3 of Prehistoric, Roman, Post-Roman, and Later Features at Cannington Park Quarry, near Bridgewater, Somerset*, Britannia Monograph Series no. 17.

Rahtz, P. and J. Musty, 1960. Excavations at Old Sarum, 1957. *Wiltshire Archaeology and Natural History Society*, 57, 353-70.

Rahtz, P. and L. Watts, 1989. Pagans Hill Revisited. *Archaeological Journal*, 146, 330-71.

Rahtz, P., A. Woodward, I. Burrow, A. Everton, L. Watts, P. Leach, S. Hirst, P. Fowler and J. Gardner, 1992. *Cadbury Congresbury 1968-73, a Late/Post-Roman Hilltop Settlement in Somerset*, Oxford: BAR British Series no. 223.

Ralston, I., 1980. *Green Castle, Portknockie, Promontory Fort*, Unpublished Report, RCAHMS MS 453/45.

Ralston, I., 1981a. *Discovery and Excavation in Scotland*, 41.

Ralston, I., 1981b. *The Green Castle, Portknockie, Moray District, Report on the Sixth Season of Excavations on Behalf of the Scottish Development Department*, Unpublished Report, RCAHMS MS 364/1.

Ralston, I., 1982. *Discovery and Excavation in Scotland*, 13.

Ralston, I. and N. Fojut, 1978. *Discovery and Excavation in Scotland*, 12.

Ralston, I. and N. Fojut, 1979. *Discovery and Excavation in Scotland*, 14.

Ralston, I. and N. Fojut, 1980. *Discovery and Excavation in Scotland*, 15.

Ralston, I. and W. Watt, 1981. *Discovery and Excavation in Scotland*, 14.

Ralston, I. and W. Watt, 1982. *Discovery and Excavation in Scotland*, 13.

Ramm, H. G., 1958. Roman Burials from Castle Yard, York. *Yorkshire Archaeological Journal*, 39, 400-18.

Ramm, H. G., 1976. The Church of St. Mary, Bishophill Senior, York: Excavations, 1964. *Yorkshire Archaeological Journal*, 48, 35-68.

Ramsay, H., 2000. *Ford Farm August 2000*, Unpublished Report, Bridgewater Archaeological Society, Somerset HER 11301.

Randall, C., 2010. *Annual Report 2010*, Unpublished Report, South Somerset Archaeological Research Group, Somerset HER 30357.

Ratcliff, M., 2008. *An Archaeological Evaluation at Watton Sewage Treatment Works, Little Cressingham, Norfolk*, Unpublished Report, NAU Archaeology Report 1950, Available on OASIS.

Ravetz, A., 1958. A Romano-British Site near Badbury, Wilts. *Wiltshire Archaeology and Natural History Society*, 57, 24-29.

Rawes, B., 1980. The Romano-British Site at Wycomb, Andoversford, Excavations 1969-1970. *Wiltshire Archaeology and Natural History Society*, 98, 11-55.

Rawes, B., 1986. The Romano-British Settlement at Haymes, Cleeve Hill, near Cheltenham. *Transactions of the Bristol and Gloucestershire Archaeological Society*, 104, 61-93.

Rawes, B., 1991. A Prehistoric and Romano-British Settlement at Vineyards Farm, Charlton Kings, Gloucestershire. *Transactions of the Bristol and Gloucestershire Archaeological Society*, 109, 25-89.

Rawlings, M., 1992. Romano-British Sites Observed Along the Codford-Ilchester Water Pipeline. *Somerset Archaeology and Natural History Society*, 136, 29-60.

Rawlings, M., 2001. Archaeological Investigations at the Roman Villa, Netheravon, 1996. *Wiltshire Archaeology and Natural History Society*, 94, 148-53.

Rawlings, M., M. J. Allen and F. Healy, 2004. Investigations of the Whitesheet Down Environs 1989-90: Neolithic Causewayed Enclosure and Iron Age Settlement. *Wiltshire Archaeology and Natural History Society*, 97, 144-96.

Rawlings, M. and A. P. Fitzpatrick, 1996. Prehistoric Sites and a Romano-British Settlement at Butterfield Down, Amesbury. *Wiltshire Archaeology and Natural History Society*, 89, 1-43.

RCAHMS, 1982. *The Archaeological Sites and Monuments of South Kincardine, Kincardine and Deeside District, Grampian Region*, Edinburgh: RCAHMS.

Read, D. W., 2007. *Artefact Classification: A Conceptual and Methodological Approach*, Walnut Creek, California: Left Coast Press.

Reynish, S., 2008. *Stonecroft, Mousetrap Lane, Bourton-on-the-Water, Gloucestershire, Archaeological Evaluation*, Unpublished Report, Cotswold Archaeology no. 08251, Gloucestershire HER 33194.

Reynish, S., S. Sheldon and J. Hart, 2010. *Park Farm, Thornbury, South Gloucestershire, Archaeological Evaluation*, Unpublished Report, Cotswold Archaeology Report 10162, Available on OASIS.

Richardson, J., 2011. Bronze Age Cremations, Iron Age and Roman Settlement and Early Medieval Inhumations at the Langeled Receiving Facilities, Easington, East Riding of Yorkshire. *Yorkshire Archaeological Journal*, 83, 59-100.

Richardson, K., 1940. Excavations at Poundbury, Dorchester, Dorset, 1939. *Antiquaries Journal*, 20, 429-48.

Richardson, K., 1951. The Excavations of Iron Age Villages on Boscombe Down West. *Wiltshire Archaeology and Natural History Society*, 54, 1-168.

Richardson, K., 1959. Excavations in Hungate, York. *Archaeological Journal*, 116, 51-114.

Richmond, I., 1932. The Four Roman Camps at Cawthorn in the North Riding of Yorkshire. *Archaeological Journal*, 89, 17-78.

Richmond, I., 1968. *Hod Hill: Volume 2, Excavations Carried out between 1951 and 1958*, London: Trustees of the British Museum.

Rickett, R., 1995. *The Anglo-Saxon Cemetery at Spong Hill, North Elmham, Part Vii: The Iron Age, Roman and Early Saxon Settlement*, Dereham, Norfolk: East Anglian Archaeology Report no. 73.

Riley, R., 2010. *6 Buttington Terrace, Beachley, Tidenham, Gloucestershire, Archaeological Watching Brief*, Unpublished Report, Cotswold Archaeology Report 10139, Available on OASIS.

Roach, M. E. and J. B. Eicher (eds.), 1965. *Dress, Adornment, and the Social Order*, New York: Wiley.

Roach-Higgins, M. E. and J. B. Eicher, 1992. Dress and Identity. *Clothing and Textiles Research Journal*, 10(4), 1-8.

Roach-Higgins, M. E. and J. B. Eicher, 1995. Dress and Identity, in *Dress and Identity*, eds. M. E. Roach-Higgins, J. B. Eicher and K. K. P. Johnson, New York: Fairchild Publications, 7-18.

Roach-Higgins, M. E., J. B. Eicher and K. K. P. Johnson (eds.), 1995. *Dress and Identity*, New York: Fairchild Publications.

Roberts, B., 2007. Adorning the Living but Not the Dead: Understanding Ornaments in Britain C. 1400 - 1100 Cal BC. *Proceedings of the Prehistoric Society*, 73, 135-67.

Roberts, I. (ed.) 2005. *Ferrybridge Henge: The Ritual Landscape, Archaeological Investigations at the Site of the Holmfield Interchange of the A1 Motorway*, Archaeological Services WYAS.

Roberts, I., 2009. A Late Iron Age and Roman-British Settlement at High Wold, Brempton Lane, Bridlington, East Yorkshire. *Yorkshire Archaeological Journal*, 81, 47-137.

Roberts, I., A. Burgess and D. Berg, 2001. *A New Link to the Past: The Archaeological Landscape of the M1-A1 Link Road*, Yorkshire Archaeology 7.

Roberts, M., 1994. *Archaeological Excavations at King's Meadow, Cirencester*, Unpublished Report, Gloucestershire HER 34570.

Robertson, A., 1970. Roman Finds from Non-Roman Sites in Scotland. *Britannia*, 1(1970), 198-226.

Robertson, A. S., 1938. A Roman Coin Hoard from Bristol. *Wiltshire Archaeology and Natural History Society*, 60, 194-97.

Robertson, D., 2003. *A Neolithic Enclosure and an Early Saxon Settlement Excavations at Broome 2001*, Unpublished Report, Norfolk Archaeological Unit 668, Norfolk HER 36289.

Robinson, G., 2009. A Romano-British Settlement at Millfield Farm, Wheldrake, near York. *Yorkshire Archaeological Journal*, 81, 139-77.

Robinson, S., 2010. *Kingsmead School, Cheltenham, Gloucestershire, Results of Additional Archaeological Trench Evaluation*, Unpublished Report, AC Archaeology no. ACW222//4/0, Gloucestershire HER 35021-24.

Rodwell, W., 1978-80. *Excavations at Wells 1978: A Summary Report*: Committee for Rescue Archaeology in Avon, Gloucestershire and Somerset, Somerset HER 15113.

Roe, A., 2009. A Roman Landscape at Moor Lane, Stamford Bridge. *East Riding Archaeologist*, 12, 70-86.

Rogers, B. and D. Roddham, 1991. The Excavations at Wellhead, Westbury 1959-1966. *Wiltshire Archaeology and Natural History Society*, 84, 51-60.

Rogerson, A., 1977. *Excavations at Scole, 1973*, Dereham, Norfolk: East Anglian Archaeology Report no. 5.

Rogerson, A. and A. J. Lawson, 1991. *The Earthwork Enclosure at Tasburgh*, Dereham, Norfolk: East Anglian Archaeology Report no. 54.

Ross, A., 1885-86. Notice of the Discovery of Portions of Two Penannular Brooches of Silver with Beads of Glass and Amber, and a Silver Coin of Coenwulf, King of Mercia (AD 795-818), at Mais of Croy, Inverness-Shire. *Proceedings of the Society of Antiquaries of Scotland*, 20, 91-96.

Rouse, I., 1960. The Classification of Artifacts in Archaeology. *American Antiquity*, 25, 313-23.

Rowe, M., 2003a. *24 Chester Crescent, Cirencester, Gloucestershire, Archaeological Evaluation*, Unpublished Report, Cotswold Archaeology 03146, Gloucestershire HER 22424.

Rowe, M., 2003b. *Land at the Old Parsonage, 30 Watermoor Road, Cirencester, Gloucestershire, Archaeological Evaluation*, Unpublished Report,

Cotswold Archaeology 03154, Gloucestershire HER 22368.

Rowe, M., 2004. *Foresters Arms, Queen Street, Cirencester, Gloucestershire, Archaeological Evaluation,* Unpublished Report, Cotswold Archaeological Trust Report no. 04002, Gloucestershire HER 22490.

Roy, M., 2000. *Discovery and Excavation in Scotland,* 52.

Roy, M., 2005. *Discovery and Excavation in Scotland,* 15.

Roymans, N. and L. Verniers, 2010. Glass La Tène Bracelets in the Lower Rhine Region, Typology, Chronology and Social Implications. *Germania,* 88, 195-219.

Russel, J., 1983. Romano-British Burials at Henbury Comp'sive School, Bristol: A Preliminary Report. *Bristol and Avon Archaeology,* 2, 21-24.

Russel-White, C. J., 1995. The Excavation of a Neolithic and Iron Age Settlement at Wardend of Durris, Aberdeenshire. *Proceedings of the Society of Antiquaries of Scotland,* 125, 9-27.

Russell-White, C. J., 1988-1989. *Wardend of Durris Settlement, Enclosures and Pits,* Unpublished Report, RCAHMS MS 1090/21-31.

Russell-White, C. J., 1990. *Discovery and Excavation in Scotland,* 18.

Russell-White, C. J., 1995. The Excavations of a Neolithic and Iron Age Settlement at Wardend of Durris, Aberdeenshire. *Proceedings of the Society of Antiquaries of Scotland,* 125, 9-27.

Russett, V., 1993. A Romano-British, Medieval and Industrial Site at Stonehill, Hanham, near Bristol. *Bristol and Avon Archaeology,* 11, 2-17.

Sackett, J., 1977. The Meaning of Style in Archaeology: A General Model. *American Antiquity,* 42(3), 369-80.

Sackett, J., 1985. Style and Ethnicity in the Kalahari: A Reply to Wiessner. *American Antiquity,* 50(1), 154-59.

Samuel, J., 2000. Watching Brief Excavations at Moat Farm, Pucklechurch South Gloucestershire, 2000. *Bristol and Avon Archaeology,* 17, 1-16.

Samuel, J., 2001. *Excavations at Nerrol's Farm During the Watching Brief Phase 2000,* Unpublished Report, Bristol and Region Archaeological Services, Somerset HER 11686.

Samuel, J., 2003. Excavations at 'Matford', Bradley Stoke Way, Bradley Stoke, South Gloucestershire, 2001. *Bristol and Avon Archaeology,* 18, 41-100.

Sasse, B. and C. Theune, 1995. Merovingian Glass Beads - a Classification Model, in *Glass Beads - Cultural History, Technology, Experiment and Analogy*, eds. M. Rasmussen, U. L. Hansen and U. Näsman, Lejre, Dennmark: Historical Archaeological Experimental Centre, 75-82.

Saunders, B. A. C. and J. Brakel, 1997. Are There Nontrivial Constraints on Colour Categorization? *Behavioral and Brain Sciences,* 20, 167-228.

Saunders, G., 2005. *1 Bell Street, Feltwell, Norfolk, Archaeological Evaluation Report,* Unpublished Report, The Heritage Network 298, Norfolk HER 41934.

Saunders, K., 2008. *Land Adjacent to 54 Barton Street, Tewkesbury, Gloucestershire, Archaeological Strip, Map and Sample,* Unpublished Report, Cotswold Archaeology Report 08061, Available on OASIS.

Saunders, K., 2010a. *Highfield Farm Tetbury, Gloucestershire, Archaeological Evaluation,* Unpublished Report, Cotswold Archaeology Report 10124, Available on OASIS.

Saunders, K., 2010b. *Land at Court Road, Brockworth, Gloucestershire, Archaeoligial Evaluation,* Unpublished Report, Cotswold Archaeology Report 10191, Available on OASIS.

Saunders, K., 2010c. *Land at Haygrove Farm, Bridgewater, Somerset, Archaeological Evalution,* Unpublished Report, Cotswold Archaeology Report no. 10204, Somerset HER 28367.

Saunders, K., 2010-11. *Cannington Bypass, Somerset, Archaeological Evaluation,* Unpublished Report, Cotswold Archaeology Report no. 11008, Somerset HER 30403.

Saunders, K., 2011. *Land to the East of Maidenbrook Farm, Taunton, Somerset, Archaeological Evaluation,* Unpublished Report, Cotswold Archaeology Report no. 11017, Somerset HER 30289.

Saunders, K. and M. Alexander, 2011. Roman and Medieval Enclosures Excavated at Beaversbrook Road, Calne, 2007. *Wiltshire Archaeology and Natural History Society,* 104, 127-34.

Saunders, P. R., 1997. The Excavation of an Iron Age Settlement Site at Stockton. *Wiltshire Archaeology and Natural History Society,* 90, 13-25.

Saville, A., 1979. *Excavations at Guiting Power Iron Age Site, Gloucestershire, 1974,* Committee for Rescue Archaeology in Avon, Gloucestershire and Somerset Occasional Papers no. 7.

ScARF, 2012. *Iron Age Scotland: Scarf Panel Report*: Scottish Archaeological Research Framework, Society of Antiquaries of Scotland.

Scarre, C., 2002. Colour and Materiality in Prehistoric Society, in *Colouring the Past: The Significance of Colour in Archaeological Research*, eds. A. Jones and G. MacGregor, Oxford: Berg, 227-42.

Scarth, P., 1888. Hoard of Roman Coins, Discovered on the Property of W.W. Kettlewell, Esq., of Harptree Court, East Harptree, on the Slope of the Mendip Hills. *Somerset Archaeology and Natural History Society,* 34, 21-8.

Schech, E. M., 2009. *Identity in Late Iron Age and Roman Britain: A Re-Examination of Glass Beads in the Tyne-Forth,* Unpublished M.A. Thesis, Durham University.

Sciama, L. D. and J. B. Eicher (eds.), 2001. *Beads and Bead Makers: Gender, Material Culture and Meaning,* Oxford: Berg.

Seaneachain, D., 2010. *Akeman Court, Cirencester, Gloucestershire, Archaeological Evaluation,* Unpublished Report, Cotswold Archaeology Report no. 10018, Gloucestershire HER 35025.28.

Seaneachain, D., 2011. *29 Watermoor Road, Cirencester, Gloucestershire, Archaeological Watching Brief,* Unpublished Report, Cotswold Archaeology Report 11084, Available on OASIS.

Seraby, W. A., 1950. The Iron Age Hill-Fort on Ham Hill, Somerset. *Archaeological Journal,* 107, 90-91.

Shanks, M. and C. Tilley, 1987. *Social Theory and Archaeology,* London: Polity Press.

Sharples, N., 1990. Late Iron Age Society and Continental Trade in Dorset, in *Les Gaulois D'armorique, La Fin De L'age Du Fer En Europe Tempérée, Actes Du Xiie Colloque De L'a.F.E.A.F. Quimper, Mai 1988,* eds. A. Duval, J. P. l. Bihan and Y. Menez, Rennes: Association pour la Diffusion des Recherches archéologiques dans l'Ouest de la France, 299-304.

Sharples, N., 1991a. *Maiden Castle: Excavations and Field Survey 1985-6,* English Heritage Report no 19.

Sharples, N., 1991b. Warfare in the Iron Age of Wessex. *Scottish Archaeological Review,* 8, 79-89.

Sharples, N., 2010. *Social Relations in Later Prehistory: Wessex in the First Millennium BC,* Oxford: Oxford University Press.

Sheldon, S., 2010. *Land at Homelands Farm, Bishop's Cleeve, Gloucestershire, Archaeological Evaluation,* Unpublished Report, Cotswold Archaeology Report 10028, Available on OASIS.

Shelley, A., 1995. *A143 Scole-Stuston Bypass,* Unpublished Report, Norfolk Archaeological Unit 129, Norfolk HER 30650.

Shelley, A., 1999. *Report of Excavations at Dunston Hall, Dunston, Norfolk,* Unpublished Report, Norfolk Archaeological Report 315, Norfolk HER 31858.

Shelley, A., 2002. *Report on an Archaeological Evaluation at 8-12 Red Lion Street, Aylsham, Norfolk, Nr11 6er,* Unpublished Report, Norfolk Archaeological Unit 750, Norfolk HER 37376.

Shelley, A. and F. Green, 2007. *An Archaeological Excavation at Myrtle Road, Hethersett: Assessment and Updated Project Design,* Unpublished Report, NAU Archaeology 1105, Norfolk HER 37645.

Sheppard, T., 1907. Note on a British Chariot-Burial at Hunmanby, in East Yorkshire. *Yorkshire Archaeological Journal,* 19, 482-88.

Sheppard, T., 1939. Excavations at Eastburn, East Yorkshire. *Yorkshire Archaeological Journal,* 34, 35-47.

Sheridan, A. and M. Davis, 2002. Investigating Jet and Jet-Like Artefacts from Prehistoric Scotland: The National Museums of Scotland Project. *Antiquity,* 76, 812-25.

Sherlock, S., 2005. *Excavations at Streethouse, Loftus, Summer 2005,* Unpublished report, NYMNP HER no number.

Sherlock, S., 2008. Excavations at Street House, North East Yorkshire NZ 7390 1965. *Prehistoric Yorkshire,* 45, 64-68.

Sherlock, S., 2012. *A Royal Anglo-Saxon Cemetery at Street House, Loftus, North-East Yorkshire,* Hartlepool: Tees Archaeology.

Shilling, C., 2003. *The Body and Social Theory,* London: Sage publications.

Signorelli, L. and M. Lightfoot, 2007. *A165 Reighton Bypass, Reighton, North Yorkshire, Excavation, Evaluation and Watching Brief, Assessment Report and Updated Project Design,* Unpublished Report, WYAS Report no. 1611, North Yorks HER S11418.

Signorelli, L. and I. Roberts, 2006. *Newbridge Quarry, Newbridge, Pickering, North Yorkshire, Interim Report,* Unpublished Report, WYS Report no. 1627, North Yorks HER S18546.

Sillwood, R. and S. Morgan, 2010. *An Archaeological Evaluation and Excavation at Mellis Road, Wortham,* Unpublished Report, NAU Archaeology Report no. 1995b, Available on OASIS.

Silvester, R. J. and J. P. Northover, 1991. An Iron Age Pit at Homebrink Farm, Methwold. *Norfolk Archaeology,* 41(2), 214-18.

Simmonds, A., 2006. *Butlers Court, Downington, Lechlade, Gloucestershire, Archaeological Evaluation Report,* Unpublished Report, Oxford Archaeological unit 6863, Gloucestershire HER 28430.

Simmonds, A., 2007a. *Cirencester Cinema, Lewis Lane, Cirencester, Gloucestershire, Archaeological Evaluation Report,* Unpublished Report, Oxford Archaeology no. 3509, Gloucestershire HER 29162.

Simmonds, A., 2007b. Excavations at Land Adjacent to the Rectory, Dymock, Gloucestershire 2002. *Wiltshire Archaeology and Natural History Society,* 125, 220-35.

Simmonds, A., 2007c. *Excavations at Stallards Place, Dymock, Gloucestershire, Draft Publication Report,* Unpublished Report, Oxford Archaeology 4001, Gloucestershire 32895.

Simmonds, A. and A. Smith, 2007. *Excavations on the Site of the Roman Forum at Cirencester,* Unpublished Report, Oxford Archaeology no. 3509, Gloucestershire HER 29699.

Simpson, D. D. A., 1996. Excavations of a Kerbed Funerary Monument at Stoneyfield. *Proceedings of the Society of Antiquaries of Scotland,* 126, 53-86.

Simpson, J. Y., 1862. Notes on Some Scottish Magical Charm-Stones, or Curing-Stones. *Proceedings of the Society of Antiquaries of Scotland,* 4, 211-24.

Simpson, M., 1968. Massive Armlets in the North British Iron Age, in *Studies in Ancient Europe: Essays Presented to Stuart Piggott,* eds. J. M. Coles and D. D. A. Simpson, Leicester: Leicester University Press, 233-54.

Sims, M., 2006. *Deerhurst House, Deerhurst, Gloucestershire, Archaeological Watching Brief,*

Unpublished Report, Oxford Archaeology Unit 2993, Gloucestershire HER 28315.

Sims, M., 2008. *New Sewer Box Vicarage, Box, Wiltshire, Archaeological Watching Brief,* Unpublished Report, Oxford Archaeology Job 3645.

Small, A., 1971. *Discovery and Excavation in Scotland,* 23.

Small, A., 1972. *Discovery and Excavation in Scotland,* 23.

Small, A. and M. B. Cottam, 1972. *Craig Phadrig, Interim Report on 1971 Excavation,* Dundee: The University Library.

Smith, A., 2007. Excavations at Neigh Bridge, Somerford Keynes, in *Iron Age and Roman Settlement in the Upper Thames Valley, Excavations at Claydon Pike and Other Sites within the Cotswold Water Park,* eds. D. Miles, S. Palmer, A. Smith and G. P. Jones, Oxford: Oxbow, 229-74.

Smith, A. T. and R. Brown, 2006. Excavations and Geophysical Survey of the Roman Settlement at Charterhouse-on-Mendip, 2005. *Somerset Archaeology and Natural History Society,* 149, 79-88.

Smith, G., 1990. Excavations at Ham Hill, 1983. *Somerset Archaeology and Natural History Society,* 134, 27-45.

Smith, L. and C. Davies, 2008. *Mangreen Hall Farm, Swardeston, Norfolk, Monitoring of Works under Archaeological Supervision and Control,* Unpublished Report, Archaeological Solutions 3131, Norfolk HER 37649.

Smith, L. F. and D. D. A. Simpson, 1964. Excavations of Three Roman Tombs and a Prehistoric Pit on Overton Down. *Wiltshire Archaeology and Natural History Society,* 59, 68-85.

Smith, R. A., 1908-09. A Hoard of Metal Found at Santon Downham, Suffolk. *Cambridge Antiquarian Society,* 8, 146-63.

Smith, R. A., 1927. Pre-Roman Remains at Scarborough. *Archaeologia,* 77, 179-200.

Smith, R. J. C., 1993. *Excavations at County Hall, Coliton Park, Dorchester, Dorset, 1988,* Wessex Archaeology Report no. 4.

Smith, R. J. C., F. Healy, M. J. Allen, E. L. Morris, I. Barnes and P. J. Woodward, 1997. *Excavations Along the Route of the Dorchester by-Pass, Dorset, 1986-8,* Wessex Archaeology Report no. 11.

Snape, M., P. Bidwell and A. Croom, 2002. Alborough Roman Town, Excavations by Miss D. Charlesworth, 1961-73, and the RCHME, 1959-60. *Yorkshire Archaeological Journal,* 74, 29-111.

Solley, T. W. J., 1966-67. Excavations at Gatcombe, Somerset, 1954. *Somerset Archaeoogy and Natural History Society,* 111, 24-37.

Sommers, M., 1998. *Archaeological Monitoring Report, Poslingford to Cavendish Water Main Renewal,* Unpublished Report, Suffolk County Council 98/13, Suffolk HER CAV 042.

Sommers, M., 1999. *Archaeological Excavation Report, Newmarket Isolation Hospital, Fordham Road, Exning,* Unpublished Report, Suffolk County Council 98/77, Suffolk HER EXG 074.

Sommers, M., 2000. *Trinity 2000 Development, Blofield Hall, Trimley St. Mary, Archaeological Assessment Report,* Unpublished Report, Suffolk County Council 2000/46, Suffolk HER TYY 026, TYY 027 and TYY 029.

Sommers, M., 2001a. *The Dairy, Hall Street, Long Melford, Archaeological Evaluation,* Unpublished Report, Suffolk County Council 2001/14, Suffolk HER LMD 130.

Sommers, M., 2001b. *Land Adjacent to 'Bramertons', Little St. Mary's, Long Melford,* Unpublished Report, Suffolk County Council 2001/49, Suffolk HER LMD 131.

Sommers, M., 2005. *Ceders Park (Phase 6a+B), Stowmarket, Archaeological Evaluation Report,* Unpublished Report, Suffolk County Council 2005/7, Suffolk HER SKT 037.

Sommers, M., 2006. *Walk Farm, Levington, Archaeological Evaluation and Monitoring Report,* Unpublished Report, Suffolk County Council 2004/151, Suffolk HER TYN 074.

Sommers, M., 2009. *Burton End Cp School, Haverhill, Archaeological Evaluation Report,* Unpublished Report, Suffolk County Council 2009, 293, Suffolk HER HVH 070.

Sørensen, M. L. S., 1991. The Construction of Gender through Appearance, in *The Archaeology of Gender,* eds. D. Walde and N. D. Willows, Calgary: University of Calgery, 121-29.

Sørensen, M. L. S., 1997. Reading Dress: The Construction of Social Categories and Identities in Bronze Age Europe. *Journal of European Archaeology,* 5(1), 93-114.

Spall, C., 2005. *Blue Bridge Land and Fishergate House, Fishergate, York, Archaeological Excavations and Watching Brief,* Unpublished Report, Field Archaeology Specialists, CYC 877.

Sparey-Green, C., 1996. Myncen Farm, Sipenny Handley, Dorset - Interim Report. *Dorset Natural History and Archaeological Society,* 118, 155-57.

Sparey-Green, C., 1998. Interim Report on Excavations at Myncen Farm, Sixpenny Handley, Dorset, 1998. *Dorset Natural History and Archaeological Society,* 120, 91-94.

Sparey-Green, C., 2007. Excavations at Mycen Farm, Sixpenny Handley, Dorset: A Summary Report. *Dorset Natural History and Archaeological Society,* 128, 53-60.

Spaulding, A., 1953. Statistical Techniques for the Discovery of Artifact Types. *American Antiquity,* 18, 305-13.

Spence, K., 1999. Red, White and Black: Colour in Building Stone in Ancient Egypt. *Cambridge Archaeological Journal,* 9(1), 114-17.

Stansbie, D. and G. Laws, 2004. Prehistoric Settlement and Medieval to Post-Medieval Field Systems at Latton Lands. *Wiltshire Archaeology and Natural History Society,* 97, 106-43.

Stansibie, D., A. Smith, G. Laws and T. Haines, 2008. Excavations of Iron Age and Roman Occupation at Coln Gravel, Thornhill Farm, Fairford, Gloucestershire, 2003-2004. *Wiltshire Archaeology and Natural History Society,* 126, 31-82.

Startin, D. W. A., 1981. Excavations at South Grove Cottage, Dorchester. *Dorset Natural History and Archaeological Society,* 103, 21-42.

Stead, I., 1988. Chalk Figurines of the Parisi. *Antiquaries Journal,* 68, 9-29.

Stead, I., 2006. *British Iron Age Swords and Scabbards,* British Museum.

Stead, I. M., 1958. Excavations at the South Corner Tower of the Roman Fortress at York, 1956. *Yorkshire Archaeological Journal,* 39, 515-38.

Stead, I. M., 1965. *The La Tène Cultures of East Yorkshire,* York: The Yorkshire Philosophical Society.

Stead, I. M., 1967. A La Tene III Burial at Welwyn Garden City. *Archaeologia,* 101, 1-62.

Stead, I. M., 1968. An Iron Age Hill-Fort at Grimthorpe, Yorkshire, England. *Proceedings of the Prehistoric Society,* 34, 148-90.

Stead, I. M., 1975. The La Tene Cemetery at Scarborough, East Riding. *East Riding Archaeologist,* 2, 1-11.

Stead, I. M., 1979. *The Arras Culture,* York: The Yorkshire Philosophical Society.

Stead, I. M., 1980. *Rudston Roman Villa,* Yorkshire Archaeological Society.

Stead, I. M., 1986. A Group of Iron Age Barrows at Cowlam, North Humberside. *Yorkshire Archaeological Journal,* 58, 5-15.

Stead, I. M., 1991a. *Iron Age Cemeteries in East Yorkshire, Excavations at Burton Fleming, Rudston, Garton-on-the-Wolds, and Kirkburn,* London: English Heritage Archaeological Report no. 22.

Stead, I. M., 1991b. The Snettisham Treasure: Excavations in 1990. *Antiquity,* 65, 447-65.

Stead, I. M., J. B. Bourke and D. Brothwell, 1986. *Lindow Man. The Body in the Bog,* London: British Museum Publications.

Stead, I. M. and V. Rigby, 1989. *Verulamium: The King Harry Lane Site,* London: Historic Buildings and Monuments Commission for England.

Stephens, M., 1991. *An Archaeological Trial Excavation at All Saints School, Mill Mount, York. April - May, 1991,* Unpublished Report, MAP Archaeological Consultancy, CYC 15.

Stephens, M., 1993. *Archaeological Excavation Along the Malton- Rillington Pumping Main,* Unpublished Report, MAP Archaeological Consultancy Ltd., North Yorkshire HER S11152.

Stephens, M., 2009. *Wykeham Quarry Proposed Extension, West Ayton, North Yorkshire, Archaeological Evaluation by Trial Trenching,* Unpublished Report, MAP Archaeological Consultancy, North Yorks HER S16288.

Stephens, M., D. Knight, N. Cavanagh and C. Rickaby, 2004. *Land at Os Field 0006, Main Road, Weaverthorpe, North Yorkshire, Archaeological Evaluation,* Unpublished Report, MAP Archaeological Consultancy, North Yorks HER S9151.

Stevenson, R. B. K., 1948. Braidwood Fort, Midlothian: The Exploration of Two Huts. *Proceedings of the Society of Antiquaries of Scotland,* 83, 1-11.

Stevenson, R. B. K., 1956. Native Bangles and Roman Glass. *Proceedings of the Society of Antiquaries of Scotland,* 88, 208-21.

Stevenson, R. B. K., 1976. Romano-British Glass Bangles. *Glasgow Archaeological Journal,* 4, 45-54.

Stillingfleet, E. W., 1848. Account of the Opening of Some Barrows on the Wolds of Yorkshire. *Proceedings of the Archaeological Institute,* 26-32.

Stirk, D., 2002. *Land at Barberry Hall Farm, Wilberfoss,* Unpublished Report, On Site Archaeology, Available on OASIS.

Stirk, D., 2003. *Clifton Garage, York., Report on an Archaeological Evaluation,* Unpublished Report, On Site Archaeology, OSA Report no. OSA03EV04, CYC 487.

Stirk, D., 2005. *Lynham's Road, Sewerby, Report on an Archaeological Watching Brief,* Unpublished Report, On Site Archaeology, OSA Report no. OSA05WB07, EHU 1187.

Stirk, D., 2006. *South Farm, Kexby, Archaeological Evaluation,* Unpublished Report, On Site Archaeology, OSA Report no. OSA05EV14, CYC 733.

Stirk, D., 2009a. *Dennington CEVCP School, Laxfield Road, Dennington, Archaeological Evaluation Report 2009/322,* Unpublished Report, Suffolk HER DNN 047.

Stirk, D., 2009b. *Land North of 7-14 Narrow Way, Wenhaston with Mells Hamlet, Suffolk, a Report on the Archaeolgoical Evaluation, 2009,* Unpublished Report, Suffolk County Council Archaeological Service, Available on OASIS.

Stirk, D., 2009c. *Land to North of the Street, Erwarton, Archaeological Evaluation Report,* Unpublished Report, Suffolk County Council Archaeological Services Report no. 2009/173, Suffolk HER ARW 064.

Stirk, D., 2010. *Site B, Priory Park, Nacton, Archaeological Monitoring Report,* Unpublished Report, Suffolk County Council Archaeology Service Report no. 2010/229, Suffolk HER NAC 105.

Stirk, D. and S. Benfield, 2010. *Land South of Sparrowhawk Road, Holton, Suffolk, Post-Excavation Assessment,* Unpublished Report, Suffolk County Council 2010/088, Suffolk HER HLN 009.

Stirk, D. and A. Fawcett, 2010. *Dennington CEVCP School, Laxfield Road, Dennington, Post-Excavation*

Assessment, Unpublished Report, Suffolk County Council Archaeological Report no. 2010/153, Suffolk HER DNN 047.

Stocks, H., 2008. *An Archaeological Watching Brief at 24 Belstead Avenue, Caister-on-Sea, Norfolk,* Unpublished Report, NAU Archaeology 17700, Norfolk HER 51057.

Stoertz, C., 1997. *Ancient Landscapes of the Yorkshire Wolds: Aerial Photographic Transcription and Analysis,* Swindon: Royal Commission on the Historical Monuments of England.

Stone, J. F. S., 1934. Three 'Peterborough' Dwelling Pits and a Double-Stockaded Early Iron Age Ditch at Winterbourne Dauntsey. *Wiltshire Archaeology and Natural History Society,* 46, 445-53.

Strachan, R., 1998. *Discovery and Excavation in Scotland,* 9.

Suddaby, I., 2001. *Inverness Southern Distributer Road, Slackbuie to Stratherrick, Inverness, Highland Region,* Unpublished Report, CFA Archaeology Ltd., RCAHMS MS 1081/23.

Sulikowska, J. and K. E. Dinwiddy, 2011. A Disturbed Romano-British Grave and Boundary Ditch at Lower Upham Farm, Ogbourne St. George. *Wiltshire Archaeology and Natural History Society,* 104, 254-56.

Sumpter, A. B. and S. Coll, 1977. *Interval Tower Sw5 and the South-West Defences: Excavations 1972-75, the Archaeology of York, Volume 3: The Legionary Fortress,* York, York Archaeological Trust for Excavation and Research.

Sunter, N. and P. Woodward, 1987. *Romano-British Industries in Purbeck,* Dorset Natural History and Archaeology Monograph no. 6.

Sutherland, M. and B. Roberts, 2003. *Land Adjoining Swanton Morley Airfield, Beetley and Hoe, Norfolk, Archaeological Investigation,* Unpublished Report, Hertfordshire Archaeological Trust 1260, Norfolk HER 37159.

Sydenham, J., 1844. On the Kimmeridge 'Coal Money'. *Archaeological Journal,* 1, 347-53.

Sykes, C. M. and G. A. Brown, 1960-61. The Wraxall Villa. *Somerset Archaeology and Natural History Society,* 105, 37-51.

Tabor, J., 2009a. Excavations at Canal Lane, Pocklington. *East Riding Archaeologist,* 12, 127-66.

Tabor, J., 2009b. Romano-British Remains at Burton Fleming. *East Riding Archaeologist,* 12, 87-96.

Tabor, J. and O. Cooper, 2007. *Scarborough Integrated Transport Scheme, Archaeolgoical Monitoring and Trial Trenching,* Unpublished Report, Northern Archaeological Associates, NAA 07/70, North Yorks HER S12170.

Tannahill, R., 2005. *Cirencester Cinema, Lewis Lane, Cirencester, Gloucestershire-Archaeological Watching Brief Interim Report,* Unpublished Report, Oxford Archaeological Unit, Gloucestershire HER 27622.

Tanner, R. M., 1975. The Iron Age and Romano-British Settlement at Barton Field, Tarant Hinton, Dorset, 1974. *Dorset Natural History and Archaeological Society,* 96, 64-66.

Tatler, S., 2004. *An Archaeological Strip and Record Excavation at Longdell Hills, Easton, Norfolk,* Norfolk Archaeological Unit 999, Unpublished Report, Norfolk HER 36414.

Tatler, S. and P. Bellamy, 2006. *Land Off Augusta Road, Portland, Dorset: Archaeological Evaluation, February 2006,* Unpublished Report, Terrain Archaeology Report no. 53211/3/1, Available on OASIS.

Tatler, S. and P. Bellamy, 2008. *Chicksgrove Quarry, Upper Chicksgrove, Tisbury, Wiltshire: Archaeological Investigation and Recording,* Unpublished Report, Terrain Archaeology Report no. 53275/3/1.

Taverner, N., 2001. *Land Adjacent to Rose Cottage and 'Winserdine', Dymock, Gloucestershire, Assessment Report on the Excavation and Watching Brief with a Project Proposal for Analysis and Publication,* Unpublished Report, Marches Archaeology series 216, Gloucestershire HER 21822.

Taylor, A., 2004. *Area 9, Manor Farm, Kempsford, Gloucestershire, a Post-Excavation Assessment,* Unpublished Report, Thames Valley Archaeological Services, Gloucestershire HER 14656.

Taylor, A., 2008. *Shorncote Quarry Footpath, Cotswold Community, Gloucestershire, 2008, Draft Publication Report,* Unpublished Report, Thames Valley Archaeological Services, CCW 05/61, Gloucestershire HER 33330.

Tester, A., 1998. *Archaeological Evaluation Report, Shakerland Hall Quarry, Badwell Ash,* Unpublished Report, Suffolk County Council 98/78, Suffolk HER BAA 013.

Tester, A., 1999. *Archaeological Evaluation Report, Low Road Debenham,* Unpublished Report, Suffolk County Council 99/30, Suffolk HER DBN 104.

Tester, A., 2002. *Land Adjacent to 'Bramertons', Little St. Mary's, Long Melford, Archaeological Monitoring Report,* Unpublished Report, Suffolk County Council 2002/116, Suffolk HER LMD 131.

Tester, A., 2006a. *Base Civil Engineering Complex, RAF Mildenhall, the Sports Field, Archaeological Evaluation Report,* Unpublished Report, Suffolk County Council 2006/050, Suffolk HER MNL 564.

Tester, A., 2006b. *RAF Lakenheath, New Dental Clinic, Archaeological Excavation and Assessment Report, 2001/2,* Unpublished Report, Suffolk County Council 2006/091, Suffolk HER ERL 101.

Tester, A., 2008. *Multi-Use Games Area, Remembrance Playing Fields, Brandon, a Report on the Archaeological Monitoring, 2006,* Unpublished Report, Suffolk County Council Archaeological Service 2008/006, Suffolk HER BRD 202.

Tester, A., 2009. *58 Little Eriswell, Eriswell, Archaeological Monitoring Report,* Unpublished Report, Suffolk County Council 2009/144, Suffolk HER ERL 043.

The Guildhouse Consultancy, 2002. The Wetwang Chariot Burial. *East Riding Archaeological Society News,* 51, 6-8.

Thistlewaite, A., 1992. *Archaeological Monitoring Report, Gravel Hill, Barnham,* Unpublished Report, Suffolk County Council, Suffolk HER BNH 043.

Thistlewaite, A., 1995. *Stuston Common, Monitoring and Evaluation Report,* Unpublished Report, Suffolk Archaeological unit 95/41, Suffolk HER SUS 023.

Thomas, A., N. Holbrook and C. Bateman, 2001. *Later Prehistoric and Romano-British Burial and Settlement at Hucclecote, Gloucestershire, Excavations in Advance of the Gloucester Business Park Link Road, 1998,* Unpublished Report, Cotswold Archaeological Trust Report no. 01137, Gloucestershire HER 20087.

Thomas, A., N. Holbrook and C. Bateman, 2003. *Later Prehistoric and Romano-British Burial and Settlement at Hucclecote, Gloucestershire, 1998,* Cotswold Archaeology, Bristol and Gloucestershire Archaeological Report no. 2.

Thomas, N., 2005. *Conderton Camp, Worcestershire: A Small Middle Iron Age Hillfort on Bredon Hill,* CBA Research Report 143.

Thompson, N. P., 1971. Archaeological Research in the Pewsey Vale. *Wiltshire Archaeology and Natural History Society,* 66, 58-75.

Thompson, P. J., 1998. *Land Adjacent to 'Clovelly', the Park, Great Barton, Archaeological Excavation Report,* Unpublished Report, Suffolk County Council Archaeological Service 98/60, Suffolk HER BRG 015.

Thompson, P. J., 1999a. *Monitoring Report, Hill Farm Tuddenham,* Unpublished Report, Suffolk County Council 99/60, Suffolk HER TDD 009.

Thompson, P. J., 1999b. *Moreton Hall East, Great Barton, Bury St. Edmunds, Archaeological Evaluation Report,* Unpublished Report, Suffolk County Council Archaeological Service 99/64, Suffolk HER BRG 024.

Tibbles, J., 1996. *An Archaelogoical Watching Brief at Main Street, Burton Agnes,* Unpublished Report, EHU 435.

Tibbles, J., 2000. *An Archaeological Evaluation on Land Adjacent to 8 Station Road, Brough, East Riding of Yorkshire,* Unpublished Report, Humber Archaeology Report no. 51, EHU 1335.

Tilliard, L., 1989. Les Bracelets Et Les Perles En Verre De Levroux (Indre), in *Le Verre Préromain En Europe Occidentale,* ed. M. Feugère, Montagnac: Monique Mergoil, 137-43.

Timble, G. L., 2003. *An Archaeological Evaluation at Bowthorpe, Land Off Bishy Barnabee Way (Ts2b, Ts3 and Ts4),* Unpublished Report, Norfolk Archaeology Unit 892, Norfolk HER 39797.

Timby, J. R., 1998. *Excavations at Kingscote and Wycomb, Gloucestershire, a Roman Estate Centre and Small Town in the Cotswolds with Notes on Related Settlements,* Cirencester: Cotswold Archaeological Trust.

Timms, S., 2000. *Report on Archaeological Works at Weybourne, Keiling and Sheringham for Anglian Water, 1999,* Unpublished Report, Norfolk Archaeological Unit 466, Norfolk HER 34702.

Timms, S. and R. Jackson, 2003. *Moss Street Dept, Moss Street, York, Archaeological Evaluation,* Unpublished Report, Field Archaeology Specialists, CYC 504.

Tinkler, B. N. and D. A. Spratt, 1978. An Iron Age Enclosure of Great Ayton Moor, North Yorkshire. *Yorkshire Archaeological Journal,* 50, 49-56.

Tipper, J., 2007. *West Stow, Lackford Bridge Quarry: A Report on a Rescue Excavation Undertaken in 1978-9,* Unpublished Report, Suffolk County Council Archaeological Service Report no. 2007/039, Suffolk HER WSW 030.

Todd, M., 1993. Charterhouse on Mendip: An Interim Report on Survey and Excavation in 1993. *Somerset Archaeology and Natural History Society,* 137, 59-67.

Todd, M., 1995. Charterhouse on Mendip: Interim Report on Excavations in 1994. *Somerset Archaeology and Natural History,* 138, 75-79.

Tongue, J., 2006. *Former Post Office Site, 12 Castle Street, Cirencester, Gloucestershire, Archaeological Evaluation,* Unpublished Report, Cotswold Archaeology Report no. 06086, Gloucestershire HER 32379.

Toop, N., 2006. *Moss Street Depot, York, Archaeological Excavation,* Unpublished Report, Field Archaeology Specialists, CYC 862.

Toop, N., 2008. Excavations at Moss Street Depot, Moss Street, York. *Yorkshire Archaeological Journal,* 80, 21-42.

Toop, N. and P. Glew, 2007. *Archaeological Watching Brief, Marriott Hotel, Tadcaster Road, York,* Unpublished Report, Field Archaeology Specialists Report FAS2007 376, North Yorkshire Moor National park YMH 299.

Topping, P. G., 1987. Typology and Chronology in the Later Prehistoric Pottery Assemblages of the Western Isles. *Proceedings of the Society of Antiquaries of Scotland,* 117, 67-84.

Town, M., 2003a. *An Archaeological Evaluation at A140 Long Stratton Bypass, Norfolk,* Unpublished Report, Norfolk Archaeological Unit 872, Norfolk HER 39671.

Town, M., 2003b. *An Archaeological Evaluation at Wattlington and Tottenhill ('Police House Field' and Conveyro Route), Norfolk,* Unpublished Report, Norfolk Archaeological Unit 852, Norfolk HER 39457.

Town, M., 2004. *Watlington Quarry, Norfolk: Preliminary Assessment of Significance (Sixty Acre*

Field - Mineral Extraction Phases 1, 1a and 2), Unpublished Report, Norfolk Archaeological Unit 956, Norfolk HER 39458.

Towrie, S., 2005. *Mesolithic Disappointment at Minehowe, but Bead Hints at Long-Distance Connections,* Accessed 8 April 2013: http://www.orkneyjar.com/archaeology/2005/08/18/mesolithic-disappointment-at-minehowe-but-bead-find-hints-at-more-long-distance-connections/.

Tremlett, S., 2002. *Report on an Archaeological Watching Brief/Strip and Excavations at Beach Road, Home-Next-the-Sea, Norfolk,* Unpublished Report, Norfolk Archaeological Unit 714, Norfolk HER 37134.

Trimble, G., 1999. *Report on an Archaeological Evaluation at Priory Road, Binham, Norfolk,* Unpublished Report, Norfolk Archaeological Unit 370, Norfolk HER 31571.

Trimble, G., 2001a. *Report on an Archaeological Excavation at 'the Oaks', Harvey Lane, Thorpe St. Andrew, Norwich,* Unpublished Report, Norfolk Archaeological Unit 584, Norfolk HER 34516.

Trimble, G., 2001b. *Report on an Archaeological Watching Brief at Aldeby Quarry, Priory Farm, Aldeby,* Unpublished Report, Norfolk Archaeological Unit 545, Norfolk HER 34099.

Trimble, G., 2002a. *Report on a Second Phase of Archaeological Evaluation at Land Adjoining Swanton Morley Airfield, Beetley, Norfolk,* Unpublished Report, Norfolk Archaeological Unit 765, Norfolk HER 37159.

Trimble, G., 2002b. *Report on an Archaeological Evaluation at Longdell Hills, Easton, Norfolk, Interim Report,* Unpublished Report, Norfolk Archaeological Unit 660, Norfolk HER 36414.

Trimble, G., 2003. *An Archaeological Watching Brief at Hungry Hill, Beetley, Norfolk,* Unpublished Report, Norfolk Archaeological Unit 860, Norfolk HER 39348.

Trimble, G., 2004a. *An Archaeological Watching Brief at Longdell Hills, Easton, Norfolk, Interim Report,* Unpublished Report, Norfolk Archaeological Unit 946, Norfolk HER 36414.

Trimble, G., 2004b. *Assessment Report and Post-Excavation Project Design, Harford Park and Ride, Harford, Norfolk,* Unpublished Report, Norfolk Archaeological Unit 938, Norfolk HER 39268.

Trimble, G., 2006. A Bronze Age and Early Romano-British Site at the Oaks, Thorpe St. Andrew, Norwich: Excavations 1999-2000. *Norfolk Archaeology,* 45(1), 41-59.

Trimble, G. and S. Underdown, 2002. *Report on an Archaeological Evaluation on Land Adjoining Swanton Morley Airfield, Beetley, Norfolk,* Unpublished Report, Norfolk Archaeological Unit 770, Norfolk HER 37159.

Trimble, R. and G. Taylor, 2005. *Archaeological Excavation on Land at Mill Drove, Blackborough End, Middleton, Norfolk, Assessment Report and Updated Project Design,* Unpublished Report, Archaeological Project Services 183/05, Norfolk HER 37396.

Trow, S., 1988. Excavations at Ditches Hillfort, North Cerney, Gloucestershire, 1982-3. *Wiltshire Archaeology and Natural History Society,* 106, 19-85.

Trow, S., S. James and T. Moore, 2009. *Becoming Roman, Being Gallic, Staying British, Research and Excavations at Ditches 'Hillfort' and Villa 1984-2006,* Oxford: Oxbow.

Turnbull, P., 1983. Excavations at Rillington, 1980. *Yorkshire Archaeological Journal,* 55, 1-9.

Turner, N., 1996. *Powell's School, Gloucester Street, Cirencester, Gloucestershire, Archaeological Evaluation,* Unpublished Report, Cotswold Archaeology Trust Report no. 96408, Gloucestershire HER 28713.

Turner, R. C. and R. G. Scaife, 1995. *Bog Bodies: New Discoveries and New Perspectives,* London: Trustees of the British Museum by the British Museum Press.

Tylecote, R. G. and E. Owles, 1960. A Second-Century Iron Smelting Site at Ashwicken, Norfolk. *Norfolk Archaeology,* 32(3), 142-62.

Underdown, S., 2002. *Report on an Archaeological Evaluation at Maytree Yard, Moor Drove, Hockwold-Cum-Wilton, Norfolk,* Unpublished Report, Norfolk Archaeological Unit 685, Norfolk HER 36961.

Unger, S. and T. Woolhouse, 2008. *Land Off Dereham Road, Hempton, Norfolk, an Archaeological Trial Trench Evaluation,* Unpublished Report, Archaeological Solutions 2985, Norfolk HER 51119.

Upson-Smith, T., 2003. *Archaeological Evaluation at the Former Watton Garden Centre, Norwich Road, Watton, Norfolk, October 2003,* Unpublished Report, Northamptonshire Archaeology, Norfolk HER 39786.

Valentin, J., 1993. An Early Iron Age Hilltop Settlement at Heron Grove, Sturminster Marshall, Dorset: First Excavation Report. *Dorset Natural History and Archaeological Society,* 115, 63-70.

Valentin, J., 2003. Manor Farm, Portesham, Dorset: Excavations on a Multi-Period Religious and Settlement Site. *Dorset Natural History and Archaeological Society,* 125, 23-69.

Valentin, J. and S. Robinson, 2002. Excavations in 1999 on Land Adjacent to Wayside Farm, Nurstead Road, Devizes. *Wiltshire Archaeology and Natural History Society,* 95, 147-213.

Vallender, J., 2005. Iron-Age Occupation at Guiting Power, Gloucestershire: Excavations at Guiting Manor Farm 1997. *Wiltshire Archaeology and Natural History Society,* 123, 17-54.

Van der Sleen, W. G. N., 1967. *A Handbook on Beads,* Musée du Verre.

Vanpeene, N., 1989. Le Verre Préromain À Epiais-Rhus (Val-D'oise), in *Le Verre Préromain En Europe*

Occidentale, ed. M. Feugère, Montagnac: Monique Mergoil, 129-36.

Vartuca, F. A., 2005. *Land to the Rear of 3, 5, 5a, 7 Ashcroft Road, Cirencester, Gloucestershire, Archaeological Evaluation,* Unpublished Report, Cotswold Archaeology Trust Report no. 05090, Gloucestershire HER 27950.

Vatcher, F. d. M. and H. L. Vatcher, 1966. An Excavation of an Earthwork near Badbury Rings, Dorset. *Dorset Natural History and Archaeological Society,* 87, 101-02.

Venclová, N., 1989. La Parure Celtique En Verre En Europe Centrale, in *Le Verre Préromain En Europe Occidentale,* ed. M. Feugère, Montagnac: Monique Mergoil, 85-97.

Venclová, N., 1990. *Prehistoric Glass in Bohemia,* Pilsen: Archeologický ústav ČSAV.

Vessey, J., 2010a. *Folly Cottage, Coln St. Aldwyns, Gloucestershire, Archaeological Watching Brief,* Unpublished Report, Foundations Archaeology Report 694, Available on OASIS.

Vessey, J., 2010b. *Williamsrip Park, Hatherop Road, Coln St. Aldwyns, Gloucestershire, Archaeological Watching Brief,* Unpublished Report, Foundations Archaeology Report 703, Available on OASIS.

Vollender, J., 2007. Excavations at Spratsgate Lane, Somerford Keynes, Gloucestersire, 1995 and 1996. *Wiltshire Archaeology and Natural History Society,* 125, 29-93.

Wacher, J. S. and A. D. McWhirr, 1982. *Early Roman Occupation at Cirencester, Cirencester Excavations I,* Cirencester: Corinium Museum.

Wainwright, G. J., 1970. An Iron Age Promontory Fort at Budbury, Bradford-on-Avon, Wiltshire. *Wiltshire Archaeology and Natural History Society,* 65, 108-66.

Wainwright, G. J., 1971. The Excavation of Prehistoric and Romano-British Settlements near Durrington Walls, Wiltshire, 1970. *Wiltshire Archaeology and Natural History Society,* 66, 76-128.

Wainwright, G. J., 1979. *Gussage All Saints: An Iron Age Settlement in Dorset*, Department of the Environment Archaeological Report no. 10.

Wainwright, J., 2002. *Oldbury Road, Tewkesbury, Gloucestershire, a Report on an Archaeological Evaluation,* Unpublished Report, Marches Archaeology 230, Gloucestershire HER 21370.

Walker, G., A. Thomas and C. Bateman, 2004. Bronze-Age and Romano-British Sites South-East of Tewkesbury: Evaluations and Excavations 1991-7. *Wiltshire Archaeology and Natural History Society,* 122, 29-94.

Wallis, H., 1996. *Watching Brief at Stanfield Quarry, Norfolk,* Unpublished Report, Norfolk Archaeological Unit, Norfolk HER 30660.

Wallis, H., 2005. *Assessment Report and Updated Project Design for an Archaeological Excavation at 3 Minstergate, Thetford,* Unpublished Report, Norfolk Archaeological Unit 1021, Norfolk HER 37356.

Wallis, H., 2011. *Romano-British and Saxon Occupation at Billingford, Central Norfolk,* Dereham, Norfolk: East Anglian Archaeology Report no. 135.

Walter, R., 1922. Some Recent Finds on Ham Hill, South Somerset. *Antiquaries Journal,* 2, 381-82.

Walters, B., 1987. Archaeological Notes. *The New Regard of the Forest of Dean,* 3, 60-63.

Walters, M., 1991. Rescue Excavations on the Roman Occupation Site at Legg House, Blakeney, Forest of Dean, Gloucestershire. *Dean Archaeology,* 3, 40-44.

Ware, K., 2008. *First Plantation, Mill Lane, Scampston, North Yorkshire, Archaeological Excavation Report,* Unpublished Report, MAP Archaeological Consultancy, North Yorkshire HER.

Ware, P., 2009. *Ebenezer Yard, Langton Road, Norton, Malton, North Yorkshire, Archaeological Evaluation,* Unpublished Report, MAP Archaeological Consultancy, North Yorkshire HER.

Warren, F. C., 1938. Excavations on a Roman Site in Brail Wood, Great Bedwyn, in 1936 and 1937. *Wiltshire Archaeology and Natural History Society,* 48, 318-20.

Watkins, K., 2002a. *An Archaeological Evaluation of a Proposed Development Site at Cricklade Road, Cirencester, Gloucestershire,* Unpublished Report, Gloucestershire County Council, Gloucestershire HER 21562.

Watkins, K., 2002b. *An Archaeological Evaluation of a Proposed Development Site at Home Farm, Ebrington, Gloucestershire,* Unpublished Report, Gloucestershire County Council, Gloucestershire HER 21515.

Watkins, K., 2003. *Land Adjacent to Ashchurch Railway Bridge, Ashchurch,* Unpublished Report, Gloucestershire County Council, Gloucestershire HER 22031.

Watkins, P. J., 2006a. *An Archaeological Evaluation at Fairswell Manor, Fincham,* Unpublished Report, Norfolk Archaeolgoical Unit 1125, Norfolk HER 42689.

Watkins, P. J., 2006b. *An Archaeological Evaluation of Land Off Spixworth Road, Old Catton,* Unpublished Report, NAU Archaeology 1191, Norfolk HER 33786.

Watkins, P. J., 2006c. *An Archaeological Excavation at Howlett Way, Thetford, Norfolk, Assessment Report and Updated Project Design,* Unpublished Report, NAU Archaeology 1171, Norfolk HER 38138.

Watkins, P. J., 2006d. *An Archaeological Excavation at the Corner House, Staithe Street, Wells-Next-the-Sea, Assessment Report and Updated Project Design,* Unpublished Report, Norfolk Archaeological Unit 1113, Norfolk HER 41754.

Watkins, P. J., 2007a. *An Archaeological Evaluation of Land Off Beacon Hill Road, Burnham Market,*

Norfolk, Unpublished Report, NAU Archaeology 1237, Norfolk HER 49125.

Watkins, P. J., 2007b. *An Archaeological Strip Map and Sample Excavation at Wimbotsham, Norfolk, Assessment Report and Updated Project Design,* Unpublished Report, NAU Archaeology 1320, Norfolk HER 48964.

Watkins, P. J., 2008. *An Archaeological Field Survey and Excavation at Little Melton, Norfolk, Assessment Report and Updated Project Design,* Unpublished Report, NAU Archaeology 1511, Norfolk HER 50209.

Watts, L., A. Jones and P. Rahtz, 2003. The Roman Villa at Blansby Park, Pickering: Excavations at the Park Gate Roman Site in 2000. *Yorkshire Archaeological Journal,* 75, 15-56.

Watts, L. and P. Leach, 1996. *Henley Wood, Temples and Cemetery; Excavations 1962-69 by the Late Ernest Greenfield and Others,* Council for British Archaeology Report 99.

Watts, M., 2009. *Ilchester to Barrington Gas Pipeline, Somerset, Post-Excavation Assessment and Updated Project Design,* Unpublished Report, Cotswold Archaeology Report no. 09022, Somerset HER 28377.

Watts, M. A., 1995. *Summary of Results from an Archaeological Evaluation of the Proposed ITT Sports Field Development Site at Ilchester, Somerset,* Unpublished Report, Exeter Archaeology Report no. 95.47, Somerset HER 55934.

Weale, A. and J. McNicoll-Norbury, 2010. *Pond Farm, Upper Wanborough, Swindon, Wiltshire, an Archaeological Evaluation,* Unpublished Report, Thames Valley Archaeological Services, PUW 10/21.

Webster, C., 2003a. *Archaeological Investigations at Yarford, Kingston St. Mary, Somerset April-July 2033,* Unpublished Report, Somerset HER 16695.

Webster, G., 1960. The Discovery of a Roman Fort at Waddon Hill Stoke Abbott, 1959. *Dorset Natural History and Archaeological Society,* 82, 88-108.

Webster, G., 1964. Further Investigations on the Site of the Roman Fort at Waddon Hill, Stoke Abbott, 1960-62. *Dorset Natural History and Archaeological Society,* 86, 135-49.

Webster, G., 1967. Excavations at the Romano-British Villa in Barnsley Park, Cirencester, 1961-66, an Interim Report. *Wiltshire Archaeology and Natural History Society,* 86, 74-83.

Webster, G., 1979. Final Report on the Excavations of the Roman Fort at Waddon Hill, Stoke Abbott, 1963-1969. *Dorset Natural History and Archaeological Society,* 101, 51-90.

Webster, J., 2001. Creolizing the Roman Provinces. *American Journal of Archaeology,* 105, 209-25.

Webster, J., 2003b. *9 Corinium Gate, Cirencester, Gloucestershire, Programme of Archaeolgoical Recording,* Unpublished Report, Cotswold Archaeolgoical Trust Report no. 03087, Gloucestershire HER 22290.

Webster, J., 2008. *9 St. Peter's Road, Cirencester, Gloucestershire, Archaeological Evaluation,* Unpublished Report, Cotswold Archaeology 08039, Gloucestershire HER 32692.

Webster, J. and N. J. Cooper (eds.), 1996. *Roman Imperialism: Post-Colonial Perspectives,* Leciester: School of Archaeological Studies, University of Leicester.

Wedlake, W. J., 1958. *Excavations at Camerton, Somerset,* Camerton Excavation Club.

Wenham, L. P., 1968. *The Romano-British Cemetery at Trentholme Drive, York,* Ministry of Public Building and Works Archaeological Reports no. 5.

Wenham, P., 1962. Excavations and Discoveries within the Legionary Fortress in Davygate, York, 1955-8. *Yorkshire Archaeological Journal,* 40, 507-87.

West, S., 1989. *West Stow, Suffolk: The Prehistoric and Romano-British Occupations,* Dereham, Norfolk: East Anglian Archaeology Report no. 48.

West, S. E., 1979. *The Roman Site at Icklingham,* East Anglian Archaeology Report no. 3.

Westall, S., 2010. *An Archaeological Strip, Map and Sample Excavation at Mangreen Travellers' Site, Harford, Norfolk,* Unpublished Report, NAU archaeology 2091, Norfolk HER 52597.

Westwood, B., 2009. Romano-British Remains at Wansford. *East Riding Archaeologist,* 12, 97-114.

Wheeler, M., 1943. *Maiden Castle, Dorset,* London: Society of Antiquaries of London research Report no. 12.

Wheeler, M., 1953. An Early Iron Age 'Beach-Head' at Lulworth, Dorset. *Antiquaries Journal,* 33, 1-13.

Wheeler, M., 1954. *The Stanwick Fortifications North Riding of Yorkshire,* London: Society of Antiquaries no. 17.

Whimster, R., 1981. *Burial Practices in Iron Age Britain: A Discussion and Gazetteer of the Evidence C. 700 BC - AD 43,* Oxford: BAR British Series no. 90.

White, D. A., 1970. The Excavations of an Iron Age Round Barrow near Handley, Dorset, 1969. *Antiquaries Journal,* 50, 26-36.

White, R. and M. Johnson, 2005. *Discovery and Excavation in Scotland,* 17-8.

Whitley, M., 1943. Excavations at Chalbury Camp, Dorset, 1939. *Antiquaries Journal,* 23, 98-121.

Whittaker, J., D. Caulkins and K. Kamp, 1998. Evaluating Consistency in Typology and Classification. *Journal of Archaeological Method and Theory,* 5(2), 129-64.

Wickstead, H. and M. Barber, 2010. A Newly Recorded Hilltop Enclosure at Myncen Farm, Michington. *Dorset Natural History and Archaeological Society,* 131, 103-12.

Wiessner, P., 1983. Style and Social Information in Kalahari San Projectile Points. *American Antiquity,* 48(2), 253-76.

Wiessner, P., 1985. Style or Isochrestic Variation? A Reply to Sackett. *American Antiquity,* 50(1), 160-66.

Wilkins, B. and B. Roberts, 2003. *Land Adjoining Swanton Morley Airfield, Beetley and Hoe, Norfolk Archaeological Investigation,* Unpublished Report, Archaeological Solutions 1435, Norfolk HER 37159.

Wilkins, B. and M. Wotherspoon, 2002. *Land Adjoining Swanton Moreley Airfield, Beetley and Hoe, Norfolk Archaeological Investigation,* Unpublished Report, Hertfordshire Archaeological trust 1161, Norfolk HER 37159.

Wilkins, J. B. and E. Herring (eds.), 2003. *Inhabiting Symbols: Symbol and Image in the Ancient Mediterranean,* London: Accordia Research Institute on the Mediterranean Volume 5, University of London.

Wilkinson, A., 2011. *Chedworth Roman Villa, Gloucestershire, Archaeological Recording and Evaluation,* Unpublished Report, Cotswold Archaeology Report 10232, Available on OASIS.

Williams, B., 2005. *45 Purley Road, Cirencester, Gloucestershire, Archaeological Evaluation,* Unpublished Report, Foundations Archaeology 443, Gloucestershire HER 28658.

Williams, B., 2007a. *An Archaeological Evaluation at 9 Prospect Place, Cirencester, Gloucestershire,* Unpublished Report, Gloucestershire County Council, Gloucestershire Her 29478.

Williams, B., 2007b. *An Archaeological Evaluation at Kyrleside, Dymock, Gloucestershire,* Unpublished Report, Gloucestershire County Council, Gloucestershire HER 29086.

Williams, D., 2010. *Newbridge Quarry Extension, Pickering, North Yorkshire, Archaeological Excavation: Phase 1, Interim Assessment Report,* Unpublished Report, WYAS Report no. 2105, North Yorks HER S16361.

Williams, J., 1999. *An Archaeological Excavation at Grange Hill Quarry, Naunton, Gloucestershire: Phase 1: Interim Statement,* Unpublished Report, Birmingham University Field Archaeology Unit 628, Gloucestershire HER 20358.

Williams, R. G. J., 1983. Romano-British Settlement at Filwood Park, Bristol. *Bristol and Avon Archaeology,* 2, 12-20.

Willis, S., 1997. Samian: Beyond Dating, in *TRAC 96: Proceedings of the Sixth Annual Theoretical Roman Archaeology Conference, Hosted by the Research School of Archaeology and Archaeological Science, the University of Sheffield, March 30th and 31st 1996,* eds. K. Meadows, C. Lemke and J. Heron, Oxford: Oxbow, 38-54.

Wilmott, T. and D. Shipp, 2006. The Romano-British Roadside Settlement of Whitewalls, Easton Brey, Wiltshire: Recent Fieldwork. *Wiltshire Archaeology and Natural History Society,* 99, 165-89.

Wilson, D., 1985. *Excavations of a Probably Roman Villa at Wortley, Gloucestershire, First Interim Report,* Unpublished Report, University of Keele Department of Adult and Continuing Education, Gloucestershire HER 2867.

Wilson, D., 1986. *Excavations of a Probably Roman Villa at Wortley, Gloucestershire, Second Interim Report,* Unpublished Report, University of Keele Department of Adult and Continuing Education, Gloucestershire HER 2867.

Wilson, D., 1987. *Excavations of a Probably Roman Villa at Wortley, Gloucestershire, Third Interim Report,* Unpublished Report, University of Keele Department of Adult and Continuing Education, Gloucestershire HER 2867.

Wilson, D., 1988. *Excavations of a Probably Roman Villa at Wortley, Gloucestershire, Fourth Interim Report,* Unpublished Report, University of Keele Department of Adult and Continuing Education, Gloucestershire HER 2867.

Wilson, D., 1989. *Excavations of a Probably Roman Villa at Wortley, Gloucestershire, Fifth Interim Report,* Unpublished Report, University of Keele Department of Adult and Continuing Education, Gloucestershire HER 2867.

Wilson, D., 1990. *Excavations of a Probably Roman Villa at Wortley, Gloucestershire, Sixth Interim Report,* Unpublished Report, University of Keele Department of Adult and Continuing Education, Gloucestershire HER 2867.

Wilson, D., 1991. *Excavations of a Probably Roman Villa at Wortley, Gloucestershire, Seventh Interim Report,* Unpublished Report, University of Keele Department of Adult and Continuing Education, Gloucestershire HER 2867.

Wilson, D., 1992. *Excavations of a Probably Roman Villa at Wortley, Gloucestershire, Eighth Interim Report,* Unpublished Report, University of Keele Department of Adult and Continuing Education, Gloucestershire HER 2867.

Wilson, D., 1993. *Excavations of a Probably Roman Villa at Wortley, Gloucestershire, Ninth Interim Report,* Unpublished Report, University of Keele Department of Adult and Continuing Education, Gloucestershire HER 2867.

Wilson, D., 1994. *Excavations of a Probably Roman Villa at Wortley, Gloucestershire, Tenth Interim Report,* Unpublished Report, University of Keele Department of Adult and Continuing Education, Gloucestershire HER 2867.

Wilson, D., 1995. *Excavations of a Probably Roman Villa at Wortley, Gloucestershire, Eleventh Interim Report,* Unpublished Report, University of Keele Department of Adult and Continuing Education, Gloucestershire HER 2867.

Wilson, D., 1996. *Excavations of a Probably Roman Villa at Wortley, Gloucestershire, Twelfth Interim Report,* Unpublished Report, University of Keele Department of Adult and Continuing Education, Gloucestershire HER 2867.

Wilson, F., 2009. Excavations at Chapel Garth, Arram. *East Riding Archaeologist,* 12, 167-71.

Wilson, K., 1966. A Survey and Excavation within the Area of Scurff Hall Farm, Drax, near Selby, Yorks. *Yorkshire Archaeological Journal,* 41, 670-86.

Wilson, N., 2006. *Archaeological Evaluation: Church Farm, Church Road, Sea Palling, Norfolk,* Unpublished Report, Archaeological Services and Consultancy 740/SPC/2, Norfolk HER 42660.

Winnett, J. and G. Williams, 2010. *An Archaeological Evaluation of Land at Brynard's Hill, Wootton Bassett, Wiltshire,* Unpublished Report, John Moor Heritage Services.

Wood, J., 1991. *Bunsen Burners...or Cheese Moulds?,* http://www.archaeologyonline.org/Bunsen%20 Burner/Bunsen%20Main%20Page.htm.

Wood, P., N.D. *Tsep Site 716 Acaster Hill, Husthwaite (Ngr Se517729) AHHOO,* Unpublished Report, Northern Archaeological Associates, North Yorkshire HER S8822.

Wood, P., 1955. Strip Lynchets at Bishopstone, near Swindon, Wilts., Excavated in 1954. *Wiltshire Archaeology and Natural History Society,* 56 , 12-6.

Wood, P., 2007. *Scarborough Integrated Transport Scheme, Fieldwork Area B and Former Play Area,* Unpublished Report, Northern Archaeological Associates NAA 07/69, North Yorks HER S512169.

Woods, H., 1991. *Moor Road, Sutton Mallet,* Unpublished Report, Somerset HER 12746.

Woodward, A. and P. Leach, 1993. *The Uley Shrines, Excavation of a Ritual Complex on West Hill, Uley, Gloucestershire: 1977-9,* London: English Heritage Archaeological Report no. 17.

Woodward, A. M., 1935. The Roman Villa at Rudston (E. Yorks), Second Interim Report: The Excavation of 1934. *Yorkshire Archaeological Journal,* 32, 214-20.

Woodward, A. M., 1938. The Roman Villa at Rudston (E. Yorks.), Third Interim Report, the Excavations of 1935. *Yorkshire Archaeological Journal,* 33, 81-86.

Woodward, P. J., 1980. A Prehistoric Burial and Roman Settlement Remains at Broadmayne, Dorset, SY 72998677. *Dorset Natural History and Archaeological Society,* 102, 100-01.

Woodward, P. J., S. M. Davies and A. H. Grasham, 1993. *Excavations at the Old Methodist Chapel and Greyhouse Yard, Dorchester, 1981-1984,* Dorset Natural History and Archaeological Society Monograph no. 12.

Woolf, G., 1993. Rethinking Oppida. *Oxford Journal of Archaeology,* 12(2), 223-34.

Woolhouse, T., N. Crummy, S. Percival and M. Tingle, 2008. A Late Bronze Age Hoard and Early Iron Age Boundary at Lodge Farm, Costessey. *Norfolk Archaeology,* 45, 370-89.

Wordsworth, J., *The Archaeological Assessment of the Ring Ditch Enclosure and Associated Features, 1990,* Unpublished Report, RCAHMS MS 730/11.

Wordsworth, J., 1991. *Discovery and Excavation in Scotland,* 41.

Wordsworth, J., 1999. A Later Prehistoric Settlement at Balloan Park, Inverness, in *Proceedings of the Society of Antiquaries of Scotland,* 129, 239-49.

Worrell, S., 2007. Detecting the Later Iron Age: A View from the Portable Antiquities Scheme, in *The Later Iron Age in Britain and Beyond,* eds. C. Haselgrove and T. Moore, Oxford: Oxbow, 371-88.

Wrathmell, S. and A. Nicholson (eds.), 1990. *Dalton Parlours: Iron Age Settlement and Roman Villa,* Yorkshire Archaeology 3.

Wright, D., 1997. Shipton Hill, Dorset, an Enigmatic Iron Age/Romano-British Enclosure. *Dorset Natural History and Archaeological Society,* 119, 103-08.

Wright, N., 2005. *An Archaeological Evaluation at Cuthamm Hill House, Cutham Hill Lane, Bagendon, Gloucestershire,* Unpublished Report, Gloucestershire County Council, Gloucestershire HER 277773.

Wright, N., 2006. *An Archaeological Evaluation at Greystones Farm, Bourton-on-the-Water, Gloucestershire,* Unpublished Report, Gloucestershire County Council, Gloucestershire HER 28526.

Wymer, J. J., 1986. Early Iron Age Pottery and a Triangular Loom Weight from Redgate Hill, Hunstanton. *Norfolk Archaeology,* 39(3), 286-96.

Yorkston, D. E. and P. J. Piper, 1994/1995. Excavations of a Romano-British Site at Stonehill, Hanham. *Bristol and Avon Archaeology,* 12, 5-17.

Young, A. C., 2003a. *The Mail Marketing Site, Bedminster, Bristol, Archaeological Trial Excavation Project,* Unpublished Report, Avon Archaeological Unit, Bristol City HER 21730.

Young, A. C., 2005a. *75 Sea Mills Lane, Sea Mills, Bristol, Archaeological Trial Excavation Project,* Unpublished Report, Avon Archaeological Unit, Bristol City HER 22202.

Young, D., 1973. An Iron Age and Romano-British Settlement at Broadmayne. *Dorset Natural History and Archaeological Society,* 95, 44-49.

Young, D., 2000. *A Prehistoric Site at the Lond Beeches Playing Fields, London Road, Cirencester, Gloucestershire, Assessment Report,* Unpublished Report, Avon Archaeological Unit, Gloucestershire HER 17205.

Young, D., 2002a. *Land at Coates Farm, Greinton, Somerset, Archaeological Evaluation Report,* Unpublished Report, Avon Archaeological Unit, Somerset HER 15679.

Young, D., 2003b. *Excavation of a Romano-British and Medieval Site on Land at Coates Farm, Greinnton, Somerset, Archaeological Excavation Report,* Unpublished Report, Somerset HER 15950.

Young, D., 2005b. The Smell of Greenness: Cultural Synaesthesia in the Western Desert. *Etnofoor,* 18(1), 61-77.

Young, D., 2006. The Colour of Things, in *Handbook of Material Cutlure*, eds. C. Tilley, W. Keane, S. Kuechler-Fogden, M. Rowlands and P. Spyer, London: Sage Publications, 173-85.

Young, D., 2008. Iron Age, Medieval and Recent Activity at Whitegate Farm, Bleadon, North Somerset. *Somerset Archaeology and Natural History Society*, 151, 31-81.

Young, D., 2010. Colouring Cars: Customising Motor Vehicles in the East of the Australian Western Desert, in *Design Anthropology*, ed. A. J. Clarke, New York: Springer, 117-29.

Young, R., 2002b. *15 Prospect Place, Cirencester, Gloucestershire, Archaeological Evaluation*, Unpublished Report, Cotswold Archaeology Trust 02072, Gloucestershire HER 21753.

Young, R., 2003c. *30 St. Peter's Road, Cirencester, Gloucestershire, Archaeological Evaluation*, Unpublished Report, Cotswold Archaeology 03013, Gloucestershire HER 22104.

Young, R. and A. Hancocks, 2006. Early Bronze Age Ring Ditches and Romano-British Agriculture at Showell Farm, Chippenham, Excavation in 1999. *Wiltshire Archaeology and Natural History Society*, 99, 10-50.

Zepezauer, M.-A., 1989. Perles À Décor Oculé Spiralé De La Tène Moyenne Et Finale, in *Le Verre Préromain En Europe Occidental*, ed. M. Feugère, Montagnac, Mergoil, 107-20.

Zepezauer, M. A., 1993. *Glasperlen Der Vorrömischen Eisenzeit III Mit Unterlangen Von Th. E. Haevernick. Mittel- Und Spätlatènezeitliche Perlen*, Marburger Studien zur vor- und Frühgeschichte Band 15.

Index

Aberdeenshire   xiii, 6, 37, 43, 45, 50, 146, 277, 288, 291, 303, 309-310, 318, 324

Age   C, i, iii, v, ix, x, xi, xii, 1-6, 9-26, 28-38, 40-41, 43, 45, 47-53, 56, 58-59, 62-63, 65-66, 68, 73-77, 79-80, 83-86, 89, 106, 139-140, 142-144, 146-147, 151, 153, 157, 159-160, 162-163, 165, 167-171, 177, 184, 186, 188-190, 192, 194-198, 208, 210, 214-217, 219, 221, 232, 239-247, 249-251, 253-254, 256, 258, 264, 276-277, 281-285, 287-291, 293-306, 308-311, 313-332, 334-335

Amber 2-3, 47, 76, 206, 213, 245, 284, 323

Anglo-Saxon   ix, 11-12, 19, 59, 65, 79, 170-171, 208, 281, 283, 287, 291, 303, 323, 325

Armlet   190, 210, 241

Banffshire 6, 308

bangle 19, 86, 168

Barrow   2, 6, 15, 26, 35, 37, 43, 48-49, 76-77, 104, 106, 140, 142, 188, 191, 198-201, 203, 206, 219, 232, 240, 243-244, 249, 254, 303, 320, 332

Bog Bodies   1, 330
   Lindow Man   1

Bone   3, 144, 188, 191-192, 216, 221, 232, 293

Bracelet   190, 197, 210, 222

Bristol xii, xiii, 6, 9, 12, 81, 147, 151, 168, 195, 255-256, 278, 280-287, 289-290, 292-304, 306, 308-309, 311, 313-317, 319-320, 322-324, 329, 333-334

Bronze Age   ix, 2-3, 11, 16, 18, 23, 25-26, 30, 37, 40-41, 43, 45, 48, 73-74, 77, 79-80, 83, 162, 165, 167, 195, 221, 245, 247, 283, 288, 299, 302-303, 309, 316, 321-322, 326, 330, 334-335

Brooch   2, 28, 47, 74-77, 192, 195, 206, 210, 217, 219, 239, 299, 304

Clay   3, 16, 18, 188, 245, 277, 290

Copper alloy   x, 2, 18, 20, 29, 31, 47, 76, 83, 89, 146, 206, 210, 216, 222, 224, 239-240

Covesea Cave   4

Cowlam   xiii, 6, 15, 35, 50, 76-77, 104, 106, 140, 147, 168, 188, 191, 198-201, 203, 240, 243, 254, 327

Culbin Sands xiii, 3-4, 6, 12, 16, 56, 58, 78-80, 147, 186, 232, 243-244, 256, 285, 291, 313

Culduthel Farm   xiii, 5, 16, 18, 45, 78, 147, 157, 185, 196, 243-244, 246

Dorset x, xii, xiii, 6, 9, 12, 16, 18, 26, 28, 38, 47, 73-74, 79-81, 89, 147, 151, 156, 159, 162, 165, 186, 189, 197, 210, 221, 232, 243, 256, 276, 279-280, 282, 284, 287-288, 291-292, 294-296, 298-305, 308-309, 311, 314-317, 319, 321, 323, 325-328, 330-332, 334

Dots   17, 52, 68, 70, 129, 134, 249, 257

Ethnicity   1, 21-23, 32-33, 295-296, 313, 324

Faience   x, 2, 16, 309

Fibre   89, 208

Finger-ring   76

Gender   2, 21-25, 32, 191, 206, 240, 282, 295, 314, 316, 324, 326

Glastonbury Lake Village   xiii, 3-4, 12, 28, 38, 75-76, 210, 256, 287, 291

Glenluce Sands   4, 12

Gloucestershire   xii, xiii, 6, 28, 38, 40, 47, 80, 162, 210, 245, 276-287, 289-291, 293-308, 310-326, 328-335

Gold   1-2, 29, 48, 216, 221-222, 297, 319

Grandcourt Quarry   xiii, 2-3, 41, 48, 76, 80, 147, 168, 172, 177, 197, 243, 245, 299, 314

Haevernick   v, 18-19, 62-63, 139, 170, 257, 296, 300, 303, 309, 335

Hair   1-2, 21, 25, 84, 197, 199, 276, 291

Hengistbury Head   xiii, 12, 16, 18, 38, 256, 279, 287, 294, 299

Identity   C, i, ii, 2, 5, 10, 13, 15, 20-26, 30-33, 41, 47, 50-51, 84-85, 103, 189, 239-240, 242-244, 246, 284, 288, 295, 301, 303, 305, 309-310, 313-314, 317, 323-324

Inverness-Shire   6, 323

Ireland   3, 5, 25, 52, 147, 256, 258, 286, 296, 301, 303, 305, 319

Jet   x, 2-3, 29, 47, 206, 213, 216, 222, 239, 245, 247, 288, 325

Materiality   2, 29, 33, 85, 146, 159, 242, 245, 324

Meare Lake Village   x, xiii, 3-4, 6, 12, 15-16, 38, 61, 63, 65, 74-80, 89, 106, 147, 151, 167, 190-191, 197, 213, 216, 243-244, 256-257, 282, 287, 319

Melon   2, 17, 66, 68, 77, 80, 85, 203, 244, 259

Mirror x, xiii, 26, 28, 35, 47, 74, 80, 89, 162, 190-191, 199, 204, 206, 208, 210, 243, 292, 299, 310

Morayshire   3-4, 6, 12, 16, 45, 56, 147, 217, 219, 243, 256, 284, 288, 291, 313

Mortuary Context
   Burial vi, x, xiii, 4, 6, 9, 13, 15, 23, 26, 28-29, 32-33, 35, 41, 43, 45, 47-51, 74, 76-77, 80-81, 84, 89, 99, 104-105, 145, 157, 162, 188-193, 195, 197-201, 203-204, 206, 208, 210, 232, 239-240, 243-246, 254, 258, 288, 293, 296, 299, 303, 306, 309-311, 314-315, 317, 327-329, 332, 334
   Cremation 26, 49, 159-160
   Enclosed   15, 37-38, 40-41, 43, 45, 48, 153, 159-160, 162, 165, 167-168, 172, 177, 194, 239, 254, 316
   Hillfort   11, 37, 165, 167, 172, 281, 287, 294, 296-297, 307, 309, 322, 329-330
   Inhumation   x, 1, 28, 35, 37, 43, 47-51, 65, 76-77, 104, 142, 159-160, 162, 168, 170, 177, 185, 188, 190, 192-193, 196-198, 200, 206, 208, 210, 212, 232, 247, 298-299

Nail cleaner   2

Necklace x, 77, 142, 189, 191, 197-201, 203-204, 208, 213, 232, 243, 245, 288

Newstead 4, 12

Norfolk   xii, xiii, 2-3, 6, 12, 34-35, 40-41, 47-48, 76, 80-81, 86, 147, 168, 196-197, 221, 243, 245, 276-

281, 283-286, 289-300, 302-303, 305-311, 314-318, 320, 322-334
Pinxi, 217, 232, 241
Pottery   2-3, 17, 24, 30-32, 37, 47, 74-76, 78-79, 143, 146, 149, 165, 168, 177, 186, 188-189, 192, 194, 196-197, 206, 210, 242, 244, 254, 281, 296, 298, 301-303, 308, 313-314, 317, 320-321, 329, 334
Roman   v, ix, xiii, 1-6, 9, 11-14, 19, 26, 30-32, 38, 40, 43, 45, 47-48, 50, 52, 59, 65-66, 73-76, 78-80, 83, 86, 151, 153, 159-160, 162-163, 165, 168, 170-172, 177, 184, 189-190, 210, 215-216, 219, 221, 232, 239, 245, 253, 255, 276-277, 281-291, 293-306, 308-327, 329-334
Settlement Context   41, 168, 177
   Enclosed   15, 37-38, 40-41, 43, 45, 48, 153, 159-160, 162, 165, 167-168, 172, 177, 194, 239, 254, 316
   Hillfort   11, 37, 165, 167, 172, 281, 287, 294, 296-297, 307, 309, 322, 329-330
   Oppida   1, 24, 38, 40, 317, 321, 334
   Open settlement   43
   Settlement   i, 1, 15, 31-32, 34-38, 40-41, 43, 45, 48-50, 75-76, 104, 159-160, 162, 165, 167-168, 172, 177, 184-185, 190, 197, 201, 213, 219, 232, 243, 246, 251, 281, 285, 287, 291-294, 296-299, 303, 305, 309-310, 312-318, 320-324, 326, 328-331, 333-334
Shale   x, 2, 213, 216, 222, 240, 288, 314
Silica   2, 16-17, 249
Silver   2, 29, 48, 216, 221, 323
Somerset   x, xii, xiii, 3-4, 6, 12, 16, 38, 47, 56, 76-77, 80, 89, 151, 190, 194, 196, 210, 213, 240, 243, 256-257, 276-284, 286-288, 290-295, 297-308, 310-319, 321-324, 326, 328-329, 331-332, 334-335
Spindle whorl 89, 144, 247
Spiral   18-19, 53, 61, 68-70, 76, 78, 80, 84, 140, 144, 193, 224, 242, 244, 255-258, 261-262, 313
Stanwick   1, 25, 332

Stone   x, 3, 17, 33, 43, 47, 76, 85, 146, 188, 190, 210, 213, 216, 250, 288, 310, 326, 328
Suffolk   xii, xiii, 6, 9, 11-12, 29, 35, 40-41, 47, 80, 168, 196, 221, 245, 276-277, 279-282, 285-290, 292-296, 298-301, 305-307, 311, 315-319, 321, 326-329, 332
Textile 1, 20, 25, 28-29, 33, 89, 143, 188, 199, 204, 206, 239, 295, 314
Tool   14, 18, 66, 81
Torc   x, 2, 25, 48, 76, 86, 177, 188, 196, 206, 221, 240, 284, 304
Tweezers   2, 28, 190, 210
Venclová   18-19, 80, 139, 240, 331
Wave   iii, 19, 56, 61, 68-69, 73, 76-77, 80, 132, 134, 137, 140, 143, 200, 203, 213, 249, 257-258, 260, 262-263
Wetwang   x, xii, xiii, 3, 6, 15, 20, 26, 35, 43, 49-50, 53, 59, 61, 73, 76-77, 80, 84, 86, 89, 99, 104, 106, 142, 147, 157, 160, 168, 190-192, 196, 198-201, 203-204, 206, 216, 232, 239-240, 243-244, 246, 286, 295, 306, 309, 328
Whirl   iv, 56, 58, 66, 70, 129, 249, 255-256, 261-262
Wiltshire   xii, xiii, 6, 35, 73-74, 79, 165, 186, 256-257, 277, 282-284, 286-291, 294, 297, 299-304, 307, 309-311, 313-326, 328-335
Woad   1, 28-30, 288
Wood   x, 3, 18, 25-26, 146, 186, 216, 256, 284-285, 288, 311, 320, 331-332, 334
Yorkshire   i, ii, v, vi, vii, viii, ix, x, xii, xiii, 1, 3, 6, 9, 11, 15, 17, 20, 25-26, 28-29, 34-37, 41, 47-52, 65, 68-70, 72-73, 76-77, 79-81, 84-85, 89-93, 96, 99-100, 104-107, 110, 116, 122, 124, 129, 132, 134, 137, 139-140, 143, 145, 147, 149, 151, 153, 159-160, 167-169, 171-172, 177, 184-188, 190, 192, 194-198, 200, 203, 206-208, 210, 217, 219, 221-222, 224, 232, 239-240, 242-245, 249, 254, 276-281, 284-286, 288, 290-291, 293, 295, 298, 300-304, 306, 309-311, 313-314, 317, 320-323, 325-334
Zepezauer 18-19, 139, 335